East and West in the Early Middle Ages

From their crystallisation in the late fifth century to their ultimate decline in the eighth, the Merovingian kingdoms were a product of a vibrant Mediterranean society with both a cultural past and a dynamic and ongoing dialogue between the member communities. By bringing together the scholarship of historians, archaeologists, art historians, and manuscript researchers, this volume examines the Merovingian world's Mediterranean connections. The Franks' cultural horizons spanned not only the Latin-speaking world, but also the Byzantine Empire, northern Europe, Sassanid Persia, and, after the seventh century, a quickly ascendant Islamic culture. Traces of a constant movement of people and cultural artefacts through this world are ubiquitous. As simultaneous consumers, adapters, and disseminators of culture, the degree to which the Merovingian kingdoms were thought to engage with their neighbours is re-evaluated as this volume analyses written accounts, archaeological findings and artefacts to provide new perspectives on Merovingian wide-ranging relations.

STEFAN ESDERS is Professor of Late Antique and Early Medieval History at the Freie Universität Berlin (Germany). He has published books and articles on the transformation of the late Roman world, on Mediterranean connectivity (sixth to ninth century), on Latin and the vernacular and on legal and social history in the early Middle Ages. He is involved in the critical edition of the Carolingian capitularies for the Monumenta Germaniae Historica (MGH).

YANIV FOX is a senior lecturer of late antique and early medieval history at Bar-Ilan University (Israel), and a member of the I-CORE Center for the Study of Conversion and Inter-Religious Encounters. He is the author of *Power and Religion in Merovingian Gaul: Columbanian Monasticism and the Frankish Elites* (Cambridge University Press, 2014).

YITZHAK HEN is Professor of Late Antique and Early Medieval History at the Hebrew University of Jerusalem, and the Director of the Israel Institute for Advanced Studies. He has published extensively on the religious, social, cultural and intellectual history of the post-Roman Barbarian kingdoms of the early medieval West.

LAURY SARTI is a lecturer of medieval history at the University of Freiburg (Germany). She is the author of *Perceiving War and the Military in Early Christian Gaul (ca. 400–700 AD)* and several articles on the early medieval military and the interconnectivities between Byzantium and the West featured in the *Journal of Medieval History*, *Early Medieval Europe*, and *Speculum*.

East and West in the Early Middle Ages

The Merovingian Kingdoms in Mediterranean Perspective

Edited by

Stefan Esders
Freie Universität Berlin, Germany

Yaniv Fox
Bar-Ilan University, Israel

Yitzhak Hen
The Hebrew University of Jerusalem, Israel

Laury Sarti
University of Freiburg, Germany

CAMBRIDGE
UNIVERSITY PRESS

Shaftesbury Road, Cambridge CB2 8EA, United Kingdom

One Liberty Plaza, 20th Floor, New York, NY 10006, USA

477 Williamstown Road, Port Melbourne, VIC 3207, Australia

314–321, 3rd Floor, Plot 3, Splendor Forum, Jasola District Centre, New Delhi – 110025, India

103 Penang Road, #05-06/07, Visioncrest Commercial, Singapore 238467

Cambridge University Press is part of Cambridge University Press & Assessment, a department of the University of Cambridge.

We share the University's mission to contribute to society through the pursuit of education, learning and research at the highest international levels of excellence.

www.cambridge.org
Information on this title: www.cambridge.org/9781009563659

DOI: 10.1017/9781316941072

© Cambridge University Press & Assessment 2019

This publication is in copyright. Subject to statutory exception and to the provisions of relevant collective licensing agreements, no reproduction of any part may take place without the written permission of Cambridge University Press & Assessment.

First published 2019
First paperback edition 2024

A catalogue record for this publication is available from the British Library

Library of Congress Cataloging-in-Publication data
Names: Esders, Stefan, editor. | Fox, Yaniv, 1975–, editor. | Hen, Yitzhak, editor. | Sarti, Laury, editor. | Minerva-Gentner Symposium (2014 : Berlin, Germany)
Title: East and west in the early Middle Ages : the Merovingian kingdoms in Mediterranean perspective / edited by Stefan Esders, Freie Universität, Berlin ; Yaniv Fox, Bar-Ilan University, Israel ; Yitzhak Hen, Ben Gurion University of the Negev, Israel ; Laury Sarti, Freie Universität Berlin.
Other titles: Merovingian kingdoms in Mediterranean perspective
Description: New York : Cambridge University Press, [2019] | Includes index.
Identifiers: LCCN 2018048889 | ISBN 9781107187153 (hardback)
Subjects: LCSH: Merovingians–France–History. | France–Relations–Mediterranean Region. | Mediterranean Region–Relations–France.
Classification: LCC DC65 .E24 2019 | DDC 303.48/244049509021–dc23
LC record available at https://lccn.loc.gov/2018048889

ISBN   978-1-107-18715-3   Hardback
ISBN   978-1-009-56365-9   Paperback

Cambridge University Press & Assessment has no responsibility for the persistence or accuracy of URLs for external or third-party internet websites referred to in this publication and does not guarantee that any content on such websites is, or will remain, accurate or appropriate.

Contents

List of Figures	*page* viii
List of Contributors	xi
Acknowledgements	xiii
List of Abbreviations	xv
Introduction STEFAN ESDERS AND YITZHAK HEN	1

I Expanding Political Horizons

1	Archaeological Perspectives on Communication and Exchange between the Merovingians and the Eastern Mediterranean JÖRG DRAUSCHKE	9
2	Anxiously Looking East: Burgundian Foreign Policy on the Eve of the Reconquest YANIV FOX	32
3	*Pax Inter Utramque Gentem*: The Merovingians, Byzantium and the History of Frankish Identity HELMUT REIMITZ	45

II Patterns of Intensification: The 580s

4	Cultural Transmission Caught in the Act: Gregory of Tours and the Relics of St Sergius PHILLIP WYNN	67
5	Hermenegild's Rebellion and Conversion: Merovingian and Byzantine Connections WOLFRAM DREWS	74

6 Early Byzantine Church Silver Offered for the Eternal Rest
    of Framarich and Karilos: Evidence of 'the Army of Heroic
    Men' Raised by Tiberius II Constantine?   87
    BENJAMIN FOURLAS

 7 Money for Nothing?: Franks, Byzantines and Lombards in
    the Sixth and Seventh Centuries   108
    ANDREAS FISCHER

III The Pope as a Mediterranean Player

 8 The Papacy and the Frankish Bishops in the
    Sixth Century   129
    SEBASTIAN SCHOLZ

 9 A One-Way Ticket to Francia: Constantinople, Rome and
    Northern Gaul in the Mid Seventh Century   138
    CHARLES MÉRIAUX

10 The Digression on Pope Martin I in the *Life of Eligius
    of Noyon*   149
    LAURY SARTI

11 Perceptions of Rome and the Papacy in Late Merovingian
    Francia: The Cononian Recension of the *Liber Pontificalis*   165
    ROSAMOND MCKITTERICK

IV Religious and Cultural Exchange

12 Relocation to the West: The Relic of the True Cross
    in Poitiers   189
    GALIT NOGA-BANAI

13 A Generic Mediterranean: Hagiography in the Early
    Middle Ages   202
    JAMIE KREINER

14 Defensor of Ligugé's *Liber Scintillarum* and the Migration
    of Knowledge   218
    YITZHAK HEN

15 Willibald in the Holy Places   230
    ORA LIMOR

V Rethinking the Late Merovingians

16 'Great Security Prevailed in Both East and West': The Merovingian Kingdoms and the Sixth Ecumenical Council (680/1) — 247
STEFAN ESDERS

17 In the Circle of the Bishop of Bourges: Bern 611 and Late Merovingian Culture — 265
DAVID GANZ

18 Contact with the Eastern Mediterranean in the Late Merovingian Period — 281
IAN WOOD

19 'Merovingian' Illuminated Manuscripts and Their Links with the Eastern Mediterranean World — 297
LAWRENCE NEES

20 'Sons of Ishmael, Turn Back!' — 318
ANN CHRISTYS

21 Carolingian Kingship, Apostolic Authority and Imperial Recognition: Pippin the Short's *Italienpolitik* and the Quest for Royal Legitimacy — 329
ERIK GOOSMANN

Index — 347

Figures

1.1	Pair of Byzantine crescent golden earrings	page 13
1.2	Distribution of early Merovingian *spathae* with gilt handles and/or cloisonné fittings	15
1.3	Diagram showing the relative frequency of Byzantine coins found in the Frankish Territory (except southern Gaul and Aquitaine)	19
1.4	Distribution of cowrie shells between Anglo-Saxon England and Austrasia, sixth/seventh century	20
1.5	Distribution of ivory rings in Merovingian southern Germany	21
1.6	The provenance of archaeological proved Mediterranean, Byzantine and South Asian imports during the early Merovingian period	25
1.7	The provenance of archaeological proved Mediterranean, Byzantine and South Asian imports between the second third of the sixth and the early eighth centuries	26
1.8	Chronological development of graves from southern Germany containing eastern Mediterranean/Byzantine and Oriental imports from the sixth until the early eighth century	27
6.1	Silver hoard at the Baden State Museum at Karlsruhe, general view	88
6.2	Censer no. 1	90
6.3	Medallion with depiction of St Constantine on the censer no. 1	91
6.4	Chalice no. 2	92
6.5	Monogram of Framarich on spoon no. 3	93
6.6	Buckles with triangular plate	100
6.7	*Solidus* of Tiberius II Constantine, Constantinople 578–82	104
12.1	Plan of the Chapel of the Holy Cross in Poitiers, after François Eygun	195

12.2	Plan of the Holy Sepulchre Church in Jerusalem, after Father Virgilio Corbo	197
12.3	Plan of the basilica of S. Croce in Rome, after Richard Krautheimer and Hugo Brandenburg	198
15.1	Willibald, the Dormition Abbey, Jerusalem, c. 1930?	231
19.1	Ornamental frontispiece, Paris BnF lat. 12190, fol. Av	301
19.2	Ornamental finispiece, Qur'an from al-Haram al-Sharif Museum	302
19.3	Qur'an manuscript with sura divider, St Petersburg, National Library of Russia	304
19.4	Title page, Paris BnF lat. 10593, fol. Av	305
19.5	Canon table page, Trier Domschatz, cod. 61, fol. 11r	306
19.6	Ornamental page, drawing by François Déroche, Kairouan Raqqada R 38	307
19.7	Ornamental page, from the Bobbio Orosius, Milan, Biblioteca Ambrosiana cod. D. 23 sup, fol. 1v	309
19.8	Paris BnF lat. 12168. Vatican City, Biblioteca Apostolica Vaticana, cod. Reg. lat. 216, fol. 3v	314
19.9	David and Musicians, London British Library MS	315
19.10	Eagle capital in the Dome of the Rock	316
21.1	Organ depicted in the Utrecht Psalter (Rheims, 825–50), illustrating Psalm 150:4: 'Praise him with strings and organs'	339

Contributors

ANN CHRISTYS, Independent scholar

JÖRG DRAUSCHKE, Member of Research Staff, Römisch-Germanisches Zentralmuseum Mainz – Leibniz-Forschungsinstitut für Archäologie and board member of the Leibniz-WissenschaftsCampus Mainz: 'Byzanz zwischen Orient und Okzident'

WOLFRAM DREWS, Professor of Medieval History, Westfälische Wilhelms-Universität Münster

STEFAN ESDERS, Professor of Late Antique and Early Medieval History, Friedrich-Meinecke-Institut für Geschichte, Freie Universität Berlin

ANDREAS FISCHER, Research Fellow, Institut für Mittelalterforschung der Österreichischen Akademie der Wissenschaften, Vienna

BENJAMIN FOURLAS, Member of Research Staff, Römisch-Germanisches Zentralmuseum Mainz – Leibniz - Forschungsinstitut für Archäologie and managing director of the Leibniz-WissenschaftsCampus Mainz: 'Byzanz zwischen Orient und Okzident'

YANIV FOX, Senior Lecturer of Late Antique and Medieval History, Bar-Ilan University

DAVID GANZ, Research Fellow, Friedrich-Meinecke-Institut für Geschichte, Geschichte der Spätantike und des frühen Mittelalters, Freie Universität Berlin

ERIK GOOSMANN, Post-doctoral Fellow, Department of History and Art History, Utrecht University

YITZHAK HEN, Professor of Medieval History, The Hebrew University of Jerusalem and Director of the Israel Institute for Advanced Studies

JAMIE KREINER, Associate Professor of History, University of Georgia

ORA LIMOR, Professor Emerita of Medieval History, The Open University of Israel

ROSAMOND MCKITTERICK, Professor Emerita of Medieval History, University of Cambridge, Fellow of Sidney Sussex College, Cambridge and Chair of the Faculty of Archaeology, History and Letters of the British School at Rome

CHARLES MÉRIAUX, Professor of Medieval History, University of Lille

LAWRENCE NEES, Professor of Art History and H. Fletcher Brown Chair of Humanities, University of Delaware

GALIT NOGA-BANAI, Associate Professor of Art History, The Hebrew University of Jerusalem

HELMUT REIMITZ, Professor of Medieval History, Princeton University

LAURY SARTI, Lecturer of Medieval History, University of Freiburg

SEBASTIAN SCHOLZ, Professor of Medieval History, University of Zurich

IAN WOOD, Professor Emeritus of Medieval History, University of Leeds

PHILLIP WYNN, Independent scholar

Acknowledgements

The present volume originated in an international Minerva-Gentner Symposium that was held in Berlin on 17–20 December 2014. This conference was the grand finale of a joint German-Israeli project – East and West in the Early Middle Ages: The Merovingian Kingdoms in Mediterranean Perspective – that was funded by the German-Israeli Foundation (GIF) for Scientific Research and Development. We wish to thank both the Minerva-Gentner Stiftung and the GIF for their generous support, as well as our host institutions – the Freie Universität Berlin and the Ben-Gurion University of the Negev – for providing a most friendly and welcoming atmosphere throughout the time of the project. We should also like to thank the speakers and audience of the Berlin conference, whose papers and comments contributed to its success and to the success of the project as a whole.

This volume could not have been published without the help and advice of many friends and colleagues. We would first wish to express our deepest gratitude to the contributors for their generous spirit and cooperation during the editorial process. We are equally indebted to the editorial team at Cambridge University Press, especially Elizabeth Friend-Smith, and our copy-editor Liz Hudson, for seeing the book through the press. Finally, warm thanks should also go to our graduate students, Lukas Bothe, Anna Gehler, Omer Glickman, Pia Lucas, Tamar Rotman, Till Stüber, and Dimitri Tarat, who formed the backbone of the GIF project and enriched our meetings in Berlin, Beer-Sheva and Leeds immensely.

This book is dedicated with warm affection and deep gratitude to Martin Heinzelmann, a laudable promoter of Merovingian studies and an inspiration to us all.

Abbreviations

AASS	Acta Sanctorum (Antwerp and Brussels, 1643–)
BM	Bibliothèque Municipale
BnF	Bibliothèque nationale de France
CAH XIII, XIV	*Cambridge Ancient History*, vol. XIII: *The Later Empire, AD 337–425*, ed. A. Cameron and P. Garnsey (Cambridge, 1998); and vol. XIV: *Late Antiquity: Empire and Successors, AD 425–600*, ed. A. Cameron, B. Ward-Perkins and M. Whitby (Cambridge, 2000)
CCCM	Corpus Christianorum, Continuatio Mediaevalis (Turnhout, 1966–)
CCSL	Corpus Christianorum, Series Latina (Turnhout, 1952–)
ChLA	*Chartae latinae antiquiores: Facsimile Edition of the Latin Charters prior to the Ninth Century*, ed. A. Bruckner and R. Marichal (Olten and Lausanne, 1954–)
CLA	*Codices Latini Antiquiores: A Palaeographical Guide to Latin Manuscripts Prior to the Ninth Century*, 11 vols with a supplement (Oxford, 1935–71; 2nd edn of vol. II, 1972)
CSEL	Corpus Scriptorum Ecclesiasticorum Latinorum (Vienna, 1866–)
MGH	Monumenta Germaniae Historica
AA	Auctores Antiquissimi (Berlin, 1877–1919)
Cap.	Capitularia regum Francorum (Hannover, 1883–97)
Epp.	Epistulae (Berlin, 1887–1939)
LNG	Leges nationum Germanicarum (Hannover, 1888–)
Poetae	Poetae latini medii aevi (Berlin, 1881–1951)

SRG	Scriptores rerum Germanicarum in usum scholarum (Hannover, 1871–)
SRL	Scriptores rerum Langobardicarum et Italicarum (Hannover, 1878)
SRM	Scriptores rerum Merovingicarum (Hannover, 1884–1951)
SS	Scriptores in folio (Berlin, 1826–)
NCMH I, II	*New Cambridge Medieval History*, vol. I: *c. 500–700*, ed. P. Fouracre (Cambridge, 2005); vol. II: *c. 700–900*, ed. R. McKitterick (Cambridge, 1995)
PG	Patrologiae cursus completus, series graeca, ed. J.-P. Migne, 161 vols (Paris, 1857–66)
PL	Patrologiae cursus completus, series latina, ed. J.-P. Migne, 221 vols (Paris, 1841–64)
SC	Sources chrétiennes (Paris, 1941–)
Settimane	Settimane di studio del Centro italiano di studi sull'alto medioevo (Spoleto, 1954–)

Introduction

Stefan Esders and Yitzhak Hen

In the autumn of 1879, a young law student, Henri Pirenne (1862–1935), joined the history class of the promising Liège professor Godefroid Kurth (1847–1916). Pirenne was captivated by Kurth's teaching, especially by his advanced medieval-history classes, which were closely modelled on the Berlin seminars of Leopold von Ranke. An enduring friendship that was nourished by mutual respect and cultivated by a lively exchange of letters developed between the master and his student, although academically they parted ways. Kurth, the romantic Catholic, became the doyen of medieval history in Belgium and one of the founding fathers of Merovingian history in Europe. Pirenne, on the other hand, became one of the most discussed historians in modern times, whose thesis, although constantly debated, changed dramatically the ways we perceive the passage from late antiquity to the Middle Ages.[1] The work of Kurth and Pirenne has been subject to endless criticism and revision in the past century or so. Yet, the influence of both on many a generation of historians was immense, not least because they had established the terms of reference for the debate about the transformation of the Mediterranean world in late antiquity and the early Middle Ages, and the role that the Merovingian kingdoms had played within that process. This volume reunites Kurth and Pirenne once again.

It should come as no surprise that Pirenne was the most eloquent advocate of the late Merovingian period as the rupture between antiquity and the Middle Ages. His posthumously published work *Mahomet et Charlemagne*, which exhibits his vision in exquisite clarity and simplicity, is a classical study, particularly if one defines as 'classic' a book that one reads and admires, realising throughout that the author is

---

[1] On Godefoid Kurth and Hénri Pirenne, see L.-E. Halkin, 'Godefcid Kurth et Henri Pirenne', *La Revue Nouvelle*, 32 (1960): 385–90; J.-L. Kupper, 'Godefroid Kurth and Henri Pirenne: An Improbable Friendship', *Journal of Belgian History*, 42 (2011): 411–26; I. N. Wood, *The Modern Origins of the Early Middle Ages* (Oxford, 2013), pp. 223–9.

wrong.² Pirenne's picture of a deep rupture that was caused by the Arab conquests and subsequently 'put an end to the Mediterranean commonwealth' has been questioned almost immediately after its first publication, by scholars such as Maurice Lombard, to mention only one of the most prominent ones.³ It is a commonplace nowadays that economic decline in the West started well before the seventh century, as has been shown by David Whitehouse and Richard Hodges in their 1983 book *Mohammed and Charlemagne: The Origins of Europe*, which made ample use of archaeological evidence, scarcely known to Pirenne.⁴ Two important volumes that originated in the ESF-funded 'Transformation of the Roman World' project, one on the sixth and one of the eighth century, took this discussion further and painted a much more nuanced picture of regional differences as well as of short- and long-term developments.⁵ More detailed studies followed suit. In his wide-ranging book *Origins of European Economy*, Michael McCormick not only advocated for an economic recovery as early as the eighth century but also introduced the slave-trade into our economic paradigm.⁶ Slaves as luxury goods calls for a reassessment of the Mediterranean exchange systems and the role played by the Arabs, who bought slaves and enslaved people in a considerable number. Pirenne, on the other hand, had focused on gold, papyrus, spices and silk as the four luxury goods that signify long-distance trade, dismissing the slave trade as insignificant for Merovingian economic activity. Similarly, Chris Wickham, in his monumental book *Framing the Early Middle Ages*, reminds us that the four luxury commodities mentioned by Pirenne 'are not reliable guides to the scale of economic activity in our period, simply because they tell us about the wrong things; indeed, historians who focus their attention on luxuries are mostly not writing economic history at all'.⁷ By contrast, Wickham calls for a more down-to-earth approach of investigation that considers the very foundations of economic activity – production and surplus – framing the

---

² H. Pirenne, *Mahomet et Charlemagne*, ed. J. Pirenne and F. Vercauteren (Paris, 1937); English trans. *Mohammed and Charlemagne* (London, 1939).
³ H. Pirenne, *Medieval Cities: Their Origins and the Revival of Trade*, trans. F. H. Halsey with a new introduction by M. McCormick (Princeton, NJ, 2014), p. 14. (Originally published in 1925.)
⁴ R. Hodges and D. Whitehouse, *Mohammed and Charlemagne: The Origins of Europe* (London, 1983).
⁵ *The Sixth Century: Production, Distribution and Demand*, ed. R. Hodges and W. Bowden (Leiden, Boston and Cologne, 1998); *The Long Eighth Century: Production, Distribution and Demand*, ed. I. L. Hansen and C. Wickham (Leiden, Boston and Cologne, 2000).
⁶ M. McCormick, *Origins of European Economy: Communications and Commerce, AD 300–900* (Cambridge 2001).
⁷ C. Wickham, *Framing the Early Middle Ages: Europe and the Mediterranean, 400–800* (Oxford, 2005), p. 701.

Introduction

question of short- and long-distance exchange in a different way. Finally, in a stimulating paper that was published recently, Bonnie Effros points at 'the enduring attraction of the Pirenne thesis', which, she argues, was fuelled by political ideology.[8] Whereas for Pirenne the Arabs were just instrumental in the destruction of Mediterranean economy, those who adhered to his thesis stressed the disrupting force not only of the Arab conquests but also of Islam as a religion. She also draws attention to Pirenne's 'Orientalism', which was rooted in the colonial discourse of the late nineteenth and early twentieth centuries, when the modern conquest of Islamic territories was perceived as part of a civilising mission to those areas which previously had been part of the Roman Empire.

Against this background, when dealing with the early medieval Mediterranean, one should perhaps be less interested in modifying Pirenne's thesis, while, at the same time, keeping in mind how influential it has been. One should try to expand one's source material and find new ways to approach the passage from late antiquity to the early Middle Ages in and around the Mediterranean. This is precisely what the various papers collected in this volume do. Their aim is to study the Merovingian kingdoms of the early Middle Ages in a broader Mediterranean context. The working hypothesis behind this enterprise is that apart from being post-Roman barbarian kingdoms, deeply rooted in the traditions and practices of the western Roman Empire, the Merovingian kingdoms had complicated and multilayered social, cultural and political relations with their eastern Mediterranean counterparts, that is, the Byzantine Empire and the Umayyad Caliphate. Not only were the Merovingians aware of the politics and culture of Byzantium and its relations with the Persians, they also had a fair amount of knowledge on the ins and outs of the Muslim East from the seventh century onwards. By analysing written accounts, as well as various archaeological findings and artefacts, the various studies in this volume offer a new perspective on the history of Merovingian Francia and its relations with the eastern Mediterranean, North Africa and Spain.

The Merovingian kingdoms were, perhaps, the most powerful and long-lasting political entities of the post-Roman world.[9] The politics of turmoil that characterised Merovingian history from the death of Clovis (d. 511) onwards led to the consolidation of three Frankish subkingdoms

---

[8] B. Effros, 'The Enduring Attraction of the Pirenne Thesis', *Speculum*, 92 (2017): 184–208.
[9] The amount of literature on the Merovingian kingdoms is enormous and cannot be listed here. For a comprehensive introduction, see I. N. Wood, *The Merovingian Kingdoms, 450–751* (London and New York, 1994). For further bibliography, see the various papers in this volume.

(*Teilreiche*, as the German call them): Neustria, Austrasia, and the south-eastern kingdom, which crystallised in the territories of the former kingdom of Burgundy. The local elite of each subkingdom developed its own political identity, which, in turn, boosted the bitter hostility and conflicts between the Merovingian rulers of Francia. Chlothar II, who, in 613 reunited the Merovingian kingdoms under his rule, must have realised the growing power of the local aristocracy, and hence allowed each of the Merovingian *Teilreiche* to have its own court under its own *major domus*.

When, in 629, Dagobert I succeeded his father as king of the Franks, he did not make any attempt to change the new political system established by his father but simply continued the policy of acknowledging local elites. Dagobert I has traditionally been seen as the last effective Merovingian king, succeeded by a series of degenerate 'do-nothing' kings (*rois fainéants*). This view, which, in the past, has poisoned the minds of many historians, was created and disseminated by the successor dynasty, the Carolingians and their advisers, who, in an attempt to justify their rise to power, developed a remarkably effective machinery of political and religious propaganda.

After the death of Dagobert I in 639, the Merovingian kingdom was indeed divided between his successors, Sigibert III and Clovis II. But this in itself must not be taken as a sign of weakness, nor is it an indication of the deteriorating authority of the Merovingian king. Dagobert was certainly not the last effective Merovingian ruler of Francia. His immediate successors, who built on their father's and grandfather's accomplishments, were no less effective as rulers, and as for the quality of their later successors, the Carolingian bias of our sources must always be taken with a pinch of salt.

The reign of Chlothar II and Dagobert I was indeed a crucial period in the formation of late Merovingian polity. The new political arrangements created by Chlothar II and bolstered by Dagobert I allowed local elites to preserve and further develop their own identities and acknowledged the increasing importance of these elites to the political system. Yet it also marked the Merovingian court as the unrivalled political centre, and it clearly set down the collaborative relationship between local aristocrats and their kings. Although cooperation was not always smooth, the political system, which was based on consensual power-sharing arrangements, was rather cohesive and largely successful. The fact that this basic structure, set down in the early seventh century, continued to define the *regnum Francorum* well into Charles Martel's day, is evidence not of an atrophied political system but rather of a stable and relatively efficient model of governance.

Introduction

The politics and culture of the Merovingian kingdoms in Gaul had most often been interpreted as a tapestry of local phenomena. The reasons for this are complex. In part, this view was due to certain nationalist historiographic traditions (especially in Germany and France) that understood the early Middle Ages as part of a national, 'Germanic' past. But it also reflects a general tendency to examine the early medieval West through a predominantly 'Western' prism, framing the early Middle Ages as an era of its own which had to be treated separately from 'Roman', that is, antique, or 'Byzantine' history.

Whereas the study of the early medieval West in general, and the study of the Merovingian kingdoms in particular, has witnessed an immense resurgence of interest in recent years, there is no monograph and only a handful of (mostly out-of-date) papers dedicated to the relations between the Merovingian kingdoms and their Eastern counterparts. These studies, more often than not, present a misleading image of the complicated and multilayered social, cultural and political relations between the Merovingians and their Mediterranean contemporaries. It is indeed extremely rare to find modern scholars asking questions about the place of the Merovingian kingdoms in the larger context of the Mediterranean world and especially about the ways the Merovingians perceived and understood both the Byzantine Empire, and the Umayyad Caliphate.[10] As the various papers in this volume demonstrate, the vibrant cultural exchanges and complex relations within the Mediterranean world render obsolete any historical interpretation that sees the Merovingian world as an isolated enclave.

The first section of this volume deals with the expanding political horizons of the Merovingian kingdoms. It begins with a survey of archaeological evidence for contact and exchange between the eastern Mediterranean and Merovingian Gaul from the end of the fifth to the eighth century (Drauschke), and it continues with an examination of the Burgundian–Merovingian relations under Sigismund and Gundobad (Fox) and the formation of a collective Frankish identity in the last decades of the sixth century vis-à-vis the rulers and elites of the Byzantine East (Reimitz).

The 580s, which witnessed a rigorous intensification in various processes that forged the vital position of the Merovingian kingdoms

[10] An exception in that respect is *Western Perspectives on the Mediterranean: Cultural Transformation in Late Antiquity and the Early Middle Ages, 400–800*, ed. A. Fischer and I. N. Wood (London, 2014). See also *The Merovingian Kingdoms and the Mediterranean World: Revisiting the Sources*, ed. P. Bockius, S. Esders, Y. Hen, P. Lucas and T. Rotman (London, 2019).

in the Mediterranean context, is the focus of the second section of this book. From various aspects of a 'Christianised culture of war' that had spread from the Byzantine East to the Merovingian West (Wynn), through Frankish involvement in political and military campaigns in Visigothic Spain (Drews) and Syria (Fourlas), up to the financial dimension in the relations between the Franks and Byzantium (Fischer), the papers in this section expose the wide horizons of the Merovingian Mediterranean.

An image of the popes as powerful cultural and political brokers in the early medieval Mediterranean emerges from the papers of the third section. During the murky times of the so-called Three-Chapters Controversy, the popes played a crucial role in securing the treaty between the Merovingian king, Childebert, and the Byzantine emperor, emphasising the immense political importance of this theological debate and the ability of the popes to negotiate power between East and West (Scholz). Similarly, a century later, Pope Martin I wrote to Amandus and King Sigibert III of Austrasia in an attempt to secure their support for the acts of the Lateran Council against the Monotheletism of the Byzantine emperor (Mériaux). Information on what was going on in the Byzantine East (Sarti) and papal Rome (McKitterick) constantly reached the Merovingian West and consequently shaped the Merovingian perception of the Mediterranean.

The vibrant cultural exchange between the East and the West during the Merovingian period is examined in the fourth section of this book through the prism of the cults of relics (Noga-Banai), hagiography (Kreiner), patristic literature (Hen) and Holy Land itineraries (Limor). This cultural effervescence continued well into the late Merovingian period, which is the focus of the fifth and final section of this book. The influx of various treatises, such as the Physiologus and Pseudo-Methodius (Ganz and Wood) and artistic models (Nees), did not stop during the period of turmoil that characterised the late Merovingian period. On the contrary, the Merovingians and their *maiores* had close religious and economic ties with Visigothic Spain, Anglo-Saxon England, Lombard Italy, the popes and the Byzantine East (Esders), which testify to their importance in the Mediterranean scene. Their pivotal role in Mediterranean politics and culture left its marks on Arabic accounts of Merovingian affairs (Christys), and it certainly paved the way for Pippin III's brand of global politics (Goosmann).

Part I

Expanding Political Horizons

1 Archaeological Perspectives on Communication and Exchange between the Merovingians and the Eastern Mediterranean

Jörg Drauschke

Archaeological artefacts with an eastern Mediterranean or even South Asian origin found in early medieval graves of middle and western Europe is a phenomenon that has been well known for a long time. By the beginning of the twentieth century, cowrie shells worn as amulets by women were already thought to come from the Indian Ocean,[1] and in 1918 some cast copper alloy vessels from Anglo-Saxon graves were identified as products of 'Coptic' Egypt.[2] Since the 1990s, the new interest in the topic of 'exotic' objects from the Merovingian area was triggered by different causes. First, the development of scientific analysing techniques offered a variety of new possibilities to more or less securely determine the provenance of materials. Second, the archaeological database of the late antique and early medieval Mediterranean was significantly improved by numerous studies dedicated to archaeological small finds.[3] This resulted in a greater amount of archaeological reference material that could be compared with the finds from middle and western Europe, which allowed for new insights concerning the transport of objects and their place of production.

The distribution of all these different object groups was often explained in terms of trade only,[4] but in the face of the many possible mechanisms of

---

[1] Cf. O. Paret, *Urgeschichte Württembergs mit besonderer Berücksichtigung des mittleren Neckarlandes* (Stuttgart, 1921), pp. 152–3, 219 (Fig. 41.8).
[2] M. Conway, 'Burgundian Buckles and Coptic Influences', *Proceedings of the Society of Antiquaries of London*, 2nd Ser., 30 (1917/18): 63–89 esp. pp. 80–2, Figs. 17–22.
[3] For an overview, see J.-P. Sodini, 'La Contribution de l'archéologie à la connaissance du monde byzantin (IVe–VIIe siècles)', *Dumbarton Oaks Papers*, 47 (1993): 139–84. A programmatic view by M. Mundell Mango, 'Action in the Trenches: A Call for More Dynamic Archaeology of Early Byzantium', in *Proceedings of the 21st International Congress of Byzantine Studies, London, 21–26 August, 2006, vol. I: Preliminary Papers*, ed. E. Jeffreys (Aldershot and Burlington, 2006), pp. 83–98 esp. 86–9. A recent survey is presented in *Byzantine Small Finds in Archaeological Contexts*, ed. B. Böhlendorf-Arslan and A. Ricci, Conference Istanbul 2008 15 (Istanbul, 2012).
[4] H. Roth, 'Zum Handel der Merowingerzeit auf Grund ausgewählter archäologischer Quellen', in K. Düwel, H. Jankuhn, H. Siems and D. Timpe (eds.), *Untersuchungen zu*

intercultural transfer, this seems to be too simple a model.[5] In addition, it was even argued that the exchange between the (eastern) Mediterranean and middle and western Europe had already stopped around AD 600.[6] Indeed it was necessary to accomplish a critical analysis of the many different materials and object groups from the Merovingian kingdoms with a supposed origin from the eastern Mediterranean. As can be seen by comparable studies for other regions,[7] an exhaustive consideration of all imported goods is a prerequisite when attempting to draw conclusions concerning the intensity and variability of exchange relations in time and space, as well as the different mechanisms responsible for the transfer of goods. To answer these questions, I have recently completed a comprehensive study for sixth- and seventh-century southern Germany and adjacent regions.[8]

The connections between Byzantium and the Merovingians have been the focus of historical research time and again.[9] This article will concentrate mainly on the archaeological perspective.

Preliminary Remarks on Archaeological Sources

The following investigation will briefly discuss the archaeological finds with a supposed origin from the eastern Mediterranean. They mainly derive from graves, where they have been laid down as component

---

Handel und Verkehr der vor- und frühgeschichtlichen Zeit in Mittel- und Nordeuropa III. Der Handel des frühen Mittelalters (Göttingen, 1985), pp. 161–92, esp. Table 1.

[5] D. Quast, 'Communication, Migration, Mobility and Trade: Explanatory Models for Exchange Processes from the Roman Iron Age to the Viking Age', in D. Quast (ed.), *Foreigners in Early Medieval Europe: Thirteen International Studies on Early Medieval Mobility* (Mainz, 2009), pp. 1–26, esp. Fig. 16.

[6] R. Hodges, *Dark Age Economics: The Origins of Towns and Trade AD 600–1000*, 2nd edn (London, 1989), pp. 31–3, Fig. 4; K. Randsborg, 'The Migration Period: Model History and Treasure', in R. Hodges and W. Bowden (eds.), *The Sixth Century: Production, Distribution and Demand* (Leiden, 1998), pp. 61–88, at pp. 82–3.

[7] J. W. Huggett, 'Imported Grave Goods and the Early Anglo-Saxon Economy', *Medieval Archaeology*, 32 (1988): 63–96; C. Pause, 'Überregionaler Güteraustausch und Wirtschaft bei den Thüringern der Merowingerzeit', *Zeitschrift für Archäologie des Mittelalters*, 29 (2001): 7–30; É. Garam, *Funde byzantinischer Herkunft in der Awarenzeit vom Ende des 6. bis zum Ende des 7. Jahrhunderts* (Budapest, 2001); J. Ljungkvist, 'Influences from the Empire: Byzantine-Related Objects in Sweden and Scandinavia, 560/70–750/800 AD', in F. Daim and J. Drauschke (eds.), *Byzanz – das Römerreich im Mittelalter* (Mainz, 2010), pp. 419–41.

[8] J. Drauschke, *Zwischen Handel und Geschenk: Studien zur Distribution von Objekten aus dem Orient, aus Byzanz und aus Mitteleuropa im östlichen Merowingerreich* (Rahden/Westf., 2011).

[9] J. Drauschke, 'Diplomatie und Wahrnehmung im 6. und 7. Jahrhundert: Konstantinopel und die merowingischen Könige', in M. Altripp (ed.), *Byzanz in Europa: Europas östliches Erbe* (Turnhout, 2011), pp. 244–75 with a collection of the relevant literature.

parts of the graves' furnishings. The sometimes huge row grave cemeteries, or *Reihengräberfelder*, are not evenly distributed over the Frankish realms: they can be found mainly between the regions of the Bavarians and Alamanni in the south-east and northern Gaul. As a result, the eastern Mediterranean imports are mainly distributed over this area.

Although the difficult process of formulating archaeological contexts cannot be discussed here, the circumstances particular to graves as an archaeological source must be taken into account. The assemblage of artefacts generally represents a deliberate choice of objects and not a representative cross section of Merovingian material culture. This choice is influenced not only by codes and values inherent in early medieval society but also by social position, sex, age, profession, ethnicity, etc., of the deceased and their family.[10]

Byzantine/Eastern Mediterranean and Oriental Imports: Different Object Groups and Their Possible Provenance

Among the objects introduced here, one can single out a group with a Byzantine or eastern Mediterranean origin in a stricter sense. Silk textiles, as high-prestige commodities imported from Byzantium and the East, often draw the most attention from scholars interested in textile remains of costume and dresses, but only a few of these belong to the Merovingian period.[11] Because of the unfavourable conditions for the preservation of organic materials, only a handful is known from archaeological contexts.[12] One of the earliest pieces of evidence is a costume made from blue silk found in a grave from the second half of the fifth century in the cemetery of Lauchheim (Baden-Württemberg).[13] Several fragments of silk textile are known from the royal burial church Saint-Denis in Paris.[14] Saint Balthild (c. 635–80), queen and wife of Clovis II

---

[10] S. Brather, 'Kleidung und Identität im Grab. Gruppierungen innerhalb der Bevölkerung Pleidelsheims zur Merowingerzeit', *Zeitschrift für Archäologie des Mittelalters*, 32 (2004): 1–58.
[11] A. Stauffer, 'Bestaunt und begehrt: Seide aus Byzanz', in *Byzanz – Pracht und Alltag*, ed. Kunst- und Ausstellungshalle der Bundesrepublik Deutschland (Bonn and Munich, 2010), pp. 94–101.
[12] A. Harris, *Byzantium, Britain and the West: The Archaeology of Cultural Identity, AD 400–650* (Stroud, 2003), p. 89, Fig. 20.
[13] J. Banck, 'Ein merowingerzeitlicher Baumsarg aus Lauchheim/Ostalbkreis. Zur Bergung und Dokumentation der Textilfunde', in L. Bender Jørgensen and Ch. Rinaldo (eds.), *Textiles in European Archaeology* (Göteborg, 1998), pp. 115–24.
[14] M. Fleury and A. France-Lanord, *Les trésors mérovingiens de la basilique de Saint-Denis* (Woippy, 1998), pp. 185–93 and the table at p. 189.

12   Jörg Drauschke

(r. 639–58), was buried in the Abbey of Chelles wearing a *casula* decorated with ornaments of a clear Byzantine style, which were stitched to the linen *casula* with silken threads.[15]

Cotton with a possible eastern Mediterranean origin is also very rarely found in archaeological contexts.[16] Gold braid textiles combined with silk have been identified in recent years, especially from high-status burials in the Austrasian part of the Frankish kingdom.[17] At present, it is still unclear whether those textiles arrived as 'finished products' or whether silk materials were processed further west in Italy or even in the Merovingian realm itself.

Only a few pieces of jewellery can be identified which could have had a Byzantine or eastern Mediterranean origin. Crescent-shaped golden earrings are typical Byzantine objects known from Mediterranean sites, especially for the end of the sixth and the first half of the seventh century. Examples have been found in the western Carpathian basin and in female tombs from the Bavarian region, altogether seven pieces from four tombs (Fig. 1.1).[18]

Strong Mediterranean affinities should be assigned to the golden pectoral cross with a central gemstone from sarcophagus 23 in Saint-Denis which belongs to the last third of the fifth century.[19] Another singular piece is a silver pectoral cross from grave 15 in Friedberg (Bavaria,

---

[15] J.-P. Laporte, 'Grab und Reliquien der Königin Balthilde in Chelles-sur-Marne', in E. Wamers and P. Périn (eds.), *Königinnen der Merowinger*, Exhibition Frankfurt 2012–13 (Regensburg, 2012), pp. 127–44.

[16] Cotton was identified in a female grave at Bülach St Laurentius, Kt. Zürich (Switzerland): H. Amrein et al., 'Neue Untersuchungen zum Frauengrab des 7. Jahrhunderts in der reformierten Kirche von Bülach (Kanton Zürich)', *Zeitschrift für Schweizerische Archäologie und Kunstgeschichte*, 56 (1999): 73–114, esp. pp. 95–6, Fig. 32–3.

[17] Cf. I. Schneebauer-Meißner, 'Technologische Untersuchungen an Goldtextilien des frühen Mittelalters', *Bericht der Bayerischen Bodendenkmalpflege*, 53 (2012): 271–336; C. Stiefel-Ludwig, 'Merowingerzeitliche Goldtextilien in Süd- und Westdeutschland im sozialen Kontext', *Bericht der Bayerischen Bodendenkmalpflege*, 53 (2012): 337–40.

[18] J. Drauschke, 'Halbmondförmige Goldohrringe aus bajuwarischen Frauengräbern – Überlegungen zu Parallelen und Provenienz', in F. Daim and J. Drauschke (eds.), *Byzanz – das Römerreich im Mittelalter* (Mainz, 2010), pp. 175–88.

[19] Fleury and France-Lanord, *Trésors mérovingiens*, pp. 272–3. A more or less contemporaneous gold cross with filigree decoration belonged to the inhumation of sarcophagus XX in Saint-Victor, Marseille (*Vie et mort à Marseille à la fin de l'Antiquité*, dir. F. Boyer [Marseille 1987] pp. 83–5). Similar golden pectoral crosses are well known 'Byzantine' types, but only two pieces from Histria (first half of sixth century) show stronger similarities to the piece from Saint-Denis: I. Barnea, *Christian Art in Romania*, vol. I: *3rd–6th Centuries* (Bucharest, 1979), pp. 228–9, pl. 96. Thus, a Mediterranean origin cannot be determined with certainty.

Communication and Exchange 13

Figure 1.1 Pair of Byzantine crescent golden earrings, grave 11 from Steinhöring (Bavaria). Original height ca. 3.2 cm. © Archäologische Staatssammlung Munich, Photograph: M. Eberlein.

Germany), dated to the third quarter of the seventh century.[20] One rare example of a *fibula* is a rectangular brooch from grave 403 in Mengen (Baden-Württemberg), which was once the central part of a diadem but which was then transformed into a *fibula* and used in a secondary way in the Merovingian world.[21]

Byzantine belt buckles found their way to the West from the end of the fifth century onwards and continued to be used in Merovingian contexts until the seventh century. Early buckles are usually of gold or gilded bronze with rectangular, D- or kidney-shaped fittings in cloisonné style; alternatively, buckles made from minerals as well as few other special forms are known.[22] It is likely that some buckles were manufactured in

---

[20] Cf. Y. Petrina, 'Kreuze mit geschweiften Hasten und kreisförmigen Hastenenden', in F. Daim and J. Drauschke (eds.), *Byzanz – das Römerreich im Mittelalter* (Mainz, 2010), pp. 257–66.
[21] S. Brather-Walter, 'Neues zu einem alten Fund – Die byzantinische "Fibel" von Mengen im Breisgau', *Archäologische Nachrichten aus Baden*, 76/77 (2008): 70–1.
[22] H. W. Böhme, 'Der Frankenkönig Childerich zwischen Attila und Aëtius. Zu den Goldgriffspathen der Merowingerzeit', in C. Dobiat (ed.), *Festschrift für Otto-Herman Frey zum 65. Geburtstag* (Marburg, 1994), pp. 69–110; M. Schulze-Dörrlamm, *Byzantinische Gürtelschnallen und Gürtelbeschläge im Römisch-Germanischen Zentralmuseum*, 2nd edn (Mainz, 2009), types A1–A7; A9–A12; B1–B14 and C1–C19.

the western Mediterranean,[23] and some are also known to have been imitated by local Frankish craftsmen. Looking at the later buckles, a change of fashion is visible as now cast copper alloy types replace the golden or gilt buckles with cloisonné-style fittings.[24]

Like the objects mentioned so far, Byzantine silver spoons have been part of the personal endowment of the deceased and were often worn like other items of costume. For the pieces found north and west of the Alps, a secular interpretation is more favourable than a Christian or liturgical one.[25] They mainly represent the types Isola Rizza, Desana, Barbing Irlmauth and Lampsakos C,[26] and were found, in so far as we are able to reconstruct their context, in very richly furnished burials. These can be dated, with few exceptions, to around AD 500. Most of them are thought to be either of Italian or western Balkan origin, or to have been produced in a late Roman context in provincial workshops with only few exceptions coming from the eastern Mediterranean, but those have been found outside the Frankish realms (e.g. the Sutton Hoo ship burial).

Craftsmen of different origins were all considered as possible producers of the swords with garnet cloisonné fittings and other items with garnet decoration from King Childeric's grave at Tournai (†481/2).[27] At some point, it was generally accepted that they had been manufactured in central Europe,[28] but Birgit Arrhenius suggested in her study on Merovingian garnet jewellery that the swords had a Constantinopolitan provenance.[29] Finally, Horst Wolfgang Böhme postulated a Mediterranean origin for

---

[23] For examples, see M. Kazanski, 'Les Plaques-boucles méditerranéennes des Ve–VIe siècles', *Archéologie Médiévale* (Paris) 24 (1994): 137–98, esp. pp. 150–1 types I.3.K, pl. 11, 18, 23.5.

[24] Schulze-Dörrlamm, *Byzantinische Gürtelschnallen*, passim.

[25] S. R. Hauser, *Spätantike und frühbyzantinische Silberlöffel* (Münster, 1992), pp. 82–7, quoting earlier studies.

[26] After Hauser, *Spätantike und frühbyzantinische Silberlöffel*. For additional finds, see J. Drauschke, 'Zur Herkunft und Vermittlung "byzantinischer Importe" der Merowingerzeit in Nordwesteuropa', in Sebastian Brather (ed.), *Zwischen Spätantike und Frühmittelalter: Archäologie des 4. bis 7. Jahrhunderts im Westen* (Berlin and New York, 2008), pp. 367–423, here p. 381, n. 40; S. Fischer, M. H. Graf, C. Fossurier, and M. Châtelet, 'An Inscribed Silver Spoon from Ichtratzheim (Bas-Rhin)', *Journal of Archaeology and Ancient History*, 11 (2014): 2–25.

[27] H. Arbmann, 'Les Épées du tombeau de Childéric', *Årsberättelse* (Lund) (1947/8): 97–137, esp. pp. 124–7 with a summary of earlier publications. Recent studies: D. Quast, *Das Grab des fränkischen Königs Childerich in Tournai und die Anastasis Childerici von Jean-Jaques Chifflet aus dem Jahre 1655* (Mainz, 2015); esp. the coins: S. Fischer and L. Lind, 'The Coins in the Grave of King Childeric', *Journal of Archaeology and Ancient History*, 14 (2015): 2–36.

[28] K. Böhner, 'Germanische Schwerter des 5./6. Jahrhunderts', *Jahrbuch des Römisch-Germanischen Zentralmuseums*, 34 (1987): 411–90, here pp. 421–51 (types B and C2–6).

[29] B. Arrhenius, *Merovingian Garnet Jewellery: Emergence and Social Implications* (Stockholm, 1985), pp. 98–101.

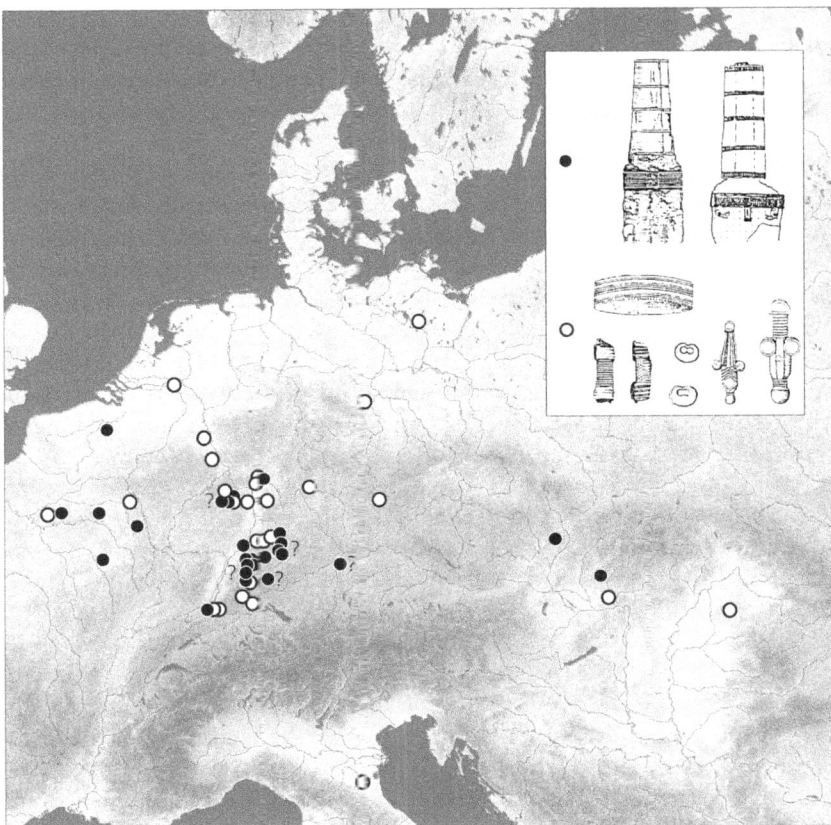

Figure 1.2 Distribution of early Merovingian *spathae* with gilt handles and/or cloisonné fittings. ©V. Kassühlke, RGZM, redrawn after Böhme, *Der Frankenkönig Childerich* Fig. 7, with additions.

most *spathae* with gilt handles and other elaborate swords with cloisonné fittings (Fig. 1.2).[30] Today, the question of which swords can be identified as Mediterranean products is still hotly debated.[31]

The grave of Childeric also contained a small, narrow *scramasax*. Seaxes were common in the region between the lower Danube and eastern France in the second half of the fifth century which may be

---

[30] Böhme, *Der Frankenkönig Childerich*, pp. 100–1.
[31] Cf. S. Brather, 'Lokale Herren um 500. Rang und Macht im Spiegel der Bestattungen', in M. Meier and St Patzold (eds.), *Chlodwigs Welt. Organisation von Herrschaft um 500* (Stuttgart, 2014), pp. 567–607, esp. pp. 580–2, Table 2, Figs. 4 and 6.

explained by the activities of the Huns. Their development in an equestrian nomadic environment is out of question, but considering of some parallels from the Byzantine Empire their use in a Byzantine military context and a subsequent transfer to the West was postulated. At the moment, however, this is anything but clear.[32]

Helmets of the Baldenheim type are rare finds, known primarily from warrior graves of the late fifth and sixth century from the *Barbaricum*, whereas the examples in the Mediterranean littoral have been found in settlement contexts. Concluding a long discussion about their origin, Joachim Werner identified them as Byzantine officer helmets in light of new finds from the destruction layers of early Byzantine cities in the Balkans. This point of view was adopted by several scholars.[33] In recent studies, a stronger typological differentiation of the helmets was carried out, resulting in only one type yielding a possible eastern Mediterranean origin and in the assumption of an Italian provenance for most other pieces.[34] A current research project at the Römisch-Germanisches Zentralmuseum is dedicated to identifying the origin of the raw material of these. Preliminary results seem to indicate the use of resources from Asia Minor, which hints at a production place in the heartland of the Byzantine Empire.[35]

Late antique amphoras and fine wares of the Mediterranean are crucial for the reconstruction of trade and exchange routes, but the archaeological record of these commodities in northern Gaul and the regions east of the Rhine disappears completely with the beginning of the sixth century. They are found, however, in the environs of southern ports like Marseille in small quantities until the early eighth century.[36] In north-west

[32] D. Quast, 'Auf der Suche nach fremden Männern: Die Herleitung schmaler Langsaxe vor dem Hintergrund der alamannisch-donauländischen Kontakte der zweiten Hälfte des 5. Jahrhunderts', in T. Fischer, G. Precht and J. Tejral (eds.), *Germanen beiderseits des spätantiken Limes*, X. Internationales Symposium 'Grundprobleme der Frühgeschichtlichen Entwicklung im Nördlichen Mitteldonaugebiet', Xanten 1997 (Cologne, 1999), pp. 115–28. With doubts about a Byzantine provenance based on convincing arguments: A. P. Kiss, 'Huns, Germans, Byzantines? The Origins of the Narrow Bladed Long Seaxes', *Acta Archaeologica Carpathica*, 49 (2014): 111–44, esp. p. 137.

[33] J. Werner, 'Neues zur Herkunft der frühmittelalterlichen Spangenhelme vom Baldenheimer Typus', *Germania*, 66 (1988): 521–8; D. Quast, *Die merowingerzeitlichen Grabfunde aus Gültlingen (Stadt Wildberg, Kreis Calw)* (Stuttgart, 1993), p. 30.

[34] F. Stein, 'Die Spangenhelme von Pfeffingen und Gammertingen – Überlegungen zur Bestimmung ihrer Herstellungsräume', *Acta Praehistorica et Archaeologica*, 35 (2003): 41–61; M. Vogt, *Spangenhelme. Baldenheim und verwandte Typen* (Mainz, 2006).

[35] Ch. Miks and F. Ströbele, 'Materialanalysen und Überlegungen zu den möglichen Fertigungsorten frühmittelalterlicher Spangenhelme des Typs Baldenheim' (in print).

[36] P. Reynolds, *Trade in the Western Mediterranean, AD 400–700: The Ceramic Evidence* (Oxford, 1995); D. Pieri, *Le Commerce du vin Oriental à l'époque byzantine (Ve–VIIe siècles): Le témoignage des amphores en Gaule* (Beyrouth, 2005).

Europe, flasks (*ampullae*) used as pilgrimage 'souvenirs' are well known, but unfortunately most of them come from museum collections and only a few derive from secure archaeological contexts,[37] so their information value concerning exchange processes is insignificant.

Silver vessels constitute another category of Byzantine items frequently 'exported' to barbarian regions, but only two finds can be named from the seventh-century Merovingian kingdoms: One silver plate from the Schelde river and two others that formed a deposit, found in Valdonne in southern France (Bouches-du-Rhône). The first one can be dated securely to the 660s due to stamps of Constans II (r. 641–68). The character of the Valdonne pieces is ambiguous, with at least one plate almost certainly produced in a Merovingian context, which may be dated to the second quarter of the seventh century.[38]

In contrast to the objects mentioned so far, so-called 'Coptic' copper alloy vessels are frequently found, especially in the Austrasian part of the kingdom, but also between Italy and Anglo-Saxon England. It has become generally accepted that the cast vessels originated in the eastern Mediterranean with a preference for Egypt, but a production in the western Mediterranean cannot be excluded for some types.[39] For example, a special type of jug that has mainly been found in the area of the Iberian peninsula and southern France was recently identified as a local product.[40] A different technological tradition is expressed by hammered copper alloy vessels that have been used broadly in the Byzantine Empire from the Balkans through Asia Minor to Palestine.[41] It

---

[37] For example, a context in Faris from the sixth century: P. Linscheid, 'Neues zur Verbreitung von Menasampullen nördlich der Alpen', in R. Harreither, P. Philippe, P. Renate and P. Andreas (eds.), *Akten des XIV. Internationalen Kongresses für Christliche Archäologie* (Vienna and PIAC Rome, 2006), pp. 911–13; W. Anderson, 'Menas Flasks in the West: Pilgrimage and Trade at the End of Antiquity', *Ancient West and East*, 6 (2007): 221–43.

[38] E. Cruikshank Dodd, 'Byzantine Silver Stamps: Supplement I – New Stamps from the Reigns of Justin II and Constans II', *Dumbarton Oaks Papers*, 18 (1964): 237–48, at p. 241, no. 78.1; J. Werner, 'Arbalco (Haribaldus), ein merowingischer *vir inluster* aus der Provence?', in P. Bastien, F. Dumas, H. Huvelin and C. Morrisson (eds.), *Melanges de numismatique d'archeologie et d'histoire offerts a Jean Lafaurie* (Paris, 1980), pp. 257–63.

[39] Recent publications: P. Périn, 'La Vaisselle de bronze dite "copte" dans les royaumes romano-germaniques d'Occident: État des la question', *Antiquité Tardive*, 13 (2005): 85–97; K. Werz, 'Sogenanntes *koptisches* Buntmetallgeschirr (Konstanz, 2005), pp. 65–6; Drauschke, *Handel und Geschenk*, pp. 126–35 and 342, list 6. For results of scientific analyses: H. Dannheimer, 'Zur Herkunft der "koptischen" Bronzegefäße der Merowingerzeit', *Bayerische Vorgeschichtsblätter*, 44 (1979): 123–47.

[40] M. Beghelli and J. Pinar Gil, 'Corredo e arredo liturgico nelle chiese tra VIII e IX secolo. Suppellettili antiche e moderne, locali e importate tra archeologia, fonti scritte e fonti iconografiche', *Jahrbuch des Römisch-Germanischen Zentralmuseums*, 60 (2013): 697–762.

[41] B. Pitarakis, 'Une production caractéristique de cruches en alliage cuivreux (VIe–VIIIe siècles): Typologie, techniques et diffusion', *Antiquité Tardive*, 13 (2005): 11–27.

is interesting to note that, apart from a very few examples, they have not been exported to the West.[42]

Byzantine coins are quite frequent, with over 400 pieces from northern Gaul and eastern territories being uncovered. Gold coins in particular were found in contexts where they had been deposited as jewellery or used as *obolus* within the graves, so their presence cannot be read as evidence for the use of these coins as currency. To compare their frequency with the general development of minting and monetarisation in Byzantium, the average number of coin finds per year under a special emperor was calculated. The resulting statistic (Fig. 1.3) shows that *siliquae* are a short-lived phenomenon under Justinian I and Justin II, issued in Italian mints. The *solidi* and other gold coins peak for the rules of Justinian I, Tiberius and Phokas, with a clear break under Heraclius around AD 626/9. Copper coins remain on a rather stable level, but also have a break after Heraclius' reign.[43]

The Merovingian finds seem to reflect some general trends of Byzantine coinage, but some crucial characteristics are missing, e.g., the continued minting of gold coins in Constantinople or the general break of copper-coin minting in the Byzantine Empire only from 668 onwards.[44] If the frequency of Byzantine coins from the Merovingian realms does not only reflect general trends of grave furnishing or phases of few coin remelting, for example, pieces of gold jewellery, then there are also clear differences compared with the money circulation in the Byzantine Empire, and therefore the 'export' of coins cannot be explained by a frequent and normal exchange only.

---

[42] S. Musteaţă, 'Unele concretizări privind vasul de metal din tezaurul monetar de la Horgeşti, jud. Bacău, România', in S. Musteaţă, A. Popa and J.-P. Abraham (eds.), *Archeologia între ştiinţă, politică şi economia de piaţă* (Chişinău, 2010), pp. 99–127.

[43] The analysis is mainly based on the catalogues of J. Lafaurie and C. Morrisson, 'La Pénétration des monnaies Byzantines en Gaule Mérovingienne et Visigotique du VIe au VIIIe siècle', *Revue Numismatique*, 6, ser. 29 (1987): 38–98; J. F. Fischer, *Der Münzumlauf und Münzvorrat im Merowingerreich. Eine Untersuchung der zeitgenössischen Münzfunde aus dem Gebiet des Reihengräberkreises* (Freiburg, 2001), cf. also J. Drauschke, 'Byzantinische Münzen des ausgehenden 5. bis beginnenden 8. Jahrhunderts in den östlichen Regionen des Merowingerreiches', in M. Wołoszyn (ed.), *Byzantine Coins in Central Europe between the 5th and 10th Century* (Kraków, 2009), pp. 279–323; Drauschke, *Handel und Geschenk*, pp. 135–46, 347–51 list 7.

[44] Cf. C. Morrisson, 'Byzantine Money: Its Production and Circulation', in A. E. Laiou (ed.), *The Economic History of Byzantium: From the Seventh through the Fifteenth Century* (Washington, DC, 2002), pp. 909–66, here pp. 917–20, Figs 6.1–6.5.

Communication and Exchange

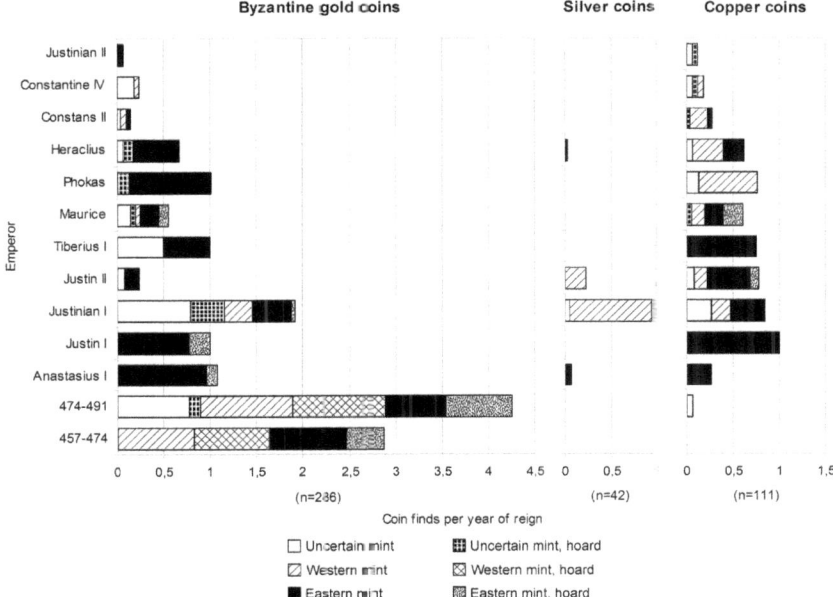

Figure 1.3 Diagram showing the relative frequency of Byzantine coins found in the Frankish territory (except southern Gaul and Aquitaine). The coins are classified by the material, the place of mint in the East or the West of the Mediterranean, and the context (grave/stray find, hoard). © J. Drauschke, RGZM.

Oriental Objects

As I have shown, the variety of Byzantine or eastern Mediterranean objects that reached the Frankish realms during the sixth and seventh centuries was indeed great, but the total number of objects remained rather small with only copper alloy vessels and coins detected in larger quantities. One might conclude that only very sporadic or coincidental contacts existed with the eastern Mediterranean region. It is, in fact, quite the opposite, as can be proven by a large group of 'Oriental' artefacts that must have arrived in the West through the eastern Mediterranean area or the Byzantine Empire. Here object groups that cannot be strictly classified as 'Byzantine' or east Mediterranean are nevertheless subsumed, having originated to the south and east. In many cases, their origin has been discovered with the help of scientific analyses.

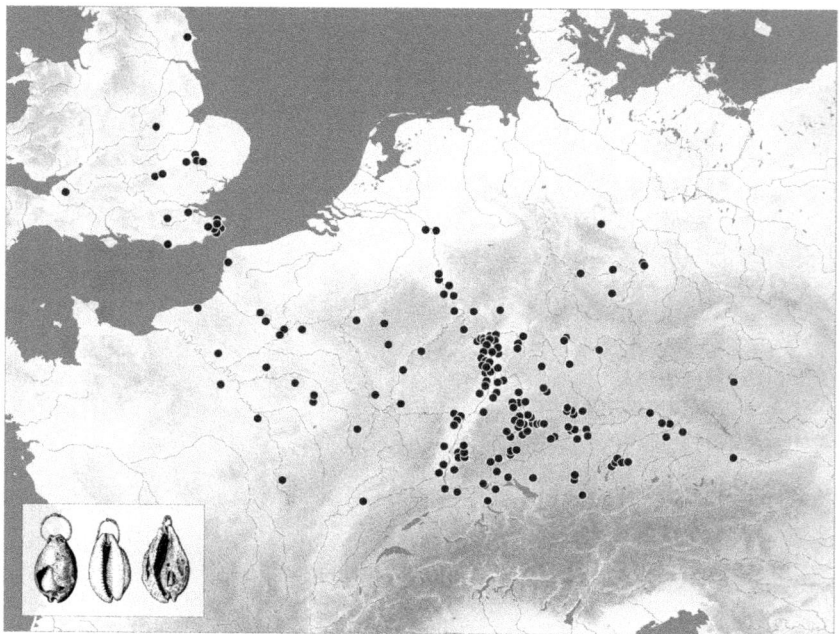

Figure 1.4 Distribution of cowrie shells between Anglo-Saxon England and Austrasia, sixth/seventh century. © M. Ober, RGZM, redrawn after Banghard, *Kaurischnecke* Fig. 180 with additions.

Due to the selective nature of archaeological evidence, Oriental artefacts are mainly known from the furnishings of women's graves and belonged to female costume. Cowrie shells, for example, were usually carried as amulets within a bail hanging down from the belt. Species from the Indian Ocean (*Cypraea tigris*) and the Red Sea (*Cypraea pantherina*) are known, but an archaeo-zoological investigation carried out some years ago proved the *Cypraea pantherina* type to be the common species used in Merovingian contexts.[45] Their distribution in western Europe stretches all over the area where row grave cemeteries can be found and more or similar equal 'fashions' can be deduced from the burial furnishings (Fig. 1.4).

[45] K. Banghard, 'Kauris im merowingerzeitlichen Europa. Ein Beitrag zur frühmittelalterlichen Fernhandelsgeschichte', *Münstersche Beiträge zur antiken Handelsgeschichte*, 20 (2001): 15–21; A. Lennartz, 'Die Meeresschnecke Cypraea als Amulett im Frühen Mittelalter: Eine Neubewertung', *Bonner Jahrbücher*, 204 (2004): 163–232; Drauschke, *Handel und Geschenk*, pp. 109–11.

Communication and Exchange 21

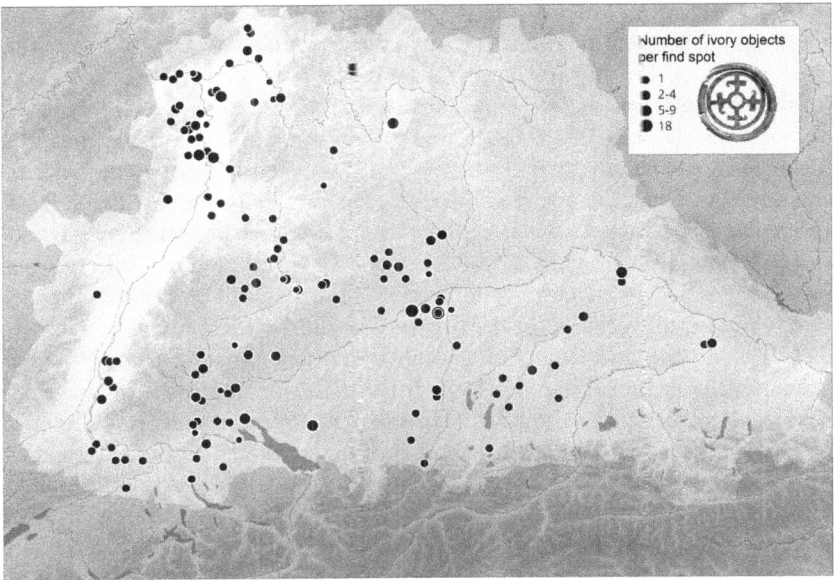

Figure 1.5 Distribution of ivory rings in Merovingian southern Germany. © M. Ober, RGZM, redrawn after Drauschke, *Handel und Geschenk*, Fig. 52.

Ivory occurs in north-west Europe mainly in the shape of rings, which served on the Continent as the enclosure rings of ornamented amulet discs that formed the end of the above-mentioned bails. Yet in Britain no such discs are found and ivory rings are interpreted as components of bags.[46] Analyses of the material confirm that they are made of African elephant ivory, which was probably imported from north-east Africa, converted in the eastern Mediterranean and then imported to middle and western Europe. The distribution of ivory rings in southern Germany alone is very dense, which can only be explained by a heavy inflow of the material (Fig. 1.5).[47]

---

[46] D. Renner, *Die durchbrochenen Zierscheiben der Merowingerzeit* (Mainz, 1970); Huggett, *Imported Grave Goods*, p. 69, Fig. 3; C. Hills, 'From Isidore to Isotopes: Ivory Rings in Early Medieval Graves', in H. Hamerow and A. MacGregor (eds.), *Image and Power in the Archaeology of Early Medieval Britain* (Oxford, 2001), pp. 131–46; Harris, Byzantium, p. 174, Fig. 61.

[47] J. Drauschke and A. Banerjee, 'Zur Identifikation, Herkunft und Verarbeitung von Elfenbein in der Merowingerzeit', *Archäologisches Korrespondenzblatt*, 37 (2007): 109–28; Drauschke, *Handel und Geschenk*, pp. 119–23, Fig. 52.

Many Oriental objects are identifiable as jewellery. We must first mention red garnet, the precious stone most appreciated by the Merovingians. During the late fifth and the sixth centuries it could be found in the form of flat inlays in a variety of 'Merovingian' objects. As early as AD 600, this fashion was abandoned, and the use of garnets increased only slowly over the course of the seventh century. As several studies of the past decade demonstrate, the raw material first came from India and Sri Lanka and was replaced in the seventh century by garnets from Bohemia, at least in Middle Europe.[48] Simultaneously, the garnet fashion reached its peak in Britain and Scandinavia. The current project 'Weltweites Zellwerk' at the Römisch-Germanisches Zentralmuseum is dedicated to the question of the seventh-century garnet's origin.[49]

Some beads found especially in the Austrasian regions also have an 'Oriental' provenance: Cylindrical beads made from sepiolithe are known from early Merovingian periods and run out by the end of the sixth century. The material was also used for belt buckles.[50] Conversely, so-called 'mother-of-pearl-beads' only occur in Merovingian tombs of the seventh through to the beginning of the eighth century. Shells from the coasts of East Africa, the Red Sea or the eastern Mediterranean were the raw material for these discoid beads that were obviously treasured for their shining surface.[51]

Beginning with the second third of the sixth and throughout the seventh century, numerous almond-shaped amethyst beads are known

---

[48] Essential: S. Greiff, 'Naturwissenschaftliche Untersuchungen zur Frage der Rohsteinquellen für frühmittelalterlichen Almandingranatschmuck rheinfränkischer Provenienz', *Jahrbuch des Römisch-Germanischen Zentralmuseums*, 45 (1998): 599–646; D. Quast and U. Schüssler, 'Mineralogische Untersuchungen zur Herkunft der Granate merowingerzeitlicher Cloisonnéarbeiten', *Germania*, 78 (2000): 75–96. Recently: P. Périn and Th. Calligaro, 'Neue Erkenntnisse zum Arnegundegrab. Ergebnisse der Metallanalysen und der Untersuchungen organischer Überreste aus Sarkophag 49 der Basilika von Saint-Denis', *Acta Praehistorica et Archaeologica*, 39 (2007): 147–79, esp. pp. 162–7; H. A. Gilg, N. Gast, and T. Calligaro, 'Vom Karfunkelstein', in L. Wamser (ed.), *Karfunkelstein und Seide. Neue Schätze aus Bayerns Frühzeit* (Regensburg, 2010), pp. 87–100.

[49] S. Greiff, A. Hilgner, and D. Quast, *International Framework: Upheaval in the Cultural Meaning of Early Medieval Jewellery in Consideration of Economic History as well as Transfer of Technology and Ideas* (working title) (forthcoming).

[50] Drauschke, *Handel und Geschenk*, pp. 55–60.

[51] F. Siegmund and M. Weiß, 'Perlen aus Muschelscheibchen im merowingerzeitlichen Mitteleuropa', *Archäologisches Korrespondenzblatt*, 19 (1989): 297–307; A. Lennartz, 'Muschelperlen – Perlmutperlen – Schneckenperlen: Drei Namen für ein Phänomen?', in Ch. Keller, H. J. Roth, H. Eckhart, A. Lennartz, B. Steinbring, and V. Zavadil, *Certamina Archaeologica*, Festschrift H. Schnitzler (Bonn, 2000), pp. 191–202. For parallels from East Africa: M. Horton, *Shanga. the Archaeology of a Muslim Trading Community on the Coast of East Africa* (London, 1996), p. 323, Fig. 246, a–b.

from north-west Europe, usually used in necklaces. Of course, amethyst is also known from deposits in the West. But given that there are numerous finds of almost identical shaped amethyst beads in the eastern Mediterranean area, which are found primarily in Byzantine necklaces, it is more convincing to assume that they were produced around the eastern Mediterranean or beyond. Admittedly the deposits' location is not clear; also, no scientific analysis has thus far been used in an attempt to identify them. South Asia or north-east Africa and/or regions around the eastern Mediterranean are all appealing possibilities.[52]

An area of research that has seen rapid development in the past two decades is the scientific analysis of antique and medieval glass. As a result, more and more connections between glass products from different areas can be established. As a consequence, it was recently suggested that glass beads of the early Merovingian period were partly produced in Egypt, the Syro-Palestine coast and Mesopotamia, a majority originating from Mesopotamia, India and Sri Lanka.[53] Still further analyses seem to indicate that certain glass bead types of the seventh century could be imports from India.[54] If these results can be confirmed by further research, it would point to a continuous transport of goods with a South Asian provenance to the West throughout the seventh century. A different type of glass bead frequently found in women's necklaces in north-west Europe, also like the amethyst beads starting from the second third of the sixth century, are millefiori beads. They have been identified as imports, but the precise place of production is still being discussed, with suggestions ranging between Italy and even Egypt.[55] In this context, prismatic millefiori beads from the collection of the Flinders Petrie Museum in London are of special interest because they have been securely identified in different locations in Egypt and show ornaments nearly identical with those known from prismatic beads from Merovingian contexts.[56]

[52] J. Drauschke, 'Byzantine Jewellery? Amethyst Beads in East and West during the Early Byzantine Period', in Ch. Entwistle and N. Adams (eds.), *'Intelligible Beauty': Recent Research on Byzantine Jewellery* (London, 2010), pp. 50–60.

[53] Preliminary report: C. Pion and O. Vrielynck, 'Le Cimetière de Bossut-Gottechain (Belgique) et son implication dans l'établissement d'une nouvelle chronologie normalisée des perles en Gaule mérovingienne', *Bulletin de Liaison*, 38 (2014): 87–91.

[54] T. Sode, B. Gratuze and J. Lankton, 'Scandinavian Opaque Red or Orange Barrel-Shaped Beads from the 7th–8th Century: Evidence for Both Long Distance Trade and Local Fabrication', in Vitrocentre Romont (ed.), *20e Congrès de l'Association Internationale pour l'Histoire du Verre, Programme et Résumés* (Romont and Fribourg, 2015), p. 176.

[55] For the discussion, see Drauschke, *Handel und Geschenk*, pp. 151–5.

[56] Necklaces with at least thirty prismatic millefiori beads unearthed in El-Lahoun and perhaps Qaw el-Kebir/Antaeopolis: inventory numbers UC 6771, UC 6772, UC 6773, UC 74003, UC 74045, UC 74066, UC 74121, UC 74605. For all information I would like to thank very much Prof. Dr. Stephen Quirke, UCL London. For parallels from Merovingian graves, see, for example, A. Volkmann and C. Theune,

An eastern origin of this special type of millefiori beads that was in use mainly in the middle and the second half of the sixth century seems absolutely possible but should nevertheless be confirmed by scientific analyses.

The Chronological, Geographical, and Social Distribution of the Imports

It is possible to distinguish between two main phases of Byzantine/eastern Mediterranean and Oriental import to the Merovingian realms. During the early Merovingian period, mainly elaborate swords, early belt buckles with either cloisonné or other fittings, helmets and silver spoons, late forms of *amphorae* and fine wares can be proven, some of which extended, to some degree into the sixth century.[57] Concurrently, there are some object groups – sepiolithe and glass beads, coins and textiles – whose import begins during this same phase but runs on to later periods. The production places and places of origin are difficult to detect but must be assumed to have been in the Mediterranean area between Italy and the East. Very few exceptions – early red garnet was not included in imported objects but used for local products, glass beads and textiles like silk – could have an origin east of the early Byzantine Empire (Fig. 1.6).

The import of most of the material begins with the second third of the sixth century. It is not only the quantity of these objects that is surprising but also the fact that they still appear in graves as late as AD 700. This second phase of import can be divided into an early part during the sixth century dominated by red garnet and further object groups like cowries, ivory amethysts, etc., and a second part starting around AD 600, when copper alloy vessels and mother-of-pearl-beads come up and the red garnet runs out (Fig. 1.7).[58]

The general chronological development shown here (Fig. 1.8) is based on the import finds in Merovingian southern Germany and adjacent areas. The number of imports increases mainly from the second third of the sixth century onwards and reaches its zenith at the end of the sixth and the beginning of the seventh century. The statistics of the sixth century are dominated by graves containing items with red garnet decoration only. Obviously, the break-off at the beginning of the seventh century

'Merowingerzeitliche Millefioriperlen in Mitteleuropa', *Ethnographisch-Archäologische Zeitschrift*, 42 (2001): 521–53, esp. p. 529, Fig. 2,4 and U. Koch, *Das Reihengräberfeld bei Schretzheim* (Berlin, 1977), colour plate 6, no. M59–M62.

[57] Drauschke, *Handel und Geschenk*, pp. 175–6.
[58] Drauschke, *Handel und Geschenk*, pp. 176–82 with the separation of a third part (c) in the late Merovingian period due to the decreasing furnishing of the graves.

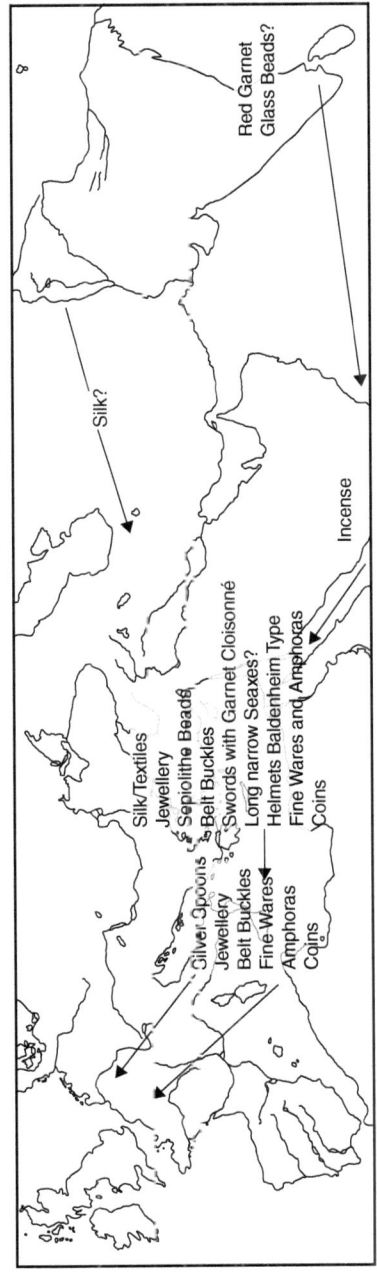

Figure 1.6 The provenance of archaeological proved Mediterranean, Byzantine and South Asian imports during the early Merovingian period. © J. Drauschke, RGZM, map by C. Pause, 'Die Franken und der Orient', *Rheinisches Landesmuseum Bonn*, 2 (1996), pp. 41–9 with additions.

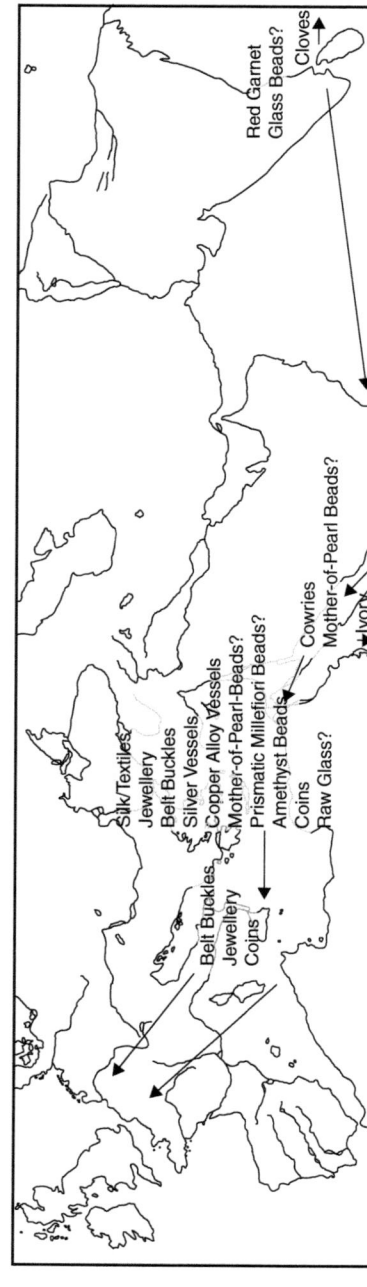

Figure 1.7 The provenance of archaeological proved Mediterranean, Byzantine and South Asian imports between the second third of the sixth and the early eighth centuries. © J. Drauschke, RGZM, map by C. Pause, *Die Franken und der Orient*, with additions.

Communication and Exchange

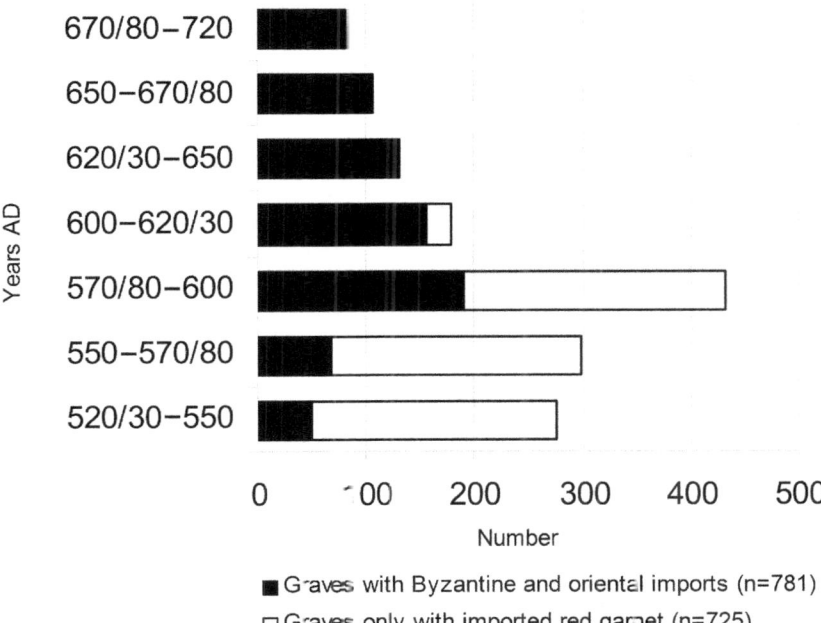

Figure 1.8 Chronological development of graves from southern Germany containing eastern Mediterranean/Byzantine and Oriental imports from the sixth until the early eighth century. © J. Drauschke, RGZM.

was not caused by general disturbances of exchange as the import of all other object groups continues, so a more finely tuned picture may be achieved by concentrating on these. Even accounting for the constant decrease of the total number of graves with imports during the seventh century, there are still over eighty from around AD 700. This seems to be a small number compared with the one for a century earlier, but it must be taken into account that in late Merovingian times the furnishing of the graves declines rapidly, and, as a result, the number of securely dated late Merovingian graves only reaches half of the amount of the graves datable to around AD 600. This effect was proven for other regions of the Merovingian realms, such as the Rhineland.[59] Thus, the percentage of graves with such imports remains more or less the same between AD 600 and 700. As a result, in my opinion, the late imports cannot be explained

[59] F. Siegmund, *Alemannen und Franken* (Berlin, 2000), p. 89, Fig. 3.

in terms of residual finds from earlier periods only but instead as clear signs of constant transactions of exchange.[60]

As far as the geographical distribution is concerned, imports reached Austrasia in particular, but Italy, England and Scandinavia are also known to have yielded frequent finds. As the objects are bound to the spread of row grave cemeteries, it cannot be concluded that the regions outside their main distribution, e.g., in some parts of Neustria and Aquitaine, did not take part in the international exchange. Perhaps the number of imports is limited there, simply because the main archaeological source (i.e. the graves with their furnishings) is less frequent. A detailed analysis conducted in southern Germany indicated that the main distribution patterns did not change from the middle of the sixth until the time around AD 700.[61]

Byzantine/eastern Mediterranean and Oriental imports are very often seen as 'luxury' items indicating the high social status of those people who have been buried with them. Some of the above-mentioned object groups are obviously of high value, especially splendour swords, helmets, silver spoons, silk textiles, etc., and it is an interesting though expectable result that they belonged mainly to the grave furnishings of high-status burials. On the other hand, a statistical analysis of the finds from southern Germany shows that between the second third of the sixth and the second third of the seventh century many other exotic objects – cowries, amethysts, brooches with red-garnet cloisonné, and even ivory rings – have also been found in graves that cannot be ranked as belonging to individuals of a high social or economic status.[62] The inflow of imports also reached the 'middle class' which must be taken into account when thinking about the possible distribution mechanisms.

Mediterranean Imports: Historical and Archaeological Sources Compared

The transfer of Mediterranean goods to the north can also be traced in the written sources that have been repeatedly analysed in this context. This is how we know about different spices (e.g., pepper, cloves, cinnamon, ginger, caraway, etc.), incense and other flavours, fruits like olives, dates or figs, almonds, pistachios, rice, papyrus, textiles, oil, and wine from Greece and the Syrian-Palestine coast that have all been exported to the Franks mainly through the ports of southern Gaul.[63] Some could

---

[60] Drauschke, *Handel und Geschenk*, pp. 182–4.
[61] Drauschke, *Handel und Geschenk*, pp. 179–81, Figs. 77–80.
[62] Drauschke, *Handel und Geschenk*, pp. 189–99.
[63] Collected after A. Verhulst, 'Der Handel im Merowingerreich: Gesamtdarstellung nach schriftlichen Quellen', *Antikvariskt Arkiv 39 = Early Medieval Studies*, 2 (1970): 2–54,

also have come from the western and not from or via the eastern Mediterranean. Except for few examples, the Mediterranean products known from archaeology and those known from historical sources do not overlap. Additionally, some raw materials must be considered that obviously have been used for the production of objects in the Frankish regions but cannot be proven in the historical or archaeological record.[64]

Altogether, a broad collection of eastern Mediterranean, Byzantine and Oriental goods that reached the Merovingian kingdoms can be compiled, even in a period when diplomatic contacts cannot be proven anymore using the historical sources. A last Byzantine embassy reached Dagobert I (r. 629/32–9) at the Frankish court in Paris in AD 634. What caused the long break that stretched until 756 is still unclear.[65] But connections on the diplomatic top level are not necessarily indicative of the relations in other areas of cultural activities. Bede mentions the case of Archbishop Theodore of Tarsus, who travelled from Rome to his new province of Canterbury through Gaul together with his companion Hadrian in 667. Ebroin the Neustrian mayor of the palace stopped them and prevented Hadrian from continuing his journey, because – to follow Bede's assumption – he suspected Hadrian of delivering a message from the Byzantine emperor to the kings of Britain that was directed against the Frankish court.[66] Stefan Esders concluded recently that this episode is able to show how connected the Mediterranean world still was even with regions far beyond its borders during the second half of the seventh century.[67] This connectivity can be proven by further sources, too. A privilege granted by King Dagobert I for Saint-Denis and another one granted by King Chlothar III (c. 650–73) for the monastery of Corbie allow, among other things, the access to oil and exotic commodities like special spices and papyrus from royal workshops in Marseille and

---

esp. p. 24; D. Schwärzel, *Handel und Verkehr des Merowingerreiches nach den schriftlichen Quellen* (Marburg, 1983), pp. 2–6; D. Claude, *Untersuchungen zu Handel und Verkehr der vor- und frühgeschichtlichen Zeit in Mittel- und Nordeuropa II: Der Handel im westlichen Mittelmeer während des Frühmittelalters* (Göttingen, 1985), pp. 83–95; H. Pirenne, *Mohammed und Karl der Große* (Frankfurt, 1985), p. 68.

[64] For example, sulphur and mercury for goldsmithing, soda for glassmaking: Drauschke, *Handel und Geschenk*, pp. 35–6.
[65] Drauschke, 'Diplomatie und Wahrnehmung', pp. 261–2.
[66] Beda Venerabilis, *Historia ecclesiastica gentis Anglorum*. Beda der *Ehrwürdige, Kirchengeschichte des Englischen Volkes*, ed. G. Spitzbart (Darmstadt, 1982), vol. IV, p. 1.
[67] S. Esders, 'Konstans II. (641–63), die Sarazenen und die Reiche des Westens. Ein Versuch über politisch-militärische und ökonomisch-finanzielle Verflechtungen im Zeitalter eines mediterranen Weltkriegs', in J. Jarnut and J. Strothmann (eds.), *Die Merowingischen Monetarmünzen als Quelle zum Verständnis des 7. Jahrhunderts in Gallien* (Paderborn, 2013), pp. 189–241, here pp. 189–90 and 211.

Fos-sur-Mer. These privileges have been confirmed again and again until the end of the seventh century, and it is believed that they remained in effect during this time, but probably not in the eighth century.[68] They show that Mediterranean goods still reached northern Gaul in the late Merovingian period, although this was perhaps now limited to privileged institutions and persons.

Mediterranean Imports: Their Transfer to and their Distribution within the Frankish Kingdoms

The detailed contextual analysis of the goods imported from and via the eastern Mediterranean provides us with crucial insights about their value and social implications, their widespread geographical distribution and their frequency on the background of the chronological development. For the purpose of identifying the possible mechanisms that were responsible for their transport, it is necessary to consider on the one hand the circumstances of long-distance exchange active in the Mediterranean since late antiquity and, on the other hand, the exchange forms known from the Frankish world.[69] Other than trade in a narrower sense, the latter might have included robbery and war booty, gift-giving between high-status clerics, aristocrats and other 'free' people, procedures of redistribution between individuals and institutions or within the emerging seigneurial systems, taxation and collection of tariffs.[70] All these mechanisms can be assigned to the categories of redistribution, reciprocity and market exchange (including trade) belonging to a model widely accepted and applied within anthropological studies.[71] But apart

---

[68] L. Levillain, *Examen critique des chartes mérovingiennes et carolingiennes de l'abbaye de Corbie* (Paris, 1902), p. 236, no 15; Gesta Dagoberti I. regis Francorum, in *Fredegarii et aliorum chronica. Vitae Sanctorum*, ed. B. Krusch. *MGH SS rer. Merov.* II (Hanover, 1888), pp. 396–425, here p. 406 cap. 18 (Saint-Denis). Claude, *Handel im westlichen Mittelmeer*, p. 75, nn. 36, 38; S. T. Loseby, 'Marseille and the Pirenne Thesis, II: "Ville Morte"', in I. L. Hansen and Ch. Wickham (eds.), *The Long Eighth Century* (Leiden, 2000), pp. 167–93, esp. pp. 186–9.

[69] Recently with previous literature: J.-M. Carrié, 'Were Late Roman and Byzantine Economies Market Economies?', in C. Morrisson (ed.), *Trade and Markets in Byzantium* (Washington, DC, 2012), pp. 13–26.

[70] Cf. Verhulst, 'Handel im Merowingerreich' and the comprehensive compilation by D. Claude, 'Aspekte des Binnenhandels im Merowingerreich auf Grund der Schriftquellen', in K. Düwel, H. Jahnkuhn, E. Ebel, H. Siems, and D. Timpe, *Untersuchungen zu Handel und Verkehr der vor- und frühgeschichtlichen Zeit in Mittel- und Nordeuropa III: Der Handel des frühen Mittelalters* (Göttingen, 1985), pp. 9–99, esp. pp. 10–14.

[71] J. Jensen, 'Wirtschaftsethnologie', in H. Fischer (ed.), *Ethnologie. Einführung und Überblick*, 3rd edn (Berlin and Hamburg, 1992), pp. 119–47, esp. 134–43; see also: C. Renfrew and P. Bahn, *Archaeology: Theories, Methods and Practice* (London, 1991), p. 310. For a survey of different exchange models discussed in archaeology, see R. Hodges, *Dark Age Economics: A New Audit* (Bristol, 2012), pp. 20–40.

from the distribution of goods using a concept of exchange, objects could have been transported over long distances by individuals, not necessarily with any intention to distribute or to exchange them. This, of course, applies particularly to migrations or exogamous procedures, as well as by itinerant craftsmen.

To conclude, the variety of possible distribution mechanisms is enormous. I would suggest the following method of classification for imports: the crucial factors driving the import of high-value objects like splendour swords, helmets, precious belt buckles, silver spoons, silver (and perhaps some copper alloy) vessels, silk and other exotic textiles, and jewellery, could have been gift exchange, personal mobility (such as by mercenaries), migration, and war booty. Some of the gold coins could have reached the Franks in the form of *subsidia*. Alternatively, imports known in high amounts like cowries, ivory objects, red garnets, amethysts, certain glass bead types, sepiolithe and mother-of-pearl beads, some of the coins and most of the copper alloy vessels seem to have been traded commodities.

It seems very improbable that merchants who travelled over the Alps or along the Rhône sold their goods by roaming from village to village, in order to exchange gemstones, cowries and ivory for the surplus products of rural activities. It seems more plausible to consider urban settlements and central places in their hinterland, perhaps also in the regions east of the Rhine, as destinations. Here one might expect to obtain an adequate price and high demand for Mediterranean goods. The subsequent redistribution of the objects from these central locations led to the distribution patterns we know from the archaeological record.[72]

The evidence of these imports points to patterns of continuous exchange and trade in the Mediterranean and beyond at least until the end of the seventh century.[73] The number of imported goods decreases jointly with the transport within the Mediterranean, but it is nevertheless possible to identify some continuity of small-scale exchange between the regions. On the other hand, it is impossible to make any definite statements about the eighth century from the 'northern' archaeological perspective, because the main source – the furnishing of the graves – was abandoned during this period

---

[72] See Drauschke, *Handel und Geschenk*, pp. 267–71, Fig. 112. The merchants who sold the goods had purchased them presumably in the ports in Italy and southern France; different merchants were responsible for the transport over the Mediterranean Sea. Claude, *Handel im westlichen Mittelmeer*, pp. 121–4.

[73] Esp. for the seventh and eighth century: J. Drauschke, 'The Development of Diplomatic Contacts and Exchange between the Byzantine Empire and the Frankish Kingdoms until the Early Eighth Century', in A. Gnasso, E. E. Intagliata and T. J. MacMaster, (eds.), *The Long Seventh Century: Continuity and Discontinuity in an Age of Transition* (Oxford, 2015), pp. 107–33.

2 Anxiously Looking East: Burgundian Foreign Policy on the Eve of the Reconquest

Yaniv Fox

Under the events of the year 534, Marius of Avenches, a Frankish chronicler working in the late sixth century in Merovingian Burgundy, wrote the following: 'the kings of the Franks Childebert, Chlothar, and Theudebert occupied Burgundy and, with King Godomar having escaped, divided the kingdom amongst themselves'.[1] And so, with a banal and unimpassioned side note, we learn how the kingdom of the Gibichungs came to meet its end. The Chronicle then quickly moves on to greater things, namely the restitution of Africa to Roman dominion after ninety-two years of Vandal rule. This impressive feat, reports Marius, was achieved by the armies of Belisarius, who also managed to take prisoner the Vandal king, Gelimer, and bring him to Constantinople to be presented before Justinian, along with his wives and treasure. It is no coincidence that the two events appear side by side; Justinian's ambitious campaigns of reconquest are very much connected to the collapse of the Gibichungs. Soon, we know, Justinian's gaze would turn northward, plunging the Byzantine armies in the protracted carnage of the Gothic wars, whose countless horrors were chronicled so studiously by Procopius. Admittedly, Burgundy's whimper could not measure up to Italy's bang. Yet it should be recognised that these tremors were all part of a tortuous process of political change affecting the Mediterranean, one in which the military accomplishments of the Merovingians in Burgundy occupy an important place.

The Frankish campaigns of 534 brought down the Burgundian kingdom and placed its territories under direct Frankish dominion. Some three years later, Justinian seems also to have acknowledged that the Burgundian kingdom was a thing of the past, with which drew to a close a fascinating political experiment.[2] The kingdom of Burgundy

---

[1] Marius of Avenches, *Chronicon*, in J. Favrod (ed. and trans.), *La Chronique de Marius d'Avenches (455–581)* (Lausanne, 1993), p. 72, s.a. 534: 'Hoc consule reges Francorum Childebertus, Chlotarius et Theudebertus Burgundiam obtinuerunt et fugato Godomaro rege regnum ipsius diviserunt'.

[2] Interpreted by Wood as an extension of the imperial recognition of Ostrogothic cessions to the Franks in Provence. See I. N. Wood, 'The Burgundians and Byzantium', in A.

had been short-lived, but it was also a unique political attempt, anchored by two, very different, ideological justifications. The first was imperial: Gundobad, the main architect of the Burgundian kingdom, received his political education in the dying days of Roman dominion over the West, under the accomplished tutelage of his uncle, Ricimer.[3] Later, the ruling family drew its legitimacy from the Byzantine court. First and foremost, the Gibichungs saw themselves as Roman officials, and attempts to secure imperial titles were pursued with great urgency, especially by Sigismund.

The second was centred on the hereditary claim of the Gibichungs to rule. In this sense, Burgundy differed little from its neighbours – here, also, the Amals[4] and Hasdings[5] come to mind – who nurtured elaborate ideologies around the royal bloodline. Even before Gundobad implemented the lessons learnt in Ravenna to his court in Lyon, the successors of Gibich were on the path to forging a successor state along characteristic post-imperial lines. Gundioc and Chilperic were not kings, however: at least nominally, they were Roman officials bearing imperial titles that would later be awarded to their successors.

As far as the terminology of kingship went, receding Roman presence occasioned varied responses throughout the West, although it is possible to identify a shared reluctance among barbarian kings to employ ethnic qualifiers to their royal titles. As pointed out by Helmut Reimitz, while Clovis appeared – disparagingly, it seems – as *rex Francorum* in Cassiodorus's *Variae*, it is difficult to see him or his officials ever using this title, usually preferring a neutral *rex* instead.[6] Yet the Gibichung family adopted a somewhat different posture, which was clearly intended to highlight their imperial affiliation and to position them, in the words of Ian Wood, as 'legitimist Roman figures'.[7]

Fischer and I. N. Wood (eds.), *Western Perspectives on the Mediterranean: Cultural Transfer in Late Antiquity and the Early Middle Ages* (London, 2014), pp. 1–16, at p. 2.

[3] For some context, see A. Gillett, 'Rome, Ravenna and the Last Western Emperors', *Papers of the British School at Rome*, 69 (2001): 131–67; P. MacGeorge, *Late Roman Warlords* (Oxford, 2002), pp. 269–93.

[4] See A. Søby Christensen, *Cassiodorus, Jordanes and the History of the Goths: Studies in a Migration Myth* (Copenhagen, 2002), pp. 124–35 for the complicated image of Gothic ancestry that emerges from the sources.

[5] A. Merrills, 'The Secret of My Succession: Dynasty and Crisis in Vandal North Africa', *Early Medieval Europe*, 18 (2010): 135–59.

[6] Cassiodorus, *Variae*, II.40: 'Cum rex francorum conuiuii nostri fama pellectus a nobis citharoedum magnis precibus expetisset, sola ratione complendum esse promisimus, quod te eruditionis musicae peritum esse noueramus'. On this, see H. Reimitz, *History, Frankish Identity and the Framing of Western Ethnicity, 550–850* (Cambridge, 2015), p. 99, and particularly his discussion of this in the present volume.

[7] I. N. Wood, '*Gentes*, Kings and Kingdoms: The Emergence of States – The Kingdom of the Gibichungs', in H.-W. Goetz, J. Jarnut and W. Pohl (eds.), *Regna and Gentes: The*

In Sigismund's day at least, it seems as though the subjects of the Burgundian kings had not yet come to describe their shared community strictly in terms of imagined ancestry.[8] We may also safely assume that the non-Roman components of this society were diverse; Alamannic, Frankish, and Alan settlements were probably quite common. The band of followers that accompanied Gundobad from Italy and later formed the nucleus of his army would also have been rather heterogeneous, ethnically speaking. In this respect, the polity was defined less by forces that sought to promote a cultural synthesis of Burgundy's constituent *gentes* and more by an allegiance to the royal family and its particular brand of imperial legitimism.[9] Royal families acting as consolidating social agents were, of course, not particular to Burgundy; given sufficient time, its ruling classes would probably have realigned around the Gibichungs in ways that were reminiscent of other barbarian kingdoms. Indeed, it seems likely that Sigismund's religious endeavours were aimed to achieve such an outcome, in many ways emulating Clovis's role as *ecclesiae catholicae filius*. Clearly, any such processes never achieved fruition.

No surprises so far; Burgundy under the Gibichungs was indeed a society in flux, undergoing transformation from a Roman province to a post-Roman kingdom. Yet without analysing its unique circumstances, it would be difficult to explain how an unfortunate series of miscalculations had fractured the Gibichung project so irreparably. My purpose is therefore to examine the external pressures that determined Burgundian foreign policy after the death of Bishop Avitus of Vienne c. 518, and its ultimate failure to adequately cope with the severe regional challenges that lay ahead.[10]

As king, Sigismund came close to realising the future emblazoned on his father's propagandistic coinage, which carried the inscription PAX ET ABUNDANTIA.[11] His religious conversion, his sponsorship of Saint-Maurice d'Agaune, and other steps taken in preparation for his

---

Relationship between Late Antique and Early Medieval Peoples and Kingdoms in the Transformation of the Roman World (Leiden, 2003), pp. 243–70, at p. 252; I. N. Wood, 'The Latin Culture of Gundobad and Sigismund', in D. Hägermann, W. Haubrichs and J. Jarnut (eds.), *Akkulturation: Probleme einer germanisch-romanischen Kultursynthese in Spätantike und frühem Mittelalter* (Berlin and New York, 2004), pp. 367–80, at pp. 376–7.

[8] Wood, 'The Burgundians and Byzantium', p. 4.

[9] Wood, '*Gentes*, Kings and Kingdoms', pp. 255–7; P. Amory, 'Names, Ethnic Identity, and Community in Fifth- and Sixth-Century Burgundy', *Viator*, 25 (1994): 1–30, at p. 4.

[10] D. Shanzer and I. N. Wood (eds.), *Avitus of Vienne: Letters and Selected Prose* (Liverpool, 2002), p. 23.

[11] On *pax et abundantia*, see I. N. Wood, 'Liturgy in the Rhône Valley and the Bobbio Missal', in Y. Hen and R. Meens (eds.), *The Bobbio Missal: Liturgy and Religious Culture in Merovingian Gaul* (Cambridge, 2004), pp. 206–18, at p. 213.

ascent to the Burgundian throne were certainly celebrated by the ecclesiastical elite of Burgundy. The optimistic vision of a king united with his church and backed by the intercessory might of St Maurice, played well on all sides. Displays of this energetic alliance peaked at the church council convened in Épaone soon after Sigismund's ascent to the throne.

Yet soon after he took the reins of power, things began to go amiss. Relations with the episcopate quickly soured after the king came to the aid of his incestuous treasurer, Stephanus. The fact that this entire affair spiralled out of control seems, above all, to be connected to Avitus' absence from the ecclesiastical scene after his death. The Burgundian episcopate's self-imposed 'exile' to the island of Sardinia was the result of a breakdown in communication between the church and the court.[12] It is not that Sigismund was particularly inclined to overlook incestuous unions; his earlier legislation and the canons of Épaone clearly demonstrate this.[13] One is made to wonder, then, whether the presence of a seasoned prelate like Avitus, who had urged leniency in similar cases in the past,[14] could have averted this collision between the king and his episcopate.

Of course, the king's shocking decision to order the killing of Sigistrix, his son by Ostrogotho-Areagni, demands an explanation that goes beyond the simplistic causality supplied by Gregory of Tours. The *Histories* sees Sigismund's new wife, who whispered conspiracies into the ear of the king, as the instigator of the murder. Sigismund nevertheless receives the lion's share of Gregory's criticism for his eagerness to believe his wife. Before we dismiss Sigismund's filicidal paranoia as being completely irrational, however, we should at least entertain the notion that behind this choice lingered a very real fear of the Ostrogoths and of their ability to threaten Gibichung rule, a notion I shall return to shortly.

A year after the murder, the kingdom was severely shaken by a Frankish invasion led by Chlodomer, which left Sigismund, his wife, and his two other sons dead. Godomar, Gundobad's younger son, rallied the Burgundian army and repelled the Franks, but in so doing was able only to forestall the inevitable. Ten years later, the successors of Clovis returned; this time around, they were able to decisively crush the Burgundians

---

[12] Recently suggested to have been the monastery of Île-Barbe, not far from Lyons. See A. Kinney, 'An Appeal against Editorial Condemnation: A Reevaluation of the *Vita Apollinaris Valentinensis*', in V. Zimmerl-Panagl, L. J. Dorfbauer and C. Weidmann (eds.), *Edition und Erforschung lateinischer patristischer Texte: 150 Jahre CSEL: Festschrift für Kurt Smolak zum 70. Geburtstag* (Berlin, 2014), pp. 157–78, at pp. 164–6.

[13] I. N. Wood, 'Incest, Law and the Bible in Sixth-Century Gaul', *Early Medieval Europe*, 7 (1998): 291–303, at pp. 297–300

[14] Avitus, *Ep.* 18.

and bring the region under Merovingian rule. From the highpoint of Sigismund's reign to the final disintegration of the kingdom span not two decades, during which the efforts of Gundobad were undone. It would be easy to view Sigismund as inept and Godomar's efforts as quixotic, yet these are evaluations reached with the benefit of hindsight. Both kings were faced with an increasingly complicated set of external pressures, and we would do well to judge their actions in this light.

A good place to begin the discussion of Sigismund's policies would be the murder of Sigistrix, an event that had calamitous consequences for the Burgundian kingdom. Our most informative source regarding the affair is Gregory of Tours,[15] who reports that the plot was masterminded by Sigismund's new wife, the mother of his two younger boys, Gundobad and Gisclahad.[16] Sigistrix, who on a certain feast day saw the new queen adorned with his late mother's finery, rebuked her for having worn the garments, stating that they had belonged to 'her mistress'.[17] Whether we are meant to infer that the queen was a servant girl who caught the king's eye or whether Sigistrix was simply speaking figuratively is unclear.[18] The fact that, unlike her predecessor, she is not mentioned by name in any of our sources, does seem to support a servile background and would doubtless be in keeping with Gregory's pronounced distaste for 'rags to riches' stories.[19] While he had his own motives for allowing the plot to unfold this way, there seems to be more to this story than Gregory lets on.

The tale of Sigistrix's murder is counterpoised in the subsequent chapter with Clothild's plea to her children that they avenge the death of her parents, slain by Gundobad, by attacking his son's kingdom.[20] Gregory's aims in doing this, I would suggest, were threefold. The first was to justify the opportunistic attack on the Burgundians by revisiting Clothild's old grudge, although in reality it is very doubtful that she held Sigismund accountable in any way.[21] Casting the Burgundian king as a

---

[15] Although Marius of Avenches reports on the murder too; see *Chronicon*, s.a. 522, p. 70: 'His consulibus Segericus filius Segimundi regis iusso patris sui iniuste occisus est'.
[16] The names of the princes are not mentioned by Gregory, and only appear in the *Passio sancti Sigismundi regis*, MGH SRM 2, ed. B. Krusch (Hanover, 1888), pp. 329–40, at c. 9, p. 338: 'Qui eum sub ardua custodia una cum coniuge et filiis Gisclaado et Gundobado vinctum ad locum cuius vocabulum est Belsa perduxerunt'.
[17] Gregory of Tours, *LH* III.5.
[18] On this, B. Kasten, 'Stepmothers in Frankish Legal Life', in P. Stafford, J. L. Nelson, J. Martindale, and P. Stafford, *Law, Laity and Solidarities: Essays in Honour of Susan Reynolds* (Manchester, 2001), pp. 47–67, at pp. 60–5.
[19] The most well-known example being Gregory of Tours, *LH* V.48.
[20] Gregory of Tours, *LH* III.6.
[21] Wood, 'Gregory of Tours and Clovis', *RBPH*, 63 (1985): 253–4.

murderous father, effortlessly duped by the wiles of a woman of questionable origins, makes the gruesome events that followed much more palatable. The second was to contrast Clothild with the 'evil stepmother', one of Gregory's more popular tropes.[22] As he himself admits, it was 'the habit of stepmothers to malign and lead astray'.[23] Here Clothild was demanding the justice due to her as a loyal daughter, while the unnamed Burgundian queen was doing very much the opposite.[24] The third, apparently, was to introduce the suspicion that Sigistrix was planning to make a bid for his father's throne, possibly with the help of his Ostrogothic connections. It is this suggestion that interests us here.

Peter Heather has noted the similarity between the story of Sigistrix and that of Amalafrida, his mother's aunt.[25] The elimination of an 'Ostrogothic link', be it by killing off Theoderic's possible heir or his sister, could have been meant as a means of distancing the court from Ravenna's influence. Memorably, Amalafrida fled the Vandal court upon Hilderic's accession to the kingship, and sheltered with the Moors of Byzacena until, in 523, she was captured and imprisoned.[26] Amalafrida later died in captivity, and an enraged Theoderic was nearly persuaded to launch a fleet to avenge her. He was ultimately dissuaded, says Procopius, by a shortage of manpower, but also because of his fear that such an attack would further escalate an already serious crisis in Gothic–Byzantine relations.[27]

This explanation certainly has several appealing features. The first is that it makes Sigismund a rational, if incredibly ruthless, player. Seeing the Vandal and Burgundian courts of the early 520s as being internally divided between two centres of gravity – Byzantine and Ostrogothic – is a useful, if somewhat reductionist, explanation. On the Vandal front, Amalafrida represented Ostrogothic interest while Hilderic, guest-friend

---

[22] Of which his Fredegund stories surely constitute the finest example. See, among many others, Gregory of Tours, *LH* V.39.

[23] Gregory of Tours, *LH* III.5: 'sicut novercarum mos est, malignari et scandalizare coepit'. On this, see also D. Shanzer, 'Marriage and Kinship Relations among the Burgundians', in J.-F. Reynaud and I. N. Wood (eds.), *The Burgundians* (forthcoming). My sincere thanks to Professor Shanzer for sending me a copy of the unpublished article.

[24] For Gregory's narrative parallels between the Franks, Burgundians and Thuringians, see Y. Fox, 'Revisiting Gregory of Tours's Burgundian Narrative', in A. Wagner and N. Brocard (eds.), *Les Royaumes de Bourgogne jusque 1032 à travers la culture et la religion* (Turnhout, 2018), pp. 227–38.

[25] P. J. Heather, *The Goths* (Oxford, 1996), p. 248; G. Halsall, *Barbarian Migrations and the Roman West, 376–568* (Cambridge, 2007), p. 302.

[26] J. Conant, *Staying Roman: Conquest and Identity in Africa and the Mediterranean, 439–700* (Cambridge, 2012), p. 40.

[27] Procopius, *BV* I.9. See also, J. Moorehead, 'The Last Years of Theoderic', *Historia: Zeitschrift für Alte Geschichte*, 32 (1983): 106–20.

of the emperor-to-be, Justinian, was allied with the empire. In Burgundy, Areagni and Sigistrix would have been the Ostrogothic partisans; the sycophantic language of Sigismund's Byzantine epistles leaves little doubt where his allegiances lay. Once Areagni was dead, very little time had elapsed before Sigismund turned against his own son, eradicating the last vestige of the hypothetical 'Ostrogothic camp' and leaving him free to side with the Byzantines.

However appealing it may be to interpret the events in Burgundy as resulting from cooling relations with the Ostrogoths, it is quite possible to imagine other explanations. First, one is made to wonder whether Sigismund's decision to marry an *anonyma* after the death of his high-profile royal bride was the result of his narrowing diplomatic horizons, or the result of internal considerations. Having read Gregory, we assume that the new Burgundian queen was in fact of common descent, although, as Danuta Shanzer has shown, this could simply be the fault of our sources.[28] Since our understanding of the story is entirely dependent on Gregory's narrative, we should acknowledge how profoundly this shapes any ensuing interpretation. The problems with the *Histories* become immediately apparent when we have other sources with which to corroborate or disprove Gregory, as in the tale of Amalasuntha's fantastical elopement with her slave Traguilla.[29] Yet even if the new queen were a commoner, Merovingian kings of the sixth century are known to have employed similar matrimonial strategies to signal confidence and strength, as shown recently by Erin T. Dailey.[30] Sigismund's case need not have been much different.

Second, the arrival of two new princes after Sigismund's remarriage would have affected his plans for partitioning the kingdom. Previous experience has shown that the king could create a sub-kingship in Geneva or elsewhere to groom an heir and to quell any princely impatience. Any other potential heirs, however, would have been left unsatisfied by such an arrangement. In fact, it seems that Gundobad was faced with a comparable challenge when it came to Godomar, who may have been considerably younger, and possibly also from a different mother than his

---

[28] Shanzer, 'Marriage and Kinship', p. 13, discussing the marriages of Sigismer and Chilperic I to royal *anonymae*.
[29] Gregory of Tours, *LH* III.31. On the similarities and differences between Gregory's, Jordanes's and Procopius's recounting, see K. Cooper, 'The Heroine and the Historian: Procopius of Caesarea on the Troubled Reign of Queen Amalasuentha', in J. J. Arnold, M. S. Bjornlie and K. Sessa (eds.), *A Companion to Ostrogothic Italy* (Leiden, 2016), pp. 296–315, esp. at pp. 309–11.
[30] E. T. Dailey, *Queens, Consorts, Concubines: Gregory of Tours and the Women of the Merovingian Elite* (Leiden, 2015), pp. 114–15.

older brother.³¹ Sigistrix's murder might have been the result of internal dynastic struggles after all, especially since the Ostrogothic alternative, which envisages an attempt to install a Burgundian prince in Italy, would have been rather difficult to implement.

We must therefore accept that the gaps in our sources are almost entirely unbridgeable and that they seriously hinder our ability to coherently explain the reasons behind Sigistrix's murder. Gregory, the only source of any substance, has demonstrated that his portrayal of Sigismund was entirely contingent upon his narrative aims,³² and this probably holds true here as well. Yet we may also conclude that, as part of a broader picture, Sigistrix's murder might be indicative of Sigismund's desire to pivot away from Ravenna.

With all of its imperfections, such an interpretation may also shed some light on the religious divisions within the Burgundian court. While Sigismund was certainly a Catholic by 515, if not much sooner,³³ it seems that his first wife and children did not immediately share his newly found conviction.³⁴ Remaining Arian in the light of such a public campaign of monastic establishment and canonical legislation should alert us to possible political overtones. Saint-Maurice d'Agaune, Sigismund's crowning achievement, was abound in imperial symbolism and with its liturgical and cultic preferences would have been understood as an unequivocal statement of allegiance with Constantinople.³⁵ We should concede that an opposite stance would have been equally laden with significance.³⁶ While it is admittedly difficult to make out who, among the members of the royal family, remained Arian after 517, it would be reasonable to assume that some in fact did.³⁷ After 522, when both direct descendants of the Amal house in Burgundy were no longer alive, our safest bet would be Godomar.³⁸

What information do we have regarding the religious preferences of Gundobad's youngest son? The evidence, in truth, is less than compelling. Gregory accuses Godegisel, Gundobad and Godomar of

---

³¹ G. Kampers, 'Caretena – Königin und Asketin: Mosaiksteine zum Bild einer burgundischen Herrscherin', *Francia*, 27 (2000): 1–32, at p. 19.
³² Compare his depiction in the *Histories* to that in the *Liber in gloria martyrum*, MGH SRM 1,2, ed. B. Krusch (Hanover 1885), c. 74, p. 87.
³³ Shanzer and Wood, *Avitus of Vienne*, pp. 220–4.
³⁴ Shanzer and Wood, *Avitus of Vienne*, p. 215 n. 1.
³⁵ On this, see Wood, 'The Burgundians and Byzantium', pp. 12–13.
³⁶ P. Amory, *People and Identity in Ostrogothic Italy, 489–554* (Cambridge, 1997), p. 309.
³⁷ On this, see the discussion in the Burgundian chapter of Y. Hen, *Western Arianism: Politics and Religious Culture in the Early Medieval West* (Cambridge, forthcoming).
³⁸ M. Heinzelmann, *Gregory of Tours: History and Society in the Sixth Century* (Cambridge, 2001), p. 126.

having been Arians. Although this claim could be taken to refer to Gundobad's brother and not his son, the subsequent statement, that heterodox observances resulted in the loss of the kingdom suggests the younger Godomar.[39] Second, in a letter composed shortly before the council of Épaone, Avitus of Vienne expressed the fear that in the event of Sigismund's death, a heretic might come to rule Burgundy.[40] If past transitions of power are anything to go by, this would again favour Godomar as the cause of Sigismund's anxiety. Finally, there is the unpopular *argumentum ex silentio*: nowhere is Godomar said to have been a Catholic. The Carolingian *Passio Sigismundi*, which circumvents Sigistrix's murder entirely by the way, makes an obscure statement about Godomar's Christianity, but that is all.[41]

Sigismund's second wife, and naturally any ensuing offspring, were certainly Catholic: the *Vita Apollinaris* has the queen beg the bishop of Valence to cure the king's illness, which he does by granting her his cloak.[42] If what we are seeing in Burgundy after the deaths of Sigistrix and Areagni is indeed a diplomatic and religious realignment, it was probably meant not only to appease Byzantine sensibilities but also to address the pressing Frankish problem by chipping away at Merovingian unity. Sigismund was allied by marriage to the Merovingian king of Rheims, Theuderic I, who had wed Sigismund's daughter, according to Gregory's account, sometime between the murder of Sigistrix and Chlodomer's invasion.[43] We would have just cause to suspect Gregory's chronology, but in many respects, this makes sense. The second generation of Merovingians was intermittently occupied with internal fighting, and Theuderic, who was not a son of Clothild, was perhaps particularly disposed to suspect his brothers and to forge an independent

---

[39] Gregory of Tours, *LH* II. 28, III.1. It is quite possible that Gregory was confused about the familial structure of the Gibichungs, as suggested by Shanzer, 'Marriage and Kinship'.

[40] Avitus of Vienne, *Ep*. 7; for dating and identification of Godomar, Shanzer and Wood, *Avitus of Vienne*, pp. 296–7.

[41] *Passio sancti Sigismundi regis*, c.4, p. 335: 'Natique ei sunt duo filii, Sigismundus et Godemarus. Et quia ipse Gundobadus omnisque gens Burgundionum leges Goticae videbantur esse cultores, tamen filiis suis christianae religionis cultum deservire visus est tradidisse'; Kampers, 'Caretena', p. 19.

[42] *Vita Apollinaris episcopi Valentinensis*, MGH SRM 3, ed. B. Krusch (Hanover, 1896), pp. 194–203, at c.6, p. 199.

[43] Gregory of Tours, *LH* III.6. Shanzer argues that Guntheuca, Chlodomer's wife – and after his death, Chlothar's – was a Burgundian, which, considering her name and that of her son (Gunthar), seems reasonable. However, Chlodomer's marriage would have been arranged much earlier, since he was Clovis's firstborn from Clothild, and contributes little to our understanding of Frankish-Burgundian relations in the late 510s and early 520s.

path. His Auvergne campaign was meant as a punitive measure against Childebert loyalists, while his Thuringian war concluded with a failed plot to murder Chlothar.[44] Theuderic was not only an outsider among the Merovingians, and in this respect somewhat more susceptible to alliance with the Burgundians, but also a voracious expansionist. One memorable attempt was made early on against the Visigoths,[45] and another against the Danish king Hygelac.[46] These were not mere acts of opportunity, and Theuderic's rationale in pursuing them conformed to his regional strategy.

To begin with, after Vouillé, Theuderic's encroachment on Aquitaine would have been understood as hostile to Ostrogothic interest.[47] Reacting to Hygelac's surprise attack was not expansion per se, and yet it is worthwhile to consider Godfrid Storms' analysis, which saw the Danish naval strike as an Ostrogothic diversionary tactic.[48] Finally, the Thuringian initiative, aggressively pursued by Theuderic, is especially significant in that it was also apparently aimed against an Ostrogothic client-state, and in this respect sits well with Sigismund's new posture. Some caution is warranted here, however; since the Christianisation of the Thuringians seems to have been a relatively recent affair, direct Ostrogothic hegemony over the Thuringians would possibly suggest Arianism, for which there is no evidence. Indeed, the Thuringians' early Catholic adherence and the shelter offered to Prince Amalfrid in Constantinople make Byzantine influence an equally reasonable option.[49]

Finally, we could apply these conclusions to the campaigns of 523 and 524. The Ostrogothic movement to capture Gallic lands between the Drôme and Durance may be understood as a reaction to Sigistrix's murder, as indeed Wolfram has done.[50] Before we rush to interpret this as a retaliatory manoeuvre, we should remember that the Ostrogoths were already present in the region after they had seized the lands captured by the Burgundians in Vouillé, and that Theoderic had spent considerable

---

[44] Gregory of Tours, *LH* III.8.
[45] *Chronica Gallica ad a. 511*, MGH AA 9, ed. T. Mommsen (Berlin, 1892), 689–690, p. 665: 'Tolosa a Francis et Burgundionibus incense et Barcinona a Gundefade rege Burgundionum capta'; I. N. Wood, *The Merovingian Kingdoms, 481–751* (London and New York: Longman, 1994), p. 48
[46] Gregory of Tours, *LH* III.3; *LHF*, c 29.
[47] Wood, *The Merovingian Kingdoms*, p. 49.
[48] G. Storms, 'The Significance of Hygelac's Raid', *Nottingham Medieval Studies* 14 (1970), pp. 3–26.
[49] I. N. Wood, 'Religion in Pre-Carolingian Thuringia and Bavaria', in *The Baiuvarii and Thuringi: An Ethnographic Perspective*, ed. J. Hines, J. Fries-Knoblach, and H. Steuer (Woodbridge, 2014), pp. 317–330, at pp. 317–318.
[50] Cassiodorus, *Variae*, VIII.10.8; H. Wolfram, *History of the Goths* (Berkeley, CA, 1988), p. 312.

resources building up his fortifications along the Durance.[51] More likely, the Goths were improving their positions as a precaution against another impulse of Frankish expansion, which in fact was on the immediate horizon.

A second possibility is that Theoderic's troops were present, to some extent, in the battle of Vézeronce. If indeed the bishop of Tours mistook the Merovingian king Theuderic I for the similarly named Italian ruler in his account of the battle,[52] this not only reconciles Gregory's confused chronology with Marius of Avenches' description but also has the added advantage of seeing the Ostrogothic king pursue in Burgundy the vendetta he was reluctant to unleash on Vandal Africa.

One interesting outcome of this theory is that the Franks, who were ostensibly closer to the Byzantines than to the Ostrogoths, were willing to consider military cooperation with Ravenna. Here, too, it is tempting to speculate that the Merovingian courts were also split in terms of their regional alignment. As previously mentioned, Theuderic I's reluctance to become involved in the Burgundian adventure hints that broader regional concerns were at play, as does the reversal of this policy under his son. Theudebert I was not related to Sigismund's daughter and thus owed the Burgundians no loyalty. When opportunity presented itself, he was only too happy to partake in his uncles' plans.

Some doubts about such a reconstruction surely remain. Once Sigismund was dead, Godomar took the reins of government. If we choose to see him as a supporter of the Ostrogoths, we would then have to explain why a detachment of Italian troops should have been sent to aid the Franks, hardly a trustworthy ally, in an attack on their own client. Now, Theoderic could have been ill informed about who held power in Lyon. Avitus' misunderstandings regarding the nature of the *Trishagion* crisis illustrate that information disseminated with some difficulty,[53] as does Theoderic's seizure of Burgundian emissaries to Constantinople,[54] although in the end, such Ostrogothic ignorance is still rather difficult to accept.

One possible way out of this conundrum is this: Chlodomer, it seems, conducted two separate campaigns against Burgundy: one in 523 in which Sigismund was captured, and one in Vézeronce, in the following year, where he himself was killed.[55] Judging by all of the evidence, if

---

[51] Cassiodorus, *Variae* III.41.
[52] I. N. Wood, 'Clermont and Burgundy, 511–534', *Nottingham Medieval Studies*, 32 (1988): 123.
[53] Avitus, *Contra Eutychianam haeresim*, Book 2.
[54] Avitus, *Ep.* 94.
[55] Wood, *The Merovingian Kingdoms*, p. 53.

the Ostrogoths became involved at some point, it would have been during the second engagement. Any preliminary negotiations between the Byzantines and the Franks that led up to this hypothetical alliance would have taken place after Sigismund's capture, so the Ostrogoths should have known that it was Godomar they would be facing on the field. This, in turn, considerably weakens the theory that Godomar was an Ostrogothic partisan.

If, as Gregory claims, it was really Theuderic, the Frankish king, who was at Vézeronce, any reluctance he may have had to fight Sigismund would have been irrelevant as it was Godomar who was leading the Burgundians into battle. Of course, we are then faced with the task of solving the chronology of the Auvergne campaign. Since it cannot have happened during the final Burgundian war, as Gregory suggests, a possible alternative would be to have Theuderic refuse to take part in Chlodomer's first battle against Sigismund, opting instead to take his armies to Clermont but later joining his half-brother at Vézeronce, which was, after all, a week's march away.

After a hard-won recovery, Godomar was faced with the complicated task of rebuilding the realm. It is possible that this took the form of a legislative effort, although recent work has called into question the assertion that the latter section of the *Constitutiones extravagantes*, entitled the *Conventu Burgundionum*, was a product of Godomar's court.[56] On the international front, adjustments were also urgently needed. Now that the intentions of the Franks were clear, conditions ripened for a closer relationship with the Ostrogoths.[57]

In Italy, too, things were changing. Theoderic had died in 526 after a period of internal unrest, and by 530, Amalasuntha was herself in a bind. Her military machine, weakened by the incorporation of Ostrogothic troops into the Visigothic army, was challenged on several fronts. That same year, she ceded her father's gains in southern Gaul to the Burgundians, in an alliance that seemed to betray a mutual panic of the Franks. Naturally, Cassiodorus depicted the Burgundian–Gothic agreement as asymmetrical, with the Gibichungs playing the part of tributaries.[58] While he was

---

[56] See *Constitutiones extravagantes*, MGH LL Nat. Germ., ed. L. R. De Salis (Hanover, 1892), XXI, pp. 119–22. On Godomar's legislation, see p. 119 n. 5; K. F. Drew, *The Burgundian Code: Book of Constitutions or Law of Gundobad* (Philadelphia, PA, 1949), p. 7; Wood, '*Gentes*, Kings and Kingdoms', p. 266; and, recently, I. N. Wood, 'The Legislation of *Magistri Militum*: The Laws of Gundobad and Sigismund', *Clio@Themis: Revue électronique d'histoire du droit*, 10 (2016): 1–16, at p. 5.

[57] U. Heil, *Avitus von Vienne und die Homöische Kirche der Burgunder* (Berlin, 2011), p. 25; A. Becker-Piriou, 'De Galla Placidia a Amalasonthe, des femmes dans la diplomatie Romano-barbare en occident', *Revue historique*, 647 (2008): 507–43, at p. 531.

[58] Cassiodorus, *Variae*, XI.I.13.

perhaps slightly exaggerating, Godomar certainly needed Amalasuntha more than she needed him. In the grander scheme, the Burgundians were clearly siding with the Ostrogoths, yet this was not a pact to which Ravenna was absolutely committed. Amalasuntha's armies watched from the sidelines as the Franks dismembered Burgundy and brought about its collapse.[59]

Godomar's fate is unknown. Ever outmatched by the Franks, he usually preferred to retreat rather than to risk destruction, and this pattern probably repeated itself here. Of all the places Godomar could have gone, Italy seems the most logical. Marius of Avenches relates that in 538, during the first phase of the Gothic wars, a Burgundian force took part in the siege of Milan.[60] Could this have been some remnant of Godomar's military? If it was, this last-ditch alliance may shed some light on the nature of the relationship between the Ostrogoths and the Burgundians in the years preceding the battle. More likely, however, these troops were not the vestiges of a Gibichung army at all but the Burgundian troops of Theudebert, who followed them into Italy the subsequent year.[61]

By this time, the regional constellation had changed dramatically. The Vandal kingdom collapsed, and Italy lay in ruins. The Justinianic wars did not usher in a *renovatio imperii*. In fact, they permanently laid to rest the notion of a barbarian West dependent on Constantinople for political validation. The fall of Burgundy was but the first contraction in the painful birth of a new West, and a new Mediterranean.

---

[59] H. Wolfram, *The Roman Empire and Its Germanic Peoples* (Berkeley, CA, 1997), p. 225.
[60] Marius of Avenches, *Chronicon*, s.a. 538.
[61] Procopius, *BG*, II.21, 25. For some discussion of post-conquest Burgundy, see Y. Fox, 'Image of Kings Past: The Gibichung Legacy in Post-Conquest Burgundy', *Francia*, 42 (2015): 1–26.

3 *Pax Inter Utramque Gentem*: The Merovingians, Byzantium and the History of Frankish Identity

Helmut Reimitz

As the chapters in this volume demonstrate, members of Merovingian society and particularly their elites continued to understand themselves as part of a wider world that was shaped as much by the horizons of the late Roman Empire as by the continuing interactions between its successor states and societies in the Mediterranean. It is important to bear in mind how consciously and confidently Merovingian rulers and elites presented and imagined themselves as part of this wider world. For a long time, modern historiography has regarded them as representing a society with shrinking cultural, political and religious horizons after the end of the western Roman Empire – a society increasingly defined by the smaller scales of barbarian, 'Northern' views of the world.[1] Studying Merovingian society in its Mediterranean contexts is an effective response to such simplifying and distorting approaches. It helps to realise how anachronistic it is to look at the Merovingian world as a world of its own, independent of broader political and social developments. It is in fact through the connections and interactions of the Merovingian world with the wider Mediterranean world that allows us study the formation and transformation of Merovingian society on its own terms.

This is particularly important for the history of Frankish identity. For a long time, scholars have assumed that a core Frankish identity was preserved and transmitted by Frankish leaders, elites and their followers. They assumed that with the establishment of Frankish rule over most of Gaul, Frankish identity spread as a by-product of the political success of the Franks. With their great political success, the Franks even came to be presented as the crown-witnesses for the idea that an ethnic mentality of the Germanic peoples (*Gentilismus*) replaced as the stronger mode of thought the Roman imperial consciousness of the provincials.[2]

---

[1] For an overview of the historiography, see I. N. Wood, *The Modern Origins of the Middle Ages* (Oxford, 2013).
[2] This idea goes back to R. Wenskus, *Stammesbildung und Verfassung: Das Werden der frühmittelalterlichen Gentes*, 2nd edn. (Vienna and Graz, 1977), p. 2: 'Der Gentilismus

However, the history of Frankish identity was not just an internal affair. As in all processes of identity construction and formation, what it meant to be 'Frankish' both transformed and gained definition in circuits of communication between insiders and outsiders.[3] In such processes of identification, Frankish identity was not just what it was. Instead, it was constantly created and recreated in debates and reflections about who the Franks were and what they should be, which have left behind a remarkably rich and surprisingly diverse evidence for the history of Frankish identity.[4]

This history is, like any other history of identities, full of breaks and contradictions. In this regard, one of the particularly interesting aspects of the history of Frankish identity is that the establishment of Frankish rulers over most of the former Gaulish provinces did not prompt the steady increase of the use and importance of the Frankish name as an identifier for individuals and groups living in the Merovingian kingdom. In fact, Clovis's rule marks a sharp break in the history of Frankish identities. By then, people and peoples who were identified and who identified themselves as Franks had a long history in late Roman Gaul. From the third century, Roman historians and authors described them as pirates and barbarian soldiers-turned-farmers in the provinces along the lower Rhine, high military officers of the Roman army and reliable federates, or treacherous enemies of the Empire.[5] While there was no consensus who the Franks actually were, the relation of these groups to each other as well as to the Roman world could be interpreted as comparable to the

---

der landnehmenden Stämme war als politische Denkform starker als das römische Reichsbewußtsein der Provinzialen.' Although this has already been proven to be a misleading perspective by H. Wolfram, *Die Goten: Von den Anfängen bis zur Mitte des sechsten Jahrhunderts*, 5th edn (Munich, 2009), Wenskus' study is still often quoted as the main impulse for new approaches in the study of late antique and early medieval ethnicity. For further discussion, see W. Pohl, 'Ethnicity, Theory and Tradition: A Response', in A. Gillett (ed.), *On Barbarian Identity: Critical Approaches to Ethnogenesis Theory* (Turnhout, 2002), pp. 221–40; and now his comprehensive overview of the historiography W. Pohl, 'Von der Ethnogenese zur Identitätsforschung', in W. Pohl and B. Zeller (eds.), *Neue Wege der Frühmittelalterforschung: Bilanz und Perspektiven* (Vienna, 2018), pp. 9–33.

[3] W. Pohl, 'Introduction: Strategies of Identification – A Methodological Profile', in W. Pohl and G. Heydemann (eds.), *Strategies of Identification: Ethnicity and Religion in Early Medieval Europe* (Turnhout, 2013), pp. 2–3.

[4] H. Reimitz, *History, Frankish Identity and the Framing of Western Ethnicity, 550–850* (Cambridge, 2015).

[5] See E. Ewig, 'Die Franken und Rom (3.-5. Jahrhundert): Versuche einer Übersicht', in E. Ewig (ed.), *Spätantikes und fränkisches Gallien, Gesammelte Schriften*, 3 vols. (Ostfildern, 2009), vol. III, pp. 121–62; E. Ewig, 'Probleme der fränkischen Frühgeschichte in den Rheinlanden', in E. Ewig, *Spätantikes und fränkisches Gallien*, pp. 75–102; U. Nonn, *Die Franken* (Stuttgart, 2010), pp. 36–67.

ancient *Germani*. Many late-antique authors even saw the Franks as the new *Germani*.[6]

This was the situation when Clovis's father, Childeric I, died in 481/2, leaving the administration of a peripheral region in north-eastern Gaul to his son who came to rule most of the former Gallic provinces, including the smaller polities held by other Frankish client-kings.[7] As king of these territories, however, he did not use the prestige of the Frankish name to legitimate his position. As a ruler of a diverse set of Gallic provinces, he seems to have preferred the absolute title *rex* without any ethnic denominator. Unfortunately, the evidence is scarce, since we only have a few extant letters that were written by or to Clovis. Nevertheless, in none of them do we find Clovis representing himself or being represented as *rex Francorum*.[8]

The two letters that Clovis received might help to understand why. Both letters were written by bishops. One was sent soon after Clovis succeeded his father by Remigius of Rheims, who congratulated Clovis on his new position.[9] The other letter was written some years later by the bishop of Vienne, Avitus. Avitus, who was one of the most important political figures in the Burgundian kingdom ruled by the Arian Gibichung kings, expressed in the letter his delight about Clovis's decision to become a 'Catholic' Christian.[10] Both bishops also used the opportunity to remind Clovis that he was now a ruler of a highly diverse and heterogeneous kingdom and should thus rule all of the different peoples with care and intelligence and that he should show equal justice towards all of them.

---

[6] For the idea of a Frankish *Stammesschwarm* or *Stammesbund*, see Nonn, *Die Franken*, pp. 15–30, with further literature; for a more complex and to my mind more accurate view, see: W. Pohl, *Die Germanen* (Munich, 2002), pp. 93–115, and G. Halsall, *Barbarian Migrations and the Roman West*, 376–568 (Cambridge, 2007), esp. pp. 120–31, and 303–10.

[7] On the question of which region Childeric and Clovis were governing, see now G. Barret and G. Woodhuysen, 'Remigius and the "Important News" of Clovis Rewritten', *Antiquite Tardive: revue internationale d'histoire et d'archeologie*, 24 (2016): 471–500. For an interesting discussion of the letter in the context of Clovis's conquest of the 'Roman' kingdom of Soissons, see M. Becher, *Chlodwig: Der Aufstieg der Merowinger und das Ende der antiken Welt* (Munich, 2010), pp. 153–8.

[8] H. Wolfram, *Intitulatio I. Lateinische Königs- und Fürstentitel bis zum Ende des 8. Jahrhunderts* (Graz, Vienna and Cologne, 1967), pp. 108–16.

[9] *Epistolae Austrasicae*, 1, ed. W. Gundlach, MGH Epistolae Merowingici et Karolini aevi, vol. I (Berlin, 1892), pp. 110–92, p. 112; on the letter, see Barret and Woodhuysen, 'Remigius', with further literature.

[10] *Avitus, Epistulae II*, 46, ed. R. Peiper, MGH AA 6, 2 (Berlin, 1883), pp. 75–7; see D. Shanzer and I. N. Wood, *Avitus of Vienne, Letters and Selected Prose* (Liverpool, 2002), pp. 362–9; for a recent discussion of the letter see U. Heil, 'Chlodwig, ein christlicher Herrscher. Ansichten des Bischofs Avitus von Vienne', in M. Meier and S. Patzold (eds.), *Chlodwigs Welt: Organisation von Herrschaft um 500* (Stuttgart, 2014), pp. 67–90.

From early on, the Merovingian kings were wise enough to take the advice of their bishops seriously. The kings positioned themselves in an equidistant relation to all the different groups and saw the successful mediation of the *regnum*'s different groupings as the foundation of just rule, peace and stability.[11] A stronger emphasis on the name of the Franks in the legitimation of their rule could well have been regarded as jeopardising the precarious balance of power in the socially, ethnically and religiously diverse regions under Clovis's rule.

The decision to use the absolute title *rex* also had international dimensions. The only surviving source that addresses Clovis as *rex Francorum* is Cassiodorus's collection of official documents written on behalf of the Gothic rulers of the Italian kingdom of Theoderic the Great, the *Variae*.[12] In his correspondence, Theoderic himself never used a title with an ethnic denominator but only referred to himself as *rex* or *patricius*.[13] It is therefore highly likely that in entitling Clovis *rex Francorum* Cassiodorus hoped to emphasise the king's subordination to the rule of Theoderic, the western *patricius* and ruler of Italy. Conversely, it is just as likely that Clovis rejected this specific attempt at subversion. He claimed a similar position to the one of Theoderic and seems to have sought recognition as ruler of his territories from the Byzantine emperor in 508, long before Theoderic's death in 526.[14] This does not mean that we should understand Clovis's strategies of legitimation as motivated exclusively by his competition with Theoderic.[15] It seems that they were rather the obvious choice for post-Roman rulers to legitimate themselves in the former Roman provinces.[16] The Gibichung kings and

---

[11] See Reimitz, *History, Frankish Identity*, pp. 98–116.

[12] See C. Kakridis, *Cassiodors Variae: Literatur und Politik im ostgotischen Italien* (Munich, 2005); M. S. Bjornlie, *Politics and Tradition between Rome, Ravanne and Constantinople: A Study of Cassiodorus and the Variae, 527–554* (Cambridge, 2013).

[13] Wolfram, *Intitulatio I*, pp. 67–76; Wolfram, *Goten*, pp. 284–90; for Theoderic's self-presentation as a Roman ruler, see M. Vitiello, *Momenti di Roma ostrogota: adventus, feste, politica* (Stuttgart, 2005) and J. Arnold, *Theoderic and the Roman Imperial Restoration* (Cambridge, 2014); for Theoderic's conception of rulership, the informative overview of U. Wiemer, 'Odovakar und Theoderich: Herrschaftskonzepte nach dem Ende des Kaisertums', in M. Meier and S. Patzold (eds.), *Chlodwigs Welt. Organisation von Herrschaft um 500* (Stuttgart, 2014), pp. 293–358.

[14] See R. Mathisen, 'Clovis, Anastasius and Political Status in 508 CE', in D. Shanzer and R. Mathisen (eds.), *The Battle of Vouillé, 507 CE: Where France Began* (Boston, MA, 2012), pp. 79–110, with the bibliography nn. 5 and 6.

[15] For Theoderic's side, see J. Arnold, 'The Battle of Vouillé and the Restoration of the Roman Empire', in D. Shanzer and R. Mathisen (eds.), *The Battle of Vouillé, 507 CE: Where France Began* (Boston, MA, 2012), pp. 118–38.

[16] See also A. Gillet, 'Was Ethnicity Politicized in the Earliest Medieval Kingdoms?', in A. Gillet (ed.), *On Barbarian Identity: Critical Approaches to Ethnicity in the Early Middle Ages* (Turnhout, 2007), pp. 85–122, who argues for a total absence of ethnic titles. However, there are examples for the use of an ethnic title (cf. Wolfram, *Intitulatio I*, pp. 77–80)

magistri militum also preferred to present themselves as *reges* rather than as *reges Burgundionum*.[17]

The minimising of ethnic affiliation, however, might have been particularly important for post-Roman rulers in Gaul. Their legitimacy was strongly tied to military control and command over the regions they came to rule.[18] Since the fourth century, the Gallic provinces were one of the most heavily militarised territories of the Roman Empire.[19] In the context of the dissolution of the Roman Empire, the regions were fertile sites for the emergence of distinct military units under the control of client leaders who eventually became independent kings and warlords.[20] When Clovis died, he controlled all of these power blocs that had been established in Gaul, including the Roman *regnum* of Soissons, and the Visigothic kingdom in the South of Gaul (the Burgundian kingdom of the Gibichungs became part of the Merovingian kingdom a generation later in the 530s).

Conquest certainly contributed to this process, but, as Stefan Esders has argued, negotiations and agreements among rulers, generals and elites in these highly militarised regions performed an equally important if not more important role in their integration into a common political framework.[21] Clovis managed to establish himself as the leader of a *militärisch konstituierten Monarchie* through the contractual recognition of a certain autonomy for the different political groups and administrative units of his kingdom.[22] These successful politics of integration were important for the accumulation of military resources and thus helped lay

---

indicating that one should allow for the possibility of different strategies of legitimation in different contexts, cf. Pohl, 'Von der Ethnogenese'; for the Merovingian kingdoms, see below, with p. 55.

[17] For the Gibichung rulers, see I. N. Wood, 'The Political Structure of the Burgundian Kingdoms', in M. Meier and S. Patzold (eds.), *Chlodwigs Welt: Organisation von Herrschaft um 500* (Stuttgart, 2014), pp. 383–96, with further references.

[18] Halsall, *Barbarian Migrations*, pp. 284–310; H. Wolfram, *Gotische Studien: Volk und Herrschaft im frühen Mittelalter* (Munich, 2005), pp. 139–54.

[19] See B. Shaw, 'War and Violence', in G. W. Bowersock, P. R. Brown and O. Grabar (eds.), *Late Antiquity: A Guide to the Postclassical World* (Cambridge, MA, 1999), pp. 130–69, here pp. 148–53; S. Esders, 'Nordwestgallien um 500: Von der militarisierten spätrömischen Provinzgesellschaft zur erweiterten Militäradministration des merowingischen Königtums' in M. Meier and S. Patzold (eds.), *Chlodwigs Welt. Organisation von Herrschaft um 500* (Stuttgart, 2014), pp. 341–5, and the study of L. Sarti, *Perceiving War and the Military in Early Christian Gaul* (Leiden, 2013); L. Sarti, 'Die spätantike Militärpräsenz und die Entstehung einer militarisierten "Grenzgesellschaft" in der nordwesteuropäischen *limes*-Region', in C. Rass (ed.), *Militärische Migration vom Altertum bis zur Gegenwart* (Paderborn, 2016), pp. 43–56.

[20] M. Kulikowski, 'The Western Kingdoms', in S. F. Johnson (ed.), *The Oxford Handbook of Late Antiquity* (Oxford, 2012), pp. 31–59; Halsall, *Barbarian Migrations*, pp. 269–72.

[21] Esders, 'Nordwestgallien um 500'.

[22] Esders, 'Nordwestgallien um 500', p. 351.

the foundation for Clovis's conquest of the largest and most powerful *regnum* of Gaul ruled by the Visigothic kings in 507. These politics might also have played a role in managing public relations between Clovis and the elites of the different regions, not least the ones in the Visigothic kingdom in the south. With the convincing flexibility and success of these political strategies, Clovis might well have been regarded as the most attractive option among the post-Roman generals and kings in Gaul.[23]

The specific features of Clovis's politics of integration had also important consequences for the limited significance of Frankish identity in the early Merovingian kingdom. This might become more obvious if we compare the situation in Merovingian Gaul with those in other post-Roman kingdoms. Even though the kings of other post-Roman kingdoms in Clovis's time preferred to present themselves as kings and not as kings of any specific ethnic *gens*, their armies provided a locus for such identities to develop. In all of these other kingdoms, military status was linked to these ethnic labels, which had their roots in the contracts of the barbarian groups' leaders with the Roman Empire when they received their imperial mandates establishing them as the commanders of an *exercitus*.[24] In contrast to these developments, Clovis's legitimacy was not primarily based on an imperial mandate for himself and his Frankish troops but rather on the contracts he concluded with the different elites in the different polities of his kingdom.[25] Such contracts were concluded by an oath of loyalty sworn by the different groups or inhabitants of regions and cities in the kingdom in exchange for the confirmation of certain privileges and rights. Clovis adapted this formula from Roman military practices where it had also been used to conclude contracts with barbarian groups who participated in joint campaigns with the Romans. In the Merovingian monarchy, this oath transformed into a means by which

---

[23] Halsall, *Barbarian Migrations*, pp. 303–10; B. Jussen, 'Chlodwig der Gallier: Zur Strukturgeschichte einer historischen Figur', in M. Meier and S. Patzold (eds.), *Chlodwigs Welt. Organisation von Herrschaft um 500* (Stuttgart, 2014), pp. 27–43; on competition with the Gibichung kings, see I. N. Wood, 'Arians, Catholics and Vouillé', in D. Shanzer and R. Mathisen (eds.), *The Battle of Vouillé, 507 CE: Where France Began* (Boston, MA, 2012); and Becher, *Chlodwig*, pp. 204–34.

[24] Halsall, *Barbarian Migrations*, pp. 473–82; W. Pohl, 'Telling the Difference: Signs of Ethnic Identity', in W. Pohl and H. Reimitz (eds.), *Strategies of Distinction: The Construction of Ethnic Communities, 300–800* (Leiden, 1998), pp. 27–35; for the example of the *exercitus Gothorum*, see Wolfram, *Die Goten*, pp. 290–305, esp. pp. 300–2.

[25] For the oath of loyalty, see S. Esders, 'Rechtliche Grundlagen frühmittelalterlicher Staatlichkeit. Der allgemeine Treueid', in W. Pohl and V. Wieser (eds.), *Der frühmittelalterliche Staat: Europäische Perspektiven, Forschungen zur Geschichte des Mittelalters* (Vienna, 2009), pp. 423–34; S. Esders, 'Sacramentum fidelitatis: Treueidleistung, Militärorganisation und Formierung mittelalterlicher Staatlichkeit', Habilitationsschrift, Univ. Bochum, 2005 (unpublished).

the entire population committed to the new ruler and acknowledged him as the highest military and legal authority.

Thus, every free person in the Merovingian kingdom was subject to military service and held the right to claim the status and privileges that came with it. Given the history of 'the Franks', it might be conjectured that Romans regarded 'Franks' as particularly qualified for military service. There is, however, no indication that one's status in the military was linked to the name of the Franks. This was very different to the situation in the Ostrogothic kingdom. When Athalaric, the grandson of Theoderic the Great, succeeded his grandfather in 526, he (or more probably his adviser, Cassiodorus) wrote to the different groups and provinces of the kingdom asking them to swear the oath of loyalty. In return, the king promised to maintain all of his grandfather's promises and guaranteed his Roman population that the *Gothi* (who had already sworn the oath of loyalty to him) would continue to protect their common state by force (*labores bellicos pro communi utilitate*).[26] There is no evidence that such a division of labour or status between 'barbarians' and Romans existed in Merovingian Gaul.[27]

This specific constitutional aspect of the Merovingian kingdoms allowed for relatively wide *Spielräume* for elites to develop strategies of identifications for the different groups and groupings in linking them to a common social or political whole. This seems to have not changed very much throughout the sixth century. When, at the end of the sixth century, Venantius Fortunatus and Gregory of Tours wrote their poems, letters, histories and hagiographical narratives,[28] they were still using the room for manoeuvre created by the Merovingian strategies of political integration and politics of identity. But the two authors' writings can also

---

[26] Cassiodorus, *Variae*, VIII, 3, ed. Th. Mommsen, MGH AA, 12 (Berlin, 1894, repr. 1981), pp. 233–4. See also VIII, 4, 5, 6 and 7, pp. 234–6, which are all letters to different regions and people regarding the oath of loyalty and include the Goths' military distinction; for the oath, see Esders, 'Rechtliche Grundlagen', and Esders, *Sacramentum fidelitatis*, pp. 70–8. For the division of labour between the two *populi* already in Theoderic's time, see Wolfram, *Die Goten*, pp. 284–90; Halsall, *Barbarian Migrations*, pp. 284–93; and Wiemer, 'Odovakar und Theoderich'.

[27] See Esders, 'Rechtliche Grundlagen'; and E. Ewig, *Die Merowinger und das Frankenreich. 6. aktualisierte Auflage, mit Literaturnachträgen von Ulrich Nonn* (Stuttgart, 2012), pp. 61–2.

[28] For Gregory, see A. C. Murray (ed.), *A Companion to Gregory of Tours* (Leiden, 2016); for Venantius, M. Roberts, *The Humblest Sparrow: The Poetry of Venantius Fortunatus* (Ann Arbor, MI, 2009); and J. George, *Venantius Fortunatus: A Latin Poet in Merovingian Gaul* (Oxford, 1992); O. Ehlen, *Venantius-Interpretationen: Rhetorische und generische Transgressionen beim neuen Orpheus* (Stuttgart, 2011).

show how differently the *Spielräume* could be employed two generations after the establishment of Merovingian rule over most of Gaul. Although Gregory and Venantius were friends and belonged largely to the same social, political and religious networks, they developed quite different ideas about what should hold the different communities and groupings in their *regnum* together.

Venantius, who grew up in northern Italy and first came to Gaul in 566 on the occasion of the marriage of Sigibert I, Austrasian king, with the Visigothic princess, Brunhild, delivered a splendid celebratory poem at their wedding ceremony.[29] The grandiose orchestration of the marriage was an important part of Sigibert's attempt to strategically position himself vis-à-vis his brothers and fellow Merovingian kings after the death of their father, Chlothar I, in 561.[30] Their constant competition and conflicts over territories, loyalties and resources is well documented in the *Histories* written by Venantius' friend, Gregory, who was, as bishop of Tours, also a protégé of Sigibert and Brunhild. In writing about the marriage in his *Histories*, Gregory contrasted Sigibert's choice with those of his brothers, who 'were taking wives that were completely unworthy of them'.[31] A rhetor like Venantius was more than welcome to further underline the royal and 'international' dimension of Sigibert's alliance, both through his own literal presence at the wedding and with his poetry.

Venantius Fortunatus knew what was expected of him. The epithalamium for Sigibert and Brunhild is full of allusions and quotations referring to Roman history, myths and imperial grandeur. The adaptation of Roman tradition for contemporary circumstances is a theme that appears again and again in Venantius' panegyrics.[32] In many of his

---

[29] On the marriage of Sigibert and Brunhild, see E. T. Dailey, *Queens, Consorts Concubines: Gregory of Tours and the Merovingian Elite* (Leiden, 2015), pp. 80–117; Dumézil, *La Reine Brunehaut* (Paris, 2008), pp. 113–30; on the poem, George, *Venantius*, pp. 153–7; and Ehlen, *Venantius-Interpretationen*, pp. 221–56.

[30] See S. Esders, 'Gallic Politics in the Sixth Century', in A. C. Murray (ed.), *A Companion to Gregory of Tours* (Leiden, 2016), pp. 429–61; M. Widdowson, 'Merovingian Partitions: A "Genealogical Charter"?', *Early Medieval Europe*, 17 (2009): 1–22; I. N. Wood, *The Merovingian Kingdoms, 450–751* (London and New York, 1994), pp. 88–101; E. Ewig, 'Die fränkischen Teilungen und Teilreiche (511–613)', in E. Ewig, *Spätantikes und fränkisches Gallien: Gesammelte Schriften (1952–1973)*, vol. I (Munich, 1976), pp. 72–113.

[31] Gregory of Tours, *Historiae*, IV, 27, ed. W. Levison and B. Krusch, MGH SS RM, 1,1 (Hanover, 1951, repr. 1992), p. 160.

[32] As Michael Roberts observed, Venantius developed 'a new kind of praise poetry well suited to the conditions of reception in Merovingian Gaul' (*The Humblest Sparrow*, pp. 38, 53–60) see also M. Reydellet, *La Royauté dans la littérature latine de Sidoine Apollinaire à Isidore de Séville* (Rome and Paris, 1981), p. 305 and E. Buchberger, 'Romans, Barbarians and Franks in the Writings of Venantius Fortunatus', *Early Medieval Europe*, 24 (2016): 293–307.

poems, we see him promoting the literary and cultural ideals of *romanitas* as the common ground upon which diverse social, cultural and political groups could be linked.

In many of his poems for the Merovingian kings, Venantius praises their eloquence as the essential element for their political and social success. This eloquence was not bound to Latin but also applied to the different languages of the Merovingian world. In a poem written for Sigibert's brother, Charibert, Venantius praises both the king's eloquence in Latin as well as in his own language.[33] Charibert brings back the joys of old in present times. For this, the barbarian world (*Barbaries*) on the one side and the Roman world (*Romania*) on the other join in applauding him. In various tongues, a single acclamation praises him (*diversis linguis laus sonat una viri*).[34] Charibert understands them all.

Not only do we find in Venantius' poetry the emphasis on the Roman virtues of eloquence and education as the keys to the kingdom's social and political integration. In a number of poems for members of the governing class such as the *dux* Lupus, or the *duces* Bodegisel and Chrodinus, Venantius constructs a similar relationship between eloquence, education and political success.[35]

While Venantius Fortunatus seemed the have used the available *Spielräume* in his poetry to articulate his post-Roman *Romanitas* as the key to a successful mediation of the different groups in the Merovingian realm, his friend and patron, Gregory of Tours, employed the same *Spielräume* in his *Histories* to place Christendom at the centre of any project to integrate the diverse Merovingian peoples. The efforts and energy with which Gregory promoted his particular vision of Christianity in hagiographical and historical writing have been discussed in a number of excellent studies in recent decades.[36] Yet, as I have tried to show at greater length elsewhere, Gregory also challenged conceptions of community other than his Christian vision in his *Histories*.[37]

---

[33] Venantius Fortunatus, *Carmina*, VI, 2, ed. Leo, p. 133.
[34] Venantius Fortunatus, *Carmina* VI, 2, ed. Leo, p. 131; trans. George, *Venantius Fortunatus*, p. 34.
[35] For a longer discussion, see Reimitz, *History, Frankish Identity*, pp. 88–97.
[36] For this, see, in part, W. Goffart, *The Narrators of Barbarian History (ad 550–800): Jordanes, Gregory of Tours, Bede, and Paul the Deacon* (Notre Dame, IN, 2005), pp. 112–234; M. Heinzelmann, *Gregor von Tours (538–594): 'Zehn Bücher Geschichte' – Historiographie und Gesellschaftskonzept im 6. Jahrhundert* (Darmstadt, 1994); P. Brown, 'Gregory of Tours: Introduction', in K. Mitchell and I. N. Wood (eds.), *The World of Gregory of Tours* (Leiden, 2002), pp. 1–28; P. Brown, *The Rise of Western Christendom: Triumph and Diversity, 200–1000*, 3rd edn (Oxford, 2013), pp. 149–79; P. Brown, *The Ransom of the Soul: Afterlife and Wealth in Early Western Christianity* (Cambridge, MA, 2015), pp. 149–79.
[37] Reimitz, *History, Frankish Identity*, pp. 51–73.

The historiographical genre confronted Gregory both with the opportunity to promote his vision of community as well as a fundamental problem. In writing the *Histories* he had to portray and talk about the different groups and peoples that came to live in the *regnum*, thus furnishing them with historical profiles and identities. But Gregory did not want to provide contemporary individuals and groups with a past that would allow them to legitimately distinguish their positions as independent from his Christian vision of community. In fact, his aim was to destabilise social roles and identities that might emerge as alternative sources of identification. In this regard, Gregory seems to have been particularly concerned with the emergence of Frankish identity as an alternative, independent, or even competing *focus* for identification. In his narrative of the history of Gaul following Clovis's establishment of Merovingian rule *per totas Gallias*[38] (which constitute eight of ten of the books in his comprehensive *Histories*), the name of the Franks appears only forty-four times.[39] In not one of these instances do the Franks represent the entire political or social framework of the Merovingian *regnum*.[40] In the *Histories*, the name describes distinct and largely disconnected social spheres. Neither in the more distant past nor in his own times did Gregory permit overlaps of social or political worlds, lest they coagulate into a shared Frankish identity. Their main connection to each other should be the same as to all other groups and individuals in the *regnum*, that is, through their decision for a shared Christian vision.

Like Venantius, Gregory built upon the relatively wide literary *Spielräume* that corresponded with the social and political rooms for manoeuvre that had been created in the first decades of Merovingian rule. However, Gregory's efforts to undermine the establishment of alternative visions of community in his *Histories* seem to indicate that the bishop of Tours recognised that they were in flux. When Gregory started to write his *Histories* is difficult to determine precisely. There is evidence that he reworked earlier parts or versions all the way up to his death.[41]

[38] Gregory of Tours, *Histories*, II, 42, ed. Krusch, p. 93.
[39] See M. Heinzelmann, 'Die Franken und die fränkische Geschichte in der Perspektive der Historiographie Gregors von Tours', in A. Scharer and G. Scheibelreiter (eds.), *Historiographie im frühen Mittelalter* (Vienna and Munich, 1994), pp. 326–44, here pp. 342–3; and cf. Reimitz, *History, Frankish Identity*, pp. 57–60, with further literature.
[40] See H.-W. Goetz, 'Gens, Kings and Kingdoms: The Franks', in H.-W. Goetz, J. Jarnut, W. Pohl and S. Kaschke (eds.), *Regna and Gentes: The Relationship between Late Antique and Early Medieval Peoples and Kingdoms in the Transformation of the Roman World* (Leiden, 2003), pp. 307–44; H.-W. Goetz, 'Zur Wandlung des Frankennamens im Frühmittelalter', in W. Pohl and M. Diesenberger (eds.), *Integration und Herrschaft: Ethnische Identitäten und soziale Organisation im Frühmittelalter* (Vienna, 2002), pp. 127–44.
[41] For a comprehensive overview, see A. C. Murray, 'The Composition of the Histories and Its Bearing on the Political Narrative', in A. C. Murray (ed.), *A Companion to Gregory of*

Nevertheless, Gregory either began or restarted the work with renewed energy sometime after the death of Chilperic in 584.[42] This was also precisely when we observe an increasing use of the name of the 'Franks' for political legitimation by competing Merovingian kings.

In 585, the Merovingian king Guntram issued the oldest clearly datable extant legal document of a Merovingian king using the title *rex Francorum*.[43] At around the same time, the nephew, adopted son and successor of Guntram, Childebert II, sent letters to the Byzantine emperor in which he presented himself as *rex Francorum*.[44] Other letters from Childebert, and more importantly those of his royal predecessors in the Austrasian kingdom, Theuderic I and Theudebert I, have come down to us in the same collection of letters: the *Epistolae Austrasicae*. But in all of them, the kings use the absolute title *rex*.[45]

Childebert's letters document more than the increasing salience of the Frankish name for political legitimation within the Merovingian kingdoms. They also show that the interaction with other polities in the Mediterranean world and, in particular, Byzantium might have played an important role in this process. In contrast to the Merovingian kings and their elites, such as Gregory and Venantius Fortunatus, most authors outside of Gaul perceived the Merovingian kingdom as the kingdom of the Franks. Comparing the reports of contemporary historians such as John of Biclaro, author of the *Chronica Caesaraugustana*, and other late-antique chroniclers with those of Gregory, illustrates this contrast in perception particularly well. Gregory frequently describes Merovingian kings' deeds and wars without mentioning the name of the Franks, and yet the corresponding entries in other chronicles *do* ascribe agency to the *Franci*.

To give just one example: whereas Gregory's text documents that Childebert I and his brother Chlothar I invaded Hispania and attacked the city of Caesaraugusta *cum exercitu*, the *Chronicle of Caesaraugusta*

Tours (Leiden, 2016), pp. 63–101, who argues for the 590s as the most important period for the extant narrative.
[42] Murray, 'The Composition of the *Histories*', pp. 83–91.
[43] *Edict of Guntram*, ed. A. Boretius, MGH Capitularia (Hanover, 1383), art. 11, p. 10.
[44] For example, *Epistolae Austrasicae* 32, 34, 38, 39 ed. Gundlach, pp. 141, 142, 144, 145; on the Austrasian letters, see the introduction of the edition and Italian translation of Malaspina in Malaspina (ed. and trans.), *Il Liber epistolarum*. Also, see I. N. Wood, 'Why Collect Letters?', in G. M. Müller (ed.), *Zwischen Alltagskommunikation und Literarischer Identitätsbildung. Kulturgeschichtliche Aspekte lateinischer Epistolographie in der Spätantike* (Stuttgart, 2018), pp. 45–62; G. Barret and G. Woodhuysen, 'Assembling the Austrasian letters at Trier and Lorsch', *Early Medieval Europe*, 24 (2016): 3–57, with further references.
[45] For Theudebert I's letter: *Epistolae Austrasicae*, 19, ed. Gundlach, p. 132; for Theudebald's letter: *Epistolae Austrasicae*, 18, p. 131; 25, p. 138; 28, p. 140; 31, p. 141.

reports that the city was besieged by the *reges Francorum*.[46] This was also the perspective held by contemporaries in the Byzantine Empire. Around the middle of the sixth century, the historian Procopius employed well-established stereotypes to reconcile the somewhat dispersed and discordant accounts of different Frankish social groups, individuals and kings.[47] For Procopius, the Franks were the 'new Germans'.[48] Procopius, who accompanied the Byzantine commander Belisarius on his campaigns, utilised a distinct mix of information in order to construct his particular image of the Franks.[49] Older stereotypes handed down by Roman ethnography certainly influenced Procopius, but he also had more recent sources, some of which may well have been western and Frankish.[50] Whatever these sources may have been, Procopius described the Franks in highly negative terms as true barbarians.[51]

A generation after Procopius, however, descriptions of the Franks were markedly more favourable. Agathias, the continuator of Procopius' histories, presented the Franks as quite Roman-like. As far as Agathias was concerned, the Franks possessed the same religion and laws as Byzantium, including sophisticated institutions and practices for conflict resolutions. Apart from their outward appearance, the Franks were nearly equals to the Romans of Agathias' time, and sometimes might have been used to show how contemporary Romans *ought* to be. Because the people

---

[46] Cf. *Chronicle of Caesaraugusta a. 541*, ed. Th. Mommsen, MGH AA, 11 (Berlin, 1894, repr. 1981), pp. 221–3, here p. 223, with Gregory, *Historiae*, III, 29, ed. Krusch, p. 125; other examples: John of Biclaro, *Chronicon*, a. 585, ed. Th. Mommsen, MGH AA, 11 (Berlin, 1894, repr. 1981), p. 217, with Gregory, *Historiae*, VIII, 30, ed. Krusch, p. 396; John of Biclaro, *Chronicon*, a. 587, ed. Mommsen, p. 218, with Gregory, *Historiae*, VIII, 45, ed. Krusch, p. 411; John of Biclaro, a. 589, ed. Mommsen, p. 218, with Gregory, *Historiae*, IX, 31, ed. Krusch, p. 450.

[47] G. Greatrex, 'Perceptions of Procopius in Recent Scholarship', *Histos*, 8 (2014): 76–121, at http://research.ncl.ac.uk/histos/documents/2014A03GreatrexPerceptionsofProcopius.pdf, plus addenda 121a–e, at http://research.ncl.ac.uk/histos/documents/2014A03aGreatrexPerceptionsofProcopiusAddendum.pdf; see also M. Meier (ed.), *A Companion to Procopius* (Leiden, 2019, forthcoming).

[48] Procopius, *Wars*, III, 3, 1, ed. H. B. Dewing, 7 vols. (Cambridge, MA, 1914–40), vol. II, p. 23, and V, 12, 7, ed. Dewing, vol., III, p. 119.

[49] A. Cameron, *Procopius and the Sixth Century* (Berkeley, CA, 1985), pp. 211–12, here pp. 214–15.

[50] See E. A. Thompson, 'Procopius on Britta and Brittania', *Classical Quarterly*, New Series, 30 (1980): 498–507; P. Schreiner, 'Gregor von Tours und Byzanz', in J. Gießauf (ed.), *Päpste, Privilegien, Provinzen. Beiträge zur Kirchen-, Rechts-, und Landesgeschichte. Festschrift für Werner Maleczek zum 65. Geburtstag* (Wien, 2010), pp. 403–18; and still for a comprehensive discussion of the sources, P. Goubert, *Byzance avant l'Islam, Byzance et l'Orient sous les successeurs de Justinien, II*, vol. I: *Byzance et les Francs* (Paris, 1955), pp. 197–8.

[51] See Cameron, *Procopius*, p. 212, for different images and function of the accounts on the Franks.

were as law-abiding as they were patriotic, and 'their kings as peaceful and ready to yield', they were able to 'keep their power secure and their laws unbroken'.[52] Agathias then introduces a series of details and stories about the history of the Merovingians and their kingdoms, which were probably not drawn from written sources and some of which came probably from more recent encounters with inhabitants of the Merovingian kingdoms. Agathias contributed some interesting details about the long hair of the Merovingian kings, their traditions of succession, the kinship ties of the last few royal generations and their soldiers' weaponry and combat techniques.[53]

Averil Cameron suggested some time ago that Agathias' choice in presenting the Frankish kingdoms as perfectly compatible with Byzantine culture reflects changing political strategies in Byzantium.[54] For Michael Maas, however, the difference between Procopius and Agathias indicate that each work originated from different arenas of encounter with other peoples, states and groups.[55] Procopius constructed his description from diplomatic sources, which reflect the Byzantine perspective that insisted on the subordination of 'barbarian' rulers in the west. Agathias, on the other hand, foregrounded the issues of Christianity and orthodoxy, which provided more space for common ground. It is well documented that both parties used and further developed this common ground in the last decades of the sixth century. The competing Merovingian kings of Gregory's time were in constant communication and diplomatic exchange with Byzantium, and Merovingian historians and their contemporaries preserved numerous anecdotes describing the exchange of embassies and presents, or relics.[56]

---

[52] Agathias, *Histories*, ed. and trans. J. D. Frendo, *Corpus Fontium Historiae Byzantinae* (Berlin, 1975), p. 11.

[53] Agathias, *Histories*, I, 3, ed. by Frendo, p. 11; I, 5, p. 12, but compare B. Bachrach, 'Procopius, Agathias, and the Frankish Military', *Speculum*, 45 (1970): 435–41.

[54] A. Cameron, 'Agathias on the Early Merovingians', *Annali della Scuola Normale Superiore di Pisa, Classe di Lettere e Filosofia*, 2 (1968): 95–140, here pp. 136–9; for a different interpretation, see A. Kaldellis, *Ethnography after Antiquity: Foreign Lands and Peoples in Byzantine Literature* (Philadelphia, PA, 2013), pp. 21–4.

[55] M. Maas, 'The Equality of Empires: Procopius on Adoption and Guardianship across the Imperial Borders', in J. Kreiner and H. Reimitz (eds.), *Motions of Late Antiquity: Essays on Religion, Politics and Society in Honor of Peter Brown* (Turnhout, 2016), pp. 175–86: this is an explanation that allows for a more complementary reading of Cameron's and Kaldellis' interpretations.

[56] S. Esders, '"Avenger of All Perjury" in Constantinople, Ravenna, and Merovingian Metz. St Polyeuctus, Sigibert I, and the Division of Charibert's Kingdom in 568', in A. Fischer and I. N. Wood (eds.), *Western Perspectives on the Mediterranean: Cultural Transfer in Late Antiquity and the Early Middle Ages, 400–800 AD* (London, 2014), pp. 23–76, with further references.

As Peter Schreiner has shown, Gregory of Tours had at his disposal different and up-to-date reports on the Byzantine Empire and its emperors too.[57] Like Agathias, he might have relied upon diplomatic envoys and embassies making the journey between Constantinople and Gaul.[58] In any case, such diplomatic encounters offered Merovingian envoys new opportunities for displaying themselves as good Christians and worthy heirs of Roman rule and culture. It seems that their partners in the Roman Empire who wanted to forge good relations with the rulers and elites of the Merovingian kingdoms were more than happy to grant the Franks a place in a shared imperial world.

One example is an Alexandrian world chronicle long known as the *Excerpta Latina Barbari*.[59] The conception of the chronicle, which is extant in an eighth-century copy from northern France, aligns well with the context of Byzantine–Merovingian connections in the last decades of the sixth century.[60] It presents Alexander the Great's empire as the prefiguration of the Christian ecumeny, while presenting the early Frankish kings with a prestigious place in Roman history, mentioning a *Francus* among the genealogy of the kings of Alba Longa.[61] Another text that might have found its way to Gaul in precisely this context is the so-called Table of Nations. The oldest manuscript from the Frankish kingdoms juxtaposes its post-Roman version of the Tacitean Mannus Genealogy with a Roman genealogy of Frankish kings.[62] The arrangement of the

---

[57] Schreiner, 'Gregor von Tours und Byzanz', pp. 403–18.
[58] For Agathias, see Cameron, 'Agathias and the Early Merovingians', pp. 136–9.
[59] *Apocalypse of Pseudo-Methodius: An Alexandrian World Chronicle*, ed. and trans. B. Garstad (Cambridge, MA, 2012).
[60] Garstad has suggested that the chronicle was compiled in the 530s as a gift for King Theudebert: see Garstad's introduction to his edition and translation of *An Alexandrian World Chronicle*; see also B. Garstad, 'Barbarian Interest in the *Excerpta Latina Barbari*', *Early Medieval Europe*, 19 (2011): 3–42. Given the integration of the Franks into early Roman history and the chronicle's stress on the empire's role as defender of orthodox Christianity, the chronicle seems more likely to be contemporary with Agathias' *Histories*. The manuscript is now preserved in Paris (BN lat. 4884; Codices Latini Antiquiores ed. by Lowe, V, no. 560).
[61] *An Alexandrian World Chronicle*, 8, 4–5, ed. Garstad, pp. 214–17.
[62] W. Goffart, 'The Supposedly "Frankish" Table of Nations', *Frühmittelalterliche Studien*, 17 (1983): 98–13; for the transmission of the text in Italy, see W. Pohl, *Werkstätte der Erinnerung: Montecassino und die Gestaltung der langobardischen Vergangenheit* (Vienna: Oldenbourg, 2001), s.v. Genealogia gentium; see also M. Stoffella, 'Tuscans as *Gens*? Shaping Local Identities and Communities in Early Medieval Tuscany', in G. Heydemann and W. Pohl (eds.), *Post-Roman Transitions: Christian and Barbarian Identities in the Early Medieval West* (Turnhout, 2013), pp. 271–295, for the oldest manuscript, St Gallen 732, see Reimitz, *History, Frankish Identity*, pp. 83 and 216–17, and W. Pohl, 'Genealogy: A Comparative Perspective from the Early Medieval West', in W. Pohl, C. Lutter and E. Hovde (eds.), *Meanings of Community in Medieval Eurasia* (Leiden, 2016), pp. 232–69, here pp. 242–4.

text and the layout of the page clearly underlines the juxtaposition of the genealogy with a catalogue of the early Frankish kings.

The historiographical export of these texts to Gaul seems to have taken place at precisely the time as Gregory's composition of his *Histories* and surely supported visions of Frankish history and identity alternative to Gregory's. Indeed, the Merovingian kings of Gregory's time might well have accepted these imported historiographical visions of 'Frankishness'. As we have seen, the grandiose orchestration of Sigibert's marriage with the Visigothic princess, Brunhild, in 566 was already intended to present the Austrasian ruler as superior to his brothers.[63] Byzantium's endorsement of this position also played an important role in the competition among the Merovingian kings, especially in the aftermath of the death of one brother, Charibert, in 567.[64] There are good reasons to assume that Sigibert concluded his peace treaty with Byzantium as early as 568. It was most likely in this fast-paced political context that the transfer of prestigious relics of the True Cross from Byzantium to Poitiers took place in the same political context.[65]

Unfortunately, the explicit evidence for accurately dating these relic-transfers is not very strong, and reconstructing a timeline demands some detective work drawing upon a number of different hints in the extant evidence.[66] Gregory of Tours is reluctant to contextualise the transfer of the relics with Sigibert's or even Radegund's relations to the Byzantine Empire under Justin II, even though his friend and protégé, Venantius, had expressed Radegund's appreciation for the relics in a poem *ad Justinum et Sophiam* in 569.[67] Gregory seems to have thought it unwise for Sigibert to form a political alliance with Justin II: the Byzantine emperor figures in his *Histories* as a heretical ruler who went insane at the end of his reign, a portrayal that has only come down to us through Gregory's reports.[68] It is very likely that Gregory, who was well connected with the Austrasian court, did not want to associate the political context with the

---

[63] Cf. above, p. 52.
[64] For the intensification of conflicts between the Merovingian kings, see above, p. 52.
[65] Esders, '"Avenger of All Perjury"'.
[66] As has been done by Esders, '"Avenger of All Perjury"'.
[67] Venantius Fortunatus, *Ad Iustinum et Sophiam* ed. Leo, pp. 275–8. Cf. Esders, '"Avenger of All Perjury"', pp. 24–5.
[68] For the contrast of Gregory's negative image of Justin with all other extant Byzantine sources on Justin who portray him in a very positive light, see Schreiner, 'Gregor von Tours und Byzanz', pp. 405–6, 413, see also S. Loseby, 'Gregory of Tours, Italy and the Empire', in A. C. Murray (ed.), *A Companion to Gregory of Tours* (Leiden, 2016), pp. 462–97, with a more comprehensive discussion concluding that 'Gregory had far more material at his disposal that he needed or wanted to incorporate into his Histories' (p. 497).

relics' translations too strongly.⁶⁹ His disapproval of Justin might have played a role, but Gregory seems to have been suspicious of too close contacts with the Byzantine Empire in other contexts as well.

This is most obvious in an episode where Gregory even more explicitly decries the Byzantine connections of another contemporary king: Sigibert's half-brother, Chilperic.⁷⁰ Gregory recounts a meeting with the king, during which Chilperic tries to impress Gregory with presents he had received from the Byzantine emperor, Tiberius.⁷¹ In stark contrast to Justin, Tiberius is presented in Gregory's *Histories* as a capable, wise and pious ruler. Tiberius was a true friend of the poor to whom he donated most of the riches Justin II had collected.⁷² Chilperic, however, was less interested in Tiberius' Christian virtues, than in imperial splendour. He shows Gregory a number of large gold coins, each of them a pound's weight, with the inscription *Gloria Romanorum*.⁷³ But Chilperic also presents Gregory with a great basin of fifty pounds' weight, which he had fashioned out of gold and gems. Chilperic had made them, he explains to Gregory proudly, for the glory of the Franks.⁷⁴ Gregory remains largely unimpressed by what he portrays as a ridiculous mockery of the Byzantine emperor and empire. That aligns well with other passages where he criticises Chilperic above all for his misguided orientation to models of Roman rule, which, according to Gregory, belonged in the past.⁷⁵

However, for Chilperic, this might not have been just an imitation of Roman imperial models but also a reformulation of these models within

---

[69] For Gregory's Austrasian connection, see Heinzelmann, *Gregor von Tours*, pp. 30–6; for his suppression of the political context of the relic transfer, see the forthcoming dissertation of Pia Lucas (Freie Universität Berlin). I am very grateful to Pia Lucas for sharing her insights with me, see also Loseby, 'Gregory of Tours'.

[70] See Heinzelmann, *Gregor von Tours*, pp. 42–9; cf. G. Halsall, 'Nero and Herod? The Death of Chilperic and Gregory's Writing of History', in K. Mitchell and I. N. Wood (eds.), *The World of Gregory of Tours* (Leiden, 2002), pp. 337–50.

[71] Gregory of Tours, *Historiae* VI, 2, ed. Krusch, pp. 266–7.

[72] Gregory of Tours, *Historiae* V, 19, ed. Krusch, p. 225.

[73] Aureus etiam singularum librarum pondere, quos imperator misit, ostendit habentes ab una parte iconicam imperatoris pictum et scriptum in circulo TIBERII CONSTANTINI PERPETUI AUGUSTI; ab alia vero parte habentes quadrigam et ascensorem contentesque scriptum GLORIA ROMANORUM. Multa enim de alia ornamenta, quae a legatis sunt exhibita, ostendit. Gregory of Tours, *Historiae* VI, 2, p. 266.

[74] 'ibique nobis rex missurium magnum, quod ex auro gemmisque fabricaverat in quinquagenta librarum pondere, ostendit, dicens 'Ego haec ad exornandam et atque nobilitandam Francorum gentem feci.' Gregory of Tours, *Historiae* VI, 2, ed. Krusch, p. 266.

[75] See Loseby, 'Gregory of Tours', pp. 483–4; and H. Reimitz, 'Contradictory Stereotypes: "Barbarian" and "Roman" Rulers and the Shaping of Merovingian Kingship', in N. Panou and H. Schadee (eds.), *Evil Lords: Theory and Representations from Antiquity to the Renaissance* (Oxford, 2018), pp. 81–98.

a distinctly Merovingian context.[76] This can also be seen in the letter exchange between Chilperic's nephew Childebert II and the Byzantine court that has survived in the letter collection of the *Epistulae Austrasicae*.[77] Childebert's letters are part of a group of letters whose precise date remains elusive, but it is very likely that they belong to the period between 584 and 590.[78] One of the letters in which Childebert is entitled as *rex Francorum* mentions the hope that relations with the *res publica* would be as strong as under the previous *reges Francorum*.[79] In contrast with the previous kings' intitulations that appear in the same letter collection,[80] Childebert presents the title of *rex Francorum* as the traditional title of the Merovingian kings. At the same time, he also reorients the relationship between the kingdom of the *reges Francorum* and the empire by emphasising his hope for friendship and peace between the two *gentes*.[81]

While the emperor and his officials addressed Childebert as *rex Francorum*, they never picked up the formulation of the Austrasian chancery about the peace between the two *gentes*. When the emperor, Maurice, reminded the Frankish king of his promise to support the Byzantine Empire against the Lombards in Italy, he took the opportunity to clarify how Byzantium saw their relationship. He was the emperor, victor over many *gentes* and ruler of a Christian *res publica*. The *gens Francorum* had to keep the promises they had made in service to the very same *res publica*.[82]

Conclusion

In the last decades of the sixth century, people like Gregory of Tours observed the increasing politicization of Frankishness with unease. The

---

[76] B. Jussen, 'Wie die post-römischen Könige sich in Selbstdarstellung übten', in B. Jussen (ed.), *Die Macht des Königs* (Munich, 2005), pp. 14–26.
[77] Cf. above, p. 55.
[78] See B. Dumezil, *La Reine Brunhaut* (Paris, 2008), pp. 575–92; and comments in *Liber epistolarum*, ed. Malaspina, p. 181. with further literature.
[79] *Epistolae Austrasicae*, 34, ed. Gundlach, p. 142.
[80] Cf. above, n. 45.
[81] 'ut inter utramque gentem copulata caritate': *Epistolae Austrasicae*, 34, ed. Gundlach, p. 143. Childebert also used this formulation in other letters to Byzantine officials, e.g., *Epistolae Austrasicae*, 35, p. 143; 37, p. 144; 38, p. 144.
[82] *Epistolae Austrasicae*, 42, ed. Gundlach, p. 148: 'In Nomine Domini Dei Nostri Iesu Christi, Imperator Caesar Flavius Mauricius Tiberius, Fidelis in Christo, Mansuetus, Maximus, Beneficus, Pacificus, Alamannicus, Gothicus, Anticus, Alanicus, Wandalicus, Erullicus, Gypedicus, Africus, Pius Felix, Incleti, Victor ac Triumphator, Semper Augustus, Childebertho, Viro Glorioso, Regi Francorum. ... Et mirum nobis videtur, si, rectam habere mentem atque priscam gentis Francorum et dicioni Romanae unitatem esse comprobatum adfirmans, nihil operis usque adhuc amicitiae congruum eminentia tua ostendens visa est: dum in scriptis pollicita atque per sacerdotis firmata et terribilibus iuramentis roborata, tanto tempore excesso, nullum effectum perceperunt.' See Goubert, *Byzance*, pp. 108–9.

increasing salience of Frankish identity, however, might not have been their most pressing concern. More important to them was the mutual stress on a shared Christian orthodoxy between the Merovingian kingdoms and Byzantium supported by Justin II's decision in favour of Chalcedonian Christianity.[83] This decision might well have been the background for Agathias' emphasis on the common religious beliefs shared by Byzantines and the Merovingians. For bishops and members of the church of Gaul, however, this may well have interfered with the definition of Christendom they had developed in the Merovingian kingdom since the time of Clovis I.[84] Gregory and his vision of Christian community present a particularly strong example of this confidence. In his various works, he employed this notion of a Gallic Christendom in order to articulate his Christian vision of community and tied it to a specific spiritual topography of Gaul that was strongly shaped by the cults and members of his own family.[85]

While the boundaries of this Christendom were in danger of becoming more permeable as a result of interaction with the Byzantine world, the same interactions increasingly defined the political boundaries of the Merovingian *regnum* as Frankish. While Gregory was unwilling to support such views, his contemporaries seem to have found their new role as members, rulers and elites of a Frankish kingdom attractive. The efforts of Byzantine politicians, diplomats and historians to offer Merovingian elites – as Franks – a prestigious place in the history and present of the Mediterranean world were certainly an important factor in this process.

For the Merovingian kings of Gregory's time, the acknowledgement of their position as *rex Francorum* by the Byzantine court was a welcome opportunity to emphasise their international reputation and imperial recognition in the context of their constant competition with each other and other post-Roman rulers.[86] Such strategies of legitimation might have

---

[83] A commonality that was repeatedly mobilised in the extant letter exchange of the Austrasian letters, see Dumezil, *La Reine Brunhaut*, pp. 575–92.

[84] Brown, *Rise of Western Christendom*, pp. 145–65; I. N. Wood, 'The Franks and Papal Theology', in C. Chazelle and C. Cubitt (eds.), *The Crisis of the Oikoumene: The Three Chapters and the Failed Quest for Unity in the Sixth-Century Mediterranean* (Turnhout, 2006), pp. 223–42; A. Suntrup, *Studien zur politischen Theologie im frühmittelalterlichen Okzident. Die Aussage konziliarer Texte des gallischen und iberischen Raumes* (Münster, 2001); R. W. Mathisen, 'Church Councils and Local Authority: The Development of Gallic Libri Canonum during Late Antiquity', in C. Harrison, C. Humfress and I. Sandwell (eds.), *Being Christian in Late Antiquity: A Festschrift for Gillian Clark* (Oxford, 2014).

[85] I. N. Wood, 'The Individuality of Gregory of Tours', in I. N. Wood and K. Mitchell (eds.), *The World of Gregory of Tours* (Leiden, 2002), pp. 29–46; Heinzelmann, *Gregor von Tours*, pp. 1–26, and cf. M. Heinzelmann, 'Gregory of Tours: Elements of a Biography', in A. C. Murray, *A Companion to Gregory of Tours* (Leiden, 2016), pp. 7–34.

[86] See E. Ewig, *Die Merowinger und das Imperium* (Opladen, 1983), pp. 26–33.

become increasingly important as more members of the Merovingian governing class came to regard Frankish identity an attractive identification for them as a community. This, however, should not be understood as the result of the persistence of Frankish identity among this class. The increasing significance of Frankish identity was as much a novelty as was the emergence of this new governing class.[87] The interaction and communication of inhabitants of the Merovingian kingdoms with the societies, states and empires of the Mediterranean world played an important role for both processes: the formation of this new governing class as well as the increasing salience of its identification as a Frankish elite.

---

[87] For the transformation of the Merovingian governing class in the second half of the sixth century, see I. N. Wood, 'The Governing Class of the Gibichung and Early Merovingian Kingdoms', in W. Pohl and V. Wieser (eds.), *Der frühmittelalterliche Staat: Europäische Perspektiven, Forschungen zur Geschichte des Mittelalters* (Vienna, 2009), pp. 11–22; and Brown, *The Ransom of the Soul*, pp. 152–4; L. Sarti, 'Eine Militärelite im merowingischen Gallien? Versuch einer Eingrenzung, Zuordnung und Definition', *Mitteilungen des Instituts für österreichische Geschichtsforschung*, 124 (2016): 271–95; H. Reimitz, 'Die Franken und ihre Geschichten', in W. Pohl and B. Zeller (eds.), *Neue Wege der Frühmittelalterforschung: Bilanz und Perspektiven* (Vienna, 2018), pp. 201–16.

Part II

Patterns of Intensification: The 580s

4 Cultural Transmission Caught in the Act: Gregory of Tours and the Relics of St Sergius

Phillip Wynn

While securing support for his rebellion in 585, Gundovald made an alliance with Bishop Bertram of Bordeaux. During his stay there, the following incident occurred, according to our source, Gregory of Tours' *Histories*:

> At that time while Gundovald was staying in the city of Bordeaux, its bishop Bertram was quite close to him. When Gundovald asked what they could provide as support for his undertaking, someone told him that there was a king in the East who had removed the thumb of Saint Sergius the martyr and attached it to his right arm. He trusted to its aid whenever he had to attack his enemies. The enemy host would take flight at the instant he raised his right arm, as though overwhelmed by the miraculous power of the martyr. When Gundovald heard this he began to make diligent inquiries as to whether there was anyone at that place who had merited to acquire relics of Saint Sergius the martyr.
>
> Meanwhile Bishop Bertram got word that the merchant Eufron had returned from another city, where he had gone to let his hair grow back, heedless of the tonsure that Bertram had earlier forced on him as an enemy whose property he lusted after. Then the bishop said, 'There is a Syrian named Eufron who has made his house into a church, where he has set up many of that saint's relics. He has seen them involved in many a helping miracle by the power of the martyr. For example, once when the city of Bordeaux had a huge fire, his house, though surrounded by flames, wasn't even singed.'
>
> (Gregory, *Hist.* 7.31)

Bertram and Gundovald's general, Mummolus, then rushed to Eufron's house, bullied their way in, and ended up hacking off a piece of bone for themselves before leaving. Although judging by Gregory's report on the fire he apparently had no doubts about the relic's power, he also clearly regarded the violent manner by which it was obtained as a profoundly sacrilegious act; in any case, it subsequently proved useless in war in the hands of profaners and sinners.[1]

---

[1] Gregory of Tours, *Libri Historiarum X*, eds. B. Krusch and W. Levison, MGH SRM 1, 1 (Hanover, 1937–51), pp. 350–1; translation by the author.

For the purpose here, this story's interest lies in its being a rare 'snapshot' of cultural transmission from the East as it is happening, and in its illuminating the westward migration of an element in what I term a Christianised culture of war that is first visible in the Byzantine Empire in the mid to late sixth century and that is found spread throughout western Europe over the course of the seventh.

Let me first specify what I'm talking about and fend off the accusation that there already existed by this point a Christianised culture of war. Philippe Contamine, author of a classic work on the history of medieval warfare, remarked of war in general, and of medieval warfare in particular, that 'it is almost never desired, experienced or conceived as pure and unlimited violence, in a crude or elementary fashion. It exists enveloped in (and also masked by) a total conceptual system springing from custom, law, morality and religion ... Put simply, war is a cultural phenomenon.'[2] What I term a Christianised culture of war refers to such an enveloping complex of ideas and practices, a cultural complex that is recognisable in the seventh century and later as almost typically 'medieval'. We see for the first time at this period deeply rooted and interconnected ideas and practices that evidence the emergence of a certain cultural 'style' of war that in its appearance has utterly effaced any sense from antiquity of a discomforting incompatibility between it and Christianity. War can now be expressed, and arguably was at least at times experienced, as a fundamentally Christian endeavour, no different in its religious aspect from other important activities in a culture deeply imbued with Christian ideas and forms.

In historical works and other sources of the period, we see, for example, a number of stories of saintly or angelic epiphanies in battle. A notable instance is the reported appearance of the Virgin Mother of God on the city walls during the Avar siege of Constantinople in 626.[3] Both Frankish and Visigothic sources of the seventh century report angels accompanying armies marching to battle.[4] More specifically as to this passage from Gregory, I want here to focus on the phenomenon of the carrying of icons and relics into battle.

Although the old idea that it is the emperor Constantine who was most responsible for linking Christianity with the politics of war is undoubtedly correct, and although Lactantius and Eusebius of Caesarea

---

[2] P. Contamine, *War in the Middle Ages*, trans. M. Jones (New York, 1984), p. 260.
[3] A. Cameron, 'Images of Authority: Elites and Icons in Late Sixth-Century Byzantium', *Past and Present*, 84 (1979): 5–6.
[4] *Liber Historiae Francorum*, 37 (MGH SRM 2, p. 307); *Historia Wambae regis* 23, ed. W. Levison (MGH: SRM 5), p. 520.

quote from prayers associated with the Roman army, A. D. Lee argues in his social history of war in late antiquity that for some decades after Constantine there is little contemporary evidence for Christian prayer in the Roman military.[5] When such practices are cited again in the late fourth century, it is significant that prayers are associated with individuals, and we rarely hear of bishops or even priests accompanying armies on campaign.[6] It is significant that as late as Gregory's late-sixth-century Merovingian Gaul, it was considered wrong for bishops to accompany armies to battle, Gregory criticising the bishops Salonius and Sagittarius for doing precisely that.[7] In the period between Constantine and the mid sixth century, the rare and sporadic references to clergy accompanying armies seem to be ad-hoc expedients.[8] Or we see Arian bishops accompanying Gothic armies in the late fourth and fifth centuries, for reasons that Ralph Mathisen has argued were purely practical.[9]

As to the later origins of the elements in this Christianised culture of war, it is surely significant that many of the earliest examples, including especially the phenomenon of priests, icons and relics present with armies on campaign, are seen first in the mid to late sixth century, in the Byzantine Empire. It is also the same area that witnesses the first appearance of liturgies that are for the first time explicitly and exclusively connected with war, and, more particularly, military liturgies conducted in the field. Significant, too, is the fact that we have relevant evidence from what has been termed the Byzantine cultural transmission zone of its Western, Latin-speaking provinces in Italy and especially North Africa.[10] It is in the last region that we see for the first time clear evidence for the regular performance of liturgies in the field. In the mid-sixth-century Latin epic poem, the *Iohannis*, a poem recounting the exploits of the Byzantine general John Troglita in North Africa fighting the Berbers, there is an account of a priest celebrating a Eucharist in the middle of

---

[5] On Constantine, P. Stephenson, *Constantine: Unconquered Emperor, Christian Victor* (London, 2009), p. 189; P. Wynn, *Augustine on War and Military Service* (Minneapolis, MN, 2013), p. 71. On the early fourth-century prayers: Lactantius, *De mortibus persecutorum*, 46.6, ed. and trans. J. L. Creed (Oxford, 1984), p. 66; Eusebius of Caesarea, *Über das Leben des Kaisars Konstantins*, IV. 19–20 (*GCS* 1/1, ed. F. Winkelmann [Berlin, 1975]), p. 160. On Christian 'military' prayers immediately after Constantine, A. D. Lee, *War in Late Antiquity: A Social History* (Malden, MA, 2007), pp. 182–3.
[6] Wynn, *Augustine on War*, pp. 76–80.
[7] *Libri Historiarum X* (n. 1 above) IV 42 (p. 175).
[8] D. S. Bachrach, *Religion and the Conduct of War, c. 300–1215* (Woodbridge, 2003), p. 17.
[9] R. W. Mathisen, 'Barbarian Bishops and the Churches "in Barbaricis Gentibus" during Late Antiquity', *Speculum*, 72 (1997): 678–81.
[10] M. McCormick, *Eternal Victory: Triumphal Rulership in Late Antiquity, Byzantium, and the Early Medieval West* (Cambridge, 1986), p. 232.

the Byzantine camp, that is, in 'officers country'.[11] That the celebration of field liturgies was or soon became generalised in the Byzantine Empire is shown in the late-sixth-century Byzantine tactical manual the *Strategikon* of Maurice, wherein the author recommended that a liturgy be performed in camp on the day of battle. Led by priests and officers, including the commander, the soldiers were to recite the *Kyrie eleison* in unison. Then, as each unit marched out of camp to battle, it was to shout three times, 'Nobiscum Deus!'[12]

Regarding this period in the Byzantine Empire, Averil Cameron has described the larger process within which these developments occurred as one of cultural integration, in which the emperors of the late sixth century through the manipulation of ceremonial and religious symbolism painted the imperial office and capital city with a more visibly Christianised palette, largely casting aside the increasingly archaic classical imagery that had informed imperial presentation up to Justinian.[13] For Cameron, the use of icons and relics in war in the late sixth century illustrates how at that time 'emperors associated themselves with a religious development already under way'.[14] Probably the most famous such war-icon was the Camuliana image of Christ, termed αχειροποίητος ('not made with human hands') for the miraculous circumstances of its creation. Its transference to Constantinople sometime in the late sixth century was a potent illustration of the emperors' efforts to enhance the religious prestige of the imperial capital.[15] The image shows up at war in 586, when the general Philippicus paraded it through the Byzantine ranks to stiffen the soldiers' courage before they engaged in battle with the Persians. In 590, there appears another powerful religious symbol in a military context: a golden imperial battle standard that preceded emperor and army and had enclosed within it a relic of the True Cross.[16]

This use of a relic of the True Cross as a battle standard provides one of the clearest indications of Byzantine influence on a developing Christianised culture of war in western Europe. A seventh-century Visigothic liturgy, the 'Ordo quando rex cum exercitu ad prelium egreditur' seems to be the earliest surviving liturgy in the West focused

---

[11] *Flavii Cresconii Corippi Iohannidos seu de bellis Libycis libri VIII*, ed. J. Diggle and F. R. D. Goodyear (Cambridge, 1970), VIII, 318–69, pp. 177–9.
[12] *Strategikon*, II 18 (*CFHB* 17, pp. 138, 140); trans., *Maurice's Strategikon: Handbook of Byzantine Military Strategy*, trans. G. T. Dennis (Philadelphia, PA, 1984), p. 9.
[13] Cameron, 'Images of Authority', *passim*.
[14] Cameron, 'Images of Authority', p. 23.
[15] E. Kitzinger, 'The Cult of Images in the Age before Iconoclasm', *Dumbarton Oaks Papers*, 8 (1954): 83–150, at p. 114; Cameron, 'Images of Authority', p. 23.
[16] Theophylactus Simocatta *Historiae*, ed. C. de Boor, P. Wirth (Stuttgart, 1972), II 3.4–8 (pp. 73–4); V 16.11 (pp. 219–20).

directly and exclusively upon war.[17] Elements in it point clearly to a basis in Byzantine precedents. Already by the late sixth century, Byzantine commanders and soldiers participated in a *profectio bellica* ceremony before setting off to battle. Particularly after Heraclius in the early seventh century revived the practice of emperors accompanying the army in war, this ceremony must have resembled that reported by Leo the Deacon in the late tenth century. There, in a rite held at Constantinople on the eve of leaving on a campaign, the emperor raised the imperial battle standard, a golden cross that contained within it a relic of the True Cross, and with it processed to the church of Hagia Sophia.[18] Likewise, during the Visigothic ceremony, the king in the church received from a deacon a royal battle standard, a golden cross that also had enclosed within it wood from the True Cross, which he handed off to a priest, who bore the cross-standard before the king and accompanied the army on its campaign. In addition, after the king had received the royal battle standard and passed it to the army priest, the army's individual standard-bearers came up and received their own standards from a priest from behind the altar ('accedentes unusquisque accipiunt de post altare a sacerdote bandos suos'). This, too, seems rooted in Byzantine practice. The *Strategikon* of Maurice notes that the army's standards were consecrated before they were given to their bearers, using the same word for the military standards (βανδον) as was used for them in the Visigothic *ordo*.[19]

As to St Sergius himself, he and his fellow martyr Bacchus, supposedly officers in the Roman army martyred during the Great Persecution when their secret Christianity was uncovered, had been venerated in the Byzantine East since the fifth century. Not long before 431, a church had been built to house Sergius' relics at Rusafa in central Syria, and the place became a popular pilgrimage site, especially after the composition of a Greek *passio* in the mid fifth century. But Sergius' fame as a specifically military saint is not attested before the mid to late sixth century. That is the estimated date for a silver flask found in the excavation of a church in north-west Syria, which, as with later objects, depicts Sergius as a soldier on horseback.[20] Even before this ideological evolution in

---

[17] *Liber ordinum*, ed. M. Férotin, Monumenta ecclesiae liturgica V 5 (Paris, 1904), 149.40–153.41: 'ordo quando rex cum exercitu ad prelium egreditur.'
[18] On the early Byzantine *profectio bellica* and its probable identification with the ceremony later described by Leo the Deacon, see McCormick, *Eternal Victory*, pp. 247, 249.
[19] *Liber ordinum*, ed. Férotin, p. 151. On the consecration of Byzantine military standards, *Strategikon* (n. 12 above), VII A 1 (p. 232).
[20] E. K. Fowden, *The Barbarian Plain: Saint Sergius between Rome and Iran* (Berkeley, CA, 1999), pp. 7, 28–43.

Sergius' reputation, however, the emperor Anastasius had had the saint's thumb translated to a shrine in Constantinople. That particular relic is not heard of again, other than in this story of Gregory's.[21]

Gregory's story is also the only source that associates this particular relic with an efficacy in war. His account is not dependent on the saint's *passio*, though, but instead resembles a biblical story that is an element in a complex of biblical narrative types that informed the imaginative representation of war in the early medieval period. In Exodus 17, while the Israelites are on their way from Egypt to Canaan, they encountered the Amalekites in the desert. Moses ordered Joshua to lead the Israelites in battle, while he carried the rod of God to the top of a nearby hill, accompanied by his brother Aaron and the otherwise little-known Hur. As long as Moses held up his hand holding the rod, the Israelites were victorious. But whenever his hand drooped, the Amalekites prevailed. So Aaron and Hur held up his hands until the Amalekites were defeated.[22]

Echoes of this story appear in Christian representations of war from early on and continuously thereafter. In the first years of the fifth century, Rufinus of Aquileia reflects it in his account of the Emperor Theodosius' prayer on a hill overlooking the battle of the Frigidus.[23] About thirty years later, the scene is depicted on one of the mosaic panels in the nave of the Roman church of Santa Maria Maggiore.[24] Later manifestations include references to the story in a war-related mass in the early eighth-century Bobbio Missal and in Pope Nicolas I's letter to the Bulgar khan in 866.[25] It therefore seems difficult to associate particularly the story told by Gregory with what is otherwise known of Sergius' hagiography. Rather, this story in Gregory is best seen as the attraction to an appropriate saint of a Christian narrative type associated with war.

Gregory's account here seems uncertain at times, but some of this vagueness may be deliberate, as with his failure to name the 'king in the East' who used the thumb relic to defeat his enemies.[26] Gregory's failure to name the king involved arguably does not exhibit ignorance but is rather a literary device to impart a folkloric and generalising exemplificative quality to the story, as we can see him doing elsewhere in

---

[21] Fowden, *The Barbarian Plain*, pp. 92, 132.
[22] Exodus XVII. 8–13.
[23] Rufinus, *Historia Ecclesiastica* XI 33 (*GCS, Eusebius Werke II*, ed. E. Schwartz [Greek], T. Mommsen [Latin] [Leipzig, 1903]), pp. 1037–8.
[24] A. Nestori and F. Bisconti (eds.), *I mosaici paleocristiani di Santa Maria Maggiore negli acquarelli della collezione Wilpert* (Vatican City, 2000), Table 33.
[25] *The Bobbio Missal: A Gallican Mass-book (MS Paris Lat. 13246)*, Henry Bradshaw Society 58, ed. E. A. Lowe (London, 1920), pp. 151–2, no. 493; Nicolas, *Epist.* 99.38 (MGH Epist. 6, p. 582).
[26] Fowden, *The Barbarian Plain*, p. 129, speculates on the identity of this king.

his oeuvre.[27] With its reminiscence of Exodus 17, the story aspires to present an archetypical portrait of God's immediately dispositive role in war mediated through the power of the saints. In the broader narrative context of the *Histories* here and Gregory's report on Gundovald's revolt, the pretender's search for a victory-giving relic from the East comes across like the quest of a Third World country for the latest high-tech weaponry from America. The story shows that Gregory in the 580s knew that the 'latest thing' in war from the holy sites of the East was the use of saints' relics in battle. So here we seem to have caught cultural transmission in the act.

---

[27] For other examples of this technique in Gregory, see P. Wynn, 'Wars and Warriors in Gregory of Tours' *Histories* I–IV', *Francia*, 28 (2001): 1–35, at p. 18 and nos.138, 140.

5 Hermenegild's Rebellion and Conversion: Merovingian and Byzantine Connections

Wolfram Drews

Hermenegild: Rebel or Saint?

The Visigothic prince Hermenegild, later called San Hermenegildo in Spanish, is an enigmatic figure who has aroused the interest of scholars from the early modern period onwards. Especially in the nineteenth century, the ideological perspective of researchers had a decisive influence on the interpretation of Hermenegild's actions.[1] However, these very diverse interpretations had their respective foundation in different early medieval sources, which are clearly divided in two, one is tempted to say, opposing camps. The two contemporary Spanish authors, John of Biclaro and Isidore of Seville, present Hermenegild as a usurper, who rebelled against his father; they do not address any religious dimension at all.[2] The two non-Spanish sources, Gregory of Tours and Gregory the Great, paint a totally different picture: Especially Pope Gregory presents a pious prince who converted from Arianism to Catholicism; this conversion is said to have been the driving motive for the prince's rebellion.

Pope Gregory goes even one step further. In his dialogues, he presents Hermenegild as a martyr for the Catholic cause, while omitting his rebellion against his father.[3] In the following centuries, this papal 'sanctification' gave rise to Hermenegild's inclusion in martyrologies, even to his

---

[1] See F. Görres, 'Kritische Untersuchungen über den Aufstand und das Martyrium des Westgothischen Königsohnes Hermenegild. Eine Kirchenhistorische Abhandlung', *Zeitschrift für Historische Theologie*, 43 (1873): 1–109 for a summary and assessment of earlier scholarship.

[2] Johannes Biclarensis, *Chronicon*, 54; 65, C. Cardelle de Hartmann (ed.) (CCL = Corpus Christianorum Series Latina 173A) (Turnhout, 2001), 71, 73; Isidorus Hispalensis, *Historia Gothorum*, 49, T. Mommsen (ed.) (MGH AA = Monumenta Germaniae Historica Auctores Antiquissimi 11) (Berlin, 1894), pp. 267–95, at p. 287: '*Hermenegildum deinde filium imperiis suis tyrannizantem obsessum exsuperavit.*'

[3] Gregorius Magnus, *Dialogues*, 3, 31, 1–8, A. de Vogüé and P. Antin (eds.) (SC = Sources Chrétiennes 260) (Paris, 1979), pp. 384–90; J. N. Hillgarth, 'Coins and Chronicles: Propaganda in Sixth-Century Spain and the Byzantine Background', *Historia: Journal of Ancient History*, 15 (1966): 483–508, at p. 486.

veneration in Byzantine, orthodox Christianity.[4] In the later Middle Ages and in the early modern period, the figure of Hermenegild returned to Spain to be remembered and venerated as a saint, which basically meant the eventual adoption of Gregory the Great's perspective by Spanish Catholicism. Finally, at the instigation of King Philip II, Pope Sixtus V officially canonised Hermenegild, 1,001 years after his death (or after his martyrdom, depending on the perspective adopted, respectively); the picture of San Hermenegildo was finalised.

Dynastic Entanglements and a Rebellious Tradition

Frankish and Byzantine connections of Hermenegild's case will become clearer by first looking at his family and at the political alliances of various family members. In 579, he married Ingund, daughter of the Merovingian Sigibert I and Brunhild. Hermenegild's mother-in-law, Brunhild, was a Visigothic princess, being the daughter of King Athanagild and Goiswinth. The figure of Athanagild is a good starting point for looking at Hermenegild's story because it presents important parallels. The Visigothic noble, Athanagild, rebelled against the legitimate king, Agila, in 551. Athanagild's centre of power lay in the province of Baetica in southern Spain, which had never been settled and controlled by the Visigoths.[5] To bolster his forces, Athanagild appealed to the Byzantines for help, who had just recently reconquered Vandal Africa and were about to deal the death blow to Ostrogothic Italy, in both cases originally pretending to interfere in dynastic struggles.[6] Athanagild's rebellion seemed to be a parallel case, a convenient starting point for the Byzantine recuperation of formerly Roman *Hispania*. King Agila was finally defeated and killed in Mérida in 555, and Athanagild was turned from usurper and 'tyrant' into the legitimate king.[7] He was the first

---

[4] W. Lackner, 'Westliche Heilige des 5. und 6. Jahrhunderts im Synaxarium Ecclesiae Constantinopolitanae', *Jahrbuch der Österreichischen Byzantinistik*, 19 (1970): 185–202, at pp. 190–2.

[5] Hillgarth, 'Coins and Chronicles', p. 495.

[6] Isidorus Hispalensis, *Chronicon*, 399a, T. Mommsen (ed.) (MGH AA 11) (Berlin, 1894), p. 475; Isidorus Hispalensis, *Historia Gothorum*, 47 (p. 286); W. Goffart, 'Byzantine Policy in the West under Tiberius II and Maurice: The Pretenders Hermenegild and Gundovald (579–585)', *Tradition. Studies in Ancient and Medieval History*, 13 (1957): 73–118, at p. 97; K. F. Stroheker, 'Leowigild', in *Germanentum und Spätantike* (Zurich, 1965), pp. 134–91, 135; Hillgarth, 'Coins and Chronicles', p. 495.

[7] J. Orlandis, 'Algunas Observaciones en torno a la "Tiranía" de San Hermenegildo', in J. Orlandis (ed.), *Estudios Visigóticos*, vol. III: *El Poder Real y la Sucesión al Trono en la Monarquía Visigoda* (Rome and Madrid, 1962), pp. 3–12, at p. 10: 'Atanagildo es el ejemplar típico del "tirano" hecho rey, de la legitimación posterior, tras el éxito, de un poder originariamente tiránico.' Cf. también J. Orlandis, 'En torno a la Noción Visigoda de Tiranía', in J. Orlandis (ed.), *Estudios Visigóticos*, vol. III: *El Poder Real y la Sucesión al*

Visigothic monarch to reside in Toledo.[8] During his reign, the standing of the Visigothic monarchy increased, even though he was unable to drive out his erstwhile supporters, the Byzantines, from the south. It is telling that when two Merovingian brothers, Chilperic and Sigibert, looked for suitable royal brides, they chose Athanagild's daughters, Brunhild and Galswinth.[9]

After Athanagild's death, the Visigothic throne was vacant for several months, until the Gothic nobles chose Liuva I as his successor. Liuva remained in Septimania, associating his brother Leovigild as co-ruler in the Spanish territories.[10] In Athanagild's steps, Leovigild consolidated the Visigothic monarchy, converting Toledo into the real centre of power, adopting Byzantine ceremonial and revising Visigothic legislation.[11] Leovigild associated his two sons by his first marriage to the throne: in 573, Hermenegild and Reccared became co-rulers (*consortes regni*).[12] To consolidate his power, Leovigild himself took Goiswinth, widow of his predecessor Athanagild, as his second wife. In order to strengthen ties with Merovingian Francia, the king married his elder son Hermenegild to Ingund, Brunhild's daughter, in 579. The relationship between Ingund and Goiswinth was thus rather complicated: On the one hand, Ingund was Goiswinth's granddaughter via Brunhild; on the other, she was her daughter-in-law, even though Hermenegild was only Goiswinth's stepson.[13]

Ingund was only about thirteen years old at the time of her marriage, and she turned out to be remarkably headstrong, sticking to her Catholic religion. Her mother Brunhild had converted from Arianism to Catholicism at the time of her marriage to Sigibert, and the Visigothic court expected Ingund to act likewise, converting to the religion of her husband. Her

---

Trono en la Monarquía Visigoda (Rome and Madrid, 1962), pp. 13–42, esp. pp. 33–6 for the application on Hermenegild's case.

[8] K. Schäferdiek, *Die Kirche in den Reichen der Westgoten und Suewen bis zur Errichtung der Westgotischen Katholischen Staatskirche* (Berlin, 1967), p. 137.

[9] Schäferdiek, *Die Kirche*, p. 137. The murder of Galswinth at the hands of Chilperic probably took place soon after Athanagild's death; see I. Wood, *The Merovingian Kingdoms, 450–751* (London, 1994), p. 170.

[10] Johannes Biclarensis, *Chronicon*, 10 (p. 61); Isidorus Hispalensis, *Historia Gothorum*, 48 (p. 268); Stroheker, 'Leowigild', 136.

[11] Cf. P. C. Díaz, 'Visigothic Political Institutions', in P. Heather (ed.), *The Visigoths: From the Migration Period to the Seventh Century – An Ethnographic Perspective* (Woodbridge, 1999), pp. 321–56, at p. 336: 'Beginning in Liuvigild's reign, the Visigoths minted their own gold coins which imitated imperial types.' On Leovigild's gold coinage, see also Stroheker, 'Leowigild', pp. 143ff.

[12] Johannes Biclarensis, *Chronicon*, 27 (p. 65); Schäferdiek, *Kirche*, p. 140; Orlandis, 'Algunas Observaciones', pp. 4ff.

[13] For a genealogical chart, see Wood, *The Merovingian Kingdoms*, p. 170.

grandmother and mother-in-law, Goiswinth, seems to have been especially fervent in trying to convert Ingund, but to no avail: the young princess remained a Catholic. Probably to alleviate tensions, Leovigild sent the young couple away from the court: Hermenegild, who was already *consors regni*, was given the province of Baetica to govern, probably residing at Seville.[14]

Hermenegild's Rebellion and Conversion

According to the Spanish sources, Hermenegild started a rebellion against his father in 579, trying to usurp the throne.[15] This would partly have been a repetition of Athanagild's actions, who had started a similar rebellion in the very same region, probably with the support of the same Hispano-Roman population who had never been really subjected by the Visigothic monarchy, which was partly due to the lack of Gothic settlement in the south. Athanagild, however, had never been *consors regni* of King Agila. On the other hand, following Athanagild's example, Hermenegild appealed to the Byzantines for help: he made contact with the Byzantine forces in southern Spain,[16] and he sent Leander, later to become bishop of Seville, to Constantinople to induce the emperor to dispatch a military expedition to support the insurrection. In this mission, Leander proved to be totally unsuccessful, but he met the future pope Gregory the Great in the Roman capital, which may have been the starting point for Gregory's later interest in Hermenegild's figure.

Meanwhile Hermenegild and Ingund had a son, who was named Athanagild after his great-grandfather, perhaps reflecting also the memory of the beginning of Athanagild's reign in a rebellion that had started in southern Spain. Hermenegild seems to have been the first Spanish ruler who used religious vocabulary on his coins: Among the very few coins that have been preserved from his reign, one issue bears the inscription: *Ermenegildi regi a deo vita*.[17] According to Díaz y Díaz,

---

[14] Johannes Biclarensis, *Chronicon*, 52 (p. 70); Gregorius Turonensis, *Libri Historiarum* 5, 38, B. Krusch and W. Levison (eds.) (MGH SS rer. Merov. = Scriptores Rerum Merovingicarum 1, 1) (Hanover, 1951), pp. 243–5; Goffart, 'Byzantine Policy', p. 87.

[15] Johannes Biclarensis, *Chronicon*, 54 (p. 71).

[16] Gregorius Turonensis, *Libri Historiarum*, 5, 38 (pp. 244ff.): 'ad partem se imperatoris iungit, legans cum praefectum eius amicitias, qui tunc Hispaniam impugnabat.'

[17] J. Vives, *Inscripciones Cristianas de la España Romana y Visigoda*, 2nd edn (Barcelona, 1969), p. 445; G. C. Miles, *The Coinage of the Visigoths of Spain Leovigild to Anchila II* (New York, 1952), p. 47 (199ff.); M. C. Díaz y Díaz, 'La Leyenda *Regi a Deo Vita* de una Moneda de Ermenegildo', *Analecta Sacra Tarraconensia. Revista de ciències historicoeclesiàstiques*, 31 (1958): 261–9; J. Vives, 'Sobre la Leyenda *a Deo Vita* de Hermenegildo', *Analecta Sacra Tarraconensia. Revista de ciències historicoeclesiàstiques*, 32

it was minted at the beginning of his insurrection when Hermenegild appears to have appealed to the support of the Catholic Roman population in southern Spain.[18] The formula may actually recall phrases used at his royal inauguration.[19] It was only later that religious legends appeared also on his father's coins, who, interestingly, did not adopt religious imagery to bolster his rule before his son's rebellion.[20] According to Hillgarth, it was also Hermenegild who first followed the Byzantine example of using religious arguments to increase his political standing:

> Hermenegild's alliance with Byzantium … is equally clearly reflected in his coinage. His first coin legend, 'regi a Deo vita', seems inspired … by a contemporary coin of Byzantine Africa, but with the very significant additions of the words 'a Deo', absent from the Byzantine bronze, stressing the orthodox character of the reign, a point, of course, unnecessary to stress in Byzantium.[21]

According to non-Spanish authors, Hermenegild converted to Catholicism before starting his revolt; in fact, Pope Gregory does not mention the rebellion at all. The influence of both his wife, Ingund, and of Leander, future bishop of Seville, is said to have been instrumental in bringing about his conversion. The influence of his wife Ingund is said to have been decisive in this respect; the young princess not only rejected all invitations to join the Arian church, she instead induced her husband to embrace the faith of the majority of the Hispano-Roman population. It is important to note that it was only after Hermenegild's conversion that Leovigild changed his religious policies:[22] he convened an Arian synod to Toledo in 580, which decisively changed the conditions under which people could convert from Catholicism to Arianism.[23] Before, any Catholic wanting to join the Arian faith had to be rebaptised; henceforth, rebaptism became unnecessary, the recitation of an Arian doxology based on early Christian theology was regarded as sufficient.[24]

(1959): 31–4 argues for the interpretation of the words *Ermenegildi regi* as being in the genitive case, usual in Visigothic numismatic usage.

[18] Díaz y Díaz, 'La Leyenda', p. 263.
[19] Cf. Díaz y Díaz, 'La Leyenda', p. 264: 'reproduce la aclamación religiosa que, quizá en el momento de su unción y consagración como rey, le fue dirigida por el clero.'
[20] Hillgarth, 'Coins and Chronicles', p. 506.
[21] Hillgarth, 'Coins and Chronicles', p. 507.
[22] Schäferdiek, *Kirche*, pp. 157–64.
[23] On his religious policies generally, see M. Mülke, 'Guter König und doch Verfolger? Die Religionspolitik des Westgotenkönigs Leovigild im Urteil der zeitgenössischen Historiker (Johannes Biclarensis und Isidor von Sevilla)', *Frühmittelalterliche Studien*, 50 (2016): 99–128; on the Arian synod cf. M. Mülke, '*Romana religio* oder *catholica fides*? Der Westgotenkönig Leovigild und das arianische Reichskonzil von 580 n. Chr. in Toledo', *Frühmittelalterliche Studien*, 43 (2009): 53–69.
[24] Stroheker, 'Leowigild', p. 174.

Hermenegild's Rebellion and Conversion

Consequently, numbers of converts to Arianism increased, which also included Catholic clergy, even Bishop Vincentius of Saragossa.[25]

Leovigild had so far been a very successful ruler, also in military terms.[26] Therefore, it is remarkable that during the first few years of his son's rebellion he did not take recourse to military means to quell the insurrection. Apparently, he tried to solve the problem by peaceful means, undermining the ideological foundations of Hermenegild's insurrection and usurpation.[27] From the Catholic perspective, this was tantamount to religious persecution, even though physical force never actually seems to have been employed against Catholics unwilling to convert; at most, they were sent into exile.[28] This happened, for instance, to the author of the major Spanish historiographical source, John of Biclaro, who lived in exile in Barcelona during the crucial years of Hermenegild's rebellion. The only relevant epigraphic source that has come down to us reflects this alleged persecution an inscription found on a marble slab at Alcalá de Guadaira, dating to 580 or 581, which reads: *In nomine Domini anno feliciter secundo regni domni nostri Erminigildi regis, quem persequitur genetor sus dom. Liuuigildus rex in cibitate Ispa. ducti aione.*[29] It is safe to assume that this inscription reflects the official perspective adopted and propagated in the territories ruled by the rebel.[30]

In addition to his ideological advance against Hermenegild and his supporters, Leovigild successfully prevented the Merovingian relatives of the young couple from providing military help. This was achieved by a number of diplomatic embassies, which incidentally also provided Gregory of Tours with part of the information he included in his *Historiae*.[31] Leovigild induced King Chilperic of Neustria to block

---

[25] Johannes Biclarensis, *Chronicon*, 57 (p. 71).
[26] Isidorus Hispalensis, *Chronicon*, 404, 407 (p. 477); Isidorus Hispalensis, *Historia Gothorum*, 49 (p. 287).
[27] Cf. Goffart, 'Byzantine Policy', p. 91: 'Leuvigild wanted to give Hermenegild every chance to change his mind and repent.'
[28] Stroheker, 'Leowigild', 178.
[29] Vives, *Inscripciones Cristianas*, p. 364; Schäferdiek, *Kirche*, pp. 143ff.
[30] Schäferdiek, *Kirche*, p. 148. In the account presented by Gregory of Tours, the alleged persecution is much more prominent, even though only exile is mentioned as a measure actually employed against Catholics: 'Magna eo anno in Hispaniis christianis persecutio fuit, multique exiliis dati ... ' (Gregorius Turonensis, *Libri Historiarum*, 5, 38 [pp. 243–5]). Later in the same chapter, Gregory has Hermenegild address his father in direct speech as follows: 'Non ibo, quia infensus es mihi, pro eo quod sim catholicus.' For Isidore's perspective, equally only mentioning banishment as the apparently only punishment imposed, see Isidorus Hispalensis, *Historia Gothorum*, p. 50 (pp. 287ff.): 'Denique Arrianae perfidiae furore repletus in catholicos persecutione commota plurimos episcoporum exilio relegavit.'
[31] Cf. Gregorius Turonensis, *Libri Historiarum*, 6, 40 (pp. 310–13).

advances from other Merovingian kingdoms, which was facilitated by the betrothal of Chilperic's daughter, Rigunth, to his second son, Reccared.[32]

Finally, Leovigild resorted to military means to subdue Hermenegild in the south (between 581 or 582 and 584); the usurper was beleaguered in Seville, which fell after a long siege. Hermenegild fled to Byzantine Cordoba, from where he was extradited to his father, who had paid the Byzantine commander substantial sums of money. The former *consors regni* was stripped of his royal garb and sent into exile at Valencia.[33] A year later, he was murdered by a certain Sisbert;[34] it is unclear whether this happened at the instigation of his father, who died a year later.

Even though this was the end of Hermenegild's rebellion, it was not the end of the Frankish and Byzantine ramifications of the matter. Ingund and her son, Athanagild, remained alive; they had stayed in Byzantine custody, being sent to Constantinople by way of Byzantine Africa. Ingund died on the way, and only Athanagild reached Constantinople, where he proved to be a very valuable hostage to the emperor. Maurice was at this time fighting the Lombards in Italy, and he had repeatedly tried to induce the Merovingians to join Byzantine forces against the invaders. Part of these designs had been the support provided to the usurper Gundovald, still under the rule of the previous emperor Tiberius.[35] Byzantine attempts to gain Frankish support had also included the payment of subsidies to Merovingian kings, who had on several occasions made incursions into Italy, without, however, achieving the results the Byzantines had wished for. When Prince Athanagild reached Constantinople, the emperor, Maurice, tried to use his hostage to induce Athanagild's grandmother Brunhild to renew Frankish military operations in Italy. According to Walter Goffart, 'Maurice's success lay in withdrawing the empire from Tiberius' Spanish diversion, while at the very same time obtaining hostages who were employed with great effectiveness to provoke Frankish expeditions against the Lombards.'[36] A few of the famous *Epistolae Austrasicae* were written in this context: Brunhild, who had never actually seen her grandson, declared her ardent desire to be reunited with Athanagild (in fact, we only know the prince's name

---

[32] Schäferdiek, *Kirche*, p. 149; Goffart, 'Byzantine Policy', p. 89; cf. Gregorius Turonensis, *Libri Historiarum*, 5, 38 (pp. 243–5).
[33] Johannes Biclarensis, *Chronicon*, 68 (p. 74).
[34] Johannes Biclarensis, *Chronicon*, 73 (p. 75).
[35] The 'Byzantine–Spanish–Gallic triangle of relations', in the years 579–82 has been thoroughly studied by W. Goffart ('Byzantine Policy', p. 73). Cf. Goffart, 'Byzantine Policy', p. 102: 'it can safely be concluded that Tiberius was in fact the imperial paymaster of Gundovald's expedition.'
[36] Goffart, 'Byzantine Policy', p. 74.

from this epistolary exchange).³⁷ Letters were sent back and forth that have been thoroughly analysed by Andrew Gillet.³⁸ In the end, Brunhild did send military forces to Italy, which however proved to be of little help to the Byzantines. Athanagild's fate remains unknown.

The Enigma of Hermenegild's Motifs

The reason of Hermenegild's rebellion remains a mystery. Being Leovigild's eldest son, already associated to the throne as a *consors regni*, he might quietly have waited for his father's demise. It is doubtful whether the intrigues of Queen Goiswinth, usually presented as a staunch and devout Arian, were sufficient to drive the young king to rebellion.³⁹ We might also ask whether the influence of Ingund was strong enough to induce her husband to start a rebellion against her own grandmother with whom she disagreed on matters of religion. Another factor that should be taken into consideration is Reccared, the final victor of the affair.⁴⁰ The relationship between the two brothers, both being *consortes regni*, was unclear.⁴¹ It was unusual for a Gothic king to associate two princes to his throne. Leovigild's brother Liuva had associated his own brother to the throne, being already king and effectively dividing the kingdom in two parts, the one in Gaul, the other in Spain. From the start, Leovigild seems to have been regarded as his brother's chosen successor, so there was little room for conflict between the two brothers in the first generation of the new dynasty.

Things were quite different with Leovigild and his two *consortes regni* of the second generation; there does not seem to have been any territorial division between the brothers, and also the succession to their

---

37 For epistolary conventions, see A. Gillett, 'Love and Grief in Post-Imperial Diplomacy: The Letters of Brunhold', in B. Sidwell and D. Dzino (eds.), *Studies in Emotions and Power in the Late Roman World: Papers in Honour of Ron Newbold* (Piscataway, NJ, 2010), pp. 127–65, esp. pp. 142–5.

38 A. Gillett, 'Ethnography and Imperium in the Sixth Century: Frankish and Byzantine Rhetoric in the Epistolae Austrasicae', in G. Nathan and L. Garland (eds.), *Basileia: Essays on Imperium and Culture in Honour of E. M. and M. J. Jeffreys* (Brisbane, 2011), pp. 67–81; Gillet: 'Love and Grief.'

39 Cf. Schäferdiek, *Kirche*, p. 148. This is the interpretation given by Gregory of Tours (Gregorius Turonensis, *Libri Historiarum*, 5, 38 [pp. 243–5]): 'Caput quoque huius sceleris Goisuintha fuit.'

40 For continuities between the reigns of Hermenegild and Reccared, for instance in chancellery usage and acclamations, see Díaz y Díaz, 'La Leyenda', p. 263.

41 Following Frankish custom, Gregory of Tours assumes that Leovigild divided the kingdom between his sons: 'regnum aequaliter divisit' (Gregorius Turonensis, *Libri Historiarum*, 4, 38 [pp. 243–5]); cf. Orlandis, 'Algunas Observaciones', p. 4; Isidore's chronicle attributes the 'division' to Hermenegild: 'Gothi per Ermenigildum Leuuigildi filium bifarie divisi mutua caede vastantur' (Isidorus Hispalensis, *Chronicon*, 405 [p. 477]).

father's throne seems to have been unclear. Regarding the association of Liuva and Leovigild, Isidore of Seville expresses a certain amount of scepticism: *dum nulla potestas patiens consortis sit*.[42] It is interesting that throughout Visigothic history there was no second instance of an association of two *consortes regni*. In the seventh century, there was only one case of co-regency, when Chindaswinth associated his son and successor, Recceswinth, to his throne in 649. The unusual and potentially dangerous installation of two *consortes regni* may have contributed to Hermenegild's decision to mount a rebellion; he was, after all, the elder son, who may have regarded the succession as his natural right. In contrast to Merovingian Francia, there was no Gothic tradition of dividing kingship between the sons of a ruler, and Hermenegild is likely to have regarded his own rights to succession as superior to those of his younger brother. Remarkably, Leovigild founded a city in honour of his second son in 577, after bestowing the title of *consors regni* to both of his sons in 572.[43] Hermenegild may quite reasonably have taken the foundation of Reccopolis as a hint that their father preferred his younger son to himself. What seems to be clear is that religion was not the primary motif, only a political argument used later in the struggle.

The Final Predominance of the *Causa Fidei*

Hermenegild's rebellion and its aftermath provide a good opportunity to study the entanglement of different Mediterranean regions in the second half of the sixth century. There were various driving forces contributing to this entanglement of political initiatives: First, there was the Byzantine Empire that had managed to regain a large part of the Mediterranean coastline. However, the empire needed barbarian allies, not only when interfering in power struggles serving as a starting point for military intervention; Walter Goffart has pointed to 'the perpetual Byzantine care to welcome dissident barbarians.'[44] Barbarian allies were also needed when other barbarians had to be driven out of certain regions; this is especially clear with regard to the Lombards in Italy, against whom Emperor Maurice tried to mobilise Merovingian allies. Since the Byzantines were increasingly unable to send troops because of other military engagements in the east, they dispatched subsidies and bribes. Skilful barbarian leaders

---

[42] Isidorus Hispalensis, *Historia Gothorum*, 48 (pp. 286ff.).
[43] Johannes Biclarensis, *Chronicon*, 27, 50 (pp. 65, 70). Isidore of Seville does not seem to relate the events of Leovigild's reign chronologically; he mentions the foundation of Reccopolis only after referring to Leovigild's religious policies and also after pointing out Hermenegild's rebellion (Isidorus Hispalensis, *Historia Gothorum*, 51 [p. 288]).
[44] Goffart, 'Byzantine Policy', p. 80 note 28.

such as Leovigild followed the example set by the Byzantines: Not only did he adopt Byzantine court ceremonial, he also copied the Byzantine example of paying bribes when he paid the Byzantine commander in Baetica in order to induce him to hand over his rebellious son.[45] The chronicle of John of Biclaro, whose author had spent seventeen years in Constantinople, shows the gradual shift within Mediterranean power structures: 'Under Leovigild there appeared to be emerging a new centre of power in the Mediterranean, which could stand against Byzantium.'[46]

A second sphere of entanglement is constituted by marriage alliances between barbarian kingdoms. Leaving out the recently established Lombards, only the Visigoths and the Franks were left among the earlier barbarian kingdoms founded on western Roman territory in the Mediterranean. From the time of Athanagild onwards, Visigothic and Frankish brides were sent across the borders, and it is not without an ironic touch that one such marriage alliance seems to have been instrumental in setting off the whole Hermenegild affair.

A third sphere of entanglement is provided by the religious field, the most remarkable one as regards change. The Visigothic kingdom itself can be considered a prime example of religious entanglements, being inhabited by people from a Catholic and Jewish Hispano-Roman as well as from a mainly Visigothic, Arian background. In view of the charges brought against the Jews in the seventh century, when they were accused of conspiring with foreign enemies of the Visigoths in order to bring about their downfall, it is worth noting that this charge was totally absent in the sixth century: Neither side in the struggle between Leovigild and Hermenegild blamed anything on the Jews. Another noteworthy fact is that the earlier rebellion of Athanagild seems to have involved no religious argument, even though his insurrection started in the very same region as later Hermenegild's; the Arian Visigothic noble Athanagild relied on the support of the Catholic Hispano-Roman population in Baetica to fight the Gothic king, Agila, without apparently appealing to religious sentiments. When Athanagild's daughters were married to Merovingian kings, both of them seem to have converted without much resistance to the Catholic faith.[47] It seems that before Hermenegild's rebellion, religion was not a major factor at all; there were even a number of Gothic converts to Catholicism, such as Bishop Masona of Mérida and the historiographer John of Biclaro, but before Hermenegild such conversions

---

[45] Gregorius Turonensis, *Libri Historiarum*, 5, 38 (pp. 243–5); Schäferdiek, *Kirche*, p. 156.
[46] Hillgarth, 'Coins and Chronicles', p 488. On Leovigild's creation of 'another, an alternative Byzantium in the West', see 'Coins and Chronicles', p. 498.
[47] Schäferdiek, *Kirche*, p. 138.

do not seem to have given rise to suspicions and apprehensions on the part of the Gothic monarchy. Even though Leovigild followed the Byzantine example in several fields, he does not seem to have done so in religious matters prior to 579.[48]

Everything changed with Hermenegild's rebellion. Suddenly, religion seems to have become an argument in the political arena. It seems probable that the rebel was the first to take recourse to religious arguments, his more conservative father only followed suit.[49] The religious argument is prominent on Hermenegild's coin discussed above, which was probably meant to appeal to the loyalty of the Catholic majority in southern Spain. Also, the inscription from Alcalá de Guadaira mentioned earlier points to the prominence of the religious argument at the very beginning of the 580s. According to Knut Schäferdiek, religion was only a secondary element in Hermenegild's rebellion, meant to bolster his support among the Hispano-Roman population. The religious argument was also prominent in Hermenegild's diplomatic endeavours meant to secure foreign aid from Catholic monarchs – first, probably, from the Merovingian relatives of his wife,[50] second from the Byzantines.

The mission of the future bishop of Seville, Leander, is very telling in this respect. While trying to gain military support without any success, he is said to have composed various writings against the Arians precisely during his stay in Constantinople. During this time, he met the papal apocrisiarius, Gregory, the future pope, who would later dedicate his *Moralia in Job* to Leander. In his dedicatory letter, the pope refers to the purpose of Leander's mission: It was the *causa fidei* that had led a Visigothic embassy to Constantinople.[51] On the one hand, these words clearly refer to Hermenegild's rebellion and conversion, but on the other, there seems to be an echo of later developments, during which the same Leander presided over the third council of Toledo in 589, at which the

---

[48] Therefore, Díaz's statement is valid only for the final period of Leovigild's reign: 'Liuvigild aspired to a unity of kingdom, law and faith, which undoubtedly was an emulation of the Empire and specifically of Justinian' (Díaz, 'Visigothic Political Institutions', p. 337); cf. already Görres, 'Kritische Untersuchungen', p. 14: 'war nämlich Leovigild im Gegensatz zu seiner früheren Regierungszeit *nach* dem Abfall seines Sohnes eifrig bemüht, die spanischen Katholiken für die arianische Staatskirche zu gewinnen.' See also 'Kritische Untersuchungen', p. 31: 'Ursprünglich scheint der Gothenkönig gar kein Vorurtheil gegen den Katholicismus gehegt zu haben; wenigstens werden *vor* 579 keine Bedrückungen der Athanasianer erwähnt'.

[49] See Schäferdiek, *Kirche*, p. 140. Before Leovigild there are no records attesting the conversion of Hispano-Romans to the Arian church; cf. Stroheker, 'Leowigild', p. 171.

[50] Hillgarth, 'Coins and Chronicles', p. 496.

[51] Gregorius Magnus, *Moralia in Iob*, ep. ad Leandrum 1, M. Adriaen (ed.), CCL 143 (Turnhout 1979), p. 1 'et te illuc iniuncta pro causis fi dei Wisigotharum legatio perduxisset'.

Goths finally converted to the Catholic faith. In Gregory's eyes, the *causa fidei* in the Visigothic kingdom started during Hermenegild's rebellion, but it gained its full momentum only during the reign of Hermenegild's brother Reccared, who converted to Catholicism ten months after succeeding their father Leovigild.

From Pope Gregory's perspective, the conversion of the Visigoths, the *causa fidei*, started at Hermenegild's time; according to Gregory's account in his dialogues, the usurper died as a martyr of the Catholic cause.[52] One may assume that this interpretation reflects a Spanish view from the time before the third council of Toledo. Originally, local Spanish Catholics may also have seen Hermenegild as a martyr, a view later officially silenced after the decisive turn decreed by Reccared.[53] When Gregory declares: *Sicut multorum qui ab Hispaniarum partibus veniunt relatione cognovimus*,[54] we may conclude that his account of the Hermenegild affair is based on Spanish oral tradition.

If this is true, Pope Gregory's perspective remained faithful to the original Catholic view from Spain. Pope Gregory in a way harmonised the achievements of the two Visigothic brothers: Hermenegild's case was taken up and brought to fulfilment by his brother Reccared through his conversion in 587, which was followed by the conversion of all the Visigoths to Catholicism two years later. In his letters to Reccared, the pope praises the king for the apostolic merit he has achieved by converting a whole people to the true faith. The *causa fidei* of the Visigoths, started by Hermenegild, was accordingly completed by Reccared. Leander of Seville seems to have played a prominent and substantial role under both of the brothers.

Strikingly, at the third council of Toledo, a meeting taking place four years after Hermenegild's death, the name of the Catholic usurper, which must have been on everybody's mind, received no mention at all. Hermenegild should be considered something like the elephant in the room. The most reasonable explanation seems to be that the rebellious *consors regni* was perceived as a potential threat to the political and religious unity achieved just recently. For this reason, both John of Biclaro and Leander's brother Isidore of Seville only refer to him as a rebel, not as a convert or martyr.[55]

---

[52] Gregorius Magnus, *Dialogues*, 3, 31, 5 (p. 386); Schäferdiek, *Kirche*, p. 154.
[53] Cf. Schäferdiek, *Kirche*, p. 154, pointing to the fact that John of Biclaro preserves the name of Hermenegild's murderer, noting also his ignominious end, both of which may be a reflection of an earlier religious veneration of the victim.
[54] Gregorius Magnus, *Dialogues*, 3, 31, 1 (p. 384).
[55] Hillgarth, 'Coins and Chronicles', pp. 497ff.

Only outside Visigothic Spain were things seen in a more nuanced way. While Gregory of Tours was more or less neutral in his assessment, disapproving of the rebellion of a son against his father,[56] Pope Gregory preserved the image of a martyr for the Catholic faith.[57] In the end, Gregory the Great's view was to prevail, as it became predominant in the wider Mediterranean world. The image of the martyr Hermenegild, which may originally also have been cherished by local Spanish Catholics, was disseminated not only through the Latin original of the Gregorian dialogues but also by way of its Greek translation, prepared by Pope Zacharias in the eighth century. From there, it seems to have found its way into the Byzantine liturgy; it was also on the basis of Gregory's dialogues that Florus of Lyons included Hermenegild in his martyrology in the ninth century.[58] Only when medieval Spain was subjected to increasing French and papal influence from the eleventh century onwards did the image of San Hermenegildo finally also come back to Spain. The 'Mediterranean' view, perhaps true to the original Spanish perspective, finally wiped out the more political interpretation proposed and cherished by Hermenegild's Visigothic contemporaries in the wake of the political and religious overthrow instigated by his brother Reccared.

---

[56] Gregorius Turonensis, *Libri Historiarum*, 6, 43 (pp. 314–16); Goffart, 'Byzantine Policy', p. 88 note 63; Görres, 'Kritische Untersuchungen', pp. 64ff. Against this interpretation, see Schäferdiek, *Kirche*, p. 153 and Hillgarth, 'Coins and Chronicles', p. 493 n. 46.

[57] Gregorius Magnus, *Dialogues*, 3, 31, 5 (p. 386): 'ad corpus eiusdem regis et martyris audiri, atque ideo veraciter regis quia martyris.' It is through martyrdom that true kingship seems to be achieved.

[58] Lackner, 'Westliche Heilige', p. 192.

6 Early Byzantine Church Silver Offered for the Eternal Rest of Framarich and Karilos: Evidence of 'the Army of Heroic Men' Raised by Tiberius II Constantine?

Benjamin Fourlas

In 1993, the Baden State Museum at Karlsruhe purchased a small complex of partly damaged early Byzantine silver objects.[1] The exact find spot and context are unknown, but the treasure was probably discovered in the Biqā valley in Lebanon in 1983.[2] The ensemble that obviously belonged to a church, consists of one cross, one censer, three chalices and a spoon (see Fig. 6.1). The composition of the hoard is not unusual, as comparable hoards consisting of a modest number of pieces of church silver are known from Greater Syria.[3]

The time frame for the burial date of the (possibly incomplete) treasure is narrowed down to the later sixth century, the latest object being the censer. The treasure was possibly hidden during the Sasanian advance towards Damascus through the Orontes valley in autumn 613, although

---

[1] This study of the silver objects was initially undertaken as part of the compilation of the collection catalogue of the late antique and Byzantine antiquities at the Baden State Museum at Karlsruhe. The project was initiated by the Leibniz-WissenschaftsCampus Mainz: Byzanz zwischen Orient und Okzident, a cooperation of the Römisch-Germanisches Zentralmuseum Mainz and the Johannes Gutenberg University at Mainz. This paper offers the preliminary results of this research. An extended version with a more in-depth discussion will be published in the Jahrbuch des Römisch-Germanischen Zentralmuseums Mainz 62, 2015. I would like to thank the following people for the fruitful discussion of various aspects of this paper and for providing valuable hints: Prof. Dr Wolfram Brandes (Frankfurt), Dr Jörg Drauschke (Mainz), Prof. Dr Denis Feissel (Paris), Dr Annette Frey (Mainz), Prof. Dr John Haldon (Princeton), Prof. Dr Wolfgang Haubrichs (Saarbrücken), Dr Christian Miks (Mainz), Prof. Dr Marlia Mundell Mango (Oxford), Prof. Dr Dieter Quast (Mainz), Prof. Dr Markus Scholz (Frankfurt) and PD Dr Alexandra Wassiliou-Seibt (Vienna).

[2] According to Prof. Dr Marlia Mundell Mango (personal communication); M. Mundell Mango, 'The Archaeological Context of Finds of Silver in and Beyond the Eastern Empire', in N. Cambi and E. Marin (eds.), *Radovi XIII: Međunarodnog Kongresa za Starokršćanscu Arheologiju II, Split – Poreč 1994* (Vatican City, 1998), pp. 207–52, at p. 215 with n. 41.

[3] M. Mundell Mango, *Silver from Early Byzantium: The Kaper Koraon and Related Treasures* (Baltimore, MD, 1986), pp. 228–50, nos. 57–76.

Figure 6.1 Silver hoard at the Baden State Museum at Karlsruhe, general view. Photograph Th. Goldschmidt/Badisches Landesmuseum Karlsruhe, numbers added.

a burial in the context of the Arab occupation of the Biqā valley in 635–7 appears more likely. Several silver treasures containing church inventories dating to the period between the sixth and the mid seventh century have been discovered in Syria, Lebanon or Turkey that were possibly hidden as a consequence of the Sasanian or the Arab invasion. The treasure in Karlsruhe fits well into this context.[4] Lack of information regarding the

---

[4] The treasures are listed by M. Mundell Mango, 'Introduction', in S. A. Boyd and M. Mundell Mango (eds.), *Ecclesiastical Silver Plate in Sixth-Century Byzantium: Papers of the Symposium Held May 16–18, 1986 at the Walters Art Gallery, Baltimore and Dumbarton Oaks, Washington, DC* (Washington, DC, 1992), pp. xxi–xxxii, at p. xxiv, n. 21. See also the survey by J. Witt, '"Hyper Euches": In Erfüllung eines Gelübdes – Untersuchungen zum Votivwesen in frühbyzantinischer Zeit', Dissertation, Univ. Erlangen-Nürnberg, 2006, pp. 109–13. On the relation between the burial of early Byzantine silver hoards during Sasanian and Arab invasions, see H. Hellenkemper, 'Ecclesiastical Silver Hoards and Their Findspots: Implications for the Treasure Found at Korydalla, Lycia', in S. A. Boyd and M. Mundell Mango (eds.), *Ecclesiastical Silver Plate in Sixth-Century Byzantium: Papers of the Symposium Held May 16–18, 1986 at the Walters Art Gallery, Baltimore and Dumbarton Oaks, Washington, DC* (Washington, DC, 1992), pp. 65–70; A. Effenberger, 'Bemerkungen zum "Kaper-Koraon-Schatz"', in *Tesserae: Festschrift für Josef Engemann* (Münster, 1991), pp. 241–77, at p. 264; J. Drauschke, 'Bemerkungen zu den

archaeological context of the Karlsruhe hoard entails that any interpretation must rely on information provided by the objects themselves. Apart from typological and stylistical criteria, the inscriptions found on three objects contained in this treasure deserve further discussion. Here, a summary of the basic data should suffice:[5]

No. 1 (Figs. 6.2–6.3): Censer (inventory no. 93/1055), height: 6 cm, diameter: c. 10.5–11 cm, weight: 183 g, date: late sixth to first third of the seventh century. Inscription at the upper rim: Μεγαλούς ύπέρ άναπαύσ(εως) Καρίλου προσένεγκ(εν) τῷ άγ(ίῳ) Κο(ν)σταντίνῳ ('Megalous offered this for the [eternal] rest of Karilos to St Constantine'). Decoration: four medallions with nimbed bust images of Christ, a veiled woman (Mother of God), an angel and an armed youthful soldier (certainly St Constantine).

No. 2 (Fig. 6.4): Chalice (inventory no. 93/1058), height: 19.7 cm, diameter: c. 13–15.5 cm, weight: 394.8 g, date: second third of the sixth to early seventh century. Inscription at the upper rim: Υπέρ μνήμης καὶ άναπαύσεως Φράμαριχ ('For the memory and [eternal] rest of Framarich').

No. 3: Spoon (inventory no. 93/1059), length: 22 cm, weight: 57 g, date: second third of the sixth to early seventh century. Inscription: on the grasp, Φύσα μὴ καῇς (blow, so that you shall not burn yourself) and a cross-shaped monogram on the disc consisting of the letters Φ, Ρ, Μ, Α (Fig. 6.5).

The inscriptions on these objects are remarkable for two reasons. First, they attest the obviously Germanic name Framarich (nos. 2–3), which is quite exceptional on early Byzantine church silver.[6] The name Karilos on the censer (no. 1) is also of Western provenance. Both names point to relations of the local community to foreigners from the West. Second, the inscription on no. 1 testifies to a saints' cult of the first

---

Auswirkungen der Perser- und Arabereinfälle des 7. Jhs. in Kleinasien', in O. Heinrich-Tamaska (ed.), *Rauben – Plündern – Morden: Nachweis von Zerstörung und kriegerischer Gewalt im archäologischen Befund*. Tagungsbeiträge der Arbeitsgemeinschaft Spätantike und Frühmittelalter 6. Zerstörung und Gewalt im archäologischen Befund (Bremen, 5.–6. October 2011) (Hamburg, 2013), esp. pp. 140–1.

[5] For a detailed description and discussion of all six objects, see B. Fourlas, 'Ein Komplex frühbyzantinischer Silberobjekte aus einer Kirche des heiligen Konstantin', in F. Daim, B. Fourlas, K. Horst and V. Tsamakda (eds.), *Spätantike und Byzanz: Bestandskatalog Badisches Landesmuseum – Objekte aus Bein, Elfenbein, Glas, Keramik, Metall und Stein* (Mainz, 2017) DOI: 10.11588/propylaeum.384, pp. 145–61, no IV.115–20.

[6] The donor inscription of Ardaburius iunior (of Alan and Gothic origin) on the silver chalice at Dumbarton Oaks is the only other example I know. A. Demandt, 'Der Kelch von Ardabur und Anthusa', *Dumbarton Oaks Papers*, 40 (1986): 113–17.

Figure 6.2 Censer no. 1. Photograph Th. Goldschmidt/Badisches Landesmuseum Karlsruhe.

Christian emperor Constantine otherwise hardly known at this period. The questions I would like to address here are why foreigners from the West are commemorated in the East and how the exceptional veneration of Constantine fits into the historical setting.

The Inscriptions

The inscriptions on the censer and the chalice have a commemorative character. The first inscription is addressed in the dative case (τῷ ἁγίῳ) to St Constantine in view of the salvation of a certain Karilos. This dedication suggests that this gift was offered to a local church dedicated to the sainted emperor. Inscriptions on early Byzantine church silver addressing other saints with τῷ ἁγίῳ, with a toponym added (e.g., 'to St Sergios of the village Kaper Koraon'),[7] confirm the supposition that the

---

[7] On dedicatory inscriptions on early Byzantine church silver naming the receiving saint, see Witt, '"Hyper Euches"', pp. 124–5, pp. 262–3 Liste 19; Mundell Mango, *Silver from Early Byzantium*, p. 5. Examples for analogies for the formula τῷ ἁγίῳ adding a village to the saint's name: D. Piguet-Panayotova, 'The Attarouthi Calices', *Mitteilungen*

Figure 6.3 Medallion with depiction of St Constantine on the censer no. 1. Drawing: M. Ober/RGZM.

mentioned dedication referred to such a church. This implies that this church was consecrated to Constantine as a warrior saint, as suggested by the figure on the medallion depicted in traditional Roman military armour (Fig. 6.3).

The formula ὑπὲρ ἀναπαύσεως is mostly believed to imply that the addressed person (in this case Karilos) had already deceased.[8] The name of the donor Megalous is considered to be female in the nominative case, and it has been assumed that she was Karilos' wife.[9] However, to my knowledge, the name Megalous is not attested anywhere in the nominative case.[10] A funerary inscription from a cenotaph in Emesa

---

zur Spätantiken Archäologie und Byzantinischen Kunstgeschichte, 6 (2009): 9–47, at p. 11 no. 3; Mundell Mango, Silver from Early Byzantium, p. 230 no. 60.

[8] Witt, '"Hyper Euches"', pp. 188–90.

[9] M. Maaß, 'Badisches Landesmuseum. Neuerwerbungen 1993: Byzanz', Jahrbuch der Staatlichen Kunstsammlungen in Baden-Württemberg, 31 (1994): 193–9, at p. 194.

[10] Prof. Dr Denis Feissel (Paris) is of the same opinion (personal communication). Maaß, Badisches Landesmuseum. Neuerwerbungen, p. 194, states that the name is widespread but

Figure 6.4 Chalice no. 2. Photograph: R. Müller/RGZM.

(sixth century) testifies Μεγαλλοῦς in the genitive case (from Μεγαλλώ or Μέγαλλης).[11] But προσήνεγκεν requires a subject in the nominative case.[12] So either the grammar of the inscription is inaccurate or Megalous is indeed a nominative form not yet explicitly attested elsewhere. As occasionally Greek female names end in -οῦς in the nominative case, this possibility is conceivable.[13]

> only refers to an inscription from Emesa (Homs). This inscription, however, is not a conclusive evidence for this name, as it is only tentatively reconstructed from a monogram: L. Jalabert and R. Mouterde, *Inscriptions grecques et latines de la Syrie* (Paris 1959), vol. V, no. 2488: 'Μεγαλοῦς (?) serait un nom féminin en -οῦς [...]. Il paraît moins probable que le 1er nom (A) soit, au génitif, le nom d'homme Μέγας, Μεγάλου'. None of the relevant prosopographical lexica contains an entry for Μεγαλοῦς.
>
> [11] *Supplementum Epigraphicum Graecum*, 44 (1994), p. 533 no. 1575; *Supplementum Epigraphicum Graecum*, 43 (1993), p. 382 no. 1020.
>
> [12] As in the inscriptions of other silver objects from sixth- to early-seventh-century Syrian treasures: Piguet-Panayotova, *Attarouthi Calices*, p. 11 no. 4; Mundell Mango, *Silver from Early Byzantium*, pp. 87–9 no. 7.
>
> [13] For example, the nominative form Μυροκαλλοῦς in a late-antique funerary inscription from Apameia in Bithynia: T. Corsten (ed.), *Die Inschriften von Apameia (Bythinien) und Pylai* (Bonn, 1987), pp. 134–5 no. 131 (advice by Prof. Dr Denis Feissel, Paris).

Early Byzantine Church Silver 93

Figure 6.5 Monogram of Framarich on spoon no. 3. Photograph: R. Müller/RGZM.

Karilos appears to be the name Carilos, a variation of Carillus that is composed of the Celtic Carus and the Latin suffix -illus. This name was widespread in Gaul during the first and until the third century.[14] The toponym Cariliacum (Charly, France Dép. Moselle), which is attested on Merovingian 'national' gold coins dating to the early seventh century, is derived from the (personal) name Carilos.[15] As far as I can see, no record of either Carilos or Carillus dates after the third century. However, the derivation Carellus is familiar in the Latin and in the post-Roman

---

[14] B. R. Hartley, *Names on Terra Sigillata: An Index of Makers' Stamps and Signatures on Gallo-Roman Terra Sigillata (Samina Ware)* (London, 2008), vol. II, pp. 249–51 (Carillus, Carilius, Carilos); E. Künzl, *Die Alamannenbeute aus dem Rhein bei Neupotz: Plünderungsgut aus dem römischen Gallien* (Mainz, 2008), vol. I., p. 398 (Carilus); A. Kakoschke, *Die Personennamen in den zwei germanischen Provinzen: Ein Katalog* (Rahden, 2007), vol. II.1, p. 213 (Carillus); D. E. Evans, *Gaulish Personal Names: A Study of Some Celtic Formations* (Oxford, 1967), pp. 326–7 (Carilos, Carillus). See also I. Kajanto, *The Latin Cognomina* (Helsinki, 1965), pp. 126–7, 284.

[15] M. Buchmüller-Pfaff, *Siedlungsnamen zwischen Spätantike und frühem Mittelalter: Die – (i)acum–Namen der römischen Provinz Belgica Prima* (Tübingen, 1990), p. 146. The 'national' gold coins (*monnaies de monétaires*) labeled *Cariliaco* are dated to 620–40. G. Depeyrot, *Le Numéraire mérovingien: L'âge de l'or* (Wetteren, 1998), vol. II, p. 60.

Romance-speaking regions.[16] The Greek equivalent Καρέλλος is attested only in very few cases for the sixth and seventh centuries; thus, the name does not seem to have been very common.[17] It therefore seems reasonable to assume that the 'Karilos' commemorated by the censer (no. 1) may have originated from a predominantly Latin-speaking part (of the empire or from one of the barbarian kingdoms in western Europe). This hypothesis is supported by the fact that Framarich, who was commemorated on the chalice no. 2, points to a Germanic background.

The first element of the name Frama- happens to be the Romanised form derived from the West Frankish Chramn-.[18] The majority of the records for this name element are to be found in the west Frankish realm and are hardly attested east of the Rhine.[19] The inscription on the chalice (no. 2) provides the oldest evidence for the name Framarich. Further early evidence for this name and its variations is attested for the ninth to the eleventh centuries in northern France and Belgium in particular.[20] Therefore, it seems likely that Framarich came from the Merovingian realm and had roots in northern Gaul or a neighbouring region. The formula Ὑπὲρ μνήμης καὶ ἀναπαύσεως is common on church

---

[16] Examples for early evidence of the name 'Carellus' are known from western Europe and the Latin-speaking areas: Paulus Diaconus, *Historia Langobadorum*, 4,47 [L. Bethmann and G. Waitz (eds.), *Pauli Historia Langobardorum: MGH SRL* (Hanover, 1878), pp. 12–219] (Italy, seventh century); L. Becker, *Hispano-romanisches Namenbuch: Untersuchung der Personennamen vorrömischer, griechischer und lateinisch-romanischer Etymologie auf der Iberischen Halbinsel im Mittelalter (6.–12. Jahrhundert)* (Tübingen, 2009), p. 321 (Spain, 943). The *magister militum* of Italy Carellus (559) possibly originated from the province *Moesia secunda* (see n. 17), which lies on the borders of the Latin- and Greek-speaking areas. I am indebted to Prof. Dr Wolfgang Haubrichs (Saarbrücken), who confirmed that the name Carilos/Carellus is restricted to the Latin-speaking regions (personal communication).

[17] There is no entry in The British Academy, *A Lexicon of Greek Personal Names* (Oxford, 1987–2013), vol. I–V, nor is there one in the Berlin-Brandenburgische Akademie der Wissenschaften (ed.), *Prosopographie der mittelbyzantinischen Zeit*, 3 vols. (Berlin, 2000–13). The best-known bearer of the name Καρέλλος held the office of *magister militum* in Italy in 559. According to two Greek epitaphs, his wife and son were buried in Odessa in the province *Moesia secunda* (Varna/Bulgaria). J. R. Martindale, *The Prosopography of the Later Roman Empire III, AD 527–641* (Cambridge, 1992), p. 272 s.v. Carellus 1. Lead seals inscribed in Latin or Greek attest further men named Carellus for the sixth or seventh century. Ibid. s.v. Carellus 2–3 dates them to the sixth century, but the seals referred to are to be dated rather to the seventh century (advice by Dr Alexandra Wassiliou-Seibt, Vienna).

[18] E. Förstemann, *Altdeutsche Personennamen*. Ergänzungsband verfaßt von H. Kaufmann (Munich, 1968), pp. 119–20 s.v. Fram–; E. Förstemann, *Altdeutsches Namenbuch*, vol. I: *Personennamen* (Munich, ²1966), p. 514 s.v. Framaricus. See also J. M. Piel and D. Kremer, *Hispano-gotisches Namenbuch* (Heidelberg, 1976), pp. 131–2.

[19] I am grateful for detailed advice given by Prof. Dr Wolfgang Haubrichs (Saarbrücken) on the regional distribution of this name.

[20] See the references compiled by Förstemann, *Altdeutsches Namenbuch*, vol. I, p. 514.

silver of the sixth century and might indicate that Framarich was already deceased.[21]

The monogram on spoon no. 3 undoubtedly refers to the same Framarich.[22] The inscription 'Blow, so that you shall not burn yourself' suggests that the spoon was originally designed to be used as part of a dinner set, not for liturgical purpose.[23] The spoon and the chalice may have been part of Framarich's personal belongings posthumously donated to the church.

The names suggest that Framarich certainly, and quite certainly Karilos as well, had foreign, i.e. non-Greek, roots. As Germanic people living in the Byzantine Empire usually adopted Greek personal names by the second or third generation at the latest,[24] it seems likely that at least Framarich had come to the East as a first-generation immigrant. Interestingly, Framarich's name most probably indicates an origin from northern Gaul, and the Gallo-Roman root of the name Karilos might point to a provenance from Gaul as well. But why had Framarich and Karilos travelled so far from home? And what was their mission in Greater Syria?

Tiberius II Recruiting Drive in 574/5: A Possible Connection?

In the sixth and seventh centuries, people from the Latin-speaking world travelled primarily for two reasons to Greater Syria: as pilgrims heading for the holy sites in Palestine or as officials or soldiers in the service of the imperial government. As there was no important supra-regional pilgrimage site in the Biqā valley, the area of discovery suggested by Mundell Mango, religious reasons seem to be a rather unlikely motive. As trade with the western Mediterranean in general and Merovingian Gaul in particular was dominated by Greeks and Syrians,[25] it seems likewise

---

[21] On the formula see Witt, '"Hyper Euches"', pp. 188–90.
[22] Maaß, *Badisches Landesmuseum. Neuerwerbungen*, p. 195.
[23] Although silver spoons were occasionally part of church treasures, an application in liturgy cannot be generally proven for the early Byzantine period. For the controversial debate see Mundell Mango, *Silver from Early Byzantium*, pp. 118–22 no. 18–19; R. F. Taft, 'Byzantine Communion Spoons: A Review of the Evidence', *Dumbarton Oaks Papers*, 50 (1996): 215–16.
[24] W. Brandes, 'Thüringer/Thüringerinnen in byzantinischen Quellen', in H. Castritius, D. Geuenich and M. Werner (eds.), *Die Frühzeit der Thüringer: Archäologie, Sprache, Geschichte* (Berlin, 2009), pp. 291–328, at p. 306.
[25] J. Drauschke, *Zwischen Handel und Geschenk: Studien zur Distribution von Objekten aus dem Orient, aus Byzanz und aus Mitteleuropa im östlichen Merowingerreich* (Rahden, 2011), p. 215; A. H. M. Jones, *The Later Roman Empire, 284–602: A Social Economic and Administrative Survey* (Oxford, 1964), pp. 865–6.

improbable that Karilos and Framarich came to the region for business reasons. What seems most likely is that they were soldiers in imperial service.[26] Two factors account for this: First, people of Germanic origin were almost exclusively hired for military service, as numerous names of Germanic origin of officers and soldiers in the sixth century attest.[27] Second, the province of *Phoenicia Libanensis*, to which most of the Biqā valley (administratively) belonged, was a frontier province with a strong military presence. In the sixth century, a striking force of c. 6,000 cavalry was stationed there, and its members seem to have been billeted in rather small units at several sites.[28] In the sixth century, this force was occasionally committed to campaigns in Syria or Mesopotamia against the Sasanians.[29]

Germanic soldiers were often deployed to fight in the wars of the sixth century against the Sasanians. They were recruited on a regular basis from the Danube region.[30] On the eastern frontier, Goths and Heruli are attested in particular for the time of the reign of Justinian I (527–65).[31] In addition, Procopius of Caesarea mentions that under the same emperor five cavalry regiments were set up of Vandal prisoners (*Vandali Iustiniani*) and were destined to be settled permanently in the cities of the praetorian prefecture of the East.[32]

---

[26] Already Maaß, *Badisches Landesmuseum: Neuerwerbungen*, p. 195, assumed that Framarich was a soldier in Roman service.

[27] For more on Germans in Roman military service in late antiquity, see Jones, *Later Roman Empire*, pp. 619–23. On the enrolment of barbarian recruits in the sixth century, see M. Whitby, 'Recruitment in Roman Armies from Justinian to Heraclius (ca. 565–615)', in A. Cameron (ed.), *The Byzantine and Early Islamic Near East*, vol. III: *States, Resources and Armies* (Princeton, NJ, 1995), pp. 103–10. On p. 109, Whitby points out that the non-Roman names of officers are a significant indication for their ethnic origin.

[28] F. Trombley, 'War and Society in Rural Syria c. 502–613 AD: Observations on the Epigraphy.' *Byzantine and Modern Greek Studies*, 21 (1997): 154–209, at p. 164; W. Liebeschuetz, 'The Defences of Syria in the Sixth Century', in *Studien zu den Militärgrenzen Roms II: Vorträge des 10. Internationalen Limeskongresses in der Germania Inferior* (Cologne, 1977), p. 497.

[29] Procopius, *Wars* I 13, 5; II 8,2; II 16,17; II 19,33 (J. Haury and G. Wirth [eds.], *Procopii Caesariensis Opera Omnia I–II* [Leipzig, 1962–3]).

[30] Whitby, *Recruitment*, pp. 107–8.

[31] Procopius, *Wars* I 13, 19; I 14, 39; II 3, 21; II 18, 24; II 21, 4; II 24, 12; II 24, 14; II 25, 26–7.

[32] Procopius, *Wars* IV 14, 17–18; Schwarze, *Römische Militärgeschichte: Rekonstruktionsver such einer römischen Truppenliste des sechsten Jahrhundert* (Pfungstadt, 2015), p. 116. On Vandal soldiers in the East, see also Procopius, *Wars* II 21, 4. M. F. D. Hoffmann, *Das spätrömische Bewegungsheer und die Notitia Dignitatum* (Düsseldorf, 1969), vol. I, p. 140, suggests that the Germanic auxiliary units deployed in the province of Phoenicia according to the *Notitia dignitatum* Or. XXXIV 35-7.41 (C. Neira Faleiro [ed.], *La Notitia dignitatum: Nueva edición crítica y comentario histórico* [Madrid, 2005]) were likewise formed from prisoners of war under the tetrarchy.

Early Byzantine Church Silver 97

After Justinian's wars, such large numbers of Germanic soldiers were only enrolled on one further occasion, according to the written sources. This was the case when war with the Sasanians broke out anew in 572 and Tiberius II was appointed Caesar by Justin II in 574 to counter the threat.[33] To this end, the Caesar conducted a major recruiting campaign in 574/5. By spending considerable sums of money, he managed to raise a large field force mainly consisting of Germanic troops.[34] The church historian Evagrius Scholasticus praises Tiberius for having recruited a multi-ethnic army of formidable cavalry:

> And he collected such an army of heroic men, by recruiting the best men both from the tribes beyond the Alps in the vicinity of the Rhine, and those on this side of the Alps, the Massagetae and other Scythian nations, and those near Paeonia, and Mysians, Illyrians and Isaurians, that he established squadrons of excellent horsemen almost 150,000 in number.[35]

These numbers are exaggerated. It appears more likely that the army numbered around 12,000–15,000 men,[36] soldiers who composed elite units of the field army serving during the last years of Justin II reign, as well as under his successors, Tiberius II Constantine (578–82) and Maurice (582–602).[37] They have left further traces in epigraphy and further written sources.[38] Obviously, Tiberius's funds were well invested, as

---

[33] Martindale, *Prosopography of the Later Roman Empire*, III, pp. 1323–6 s.v. Tiberius Constantinus 1. On outbreak and course of the Persian war under Justin II and Tiberius II: M. Whitby, *The Emperor Maurice and His Historian: Theophylact Simocatta on Persian and Balkan Warfare* (Oxford, 1988), pp. 250–75.

[34] Whitby, *Recruitment*, pp. 108–9; Whitby, *Emperor Maurice*, pp. 258–9; H. Ditten, *Ethnische Verschiebungen zwischen der Balkanhalbinsel und Kleinasien vom Ende des 6. bis zur zweiten Hälfte des 9. Jahrhunderts* (Berlin, 1993), pp. 126–7, at p. 381.

[35] Evagrius Scholasticus V 14 (A. Hübner [ed.], *Evagrius Scholasticus, Historia Ecclesiastica Kirchengeschichte* (Turnhout, 2007]). English translation according to M. Whitby, *The Ecclesiastical History of Evagrius Scholasticus* (Liverpool, 2000), pp. 273–4. This major recruiting drive among foreign people is also attested by Theophylact Simocatta III 12, 3–4 (C. de Boor and P. Wirth [ed.], *Theophylacti Simocattae Historiae* [Stutgardiae 1972]). See also John of Ephesus, *Ecclesiastical History* III 3,26 (E. W. Brooks [ed.], *Iohannis Ephesini Historiae ecclesiasticae pars tertia* [Louvain, 1935]) and John of Epiphania fragment 5 ('Joannes Ephiphaniensis', in C. Müller [ed.], *Fragmenta Historicorum Graecorum* [Paris, 1851], vol. IV, pp. 272–6).

[36] J. F. Haldon, *Byzantine Praetorians: An Administrative, Institutional and Social Survey of the Opsikion and Tagmata, c. 580–900* (Bonn, 1984), 97. Schwarze, *Römische Militärgeschichte*, p. 122, recently suggested that these so-called *Tiberiani* comprised of fifteen *alae* of approximately 500–600 men each.

[37] Haldon, *Byzantine Praetorians*, pp. 96–101.

[38] Several officers and soldiers with Germanic names are attested for the later sixth and the early seventh century. Martindale. *Prosopography of the Later Roman Empire*, vol. III, p. 120 s.v. Ariulph; p. 435 s.v. Eiliphredas; pp. 512–13 s.v. Gentzon; p. 536 s.v. Gibimer 2; pp. 561–5 s.v. Guduin 1; p. 1237 s.v. Theodericus 2. John of Ephesus, *Ecclesiastical History*, VI 13 mentions an army of 60,000 Lombards commanded by the *magister utriusque militae per Orientem* Justinian in 575 (Martindale, *Prosopography of the Later*

the Sasanians suffered a decisive defeat in Armenia once the army had been put into action in 576.[39]

It is generally assumed that apart from residents within the empire, Franks, Burgundians and possibly Saxons from beyond the Alps, Goths and Lombards from Italy, as well as Bulgars and Gepids from Pannonia and along the Danube were among the newly levied troops.[40] Referring to Evagrius' account, some scholars stress the probability of Frankish mercenaries in the army because of the good relationship between the Austrasian kingdom and Constantinople in the 570s and 580s.[41] Archaeological remains of Frankish provenance in the Byzantine Empire have not yet been studied systematically, but some objects seem to corroborate the presence of people from north of the Alps in the East in the later sixth century or the early seventh century. I am especially referring to a (belt?) buckle with triangular plate from Anemurium dating from around the late sixth to the first third of the seventh century (Fig. 6.6a), a type that is widespread in the Frankish realm (Fig. 6.6d–e).[42] Although

---

Roman Empire, III, pp. 744–7 s.v. Ivstinianvs 3). John of Ephesus, *Ecclesiastical History*, III 13, 26 also attests to Arian Goths leaving their families at Constantinople while being sent on campaign to the East. R. Scharf, *Foederati: Von der völkerrechtlichen Kategorie zur byzantinischen Truppengattung* (Vienna, 2001), pp. 101–4 suggested that they were probably *foederati* withdrawn from the Danube region to Constantinople. He links the testimony of John with some funerary inscriptions of *foederati* with Germanic names from Constantinople dated ca. 580–620.

[39] Theopylact Simocatta III 12–14; John of Ephesus, *Ecclesiastical History*, VI 8. On the date of the Persian invasion of Armenia in 576 and their defeat, see Whitby, *Emperor Maurice*, pp. 262–8.

[40] Whitby, *Evagrius Scholasticus*, p. 274 n. 52; Whitby, *Recruitment*, p. 89; Ditten, *Ethnische Verschiebungen*, p. 127.

[41] Ditten, *Ethnische Verschiebungen*, p. 127; E. Stein, *Studien zur Geschichte des byzantinischen Reiches vornehmlich unter den Kaisern Justinus II. u. Tiberius Constantinus* (Stuttgart, 1919), p. 59. On the tight diplomatic relations between Constantinople and the Merovingian realm, especially from the late 560s to the 580s, see J. Drauschke, 'Diplomatie und Wahrnehmung im 6. und 7. Jahrhundert: Konstantinopel und die merowingischen Könige', in M. Altripp (ed.), *Byzanz in Europa: Europas östliches Erbe* (Turnhout, 2011), pp. 252–7 with further bibliography. In addition, the Frankish prince, Gundovald, spent his exile from the 570s to 581 in Constantinople (Martindale, *Prosopography of the Later Roman Empire*, vol. III, pp. 566–7, s.v. Gundovaldus 2). He surely went there with some followings, and he might have been able during his long stay in Constantinople to set up a stable network of contacts with the Frankish realm. This may have attracted mercenaries to enter imperial service. A fragmentary papyrus letter from Hermoupolis (P. Vindob. G 14307) dated to the second half of the sixth century also attests Franks. But these are considered to be soldiers of a late-Roman military unit labeled as *Franci* (see n. 46), not ethnic Franks. R. S. Bagnall and B. Palme, 'Franks in Sixth-Century Egypt', *Tyche*, 11 (1996): 4–7.

[42] J. Russell, 'Byzantine Instrumenta Domestica from Anemurium: The Significance of Context', in R. L. Hohlfelder (ed.), *City, Town and Countryside in the Early Byzantine Era* (New York, 1982), pp. 144–5, Fig. 8.28. He refers to some comparable buckles from Switzerland (n. 48). This type of buckle is widespread in the Frankish realm in the period of the last third of the sixth to the first half of the seventh centuries. On the type and its

it is unclear how this buckle reached Anemurium. Russell assumed that it might have been 'left behind by some wandering mercenary'.[43] To this find, a comparable West Frankish example (dated to the second half of the sixth century) (Fig. 6.6b) and the loop of another belt buckle (later sixth–early seventh centuries), likewise of West Frankish provenance, should be added. These pieces are part of the collection of Byzantine belt buckles at the Römisch-Germanisches Zentralmuseum in Mainz, a former private collection that has been compiled in the vicinity of Constantinople.[44] A fourth buckle of this type in the aforesaid museum was found at the late Roman fortress of Sadovec (Bulgaria) that was occupied until the late sixth century (Fig. 6.6c).[45]

Although Evagrius's account is merely indirect evidence, it seems to be the only reference to Franks (i.e. people from the Frankish realm) in the service of the early Byzantine army to be found in the narrative source material after the fourth century.[46] Apart from the recruiting campaign of 574/5, enlistment of Germanic soldiers (especially Lombards) probably continued to a lesser degree in the later 570s and under the emperor Maurice in the 580s.[47] Still, for the early Byzantine period, there

chronology, see U. Müssemeier, E. Nieveler, R. Plum and H. Pöppelmann, *Chronologie der merowingerzeitlichen Grabfunde vom linken Niederrhein bis zur nördlichen Eifel* (Bonn, 2003) p. 19, Gür3A–B. D Fig. 7. 9; U. Koch, *Das alamannisch-fränkische Gräberfeld bei Pleidelsheim* (Stuttgart, 2001), p. 87, Fig. 24 Phase SD 7; pp. 284–5 Fig. 115; p. 576 Fundliste 35; F. Siegmund, *Merowingerzeit am Niederrhein: Die frühmittelalterlichen Funde aus dem Regierungsbezirk Düsseldorf und dem Kreis Heinsberg* (Cologne, 1998), p. 25; pp. 204–5 Fig. 81 Phase 6.8. The comparatively small size of the buckle indicates that it may not have belonged to a belt but rather a sword harness or maybe a leg binding (*Wadenbindengarnitur*).

[43] Russell, *Instrumenta Domestica*, p. 145.

[44] M. Schulze-Dörrlamm, *Byzantinische Gürtelschnallen und Gürtelbeschläge im Römisch-Germanischen Zentralmuseum* (Mainz, 2009), vol. II., pp. 279–81 nos. 586–7.

[45] Inventory no. O.39877. S. Uenze, *Die spätantiken Befestigungen von Sadovec (Bulgarien): Ergebnisse der deutsch – bulgarisch – österreichischen Ausgrabungen 1934–1937* (Munich, 1992), p. 176; p. 422 no. B 36 p. 9,16; pl. 126,9. The unstratified buckle is wrongly dated to the fourth or fifth century, but, according to its typology, it certainly belongs to the sixth-century settlement. Like the piece from Anemurium it seems to be too small for a belt buckle

[46] On Franks in Roman military service in the fourth century in general, see E. Zöllner, *Geschichte der Franken bis zur Mitte des sechsten Jahrhunderts* (Munich, 1970), pp. 15–16. The name of four Eastern military units suggests that these were raised among the Franks. They were deployed before c. 400 in the East according to the *Notitia dignitatum*: under the command of the *dux Thebaidis* a *cohors VII Francorum* (Or. 31,51) and an *ala I Francorum* (Or. 31,32) Under the command of the *dux Phoenicis* an *ala I Francorum* (Or. 32,35). Under the command of the *dux Mesopotamiae* an *ala VIII Flavia Francorum* (Or. 36,33).

[47] Whitby, *Emperor Maurice*, pp. 147, 267. According to Menander the Guardsman fragment 22 (R. C. Blockley [ed.], *The History of Menander the Guardsman: Introductory Essay, Text, Translation and Historical Notes* [Liverpool, 1984]), Caesar Tiberius II in 577 or 578 sent the Roman *patricius* Pamphronius to Italy with a large amount of gold in

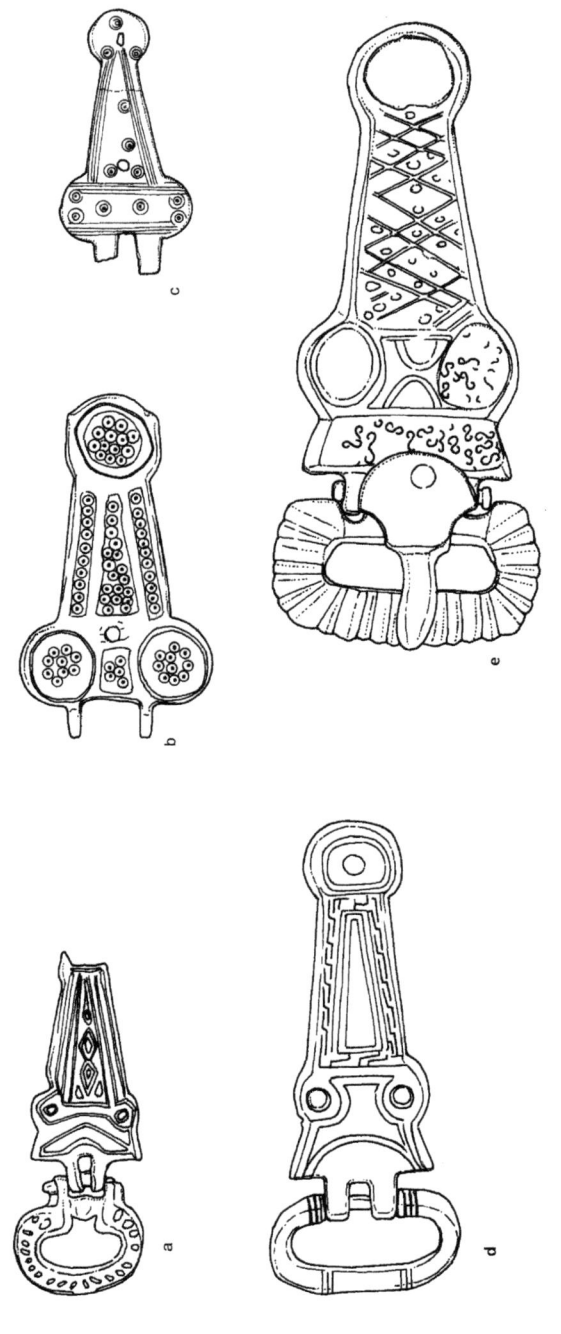

Figure 6.6 Buckles with triangular plate: (a) Anemurium (Anamur/TR), stray find (redrawn after Russell, *Instrumenta Domestica*. Fig. 8.28). (b) Mainz, RGZM Inv. O.40054 (presumably from Asia Minor). (c) Sadovec/BG, unstratified find, Mainz, RGZM Inv. O.39877 (after Uenze, *Die spätantiken Befestigungen von Sadovec*, pl. 9,15). (d) Forstfeld/F, stray find (redrawn after B. Schnitzler/A. Frey, *Les Trouvailles mérovingiennes en Alsace* 1: Bas-Rhin, Kataloge Vor- und Frühgeschichtlicher Altertümer 41,1 (Mainz, 2009), Fig. 100). (e) Pleidelsheim/D, grave no. 64 (redrawn after Koch, *Das alamannisch-fränkische Gräberfeld bei Pleidelsheim*, pl. 25). Drawing M. Ober/RGZM.

is no evidence for any large-scale recruitment in the West after 575, and later recruitment campaigns were carried out among other peoples (e.g., Armenians).[48] A look into the Prosopography of the later Roman Empire confirms this. Until the later sixth century, officers bearing Germanic names are quite often attested in Roman military service, but evidence hardly exists for the seventh century or later.[49]

The above suggests that the presence in Syria or Lebanon of men from the Latin West, and especially from the Frankish realm, is not surprising in the last quarter of the sixth century. It seems reasonable to hypothesise that Karilos and Framarich were part of the military force raised by Tiberius II Constantine in 574/5 or the following years. They may have been part of the force stationed in the province of *Phoenicia Libanensis* and maybe based somewhere in the Biqā valley. The presence of a large number of soldiers from the Merovingian kingdoms in the late-sixth-century Byzantine Empire may have influenced the eulogy of the Franks presented in Agathias's *Histories* written in the 570s. Alongside some Frankish envoys, these soldiers may have been one of Agathias's sources. The information on Frankish weapons, in particular, might go back to the first-hand witness of a soldier from the Merovingian kingdoms recruited for imperial service.[50]

The Cult of St Constantine

I would now like to briefly discuss what significance St Constantine may have had for the community that used the silver objects. The discussion of this question is closely connected to the problem whether this saint is

---

order to hire some Lombard rulers and their followers for Roman service in the East. Scharf, *Foederati*, p. 102; Stein, *Studien*, p. 106. As a consequence of the good diplomatic relations between the emperor at Constantinople and the Austrasian king, Childebert II, the latter acted as an important confederate of the Byzantines and conducted several campaigns against the Lombards in Italy in the 580s (Drauschke, *Diplomatie*, pp. 254-7). It is conceivable that in this context some Frankish chiefs and their followers might have been brought into Roman service and found their way to the East.

[48] Ditten, *Ethnische Verschiebungen*, pp. 127-8; J. F. Haldon, *Recruitment and Conscription in the Byzantine Army ca. 550–950: A Study of the Stratiotika Ktemata* (Vienna, 1979), p. 22. See also Stein, *Studien*, pp. 119-20.

[49] See Brandes, *Thüringer*, p. 306, on the difficulties of tracing Germanic people in Byzantium after the sixth century.

[50] Text, translation and commentary, A. Cameron, 'Agathias on the Early Merovingians', *Annali della Scuola Normale Superiore di Pisa. Classe di lettere e filosofia* ser. 2, 37 (1968): 95-140. On Agathias' sources and his positive attitude towards the Franks, see Cameron, 'Agathias on the Early Merovingians', pp. 133-4, pp. 136-9. She supposed an envoy of Sigibert's embassy in 571 as a possible source, but also suggested (p. 131) that Agathias' accurate description of the two-edged *ango* (II 5) was based on information by someone who had actually used one.

identical with the first Christian emperor. For Marlia Mundell Mango, providing a first brief presentation of the censer (no. 1), there is no doubt that it is 'the earliest evidence of the cult of the first Christian emperor'.[51] Denis Feissel, on the other hand, refuses in his brief comments on the inscription to identify the figure as Constantine the Great, as he considers it too early for this cult.[52] How should this problem be approached?

Only very little evidence for the early formation of the cult of St Constantine has survived. Feissel's assessment is obviously based on the assumption, shared by many scholars, that the veneration of Constantine was not established before the late eighth century.[53] I will not be able to discuss the origin of the cult of St Constantine the Great here. However, depictions of Constantine and his legend already appear in monumental church decorations since the sixth century.[54] Furthermore, some scattered epigraphical evidence suggests that Constantine was considered a patron saint at least since the seventh century, if not as early as the sixth.[55]

The iconography of the depiction of Constantine on the censer (Fig. 6.3) supports its identification with the first Christian emperor. The helmet is an unusual feature for warrior saints, which, in early and

---

[51] M. Mundell Mango, 'Imperial Art in the Seventh Century', in P. Magdalino (ed.), *New Constantines: The Rhythm of Imperial Renewal in Byzantium, 4th–13th Centuries – Papers of the Twenty-Sixth Spring Symposium of Byzantine Studies, St Andrews March 1992* (Aldershot, 1994), pp. 109–38, at p. 136.

[52] *Revue des Études Grecques*, 108 (1995), 564 no 710; *Supplementum Epigraphicum Graecum*, 44 (1994), 533 no 1575.

[53] For example, M. Grünbart, 'Konstantins Nachwirken im oströmischen Kaiserreich', in M. Grünbart (ed.), *Gold und Blei: Byzantinische Kostbarkeiten aus dem Münsterland* (Vienna, 2012), p. 33; U. Peschlow and G. Schmalzbauer, 'Konstantin als heiliger der Ostkirche', in A. Demandt and J. Engemann (eds.), *Konstantin der Große: Imperator Caesar Flavius Constantinus* (Mainz, 2007), pp. 420–4, at p. 420; R. Janin, *La Géographie ecclésiastique de l'empire byzantin 3. Le Siège de Constantinople et le Patriarcat oecuménique 3. Les églises et les monastères* (Paris, ²1969), p. 295.

[54] The picture cycle referred to in the famous epigram of the Church of Saint Polyeuctus in Constantinople *Anthologia Graeca*, I 10 (H. Beckby [ed.], *Anthologia Graeca* [Munich, ²1965]) is the earliest evidence known to me for a reception of Constantine as a saintly figure and the legends associated with him. On the cycle, see C. Milner, 'The Image of the Rightful Ruler: Anicia Juliana's Constantine Mosaic in the Church of Hagios Polyeuktos', in P. Magdalino (ed.), *New Constantines: The Rhythm of Imperial Renewal in Byzantium, 4th–13th Centuries. Papers from the Twenty-sixth Spring Symposium of Byzantine Studies, St Andrews, March 1992* (Aldershot, 1994), pp. 73–81; P. Speck, 'Juliana Anicia, Konstantin der Grosse und die Polyeuktoskirche in Konstantinopel', *Poikila Byzantina* 11 *(Varia III)* (Berlin, 1993), pp. 134–47. Mural fragments attest a further picture cycle in the church at Karm Al-Ahbarīya in Egypt (second half of sixth century): J. Witte Orr, *Kirche und Wandmalereien am Karm Al-Ahbarīya* (Münster, 2010), pp. 78–84, pp. 147–51 pls. 2, 7, 26–7.

[55] For a discussion of the epigraphical evidence, see Fourlas, *Ein Komplex frühbyzantinischer Silberobjekte*, p. 159 no. IV.120 and the above-mentioned (n. 1) extended version of this paper.

middle Byzantine iconography, are bareheaded without exception.[56] The absence of the pearl diadem, a feature common since the time of Constantius II (337–61) on coin images depicting a helmeted emperor, might be explained by supposing that the artist adhered to iconographical prototypes predating its introduction.[57] Constantine the Great is the last emperor who wore an attic helmet similar to the one worn by the saint on the censer, which can be found in particular on coin issues struck between 318 and 322.[58] Constantine's helmet was connected to the story of the vision of the Cross and thereby part of the ideology of Christian victory. After describing the monogram of Christ consisting of the letters Chi and Rho fixed to the *labarum*, Eusebius briefly states that subsequently the emperor was bearing these letters on his helmet.[59] Constantine's military equipment was also connected to the legend of the discovery of the True Cross: nails of the True Cross had been incorporated into the helmet and the bridle of his horse.[60] This symbolic reference to Constantine's helmet would help explain the unusual iconography on the censer, including the warrior saint with a helmet and would strengthen the identification of the depicted saint with the first Christian emperor. There are thus no serious reasons why the identification of the figure proposed by Marlia Mundell Mango should be doubted. What is more, we know of no other homonymous warrior saint who was already venerated in the early Byzantine period.

Constantine as an imperial model was revived in the later sixth century. Tiberius II was the first Caesar (and later emperor) who took up the programmatic name 'Constantine' after 150 years.[61] He also was the

---

[56] P. Ł. Grotowski, *Arms and Armour of the Warrior Saints: Tradition and Innovation in Byzantine Iconography (843–1261)* (Leiden, 2010), p. 89, points out that the helmet is unusual in the iconography of warrior saints.

[57] On the pearl diadem on the emperors' helmet, see P. Bastien, *Le Buste monétaire des empereurs romains* (Wetteren, 1992), vol. I, p. 223. For a discussion of the iconography, see also Fourlas, *Ein Komplex frühbyzantinischer Silberobjekte*, pp. 159–60 no IV.120 and the extended version of this paper (n. 1).

[58] Bastien, *Le Buste monétaire*, vol. I, pp 209–10 pl. 170,10; P. M. Bruun, *Roman Imperial Coinage VII: Constantine and Licinius AD 313–337* (London, 1966), pp. 56–9; p. 112 no 231 pl. 4; p. 438 no 119 pl. 13; p. 508 no 82 pl. 16.

[59] Eusebius, *Vita Constantini*, I, 31 (P. Dräger [ed.], *Eusebios über das Leben des glückseligen Kaisers Konstantin* [Oberhaid, 2007])

[60] The sources referring to the nails incorporated into Constantine's helmet and bridle are summarised by J. W. Nesbitt, 'Alexander the Monk's Text of Helena's Discovery of the Cross (BHG 410)', in J. W. Nesbitt (ed.), *Byzantine Authors: Literary Activites and Prepoccupations* (Leiden, 2003), pp. 35–6.

[61] M. Whitby, 'Images for Emperors in Late Antiquity: A Search for New Constantine', in P. Magdalino (ed.), *New Constantines: The Rhythm of Imperial Renewal in Byzantium, 4th–13th Centuries – Papers from the Twenty-Sixth Spring Symposium of Byzantine Studies, St Andrews, March 1992* (Aldershot, 1994), pp. 83–93.

(a)   (b)

Figure 6.7 *Solidus* of Tiberius II Constantine, Constantinople 578–82, Münzkabinett der Staatlichen Museen zu Berlin 18204093. Photograph: Lutz-Jürgen Lübke.

last sovereign of the early Byzantine period to recruit large numbers of western barbarians. This raises the question of whether it really can be a coincidence that Framarich and Karilos belonged to a community venerating a warrior saint named Constantine, or whether this was the result of a contemporary imperial policy.

Tiberius II was given the name 'Constantine' (by Emperor Justin II) during his promotion to the rank of Caesar in December 574 as he was expected to renew the empire of Constantine the Great.[62] This stylisation of Tiberius II as a new Constantine appears to have been part of a purposeful propaganda campaign connected to the war against the Sasanians that broke out in 572 (and lasted until 591).[63] This anti-Persian campaign is mainly articulated in coinage (Fig. 6.7a–b). During his reign as sole emperor (578–82), a new iconography was introduced on the back side of the gold coinage: the Cross on a stepped base with the legend *Victoria Augusti* (Fig. 6.7b).[64] The motif of the Cross alludes to the memorial cross on the Rock of Golgotha[65] beside the Church of the Holy Sepulchre built by Constantine I and its significance as instrument of imperial victory.[66] According to John of Ephesus, the emperor was spreading the story that he had received a vision of the new reverse imagery of the coins, an explicit hint to Constantine's vision of the Cross

---

[62] According to John of Ephesus, *Ecclesiastical History*, III 5; Whitby, *Images*, p. 83.

[63] A. Grabar, *L'iconoclasme Byzantin* (Paris, ²1984), pp. 34–5. On the Persian war of 572–91, see Whitby, *Emperor Maurice*, pp. 195–304.

[64] On the introduction of the new motive, see A. R. Bellinger and P. Grierson, *Catalogue of the Byzantine Coins in the Dumbarton Oaks Collection and in the Whittemore Collection* (Washington, DC, 1966–93), vol. I, pp. 94–5; Grabar, *Iconoclamse*, pp. 34–5, Figs. 2–3. On the coins, see Bellinger and Grierson, *Catalogue of the Byzantine Coins*, vol. I, pp. 266–8.

[65] E. Dinkler and E. Dinkler-von Schubert, 'Kreuz I', *Reallexikon zur byzantinischen Kunst*, vol. V (Stuttgart, 1995), p. 47; Bellinger and Grierson, *Catalogue of the Byzantine Coins*, vol. II, pp. 95–6.

[66] K. Wessel, Kaiserbild, *Reallexikon zur byzantinischen Kunst III* (1978), pp. 784–5.

before the battle at the Milvian Bridge.⁶⁷ In addition, quite a few of Tiberius' coins only bear the name Constantine and omit Tiberius.⁶⁸

The new reverse type introduced by Tiberius II only reappeared under Herakleios (610–41) and his successors.⁶⁹ Herakleios used Constantine as a model for his self-representation during the war against the Sasanians and founded a 'Constantinian' dynasty by naming three of his sons Constantine.⁷⁰

A major characteristic of the Constantinian indications in imperial self-representation, especially of Tiberius II, Herakleios and his sons, is its military content. The coin imagery and circumscriptions refer to Christian imperial victory, which is based upon divine support for Constantine's campaigns.⁷¹ This concept emerged from the legend of Constantine's vision of the Cross,⁷² and it was linked to Constantine's imperial standard, the *labarum*,⁷³ as well as with his helmet and the bridle of his horse, as has been explained above.

According to Haldon, wars with the Persians were 'frequently presented both to soldiers of the Roman armies and to the wider populace in the light of a struggle between Christianity and the forces of evil'.⁷⁴ Thus, it is not surprising that in the Byzantine Empire Constantine was employed as a programmatic model in conflicts with the Sasanians. Middle

---

⁶⁷ John of Ephesus, *Ecclesiastical History*, III 14.

⁶⁸ Bellinger and Grierson, *Catalogue of the Byzantine Coins*, vol. I, p. 256 nos. 1–2; p. 268 nos. 5–6; p. 269 no. 8; pp. 271–2 nos. 12b.2–14c.

⁶⁹ Whitby, *Images*, pp. 92–3, emphasised that Constantine had a 'false start' as an imperial model under Tiberius II and became firmly established by the seventh century.

⁷⁰ On Constantine as model for Herakleios, see J. W. Drijvers, 'Heraclius and the *Restitutio Crucis*: Notes on Symbolism and Ideology', in G. J. Reinik and B. H. Stolte (eds.), *The Reign of Heraclius (610–641): Crisis and Confrontation* (Leuven, 2002), pp. 181–4.

⁷¹ The gold coins of Herakleios depicting the cross on stepped base bear the legend *Victoria Augusti* and on the silver double *miliaresia* the war cry of the Roman army *Deus Adiuta Romanis* appeared. Dinkler and Dinkler von Schubert, *Kreuz*, p. 48; Bellinger and Grierson, *Catalogue of the Byzantine Coins*, vol. II, p. 94; Grabar, *Iconoclasme*, pp. 35–6, fig. 6. During the reign of Constans II (641–68), Folles with the image of the emperor were struck bearing the legend ἐν τούτῳ νίκα, a quote from the narration of Constantine's vision of the cross according to Eusebios of Caesarea. Eusebius, *Vita Constantini*, I 28, 2. Dinkler und Dinkler von Schubert, *Kreuz*, pp. 48–9; Bellinger and Grierson, *Catalogue of the Byzantine Coins*, vol. II, p. 406.

⁷² A. Grabar, *L'Empereur dans l'art byzantine* (London, 1971), pp. 32–9; J. Gagé, 'Σταυρὸς νικοποιός.: "La Victoire impérial dans l'empire chrétien"', *Revue d'histoire et de philosophie religieuses*, 13 (1921): 370–400, esp. pp. 382–91. The different traditions of Constantine's vision of the cross are discussed by A. Kazhdan, '"Constantine Imaginaire": Byzantine Legends of the Ninth Century about Constantine the Great', *Byzantion*, 57 (1987): 218–30.

⁷³ Eusebius, *Vita Constantini*, I, p. 31. On the *labarum*, see Dinkler and Dinkler-von Schubert, *Kreuz*, pp. 24–5; H. Kruse, *Studien zur offiziellen Geltung des Kaiserbildes im römischen Reiche* (Paderborn, 1934), pp. 68–79.

⁷⁴ J. Haldon, *Warfare, State and Society in the Byzantine World, 565–1204* (London, 1999), p. 18.

Byzantine *vitae* of Constantine also include the unhistorical narration that the emperor had campaigned against the Persians and defeated them.[75] Reference to Constantine fighting the Persians already occurs in seventh-century Coptic texts, where Constantine's vision of the Cross is connected to a battle against the Persians.[76]

In the context of the war against the heathen Sasanians, Constantine thus would have been a most suitable patron saint. This is particularly true for a community partly consisting of non-Roman members of the military. The veneration of the first Christian emperor, attested by the inscription on the censer, could be the expression of a specific group identity with strong ideological ties to Constantinople, the empire and the emperor. Maybe Constantine was purposefully chosen as a patron of the local church because he was able to represent Roman Christian identity like no other saint, alongside loyalty to the emperor (the new Constantine), while his adherents were hoping for divine support during the war against heathen enemies.[77]

Conclusion

It is most unfortunate that the hoard discussed here was not properly excavated and that no further data regarding the original context is available today. As a consequence, some of the conclusions drawn here are inevitably based upon assumptions. In any case, the material presented above provides valuable insights into the relations between the East and the West during the later sixth century and the social life of early

---

[75] The core of this narration is considered to be a reflection of the successful campaigns of Herakleios: S. N. C. Lieu, 'Constantine in Legendary Literature', in N. Lenski (ed.), *The Cambridge Companion to the Age of Constantine* (Cambridge, 2006), pp. 313–17.

[76] T. G. Wilfong, 'Constantine in Coptic: Egyptian Constructions of Constantine the Great', in S. N. C. Lieu and D. Montserrat (eds.), *Constantine: History, Historiography and Legend* (London, 1998), pp. 181, 185–6; P. Buzi and A. Bausi, 'Tradizioni ecclesiastiche e letterarie copte ed etiophiche', in *Costantino I. Enciclopedia costantiniana sulla figura e l'immagine dell'imperatore del cosidetto editto do Milano 313–2013* (Rome, 2013), pp. 409, 412.

[77] Contemporary Byzantine authors regularly define their own side as 'the Christians' or 'the Romans', in contrast to the Sasanian enemies. Haldon, *Warfare*, pp. 18–19. G. Greatrex, 'Roman Identity in the Sixth Century', in G. Greatrex and S. Mitchell (eds.), *Ethnicity and Culture in Late Antiquity* (London, 2000), pp. 268, 274 stresses that loyalty to the emperor and not ethnic origin was the determining factor of Roman identity especially of soldiers in the sixth century. See also H. Leppin, 'Roman Identity in a Border Region: Evagrius and the Defence of the Roman Empire', in W. Pohl (ed.), *Visions of Community in the Post-Roman World: The West, Byzantium and the Islamic World, 300–1000* (Farnham, 2012), pp. 252–4, especially on the Roman identity of the multiethnic army raised by Tiberius II.

Byzantine society in Greater Syria, allowing us to draw the following conclusions.

With high probability, the inscriptions found on the objects bear witness to the migration to Greater Syria of at least two individuals originating from Latin-speaking regions in the second half of the sixth century. It is likely, however, that Framarich and Karilos had been part of a larger group from the Frankish kingdoms who served as soldiers in the imperial forces.

The Karlsruhe silver hoard thus helps to better understand important aspects of the (intensified) relations between Constantinople and the Frankish kingdoms in the 560s–80s. The presence of Framarich and probably Karilos in the East as well as the auspicious discovery in Asia Minor and Bulgaria of buckles of a type widespread north of the Alps affirm earlier hypotheses that people from the Frankish realm were among the soldiers of the 'army of heroic men' raised by Tiberius II Constantine. Apparently, many more 'Franks' were present in the Byzantine Empire in the later sixth century than is usually assumed.

Framarich and Karilos were obviously fully integrated in the commemorative practice of a Greek-speaking community as attested by the existence of family or relatives commemorating them. The evidence pointing to the cult of Constantine suggests that the idea of the Christian Roman Empire and imperial victory was an important part of this community's identity.

7 Money for Nothing?: Franks, Byzantines and Lombards in the Sixth and Seventh Centuries

Andreas Fischer

Taking a long-term perspective, the Byzantine emperor Maurice (r. 582–602) was very much in line with the traditions of foreign Roman imperial policy when he paid 50,000 *solidi* to King Childebert II (r. 575–96) for the attack on the Lombards in Italy in 582 or 583. The results of his financial efforts, however, left him disappointed and embarrassed, as both Gregory of Tours and subsequently Paul the Deacon noted.[1] According to the bishop of Tours, the Frankish campaign against the invaders of the Apennine peninsula which took place in 584 ended with submission of the enemy that gave gifts to Childebert. Having learnt about this arrangement, Maurice, understandably so, demanded the return of the money he had spent to make sure the Merovingian

---

[1] Gregory of Tours, *Historiae*, VI, 42, ed. by B. Krusch and W. Levison, MGH SRM 1, 1 (Hanover, ²1951), p. 314; and Paul the Deacon, *Historia Langobardorum*, III, 17, ed. L. Bethmann and G. Waitz, MGH SRL 1 (Hanover, 1878), pp. 12–187, at p. 101. See W. Pohl, 'Gregory of Tours and Contemporary Perceptions of Lombard Italy', in K. Mitchell and I. Wood (eds.), *The World of Gregory of Tours* (Leiden, 2002), pp. 131–43, at pp. 137–9, on the differences in their views. Fredegar, *Chronicae*, IV, 45, ed. B. Krusch, MGH SRM 2 (Hanover, 1888), pp. 1–168, at p. 143, has a different perspective on the events, on which see C. Wickham, *Early Medieval Italy: Central Power and Local Society, 400–1000* (Basingstoke, 1981), pp. 32–3; I. Wood, *The Merovingian Kingdoms, 450–751* (Harlow, 1994), p. 168. On the Roman policy of payments in general, see C. D. Gordon, 'Subsidies in Roman Imperial Defence', *Phoenix*, 3 (1949): 60–9, esp. pp. 64 and 67; for payments of armed forces and tributes in the sixth century, see W. Pohl, 'The Empire and the Lombards: Treaties and Negotiations in the Sixth Century', in W. Pohl (ed.), *Kingdoms of the Empire: The Integration of Barbarians in Late Antiquity* (Leiden, 1997), pp. 75–133, at pp. 80–3, 88, 90, 93–8; H. Börm, '"Es war allerdings nicht so, dass sie es im Sinne eines Tributes erhielten, wie viele meinten ... ": Anlässe und Funktion der persischen Geldforderungen an die Römer (3. bis 6. Jh.)', *Historia*, 57 (2008): 327–46; S. T. Loseby, 'Gregory of Tours, Italy, and the Empire', in A. C. Murray (ed.), *A Companion to Gregory of Tours* (Leiden, 2016), pp. 462–97, at pp. 489–90; on Maurice, see M. Whitby, *The Emperor Maurice and His Historian: Theophylact Simocatta on Persian and Balkan Warfare* (Oxford, 1988), p. 12; on the sources, Whitby, *The Emperor Maurice and His Historian*, pp. 126–7. I would like to thank Francesco Borri and Stefan Esders for their comments. The research leading to these results has received funding from the European Research Council under the European Union's Seventh Framework Programme (FP7/2007–13)/ ERC grant agreement No. 269591.

expelled the Lombards from Italy. At first, Childebert did not respond to the emperor's demand at all, but one year later he agreed to another campaign.[2] The money already given to him or another subsidy paid by Maurice clearly worked as an incentive in this case, and Byzantine gold might have done so in further interventions by the Frankish king in 589/90, although other determinants also had their share in the campaigns of Childebert. The king's sister, Ingund, and his nephew, Athanagild, had been captured by the Byzantines, and the latter was kept in Constantinople after his mother's death. Even religious arguments seem to have induced Childebert to wage war against the Lombards: in 580, Pope Pelagius II (r. 579–90) had referred to the orthodoxy of the Frankish kings to win them over against the Lombards, and apparently there were reservations about Lombard faith in parts of the Frankish episcopacy that were helpful in this respect.[3] From the Byzantine perspective, however, these military interventions led to nothing: the one in 585 failed because the *duces* of the army sent against the Lombards were at odds with one another,

---

[2] Gregory of Tours, *Historiae*, VIII, 18 ed. Krusch and Levison, p. 384 and Paul the Deacon, *Historia Langobardorum* III, 22, ed. Bethmann and Waitz, p. 104. G. Reverdy, 'Les Relations de Childebert II et de Byzance', *Revue historique*, 114 (1913): 62–86, at pp. 66–70; P. Goubert, *Byzance avant l'Islam, Byzance et l'Orient sous les successeurs de Justinien, II, 2: Rome, Byzance et Carthage* (Paris, 1965), pp. 20–6.

[3] For the campaigns see Gregory of Tours, *Historiae* IX, 25 and X, 3, ed. Krusch and Levison, pp. 444–5 and 483–6; and Paul the Deacon, *Historia Langobardorum* III, 28–9 and 31, ed. Bethmann and Waitz, pp. 108 and 110–12; G. Löhlein, *Die Alpen- und Italienpolitik der Merowinger im VI. Jahrhundert* (Erlangen, 1932), pp. 65–9; Loseby, 'Gregory of Tours', p. 489. For the role of Ingund and Athanagild see Loseby, 'Gregory of Tours', pp. 491–2; B. S. Bachrach, *The Anatomy of a Little War: A Diplomatic and Military History of the Gundovald Affair (568–586)* (Boulder, CO, 1994), pp. 84–5; S. Scholz, *Die Merowinger* (Stuttgart, 2015), p. 150; W. Goffart, 'Byzantine Policy in the West under Tiberius II and Maurice: The Pretenders Hermenegild and Gundovald (579–585)', *Traditio*, 13 (1957): 73–118, at pp. 116–17. The letter from Pelagius II: *Epistolae aevi Merowingici collectae*, ed. W. Gundlach, MGH Epp. 3: Merowingici et Karolini aevi 1 (Berlin, 1892), pp. 434–68, no. 9 pp. 448–9, at p. 449; Loseby, 'Gregory of Tours', p. 493. The letter of Nicetius of Trier echoes religious resentments against the Lombards; *Il Liber epistolarum della cancelleria austrasica (sec. V–VI)*, ed. E. Malaspina (Rome, 2001), no. 8 pp. 86–97, at p. 92. Pohl, 'Gregory of Tours', pp. 134–5; W. Pohl, 'Deliberate Ambiguity: The Lombards and Christianity', in G. Armstrong and I. N. Wood (eds.), *Christianizing Peoples and Converting Individuals* (Turnhout, 2000), pp. 47–58, at p. 53; see also A. Gillett, 'Ethnography and Imperium in the Sixth Century: Frankish and Byzantine Rhetoric in the Epistolae Austrasicae', in G. Nathan and L. Garland (eds.), *Basileia: Essays on Imperium and Culture in Honour of E. M. Jeffreys and M. J. Jeffreys* (Leiden, 2011), pp. 67–81, esp. pp. 72–3. For the background see W. Pohl, 'Die langobardische Reichsbildung zwischen Imperium Romanum und Frankenreich', in M. Becher and S. Dick (eds.), *Völker, Reiche und Namen im frühen Mittelalter* (Munich, 2010), pp. 223–43, at pp. 236–7; M. Dunn, 'Lombard Religiosities Reconsidered: "Arianism", Syncretism and the Transition to Catholic Christianity', in A. P. Roach and J. R. Simpson (eds.), *Heresy and the Making of European Culture: Medieval and Modern Perspectives* (Abingdon and New York, 2016), pp. 89–109, at pp. 95–6.

while in 590 the army sent to northern Italy was nearly destroyed by dysentery.[4] Afterwards, Maurice had to accept the Lombards as the new masters of vast areas of the Italian peninsula and indeed did so after 590 when the Frankish relations to the Lombards were moulded by marriage alliances and the payment of tribute rather than warfare.[5] It seemed as if the emperor had spent his money for nothing.[6]

This short description of an episode of Byzantine 'chequebook diplomacy' that was meant to turn the tide in the military confrontation between the empire and the Lombards in Italy at the beginning of Maurice's reign owes a lot to Gregory of Tours' biased perspective: to be sure, the bishop was critical about the effects the military adventures in Italy had on Frankish soil.[7] He was also willing to admit the last of Childebert's campaigns had been real setbacks for the Franks. But, at the same time, he seems to have embellished the real course and outcome of the intervention in 584. Another contemporary source, the chronicle written by John of Biclaro, gives a different account of what took place in this year. According to this text, in the second year of his reign, the 'emperor Maurice paid the Franks to attack the Lombards and thus inflicted no small damage on both peoples'.[8] The chronicle from Spain therefore presents a different story: Rather than the clear Frankish victory Gregory of Tours presented, John of Biclaro emphasised the detrimental effect the payment had to both the Lombards and the Franks.

---

[4] Gregory of Tours, *Historiae*, VIII, 18, and X, 3, ed. Krusch and Levison, pp. 384 and 485–6; Paul the Deacon, *Historia Langobardorum*, III, 22 and III, 31, ed. Waitz, pp. 104 and 111–12. Wood, *Merovingian Kingdoms*, p. 168; Pohl, 'Gregory of Tours', p. 140.

[5] Acceptance: Wickham, *Early Medieval Italy*, p. 33. On the marriage alliances, see Wood, *Merovingian Kingdoms*, pp. 165–8; on the payment of tributes see Fredegar, *Chronicae*, IV, 45, ed. Krusch, p. 143.

[6] See, for instance, Reverdy, 'Relations', p. 84, who considered the emperor's efforts 'aboutirent à un échec'.

[7] Gregory of Tours, *Historiae*, X, 3, ed. Krusch and Levison, pp. 483–4; W. Goffart, 'Foreigners in the *Histories* of Gregory of Tours', *Florilegium*, 4 (1989): 80–99, at p. 89. On his perspective in general see now Loseby, 'Gregory of Tours', esp. p. 496.

[8] John of Biclaro, *Chronicon* 69, in *Victoris Tunnunensis Chronicon cum reliquiis ex Consularibus Caesaraugustanis et Iohannis Biclarensis Chronicon*, ed. Carmen Cardelle de Hartmann, comm. Roger Collins, CCSL 173A (Turnhout, 2001), p. 74 ll. 56–9: *Mauritius imperator contra Longobardos Francos per conductelam mouet. Que res utrique genti non parua intulit damna*; the translation quoted from *Conquerors and Chroniclers of Early Medieval Spain*, translated with notes and introduction by K. B. Wolf (Liverpool, ²1999), p. 61 no. 70. On John's biography and work, see J. N. Hillgarth, 'Historiography in Visigothic Spain', in *La Storiografia Altomedievale*, 10–16 April 1969, vol. I (Spoleto, 1970), pp. 261–311, at pp. 266–9, 276–7, 280–3, 289–91, 308–10; M. Pozo Flores, 'Las fuentes en Juan de Biclaro', *Studia histórica: Historia medieval*, 32 (2014): 161–85; Whitby, *Emperor*, p. 126; A. Kollautz, 'Orient und Okzident am Ausgang des 6. Jh. Johannes, Abt von Biclarum, Bischof von Gerona, der Chronist des westgotischen Spaniens', *Byzantina*, 12 (1983): 463–506, esp. pp. 465–8 and 473–4.

Here the chronicler might not, as in other parts of his work, rely on Byzantine sources in this passage, and his view certainly does not echo the imperial view.⁹ Nevertheless, the report brings up the issue whether the damage done to both peoples was the intended effect of the empire's financial intervention. Did Maurice try to use his money in order to ensnarl the Franks and Lombards in a war of attrition?

Although both versions – Gregory's and John's – could imply different views on the real purpose of Byzantium's financial intervention, they also have some characteristics in common. They correspond, for instance, with regard to the contractual nature of the agreement between the emperor and the Franks: the latter were hired to fight against the Lombards. The reports also share the common view of *gentes* as military agents and addressees of Byzantium's diplomacy alike.¹⁰ On the whole, they raise questions such as what Byzantine gold actually was meant to accomplish in the West and how, that is among whom, it actually was distributed. This paper therefore deals with the influx of Byzantine money and its intended effect on the stability of a political formation such as Merovingian and Lombard rule. It tries to look beyond the *gentes*, which ostensibly feature as the political agents in contemporary historiography: as groups, as personified social bodies, they were shaped, to a large extent, by the distribution and redistribution of wealth and money which worked as instruments of external connections and internal distinction, used to set up hierarchies. The results of a closer analysis of the sources should shed light on the Byzantine strategies for the use of money as a political tool. It is supposed to gain insights into the interference of the Mediterranean East with the West and Byzantium's financial share in the formation of Frankish and Lombard power structures. We start with the Byzantine policy towards the Lombards before we pass on to the situation in the Merovingian kingdoms.

A decisive determinant for the use of money as a political instrument against Byzantium's enemies on the Italian peninsula was the fragmentation of the Lombards.¹¹ The Byzantines had to face not one single but many different small groups when they tried to counteract the invasion in Italy, and, according to Paul the Deacon, not all of them were Lombards. Immediately after the heterogeneous host led by Alboin (r. 560/5–72/3) had gained a foothold in Italy and the king was laying siege to Pavia, his army dissolved, and Lombard warriors turned south and

---

⁹ On the sources, see Pozo Flores, 'Fuentes', esp. pp. 165–70.
¹⁰ On Gregory's view on the Franks as a *gens*, see now H. Reimitz, *History, Frankish Identity and the Framing of Western Ethnicity, 550–850* (Cambridge, 2015), esp. pp. 116–23.
¹¹ Pohl, 'Empire', pp. 76, 99–100.

west to pillage Byzantine Italy and Frankish Burgundy.[12] The subsequent foundation of the Lombard duchies in Spoleto and Benevento attests to the territorial fragmentation of the invaders' rule over the peninsula while rebellions in the north indicate the lack of cohesion that led to the killing of Alboin and his successor, Cleph (r. 572/3–4) and, eventually, resulted in a decennial *interregnum*. Between 574 and 584, Lombard *duces* governed the north of Italy before some of them agreed to elect a king again.[13] But also the new ruler Authari (r. 584–90) had to grapple with the resistance of several dukes. All in all, the first decades after the Lombard invasion of Italy were a period of constant rivalries and continuous conflicts between different groups and their leaders.

Lombard historiography, however, glossed over the fact that the kingship of Authari and even Agilulf (r. 590–616) were challenged by local powers: to be sure, Paul the Deacon used the period of ducal rule as a projection screen against which he could display the shortcomings of a time without a king, because the image of Lombard kingship as the institutionalised representation of order was a major concern of his

---

[12] For the army's composition, see Paul the Deacon, *Historia Langobardorum* II, 26, ed. Bethmann and Waitz, p. 87. W. Pohl, 'Invasions and Ethnic Identity', in Cristina La Rocca (ed.), *Italy in the Early Middle Ages: The Short Oxford History of Italy* (Oxford, 2002), pp. 11–33, at p. 21; Pohl, 'Empire', p. 99; S. Gasparri, 'The Aristocracy', in Cristina La Rocca (ed.), *Italy in the Early Middle Ages: The Short Oxford History of Italy* (Oxford, 2002), pp. 59–84, at p. 64. On Alboin, see F. Borri, *Alboino: Frammenti di un racconto (s. VI–XI)* (Rome, 2016).

[13] S. Dick, '*Langobardi per annos decem regem non habentes, sub ducibus fuerunt*. Formen und Entwicklung der Herrschaftsorganisation bei den Langobarden. Eine Skizze', in W. Pohl and P. Erhart (eds.), *Die Langobarden: Herrschaft und Identität* (Vienna, 2005), pp. 335–43, esp. pp. 341–2; J. Jarnut, '*Gens, rex* and *regnum* of the Lombards', in H.-W. Goetz, J. Jarnut and W. Pohl with the collaboration of S. Kaschke (eds.), *Regna and Gentes: The Relationship between Late Antique and Early Medieval Peoples and Kingdoms in the Transformation of the Roman World* (Leiden, 2003), pp. 409–27, at p. 415; Wickham, *Early Medieval Italy*, pp. 31–2; see also the biased account of Fredegar, *Chronicae*, IV, 45, ed. Krusch, p. 143. According to Paul the Deacon, the *interregnum* was a period of war motivated by greed; *Historia Langobardorum*, II, 32, ed. Bethmann and Waitz, p. 90, ll. 18–19: *His diebus multi nobilium Romanorum ob cupiditatem interfecti sunt*. Pohl, 'Empire', p. 113; see also W. Pohl, '*Per hospites divisi* – Wirtschaftliche Grundlagen der langobardischen Ansiedlung in Italien', *Römische Historische Mitteilungen*, 43 (2001): 179–226, at pp. 189 and 224–5. For a different reading of the passage, see Gasparri, 'The Aristocracy', p. 62. According to other sources such as the *Continuatio Havniensis Prosperi* 7, in *Chronica minora saec. IV.V.VI.VII*, ed. T. Mommsen, vol. I, MGH AA 9 (Berlin, 1892), pp. 337–9, at p. 338, the *Origo gentis Langobardorum* 6, ed. G. Waitz, MGH SRL 1 (Hanover, 1878), pp. 1–6, at p. 5; and Fredegar, *Chronicae*, IV, 45, ed. Krusch, p. 143 from the seventh century, the *interregnum* lasted for twelve years. On the *interregnum*, see F. Borri, 'Dieci anni, trentacinque duchi: I Longobardi nel periodo dell'interregno (574–584)', in G. Albertoni (ed.), *577: I Longobardi nel Campo Rotaliano* (forthcoming).

historiographical efforts.[14] The rebellions of the dukes before and after the *interregnum* were marginalised in his account. In doing so, Paul intentionally covered a more complex power structure under the euphemised description of a hierarchical regime represented by a king at the top of it.

Unlike the eighth-century accounts of Lombard history, contemporary Byzantine diplomacy attentively acknowledged the mosaic of different groups that held sway over Italy. The empire consequently tried to benefit from the situation and bought some *duces* off to join the imperial side. Menander the Guardsman, a contemporary Byzantine author, reports that, responding to a cry for help from the Roman senate and the pope, the emperor, most probably Tiberius (r. 578–82), spent money to win over a group of Lombard leaders on two different occasions at the end of the 570s. Menander does not inform us about the results of the first time the emperor tried to use his gold this way. But the second time, according to the chronicler, the strategy worked just fine: many of the chiefs, the *hegemones*, accepted the promised gifts and rewards and changed sides.[15] With no king left to deal with, the *interregnum* made the dukes the preferred targets of Byzantium's financial approach. And some of them willingly accepted, because the subsidies paid by the emperor could give the recipient the upper hand in the conflict with his ducal rivals.[16]

---

[14] See his conclusion with regards to the election of Authari: 'Erat sane hoc mirabile in regno Langobardorum: nulla erat violentia, nullae struebantur insidiae; nemo aliquem iniuste angariabat, nemo spoliabat; non erant furta, non latrocinia; unusquisque quo libebat securus sine timore pergebat'; Paul the Deacon, *Historia Langobardorum*, III, 16, ed. Bethmann and Waitz, p. 101, ll. 6–8; see also *Historia Langobardorum*, II, 32, ed. Bethmann and Waitz, p. 91. For his stance on kingship, see also *Historia Langobardorum*, I, 14, ed. Bethmann and Waitz, p. 54; Jarnut, '*Gens*', pp. 411 and 413. See also Pohl, 'Gregory of Tours', pp. 135 and 141; Pohl, 'Empire', p. 125; Pohl, '*Per hospites divisi*', pp. 189 and 200 (here referring to the view of Secundus of Trient, Paul's presumable source on the events).

[15] *The History of Menander the Guardsman: Introductory Essay, Text, Translation and Historiographical Notes*, ed. and trans. by R. C. Blockley (Cambridge, 2006), fr. 22 and 24, pp. 196–7 and 216–17; on the dating see *History of Menander the Guardsman*, pp. 281 and 283, nn. 267 and 293. Both fragments refer to the *hegemones* of the Lombards and, thus, most probably to the ducal level of the Lombard power structures. Wickham, *Early Medieval Italy*, p. 31. See also Loseby, 'Gregory of Tours', pp. 486–8; Pohl, 'Empire', pp. 130–1, n. 192; and H. Krahwinkler, *Friaul im Frühmittelalter: Geschichte einer Region vom Ende des fünften bis zum Ende des zehnten Jahrhunderts* (Vienna, 1992), p. 36; on Menander and his work in general, see B. Baldwin, 'Menander Protector', *Dumbarton Oaks Papers*, 32 (1978): 99–125.

[16] This argument also stands if we assume the dukes earned a possible surplus through the king's absence. According to Jean Durliat, they received the third part of the tribute which, originally, was meant for the royal court; J. Durliat, 'Le Salaire de la paix sociale dans les royaumes barbares (Ve–VIe siècles)', in H. Wolfram and A. Schwarcz (eds.), *Anerkennung und Integration: Zu den wirtschaftlichen Grundlagen der Völkerwanderungszeit 400–600* (Vienna, 1988), pp. 21–72, at p. 49 with n. 147, but see also the critique by Pohl, '*Per hospites divisi*', pp. 193–4. Even if this were so, this additional income must

Duke Droctulf of Brescello was certainly one of the beneficiaries of the Byzantine economic intervention, even though Paul the Deacon does not mention that any kind of payment or gift was involved when he defected to the enemy. Ethnically a Sueve or possibly an Alaman, the former commander of a part of the Lombard army went over to the Byzantines, where he served as a member of the imperial troops. It was Authari who had to lay siege on Droctulf in Brescello and made him retreat to Ravenna where he remained an active participant in the fight 'against his own people', as his epitaph put it.[17] Others did the same and joined the Byzantines:[18] Nordulf was a Lombard noble who went over to the enemy and later even became an important adviser on Italian affairs to the emperor.[19] Like him, another *dux* called Auctarit (Autharius) had submitted to the empire, probably in 584.[20] Both obviously had paid their troops with Byzantine gold: this is at least what a demand of *dux* Ariulf of Spoleto on Gregory the Great (r. 590–604) in June 592 suggested. The Lombard duke requested the *precaria* of Nordulf's and Auctarit's armies as a precondition for peace.[21] In the sixth century, this term was used to refer to payments made in the context of short-time treaties concluded with leading men and their military retinues to make them fight for the empire: the *duces* who received the *precaria* redistributed the money

---

have been divided on equal terms, whereas Byzantine money was not, thus offering a financial advantage in the strife for power.

[17] Paul the Deacon, *Historia Langobardorum*, III, 18–19, ed. Bethmann and Waitz, pp. 101–3, the quotation from the epitaph from p. 102 l. 16: ... *Vastator genti adfuit ipse suae.* Wickham, *Early Medieval Italy*, pp. 31–2; Pohl, 'Empire', pp. 99 and 132; Reverdy, 'Relations', p. 73; N. Everett, *Literacy in Lombard Italy, c. 568–774* (Cambridge, 2003), pp. 71–2.

[18] For the following, see T. S. Brown, *Gentlemen and Officers: Imperial Administration and Aristocratic Power in Byzantine Italy, AD 554–800* (London, 1984), pp. 70–3; W. Pohl, 'L'Armée romaine et les Lombards: stratégies militaires et politiques', in F. Vallet and M. Kazanski (eds.), *L'Armée romaine et les barbares du IIIe au VIIe siècle* (Paris, 1993), pp. 291–5, at p. 293; Krahwinkler, *Friaul im Frühmittelalter*, p. 37.

[19] This is implied in *S. Gregorii Magni Registrum epistularum* V, 36, ed. D. Norberg, 2 vols., CCSL 140 and 140A (Turnhout, 1982), p. 305. Pohl, 'Empire', p. 132; Pohl, 'Reichsbildung', p. 241; F. Borri, 'Swollen with Their Accustomed Pride: Solidarity, Hegemony, and Defiance in the Roman Army of Italy, 584–727', in W. Pohl and A. Fischer (eds.), *Social Cohesion and Its Limits* (forthcoming).

[20] Fredegar, *Chronicae*, IV, 45, ed. Krusch, p. 143. *The Prosopography of the Later Roman Empire*, ed. J. R. Martindale, vol. IIIA 527–641 AD (Cambridge, 1992), p. 158 s.v. Autharius 1. See also J. Jarnut, *Prosopographische und sozialgeschichtliche Studien zum Langobardenreich in Italien 568–774* (Bonn, 1972), p. 346, no. 33. For Auctarit, see *The Prosopography of the Later Roman Empire*, ed. J. R. Martindale, vol. IIIA 527–641 AD (Cambridge, 1992), p. 150 s.v. Auctarit; for the possible identity of Autharius/Auctarit see *The Prosopography of the Later Roman Empire*, p. 158 s.v. Autharius 1.

[21] Gregory the Great, *Registrum epistularum*, II, 38, ed. Norberg, p. 123. See also Pohl, 'Reichsbildung', p. 241; Pohl, 'Empire', pp. 103–4.

among their followers.²² The episode indicates that Byzantine gold did not fall into desuetude after the ascension of Authari. On the contrary, even after the *interregnum*, money was still employed to bind military groups and their leaders to the empire, which had to assure the constant flow of subsidies to keep up the loyalties they generated.

In an impoverished land such as Italy in the sixth century, a peninsula devastated by decades of warfare, the influx of gold and valuables as subsidies and gifts must have had an enormous effect. As a component of the larger Byzantine strategy, it was likely meant to topple the Lombard regime: the fragmentation of Lombard rule was supposed to weaken the enemy by splitting up its military force and turning it against itself.²³ In doing so, the Byzantines certainly tried to meet the challenges posed by the multifarious accumulation of groups that were dubbed as 'Lombard', but they were equally involved in the production of groups self-identifying as such. To be sure, there is no chance to solve the causality dilemma of the sequence of Lombard dissolution and Byzantium's financial interventions: the reciprocal nature of the redistribution of wealth and social cohesion in terms of offer and demand does not allow for a deeper insight into the process. All the same, the fact needs to be stressed that Byzantium continued its financial support for some dukes even after other nobles had agreed on the re-establishment of the kingdom in 584, as the cases of Auctarit and Nordulf prove. The end of the *interregnum* did not change the strategy of the emperor and his local representatives, who refused to make peace with the Lombard king, to the grief of the bishops of Rome. Gregory the Great, for instance, saw the Lombard kingdom as an institution capable of domesticating and controlling the Lombard dukes, if Byzantine diplomacy would back the monarch rather than the centrifugal tendencies represented by the dukes.²⁴ But the existence of a settled hierarchy seems to have been what the Byzantines tried to prevent. Contrary to the pope's intentions, they did not want to come to terms with a single representative of a stable political entity. Instead, they used their money to establish cohesion on a small-scale level to keep the Lombards in a state of permanent rivalry. Hence, even after 584, Byzantium and its local authorities still tried to prey on the disputed position of the new king and watch the enemy tear itself apart through continuous war.

---

²² Pohl, 'Empire', p. 113.
²³ Pohl, 'Empire', p. 112.
²⁴ Gregory the Great, *Registrum epistularum*, IX, 66, ed. Norberg, p. 622. Pohl, 'Empire', pp. 109–10; see also Whitby, *Emperor*, pp. 23–4 and 114.

The strategy employed by the emperor Tiberius and his successor Maurice towards Lombard Italy provokes thoughts about what the Byzantine gold paid to the Franks actually did to the power structures in the Merovingian kingdoms in these years. On the face of it, there seems to have been a clear top-down approach: the Burgundian or the Austrasian kings, as the major protagonists of Merovingian policy in Italy, were those to be addressed through embassies they exchanged with Constantinople.[25] As the episode about Childebert and Maurice paraphrased at the beginning of this article suggests, it was they who had to be paid to get a Frankish army moving against the Lombards. In fact, especially the Austrasian kings had a long history of military campaigns in northern Italy in the sixth century. Theudebert I (r. 533–47/8) brought Raetia, Noricum and large parts of Venetia under his control between 540 and 545.[26] Back then, he was allied with the Lombards. According to Gregory of Tours, Sigibert I (r. 561–75) also held sway over some unfortunately undefined parts of the northern peninsula. His son Childebert II had inherited his realm and, with it, Sigibert's interest in Italy.[27] Unsurprisingly, it was he who was approached by Maurice to battle the Lombards.

There were, of course, Frankish dukes directly involved in the Italian campaigns, such as Leuthari or Amingus: Paul the Deacon reports that they fought alongside Butilinus, who possibly was an Aleman, and that they acted on behalf of the Merovingian king, Theudebert, who, as we are told, tried to conquer parts of the peninsula.[28] The unfolding of the intervention, however, suggests that a certain degree of independent

---

[25] On the embassies, see E. Ewig, *Die Merowinger und das Imperium* (Opladen, 1983), pp. 5–62, at pp. 26–48; P. Schreiner, 'Gregor von Tours und Byzanz', in J. Gießauf, R. Murauer and M. P. Schennach (eds.), *Päpste, Privilegien, Provinzen: Beiträge zur Kirchen-, Rechts- und Landesgeschichte – Festschrift für Werner Maleczek zum 65. Geburtstag* (Vienna, 2010), pp. 403–18, at pp. 408–9; P. Schreiner, 'Eine merowingische Gesandtschaft in Konstantinopel (590?)', *Frühmittelalterliche Studien*, 19 (1985): 195–200.

[26] Ewig, *Die Merowinger und das Imperium*, pp. 20–1; on his expansionist politics in general, see R. Collins, 'Theodebert I, "Rex Magnus Francorum"', in P. C. Wormald, D. A. Bullough and R. Collins (eds.), *Ideal and Reality in Frankish and Anglo-Saxon Society: Studies Presented to John Michael Wallace-Hadrill* (Oxford, 1983), pp. 7–33, at pp. 9–12.

[27] Gregory of Tours, *Historiae*, IX, 20, ed. Krusch and Levison, p. 440. Ewig, *Die Merowinger und das Imperium*, p. 28.

[28] Paul the Deacon, *Historia Langobardorum*, II, 2, ed. Bethmann and Waitz, pp. 72–3; see also Gregory of Tours, *Historiae*, III, 32 and IV, 9, ed. Krusch and Levison, pp. 128 and 140–1; Menander fr. 3, 1, ed. Blockley, pp. 44–5 (Baldwin, 'Menander Protector', p. 120); H. Keller, 'Fränkische Herrschaft und alemannisches Herzogtum im 6. und 7. Jahrhundert', *Zeitschrift für die Geschichte des Oberrheins*, 124 (1976): 1–30, at pp. 6–9; D. Geuenich, *Geschichte der Alemannen* (Stuttgart, 1997), pp. 93–4 and 113; see also Pohl, 'Gregory of Tours', pp. 137–9; Löhlein, *Alpen- und Italienpolitik*, pp. 35 and 46–8.

military entrepreneurship was at the heart of the dukes' motivation.[29] A contemporary Byzantine writer, Agathias, alleged their plan was simply to plunder Italy rather than to conquer it, and it might well be that the Ostrogothic treasure Totila had stored in Cumae was the primary goal of their efforts.[30] Paul the Deacon also tells us that Butilinus took rich presents from the booty he had obtained and gave them to Theudebert, which implies that he kept the remainder for himself, for obvious reasons.[31] In the next decades, the chance to gather riches in the theatre of war lured other Frankish magnates to northern Italy, such as Chramnichis, who finally lost his life and all the booty he had collected on his campaign thus far to his Lombard enemies.[32] Rather than being a part of a combined Byzantine–Frankish campaign, his intervention appears to have been a quite independent act. This is not to say that the Merovingian king was not in control, but, like many other war zones, Lombard Italy obviously was a grey area for soldiers of fortune (in a literal sense) who fought as much for their own account as on behalf of their ruler.[33]

Given the involvement of Frankish military men, it does not come as a surprise that the Byzantines also thought them to be a worthwhile target

---

[29] Löhlein, *Alpen- und Italienpolitik*, pp. 47–8; Ewig, *Die Merowinger und das Imperium*, p. 24. For the general background, see B. S. Bachrach, 'Merovingian Mercenaries and Paid Soldiers in Imperial Perspective', in J. France (ed.), *Mercenaries and Paid Men: The Mercenary Identity in the Middle Ages – Proceedings of a Conference held at University of Wales, Swansea, 7th–9th July 2005* (Leiden, 2008), pp. 167–92, esp. p. 183.

[30] *Agathiae Myrinaei Historiarum libri quinque* II, 2, 1–3, ed. R. Keydell (Berlin, 1967), pp. 41–2; M. Hardt, *Gold und Herrschaft: Die Schätze europäischer Könige und Fürsten im ersten Jahrtausend* (Berlin, 2004), p. 36.

[31] Paul the Deacon, *Historia Langobardorum*, II, 2, ed. Bethmann and Waitz, p. 73 ll. 1–3: *Qui Buccelinus cum pene totam Italiam direptionibus vastaret et Theudeperto suo regi de praeda Italiae munera copiosa conferret ...* ; cf. the different version in Gregory of Tours, *Historiae*, III, 32, ed. Krusch, p. 128 ll. 14–15: *thesauros vero magnus ad Theudobertum de Italia dirixit*. The dating of this episode might be wrong; see Löhlein, *Alpen- und Italienpolitik*, p. 47 n. 152 on this issue. But there is no reason to dismiss the whole story: in any case Butilin certainly shared his prey with the current Merovingian king. For the distribution of booty in general, see J.-P. Bodmer, *Der Krieger der Merowingerzeit und seine Welt: Eine Studie über Kriegertum als Form der menschlichen Existenz im Frühmittelalter* (Zurich, 1957), pp. 100–1.

[32] Paul the Deacon, *Historia Langobardorum*, III, 9, ed. Bethmann and Waitz, p. 97.

[33] On the issue of plundering in general and its social implications, see also Bodmer, *Krieger*, pp. 68–72; G. M. Berndt, 'Beute, Schutzgeld und Subsidien: Formen der Aneignung materieller Güter in gotischen Kriegergruppen', in H. Carl and H.-J. Bömelburg (eds.), *Lohn der Gewalt: Beutepraktiken von der Antike bis zur Neuzeit* (Paderborn, 2011), pp. 121–47, esp. pp. 128–9; L. Sarti, *Perceiving War and the Military in Early Christian Gaul (ca. 400–700 AD)* (Leiden, 2013), esp. pp. 194–8; G. Halsall, 'Predatory Warfare: The Moral and the Physical', in R. Keller and L. Sarti (eds.), *Pillages, tributs, captifs: Prédation et sociétés de l'Antiquité tardive au haut Moyen Âge – Tributzahlungen, Plünderungen, und Gefangennahmen. Die Aneignung von fremdem Eigentum von der Spätantike zum frühen Mittelalter* (Paris, 2018), pp. 53–68, esp. pp. 57–60.

of financial efforts. In his account of Tiberius's aforementioned attempt to buy off Lombard nobles in the late 570s, Menander reports the emperor's plan to spend the money on magnates in the Merovingian kingdoms. If, as he expected, the Lombards declined the offer, the money was supposed 'to buy the alliance of some of the Frankish chiefs, and by this means to wear down and wipe out the power of the Lombards'.[34] To be sure, we do not know whether the imperial envoy approached one of the Franks and if someone accepted the gold offered to them in the end. But the strategy made perfect sense against the backdrop of the minority of Childebert II, the ruler of the eastern part of the Merovingian kingdom, that is, at a time when Frankish dukes and aristocrats dominated the court after Sigibert had passed away in 575.

Interestingly enough, it was there and then that a member of the court broached the issue of Byzantine money. A letter written by Gogo, a high official, probably the mayor at Sigibert's court and the *nutricius* of Childebert II between 575 and 581, on behalf of the minor king to the Lombard duke, Grasulf, dealt with the prospect of subsidies. The text implied that the complete sum of money for this conflict, that is the war against the Lombards, would be paid, if Grasulf was able to conclude the necessary treaties on behalf of the empire.[35] Obviously the *nutricius* talked about imperial gold, and Grasulf was supposed to be able to regulate its influx to Francia: he was the mediator for the other side, the Byzantine one, while Gogo played the negotiator on behalf of the Merovingian king.[36] The fact that Gogo writes 'De Nomen Regis'

---

[34] Menander fr. 22, ed. Blockley, pp. 196–7.

[35] *Liber epistolarum*, 48, ed. Malaspina, pp. 218–21, with the crucial phrase on p. 218. On Grasulf see Pohl, 'Empire', p. 132; P. Goubert, *Byzance avant l'Islam, Byzance et l'Orient sous les successeurs de Justinien, II, 1: Byzance et les Francs* (Paris, 1955), pp. 197–8; and the literature cited in the following note. The dating of the letter is controversial: Goffart, 'Policy', pp. 77–80 dates it to 571, while Bachrach, *Anatomy*, pp. 155–9, gathered convincing arguments for a later date at the end of the 570s. On this issue, see also Ewig, *Die Merowinger und das Imperium*, pp. 28–9 n. 111. On Gogo, see also H. D. Williard, 'Letter-Writing and Literary Culture in Merovingian Gaul', *European Review of History*, 21 (2014): 691–710, esp. pp. 695–9; on the collection of letters in general, see B. Dumézil and T. Lienhard, 'Les *Lettres austrasiennes*: dire, cacher, transmettre les informations diplomatiques au haut Moyen Âge', in *Les Relations diplomatiques au Moyen Âge: Formes des enjeux*, XLIe Congrès de la SHMESP, Lyon, 3–6 June 2010 (Paris, 2011), pp. 69–80, R. Jakobi, 'Redaktion als Literarisierung und politisches Programm: Die Sammlung der "Epistulae Austrasicae"', *Mittellateinisches Jahrbuch*, 50 (2015): 91–105, esp. pp. 96–9; and G. Barrett and G. Woudhuysen, 'Assembling the *Austrasian Letters* at Trier and Lorsch', *Early Medieval Europe*, 24 (2016): 3–57.

[36] Reverdy, 'Relations', pp. 63–4 and 78; B. Dumézil, 'Gogo et ses amis: écriture, échanges et ambitions dans un reseau aristocratique de la fin du VIe siècle', *Revue historique*, 309 (2007): 553–93, at p. 578; Krahwinkler, *Friaul*, p. 36; Brown, *Gentlemen*, p. 72. For a different interpretation of the letter and Grasulf's role, see Pohl, 'Empire', pp. 100–1; Pohl, 'Reichsbildung', pp. 237–8; Everett, *Literacy*, pp. 69–70.

deserves some attention in this context: it is an exceptional case in the collection of the *Epistolae Austrasicae* in that the formula refers to the writer of the letter, Gogo, and the king, Childebert II, at the same time.[37] This could be read as an expression of Childebert's weakness, but the way Gogo explicitly mentioned the king emphasised his role as a representative of the Merovingian. One wonders therefore whether this was meant to contrast the activities of other Frankish magnates to act on behalf of this king – or for the benefit of theirs.

In fact, Gogo had excellent qualifications to negotiate between both sides, the Franks and the Byzantines. As a high official at the court, he was one major pillar of a network that extended to northern Italy and Constantinople.[38] Among its members were Venantius Fortunatus, coming from Italy, although most probably not as a Byzantine agent, who turned to Gogo in five of his poems.[39] Another one was *dux* Chamingus, possibly identical with the Amingus mentioned above, who had fought in Italy during the reign of Theudebert and afterwards.[40] He lobbied for Gogo at the Austrasian court. Some members of the circle who patronised each other built connections to Byzantium. One of them, an unnamed magnate, wrote a letter to the emperor asking for the release of one of his relatives from custody around 585. Other friends of Gogo at the Austrasian court might have been present when Byzantine ambassadors arrived in the Merovingian kingdoms. Recently it has also been suggested that members of the group around the supposed mayor were among those who had supported Gundovald. According to Gregory of Tours, several magnates of Childebert II were responsible for calling the pretender in. If so, Gogo's affiliates might indeed have taken a hand in Gundovald's upheaval, after the network had lost its centre following the *nutricius*'s death.[41] Finally,

---

[37] Dumézil, 'Gogo', pp. 578–9.
[38] On the network, see Dumézil, 'Gogo', esp. pp. 557–77, 581–4 and 587–90.
[39] *Venanti Honori Clementiani Fortunati carminum epistolarum expositionum libri undecim*, VI, 8 and VII, 1–4, ed. F. Leo, MGH AA 4, 1 (Berlin, 1881), pp. 148–9 and 153–6. Dumézil, 'Gogo', pp. 553 and 579; B. Brennan, 'Venantius Fortunatus: Byzantine Agent?', *Byzantion*, 65 (1995): 7–16; Y. Hen, *Roman Barbarians: The Royal Court and Culture in the Early Medieval West* (Basingstoke, 2011), p. 99; A. Bayard and S. Joye, 'Les Élites d'Austrasie, des aristocrates raffinés?', in *Austrasie: Le royaume mérovingien oublié* ed. V. Dupuy (Milan, 2016), pp. 60–7, at p. 65; Y. Hen, 'Les Élites culturelles', in B. Dumézil and S. Joye (eds.), *L'Austrasie: pouvoirs, espaces et identité a la charnière de l'Antiquité et du Moyen Âge* (forthcoming).
[40] For the identification, see Goffart, 'Policy', p. 76 n. 11; see also K. Selle-Hosbach, *Prosopographie merowingischer Amtsträger in der Zeit von 511 bis 613* (Bonn, 1974), p. 42 no. 10 (Amingus) and p. 67 no. 52 (Chamingus).
[41] Dumézil, 'Gogo', pp. 583–4; Goffart, 'Policy', pp. 93–4 and 102–3.

Dynamius, *patricius* and *rector* of the Provence, also belonged to the group.[42]

Dynamius was the member of the group who, due to his position, got in touch with Byzantium easily. Residing in Marseille, he controlled the interface through which Mediterranean goods made their way into Francia.[43] Byzantium's presence must have been felt strongly in the city whose economic turnover fed the treasures of the Burgundian or the Austrasian kings respectively. Its *rector* had also built his own tiny network in Provence, including Uzès, another important city in terms of transportation.[44] Both places of trade were among few cities in southern Gaul where so-called 'quasi-imperial' coins were minted.[45] Between 565 and 641, the beginning of the rule of Justin II (565–78) and the end of Heraclius's reign (610–41), but probably starting under Tiberius at the beginning of the 580s with a peak under Maurice, *solidi* and *tremisses* (⅓ *solidus*) were issued that were anomalous in style compared to the Merovingian and imperial standards. As a matter of fact, all of them bore the portrait of the current emperor, but rather than just imitating the iconography of older types of imperial coins, the *solidi* issued in Provence during the reign of Maurice were stylised according to local traditions.[46] Since archaeological

---

[42] On him, see B. Dumézil, 'Le Patrice Dynamius et son réseau: Culture aristocratique et transformation des pouvoirs autour de Lérins dans la seconde moitié du VIe siècle', in Y. Codou and M. Lauwers (eds.), *Lérins, une île sainte dans l'Occident médiéval* (Turnhout, 2009), pp. 167–94; M. Manitius, 'Zu Dynamius von Massilia', *Mitteilungen des Instituts für Österreichische Geschichtswissenschaften*, 18 (1897): 227–32. See also Selle-Hosbach, *Prosopographie*, pp. 80–2 no. 74; and Williard, 'Letter-Writing', pp. 699–702; Hen, *Roman Barbarians*, p. 99; Bayard and Joye, 'Les Élites d'Austrasie', p. 65.

[43] For his connection to the city, see also Gregory the Great, *Registrum epistularum*, VII, 12, ed. Norberg, pp. 461–2.

[44] Gregory of Tours, *Historiae*, VI, 7, ed. Krusch and Levison, pp. 276–7; Dumézil, 'Gogo', pp. 581 and 583; Dumézil, 'Patrice', p. 177. For Uzès as a transfer site, see S. Loseby, 'Marseille: A Late Antique Success-Story?', *Journal of Roman Studies*, 82 (1992): pp. 165–85, at p. 177 with n. 83.

[45] S. E. Rigold, 'An Imperial Coinage in Southern Gaul in the Sixth and Seventh Centuries?', *The Numismatic Chronicle*, 14 (1954): 93–133; P. Grierson, 'The "Patrimonium Petri in illis partibus" and the Pseudo-Imperial Coinage in Frankish Gaul', *Revue belge de numismatique et de sigillographie*, 105 (1959): 95–111; K. Uhalde, 'The Quasi-imperial Coinage and Fiscal Administration of Merovingian Provence', in R. W. Mathisen and D. Shanzer (eds.), *Society and Culture in Late Antique Gaul: Revisiting the Sources* (Aldershot, 2001), pp. 134–65; M. F. Hendy, 'From Public to Private: The Western Barbarian Coinages as a Mirror of the Disintegration of Late Roman State Structures', *Viator*, 19 (1988): 29–78, at pp. 68–70; J. Lafaurie and C. Morrisson, 'La Pénétration des monnaies byzantines en Gaule mérovingienne et visigotique du VIe au VIIIe siècle', *Revue numismatique*, 6e série, 29 (1987): 38–98, at pp. 42–3, 52; S. Loseby, 'Marseille and the Pirenne Thesis, I: Gregory of Tours, the Merovingian Kings and "Un Grand Port"', in R. Hodges and W. Bowden (eds.), *The Sixth Century: Production, Distribution and Demand* (Leiden, 1998), pp. 203–29, at pp. 223–5. For the denomination as 'quasi-imperial' rather than 'pseudo-imperial' see Loseby, 'Marseille', p. 177 n. 80.

[46] Uhalde, 'Quasi-imperial Coinage', pp. 7–8. For the dating see Uhalde, 'Quasi-imperial Coinage', pp. 3–4 and Lafaurie and Morrisson, 'Pénétration', pp. 49–50 and 52.

surveys have rarely unearthed Byzantine gold in France (although more *solidi* have been found in the south due to its higher level of integration into the Mediterranean economy), while there is a lot of evidence for imperial coins beyond its borders, it has been assumed that the precious metal had been reused for striking new coins.[47] Against this backdrop, imperial payments (in particular those made by Maurice) could therefore also have formed the material basis for the 'quasi-imperial' coinage.[48]

The practice of simultaneously minting a specific coinage in several cities of the region, however, bespeaks the existence of a unitary organisation in an area that was torn apart by many different and competitive local sovereignties and political allegiances to the Merovingian kings, Guntram (r. 561–92) and Childebert II.[49] Dynamius was not only involved in the conflict that broke out over Marseille.[50] Representing the most eminent office-holder in the area that the 'quasi-imperial' coinage covered, he, possibly together with other members of his network, may also well have been the person behind the production of this type of money, the more so because he was adept in monetary politics. Due to his function as a patrician, which made him the administrator of the papal estates in Provence, Dynamius was in charge of collecting the revenues from these lands, as his correspondence with Gregory the Great

---

[47] Lafaurie and Morrisson, 'Pénétration', pp. 44–6 and 55; M. McCormick, *Origins of the European Economy. Communications and Commerce, AD 300–900* (Cambridge, 2001), pp. 321 and 351; D. M. Metcalf, 'Monetary Circulation in Merovingian Gaul, 561–674. A propos des Cahiers Ernest Babelon, 8', *Revue numismatique*, 6e série, 162 (2006): 337–93, at p. 338; M. McCormick, 'Coins and the economic history of post-Roman Gaul: testing the standard model in the Moselle, ca. 400–750', in J. Jarnut and J. Strothmann (eds.), *Die Merowingischen Monetarmünzen als Quelle zum Verständnis des 7. Jahrhunderts in Gallien* (Paderborn, 2013), pp. 337–376, at pp. 352–3. For Byzantine coinage in the area east of the Rhine, see also J. Drauschke, 'Byzantinische Münzen des ausgehenden 5. bis beginnenden 8. Jahrhunderts in den östlichen Regionen des Merowingerreiches', in M. Wołoszyn (ed.), *Byzantine Coins in Central Europe between the 5th and the 10th Century* (Krakow, 2009), pp. 279–323, esp. 293–5; Drauschke, 'Zur Herkunft und Vermittlung "byzantinischer Importe" der Merowingerzeit in Nordwesteuropa', in S. Brather (ed.), *Zwischen Spätantike und Frühmittelalter: Archäologie des 4. bis 7. Jahrhunderts im Westen* (Berlin, 2008), pp. 367–423, at pp. 385 and 393–4.

[48] Lafaurie and Morrisson, 'Pénétration', p. 44. Rigold, 'Imperial Coinage', p. 98, considers a connection between the minting of the 'quasi-imperial' coinage and the politics of subsidising the Franks for waging war against the Lombards.

[49] Hendy, 'From Public to Private', pp. 68–70; M. F. Hendy, 'East and West: The Transformation of Late Roman Financial Structures', in *Roma fra Oriente ed Occidente*, 19–24 April 2001, vol. II, Settimane 49 (Spoleto, 2002), pp. 1307–70, at p. 1345; Uhalde, 'Quasi-imperial Coinage', p. 7; Rigold, 'Imperial Coinage', pp. 102 and 122, but see p. 105.

[50] For Marseille as a bone of contention between the Merovingians, see Loseby, 'Marseille', p. 174; Loseby, 'Marseille and the Pirenne Thesis', pp. 225–7. For Dynamius's position in the conflict, see Gregory of Tours, *Historiae*, VI, 11 and IX, 11, ed. Krusch and Levison, pp. 280–2 and 426; Duméz.l, 'Patrice', p. 180; Wood, *Merovingian Kingdoms*, pp. 85 and 101.

shows.⁵¹ It has been assumed that his fiscal responsibilities might have extended to several cities in Provence where his staff members possibly gathered taxes for the Merovingian kings.⁵² With the whole region tied in with the Mediterranean trading network via Marseille as the hegemonic centre in Provence and, thus, linked with Byzantium, the 'quasi-imperial' coinage testifies to a thriving economy in the area that saw the need for coinage of higher denomination for major transactions.⁵³ Some of the coins might have been used as payment to the papal see, if the coinage is identical with the *solidi Gallicani* or *solidi Galliarum* that Dynamius sent to Rome during the pontificate of Gregory the Great, who later refused them due to the lack of consumer acceptance.⁵⁴ Since the currency did not meet with imperial gold standards in terms of weight, the distribution remained limited, and the coins therefore seem to have been originally meant for use on the markets in Merovingian Gaul rather than in the Mediterranean area.⁵⁵ At the same time, they conveyed a political message, demonstrating close ties to the empire.⁵⁶ Regional traders and merchants passed on the coinage and the information about it, and this way or other news about the emperor's icon circulating on coins in Provence and beyond must have reached the court in Constantinople. All the same, minting the coinage seems to have been intended to express the discrete status of the region in a Frankish realm that used completely different coinage elsewhere. And there are good reasons to believe Dynamius was behind these efforts.

That the patrician had deeper personal interests in a lasting connection with Byzantium becomes evident from the information on an embassy sent to Constantinople at the end of the 580s. At that time, Dynamius seemed to have tried to pass on this linkage with Constantinople to his son: Evantius was one of the envoys who travelled to the Byzantine

---

[51] Gregory the Great, *Registrum epistularum*, III, 33, ed. Norberg, p. 179; see also Gregory the Great, *Registrum epistularum*, IV, 37 and VI, 6 pp. 259 and 374.

[52] Uhalde, 'Quasi-imperial Coinage', pp. 10–11; Dumézil, 'Patrice', p. 168; Hendy, 'From Public to Private', p. 70; Loseby, 'Marseille and the Pirenne Thesis', p. 224 n. 63.

[53] Loseby, 'Marseille', esp. pp. 171–2 and 177 and Loseby, 'Marseille and the Pirenne Thesis', esp. p. 221.

[54] Gregory the Great, *Registrum epistularum*, VI, 10, ed. Norberg, p. 378. Dynamius had sent *solidi Gallicani* as earnings from the papal patrimony to Rome; Gregory the Great, *Registrum epistularum*, III, 33, ed. Norberg, p. 179. Loseby, 'Marseille and the Pirenne Thesis', p. 224, considers the 'quasi-imperial' coins and the *solidi Galliarum/Gallicani* identical, while Uhalde, 'Quasi-imperial Coinage', p. 9 n. 23, seems to have reservations on this issue.

[55] Loseby, 'Marseille', pp. 177–8; Loseby, 'Marseille and the Pirenne Thesis', pp. 223–4.

[56] For coins as markers of distinction, see W. Pohl, 'Münzen als Identitätsträger', in J. Jarnut and J. Strothmann (eds.), *Die Merowingischen Monetarmünzen als Quelle zum Verständnis des 7. Jahrhunderts in Gallien* (Paderborn, 2013), pp. 21–31, esp. pp. 30–1.

court in 589 to negotiate the terms of another intervention in Italy, as Gregory of Tours suggests.[57] To be sure, the son of Dynamius was sent to Constantinople on behalf of Childebert II, who had attained majority in 584/5. But most certainly, he also represented his father's interests, as probably did another member of the embassy, Bodegisel, the son of Mummolinus of Soissons, who had also been an ally of Gogo once. The old network (or the remnants thereof) was still operating: the young King Childebert relied on the next generation of magnates, who had built up relations with the emperor in the past years. He intended to benefit as much from their connections to the imperial court as the aristocrats who tried to hand over their social capital, the relations to Byzantium, to the next generation. Maybe it is not wrong to assume that Byzantine gold had its effect on this circle and its politics as it might have had on Gogo.

To be sure, the sources do not reveal whether the members of the network had any share in Byzantine gold directly flowing into Merovingian France, and, if so, to what extent. But Gogo's letter to Grasulf suggests that he had a strong interest in Byzantine subsidies. Therefore, it does not seem to be too far-fetched to conclude that imperial gold had its effect on the diplomatic efforts of the Frankish magnate. The same seems to hold true for Dynamius, possibly also for the latter's son and the progeny of other members of the network in the next generation. As high officials, Dynamius and Gogo could well have been among the Frankish chiefs Tiberius wanted his envoy to pay at the end of the 570s. But while there are good reasons to speculate that the patrician might have used Byzantine gold for his own ends, possibly using imperial subsidies to issue 'quasi-imperial' coinage in order to express his territory's peculiar position and its ties to Byzantium, Gogo seems to have dealt with the emperor's money in a different way. It might be more plausible to suppose that his communication with Grasulf was a deliberate attempt to monopolise the negotiations about the Frankish–Byzantine–Lombard relations. If we take seriously that Gogo wrote 'in the name of the king', as his letter to Grasulf states, it would mean that he tried to keep the influx of subsidies under control and, thus, the economic resources

---

[57] Gregory of Tours, *Historiae*, X, 2, ed. Krusch and Levison, p. 482–3; Wood, *Merovingian Kingdoms*, p. 101; Dumézil, 'Patrice', p. 182; Dumézil, 'Gogo', pp. 588 and 590; for the background, see also Loseby, 'Gregory of Tours', pp. 494–5. I follow the convincing argument by Manitius, 'Dynamius', pp. 231–2 in the assumption that the Dynamius of Arles Gregory mentions is identical with the *patricius* of the Provence, this making Evantius his son. See also Wood, *Merovingian Kingdoms*, p. 101 and Dumézil, 'Gogo', p. 586 with n. 204, but Reverdy, 'Relations', p. 79 with n. 1, who considers him a different person; R. Buchner, *Gregor von Tours, Zehn Bücher Geschichten*. Vol. II (Darmstadt, 2000), p. 329 n. 8 expresses reservations on their identity.

firmly in hand. He did so certainly to the benefit of his position and that of his own network, but he also strengthened the position of the minor king whom he controlled. In a world in which riches and wealth meant power, this policy of concentration of the Byzantine payments to the king must have weakened the influence of other magnates. This is where the interests of Gogo, his followers and Childebert II met.

And the young king obviously needed the money Byzantium had to offer. Years after Gogo had written his letter, financial issues seem to have beset Childebert on all fronts. At the end of the 580s, the Merovingian wanted to produce new lists of taxation in rich cities such as Tours, Poitiers and in Clermont, where in 589 he abated the debts of the taxpayers belonging to the church.[58] He tried to make his system more efficient, while he was also searching for new funds, like other Merovingian kings had tried before, meeting with the same resistance his predecessors had encountered.[59] His willingness to comply with the emperor's request to fight the Lombards could have been motivated by the same financial demand which generated his commitment to tax collection. Competitive rivalries between king and magnates certainly urged Childebert, or Gogo on his behalf, to gather wealth in order to maintain a treasure constantly diminished by privileges and royal largesse.[60] Byzantine subsidies could work as an economic counterweight to the booty the freelancing dukes collected on their campaigns, even if they gave parts of it to the king. At the same time, spending money had also a cultural dimension: the king had to demonstrate his wealth to assure his superior position.[61] Constantinople's gold was certainly helpful in this respect, too.

---

[58] Gregory of Tours, *Historiae*, IX, 30 and X, 7, ed. Krusch and Levison, pp. 448–9 and 488. M. Hardt, 'Was übernahmen die Merowinger von der spätantiken römisch-byzantinischen Finanzverwaltung?', in J. Jarnut and J. Strothmann (eds.), *Die Merowingischen Monetarmünzen als Quelle zum Verständnis des 7. Jahrhunderts in Gallien* (Paderborn, 2013), pp. 323–36, at p. 330; W. Goffart, 'Old and New in Merovingian Taxation', *Past and Present*, 96 (1982): 3–21, at p. 13.

[59] Gregory of Tours, *Historiae*, IV, 2 and V, 28 and 34, ed. Krusch and Levison, pp. 136, 233–4 and 239–40. Goffart, 'Old and New', p. 11 with n. 35 and p. 14; R. Kaiser, 'Steuer und Zoll in der Merowingerzeit', *Francia*, 7 (1979): 1–17, at pp. 4–5; J. Führer, 'Verbrannte Steuerliste oder zerstörte Verwaltung? Zum Umgang mit Verwaltungswissen im merowingischen Frankenreich', in S. Dusil, G. Schwedler and R. Schwitter (eds.), *Exzerpieren – Kompilieren – Tradieren: Transformationen des Wissens zwischen Spätantike und Frühmittelalter* (Berlin, 2017), pp. 177–97, at pp. 188–91.

[60] Hardt, *Gold*, pp. 236–48; D. C. Pangerl, 'Der Königsschatz der Merowinger: Eine interdisziplinäre historisch-archäologische Studie', *Frühmittelalterliche Studien*, 47 (2013): 87–127; see also Collins, 'Theodebert I', p. 14.

[61] M. Hardt, 'Gold und Silber: Über die veränderten Möglichkeiten der Herrschaftsbildung und -sicherung durch Edelmetallschätze im frühen und hohen Mittelalter', in F. Bougard, L. Feller and R. Le Jan (eds.), *Les Élites au haut Moyen Âge: Crises et renouvellements* (Turnhout, 2006), pp. 457–68, at p. 460 (quoting Marcel Mauss); see also Pohl, 'Empire', p. 133 ('prestige economy').

Either way, the influx of gold widened the king's scope of action and strengthened the men who benefited from its redistribution. Especially the one who held the office of the mayor seems to have drawn profit from this kind of top-down payout in the long run. After the last campaign of Childebert II, the Lombards under Agilulf agreed to pay 12,000 *solidi* to the Franks each year. After their kingdom had been stabilised by a lasting peace and marriage alliances with their neighbours, they tried to buy off the obligation to remit the tribute with a lump sum during the reign of Chlothar II (584–629) at the beginning of the seventh century (617/18). On this occasion, the Lombard envoys turned to the king and the three mayors of Austrasia, Neustria and Burgundy, and paid off the magnates with 1,000 *solidi*.[62] Apart from the king, these were the only officials that mattered now. But Gogo's action on behalf of the king foreshadowed this later stage of importance of the mayor's office.

To conclude: the distribution of Byzantine money among military men in Italy with a considerable retinue moulded the power structures of Lombard rule especially by preventing the group from establishing a king at the top of a hierarchy. One intention certainly was to downsize the enemy. Small groups seemed more opposable, the more so when one could buy off military leaders and turn them against their former allies. The Byzantine strategy worked out, if it was meant to break the power of the Lombards, as Menander put it. The downside of it was the necessity to assure a constant flow of money in order to refresh the loyalties once they were built.

As a spin-off, the payments also affected the power structures of the Merovingian kingdoms. Northern Italy became a theatre of war that invited activities of Frankish kings and magnates alike. All of them were searching for booty and tribute – in short: wealth, either by plundering or by receiving payments from Byzantium. The influx of money seems to have narrowed the gap between the Merovingian kings and the Frankish aristocracy: the latter, however, benefiting from the privileges it gained, started to outgrow the financial potential of the Merovingian king. Their expanding resources added to the magnates' ability to clip the power of the Merovingian kings, which became even more visible if the ruler in question was still of minor age. The way Gogo communicated with Grasulf shows that the *nutricius* of the young king had to make an effort to retain control over the flow of subsidies. These were a powerful political instrument: due to the Frankish aristocracy's commitment to the Italian theatre of war, Gogo's endeavour could have resulted from a competitive situation between the kings and the magnates.

---

[62] Fredegar, *Chronicae*, IV, 45, ed. Krusch, p. 144. Wickham, *Early Medieval Italy*, pp. 32–3.

This said, it seems remarkable that both the *interregnum* in Lombard Italy and the minority of Childebert II span almost the same period of ten years between 574/5 and 584/5. In this space of time, the magnates of the Lombards and the Franks alike could prey on the benefits wartime economy offered and, thus, expand the material basis of their power. When the kings returned on the scene, in both cases they had to win back the position their precursors had obtained. While Authari fought those dukes who did not vote for him, Childebert started to battle the Lombards in return for money consideration. This way he tried to compensate for his losses – and the rewards his aristocratic opponents had gained. The emperor seems to have known about the Merovingian's financial distress, since he appears to have deliberately and quite successfully exerted pressure on Childebert to intervene in Italy because of the subsidies he had received – although other factors were also involved. Rather than toppling the hierarchical structures in the Frankish realm, Maurice's gold was invested to benefit from them. It was like putting a leash on the Merovingian dog.

There are, however, good reasons to assume that this was not the only strategy applied to Merovingian France. The 'quasi-imperial' coinage in southern Gaul seems to indicate that Byzantium also directly addressed the Frankish political elites. There is, of course, currently no way to prove that imperial gold formed the material basis for this local money nor that Dynamius was the direct beneficiary of Byzantine subsidies. But the fact that the coins were minted in an area he controlled implies that he was involved in their production. The *patricius* certainly had a say in the appropriation, distribution and use of the gold that poured in. If it was, as is much likely, imperial gold, the minting of coins carrying the images of Byzantine emperors represents the expression of Dynamius's loyalty and that of his followers bought by Constantinople's wealth.

Western sources saw this differently. Rather than presenting the influx of Byzantine gold as an issue that affected and split the upper strata of Merovingian society in a rivalry between kings and magnates, contemporary historians such as Gregory of Tours and John of Biclaro considered the kings and *gentes* as the addressees of imperial subsidies. Even an observer as close to the events as the bishop of Tours emphasised the role of the peoples as historical agents in this respect: he was not concerned with the social diversity of the groups labelled as peoples. The plurality of agents, however, was a decisive element in the relations between East and West in that the social and 'constitutional' structures they represented determined the connections with other political entities in the Mediterranean and were governed by them in turn. In this respect, the issue of money means a lot: with its connective and differing force it was never for nothing.

Part III

The Pope as a Mediterranean Player

8 The Papacy and the Frankish Bishops in the Sixth Century

Sebastian Scholz

The so-called *Epistolae Arelatenses genuinae* contain fifty-six letters, which date from the period between 417 and 557. Their particular concern is the status and rights of the bishop of Arles, who was vicar to the pope in Gaul at that time.[1] Besides these letters, few sixth-century sources are available about the relationship between the pope and the Franks. This creates a one-sided view of Frankish-papal relations, which concentrates, for the sixth century, on the Three-Chapters Controversy. The *Epistolae Arelatenses genuinae* nonetheless provide important insights into a quadripartite relationship that involved the pope, his vicar (the bishop of Arles), the Frankish king and the emperor. In what follows, I shall examine the importance of this quadripartite relationship and consider how communication took place in this quartet during the Three-Chapters Controversy.

In the year 535, war broke out in Italy between the Ostrogoths and the Roman Empire. Since 536, Rome was in the hands of the Roman general, Belisarius, and therefore directly under Emperor Justinian's rule again.[2] Vigilius had been pope since 537, and the new situation in Italy is also reflected in the letters, which he sent to his vicar in Arles. When Bishop Caesarius of Arles died in 542, his successor, Auxanius, informed the pope about his consecration, requested from him the pallium and presented other matters to him to preside over. In his response of 18 October 543, Pope Vigilius declared in his letter:

---

[1] No early collection of the letters has survived, but seventeen letters are known from three canon-law collections made in Francia in the sixth and early seventh centuries; other collections of the letters are compiled in the ninth century, see R. W. Mathisen, 'Between Arles, Rome and Toledo: Gallic Collections of Canon Law in Late Antiquity', *Ilu. Cuadernos*, 2 (1999): 33–46; I. Wood, 'The Franks and Papal Theology', in C. Chazelle and C. Cubitt (eds.), *The Crisis of the Oikoumene: The Three Chapters and the Failed Quest for Unity in the Sixth-Century Mediterranean* (Turnhout, 2007), p. 226; I. Wood, 'Between Rome and Jarrow: Papal Relations with Francia and England, From 597 to 716', *Chiese locali e chiese regionali nell'alto medioevo* (Spoleto, 4–9 April 2013), pp. 314–15.

[2] W. Giese, *Die Goten* (Stuttgart, 2004), pp. 128–9.

Yet concerning the things, which your love requests us to grant you, regarding the use of the pallium as well as other things, we could freely do this now without delay, if we did not want, as reason demands, to do so with the knowledge of the most Catholic lord, our son, the emperor, so that what has been granted you will be more welcome, since what you have requested will be given with the consent of the most Catholic Prince, and we will be judged as having kept the honour of his faith with the necessary reverence.[3]

This passage has been interpreted many times to suggest that after Justinian's conquest of Italy the pope could only have bestowed the pallium with the emperor's consent.[4] However, one must ask what interest Justinian could have taken in the bestowal of a pallium. As a matter of fact, the text says something different. Vigilius explicitly emphasises that he could grant Auxanius the use of the pallium 'now without delay', yet reason demands that he do so with the emperor's knowledge. The pope also reveals the reason for his hesitation: he would like the emperor to regard him as the individual who has 'kept the honour of his faith with the necessary reverence'. The pope was presumably much less concerned about Auxanius than about his own relationship with the emperor. He was apparently worried about making an important decision about a new ecclesiastical appointment without securing the approval of the imperial court. Auxanius should no longer merely be, as were his predecessors, the extended arm of the pope in Gaul. Instead, he should also perform duties of communication between the imperial court and the Frankish king.

This is evident in a letter from Vigilius to Auxanius dated 22 May 545, in which the pope asks the bishop continually to pray for Emperor Justinian and his wife Theodora, so that God may protect them. Through Belisarius's action as intermediary, they had consented to the pope's proposed appointment of Auxanius as papal vicar. Now Auxanius should call on King Childebert I, whose capital city was Paris and who, at that time, reigned together with the kings Theudebert I and Chlothar I,[5] 'by fatherly exhortation' to keep to the established alliance with Justinian.[6]

---

[3] *Epistolae Arelatensis genuinae*, 39, ed. Wilhelm Gundlach, MGH Epp. 3 (Berlin, 1892), pp. 58–9: 'De his vero, quae caritas vestra tam de usu pallii quam de aliis sibi a nobis petiit debere concedi, libenti hoc animo etiam in praesenti facere sine dilatione potuimus, nisi cum christianissimi domni, filii nostri, imperatoris, hoc, sicut ratio postulat, voluissemus perficere, Deo auctore, notitia, ut et vobis gratior praestitorum causa reddatur, dum, quae postulastis, cum consensu christianissimi, principis conferuntur, et nos honorem fidei eius servasse cum conpetenti reverentia iudicemur.'

[4] E. Caspar, *Geschichte des Papsttums II* (Tübingen, 1933), p. 235; G. Langgärtner, *Die Gallienpolitik der Päpste im 5. und 6. Jahrhundert* (Bonn, 1964), pp. 150–2; and already correctly J. Braun, *Die liturgische Gewandung im Occident und Orient.* (Freiburg, 1907), pp. 634–8.

[5] S. Scholz, *Die Merowinger* (Stuttgart, 2015), pp. 82 f.

[6] *Epistolae Arelatensis genuinae*, 41, MGH Epp. 3, p. 62: 'Oportet ergo fraternitatem vestram incessantibus supplicationibus Deo nostro preces effundere, ut domnos filios

Conspicuously, King Theudebert I and his successor, Theudebald, were included in Justinian's system of alliances, but they played no role in the communication in connection with the Three-Chapters Controversy.[7]

Here, Auxanius was immediately under a double obligation to the imperial court. On the one hand, he should pray for the imperial couple, and, on the other hand, he should motivate Childebert not to give up the alliance with Justinian. This alliance probably ranked among those alliances that, according to Procopius, Justinian also formed with the other Frankish kings against the Ostrogoths.[8] Thus, in no sense was the focus on the bestowal of the pallium but on the papal vicar's position in Gaul. The vicar was assigned a new role, since as the agent of the pope he was supposed to act not only as the intermediary man between Rome and the Gallic bishops but also between the emperor and King Childebert. Therefore, it was important for the emperor to consent to his nomination. Belisarius's role as intermediary shows what value was placed on this process not only in Rome but also in Constantinople. Yet with the novel role for the bishop of Arles, the pope also acquired a new duty because he now became a link in the relationship between the emperor and the Frankish king.

The emergence of the Three-Chapters Controversy further augmented the significance of the bishop of Arles for the pope. Around the turn of the year 544/5, Emperor Justinian had issued an edict against the 'Three Chapters' that refer to the person and writings of Theodore of Mopsuestia, the writings of Theodoret of Cyrus as well as the letter of Ibas of Edessa to the Persian Maris. The Council of Chalcedon (451) had issued no statement about Theodore of Mopsuestia, but Theodoret and Ibas had been acknowledged at the council as orthodox.[9] However, all three represented a particular problem for the Monophysites, since they had opposed their much revered Cyril of Alexandria and represented a pronounced form of Dyophysitism. Through the anathematisation of the

---

nostros, clementissimos principes Iustinianum atque Theodoram, sua semper protectione custodiat, qui pro his nobis vestrae caritati mandandis, suggerente gloriosissimo et excellentissimo viro, filio nostro, patricio Belisario, quo pro idem vos convenit exorare, pia praebuerunt devotione consensum. Hortamur quoque, ut sacerdotali opera inter gloriosissimum virum, Childebertum regem, sed et antedictum clementissimum principem conceptae gratiae documenta paterna adhortatione servetis.'

[7] Scholz, *Merowinger*, pp. 91–3 and 98. Nothing can be said about Chlothar I in this regard.
[8] Procopius of Caesarea, *History of Wars*, Books V–VI.15. *The Gothic War*, ed. with an English translation by H. B. Dewing (Cambridge, MA, 1919, reprinted 1993), V.5, p. 47; V.13, p. 141.
[9] R. Price, 'The Second Council of Constantinople (553) and the Malleable Past', in R. Price and M. Whitby (eds.), *Chlacedon in Context: Church Councils, 400–700* (Liverpool, 2011), pp. 120–9.

'Three Chapters', Justinian wanted to release the Council of Chalcedon from any appearance of Nestorianism. However, Justinian's edict was rejected in the West, since it was viewed as an attack on the decrees of Chalcedon, nor did it meet with undivided approval in the East.[10] In this context, a letter that the pope addressed to King Childebert's bishops on 22 May 545 is significant. In it, the pope informed the bishops that he had appointed Auxanius as the papal vicar, briefly explaining his vicar's privileges and then emphasising the particular privileges of the Holy See:

> As the divine power has decreed that we hold the chair of the First Apostle not on grounds of our merits, but on grounds of the ineffable love of his mercy, so it has pleased it that we should secure the order, peace and stability of all churches ... Yet if, and may God prevent it, disputes were to affect questions of faith, or perhaps such a matter were to arise, it should be ended by virtue of its magnitude by the judgement of the Apostolic chair and brought to our attention without delay, in order for the truth to be examined.[11]

The point is striking because in the foregoing correspondence between the popes and their Gallic vicars since the time of Symmachus (r. 498–514), the primacy of the pope played no role in matters of faith, albeit in 515, Pope Hormisdas had informed Caesarius of Arles at length about the heresies of Nestorius, Eutyches as well as Acacius.[12] Possibly, there is a connection here to the imperial edict against the 'Three Chapters'. At first, Vigilius had not openly opposed the edict, but neither did he sign it. This awkward situation for the pope may be why he so clearly emphasised the primacy of his doctrine towards the Frankish bishops. Regardless of how his decision turned out, he had to be able to defend it in the Western church.

Auxanius died in 546. On 23 August 546, Pope Vigilius introduced his successor, Aurelian, to the bishops in King Childebert's kingdom as the new apostolic vicar. At the very start of the letter, the pope emphasised his primacy, as well as his concern for the peace of the church and warned against disputes that the Devil would try to bring into the

---

[10] Caspar, *Papsttum*, II, pp. 242–4; P. Maraval, 'Die Rezeption des Chalcedonense im Osten des Reiches', in *Die Geschichte des Christentums*, Altertum vol. III (Freiburg, Basel and Wien, 2005), pp. 448–50.

[11] *Epistolae Arelatensis genuinae*, 40, MGH Epp. 3, pp. 59–60: 'Quantum nos divina potentia apostolorum primi sedem non pro nostris meritis, sed pro ineffabili suae misericordiae pietate habere constituit, tantum nos de universarum ecclesiarum dispositione et pace et statu convenit esse sollicitos. ... Contentiones vero si quae, quas Dominus auferat, in fidei causa contigerint, aut tale emerserit forte negotium, quod pro magnitudine sui apostolicae sedis magis iudicio debeat terminari, ad nostram, discussa veritate, perferat sine dilatione notitiam.'

[12] *Epistolae Arelatensis genuinae*, 30, MGH Epp. 3, pp. 43–4.

church.[13] Thus, he again alluded to the tense situation caused by the Three-Chapters Controversy. In a further letter to Aurelian of the same date, the pope demanded of him, as he had once demanded of his predecessor, Auxanius, that he may like to keep 'with priestly fervour' to the alliances between the imperial couple and King Childebert.[14] This time, as before, the emperor again confirmed Aurelian's appointment as papal vicar, with Belisarius acting as intermediary. The new vicar was also supposed to act as an intermediary between the imperial court and the Frankish king. At the same time, it was obviously the pope's intention, with the help of his vicar, for papal opinion to prevail in Gaul about the Three-Chapters Controversy. Yet things happened differently. When Pope Vigilius wrote both letters, he was no longer staying in Rome but had been forcibly transported to Sicily by order of the emperor. The reason lay in his refusal to sign the edict against the 'Three Chapters'. At the end of 546, he was transferred from Sicily to Constantinople, where he arrived in January 547, and on the advice of Deacon Pelagius at first protested against the condemnation of the 'Three Chapters'.[15]

King Childebert and the bishops in the Frankish kingdom seemed to have anxiously followed the development in the East. The bishop of Arles was again used as intermediary, yet this time by the Frankish king! In consultation with the king, Aurelian sent an ambassador with a letter for the pope to Constantinople, where he arrived in July 549. He was to question the pope about his position on the Three-Chapters Controversy.[16] In a letter from April 550, which the pope again sent to Aurelian and not directly to the Frankish king, Vigilius vehemently denied having abandoned anything that was taught and decided by his predecessors or the councils of Nicaea, Constantinople, Ephesus and Chalcedon. He claimed to honour these councils and to adhere to their decrees. Besides, he also maintained he would firmly comply with the

---

[13] *Epistolae Arelatensis genuinae*, 43, MGH Epp. 3, pp. 63–4.

[14] *Epistolae Arelatensis genuinae*, 44, MGH Epp. 3, p. 66: 'Oportet ergo caritatem vestram sacerdotali semper studio inter domnos filios nostros, clementissimos principes, et gloriosissimum virum, id est filium nostrum Childebertum regem, gratiae initae federa custodire.'

[15] Caspar, *Papsttum II*, pp. 243–9; W Ensslin, 'Justinian I. und die Patriarchate Rom und Konstantinopel', *Symbolae Osloenses*, 35 (1959): 124–6; J. Richards, *The Popes and the Papacy in the Early Middle Ages, 476–752* (London, 1979), pp. 143–6; Maraval, 'Religionspolitik', pp. 448–50; M. Maser, 'Die Päpste und das oströmische Kaisertum im sechsten Jahrhundert', in K. Herbers and J. Johrendt (eds.), *Das Papsttum und das vielgestaltige Italien. Hundert Jahre Italia Pontificia* (Berlin, 2009), pp. 59–60; S. Scholz, 'Das Papsttum und die theokratischen Ansprüche der Herrscher im frühen Mittelalter', in K. Trampedach and A. Pečar (eds.), *Theokratie und theokratischer Diskurs* (Tübingen, 2013), pp. 267–8.

[16] *Epistulae Arelatensis genuinae*, 45, MGH Epp. 3, p. 67.

professions of faith, which were issued by Cyril of Alexandria and Pope Leo the Great, and had been confirmed in Chalcedon. Aurelian should convey to the other bishops that false writings as well as lying words and messengers should not deceive them.[17]

Vigilius kept quiet in this letter about how, in June 547, under pressure from the emperor, he had already relinquished and had condemned the 'Three Chapters' in two secret letters to Justinian, and had published the anathemisation in his *Iudicatum* of April 548.[18] Probably it was precisely this behaviour that led to the Frankish enquiry of 549. In October 549, the Frankish bishops adopted a clear position on the Three-Chapters Controversy after King Childebert I assembled them for a council in Orléans.[19] The first canon issued by the council read as follows:

And thus the impious sect once founded by Eutyches, the sacrilegious originator, conscious of his evil, and departing from the living fount of Catholic faith, as well as whatever was set forward by the similarly venomous and impious Nestorius, both of which sects the Holy See condemns, so too we execrate them, their founders and followers and we anathematise and condemn them by the power of this present constitution, preaching the right and apostolic order of faith in the name of Christ.[20]

Those attending the council therefore proved well informed about the current dispute in Constantinople when – in support of the decrees of Chalcedon – they condemned Eutyches as one of the main representatives of Monophysitism and Nestorius as his counterpart. In doing so, they emphasised their agreement with the Holy See, for Pope Leo the Great was considerably involved in the decrees of Chalcedon. It is notable that the council formulated the decree without waiting for the pope's response. Perhaps this stance was supposed to encourage Vigilius not to deviate from the position of his papal predecessors. Since initially in his response the pope underlined how he was not deviating from a single of his predecessor's decisions prior to announcing his loyalty to the

---

[17] *Epistolae Arelatensis genuinae*, 45, MGH Epp. 3, pp. 67–8.
[18] *Acta Conciliorum Oecumenicorum*, 4,1; *Concilium universale Constantinopolitanum sub Iustiniano habitum*, ed. Johannes Straub (Berlin, 1971), pp. 184–8; Richards, *Popes*, pp. 146–7; Maraval, 'Religionspolitik', pp. 450–1.
[19] Scholz, *Merowinger*, pp. 101–2.
[20] Council of Orléans (549), can. 1, CCSL 148 A, pp. 148–9: 'Itaque nefariam sectam, quam auctor male sibi conscius et a uiuo sanctae fidei catholicae fonte discedens sacrilegos quondam condidit Euthicis, uel si quaequae a uenefico similiter impio sunt prolata Nestorio, quas etiam sectas sedes apostolica sancta condemnat, similiter et nos easdem cum suis auctoribus et sectatoribus execrantes praesentis constitutionis uigore anathematizamus adque damnamus, rectum adque apostolicum in Christi nomine fidei ordinem praedicantes'; Translation by Wood, 'The Franks and Papal Theology', pp. 223–4.

four ecumenical councils, he could still have been potentially informed about the first canon issued by the 549 Council of Orléans before having compiled his response.

One must ask who was responsible for the Council of Orléans being preoccupied at all with the Three-Chapters Controversy. In the prologue to the council's decrees, it is stated that King Childebert had assembled the council in Orléans 'out of love for the sacred faith and because of the state of religion'.[21] No comparable phrase exists earlier than this date in the prologues to the Frankish imperial councils and, after all, at least three councils, namely Orléans 533, Orléans 538 and Orléans 541, were held with Childebert's approval. This leads to the conclusion that the matter of faith was in fact not only crucial for the bishops but also for the king. Obviously, from the outset, the central focus was on the pope's position and not the emperor's position, since the letters sent by the bishops and the king were always addressed to the pope. In this case, the contacts were established via the papal vicar in Arles.

This is also shown in a letter to a Frankish king in 552, possibly to Childebert, written by clerics from Milan. However, the addressee is missing in this source. The letter mentions a further delegation of the Frankish king to Constantinople. With their letter, the Milanese clerics wanted to ensure that the Frankish embassy was correctly informed about how badly Pope Vigilius and Bishop Datius of Milan, who had accompanied the pope to Constantinople, had been treated. Furthermore, they requested support for the pope and asked for the bishop's return to Milan:

Therefore, we ask and entreat your glory, by the future judgement of God, of which the whole of humanity is afraid, that you swiftly communicate all this in your provinces, so that neither those who were sent out secretly return, nor that Anastasius, whom the holy Bishop Aurelian of Arles sent to the holiest pope two years ago, spreads any lies in Gaul, because he himself, when he couldn't leave Constantinople, devised the plan to induce all Gallic bishops to condemn the chapters about which this controversy arose.[22]

---

[21] Council of Orléans (549), Prologue, CCSL 148 A, p. 148: 'Childeberthus rex pro amore sacrae fidei et statu religionis in Aurelianinsi urbi congregasset'.

[22] *Epistolae aevi Merovingici collectae* 4, MGH Epp. 3, p. 441: 'Unde rogamus et contestamus gloriam vestram per futurum Dei nostri iudicium, quod omnis conditio humana formidat, ut ad provincias vestras haec omnia velociter indicetis, ne aut isti subripiant qui missi sunt, aut Anastasius quidam, quem sanctus episcopus Aurilianus Arelatinsis civitatis ad beatissimum papam ante hoc biennium direxerat, ibidem in Grallias aliqua mentiatur, quia et ipse, cum de Constantinopole exire non posset, usus est consilio, ut promitterit, se omnium episcoporum Gallicanorum ad damnanda capitula, pro quibus haec scandala orta sunt, animus inclinare.'

The letter of clerics from Milan reinforces the important role of Bishop Aurelian concerning the communication with the pope. Moreover, it demands letters from the king and the Frankish bishops to the pope and to Bishop Datius, but not to the emperor. Here too, the focus is clearly on the position of the pope.

At the end of 553, Vigilius had agreed to a condemnation of the 'Three Chapters' by the Council of Constantinople.[23] After his death in 555, Justinian offered the former papal adviser, Pelagius, the office of pope, yet in return demanded of him that he also agree to the condemnation of the 'Three Chapters'. Pelagius (r. 556–61) accepted the offer, which led to a schism with the northern Italian bishops, who broke up their community with Rome. In 556, King Childebert and his bishops also accused the pope of having opposed the decrees of Chalcedon and the doctrines of Pope Leo the Great, and threatened him with excommunication, should their fears prove valid. In this instance, the letter was not delivered by the papal vicar but by a legate of the king, and the pope's response was also dispatched directly to the king.[24] This could have been due to the explosiveness of the situation as well as the fact that Aurelian had died in 551 and no successor had been appointed to the office of vicar. The pope rejected the criticisms and described them as fables and malicious gossip.[25] However, Childebert and his bishops insisted on a clear profession of faith from the pope.[26] In a letter to Childebert of 3 February 557, the pope gave an elaborate profession of faith in which he attested to his agreement with the four ecumenical councils as well as the declarations issued by former popes. However, he avoided any reference to the decrees from Constantinople.[27] In a further letter, which the pope probably addressed to all orthodox believers in April 557, he explicitly professed his agreement with the four councils, the papal doctrines as well as the orthodoxy of Theodoret and Ibas of Edessa. He therefore disavowed the Council of Constantinople of 553 without openly condemning it.[28]

The events reveal how important the pope's professions of faith were for the Franks, yet also how important the attitude of the Franks was for the pope. In view of the schism with the northern Italian bishops, he

---

[23] Caspar, *Papsttum II*, pp. 269–83; Richards, *Popes*, pp. 152–3; Maraval, 'Religionspolitik', pp. 453–7; Maser, 'Päpste', pp. 60–1. Scholz, 'Papsttum', pp. 268–9.
[24] Scholz, 'Papsttum', p. 269; Scholz, *Merowinger*, pp. 103–4.
[25] *Pelagii I papae epistulae quae supersunt* (556–61), Ep. 3, ed. P. M. Gassó and C. M. Battle (Montserrat, 1956), pp. 6–9; Wood, 'The Franks and Papal Theology', pp. 226–30.
[26] Pelagius I, Ep. 7, ed. Gassó and Battle, p. 21.
[27] Pelagius I, Ep. 7, ed. Gassó and Battle, pp. 21–5.
[28] Pelagius I, Ep. 11, ed. Gassó and Battle, pp. 35–40.

had to strive to prevent yet another schism emerging with the Frankish bishops. Here, the entire communication situation was altered. On the one hand, as has been shown, a direct correspondence emerged between Childebert and Pelagius I. On the other hand, the role of the papal vicar in Arles changed. Bishop Sapaudus was appointed as the new vicar in 556; however, the pope no longer sought confirmation of the vicar's appointment from the emperor. This time, King Childebert's request was enough.[29] The relationship between Childebert and Justinian was also no longer an issue. After the crushing defeat of the Ostrogoths and the integration of Rome into the empire, obviously it was no longer important to establish diplomatic contacts through the pope and his vicar.

However, for the pope, the vicar remained pivotal for his relations with the Franks. On 4 July 556, Pelagius already informed Sapaudus that he was chosen as the pope and invited him to a mutual exchange of ideas.[30] On 16 September 556, the next papal epistle already followed in which the pope expressed thanks for the messages of congratulations on his nomination.[31] And, on 14 December, Pope Pelagius agreed to send Sapaudus the relics of Peter and Paul and other saints, which King Childebert had requested from him. In the same letter, the pope asked Sapaudus to ensure that his father, the patricius Placidus, would soon send everything, especially clothing, which had been collected and was in the possession of the church of Rome in Gaul, to be sent as soon as possible to Rome to support the people in desperate need there.[32]

Since the *Epistolae Arelatenses genuinae* break-off in the year 557, for the period up to the papacy of Gregory the Great we learn hardly anything more about the communication between the popes and the Frankish bishops and the role that the vicar played in this. Yet his central role in the communication process should have become clear enough during the period of the Three-Chapters Controversy. Nevertheless, under Pelagius, the quadripartite communication between Constantinople, Rome, Arles and Paris had already collapsed. The bishop of Arles was no longer a linkman for communication on behalf of Constantinople.

---

[29] Pelagius I, Ep. 5, 6, ed. Gassó and Battle, pp. 14–19.
[30] Pelagius I, Ep. 1, ed. Gassó and Battle, pp. 1–2.
[31] Pelagius I., Ep. 2, ed. Gassó and Battle, pp. 3–5.
[32] Pelagius I., Ep. 4, 9, ed. Gassó and Battle, pp. 11–12, 29–30.

9 A One-Way Ticket to Francia: Constantinople, Rome and Northern Gaul in the Mid Seventh Century

Charles Mériaux

In the middle of the twelfth century, the monks of the abbey of Saint-Amand, in what is now northern France, copied out a collection of ancient documents compiled in the mid ninth century by a predecessor of theirs named Milo. The illuminations that decorate the manuscript they made, today housed at the Bibliothèque municipale of Valenciennes, rank among the region's most celebrated works of Romanesque art.[1] Among the documents is a peculiar *petitio*, through which St Amandus himself supposedly requested to be buried in the monastery that he had founded, known at the time as Elnone.[2] Though Amandus is today best known as the founder of a considerable number of monasteries in northern France and Belgium, his *petitio* nevertheless reminds us that his missionary work had a much wider frame and that he travelled the Christian world and its borders during his lifetime, *longe lateque per universas provintias seu gentes propter amorem Christi*.[3]

Although the links between the *regnum Francorum* and the Eastern empire had been relatively tight in the sixth century, it has generally been considered in the wake of Henri Pirenne that they almost ceased

---

[1] My thanks to Stefan Esders, Yitzhak Hen, Yaniv Fox and Laury Sarti for helpful comments and to Charles West for translating this paper. Valenciennes BM 501, esp. fol. 58v–60r for images of witnesses to the *petitio*; on these illuminations, see B. Abou-El-Haj, *The Medieval Cult of Saints: Formation and Transformations* (Cambridge, 1994), pp. 107–29. Concerning the collection of Milo, edited by Bruno Krusch under the title of *Vita Amandi secunda* in MGH SRM V (Hanover and Leipzig, 1910), pp. 450–83, see C. Mériaux, 'Hagiographie et histoire à Saint-Amand: la collection de Milon (d. 872)', in *Rerum gestarum scriptor: Histoire et historiographie au Moyen Âge – Mélanges Michel Sot*, ed. M. Coumert, M.-C. Isaïa, K. Krönert and S. Shimahara (Paris, 2012), pp. 87–98. Saint-Amand-les-Eaux: Fr., dép. Nord, arr. Valenciennes, *chef-lieu* of the canton.

[2] On the monastery of Elnone and the circumstances of its foundation, see H. Platelle, *Le Temporel de l'abbaye de Saint-Amand des origines à 1340* (Paris, 1962); on its founder, see É. de Moreau, *Saint Amand apôtre de la Belgique et du nord de la France* (Louvain, 1927), with the updates by A. Dierkens, 'Notes biographiques sur saint Amand, abbé d'Elnone et éphémère évêque de Maastricht (mort peu après 676)', in E. Bozóky (ed.), *Saints d'Aquitaine: Missionnaires et pèlerins du haut Moyen Âge* (Rennes, 2010), pp. 63–80.

[3] 'Far and wide through all provinces and peoples for the love of Christ': *Vita Amandi secunda*, p. 484.

to exist in the seventh century, as the disappearance of gold coinage and the definitive abandoning of papyrus by the chanceries of the later Merovingian kings demonstrate.[4] From a theological perspective, the decline of Frankish interest in the East began even earlier, perhaps as early as the sixth century, when the Three-Chapters Controversy ceased to find any resonance in Gaul, outside of Provence.[5] It is therefore all the more surprising to note that in the middle of the seventh century Amandus appears as one of the few Frankish interlocutors of the pope on Eastern matters, as revealed by a letter sent by Pope Martin I in the wake of the Lateran Council of October 649.

After a brief presentation of this well-known and much-studied letter,[6] I shall seek to demonstrate that it attests to the interest in the Eastern empire previously shown by King Dagobert (629–39) and his entourage, but that this interest was not maintained by his successors, notably those kings of the Austrasian court with which Amandus was familiar in the early 650s. By that date, the East no longer figured on the horizon of the Merovingian political elites, which henceforth extended no further than Rome.

The Letter of Pope Martin to Amandus

The circumstances through which the letter of Pope Martin to Amandus has been preserved are no less interesting than its contents. It has been transmitted in two separate ways. To begin with, it is copied in manuscript 199 of the Bibliothèque municipale of Laon (fol. 135v–7v), which includes the complete set of acts of the Roman council of 649. The Laon manuscript, which conserves the oldest and best text of the Latin version of the Roman conciliar acts, was produced at the monastery of Saint-Amand between the years 830 and 850, before passing into the library of Bishop Dido of Laon at the very end of the ninth century.[7] For Rudolf Riedinger, this version of the acts might go back to the copy that Pope Martin's letter mentions he was sending to Amandus. But Riedinger did not rule out the possibility that the text of the Laon manuscript could

---

[4] H. Pirenne, *Mahomet et Charlemagne* (Brussels, 1937); M. McCormick, *Origins of the European Economy: Communications and Commerce, AD 300–900* (Cambridge, MA, 2001).
[5] I. N. Wood, 'The Franks and Papal Theology, 550–660', in C. Chazelle and C. Cubitt (eds.), *The Crisis of the Oikoumene: The Three Chapters and the Failed Quest for Unity in the Sixth-Century Mediterranean* (Turnhout, 2007), pp. 223–41.
[6] G. Scheibelreiter, 'Griechisches-lateinisches-fränkisches Christentum: Der Brief Papst Martins I. an den Bischof Amandus von Maastricht aus dem Jahre 649', *Mitteilungen des Instituts für österreichische Geschichtsforschung*, 100 (1992): 84–102.
[7] B. Bischoff, *Katalog der festländischen Handschriften des neunten Jahrhunderts*, vol. II, *Laon-Paderborn* (Wiesbaden, 2004), no. 2089, p. 29: 'Saint-Amand, IX Jh., ca 2. Viertel'.

also have come from a version subsequently obtained by the famous Arn, bishop of Salzburg and abbot of Saint-Amand at the end of the eighth century.[8]

The second path through which this letter has been preserved is via the collection of the monk Milo, intended to supplement the *Vita Amandi prima*. The oldest manuscript of this collection, in 'Franco-Saxon' style, is contemporary with Milo's death in 872.[9] Before giving a transcription of Pope Martin's letter, Milo provided a brief description of its contents and noted that he had copied it from a papyrus exemplar (*exemplar in papireis scedis editum*). This in turn was to be found at the end of a *volumen* of the acts of the 649 council arranged in five books, corresponding to the five sessions of this meeting.[10] As noted above, this same volume might well also have served as the model for the Laon manuscript.

Let us turn now to the contents of Pope Martin I's letter. It was written in response to a letter from Amandus, no longer extant, in which the latter informed the pope that he wished to give up his episcopal duties and retire to a monastery, presumably the monastery of Elnone that he had founded during the reign of Dagobert I. Martin's letter stated that Amandus had complained in particular about the priests of his diocese. In response, the pope encouraged the bishop of Maastricht to persevere and not to hesitate to depose recalcitrant clerics.[11]

The second part of the letter dealt, however, with a quite different matter, that of 'the detestable and abominable heresy' (*exsecranda et abominanda heresis*) that had been spread for a dozen years by Sergius, patriarch of Constantinople (610–38), with the support of the emperor Heraclius (610–41).[12] Martin I said nothing about the extremely tense political context of these years, during which the Byzantine political

---

[8] *Concilium Lateranense a. 649 celebratum*, ed. R. Riedinger, ACO II 1 (Berlin, 1984), p. xiii; *Concilium Lateranense a. 649 celebratum*, pp. 422–4 for the edition of Martin I's letter from the Laon manuscript.

[9] Ghent University Library 224; cf. B. Bischoff, *Katalog der festländischen Handschriften des neunten Jahrhunderts*, vol. I, *Aachen–Lambach* (Wiesbaden, 1998), no. 1361, p. 286: 'Saint-Amand, IX. Jh., 3 Drittel'. For later copies of the collection, see above, note 1. For an edition of the letter from the collection of Milo, see *Vita Amandi secunda*, pp. 452–6 and, from the Laon manuscript, *Concilium Lateranense a. 649 celebratum*, pp. 422–4. An English translation can be found in *The Acts of the Lateran Synod of 649*, trans. R. Price (Liverpool, 2014), pp. 408–12.

[10] *Vita Amandi secunda*, p. 452.

[11] *Vita Amandi secunda*, pp. 452–4; *Concilium Lateranense a. 649 celebratum*, pp. 422–3. On Amand's difficulties as bishop of Maastricht, see C. Mériaux, 'Qui verus christianus vult esse: christianisme et "paganisme" en Gaule du Nord à l'époque mérovingienne', in H. Inglebert, S. Destephen and B. Dumézil (eds.), *Le Problème de la christianisation du monde antique* (Paris, 2010), pp. 359–73, at pp. 362–3.

[12] For what follows here, see *Vita Amandi secunda*, pp. 454–6 et *Concilium Lateranense a. 649 celebratum*, pp. 423–4.

and religious authorities had attempted to reconcile contradictory theological positions – Chalcedonians and monophysites – under the banner of Monoenergism, in order to re-establish the empire's unity in the face of the double threat represented by the Avars and the Persians. Without any reference to the theological debates underway, the pope reminded Amandus that Sergius had promoted old ideas previously developed by the disciples of Apollinaris of Laodicea (d. c. 390) and by Severus and Eutyches (d. c. 450) as well as by the Manicheans. These ideas, argued Martin, had subsequently been supported by Sergius's successors on the see of Constantinople, Pyrrhus (638–41) and then Paul (641–53), inspiring the promulgation of an imperial decree (*imperialis typus*) in 648 by Constans II (641–68).

Martin explained to Amandus that this was why he had gathered a council at Rome (*coetus generalis fratrum et coepiscoporum nostrorum*), after having tried to persuade the Eastern authorities to renounce these ideas. The council had proceeded to examine these views and had condemned them. The pope declared to his correspondent that he had arranged to send him the conciliar acts as well as its 'encyclical' (*praevidimus volumina gestorum synodalium in praesenti vobis dirigere una cum incyclia nostra*), so that he too could combat this heresy. The pope further asked Amandus to call an assembly of the bishops of those regions (*synodalis conventio omnium fratrum et coepiscoporum nostrorum partium illarum*) to reaffirm the decisions taken at Rome, and requested that he be sent a written report of this assembly, furnished with the subscriptions of the participants. Moreover, the pope hoped that Amandus would intervene with King Sigibert III of Austrasia (633–56) so that he might send some bishops to Rome to join an embassy to the emperor. This embassy was to take the texts of the Roman council to Constantinople. The pope finally stated that the letter-bearer was bringing relics, but not the manuscripts that Amandus had asked for, because he had to leave the city in haste.

The letter is not precisely dated. Alain Dierkens has suggested that it is very likely Pope Martin who drafted and sent it in the days following the end of the council, probably during the fifth and final session, convened on 31 October 649. The onset of winter could explain the messenger's hurry, who might therefore have delivered it to Saint-Amand at the end of 649 or at the very beginning of 650. Such a date fits with the little that we know of Amandus's three-year episcopate at Maastricht.[13]

In 1996, Rudolf Riedinger argued that the letter had been drafted by the Greek entourage of the pope who, grouped around Maximus

---

[13] A. Dierkens, 'Notes biographiques', pp. 72, 74.

the Confessor, had redacted the acts of the 649 council first in Greek and then in Latin, before they were submitted to the participants for approval.[14] This hypothesis was proven wrong by Richard M. Pollard and Richard Price.[15] Though part of the letter could have been used to inform other correspondents of the decisions taken at the Lateran Council, there is no doubt that the first part, encouraging Amandus not to abandon his diocese, indicates that the pope had an accurate understanding of Amandus's position at Maastricht, and, to judge by the evidence, also suggests that the latter was himself familiar with Eastern affairs, a familiarity for which we shall now seek to account.

King Dagobert, the Neustrian court and the East

The letter of Pope Martin I has above all been interpreted as proof of close links between Amandus and Rome, as is also suggested, though with less detail, by certain passages of the *Vita Amandi prima*. This *Vita* refers to at least two visits by Amandus to Rome. The first took place in his youth, after he had spent five years as a hermit at Bourges, and was marked by a vision of St Peter who encouraged him to return to Gaul to preach.[16] On the way back from a second visit, Amandus was miraculously saved from a storm.[17] He might have brought manuscripts back with him, according to a later *Vita* contained in the legendary of the Dominican Bernard Gui (d. 1331), but which could be based on an older, now lost text.[18]

Amandus was not the only recipient of a papal letter accompanied by a copy of the Lateran Council acts. These missives were part of a

---

[14] R. Riedinger, 'Wer hat den Brief Papst Martin I. an Amandus verfasst?', *Filologia mediolatina*, 3 (1996): 95–104.

[15] R. M. Pollard, 'The Decline of the Cursus in the Papal Chancery and Its Implications', *Studi Medievali*, 50–1 (2009): 1–40, and *The Acts of the Lateran Synod of 649*, pp. 391–3.

[16] *Vita Amandi prima*, c. 6–7, p. 434; for the dating of this *Vita* to the second half of the eighth century, see A. Dierkens, 'Notes biographiques', pp. 65–8. An English translation is published in *Christianity and Paganism, 350–750: The Conversion of Western Europe*, ed. J. N. Hillgarth (1969; revised ed. Philadelphia, PA, 1986), pp. 139–48.

[17] *Vita Amandi prima*, c. 10, p. 435.

[18] *Alia Vita auctore Aquitano anonymo*, ed. G. Hensken, AA SS Februarii I (Anvers, 1658), pp. 854–5, c. 5, p. 854. The significance of this *Life* derives from the discovery of an ancient fragment of a *Vita Amandi* linked to it; cf. J. Riedmann, 'Unbekannte frühkarolingische Handschriftenfragmente in der Bibliothek des Tiroler Landesmuseums Ferdinandeum', *Mitteilungen des Instituts für österreichische Geschichtsforschung*, 84 (1976): 262–89 (esp. p. 282 for the mention of a journey to Rome *ad uisitanda sanctorum apostolorum ac martyrum patrocinia*) and G. Declercq and A. Verhulst, 'L'Action et le souvenir de saint Amand en Europe centrale: À propos de la découverte d'une *Vita Amandi antiqua*', in R. Demeulenaere and M. Van Uytfanghe (eds.), Aevum inter utrumque. *Mélanges offerts à Gabriel Sanders* (Steenbrugge-La Haye, 1991), pp. 503–26. See below, note 41.

wider initiative that aimed to gather the Western bishops around the pope in the struggle that pitched him against the emperor and the patriarch of Constantinople. In fact, another Merovingian source, the *Life of Saint Eligius*, records that another, similar message was sent to the court of the Frankish kingdom of Neustria, ruled at the time by Clovis II, son of Dagobert. Clemens Bayer has recently shown that this *Life* was entirely the work of Saint Audoin (Ouen), metropolitan bishop of Rouen between 641 and 684, and not a work interpolated in the first half of the eighth century, as Bruno Krusch thought.[19] At the end of its first book, this *Vita Eligii* mentions the development of Monotheletism in the reign of Constans II, and provides a short summary. It then mentions the summoning of a council by Pope Martin, and the dispatch to Gaul of the conciliar acts together with a letter to the king, asking him to send 'catholic and erudite men' (*viri catholici eruditi*) to Rome, which would have included Eligius and Audoin 'impeded by a certain thing'.[20] Audoin then presented what he knew of subsequent events, including the exile of Martin, which he claimed he had learnt from 'a brother arrived from the East'.[21] Judging by the evidence, Eligius and Audoin, the first a former moneyer and the second a former *referendarius* of Dagobert, were very well informed of what was happening in the East.

There are a number of reasons to suppose that the letter sent to Amandus was quite different from the one received by the king of Neustria, although Amandus's position as bishop of Maastricht did not *a priori* make him a prominent figure in the Austrasian episcopate. Georg Scheibelreiter emphasised the 'personal tone' of the letter to Amandus.[22] It is nevertheless unlikely that the two men were genuinely very close. Originally from Umbria, Martin had spent much time as an *apocrisarius* at Constantinople and had not had the opportunity to meet Amandus before his pontifical election in July 649. It remains the case, however, that Amandus was not unknown to the Lateran *scrinium*. It was with this

---

[19] On Bruno Krusch's dating, cf. C. M. M. Bayer, 'Vita Eligii', *Reallexikon der Germanischen Altertumskunde*, 35 (2007), cols. 461–524.

[20] *Vita Eligii*, ed. B. Krusch, MGH SRM IV (Hanover and Leipzig, 1902), pp. 663–741, I, 33, p. 690: 'In quo concilio, omnibus orthodoxis consentientibus, edidit contra hereticos fidem magnifice valde atque accurate, quam etiam cum subiunctam epistolam Galliarum partibus destinavit, mandans et obtestans regi Francorum, ut si essent in regno eius viri catholici eruditi, hos sibi adminiculum ob eresim conprimendam faceret destinari. Ubi tunc Eligius cum sodale libentissime perrexisset, nisi ei quaedam causa inpedimenti fuisset'; cf. C. M. M. Bayer, 'Vita Eligii', above all col. 466, 469–70 and 485–6 for a refutation of Bruno Krusch's dating. On all this, see also Laury Sarti's chapter in this volume.

[21] *Vita Eligii*, I, 34, ed. B. Krusch, p. 691: *Novimus quendam fratrem a partibus Orientis venientem, qui ea quae narro se coram posito gesta esse testabatur.*

[22] G. Scheibelreiter, 'Griechisches-lateinisches-fränkisches Christentum', p. 85.

in mind that the Roman notaries prepared a copy of the decisions of 649 for his attention.

In Rome in 649, one could hardly not have been aware of Amandus's high-profile connections with King Dagobert I ten years earlier, between 629 and 639, of which the *Vita prima* gives some indication. Amandus is described as the godfather of Dagobert's son, Sigibert III, born shortly after 630.[23] What is more, Amandus seems to have obtained permission from the king to preach (the *licentia praedicandi*) throughout the kingdom, and especially among the neighbouring peoples whom Dagobert was in the process of subjugating.[24] Another passage of the *Vita Amandi prima* mentions a royal letter authorising the bishop to carry out compulsory baptism in the Scheldt valley.[25] This passage has long been considered to be an echo, introduced by a Carolingian interpolator, of Charlemagne's conversion of the Saxons. Stefan Esders, however, has recently shown that the passage can be put into context with two other sources: One is Fredegar's account of the perpetual peace between Emperor Heraclius and Dagobert and the embassy sent by the emperor asking (with success) for the compulsory baptism of the Jews of the *regnum Francorum*, in imitation of Heraclius's programme in the Byzantine Empire.[26] The second is the *Vita Sulpicii*, referring to the forced baptism of Jews carried out by Sulpicius of Bourges, whom Amandus had known at the beginning of his career.[27]

While Wolfgang Fritze insisted on the role of Rome and the papacy as the inspiration for the politics of the universal mission of Amandus and other bishops close to Dagobert,[28] Stefan Esders prefers to emphasise the *imitatio imperii* practised by the Merovingian king and his entourage at the beginning of the 630s: 'the treaty of 629 provides the best explanation why Dagobert should have adapted religious policies which were basically connected with events happening in the Near East'.[29] In

---

[23] *Vita Amandi prima*, c. 17, p. 441.
[24] *Vita Amandi prima*, c. 17, p. 441.
[25] *Vita Amandi prima*, c. 13, p. 437.
[26] *Chronicarum quae dicuntur Fredegarii scholastici*, ed. B. Krusch, MGH SRM II (Hanover, 1888), pp. 18–168, IV, 62, p. 151 and IV, 65, p. 153; *The Fourth Book of the Chronicle of Fredegar with Its Continuations*, trans. with introduction and notes by J. M. Wallace Hadrill (London, 1960), pp. 51 and 53–4.
[27] *Vita Sulpicii*, ed. B. Krusch, MGH SRM IV (Hanover and Leipzig, 1902), pp. 371–80, c. 4, p. 374–5; on Amand's stay at Bourges while Sulpicius was still archdeacon there, see *Vita Amandi prima*, c. 5, p. 433.
[28] W. H. Fritze, '*Universalis gentium confessio*. Formeln, Träger und Wege universalmissionarischen Denkens im 7. Jahrhundert', *Frühmittelalterliche Studien*, 3 (1969): 78–130.
[29] S. Esders, '*Nationes quam plures conquiri*: Amandus of Maastricht, Compulsory Baptism and "Christian Mission" in 7th-Century Gaul', in *Motions of Late Antiquity: Essays on Religion, Politics, and Society in Honour of Peter Brown*, eds. J. Kreiner and H. Reimitz

this way, the missionary politics ascribed to Dagobert can be seen as a reflection of the religious politics imposed by the emperor in the East, which aimed to repress heresies and religious deviance as much as to convert pagans. Some years later, Clovis II was still concerned with the religious unity of the *regnum Francorum* and with the suppression of heresy, if we are to believe the *Vita Eligii*.[30] In other words, if Amandus was solicited by Martin, it was because it was believed at Rome, where he was well known, that he had the ear of his godson, the Austrasian king, Sigebert III, and also because of his former intimacy with Dagobert in the early 630s, when he had been closely involved with the Merovingian king's policies inspired by Emperor Heraclius.

Beyond the role that Amandus played in northern Gaul along the Scheldt valley, the *Vita prima* mentions his episcopate at Maastricht, and then a mission to the *Wascones*.[31] But before this, it also mentions a spell of missionary activity among the Slavs in the Danube valley.[32] The discovery of another ancient *Life of Amand* has led historians to re-evaluate the value of the later *Life* preserved in the legendary of Bernard Gui, which also refers to missionary work among the Slavs.[33] For Georges Declercq and Adriaan Verhulst, this mission was by no means imaginary. It might explain why a century and a half later, at the end of the eighth century, the Bavarian Arn became monk then abbot of the monastery of Saint-Amand before becoming bishop of Salzburg (785) and architect of the mission to the Avars.[34] Furthermore, Amandus's presence among the Slavs might be related to the attention that first Chlothar II then Dagobert had paid to this region, as demonstrated by the references Fredegar makes to the Frankish merchant Samo between 623 and 632.[35] Samo ended up taking charge of a Slavic kingdom, against which Frankish and Lombard armies both fought.

(Turnhout, 2016), pp. 269–307; see also S. Esders, 'Heraklios, Dagobert und die "beschnittenen Völker": Die Umwälzungen des Mittelmeerraums im 7. Jahrhundert in der fränkischen Chronik des sog. Fredegar', in A. Goltz, H. Leppin and H. Schlange-Schöningen (eds.), *Jenseits der Grenzen: Studien zur spätantiken und frühmittelalterlichen Geschichtsschreibung* (Berlin and New York, 2009), pp. 239–311.

[30] See below, note 35.
[31] *Vita Amandi prima*, c. 18, pp. 442–3 and c. 20–1, pp. 443–5.
[32] *Vita Amandi prima*, c. 16, p. 440: *transfraetato Danubio, eadem circumiens loca, libera voce euangelium Christi gentibus praedicabat*.
[33] *Alia Vita auctore Aquitano anonymo*, c 9, p. 855; see above, note 18.
[34] Verhulst and Declercq, 'L'Action et le souvenir de saint Amand en Europe centrale', pp. 522–5, acknowledge, however, that it is difficult to distinguish traces of the cult that could have developed after the saint's visit from attestations brought by Arn at the end of the eighth century.
[35] *Chronicarum quae dicuntur Fredegarii scholastici*, IV, 48, 68 and 75, pp. 144–5, 154–5 and 158–9; *The Fourth Book of the Chronicle of Fredegar*, pp. 39–40, 56–8 and 63.

To return to our topic, all this could indicate that Amandus had obtained precise knowledge of the Byzantine situation during his visit to the Danube region, a region certainly occupied by the Slavs, but in which Byzantine missionaries were very active in the seventh century, after the disturbance provoked by the Avars (who besieged Constantinople in 626) had subsided.[36] In addition to the knowledge that Amandus had gained of Eastern realities at Dagobert's court, therefore, we might need to add personal experience of the Byzantine world acquired through a short mission to the Slavic borderlands.

Rome and the North of Gaul in the Mid Seventh Century

As is well known, the aftermath of the Roman council of 649 were dramatic for Pope Martin. Seized at Rome in 653 on the order of Constans II, he was judged and exiled to Cherson on the Black Sea, where he died in 655. The consequences of this tragic event in the West did not, however, match the energies formerly devoted by the pope to its bishops. True, the *Life of Saint Eligius* mentions a council held at Orléans to deal with a mysterious heretic who had 'come from the other side of the sea' (the Mediterranean?), and who had been especially active at Autun.[37] Furthermore, the first canon of the council of Chalon (held on a 24 October between 647 and 653), subscribed by Audoin and Eligius, proposed a fresh affirmation of Trinitarian dogma and of the Nicene faith, which might implicitly refer to the Monothelete crisis, though its formulation is very generic.[38] But there was no question of Frankish bishops travelling either to Rome or to Constantinople. The *Life of Eligius* specifies that Eligius and Audoin were retained in Gaul by other business.[39] Tempting though it may be, the proposal of André Borias that St Wandrille, the founder of the monastery of Fontanelle, might have been sent to Pope Martin to represent St Audoin remains entirely hypothetical.[40] All this attests to the limits of the Neustrian kingdom and

---

[36] *Histoire du Christianisme*, ed. J.-M. Mayeur, Ch. and L. Pietri, A. Vauchez and M. Venard, vol. IV (Paris, 1993), pp. 10–13 and 18–22.

[37] *Vita Eligii*, I, 35, p. 691: *unus hereticorum pulsus a partibus transmarinis Galliarum provintiam petiit*; this council of Orléans is not attested elsewhere.

[38] *Les Canons des conciles mérovingiens (VIe–VIIe siècles)*, ed. J. Gaudemet and B. Basdevant (Paris, 1989), vol. II, pp. 550, 560 and 562.

[39] See above, note 19.

[40] A. Borias, 'Saint Wandrille et le crise monothélite', *Revue bénédictine*, 97 (1987): 42–67, is based on the mention of *pixides duae ex ebore quas fuerunt a sancto Wandregisilo ab urbe Roma delatas* in the list of relics taken from Fontanelle to the monastery of Saint-Pierre of Gand in 944: ed. N.-N. Huyghebaert, *Une translation de reliques à Gand en 944, Le Sermo de adventu sanctorum Wandregisili, Ansberti et Vulframni in Blandinium*, Commission royale d'histoire. Recueil de textes pour servir à l'étude de l'histoire de la

episcopate's interest in Eastern matters. As for Austrasia, it is impossible to know what answer Amandus gave to the pope. But thirty years later, in 680, the episcopate of the *regnum Francorum* simply ignored a comparable consultation initiated by Pope Agatho.

If in the short-term the Eastern question found little echo in Gaul, the links thereby established with Rome in contrast do seem to have been put to use. Pope Martin's letter reveals that Amandus obtained relics and that he was also looking for manuscripts.[41] Even if these could not be provided in the autumn of 649, we might wonder whether the abbot of Elnone's request was as fruitless as the anonymous Aquitainian life suggests.[42] Other initiatives in the direction of Rome came from Amandus's circle. A few years later, around 651, he was involved in the foundation of the monastery of Nivelles by Itta and Gertrude, respectively the mother and sister of Grimoald, mayor of the palace.[43] The *Vita Geretrudis* underlined the relations with Rome, since relics and books were brought from there to Nivelles following the monastery's foundation.[44] Amandus was also in touch with another holy woman, Aldegundis, founder of the monastery of Maubeuge in the early 660s.[45] Curiously enough, this Aldegundis subsequently appeared as the only saint from northern Gaul whose relics were sent to Rome at the beginning of the eighth century, if one trusts the dating of a relic label or *authenticum*

Belgique (Brussels, 1978), p. 32. The *Gesta abbatum Fontanellensium* mention a journey to Rome by Wandrille's nephew, Gond, during the pontificate of Vitalien (657–72), after which he brought back relics and manuscripts: *Gesta sanctorum patrum coenobii Fontanellensis: Chronique des abbés de Fontenelle*, ed. P. Pradié (Paris, 1999), I, 6, p. 18.

[41] *Vita Amandi secunda*, p. 456, and *Concilium Lateranense a. 649 celebratum*, p. 424: 'Reliquias vero sanctorum, de quibus praesentium lator nobis ammonuit, dare praecipimus; nam codices iam exinaniti sunt a nostra bybliotheca, et unde dare ei nullatenus habuimus. Transscribere autem non potuit, quoniam festinanter de hac civitate regredi properavit. Haec igitur ita praelibatis, quae a nobis per epistolam vobis scripta sunt, effectui mancipari fraternitatem vestram hortamur.'

[42] See above, note 18.

[43] *Vita Geretrudis*, ed. B. Krusch, MGH SRM II (Hanover, 1898), pp. 453–64, c. 2, p. 455; trans. P. Fouracre and R. Gerberding, *Late Merovingian France: History and Hagiography (640–720)* (Manchester, 1996), pp. 319–29, here at p. 321. On the date of Nivelles's foundation, see A. Dierkens, 'Saint Amand et la fondation de l'abbaye de Nivelles', *Revue du Nord*, 68 (1986): 325–34.

[44] *Vita Geretrudis*, c. 2, p. 457: *sanctorum patrocinia vel sancta volumina de urbe Romana*; trans. P. Fouracre and R. Gerberding, *Late Merovingian France*, p. 322.

[45] *Vita Aldegundis prima*, ed. J. Mabillon, Acta Sanctorum ordinis sancti Benedicti, II (Paris, 1669), pp. 807–15, c. 14, p. 81: *quidam episcopus nomine Amandus, amicitia spirituali familiaritate adnexus*; ibid., c. 18, p. 812 for a mention of abbot Subinus of Nivelles; cf. trans. J. A McNamara, J. E. Halborg and E. Gordon Whatley, *Sainted Women of Dark Ages* (Durham, NC, 1992), pp. 237–54, here at pp. 247–8; on all this, see A.-M. Helvétius, 'Sainte Aldegonde et les origines du monastère de Maubeuge', *Revue du Nord* 74 (1992): 221–37.

preserved until 1905 in the Sancta Sanctorum, the treasure of the chapel of San Lorenzo-in-Palatio at the Lateran.[46] Other sources too attest to the interest that Martin's successors maintained in the Western bishoprics, and especially the Frankish Church, long before the rise to power of Charlemagne's ancestors.[47]

St Amandus appears to have been an essential link in the chain not only for our knowledge of the circumstances in which the acts of the Council of 649 were sent to Gaul (thanks to the letter of Martin I) but also for our knowledge of the acts themselves (copied into the Laon manuscript). Amandus was without doubt one of the few bishops of Gaul capable at the time of understanding the stakes of the Monothelete crisis. He had known the united reign of Dagobert, who had practised a kind of *imitatio imperii*; it is possible that the mission to the Slavs had put him in contact with Byzantium; and he was also familiar with Rome. All these are reasons for Martin to have contacted him, and they explain too why the documents were preserved at Elnone.

But, by the end of the 640s, Amandus was no longer a typical Frankish bishop: he was yesterday's man. He would soon leave the see of Maastricht to return to his monastery of Elnone, maybe because the Austrasian court remained cautious towards Byzantium and preferred not to follow the papal position on Monotheletism. Just as the papyrus on which Martin's letter was written was destined to vanish definitively from the West, so the horizon of Eastern affairs became ever more distant. From this point of view, Martin's unanswered letter to Amandus was another swansong of antiquity. Yet at the same time, from a Roman perspective, it represented a first effort at the rapprochement with the Austrasian political and religious elites whose future is so well known. That, however, is another story.

---

[46] B. Galland, *Les Authentiques de reliques du Sancta Sanctorum* (Vatican City, 2004), p. 103; cf. J. M. H. Smith, 'Care of Relics in Early Medieval Rome', in V. L. Garver and O. M. Phelan (eds.), *Rome and Religion in the Medieval World: Studies in Honor of Thomas F. X. Noble* (Farnham, 2014), pp. 179–205, esp. p. 198.

[47] I. N. Wood, 'Between Rome and Jarrow: Papal Relations with Francia and England, from 597 to 716', in *Chiese locali e Chiese regionali nell'alto Medioevo* (Spoleto, 2014), vol. II, pp. 865–94.

10 The Digression on Pope Martin I in the *Life of Eligius of Noyon*

Laury Sarti

The sources suggest that, in contrast to the earlier Merovingian period, diplomatic and other official contacts between the West and the eastern Roman Empire drastically decreased since the seventh century, having ceased almost completely after the 630s and until the year 756. Evidence referring to the movement of more ordinary people or even the exchange of simple knowledge of events in the other part of the Mediterranean is also very meagre. The latest source testifying to a more intensive interchange is the *Chronicle of Fredegar*, written until around the year 660.[1] Beyond this, the Western sources only contain most sporadic mentions of the East, which includes dates according to Roman standards (and thus referring to the Byzantine emperors[2]), nondescript mentions of 'Greeks' as opposed to other groups such as 'Romans' or 'Franks',[3] or, for example, a reference to an ecumenical synod in Constantinople in a letter written by Bishop Chrodebert of Tours.[4] Any further evidence thus is important to understand the relations between these major regions. This study focuses on an enigmatic digression found in the *Life of Eligius of Noyon*, which contains some noteworthy late-seventh-century evidence that has not yet received the attention it deserves.[5]

---

[1] *Chronicarum quae dictuntur Fredegarii scholastici Libri IV*, ed. B. Krusch, MGH SRM 2 (Hanover, 1888), pp. 1–193.
[2] See, for example, Boniface, *Epistolae* 45, ed. M. Tangl, MGH Epp. selectae 1 (Berlin, 1916), p. 74.
[3] Boniface, *Epistolae* 78, p. 171.
[4] Epist. coll. 16, in 'Epistolae aevi Merowingici collectae' ed. W. Gundlach, *Epistolae Merowingici et Karolini aevi*, MGH Epp. 3 (Berlin, 1892), vol. I, pp. 434–68, at p. 461. See also Adomnán's *De locis sanctis* and Willibald's *Hodoeporicon*.
[5] 'Vita Eligii episcopi Noviomagensis', ed. B. Krusch, *Passiones vitaeque sanctorum aevi Merovingici*, MGH SRM 4 (Hanover, 1904), pp. 663–742. Complete edition in 'Audoenus Rothomagensis. Vita S. Eligii', ed. J.-P. Migne, *PL*, 87 (Paris, 1851), pp. 477–592. I would like to thank Stefan Esders for suggesting that I have a closer look at this piece of evidence. Yaniv Fox kindly improved my English.

The *Life of Eligius of Noyon*

The *Life of Eligius* is composed of two books, the first of which is dedicated to the saint's life before his consecration as a bishop and the second to his life afterwards. It is remarkable for its length and richness in detail. Given that this extraordinary piece of evidence is also one of the most abundant sources for the particularly gloomy decades of the late-seventh-century West, it has not been accorded adequate importance. The reason for this neglect is its dubious date of composition. A letter addressed to a bishop named Rodobert (Chrodobert) is appended to the *Life* to claim that it had been written shortly after the saint's death and under the guidance of his long-time friend and colleague, Bishop Audoin of Rouen.[6] This claim of a near-contemporary redaction is supported by features like a detailed description of the saint's outer appearance,[7] or the occasional use of the first person by the author in his narration.[8]

Several inconsistencies, however, cast doubt on the thesis of a near-contemporary redaction. The *Life* contains mentions that suggest that a longer period of time had already passed between Eligius' lifetime and its composition,[9] and the prologue even speaks of the existence of earlier (contemporary) *Lives* written in too much haste.[10] The author occasionally calls Audoin a saint, a denomination that appears unusual as a self-designation.[11] Moreover, alongside the mentioned use of the first person, the *Life* contains as many cases where the third person is used to refer to the same alleged author.[12] In Book 2, the first and third person are both used at the same time (provided that Audoin is the author).[13] The sporadic use of the third person cannot be explained as the result of modesty,

---

[6] 'Epistola Dadonis ad Rodobertum', ed. Krusch, *Passiones vitaeque* (1904), p. 741. Its authenticity has never been questioned, see M. Heinzelmann, '*Eligius monetarius*. Norm oder Sonderfall?', in J. Jarnut and J. Strothmann (eds.), *Die Merowingischen Monetarmünzen als Quelle zum Verständnis des 7. Jahrhunderts in Gallien* (Munich, 2013), pp. 243–91, at pp. 250–1.

[7] For example, *Vita Eligii*, 1.12.

[8] For example, *Vita Eligii*, 1.6, 1.11.

[9] For example, *Vita Eligii*, 2.5.

[10] *Vita Eligii*, praef., p. 664. See also Heinzelmann, '*Eligius monetarius*', p. 255.

[11] For example, *Vita Eligii*, 2.1, p. 694: *sancti viri Eligius et Audoinus*. See also C. M. Bayer, Art. 'Vita Eligii', *Reallexikon der Germanischen Altertumskunde*, 35 (2007): 461–524, at p. 473, challenged by Heinzelmann, '*Eligius monetarius*', pp. 252–3. The response letter, 'Rescriptum ad domnum Dadonem a Rodoberto', ed. Krusch, *Passiones vitaeque* (1904), p. 741, refers to Audoin as *sanctitatis tuae*, suggesting that such a denomination was at least feasible for a living person.

[12] See *Vita Eligii*, 1.8, p. 675: *Quod cum vir sanctus sodali suo Audoino nomine, cognomento Dadone*. Similarly, *ibid*. 1.12, 2.2.

[13] See *Vita Eligii*, 2.2, p. 696: *Autoino de partibus Transligeritanis reducto* […] *ego Rodomo, ille vero Noviomo*.

since Audoin is frequently worked into the narrative, even in instances where his mention seems superfluous.[14] In addition, the *Life* contains sections that apparently were copied from the *Vita sancti Remedii*.[15] Some scholars have dated this *Life of Remigius* to the eighth century,[16] which is one reason why historians tend to assume that, while the *Life of Eligius* might date back to an earlier version written by Audoin himself, the text as it is preserved today had been significantly rewritten, altered and complemented at a later stage.[17] A possible *terminus ante quem* for this latter redaction is the year 743, the supposed year of composition of the *Life of Lambert*, which refers to the *Life of Eligius*.[18]

The thesis of an eighth-century dating and revision of the *Life of Eligius* has lately come into question. Clemens Bayer argued in a large article in the *Reallexikon der Germanischen Altertumskunde*, emanating from his dissertation, that for the most part the current version of the *vita* is the work composed by Audoin himself. He refuted the assumption of a significant late Merovingian rewriting and the thesis of a Carolingian revision, claiming that the importance of any supplementary reworking or edition has been overestimated. The alternation between the first and third person is explained through an intentional change in the author's narrative perspective.[19] The thesis of a late-seventh-century redaction is supported by sematic evidence. As I could show more recently, the *Life* uses the words *miles* (with the meaning custodian of prisoners) and

---

[14] See the examples in note 12. Compare to Gregory of Tours, who only mentions himself in the context of events where he had been actively involved.

[15] 'Vita sancti Remedii', ed. B. Krusch, *Venanti Honori Clementiani Fortunati presbyteri Itallica opera pedestria*, MGH AA 4.2 (Berlin, 1885), pp. 64–7.

[16] See I. Westeel, *Vie de saint Eloi: Présentation et traduction* (Noyon, 2006), p. 14. Challenged by K. Schäferdiek, 'Remigius von Reims. Kirchenmann einer Umbruchszeit', in H. C. Brennecke (ed.), *Schwellenzeit: Beiträge zur Geschichte des Christentums in Spätantike und Frühmittelalter* (Berlin, 1996), pp. 305–28, at p. 305.

[17] Krusch, '*Vita Eligii*', pp 644–62. Adopted, for example, in P. Fouracre, 'The Work of Audoenus of Rouen and Eligius of Noyon', in D. Baker (ed.), *The Church in Town and Countryside* (Oxford, 1979), pp. 77–91; Y. Hen, *Culture and Religion in Merovingian Gaul AD 481–751: Cultures, Beliefs and Traditions* (Leiden, 1995), p. 196 and n. 245; R. Le Jan, 'Die Sakralität der Merowinger oder: Mehrdeutigkeiten der Geschichtsschreibung', in St Airlie, W. Pohl and H. Reimitz (eds.), *Staat im frühen Mittelalter* (Vienna, 2006), pp. 73–92, at p. 80, n. 46.

[18] Westeel, *Vie de saint Eloi*, p. 10 and pp. 151–2, n. 36. See also J. Howe, 'The Hagiography of Saint-Wandrille (Fontenelle)', in M. Heinzelmann (ed.), *L'Hagiographie du haut Moyen âge en Gaule du nord: Manuscrits, textes et centres de production* (Stuttgart, 2001), pp. 127–92, at p. 140 and pp. 152–3. The oldest MS, Bruxelles BR 5374–5, dates to the second quarter of the ninth-century, see Westeel, *Vie de saint Eloi*, pp. 11–12. It can be viewed online via https://uurl.kbr.be/1449093 (accessed 30 October 2018). See also Heinzelmann, '*Eligius monetarius*', p. 254, n. 35.

[19] Bayer, 'Vita Eligii', pp. 469–70. This still does not adequately explain the simultaneous use of both in *Vita Eligii*, 2.2.

Romanus (either referring to Christians or the Byzantine Empire) in a manner that is very specific to Merovingian sources, which means that their uses perfectly match related semantic evidence found in other contemporary sources.[20] Bayer argued that the original version of the *Life* had been composed before the year 684.[21] Walter Berschin more recently supported this thesis and assumed that, subsequent to Audoin, Carolingian scribes only added minor changes in grammar and wording to the text.[22] He suggested that the *Life* was penned between the years 675 and 680.[23]

Considering these many inconsistencies,[24] the discussion of the date of composition of the *Life* certainly is not closed yet, and it may never be solved completely. Still, the recent re-evaluation of the date of this important text necessitates a reassessment of its potential significance as a seventh-century testimony.[25] In this regard, a digression contained in the *Life of Eligius* deserves some particular consideration. It may be considered one of the most extensive accounts on the Byzantine world in a Merovingian source – other than pilgrimage reports – that post-dates the *Chronicle of Fredegar*.

The Digression

The digression is included as part of the sections 33 and 34 in Book 1 of the *Life of Eligius*. It begins with a description of how, during the early

---

[20] On the use of *Romanus* in *Vita Eligii*, 1.10, 1.33, 2.20, see L. Sarti, 'Frankish Romanness and Charlemagne's Empire', *Speculum*, 91 (2016): 1040–58, at p. 1049 and 'From *Romanus* to *Graecus*: The Identity and Perceptions of the Byzantines in the Frankish West', *Journal of Medieval History*, 44 (2018): 131–50. On the use of *miles* in *Vita Eligii*, 2.15, see L. Sarti, 'Der fränkische *miles*: weder Soldat noch Ritter', *Frühmittelalterliche Studien* 52.1 (2018): 99–117, at p. 103.

[21] Bayer, 'Vita Eligii', pp. 462–75. Heinzelmann, '*Eligius monetarius*', pp. 249–56 supports the thesis of a contemporary redaction.

[22] W. Berschin, 'Der heilige Goldschmied: Die Eligiusvita – ein merowingisches Original?' *Mitteilungen des Instituts für österreichische Geschichtsforschung*, 118 (2010): 1–7. See also Bayer, 'Vita Eligii', pp. 461–524. Similarly, M. Banniard, 'Latin et communication orale en Gaule franque: Le témoignage de la Vita Eligii', in J. Fontaine and J. N. Hillgarth (eds.), *Le Septième siècle: changements et continuités* (London, 1992), pp. 62–7, challenged by Hen, *Culture and Religion*, p. 196, n. 245. This was contested by Heinzelmann, '*Eligius monetarius*', p. 253.

[23] Berschin, 'Der heilige Goldschmied', pp. 1–7. Westeel, *Vie de saint Eloi*, p. 11, suggests a date between 673 and 675.

[24] Interestingly, the 'Epistola Dadonis ad Rodobertum' already mentions that errors might have emerged during the redaction or copying. Similar *Vita Eligii*, praef., p. 665.

[25] See the recent assessment by S. Patzold, 'Eliten um 630 und um 700: Beobachtungen zur politschen Desintegration des Merowingerreichs im 7. Jahrhundert', in J. Jarnut and J. Strothmann (eds.), *Die Merowingischen Monetarmünzen als Quelle zum Verständnis des 7. Jahrhunderts in Gallien* (Munich, 2013), pp. 551–61, at pp. 560–1.

reign of Clovis II, 'the Roman Empire being headed by Constantine, a wicked heresy which originated in eastern lands began to pullulate'.[26] Unnamed 'heresiarchs' spread the false information that Christ had never been born in true flesh, which caused great trouble throughout the entire Christian world by infecting people in Byzantium as well as Rome. It continues that the emperor was attracted to the heretic doctrine now opposed by Pope Martin I, who arranged a synod to discuss the matter and to 'destroy this despicable dogma'. During this convention, a statement was set up that was sent to Gaul together with a letter to the Frankish king, encouraging the episcopate to support the prelate's fight against the heresy. Although Eligius was among those approached in this context, he was finally impeded from joining the pope's cause. The second section of the digression mentions imperial decrees asking Martin to abandon his faith and, as a consequence of his refusal, an attempt to have him removed from his episcopal see. His deposition and subsequent arrest are not attributed to a specific person or group but to the Devil, whom the Roman prelate is said to have virtuously resisted. The author specifies that Martin preferred martyrdom to heresy, and that his hands were bound until he was driven out of his episcopal city. He was first taken to Constantinople and then to exile, where he miraculously cured a blind man, before dying a martyr. The author insists that Martin did not kill himself, nor did he die by the sword, adding that, in death, he finally defeated his adversaries.

The digression has not attracted much attention among modern scholars.[27] An obvious reason is the particularly problematic role of these two sections inside the *Life*. They are occasionally understood to be a later interpolation, not an original part of the hagiographic composition.[28] This assumption is based on inconsistencies like potential anachronisms, as when Martin's pontificate of 649 is supposed to be associated with the accession to the throne of Clovis II ten years before, or the digression's

---

[26] Trans. J. A. McNamara, 'Life of St Eligius of Noyon, 588–660', *Medieval Sourcebook*, with an entire translation only here: www.fordham.edu/halsall/basis/eligius.asp (accessed 1 December 2014). Partly published in T. Head (ed.), *Medieval Hagiography: An Anthology* (London and New York, 2001), pp. 137–67.

[27] Some credit is given to its contents, for example, in *The Acts of the Lateran Synod of 649*, trans. R. Price (Liverpool, 2014), p. 80; Bayer, 'Vita Eligii'. See also the forthcoming study by Catherine Cubitt on 'The Impact of the Lateran Council of 649 in Francia: The "Martyrdom" of Pope Martin and the Life of St Eligius', kindly shared with me after work on the present manuscript had already been concluded. It also argues for a seventh-century redaction of the *Life of Eligius*.

[28] See Krusch, 'Vita Eligii', pp. 651–2; G. Scheibelreiter, 'Griechisches – lateinisches – fränkisches Christentum: Der Brief Papst Martins I. an den Bischof Amandus von Maastricht aus dem Jahre 649', *Mitteilungen des Instituts für österreichische Geschichtsforschung*, 100 (1992): 84–102, at p. 102.

inclusion in the first book of the *Life*, which is dedicated to Eligius' life before his consecration in 641 as bishop of Noyon.[29] Moreover, these sections are lacking in some manuscript classes, such as the thirteenth-century MS 5287 from the Fonds latin of the Parisian Bibliothèque nationale.[30]

There are, however, also reasons to believe that the digression was indeed an original piece and thus an integral part of the *Life*. At the end of the digression, the author adds that:

> These few words about so excellent a man have been inserted into the life of Eligius because Martin did so much to brighten the faith in the part of the world where he lived. And it suffices us to have narrated it for love of grace so that the memory of that special man who impended much good to my colleagues in Rome shall not be forgotten in the West although he was brought to the East.[31]

Although this explanation does not provide any indication that helps to determine whether the author or a later compiler had added the digression, it appears more likely that this account was part of the *Life* as it had been designed by its creator. It is difficult to envisage a later scribe or editor adding this account to this *vita* dedicated to Eligius, a saint unrelated to Martin. It also appears implausible that the digression was mistakenly integrated to the first book, as this is clearly identified as referring to Eligius' life before his ordination.[32] The report that Eligius was asked to support Pope Martin only makes sense if the saint was a bishop already.[33] The digression also (correctly) refers to the time after 641, which is why the evidence brought forward to argue against a contemporary redaction, stating that the digression falsely claims that the royal request would have reached Eligius while still a layman, only emerges implicitly from its position in Book 1 and its insertion directly before Chapter 35, which discusses the pre-clerical phase of Eligius' life.[34] If the author consciously added this association of Eligius as a layman with

---

[29] See E. Vacandard, *Vie de saint Ouen: Évêque de Rouen (641–684) – Étude d'histoire mérovingienne* (Paris, 1902), p. 223, n. 2. See also the discussion (including some unfounded presuppositions) in K. J. Hefele, *A History of the Councils of the Church from the Original Documents*, vol. III: AD 626 to the Close of the Second Council of Nicea, AD 787 (Edinburgh, 1896), pp. 69–70 and pp. 97–8.

[30] Paris BnF Lat 5287. See Vacandard, *Vie de Saint Ouen*, pp. 73–4, n. 1. On further inconsistencies, see Bayer, 'Vita Eligii', pp. 467–9.

[31] Trans. McNamara. *Vita Eligii*, 1.34, p. 691: *Haec pauca de tanto viri memoria Eligii vita sibi contineat subnexa, loquatur et, ubi pergit cumque per saecula, quanta Martinus claruerit fidei dogma: quae nos dilectionis gratia hucusque narrasse sufficiat, ut tam eximii viri memoria, qui utique collegis meis in urbe Romana multa inpendit bona, quamvis in Oriente frequentetur, non usquequaeque in Occidente oblivione tradatur.*

[32] *Vita Eligii, praef.*, 2.2.

[33] See also Scheibelreiter, 'Griechisches – lateinisches – fränkisches Christentum', p. 101, n. 76.

[34] *Vita Eligii*, 1.35.

what would have been an exclusively ecclesiastical duty, he must have done so to further enhance the idealisation of the saint's sanctity, and not because this was a fact. There is, however, no reason to question that the royal request had been addressed to Eligius, not least because this is the only explicit association provided between the saint and the content of the digression. Thus, this particular detail also helps to explain why the account on the fate of Pope Martin had been included in the *Life* in the first place. Although the position of the digression remains difficult to explain, this is made somewhat easier if we accept that it was a (conscious) decision by the author himself.

As indicated above, the second chapter deals with Martin's stay in Constantinople and exile, which, according to other sources, took place in the ancient city of Cherson(es), in the near vicinity of the modern city of Sevastopol in Crimea.[35] Speaking of his time after leaving Rome, the author claims that: 'We know a certain brother from eastern parts who witnessed all these deeds that I now report in his own presence.'[36] He thus asserts that his account is based on the direct testimony of a clerk who had accompanied Martin to Constantinople and the Crimea and who, some years later, would have travelled to Gaul, where he met the *Life*'s author. A possible context for this visit would be the preparations to the third ecumenical synod of 680 in Constantinople.[37]

This is not an unlikely scenario. Such an encounter, and maybe the author's enthusiasm about what he had learnt, could further explain why he added the account of Martin to his *Life* – especially as Eligius had almost been involved in what had happened. This would also help clarify why the author felt the need to provide an explanation for why this was not eventually the case.[38] Was the author so impatient and enthusiastic to

---

[35] *Liber Pontificalis*, 76.8, in L. Duchesne (ed.), *Le Liber Pontificalis: Texte, introduction et commentaire*, vol. I (Paris, 1886). See also E. Michael, 'Wann ist Papst Martin I. bei seiner Exilierung nach Constantinopel gekommen?' *Zeitschrift für katholische Theologie*, 16 (1892): 375–80; J. Srutwa, 'The Exile and Death of Pope Martin I on Crimea', *Antiquitas: Acta Universitatis Wratislaviensis*, 18 (1993): 203–9. Martin sent four letters from exile, see Price, *The Acts of the Lateran Synod*, pp. 179–94; W. Brandes, '"Juristische" Krisenbewältigung im 7. Jahrhundert? Die Prozesse gegen Papst Martin I. und Maximos Homologetes', in D. Simon (ed.), *Fontes minores* (Frankfurt, 1998), pp. 141–212, at p. 159.

[36] *Vita Eligii*, 1.34, p. 690: *Novimus quondam fratrem a partibus Orientis venientem, qui ea quae narrow se coram posito gesta esse testabatur.* Trans. McNamara. See also Scheibelreiter, 'Griechisches – lateinisches – fränkisches Christentum', p. 101, n. 77; R. G. Hoyland and S. Waidler, 'Adomnán's *De locis sanctis* and the Seventh-Century Near East', *English Historical Review*, 129 (2014): 787–807, at p. 805.

[37] See the chapter by Stefan Esders in this volume.

[38] I. N. Wood, 'The Franks and Papal Theology, 550–660', in C. M. Chazelle and C. Cubitt (eds.), *The Crisis of the Oikoumene: The Three Chapters and the Failed Quest for Unity in the*

put down what he had learnt that he added his report where he had just stopped writing? This could indeed have been the later part of book one, in which case we would not only have an explanation for the digression's position but also an interesting testimony for the author's writing process and progress. Suggesting that the digression is a later addition, on the other hand, would imply that a later scribe or author made false assertions of authenticity, by adding the mention of this traveller, which would be a consciously misleading claim. Although such things do happen, it is difficult to explain what would have occasioned such interference in a *Life* that was not dedicated to Pope Martin himself, and that thus hardly aimed to promote his cult.

The assumption that the account derives from an oral report is supported by the fact that the content of the digression diverges significantly from other written sources. The *Commemoratio*, an account of Martin apparently written by a contemporary admirer of the pope,[39] possibly Theodorus Spudaeus, and the *Hypomnesticum*, probably written by the same author,[40] differ considerably in scope and content from the digression. As I will argue below, there is also no proof for direct copying from neither the *Liber Pontificalis* nor any of Martin's letters that were available in the West. More or less explicit citation of earlier written testimony, however, would be expected of a later composition in particular. The *Liber Pontificalis* only calls Martin a confessor and specifies that he died in peace,[41] while the idea of martyrdom is only contained in the slightly later appendix to the *Commemoratio*.[42] Beyond this, the digression mentions the miraculous curing of a blind man during the pope's exile,[43]

Sixth-Century Mediterranean (Turnhout, 2007), p. 240, suggests that Wandregisel travelled to Rome instead of Eligius.

[39] 'Commemoratio eorum saeviter et sine Dei respectu acta sunt', ed. Migne, *Saeculum 9. Anastasii abbatis. Sanctae Romanae ecclesiae presbyteri et bibliothecarii. Opera omnia*, vol. III, PL 129 (Paris, 1853), pp. 591–9. F. Winkelmann, *Der monenergetisch-monotheletische Streit* (Frankfurt, 2001), pp. 145–6 dates it to early summer 655. An appendix, however, must date after Martin's death, which it mentions, Winkelmann, *Der monenergetisch-monotheletische Streit*, pp. 599–600. See also Brandes, '"Juristische" Krisenbewältigung', pp. 154–5.

[40] 'Scholion sive Hypomnesticum', ed. Migne, PL 129 (Paris, 1853), cols. 681–90. See also R. Devreese, 'Le Texte grec de l'Hypomnesticum de Théodore Spoudée: Le supplice, l'exil et la mort des victimes illustres du monothélisme', *Analecta Bollandiana*, 53 (1935): 49–81. Both texts are preserved in Anastasius Bibliothecarius' *Collectanae*. See also Brandes, '"Juristische" Krisenbewältigung', pp. 156–8.

[41] *Liber Pontificalis*, 76.8.

[42] *Commemoratio*, p. 592. A Greek *Passio*, probably penned or rewritten after 726, uses the *Commemoratio* and some of Martin's letters to Theodorus Spudaeus. Its content significantly differs from the digression, its poor Greek suggests a Latin original. P. Peeters, 'Une vie grecque du pape S. Martin I', *Analecta Bollandiana*, 51 (1933): 225–62.

[43] *Vita Eligii*, 1.34.

which is unmentioned in the other source material. It also remains very vague and often appears consciously inexplicit, which further supports the impression of a contemporary account, given that such sources tend to be more considerate of current constellations than accounts set up some generations later.

Assuming that the digression is an original part of the *Life* requires refutation of the arguments opposed to this thesis. The digression in fact does not explicitly associate the time of consecration of Pope Martin with the accession of Clovis II. It only states in reference to Clovis (639–58) that it was *sub huius regni* that Martin had been pope and organised a council in Rome. The reference to the reign of an emperor 'Constantine' is also correct. It does not refer to the son of Heraclius, Heraclius Constantine III, who was emperor in 641 during only a few months,[44] but to his immediate successor, who ruled until 668. Although this emperor was popularly known as Constans II, he had received the name *Constantinus* at his coronation,[45] a name that is also used on his coins.[46] The date provided by the digression for Martin's episcopate (649–53/5), which is located between the years 641 and 658, is therefore not false but only imprecise. This is nothing unusual in hagiography. The absence of the digression in some manuscript classes neither is conclusive proof for a later date of composition, since it is extremely likely that at some later point one unknown copyist chose to skip what could be considered an unnecessarily tangential episode of the *Life*, so as to reduce its extraordinary length. The likeliness of such a subsequent omission is supported by the fact that the earliest manuscript does, in fact, contain the digression.[47]

The last problem I shall address here is the author's simultaneous use of the third and first person, a phenomenon that is not limited to this part of the *Life* and thus should not be considered as a particular problem found only in the digression. It is still worth mentioning here that in the one sentence contained in the digression, which is generally considered as an example in which the author is mentioned in the third person,[48] this is less clear than expected. In this particular section, the text does not explicitly refer to Audoin but only speaks of Eligius' 'comrade' (lat. *sodale*). The sentence is enigmatic in itself, as Audoin explains

---

[44] A. H. M. Jones, J. R. Martindale and J. Morris (eds.), *The Prosopography of the Later Roman Empire*, vol. III: *AD 527–641* (Cambridge, 1980, 1992), p. 588.
[45] Jones et al., *The Prosopography*, p. 333. See also Vacandard, *Vie de saint Ouen*, p. 74, n. 1.
[46] See W. W. Warwick (ed.), *Catalogue of the Imperial Byzantine Coins in the British Museum*, vol. I (London, 1908), pp. 255–311.
[47] Bruxelles, BR 5374–75, fol. 16v–19r, at https://uurl.kbr.be/1449093.
[48] Westeel, *Vie de saint Eloi*, p. 10. See also Scheibelreiter, 'Griechisches – lateinisches – fränkisches Christentum', p. 101, n. 76

that both men were impeded from complying with Martin's request. The author does not provide any further detail, and only mentions *quaedam causa*.[49] Obviously, he did not want to be more precise. If Audoin himself is indeed the author, it appears likely that this unspecified *causa* is the reason why he chose not to refer to himself explicitly in the digression. Thus, most of the evidence used to disprove that the digression is an original part of the *Life of Eligius* may be overcome without resorting to a theory that casts the digression as a later addition. This means that we may surmise that it is, in all likelihood, a part of the original *Vita Eligii* and the result of a near-contemporary account.

The *Vita Eligii* as a Seventh-Century Testimony

The above-mentioned council, organised by Pope Martin to contain the 'unnamed heresy', can be identified beyond reasonable doubt as the Lateran Council held in Rome in 649 to oppose the Monothelete dogma.[50] The information provided in the digression on the controversy, however, is vague and in places inaccurate. For example, contrary to what is stated in the digression, the emergence of Monotheletism predated the reign of Constans II. The Monothelete doctrine, which initially aimed at reconciling the Chalcedonian with the Monophysite view, was elaborated under the rulership, and probably guidance, of Emperor Heraclius.[51] The author of the *Vita Eligii* obviously was not interested in presenting a detailed chronology of events that predated his own account, and therefore these inaccuracies might just be due to his attempt at a hurried summary. Perhaps the author also simply did not know when Monotheletism had emerged or was not aware of the long process of development that had preceded Martin's episcopacy and the Lateran Council. In any case,

---

[49] *Vita Eligii*, 1.33, p. 690: *Ubi tunc Eligius cum sodale libentissime perrexisset, nisi ei quaedam causa inpedimenti fuisset.*

[50] See E. Caspar, 'Die Lateransynode von 649', *Zeitschrift für Kirchengeschichte*, 51 (1932): 75–137; Winkelmann, *Der monenergetisch-monotheletische Streit*. The first synod to ban the Monothelete heresy was probably held in Rome in 641, see W. Brandes, 'Orthodoxy in the Seventh Century: Prosopographical Observations on Monotheletism', in A. Cameron (ed.), *Fifty Years of Prosopography: The Later Roman Empire, Byzantium and Beyond* (Oxford, 2003), pp. 103–18, at p. 107 and n. 18.

[51] Brandes, 'Orthodoxy and Heresy', pp. 105–6. On the Monothelete controversy, see H.-G. Beck, *Geschichte der orthodoxen Kirche im byzantinischen Reich* (Göttingen, 1980), pp. 54–62; A. J. Ekonomou, *Byzantine Rome and the Greek Popes: Eastern Influences on Rome and the Papacy from Gregory the Great to Zacharias, AD 590–752* (Lanham, MD, 2007), pp. 79–198. Heraclius's role in all this is disputed, see A. Alexakis, 'Before the Lateran Council of 649: The Last Days of Herakleios the Emperor and Monotheletism', *Annuarium historiae conciliorum*, 27/28 (1996): 93–101, at pp. 95–6.

as already indicated, imprecisions of chronology are hardly unusual in hagiography.

More interesting is the representation of the role of the emperor. When speaking of the Monothelete heresy and its supporters, the digression does not explicitly mention an emperor by name but only refers to impersonal 'imperial decrees'. It also specifies that the 'emperor', like many others, was receptive to the assertions of the 'heresiarchs'. Where the author refers to Martin's removal, the only active figure is the Devil. Heraclius, under whose rulership Monotheletism had been established, remains unmentioned, whereas the name of Constans only appears as a reference used to date the account at the beginning of the digression. Whether the author was aware of Heraclius' significance in the establishment of Monotheletism remains unclear. The very vague and seemingly deliberate impersonal reference to Constans, on the other hand, leaves the impression that this depiction was not unintentional.

A comparable attitude can be found in the *Liber Pontificalis*, which, like the digression, does not mention the process dealing with Martin's case in Constantinople. It only alludes to the binding of Martin's hands.[52] The *Liber* also insists that it was not Constans who was the real instigator of the *Typus*, a proclamation issued in 648 to ban discussions of the will(s) of Christ and that was heavily criticised by Martin,[53] but the patriarch (*sic* 'bishop') Paul of Constantinople, who perfidiously seduced him to do so.[54] Neither is Heraclius explicitly associated with the *Ekthesis*, an edict published in 638 to promote the Monothelete doctrine.[55] An active role is attributed to the emperor, nevertheless, where the *Liber Pontificalis* accounts for the instructions given to the exarch Olympius on his way to Italy in order to enforce the *Typus*.[56] Considering the fact that in early eighth-century Britain Bede had been able to use a *Life* of a pope who then was still alive,[57] and given that the *Life of Pope Martin* in the *Liber Pontificalis* was probably penned only shortly after his death, this *Life of Pope Martin* could have been available to the author of the digression

---

[52] See Brandes, '"Juristische" Krisenbewältigung', pp. 141–212; Srutwa, 'The Exile and Death of Pope Martin I', pp. 204–5.
[53] See Martin, 'Epistula encyclica', in R. Riedinger (ed.), *Concilium Lateranense a. 649 celebratum* (Berlin, 1984), pp. 404–21, at p. 411; and 'Martinus ad Amandum', in R. Riedinger (ed.), *Concilium Lateranense a. 649 celebratum* (Berlin, 1984), pp. 422–4, at p. 423.
[54] *Liber Pontificalis*, 76.1. In 76.4 he is called *Paulus patriarcha*.
[55] *Liber Pontificalis*, 76.2. See also 72.1–5.
[56] *Liber Pontificalis*, 76.4.
[57] R. Davis, *The Book of Pontiffs: The Ancient Biographies of the First Ninety Roman Bishops to AD 715*, 2nd edn (Liverpool, 2000), p. xiii.

already. The parallels, however, are inconclusive and due to lack of verbatim quotations this cannot be proven.

A more likely source for the author of the *Life of Eligius* is Martin himself. As mentioned in the digression, the pope sent letters to Gaul after the Lateran synod, together with the synodal acts.[58] Two of these letters have been preserved, together with appended files. It is an encyclical addressed to the entire Christian population and a letter sent to the bishop Amandus in response to a previous inquiry.[59] Similar to the digression and the *Liber Pontificalis*, the encyclical exculpates the emperor of heresy by underlining that he had been perfidiously betrayed into acquiescence.[60] The same view is repeated in reference to Constans in the letter to Amandus.[61] In opposition to Constans, Emperor Heraclius is explicitly mentioned, together with the patriarch Sergius as being responsible for the spread of the heresy. It is also interesting to note that Martin assumed that Amandus had already heard of this.[62] Apart from the reservations in blaming Constans, however, there is no indication proving that the author did have one of these letters at hand when writing his *Life of Eligius*.

The letter to Amandus mentions another letter to the Austrasian king Sigibert III.[63] While Georg Scheibelreiter argued that Amandus was not the ideal candidate for an overall dissemination of the papal news,[64] Charles Mériaux stressed that Chapter 17 of the *Vita Amandi prima* refers to Amandus as Sigibert's III godfather,[65] a circumstance that would indeed make him a useful intermediary for those aiming at making contact with the king. Amandus was not the only recipient addressed by Martin subsequent to the Lateran Council. As already mentioned, the digression refers to letters sent by Martin to request

---

[58] *Liber Pontificalis*, 76.3 confirming their distribution.
[59] Ed. Riedinger, *Concilium Lateranense*, pp. 404–24. See also Scheibelreiter, 'Griechisches – lateinisches – fränkisches Christentum', pp. 84–102; C. Mériaux, *Gallia irradiata: Saints et sanctuaires dans le nord de la Gaule du haut Moyen Âge* (Stuttgart, 2006), pp. 69–70.
[60] Martin, *Epistula encyclica*, p. 409: 'impiissimum Typum, qui ex maligna instigatione illorum factus est contra inmaculatam nostram Christianorum fidem a serenissimo principe'. See also B. Neil, 'From *Tristia* to *Gaudia*: The Exile and Martyrdom of Pope Martin I', in L. Johan (ed.), *Martyrdom and Persecution in Late Antique Christianity. Festschrift Boudewijn Dehandschutter* (Leuven, 2010), pp. 179–94, at p. 190.
[61] *Epistula Martini ad Amandum*, ed. Riedinger, *Concilium*, pp. 423–4: 'a decessoribus suis [Heraclius] haereticae exposita fuerant distruens, et imperialem Typum sacrilego auso totius plenum perfidiae a clementissimo principe nostro fieri persuasit, in quo promulgatum est, ut omnes populi Christiani credere debuissent.'
[62] *Epistula Martini ad Amandum*, p. 423: *credimus etenim ad uos peruenisse.*
[63] *Epistula Martini ad Amandum*, p. 424. See also Scheibelreiter, 'Griechisches – lateinisches – fränkisches Christentum', p. 99.
[64] Scheibelreiter, 'Griechisches – lateinisches – fränkisches Christentum', p. 99.
[65] See the chapter by Charles Mériaux in this volume.

an unnamed Frankish king to assign his clergy to support his struggle against the heresy. The fact that Eligius was allegedly approached in this context suggests that another letter was addressed to the Neustrian king, Clovis II.

Amandus' letter is the only known correspondence preserved from the West. However, more letters have survived that were sent in the same context from Rome to the eastern regions.[66] They give an idea of the different types of letters and their potential variances. The contents of those letters mentioning that the synodal acts had been attached as addendum[67] do not differ significantly in those sections that refer to the heresy and the council in Rome. It thus seems likely that the content of the letters sent to Gaul neither differed significantly from those sections of the letter to Amandus that deal with the heresy.

Although the author of the *Life of Eligius* did not necessarily have a copy of Amandus' epistle, it appears likely that he had read a similar letter. Maybe he knew the letter sent by Martin to Clovis II, which might have been handed over to Eligius when he was asked to comply with the pope's requests.[68] It is likely that this letter did not mention Heraclius as supporter of Monotheletism but adopted the position expounded in the encyclical. The very personal formulation used in this particular section by Martin and the expressed assumption that Amandus had already heard of Heraclius' participation in the establishment of the Monothelete doctrine, fifteen years earlier, suggest that this formulation was specific to this letter. Martin obviously had reasons to assume that Amandus had heard of the troubles in Byzantium. Maybe he had the opportunity to inform Amandus personally, be it with a letter or perhaps even during the bishop's stay in Rome in the late 630s, before Martin had been appointed as *apocrisiarius* in Constantinople.[69]

The *Liber Pontificalis* suggests that the position that the Byzantine emperors were not to be explicitly blamed for the spread of Monotheletism corresponds to the official papal position. Although the popes were not necessarily in agreement with the emperors and could not entirely draw the curtain over their role in view of the Monothelete crisis, the papal

---

[66] Ed. Migne, PL 87 (Paris, 1863), cols. 145–98. See the summaries in Price, *The Acts of the Lateran Synod*, pp. 394–6.
[67] *Letters* 4, 5, and 6.
[68] Stefan Esders will be arguing in a forthcoming paper on 'Chindasvinth, the "Gothic Disease", and the Monothelete Crisis' that Clovis II in fact was much more in favour of the Lateran synod than his brother Sigibert III.
[69] See *Liber Pontificalis*, 1.2, 1.4. On Amandus' stay in Rome, see *Vita Amandi* 6–7, ed. B. Krusch, 'Vita Amandi episcopi I', MGH SRM 5 (Hanover and Leipzig, 1910), pp. 395–449, at p. 434.

sources did not expose too prominently potential oppositions, preferring instead to broadcast an image of consensus. Moreover, Pope Martin must have been aware of the emperor's displeasure when he accepted the papal nomination without waiting for the imperial approval,[70] or when he excluded the emperor from participating in the organisation of the synod of 649,[71] which was considered of ecumenical importance.[72] Although according to the pope the emperors were promoters of heresy, it must have been important to him not to unnecessarily emphasise such elements of discord. The emperor was a central and most important integrative figure, which was not only significant from a political perspective, but also from a religious point of view.[73] Demonstration of concord in the fight against heresy thus was certainly a more important aim than personal enmity or incrimination towards the respective emperor – even when the emperor had promoted the heresy himself.[74]

I have argued above that this is also the position that was largely adapted by the author in his digression. Assuming that he did have one of Martin's letters at hand raises further questions. Contrary to the papal epistles, the synodal acts and the *Liber Pontificalis*, mentioning men like Theodore of Pharan, Cyrus of Alexandria or Sergius, Pyrrhus and Paul of Constantinople,[75] the digression does not specifically assign blame to any individual for the establishment and spread of Monotheletism. It only refers to 'heresiarchs'. Did Audoin consciously neglect to mention them, maybe because he assumed that these names were superfluous in the context of his *Life*? Or did he not have them at hand? Even if the author was aware of the existence of Martin's letters and might have read them in 649/50, they were not necessarily available to him when he wrote his *Vita Eligii* three decades later. There is no evidence that proves

---

[70] Srutwa, 'The Exile and Death of Pope Martin I', p. 203.
[71] Scheibelreiter, 'Griechisches – lateinisches – fränkisches Christentum', p. 94. See also Caspar, 'Die Lateransynode', p. 135.
[72] Scheibelreiter, 'Griechisches – lateinisches – fränkisches Christentum', p. 96. See also C. Gantner, *Freunde Roms und Völker der Finsternis. Die päpstliche Konstruktion von Anderen im 8. und 9. Jahrhundert* (Vienna, 2014), p. 77. The synod was confirmed in Britain, see Bede, *Ecclesiastical History*, 4.17–18, ed. G. Spitzbart, *Venerabilis Bedae Historia ecclesiastica gentis anglorum*, 2nd edn (Darmstadt, 1982), pp. 366–74.
[73] See, for example, W. Ullmann, *Kurze Geschichte des Papsttums im Mittelalter* (Berlin, 1978), pp. 24–45 and pp. 53–8; D. M. Nicol, 'Byzantine Political Thought', in J. H. Burns (ed.), *The Cambridge History of Medieval Political Thought, c. 350–c. 1450*, 6th edn (Cambridge, 2007), pp. 51–82, especially pp. 63–71.
[74] Similarly, E. Rubery, 'Conflict or Collusion? Pope Martin I (649–54/5) and the Exarch Olympius in Rome After the Lateran Synod of 649', *Studia Patristica*, 52 (2012): 339–74.
[75] For example, Martin, *Epistula encyclica* 18; *Epistula Martini ad Amandum*; *Liber Pontificalis* 76.3; see also the version B and C of the *Life of Audoin*, Vacandard, *Vie de saint Ouen*, 74, n. 1; Beck, *Geschichte der orthodoxen Kirche*, pp. 54–62.

that Martin sent a personal invitation to Eligius, which means that the letter would have remained in royal possession until 680. It is also conceivable that the author did not remember their names, and, if indeed he wrote the digression more spontaneously in the presence of the unnamed Eastern clerk, he might have had no occasion to have a second look at Martin's letter before setting up his own report.

Conclusion

The present investigation has argued that the digression is an original part of the *Vita Eligii* rather than a later addition. It contains independent information that, all in all, appears authentic and corresponds well to what could be expected from a primarily oral testimony given by a traveller from the East.[76] Keeping this scenario in mind when reading the digression also helps to explain the shortcomings that have provoked suspicion of its fabrication. Although definite proof is obviously impossible to provide, it appears reasonable that the digression is a largely independent account based on an oral source with regard to Martin's fate. This thesis is backed not only by the lack of quotations or borrowings from other sources that would have been available to a later author or compiler but also by several pieces of information unknown from later sources. This includes the miraculous cure of a blind man, possibly in Crimea, and the author's insistence that Martin died a martyr, which is only vaguely alluded to in later sources. This independent mention of Martin's death in the far East noted in a Western source is an interesting indication of knowledge exchange that took place between these regions during the later seventh century.[77]

This does not mean that the digression had been composed without any knowledge of written sources. It betrays influence from several texts, among which some are still extant, like the encyclical or the synodal acts. Other letters are now lost, but with the epistle to Amandus we still have proof for a comparable text. Basic details such as the date of Martin's episcopacy are correct. What it lacks are the names of the prelates responsible for the Monothelete doctrine and information about Martin's trial in Constantinople or the place of his exile. These shortcomings, however, are neither unusual in view of the hagiographic nature of the text, nor in consideration of its dependence on a primarily oral source, as

---

[76] Srutwa, 'The Exile and Death of Pope Martin I', p. 208, suggests that the *Scholion sive Hypomnesticon*, PL 129, pp. 686–8 testifies for a second eyewitness in Cherson soon after Martin's death.

[77] See also Peeters, 'Une vie grecque', p. 250.

they mainly come about as a result of imprecision, not misinformation. It is interesting to note, however, that those details that can be traced back to Byzantium, like the miracle and Martin's death, can be mainly attributed to an oral source. This again matches well with the indication of the unnamed traveller. Although the testimony given by the digression appears rather independent, it is also interesting to note that the view given of the Byzantine emperor does not differ significantly from papal sources. If this is not the result of the author's reading of Martin's letters, this could also be explained by the fact that the traveller was a clerk himself and that he adhered to a papal view.

11 Perceptions of Rome and the Papacy in Late Merovingian Francia: The Cononian Recension of the *Liber Pontificalis*

Rosamond McKitterick

One of the peculiarities of the manuscript transmission of the Roman *Liber pontificalis*, the serial biography of the popes from St Peter to the end of the ninth century, is that most of the earliest copies of the text are Frankish and produced in the Carolingian period.[1] Apart from fragments in Naples, Turin and Verona, and the famous version of the entire text produced in Lucca c. 800 (Lucca, Biblioteca Feliniana 490),[2] the surviving eighth- and ninth-century codices containing full versions of the papal biographies up to the eighth century at least were copied in such Carolingian centres as Saint-Amand, Rheims, Tours, Cologne, Laon, Auxerre and Flavigny. A further peculiarity is that the extant manuscripts appear to witness to the episodic production and continuation of the *Liber pontificalis*, and its circulation in increasingly augmented form at different points in its history. These production episodes can be shown, as I have argued elsewhere, to correspond to particularly crucial moments in the history of the early medieval papacy.[3] That the reconstruction of such moments has to be from manuscripts copied from now-lost exemplars is an extra complication. Another, of course, is determining the motives for the copying and construction of codices containing the *Liber pontificalis* in the Frankish world. Such codices, therefore, may throw light both on the textual history of the *Liber pontificalis* itself, as well as on the context in

---

[1] *Liber pontificalis*, ed. L. Duchesne, *Le Liber pontificalis: Texte, Introduction et Commentaire*, 2 vols. (Paris, 1886–92, repr. 1955; hereafter Duchesne, *LP*.
[2] Verona, *Biblioteca Capitolare*, XXII (20) s.VI^{med}, *CLA*, III.490; Naples, Biblioteca Nazionale IV.A.8,(8 palimpsested folios) s.VII^{ex} *CLA* III. 403; Turin, Biblioteca Nazionale F.IV.18 (2 palimpsested folios), s.VIII/1, Hormisdas and John I, *CLA* Supplement, 1810; see also Alessandro Zironi, *Il Monasterio Longobardo di Bobbio: Croceva du uomini, manoscritti e culture* (Spoleto, 2004), pp. 135 and 164.
[3] L. Duchesne, *Etude sur le Liber pontificalis* (Paris, 1877); R. McKitterick, 'The Papacy and Byzantium in the Seventh- and Early Eighth-Century Sections of the *Liber Pontificalis*', *Papers of the British School at Rome*, 84 (2016): 241–73. On the later sections, see F. Bougard, 'Composition, diffusion et réception des parties tardives du *Liber pontificalis* romain (VIIIe–IXe siècles)', in F. Bougard and M. Sot (eds.), *Liber, gesta, histoire: Écrire l'histoire des évêques et des papes, de l'Antiquité au XXIe siècle* (Turnhout, 2009), pp. 127–52.

which the text was received and its contents digested in late Merovingian Francia. They may mirror contemporary Frankish perceptions of Rome and the history of the popes. They may also provide important evidence for the essential foundations laid in the Merovingian period for subsequent cultural developments and preoccupations in the early Carolingian period.

This paper therefore will focus on the content and implications of one codex, Paris BnF lat. 2123. The manuscript is usually dated to the late eighth or the early ninth century and contains on fols. 29v–52r a text headed: INCIPIT ORDO EPISCOPORUM ROMAE.[4] This text is actually an epitome of the *Liber pontificalis*, known as the 'Cononian epitome' or 'Cononian recension', for the simple reason that the entries up to Pope Conon (d. 687) are quite full. Thereafter, the entries from Stephen II to Hadrian I (d. 795) are simply short notes of the length of each pope's reign in years, months and days in order to document the succession. It is of particular interest that Pope Constantine II is included in this list, and the length of his reign is correctly given as one year. Other copies of the *Liber pontificalis* follow the decisions of the Synod of Rome in 769 and delete Constantine II from the succession record.[5]

Duchesne assumed that the full text of the original exemplar stopped at Conon, that is, the point at which an abridged version was made. It was then the later copyist of this abridged text in Paris, BnF lat. 2123 who added the names and reign dates of subsequent popes up to his own day. There is one other manuscript of the Cononian epitome, Verona, Biblioteca capitolare LII (50), with which to compare the Paris codex. Like Paris BnF lat. 2123, it is from the Burgundian region, again possibly Flavigny itself, and of a similar date. The Verona manuscript is written in a pre-Caroline minuscule described by E. A. Lowe as a 'curious type of minuscule in a transitional stage with use of uncial D N R and S'.[6] The manuscript appears to have reached Verona by the second quarter of the ninth century, for two notes in the hand of Pacificus (d. 846) on f. 266v have been identified.

Both manuscripts raise questions not only about the copying of the Cononian epitome but also about whether the actual redaction of this

---

[4] B. Bischoff, *Katalog der festländischen Handschriften des neunten Jahrhunderts (mit Ausnahme der wisigotischen)* (hereafter Bischoff, *Katalog*), Teil III, Padua–Zwickau (Wiesbaden, 2014), no. 4134, p. 62.

[5] I return to the possible significance of this inclusion briefly below. See also R. McKitterick, 'The *Damnatio Memoriae* of Pope Constantine II (767–768)', in R. Balzaretti, J. Barrow and P. Skinner (eds.), *Italy and Medieval Europe: Papers for Chris Wickham on the Occasion of his 65th Birthday* (Oxford, 2018), pp. 231–48.

[6] CLA IV.550.

version of the *Liber pontificalis* might have been made in Merovingian or even Carolingian Francia. If so, the Cononian epitome may be a witness to the early dissemination of the first version of the *Liber pontificalis* north of the Alps and adjustments made to the text thereafter. The text, and its codicological context in the Paris codex as a whole, therefore, merit further examination.[7]

The Cononian and Felician Epitomes and Their Place in the Compilation of the *Liber Pontificalis*

A fuller explanation of the Cononian epitome and how it fits into the current understanding of the process of the production and transmission of the *Liber pontificalis* may be helpful. First of all, the *Liber pontificalis* was undoubtedly composed in stages, and these can be set out schematically as follows:

> **LP I (1st redaction)** Surmised from the existence of the Felician and Cononian epitomes,[8] c. 530, Lives 1–56: Peter to Felix IV
> **LP I (2nd redaction)** c. 535 Lives 1–59/?60: Peter to Agapitus/ Silverius
> **LP IIA** Lives 60–71: Silverius to Boniface V
> **LP IIB** Lives 72–8: Honorius to Eugene I
> **LP IIC** Lives 79–81, 82–90: Adeodatus to Agatho; Leo II to Constantine I
> **LP III** Eighth-century Lives 91(2 versions), 92, 93, 94 (three versions), 95, 96, 97 cc. 1–44, 97 cc. 45 to end: Gregory II to Hadrian I
> **LP IV** Ninth-century Lives 98–112: Leo III; Eugenius to Stephen V.

Most versions of the *Liber pontificalis* stem from the second edition (LP I, 2nd redaction) produced no later than the 540s, possibly early in the pontificate of Silverius d. 537 or of Vigilius (537–55). The life of Vigilius itself was probably part of the seventh-century continuation (LP IIA above), though this remains both debated and debatable.[9] Scholars are so far agreed that both editions of the *Liber pontificalis* are post-514 and that it was completed by 540, but the context of production and the complex

---
[7] Duchesne, *LP*, I, p. lv. See also T. Mommsen, *Liber pontificalis, pars prior*, MGH Gesta Pontificum Romanorum I.1 (Berlin, 1898), p. lxxi.
[8] On Epitomes F and K, see *LP*, I, xlvix–lvii.
[9] I discuss these fully in McKitterick, 'The Papacy and Byzantium'.

of motives that governed the compilation of this remarkable narrative are disputed, with the Laurentian schism, the Acacian schism and the reorientation of Rome's self-perception and representation consequent on the Gothic wars of Justinian, all being invoked.[10] My own recent work has stressed the political agenda and historiographical context of the *Liber pontificalis*. I have argued that the text effectively Christianised the history of Rome and presented the popes as substitutes for the emperors. It did so by the simple device of presenting the history in the form of serial biography in the manner of the imperial histories and biographies by Suetonius and the author(s) of the *Historia Augusta*.[11] The next portion of the *Liber pontificalis* continued the themes already established. It was begun in the context of the dispute about Monotheletism and preparations for the Lateran synod of 649 and disseminated from Rome in the 680s as a triumphant vindication of the popes' championing of orthodoxy. This section (LP IIA and IIB) was further augmented up to the *Life of Pope Constantine I* (LP IIC) and disseminated early in the reign of Pope Gregory II.[12]

The early editions and versions of the *Liber pontificalis* are arguably local redactions reflecting local concerns or loyalties. An obvious example is the so-called Laurentian fragment that survives in a sixth-century manuscript in Verona.[13]

---

[10] Most recently, H. Geertman, 'Documenti, redattori e la formazione del testo del *Liber pontificalis*', in H. Geertman (ed.), *Il Liber pontificalis e la storia material* (Assen, 2003), pp. 267–84, repr. in H. Geertman, 'Hic fecit basilicam', in *Studi sul Liber pontificalis e gli edifice ecclesiastici di Roma da Silvestro a Silverio* (Leuven, 2004), pp. 149–68. See also H. Geertman, 'La genesi del *Liber pontificalis* romano: un processo di organizzazione della memoria', in F. Bougard and M. Sot (eds.), *Liber, gesta, histoire: Écrire l'histoire des évêques et des papes, de l'Antiquité au XXIe siècle* (Turnhout, 2009), pp. 37–108, K. Blair-Dixon, 'Memory and Authority in Sixth-Century Rome: The *Liber Pontificalis* and the *Collectio Avellana*', in K. Cooper and J. Hillner (eds.), *Religion, Dynasty, and Patronage in Early Christian Rome, 300–900* (Cambridge, 2007), pp. 59–76; R. McKitterick, 'La Place du *Liber Pontificalis* dans les genres historiographiques du haut moyen âge', in F. Bougard and M. Sot (eds.), *Liber, gesta, histoire: Écrire l'histoire des évêques et des papes de l'antiquité au XXe siècle* (Turnhout, 2009), pp. 23–36; R. McKitterick, 'Roman Texts and Roman History in the Early Middle Ages', in C. Bolgia, R. McKitterick and J. Osborne (eds.), *Rome Across Time and Space: Cultural Transmission and the Exchange of Ideas c. 400–1400* (Cambridge, 2011), pp. 19–34; L. Capo, *Il* Liber pontificalis, *I Longobardi e la nascità del dominio territoriale della chiesa Romana* (Spoleto, 2009), pp. 23–48; D. Mauskopf-Deliyannis, 'The Roman *Liber Pontificalis*, Papal Primacy, and the Acacian Schism', *Viator*, 45 (2014): 1–16.

[11] McKitterick, 'Roman Texts and Roman History'.

[12] For a useful summary, see Capo, *Liber pontificalis*, pp. 58–88; See also McKitterick, 'The Papacy and Byzantium'.

[13] *CLA* IV.4909. On the Laurentian fragment, see Blair Dixon, 'Memory and Authority'. I have yet to see this manuscript.

As well as the apparent local adaptations of the *Liber pontificalis*, there are other meagre indications of the dissemination from Rome of the *Liber pontificalis* from time to time, in that each of these early copies may indicate the text up to that point having formed the exemplar. One early manuscript witness to this is the Naples palimpsest, mentioned above, of the late seventh century or early eighth century in which the list of popes ends with Conon.[14] Apart from this there is the clear knowledge of the *Liber pontificalis*, whether in an abbreviated or full version, displayed by Gregory of Tours at the end of the sixth century in offering a brief history of the bishops of Tours in Book 10 of his *Historiae*, and by Bede with the many phrases he incorporates into his Chronicle in c. 66 of the *De temporum ratione*. These suggest, first of all, dissemination to Gaul by the end of the sixth century and, second, a version that went up to the beginning of the reign of Pope Gregory II (after 715) and had reached Northumbria by the early eighth century.[15]

It is in the context of local adaptations of the *Liber pontificalis*, therefore, that both the 'Cononian' and 'Felician' epitomes need to be considered. They have been regarded since Louis Duchesne's reconstruction of the different editions and production of the initial section of the *Liber pontificalis* (LP I, 1st redaction, see above) as witnesses to a first edition of the *Liber pontificalis*, even though both survive in late-eighth-century manuscripts.[16] Duchesne argued that the Felician epitome ended with the Life 56 of Felix IV (526–30). The Cononian continued beyond the reign of Felix IV. In Duchesne's opinion, it also abbreviated this first edition, but for the Lives after Felix IV abbreviated the standard text (LP I 1st and/or 2nd redaction, II A–C above) up to Life 85 of Conon.[17]

Obvious questions arise. Did the Cononian epitome simply use the Felician epitome before continuing, and does it therefore witness to a compiler making use of two different presentations of the text of the

---

[14] Naples Biblioteca Nazionale IV.A.8 (ff. 4C–7), *CLA* III. 403.

[15] See R. McKitterick, 'Rome and the Popes in the Construction of Institutional History and Identity in the Early Middle Ages: The Case of Leiden Universiteitsbibliotheek Scaliger MS 49', in O. Phelan and V. Carver (eds.), *Rome and Religion in the Medieval World: Studies in Honor of Thomas F. X. Noble* (Aldershot, 2014), pp. 207–34.

[16] L. Duchesne, 'L'Abrège Cononien', in *LP*, pp. liv–lvii, and pp. 47–113. For another edition of both the Felician and Cononian recensions, see Mommsen, *Le Liber Pontificalis*. His notes on the manuscripts are pp. xxi–lxxiv.

[17] Mommsen only printed the first part of these two epitomes in parallel columns, to *Life* 61 (Felix IV, 227–63), to facilitate comparison of the two, and without an *apparatus criticus*. Duchesne's edition adds the rest of the text from *Lives* 57–85 and the notes thereafter to *Life* 98, *LP*, I, pp. 108–13.

Liber pontificalis? The possible scenarios can be set out schematically as follows:

1.   **LP 1st edition** c. 530
                         /   \
Felician (to Felix IV *Life* 56 526–30)   Cononian (to Felix IV)
+ **LP II** epitomised

2. Felician + **LP 2nd edition** from *Life* 57 Boniface II (530–2) – *Life* 85 Conon (686–7) epitomised = Cononian recension

If the Felician and Cononian recensions are compared, the relationship between them appears to be very close, and the second scenario is usually thought to be the most likely.[18] Like the Cononian epitome, the Felician may be a Frankish creation, based on whatever was transmitted to Gaul from Rome in the brief period between 530 and 536, before the murder of Amalasuntha and the succession of Witigis precipitated the military intervention of Belisarius and the Byzantine armies. Gregory of Tours could have been inspired by the example of the *Liber pontificalis* either in its full first edition, its second, or in the Felician epitome, if the last named was indeed made in the sixth century.[19] The Felician epitome survives in two Frankish manuscripts: Paris BnF lat. 1451 from the Tours region is usually dated before 816 because the list of popes includes Hadrian I (d. 795) and the name of Leo III is added without the end of his reign being indicated.[20] It is apparently a direct copy of The Hague Museum Meermanno-Westreeanum, MS 10.B.4 of c. 800. We should heed the fact that there is no trace of the supposed first edition of the *Liber pontificalis* or of the Felician epitome thereof until the production of MS 10.B.4. I leave aside further consideration of both manuscripts and of the Felician epitome itself in response to the arguments of both Simperl and Varadi, for another occasion.[21]

---

[18] See Capo, *Il Liber pontificalis*, especially pp. 24–41.
[19] Since I wrote this suggestion, Matthias Simperl's excellent article has appeared: M. Simperl, 'Ein gallische *Liber Pontificalis*: Bermerkungen und Überlieferungsgeschichte des sogenannten Catalogus Felicianus', *Römische Quartalschrift*, 111 (2011): 272–87, which also offers a critique of A. Verardi, *La memoria legittimante: il* Liber Pontificalis *e la Chiesa di Roma del secolo VI* (Rome, 2016).
[20] *CLA* V (Paris, 1950), no. 528; and Bischoff, *Katalog*, Teil III, *Padua –Zwickau*, no. 4011.
[21] For older comments on the manuscripts, see E. K. Rand, *Studies in the Script of Tours*, vol. I: *A Survey of the Manuscripts of Tours* (Cambridge, MA, 1929), pl. 56 (no. 44), H. Mordek, *Bibliotheca capitularium regum Francorum manuscripta: Überlieferung und Traditionszusammenhang der fränkischen Herrschererlasse* (Munich, 1995), p. 413. L. Kéry, *Canonical Collections of the Early Middle Ages (ca. 400–1140): A Bibliographical Guide to the Manuscripts and Literature, History of Medieval Canon Law* (Washington, DC, 1999), pp. 45–6. See also Bischoff, *Katalog*, I Aachen-Lambach (Wiesbaden, 1998), no. 1442a. The *Collectio sancti Mauri* it contains was dated by F. Maassen, *Geschichte der Quellen und der Literatur des canonischen Rechts im Abendlande bis zum Ausgange des Mittelalters* (Graz, 1871) to s.VI/2 and located to southern Gaul.

The Cononian Epitome in BnF Lat. 2123: A Local Adaptation of the *Liber Pontificalis*

I turn now to the Cononian epitome in Paris, BnF lat. 2123. It is certainly a synopsis, but the process of selection and deletion of sections from the original text creates a very particular emphasis. It offers the chronological succession and brief historical notes on each pope in a manner that distils what this epitomiser apparently regarded as essential. In this respect, the omissions are as significant as what is retained, so it may be helpful to offer a brief indication of these here.

The supposed exchange of letters between Jerome and Damasus present in ninth-century copies of the *Liber pontificalis* is absent in the Paris manuscript, though it was included in the Verona version. The *Life of Peter* offers the biographical details about his career and his alleged writings, including the attribution to Peter of the writing up of Mark's Gospel and 'confirmation' of the Gospel texts. Oddly enough, the information that the apostle Andrew was Peter's brother is omitted, as are the provisions Peter made for his succession and the debates with Simon Magus. Most of the details for the next twenty-eight popes are preserved in full, up to the *Life of Marcellinus*. This includes the note of many of them receiving the 'martyr's crown'. For Marcellinus and Marcellus most of the other details are pared away to highlight their deaths during the persecutions of Diocletian.

It is particularly striking that the liturgical innovations credited to many of these early popes are retained. This has the effect of throwing into even greater relief the way in which the *Liber pontificalis* constructed a chronology for liturgical development in terms of feasts to be observed, the introduction of particular rituals and prayers, and the establishment of the clerical hierarchy and organisation in Rome. Thus, such details as Telesphorus' regulation of the Christmas Mass, and the singing of the *Gloria*, and Sixtus I's institution of the *Sanctus*, the other innovations and requirements allegedly made by Popes Alexander, Zephyrinus, Sixtus, Callistus, Felix, Eutyches and Miltiades are all retained. Similarly, the designation of Easter to be celebrated on a Sunday referred to in the Lives of Pius and Victor, and the contributions Popes Clement, Evaristus, Anicetus, Soter, Victor, Zephyrinus, Fabian, Lucius, Stephen I, Dionysius, Gaius and Leo I made to the organisation and conduct of the clergy in Rome are also preserved, though the specification of the ecclesiastical grades the full *Liber pontificalis* credits to Gaius is absent.

Julius's description of the range of documents that were the responsibility of the *primicerius notariorum* is not retained; only the requirement that no cleric should take part in any lawsuit in a public court is included. Writings attributed to the popes are also usually noted, such as Gelasius and Gregory. Details, such as the letter Pope Eleutherius allegedly received from the British king Lucius,[22] as well as the various efforts made during the reigns of Anteros and Fabian to ensure the *Gesta* of the martyrs and aspects of Rome's administration for the care of the martyrs' shrines are preserved. The curious story of the translation of St Peter's body from the catacomb on the Via Appia to a new resting place near the place of his execution, later the site of St Peter's basilica, and the parallel translation of Paul to the place on the Via Ostiense where he had been beheaded, later the site of San Paolo fuori le mura, is offered with almost nothing omitted.[23] Laurence's martyrdom in the time of Decius and the reign of Pope Sixtus II is included.

The absent details are consistently those that refer to the papal office. Thus, the designated succession from St Peter in the *Life of Clement* (Life 4) is omitted, even though the *Life of Linus* had highlighted his burial close to Peter. Clement's life also refers only to his martyrdom and the division of Rome into regions for better investigation of the *gesta* of the martyrs and does not include the elaborate paragraph reinforcing the apostolic succession though Linus and Cletus to Peter.[24]

The *Life of Silvester* is the longest in the early section of the *Liber pontificalis* and in the full edition is replete with lists of estates and precious ecclesiastical vessels and furniture donated to the new churches, all credited to Constantine's generosity. Given how much else is omitted by the compiler, a substantial amount was retained. The compiler omitted reference to Constantine's leprosy and persecution as well as the account of Silvester's own church, the attribution of the advice for a Synod of Rome to Constantine, and the reference to the reconciliation of an Arian who had had a change of heart. It included the biographical section about Silvester himself in Chapters 5–8 but most of the copious detail given in the list of gifts in Chapters 9–32 is left out. This has the effect of retaining the narrative thread, for the next part of the story

---

[22] *Life* 14, Duchesne, *LP*, I, p. 136. On the comment, see Duchesne, *LP*, p. xcii. This letter was one of the details Bede repeated in his *Historia ecclesiastica*, which led to significant claims for the new Protestant church of England in the course of the Reformation: see F. Heal, 'What Can King Lucius Do for You? The Reformation and the Early British Church', *The English Historical Review*, 120 (2005): 593–614, and extravagant support in the sixteenth century for the antiquity of the University of Cambridge, allegedly granted a privilege by Pope Eleutherius in the second century: John Caius, *De antiquitate Cantebrigiensis academiae libri duo*, 2nd edn (London, 1574), p. 76.

[23] Rosamond McKitterick, 'The Representation of Old Saint Peter's Basilica in the *Liber Pontificalis*', in R. McKitterick, J. Osborne, C. Richardson and J. Story (eds.), *Old St Peter's Rome* (Cambridge 2013), pp. 95–118.

[24] Compare Duchesne, *LP*, I, Life, 4 c. 3, p. 123.

preserved is that of Silvester baptising Constantine. The story is rounded out with the formulaic ending of Silvester's ordinations and his burial in the cemetery of Priscilla on the Via Salaria. Of great interest is the inclusion of the note in Chapter 16 that the basilica of St Peter was built at Silvester's request. This is otherwise recorded only in the 'E' group of *Liber pontificalis* manuscripts, none of which is earlier than the eleventh century and all of which are Italian and thought to represent a version of the text emanating from Rome.[25] The compiler apparently decided not to include the list of the estates granted to the churches of St Peter and St Paul but did retain the lists of endowments in the form of supplies of nard oil, balsam, papyrus, storax and spices, as well as the church in the Sessorian palace and the wood of the Cross, whose discovery had been signalled in Life 32 of Eusebius. From Chapter 23 in Life 34 onwards, however, this Life simply lists Constantine's foundations by reference to the saints, introduced as 'many churches dedicated to saints: Agnes, Laurence, Marcellinus and Petrus (where Constantine's mother was buried) and St John the Baptist'.

From the *Life of Mark* (Life 35) onwards, the epitomiser usually omitted all the details about the gifts and buildings in Rome; exceptions are the *Life of Sixtus III* and Hilarus. For the most part, the epitomiser concentrated on providing a compressed narrative. The editorial work is particularly evident in the *Life of Felix II* (Life 38), which is systematic in omitting a succession of phrases, such as the details of death. It states simply that he built a basilica on the Via Aurelia and was buried there and notes his ordinations. Nevertheless, there is a curious inconsistency in the details picked out. Sometimes the work of the epitomiser has the appearance of inept summary. In the truncating of the *Life of Siricius* (Life 40), for example, only the phrases concerning the decree he broadcast about the church, the necessity for episcopal consecration without specifying the *fermentum*, and the reconciliation of a heretic by the laying on of hands are preserved.

Although these later lives in the *Liber pontificalis* generally report less about liturgical innovation, it is nevertheless the details relating to the various facets of the episcopal ministry that continue to attract the attention of the epitomiser. John III's Life refers to the restoration of the cemeteries of the martyrs and that he completed the church of the apostles Peter and James. Most of the short *Life of Gregory I* is reproduced. Thus, the list of his writings, the mission to the English and the mention of his establishing his own house as a monastery are all

---

[25] One early manuscript from ninth-century Farfa is now lost: Duchesne, *LP*, I, p. 176.

preserved. So too are the records of Gregory's addition to the canon of the mass, his devotion to the shrines of St Peter and St Paul and his dedication of the church of the Goths in the *subura* to St Agatha. A further significant detail contributed is the method for electing a successor to the pope that comprises most of the *Life of Boniface III*, complemented by the further provision in the *Life of Benedict III*, saying that the person elected to the apostolic see should be ordained immediately without the need to wait for the imperial mandate. Boniface IV's Life, with the momentous conversion of the Pantheon into a church dedicated to St Mary and his conversion of his own house into a monastery is almost completely reproduced. The *Life of Deusdedit* refers to the 'second mass' among the clergy. The *Life of Boniface V* specifies the conduct of baptism by deacons and subdeacons in the Lateran. Donus's biography records his honouring of various ranks of the clergy with preferments. All these serve to augment the reader's sense of the bishop of Rome's care for his clergy.

A number of the Lives address further topics. The *Life of Honorius*, for example, also includes the detail about the pope's attention to the decoration of the shrine of St Peter and his decree concerning the Saturday litany from St Apollinaris to St Peter, his building of Sant'Agnese fuori le mura and St Pancratii are briefly mentioned among the 'many others he built'. The epitomiser also seems anxious to maintain the reader's understanding of the virtues of the pope, with praise offered for the special virtues of Severinus, John IV, Theodore, Agatho, Leo II and Benedict III in particular. Papal attention to ensuring grain supply within the city and to the welfare of the citizens is also noted.

Features of various popes are somewhat haphazardly thrown into relief. In the *Life of Liberius* (Life 37), the epitome omits Liberius' construction of a basilica but includes all of the story of his support of the emperor, Constantius. For Damasus (Life 39), the focus is on his attention to the burial place of St Paul and St Peter and the fact that he was acquitted of the charges against him. For Boniface I (Life 44), the account of the rival election of Eulalius is retained but drastically summarised so that the imperial intervention is not mentioned, only the reference to the synod that deposed Eulalius and sent him to be bishop of the city of *Nephisana* (the city's name is actually a detail not included in the full version of the *Liber pontificalis*). Boniface's prohibitions of a slave becoming a cleric and women handling the consecrated pall or the incense form the bulk of the entry. The account of Leo I's career states merely that he revived the church of Rome in the aftermath of the Vandal war and that he made a statement about the orthodox faith, now kept in the archive. It alludes briefly to the heresies of Eutyches and Nestorius, to Leo's role as legate to the Huns, and to the foundation of a monastery at St Peter's. The *Life of Hormisdas* also differs markedly from that in the Felician epitome, in omitting the detail about Hormisdas's dealings with Byzantium. On the other hand, the lively account of the disputed election of Laurentius recounted in the *Life of Symmachus* is largely preserved. Lest one think the epitomiser is not interested in events in Byzantium, the *Life of John I* (Life 55) retains the detail about John's reception in Constantinople, with the emperor abasing himself before John and John crowning the emperor. It also records the death of John in Theodoric's prison and the death of Theodoric himself. Interestingly, the epitome adds the claim that Theodoric ordered the consecration of Felix IV (Life 56), a phrase that is absent in the full version of the *Liber pontificalis*.

Whether another, and later, link with Rome is reflected in the seventh-century sections of this epitome is not obvious. The degree to which information about Byzantium is included, for example, is capricious. Thus, the extract from the *Life of John II* (Life 58) merely reports the emperor's letter protesting his orthodoxy, and the *Life of Agapetus* (535–6) (Life 59) is boiled down to Agapetus' membership of the legation sent to Constantinople, where he died. Although Silverius' nomination by Belisarius is retained, the *Life of Vigilius* omits the extensive passages about Belisarius, and the passage makes it seem as if Vigilius were simply persecuted by the Byzantine emperor. Similarly, Narses' role in Pelagius I's remorseful litany (Life 62) is simply not reported, and John III's biography (Life 63) omits all the narrative about Narses. The negative emphasis about the visit of the Emperor Constans to Rome and his depredations there as well as in Calabria and Sicily, and the murder of Constans in his bath, are all maintained. Most of the detail concerning the problematic relationship between the popes and Ravenna, notably the disgraceful depredations of Maurice the *cartularius*, is omitted. But the *Life of Conon* retains the abolition of imperial taxes in Bruttium and Lucania.

The retention of references to doctrinal dispute is generally notably meagre, not just in Leo's Life but also in the Lives of popes concerned in the Acacian schism, namely, Hilary, Simplicius, Felix III, Gelasius, and Anastasius. The Lateran synod summoned by Pope Martin is simply mentioned in passing. An important exception to the otherwise brief allusions to doctrine is the full account of the Council in Trullo from the *Life of Agatho*. Further, the epitomiser added the note from the *Life of Leo II* about his receipt of the *Acta* of the sixth ecumenical council, and Justinian II's eventual undertaking to uphold these same *Acta* recorded in the *Life of Conon*.[26]

---

[26] See, however, further below, pp. 180–2.

The inclusion of details about local Roman politics is only occasional and is mostly in the context of disputed papal elections. In the *Life of Boniface II* (530–2) (Life 57) there is a marked emphasis on the disputed election of Dioscorus and Boniface's own repudiation of his attempt to appoint his own successor. John V's election is recorded in full, and that he had been sent to Constantinople as a deacon by Agatho. The epitomiser chose to preserve too the account of Conon's archdeacon's plot with the exarch, John of Ravenna, to secure the papal throne. The turmoil of the disputed election of Conon's successor Sergius, however, is absent, and it is at this point, presumably, that the exemplar's text stopped.

This epitome, therefore, is markedly interested in the *Liber pontificalis*'s presentation of the liturgy and the role of the pope as a bishop. The marginal summary headings inserted in the manuscript, apparently by the scribe or a contemporary reader, furthermore, reinforce these themes. They are strikingly consistent in what they choose to highlight in a way that serves to emphasise still further the way the epitomiser has chosen to concentrate the message of the original text of the *Liber pontificalis*. Thus, the reference in the *Life of Alexander* (Life 7) to the blessed water being sprinkled in dwellings of the people, receives a marginal summary heading about blessing of the water (fol. 30v). In the *Life of Sixtus I* (Life 8), the liturgical phrase about the consecrated objects only being touched by ministers is singled out with a marginal note (fol. 31r), as is the introduction of the Mass on Christmas night under Telesphorus (fol. 31r), and the requirement that Easter be on a Sunday associated with Pius (fol. 31v). In the *Life of Eleutherius*, the marginal heading also draws attention to this pope's decree about food to be shunned (fol. 32r), while for Lucius the clause signalled is the decree about the number of deacons and priests to be with the bishop (fol. 34v). For Pope Stephen I, it is the clause about consecrated vestments (fol. 35r). Attention is also drawn to the creation of parishes and dioceses by Pope Dionysius (fol. 35r). The most important thing to note in the *Life of Eusebius* is that it was during his reign that the True Cross was discovered (fol. 36v),[27] and for Silvester (fol. 37r) it is the specification that the bishop should consecrate the chrism that is noted. For Mark, the marginal note highlights the *pallium* and consecration of the bishop of Rome by the bishop of Ostia (fol. 39r). For Innocent I, the marginal note emphasises his decree that a fast should be observed on Saturdays (fol. 40v). A similar interest

---

[27] See E. Ó Carragáin, 'Interactions between Liturgy and Politics in Old St Peter's, 670–741', in R. McKitterick, J. Osborne, J. Story and C. Richardson (eds.), *Old St Peter's, Rome* (Cambridge, 2013), pp. 177–89, at pp. 184–8.

is indicated for the *Life of Celestine*, with the marginal note drawing attention to Celestine's decree concerning the antiphonal singing of the Psalms in the mass (fol. 41r) Next to the *Life of Sixtus III*, the heading draws attention to his exoneration by the synod (fol. 41r). For the most part, therefore, these headings highlight the liturgical changes and papal attention to the organisation of the clergy.

The characteristics of the Cononian epitome in Paris BnF lat. 2123 can therefore be summarised as follows: the epitome includes a notice about each pope from St Peter to Conon, but the narrative generally retains particular elements of the original full text. First of all, every life repeats the formulaic references to where each pope was from, his father and the enumeration of his ordinations. He or she altered the *natus* describing the origin of each pope to *nationem* throughout the text. Second, the epitomiser cut the long descriptions of gifts and the details about the churches of Rome. Generally too, he or she omitted details about martyrs though there are, as we have seen, some important exceptions to this. Such cuts serve to highlight the details concerning innovations in the liturgy and the papal role in determining the clerical and ecclesiastical grades. These elements, especially those concerning the liturgy, are further emphasised by the annotator or corrector who added notes in the margin, most of which summarise the liturgical comments.

The Cononian epitome, therefore, presents more than a slimmed-down version of the *Liber pontificalis*. It preserves to some degree the emphasis on apostolic succession from St Peter that is to be found in the full text. Above all, it epitomises the text in such a way as to emphasise the history of the liturgy and the popes' role therein to concentrate attention on the pope's role as a bishop and on papal orthodoxy.

The question remains as to whether this epitome was something used and reproduced by the compiler of Paris BnF lat. 2123 or whether the compiler himself was the epitomiser. That is, is this epitome to be dated to the late seventh or to the late eighth century? That the compiler of Paris BnF lat 2123 lacked a text of the *Liber pontificalis* that extended much beyond Conon's reign seems clear. The indications that the text was corrected from an exemplar, such as those on fol. 42v correcting *presbyter* to *episcopus*, and the nonsensical suggested expansion of the Y of Ygenus (Hyginus: Life 10) misread as 'V' to Vigilius on fol. 31r, could be from either the epitome or the full text. In the list of popes after Conon recording the length of reigns (and from John VI the length of the vacancy) there is a slightly longer reference in the *Life of Constantine I* (Life 90) to dating by the Victorine cycle that is not in any other recension of the *Liber pontificalis*. This seems to indicate that the epitome did indeed end with Conon and that the rest was added by the compiler. Given the interest in liturgical matters, moreover, it does not seem likely that the epitomiser would have omitted either the innovation of the *Agnus Dei* made by Sergius I or Stephen II's inauguration of Saturday litanies and restoration of the daytime office, had he had access to the later section of the *Liber pontificalis* that provides such details. The meagre details about each pope after Conon could conceivably have been derived from a simple list rather than a full text of the *Liber pontificalis*.

A tentative conclusion, therefore, is that the *Liber pontificalis* with the seventh-century portion (up to Conon d. 685) had reached Gaul where this abbreviated version, preserved in Paris, BnF lat. 2123, was produced. The epitome could be interpreted, furthermore, as a response to the papal determination to disseminate this representation of its past and its leading position within the Western church as well as its championship of orthodoxy. This culminated in the statement of the orthodox faith concerning the person and natures of Christ articulated at the Council of Trullo in the *Life of Agatho* and preserved by the epitomiser more or less in full. At this point, the remaining contents of the codex and what these suggest about its place and context of production may be helpful.

Paris, BnF Lat. 2123: A Frankish Compilation from the Diocese of Autun?

The production of Paris BnF lat. 2123 is to be dated between 795 and 816, though the script would suggest closer to 795.[28] The list of popes on fol. 52r includes the pontificate of Hadrian I, but the supplementary list of popes from Leo III onwards was clearly added in the early eleventh century, during the reign of Pope John XVII (d. 1003). The codex comprises 156 leaves (219 × 160 mm) written in two columns of 26–31 lines. The script itself, by more than one hand, is certainly a very early form of Caroline minuscule with headings in a confident uncial and enlarged coloured (green and ochre) initials. Bernhard Bischoff identified the scribes as from Flavigny and dated the manuscript to the early ninth century, prompted by the list of popes already mentioned, to after the death of Hadrian (d. 795).[29] Bischoff also noted that the script of 'fols. 45ff' (actually fols. 44v ff.) is identical to that of 's-Gravenhage (Den Haag) Koninklijke Bibliotheek MS 130 E 15, fols. 8v–24v. This is a codex containing, among other texts, a copy of Jerome, *Liber quaestionum Hebraicarum in Genesim* and pseudo-Jerome *Expositio IV evangeliorum*; it

---

[28] Bischoff, *Katalog*, III, no. 4134, p. 62.
[29] Bischoff, *Katalog*, III, p. 62, no. 4134, p. 62.

has also been located to Flavigny.³⁰ Another close association with the Paris codex can be found in the second copy of the Cononian recension, extant in Verona Biblioteca Capitolare LII already mentioned above.³¹ According to the description in *Codices Latini Antiquiores*, Verona LII (50) assembles a rather different assortment of texts to accompany the epitome, such as *Homiliae* and the Rule of St Benedict. Although the current Verona codex appears to be chunky, with 277 leaves, it is of a modest size – 225 × 104 mm (185 × 79 mm) – and layout (22–8 long lines). The new series of quire marks on fol. 100 and another series marked with letters on fol. 226 suggest, however, that three different sets of quires have been bound together into one codex at a later stage of its history. Given the uncertainty as to when this might have happened, Verona LII has less to reveal as a composite manuscript than Paris, BnF lat. 2123. Paris, BnF lat. 2123 in comparison was arguably designed as a coherent collection, or so its contents would suggest. Alice Rio, indeed, has characterised the codex as an 'ecclesiastical reference book'.³² The contents are as follows, in summary form for the purposes of this chapter, for all the other sections of the codex in addition to the epitome of the *Liber pontificalis* considered in this chapter and the Formulary known as the *Collectio Flaviniacenis* on fols. 105v–153v, which has been studied in detail by Warren Brown,³³ require further work.³⁴

Paris, BnF lat. 2123 Contents

1r–v First Council of Ephesus, Chapters 1–4 with the declaration on original sin.

2r–5v Lateran Council, 649. The extract is apparently from two different and incomplete versions (because of the loss of leaves between fols. 1v and 2r and between 5v and 6r) of

---

[30] Bischoff, *Katalog*, I, no. 1436, p. 300.
[31] Above, p. 166. See also Bischoff *Katalog*, III, no. 7043, p. 467, but referring to *CLA* IV, no. 550, so no change of mind from the s.VIII/IX date is indicated.
[32] A. Rio, *Legal Practice and the Written Word in the Early Middle Ages: Frankish Formulae, c. 500–1000* (Cambridge, 2009), pp. 96–9 and 252.
[33] Warren C. Brown, 'Laypeople and Documents in Frankish Formulary Collections', in W. C. Brown, M. Costambeys, M. Innes and A. J. Kosto (eds.), *Documentary Culture and the Laity in the Early Middle Ages* (Cambridge, 2013), pp. 125–51, especially pp. 143–9. See also W. C. Brown, 'The *Gesta Municipalia* and the Public Validation of Documents in the Frankish Europe', in Brown et al (eds.), *Documentary Culture and the Laity*, pp. 95–124, at pp. 108–12.
[34] For a brief but inadequate description, see P. Lauer, *Catalogue général des manuscrits Latins 2 (nos. 1439–2692)* (Paris, 1940), p. 329, reproduced in Rio, *Legal Practice*. It includes further details concerning the availability in 1940 of editions of the various texts. Here I have adapted the description to say more about the contents.

the final 'canons' or 'anathemas' of the Synod at the Fifth Session of the Lateran synod of 649, defining and professing the orthodox and Chalcedonian definition of the Trinity and specially the person and natures of Christ.[35]

6r–17r *Incipit dogma id est doctrina uel definitio de fide* (Gennadius of Marseilles, *De ecclesiasticis dogmatibus*). Gennadius' tract on Christian doctrine, with expository comments on the creed, is regarded as 'semi-Pelagian' in character. It also contains the statement of the single rather than double procession of the Holy Spirit. Yet it was very widely disseminated in the early Middle Ages and is to be found in a great many early Carolingian manuscripts. In this copy it is not attributed to any author.[36] The text lacks the first seventeen chapter headings in the table of contents because of the missing leaves in the first quire before fol. 6r, and organises the text into fifty-one chapters.

17r–24v Described by Lauer in 1940 as 'Ps-Augustine's *Sermones de Symbolo*', this section of the codex in fact comprises a number of different commentaries on the Creed, and thus statements of orthodoxy centring on the persons of the Trinity, listed by Susan Keefe as her hand list of Commentaries on the Creed as nos. 58, 254 (which includes the text of the Apostle's Creed with each verse attributed to a different apostle), 309, 386 (often added to Pope Leo I's Letter 165 as *testimonia de fide*.[37]

24v–29r Leo the Great, Ep. 165, that is, as noted by Lauer, Leo's detailed statement of the doctrine of the Incarnation. This section, however, also includes texts attributed by the scribe to Hilary of Poitiers, Ambrose of Milan, John of Constantinople and others on the same topic.

29v–51r The Cononian Epitome of the *Liber pontificalis* (discussed above).

---

[35] See the discussion by R. Price, P. Booth and C. Cubitt, *The Acts of the Lateran Synod of 649* (Liverpool, 2014), pp. 300–1, and also pp. 376–83 especially p. 376, note 471.

[36] See C. H. Turner, 'The *Liber ecclesiasticorum dogmatum* Attributed to Gennadius of Marseilles', *Journal of Theological Studies*, 7 (1905): 78–99; and C. H. Turner, 'The *Liber ecclesiasticorum dogmatum*: Supplenda to J.T.S. vii 78–99', *Journal of Theological Studies*, 8 (1906): 103–14.

[37] S. Keefe, *A Catalogue of Works Pertaining to the Explanation of the Creed in Carolingian Manuscripts* (Turnhout, 2012), no. 58, pp. 83–4 (probably Gallican, s.v.); no. 254, pp. 148–9; no. 309, p. 169; no. 386: pp. 194–5.

52v–54v Polemius Silvius's *Laterculus* (*nomina provinciarum*) with *Notitia Galliarum* comprising ancient lists of the Gallic provinces, in which the province of Lyon heads the list of the provinces of Gaul after a brief enumeration of the number of ecclesiastical provinces in Italy (there is no reference to Rome). After Gaul, the rest of the known world's provinces are listed, and on fol. 54r, the scribe sets out all the ecclesiastical provinces of Gaul once more. Lyons is cited as the metropolitan at the beginning, and many of the suffragan dioceses within them, quite clearly before the Carolingian reorganisation.[38]

54v–64r In the manuscript, this section is labelled as Gregory the Great's *canones*, recorded by Lauer as identified by Schmitz as Theodore of Canterbury's *Dicta* but now better known as the *Canones Gregorii* version of the *Iudicia Theodori*.[39]

64v–104v *Decreta maiorum* (= *Collectio canonum Herovalliana*). There is some prefatory material, not recorded in the Paris catalogue, succeeded by a list of contents (fol. 65v) headed *canones grecorum*. This starts with a short account of the ecumenical councils up to Chalcedon, explicitly referring to Isidore of Seville as a source, drawing mostly verbatim from Isidore, *Etymologiae* VI.16 (*De canonibus Conciliorum*) (fols. 66r–67r), but extending it to provide essentially a summary history of the councils and their decisions about doctrine (fols. 67r–68v). The seventy-one chapter headings of the *Collectio canonum Herovalliana* are then set out (fols. 68v–70r). This 'systematic' collection of excerpts from ecumenical and Gallican conciliar records (that is, organised thematically rather than chronologically) is thought to have been compiled in the late Merovingian period, that is, late seventh or early eighth century. Kery, following Mordek, has noted that the *Herovalliana* in Paris, BnF lat. 2123 on which Maassen relied for his description of contents is actually an 'extensive excerpt'

---

[38] See T. Mommsen (ed.), *MGH Auctores Antiquissimi* IX (Berlin, 1892), pp. 512, 524, 535–42, 570, 575, 584–612.

[39] H. J. Schmitz, *Die Bussbücher und das kanonische Bussverfahren nach handschriftlichen Quellen* 2 (Düsseldorf, 1898), pp. 522–42. See the discussions by T. Charles-Edwards, 'The Penitential of Theodore and the Iudicia Theodori', in M. Lapidge (ed.), *Archbishop Theodore* (Cambridge, 1995), pp 141–74; and the website ASCL Iudicia Theodori entry constructed and transcription for other manuscripts by M. Elliot, available at http://individual.utoronto.ca/michaelelliot/manuscripts/texts/transcriptions/pthg.pdf (accessed 24 February 2016).

from the *Collectio*. Mordek was slightly misleading in this respect for the compiler has apparently abridged some of the individual *capitula* rather than omitting any of the topics.[40] Another copy of the *Herovalliana* is apparently in BnF lat. 3848B sVIII/IX fols. 70r–178v, also from Flavigny.[41] In the light of the other contents of the Paris BnF lat. 2123 codex, it is significant that this compilation starts with the statement about the Catholic faith and the creed, defines the canon of scripture and the biblical apocrypha and then inserts the decree *De libris recipiendis et non recipiendis* usually attributed to Gelasius (fols. 73v–76r).[42] The *Herovalliana* also includes the requirements for the convening of synods, episcopal ordination, definitions of episcopal jurisdiction and particular laws relating to the clergy, social crimes such as incest, adultery, homicide, clauses on the mass, relics, oratories, altars, baptism, the observance of fasts and Easter, the necessity for preaching, tithe, care of widows and the poor, organisation of parishes, clerical behaviour and hierarchy, abbots and monks, liturgical feasts, penance, the position of the Jews, burial of the dead and observance of the canons.

105r Council of Carthage, 418 Chapter 1. This, like the extract from the Council of Ephesus at the beginning of the compilation, concerns original sin. This page also includes a brief account of the ages of the world up to Charlemagne.

105v–153v *Collectio Flaviniacensis*.[43] This collection of legal formulae appears to have been compiled and adapted partly from formulae from the *Formularies* of Marculf and Tours and partly from material relating to the monastery of Saints Praeiectus and Peter of Flavigny, notably the donation and confirmation charters of the original donor of the abbey,

---

[40] L. Kéry, *Canonical Collections of the Early Middle Ages (ca. 400–1140): A Bibliographical Guide to the Manuscripts and Literature* (Washington, DC, 1999), pp. 54–5. Another Burgundian copy is Paris, BnF lat. 4281, fols. 1r–63v s.IX¼; Mordek thought that the version in this manuscript came closest to the original form of the *Herovalliana*. Another version is Ivrea, *Biblioteca Capitolare* XLII s.IX1/4 from northern Francia, fol. 57r–111v. This also contains an incomplete (!) copy of Bede's *De temporum ratione*, computistic texts: see Bischoff, *Katalog*, I, no. 1569 and H. Mordek, *Kirchenrecht und Reform im Frankenreich. Die Collectio Vetus Gallica Kanonessammlung des fränkischen Gallien. Collectio frisingensis secunda* (Berlin, 1975), pp. 114–17.

[41] *CLA* V, no. 555 and compare *CLA* Suppl. p. 54.

[42] E. von Dobschütz, *Das Decretum Gelasianum de libris recipiendis et non recipiendis in kritischem Text* (Leipzig, 1912). For discussion, see R. McKitterick, *The Carolingians and the Written Word* (Cambridge, 1989), pp. 200–5.

[43] MGH Formulae, ed. K. Zeumer, pp. 471–92.

Wideradus, from 717 and 719.[44] Consequently it has been identified as the Flavigny Formulary and dated to the second half of the eighth century. The charter formulae it contains concern property (sales, inheritance, benefices, episcopal rights and privileges), but the collection also includes extracts from letters relating to the ordination of bishops between Emperor Constantine and his mother, Helena, and from Pope Julius to the clergy and people of Alexandria, and part of a speech credited to the Emperor Valentinian II on the election of Ambrose as Bishop of Milan. All these are excerpted from the *Acta Sancti Silvestri* and the *Historia ecclesiastica tripartita* of Cassiodorus-Epiphanius. The collection also contains a selection of twelve sets of opening letters from bishops to a variety of recipients, two of which, as Brown has shown, were extracted from Eusebius-Rufinus' *Historia ecclesiastica*. These are unique to the Flavigny collection.[45]

153v–156v Isidore of Seville, *Etymologiae*, XVI, 25–6 and II, 10. The former extract comprises Isidore's catalogue of weights and measures. The latter extract is Isidore's famous discussion of law with definitions of *lex, constitutio, edictum* and *mos*.

The entire contents of this codex, therefore, are consistent with the themes highlighted in the Cononian recension. The emphasis on doctrine and on episcopal function is particularly striking, with many apparently unique presentations of the history of the councils and guidance to orthodox doctrine. In its codicological context, the Cononian recension effectively provides the historical and specifically Roman and Western framework, within which the statements the Eastern church councils as well as the definitions of the bishops' diverse responsibilities, and texts to assist a bishop in the discharge of these responsibilities, are to be understood. Each separately appears to be the product of late Merovingian ecclesiastical preoccupations and reception of earlier Christian historical, doctrinal and didactic texts from southern Gaul, Italy and Rome, and the eastern Mediterranean. Is it then possible to determine whether

---

[44] C. Brittain Bouchard (ed.), *The Cartulary of Flavigny 717–1113* (Cambridge, MA, 1991), charters 1 and 2, pp. 19–30 and compare charters 57 and 58, pp. 135–44 and K. Zeumer, MGH Formulae, pp 476–7 (no. 8): *Ad testamentum faciendum*, and pp. 480–1, no. 43: *Qui monasterio in proprio edificat, qualiter cartam faciat*. See also U. Nonn, 'Merowingische Testamente: Studien zum Fortleben einer römischen Urkundenform im Frankenreich', *Archiv für Diplomatik*, 18 (1972): 1–129.

[45] Brown, 'Lay People and Documents', and compare P. Depreux, 'La Tradition manuscrite des "Formules de Tours" et la diffusion des modèles d'actes aux VIIIe et IXe siècles', *Annales de Bretagne et des pays de l'Ouest*, 111 (2004): 55–71, at pp. 61–3.

this distinctive compilation is a late Merovingian creation as a whole or whether it is rather a case of an early Carolingian scribe taking advantage and seeing the potential of assembling a set of very useful locally produced late Merovingian texts? Here the context of the production of the manuscript itself, and the clear association with Flavigny in the diocese of Autun, may provide some clues.

The Flavigny–Autun Context

Most germane to the context in which Paris BnF lat 2123 appears to have been produced is the notable energy with which scribes, compilers and highly creative liturgists contributed to the liturgy and canon law in the diocese of Autun in the later seventh and the eighth centuries. The manuscripts attesting to this creative liturgical activity at Autun comprise, first of all, the set of episcopal benedictions now in Munich, Bayerische Staatsbibliothek Clm 6430. These were apparently copied between 811 and 836 from an exemplar from Saint Symphorien of Autun, possibly first compiled between 760 and 785. Yet they are linked by distinctive language to the *Missale gothicum* (Vat reg. lat. 317), also probably to be located to Autun at the end of the seventh century.[46] Deshusses also located the compilation of the eighth-century Gelasian sacramentary to Flavigny c. 760 and posited an Autun assembly of texts, such as the *Missale gallicanum vetus* of the late seventh century incorporated into the eighth-century Gelasian sacramentary.[47] Deshusses then went on to suggest a sequence of liturgical texts produced at Flavigny in the middle of the eighth century, including the Benedictions and the *Missale gallicanum vetus* (Vat. reg. pal. lat. 493). The activity in canon law is attested not only by the *Collectio Herovalliana* discussed above but also the famous *Collectio vetus gallica* on which it drew, compiled in the archdiocese of Lyon at the beginning of the seventh century.[48] Further knowledge and witnesses to the intellectual and cultural resources in the diocese of Autun can be assembled on palaeographical grounds, for the distinctive script of the Cononian recension in the Verona manuscript is also to be observed in a

---

[46] J. Deshusses, 'Le Bénédictionnaire gallican du VIIIe siècle', *Ephemerides Liturgicae*, 67 (1963): 167–87; E. Rose (ed.), *Missale gothicum: e codice Vaticano Reginensi latino 317 dictum* (Turnhout, 2005); and Y. Hen, *The Royal Patronage of Liturgy in Frankish Gaul to the Death of Charles the Bald (877)* (London, 2011), pp. 21–41.

[47] See also B. Moreton, 'A Patronal Festival? St Praiectus and the Eighth-Century Gelasian Sacramentary', *Journal of Theological Studies*, 27 (1976): 370–80 and Hen, *The Royal Patronage of Liturgy*, especially pp. 57–61.

[48] Mordek, *Kirchenrecht und Reform*. See also G. I. Halfond, *Archaeology of Frankish Church Councils, AD 511–768* (Leiden, 2010).

number of other codices, all from the later eighth century, many now in the Bibliothèque municipale, Autun.[49] Earlier books from Italy survive in palimpsested codices. These books were apparently written in the same Burgundian centre, probably Flavigny, that had, as we have seen, access to major patristic works as well as scripture, canon law and history.[50]

The charters of Flavigny, moreover, reflect how securely the monastery, dedicated to Saints Praiectus and Peter, was anchored from its foundation by Wideradus in 717 on land given by the Merovingian king, Theuderic III (673–90), in the local community within the diocese of Autun. The confirmation charter of 719 that committed the community to observance of the Benedictine rule, moreover, was witnessed by no less a person than Moderannus, bishop of Autun.[51] The monastery also very soon came under Carolingian patronage, even before Pippin III became king.[52] Thereafter, Manasses, abbot from 755 to 787, for example, attended Pippin III's council of Attigny in 760/2, and in 775 the monastery received from Charlemagne a grant of freedom from a great variety of tolls. After Adalbert and Zacho had held office briefly (791–5 and 795–802), Alcuin was made abbot while also abbot of Tours. Apollinaris, abbot from 802, received the abbacy from Charlemagne, and, like Alcuin, held other abbacies as well, notably Saint-Benigne de Dijon.

Conclusions

Autun was a suffragan bishopric within the archdiocese of Lyon, and Lyon was one of the provinces or sees present at the Synod of Rome in 769, and therefore its bishop was among those selected by the young Carolingian rulers Carloman and Charlemagne to attend the synod.[53]

---

[49] G. Lanoë (ed.), 'Histoire de la bibliothèque d'Autun', *Regards sur les Manuscrits d'Autun VIe-XVIIIe siècle* (Autun, 1995), pp. 13–25.

[50] G. Lanoë, 'Les Plus Anciens Manuscrits d'Autun', in *Manuscrits d'Autun*, pp. 41–55. See also J. Marilier, 'Le Scriptorium de l'abbaye de Flavigny au VIIIe siècle', *Annales de Borgogne* 55 (1983): 30–3.

[51] Constance Brittain Bouchard (ed.), *The Cartulary of Flavigny, 717–1113* (Cambridge MA, 1991), charters 1 and 2 (the foundation charters), 3 (Pippin's grant to Gayroinus, the document recording which was conveyed in a pair of ivory tablets, *mittimus tibi istas tabulas eburneas ad honorem, Sancti Petri et Sancti Praiecti*), 4 (Charlemagne's charter issued 3 May 775); 5 (Louis the Pious's reference to Apollinaris as abbot), pp. 19–37.

[52] Brittain Bouchard, *The Cartulary of Flavigny*, nos. 57 and 58, pp. 135–44. Compare K. Zeumer, MGH Formulae, pp. 476–7 (no. 8): *Ad testamentum faciendum*, and pp. 480–1, no. 43: *Qui monasterio in proprio edificat, qualiter cartam faciat*. See also U. Nonn, 'Merowingische Testamente: Studien zum Fortleben einer römischen Urkundenform im Frankenreich', *Archiv für Diplomatik*, 18 (1972): 1–129.

[53] R. McKitterick, *Charlemagne: The Formation of a European Identity* (Cambridge, 2008), pp. 299–301.

Nevertheless, the regnal year of Pope Constantine II is retained in the papal list in Paris BnF lat. 2123, otherwise expunged from the record in other Frankish manuscripts of the *Liber pontificalis*.[54] Whether the compiler of Paris BnF lat. 2123 expressed his own disaffection from the decision of the Synod of Rome in this way, that of his bishop of Autun (Hiddo or Reginald) and/or of his metropolitan Ado of Lyon remains uncertain. Whether this might be one indication of the maintenance of a certain degree of independence, or of different cultural, intellectual or liturgical preoccupations from those of other Frankish sees in the later eighth century, also requires further investigation. As far as the evidence for Paris BnF lat. 2123 is concerned, however, the Cononian recension of the *Liber pontificalis* certainly mirrors the intensely creative reception of older texts from the Merovingian past and from Italy in Francia, and how these were digested and presented in a new context deemed to be the most useful for use within the diocese of Autun, if not Flavigny itself. That is to say, the separate contents of the codex as well as the total assembly thereof accord with the period of intense liturgical and legal creativity associated with Autun in the last years of the seventh century and first few decades of the eighth century. It represents a crucial piece of evidence for the way in which the later Merovingian achievements and a particular presentation of the Roman and Christian past, extending to the Greek councils convened in Asia Minor, were subsequently assimilated in the early Carolingian period and given a new lease of life.

---

[54] Rosamond McKitterick, 'The *damnatio memoriae* of Pope Constantine II (767–768)', in R. Balzaretti, J. Barrow and P. Skinner (eds.), *Italy and Medieval Europe: Papers for Chris Wickham on the Occasion of his 65th birthday* (Oxford, 2018), pp. 231–48.

Part IV

Religious and Cultural Exchange

12 Relocation to the West: The Relic of the True Cross in Poitiers

Galit Noga-Banai

Radegund (Radegundis, c. 525–87), a Thuringian princess and wife of King Chlothar I, was a woman who maintained social contacts with leading figures in the church and with the secular reigning classes.[1] In what was perhaps her most significant achievement, she was the recipient of the relic of the True Cross for the monastery she founded in Poitiers. The relic of the Cross was given to her by none other than the imperial couple of the Byzantine Empire, Justin II (565–74) and his wife Sophia, after Radegund sent an envoy to Constantinople in 568.[2] Radegund received the relic in 569 in one of the earliest recorded translations of the relic of the True Cross to the western end of the world.[3] It was most

---

[1] Radegund's biography and deeds were recorded by Venantius Fortunatus, an Italian poet who later became bishop of Poitiers, and by the nun Baudonivia. Venantius Fortunatus, *Vita sanctae Radegundis*, liber I, c.2, and Baudonivia, *Vita sanctae Radegundis*, liber II, c.16, MGH SRM 2, ed. B. Krusch (Hanover, 1888), pp. 364–77, 378–95; J. A. McNamara, J. E. Halborg and E. Gordon Whatley (eds.), *Sainted Women of the Dark Ages* (Durham, NC, 1992), pp. 70–103. An English translation of Baudonivia's work may be found also in M. Thiébaux, *The Writings of Medieval Women*, 2nd ed. (London and New York, 1994), pp. 106–20. Much has been written on Radegund and references will be given accordingly in the notes. Most recently, see J. Schulenburg, 'Female Religious as Collector of Relics, Finding Sacrality and Power in the "Ordinary"', in M. Frassetto, J. Hosler and M. Gabriele (eds.), *Where Heaven and Earth Meet: Essays on Medieval Europe in Honor of Daniel F. Callahan* (Leiden, 2014), pp. 152–77; L. Jones, 'Perceptions of Byzantium: Radegund of Poitiers and Relics of the True Cross', in Lynn Jones (ed.), *Byzantine Images and Their Afterlives: Essays in Honor of Annemarie Weyl Carr* (Farnham, 2014), pp. 105–24; E. T. Dailey, 'Misremembering St Radegund's Foundation of Sainte-Croix in Poitiers', in H. Brandt, B. Pohl, W. M. Sprague and L. K. Hörl (eds.), *Erfahren, Erzählen, Erinnern: Narrativ Konstruktionen von Gedächtnis und Generation in Antike und Mittelalter* (Bamberg, 2012), pp. 117–40; E. T. Dailey, *Queens, Consorts, Concubines. Gregory of Tours and Women of the Merovingian Elite* (Leiden, 2015), pp. 68–72.

[2] Radegund may have heard about a recent addition of a relic of the True Cross to the collection of relics in Constantinople, translated in 566 from Apamea. See W. Brandes, 'Thüringer/Thüringerinnen in byzantinischen Quellen', in H. Castritius, D. Geuenich, M. Werner and T. Fischer (eds.), *Die Frühzeit der Thüringer: Archäologie, Sprache, Geschichte* (Berlin, 2009), pp. 302–5, suggesting that Radegund got word of this through her cousin Amalafrid, who was *magister militum* in Constantinople at that time.

[3] For the translation of the relic of the Cross from Constantinople to Poitiers, see Gregory of Tours, *Libri Historiarum*, IX, 40, MGH, SRM 1, ed. B. Krusch (Hanover, 1885), pp. 396–7 (cf. X, 15, 425–6), trans. L. Thorpe, *The History of the Franks* (London,

likely the occasion of the *adventus* of the relic of the Cross to Poitiers for which the poet (and later bishop of Poitiers) Venantius Fortunatus composed the two hymns adopted by the church: the *Vexilla Regis* and the *Pange Lingua*.[4]

We have no records of the original reliquary received by Radegund. A hint appears in her biography, composed between 609 and 614 by Baudonivia, a nun in the convent at Poitiers. Baudonivia reports that Radegund 'got what she had prayed for: that she might glory in having the blessed wood of the Lord's cross enshrined in gold and gems and many relics of the saints that had been kept in the East living in that one place'.[5] Gregory of Tours mentions a chest (*arca*) when describing the search for the abbess, Leubevera, following the revolt of the nuns several years after the deaths of Radegund and the first abbess, Agnes. The men sent by the princess and nun Chlothild 'went into the oratory and found her [Leubevera] lying on the ground before the chest (*arca*) of the Holy Cross'.[6] In another place Gregory specifies that it was a silver chest (*arca argentea*).[7]

While the reliquary's form and appearance are unclear, there is no doubt that the Byzantine imperial patrons (Justin II and Sophia) and its established Constantinopolitan source authenticated the relics received by Radegund and contributed to its reputation as well as to

---

1974), p. 530; Gregory of Tours, *De Gloria Martyrum*, 5, ed. B. Krusch, MGH, SRM 1,2 (Hanover, 1885), 489–90, trans. R. Van Dam, *Glory of the Martyrs* (Liverpool, 1988), p. 22; Baudonivia, *Vita sanctae Radegundis*, 16, 377–95; Venantus Fortunatus, *Ad Justinum et Sophiam Augustos*, vv. 59–91, MGH, Auct. Antiqu., ed. F. Leo (Berlin, 1881) IV, 1, p. 277; A. Frolow, *La Relique de la Vraie Croix* (Paris, 1961), pp. 179–80; Yvonne Labande-Mailfert, 'Les Débuts de Sainte-Croix', in Y. Labande-Mailfert (ed.), *Histoire de l'abbaye Sainte-Croix de Poitiers: quatorze siècles de vie monastique* (Poitiers, 1986), pp. 21–116, esp. the first chapter, which deals with the founding of the monastery. An earlier recorded *translatio* of a relic of the Cross to Gaul is reported in a letter that Paulinus of Nola sent to his friend Sulpicius Severus in 404. Paulinus of Nola, Ep.31.1 (CSEL, 29.268); D. E. Trout, *Paulinus of Nola, Life, Letters and Poems* (Berkeley, CA, 1999), p. 151.

[4] Venantius Fortunatus, *Opera poetica*, ed. F. Leo, MGH, AA, IV/1 (Berlin, 1881), pp. 34–5; *Vexila regis Prodeunt and Pange lingua gloriosi, ed Bulst. Hymni latini antiquissimi* LXXV (Heidelberg, 1956); for English trans., see L. van Tongeren, *Exaltation of the Cross: Towards the Origins of the Feast of the Cross and the Meaning of the Cross in Early Medieval Liturgy* (Leuven, 2000), pp. 236–45.

[5] Baudonivia, *VR*, II, 16, trans. McNamara et al., *Sainted Women*, p. 97. More recently, on Baudonivia's description of Radegund with an emphasis on her collection of relics, see M. A. Mayeski, *Women at the Table: Three Medieval Theologians* (Collegeville, MN, 2004), esp. pp. 127–36.

[6] '*introeuntes in oraturium, repperierunt iacentem super humum ante arcam sanctae crucis*', Gregory of Tours, *Historia Francorum* 10:15, trans. in Thorpe's *The History of the Franks*, p. 567; for a narration of the rebellion in the convent, see Dailey, *Queens, Consorts, Concubine*, pp. 64–79.

[7] Gregory of Tours, *De Gloria Martyrum*, 5, trans. Van Dam, *Glory of the Martyrs*, p. 22.

her community. Baudonivia does not bother to identify the saints' relics that accompanied the relic of the True Cross on the *translatio* from the Byzantine capital;[8] they paled in comparison to the most precious relic in Radegund's collection. The relics of the saints might have had a similar reputed biography. They were translated under imperial patronage, and their source could have been, for instance, the relics kept in the church of the Holy Apostles in Constantinople, founded by Constantine, completed by his son Constantius and rebuilt by Justinian I.[9] But, as is clear from Baudonivia's description of Radegund's pertinacious efforts to obtain a relic of the Cross, no item could compete with it: 'After having collected many relics of the saints, had it been possible, she would have petitioned the Lord himself in the seat of His Majesty to dwell here in sight of all.' The relic was evidence of Christ's presence in the monastery. According to Baudonivia's description of its arrival, the holy fragment brought Poitiers into direct contact with the most important *locus sanctus*, signifying Christ's triumph over death: 'And the wood where once hung the salvation of the world came with a congregation of saints to the city of Poitiers ... ' Afterwards, Baudonivia conveys its ability to work miracles: 'Anyone who comes in faith, whatever the infirmity that binds them, goes away healed by the virtue of the Holy Cross.'[10]

After the arrival of the precious relic in 569, the monastery formerly dedicated to Mary was rededicated to the Holy Cross.[11] A special chapel was built within it for the Holy Cross, and the relic was venerated every Wednesday and Friday.[12] We do not know much about the liturgy in Poitiers specifically, but we may assume that the feasts associated with the cult of the Cross were celebrated with great enthusiasm. The *inventio* of the Cross is listed under the third of May in the Merovingian Martyrologium Hieronymianum: *In Hierusalem inventio sanctae crucis Domini nostri Iesu Christi ab Helena regina in monte Golgotha post passionem Domini anno ducentesimo trigesimo tertio regnante Constantino imperatore.*[13]

---

[8] Y. Hen, *Culture and Religion in Merovingian Gaul, AD 481–751* (Leiden, 1995), pp. 100–2.
[9] C. Mango, 'Constantine's Mausoleum and the Translation of Relics', *Byzantinische Zeitschrift*, 83 (1990): 51–62, and 'Addendum', 434.
[10] Baudonivia, *VR*, II, 16, trans. McNamara et al., *Sainted Women*, p. 97.
[11] Labande-Mailfert, 'Les Débuts de Sainte-Croix', pp. 33–41; Cynthia Hahn, 'Collector and Saint: Radegund and Devotion to the Relic of the True Cross', *Word and Image*, 22 (2006): 268–74, n. 3.
[12] Gregory of Tours, *De Gloria Martyrum*, 5, trans. Van Dam, *Glory of the Martyrs*, p. 22.
[13] G. B. de Rossi and L. Duchesne (eds.), *Martyrologium Hieronymianum, Acta Sanctorum Novembris*, t.2/1 (Brussels, 1894), p. 227; The Gothic missal lists a mass for the invention of the cross in May, and the Old Gelasian Sacramentary records a celebration of the holiday in May. H. M. Bannister (ed.), *'Missale Gothicum'*, *a Gallican Sacramentary ms. Vatican. Regin. Lat. 317* (London, 1917), p. 92; H. A. Wilson (ed.), *The Gelasian*

In Jerusalem, the Finding of the Cross was celebrated together with the inauguration of the church on the 13th and 14th of September. The May celebration reflects the celebration of the Recovery of the Cross in Rome (probably as early as the fifth century; certainly by the sixth). It is then reasonable to assume that the Roman feasts of the Cross were adopted in Gaul, possibly already during Radegund's time in Poitiers.

As I intend to demonstrate, although little is known about the portable reliquary of the Cross in Poitiers or about the local liturgy related to it, we may have just enough evidence to analyse the structure of the chapel of the Cross. I will suggest that Radegund could have been the inspired architect behind what may be seen as a monumental reliquary of the Cross, visually reconstructing the biography of the reputed relic and the ideal and admirable exemplar of its royal patron. My point of departure will be Baudonivia's description of Radegund's efforts to obtain the relic of the Cross; from there, I will turn to the question of the chapel's possible model and its consequent potential contribution to the field of architectural history.

Thus like Saint Helena, imbued with wisdom, full of the fear of God, glorious with good works, she eagerly sought to salute the wood ... When she had found it, she clapped both hands. When she recognized that it was truly the Lord's cross that had raised the dead to life with its touch, she knelt on the ground adoring the Lord and said: 'In truth, you are Christ, the Son of God, who came into the world and with your precious blood you have redeemed your own people, whom you created, from captivity.' What Helena did in Oriental lands, Radegund the blessed did in Gaul![14]

Studying Baudonivia's comparison of Radegund with Helena, E. Gordon Whatley has noted that she freely combines isolated episodes and contexts of the *Inventio sanctae Crucis* into her description of Helena, based on intimate knowledge and possibly liturgical texts.[15] For instance, the clapping of the hands and the kneeling on the ground in

---

Sacramentary, Liber sacramentorum Romanae Ecclesiae (Oxford, 1894), p. 172. For the various celebrations of the cross, see Van Tongeren, *Exaltation of the Cross*.

[14] 'Ut sicut beata Helena sapientia inbuta, timore Dei plena, bonis operibus gloriosa lignum salutare, ubi precium mundi pro nostra salute appensum fuerat ... ita ut invento ambabus manibus plauderet et, in terra genu flexo, Dominum adoraret, ubi ipsam in mortuo suscitato dominicam crucem suprapositam agnovit, dicens: "In veritate tu es Christus, filius Dei, qui in mundum venisti tuosque captivos, quos creasti, precioso sanguine redemisti." Quod fecit illa (Helena) in Orientali patria, hoc fecit beata Radegundis in Gallia'; Baudonivia, *VR*, II, 16; the English translation is in McNamara et al., *Sainted Women*, p. 97.

[15] E. Gordon Whatley, 'An Early Literary Quotation from the *Inventio S. Crucis*: A Note on Baudonivia's *Vita Radegundis* (BHL 7049)', *Analecta Bollandiana*, 111 (1993): 81–91.

adoration after the resuscitation miracle are both attributed to Judas in the Legend of the True Cross.[16] Baudonivia's adaptation of elements from the *Inventio* story naturally suggests itself; Empress Helena's reputation had great potential as a forerunner of Queen Radegund's efforts to obtain a relic of the True Cross for her monastery in Poitiers. The emperor's mother found the True Cross in Jerusalem and was responsible for its *translatio* to Constantinople.[17] Whether the relic Radegund received from the imperial couple was a chip of the relic sent by Helena to Constantinople or had another origin, Helena was believed to be the ultimate source for the relic which eventually arrived in Poitiers thanks to another noble woman: Radegund.

Helena was not always acknowledged as the one who found the True Cross. When the legend of the *Inventio* was composed – probably in Jerusalem sometime during the second half of the fourth century, under the episcopate of Cyril – credit was given to Constantine.[18] In 395, the Legend of the True Cross was included in Ambrose's funeral oration for the Emperor Theodosius; there, Helena was recognised as the finder.[19] By the sixth century, as we are also told by Baudonivia, the primary tradition crowned Helena as the main protagonist; various versions of it existed. Baudonivia's emphasis of Helena's piety is understood with her declaration, '*Quod fecit illa (Helena) in Orientali patria, hoc fecit beata Radegundis in Gallia*'. Radegund's devotion to God is in direct line with

---

[16] Whatley, 'Early Literary Quotation', p. 88; Baudonivia may hint once more towards the Legend of the Finding of the True Cross when she makes an analogy between the bishop of Poitiers, refusing to receive the relic in his city, and the role of the Jews, which is not part of our story. Inserting the Jew in the context of the negative bishop may recall the Jews who refused to assist Helena in finding the True Cross. See McNamara et al., *Sainted Women*, p. 98, n. 118.

[17] It is not certain where the relic was kept in Constantinople. See H. A. Klein, 'Sacred Relics and Imperial Ceremonies at the Great Palace of Constantinople', in F. A. Bauer (ed.), *Visualisierungen von Herrschaft*, Frühmittelalterliche Residenzen – Gestalt und Zeremoniell, Istanbul: Ege Yayınlar. 2006, pp. 79–99, esp. pp. 81–2, 89.

[18] Cyril of Jerusalem, *Epist. ad Const.* 3; Cyril of Jerusalem, *Catech.* 4.10, 10.19, 13.4. See S. Heid, 'Der Ursprung der Helena legende im Pilgerbetrieb Jerusalems', *Jahrbuch für Antike und Christentum*, 32 (1989): 41–71; S. Borgehammar, *How the Holy Cross was Found: From Event to Medieval Legend* (Stockholm, 1991), pp. 87–92; H. J. W. Drijvers and J. W. Drijvers, *The Finding of the True Cross: The Judas Kyriakos Legend in Syriac – Introduction, Text and Translation* (Leiden, 1997), p. 13; B. Baert, *A Heritage of Holy Wood: The Legend of the True Cross in Text and Image* (Leiden, 2004), pp. 15–53; J. W. Drijvers, 'Helena Augusta, The Cross and the Myth: Some New Reflections', *Millennium*, 8 (2011): 23–4.

[19] Ambrose, *De obitu Theodosii*, c.40–7, ed. O. Faller, CSEL 73 (Vienna, 1955), pp. 393–6; for all sources, versions, and chronology, see J. W. Drijvers, *Helena Augusta: The Mother of Constantine the Great and the Legend of Her Finding of the True Cross* (Leiden, 1992), pp. 95–180; Drijvers, 'Helena Augusta. The Cross and the Myth'; Borgehammar, *How the Holy Cross Was Found*, pp. 60–6.

the pious first Christian empress who became a saint.[20] Gregory of Tours compares the two noble women as well 'in both merit and faith'.[21] In addition to the biographical details and past narrative tradition related to the Cross, Baudonivia's comparison of Radegund with Helena may have a formative element. I intend to take Helena's reputation a step further, suggesting that the analogy could benefit the monumental dimension by linking the chapel in Poitiers with the shrine for the Holy Cross in Rome, strongly associated with Helena.

Excavations at the site of Sainte-Croix in Poitiers were conducted by François Eygun in 1962. He reconstructed a small chapel dating to the Merovingian period. It is composed of wide walls (0.50 m) enclosing a 5.5 m space. The walls end on the eastern side with an apse (Fig. 12.1). Inside the chapel, various fragments of decorative mosaic were found, including an inscription, 'O CRUX A[VE]', which, although added later in the Middle Ages, helps to identify the church as the chapel of the Holy Cross. Behind the apse, and attached to it, there was a small exterior rectangular room (1.90 × 1.80 m) with an opening on its southern side.[22] This was most likely the oratory described by Gregory of Tours on the same occasion when he mentions the chest (*arca*) of the Holy Cross.[23]

It was not often that relics were enshrined in a small room behind the apse. The plan of Sainte-Croix, then, was exceptional in Gaul. For instance, the basilica of St Martin in Tours, a church not far from Poitiers and closely associated with Radegund, seems to have had an atrium behind the apse. As suggested by Werner Jacobsen, the pilgrims wishing to venerate St Martin could see his tomb by looking towards the altar

---

[20] For Helena as model of medieval queenship, see J. A. McNamara, 'Imitatio Helenae: Sainthood as an Attribute of Queenship in the Early Middle Ages', in S. Sticca (ed.), *Saints: Studies in Hagiography* (Binghamton, NY, 1996), pp. 51–80; in his thanksgiving poem to the imperial couple in Constantinople, for sending the generous sacred gift to Radegund, Venantius Fortunatus compared the Byzantine empress Sophia to Helena; see his *Ad Justinum et Sophiam Augustos*, vv. 59–91, 277; A. Cameron, 'The Early Religious Policies of Justin II', *Studies in Church History*, 13 (1976): 51–67, esp. pp. 55–67; I. Moreira, 'Provisatrix Optima: St Radegund of Poitiers' Relic Petitions to the East', *Journal of Medieval History*, 19 (1993): 285–305, esp. pp. 300–1.

[21] '*et merito et fide Helenae conparanda regina Radegundis*', Gregory of Tours, *De Gloria Martyrum*, 5, trans. Van Dam, *Glory of the Martyrs*, p. 22.

[22] F. Eygun, 'Circonscription de Poitiers', *Gallia*, 21 (1963): 433–84, esp. pp. 469–73, Fig. 49; Labande-Mailfert, 'Les Débuts de Sainte-Croix', p. 70, Fig. 2. For a different version of the plan, leaving the room behind the apse open towards the eastern side, see S. Ristow, 'Gräber der merowingerzeitlichen Elite in und bei Kirchen', in E. Wamers and P. Périn (eds.), *Königinnen der Merowinger* (Regensburg, 2012), pp. 59–76, esp. p. 71. I thank Sebastian Ristow for responding to my queries and for his generosity regarding the pictures of the place as seen today.

[23] See above, n. 6.

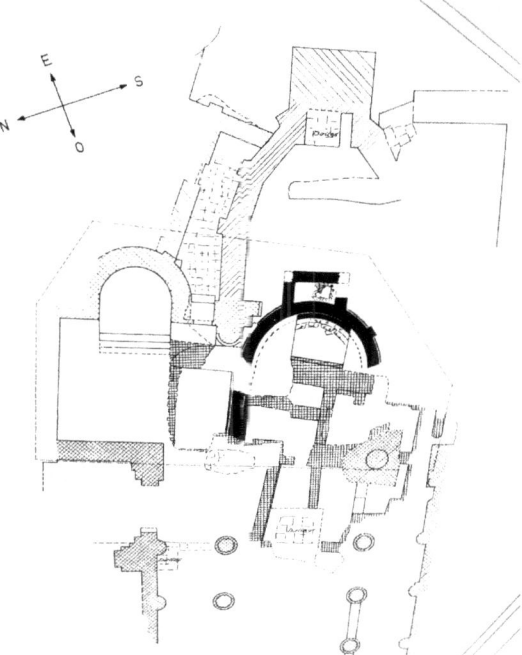

Figure 12.1 Plan of the Chapel of the Holy Cross in Poitiers, after François Eygun.

of the basilica through an opening in the wall. The tomb was located between the hemisphere wall of the apse and the altar, thus sharing the same space.[24] Alternative spatial relations included a tomb chamber below the altar, known especially from cemetery churches in Rome, and a chamber adjacent to the church.[25] Layouts vary, but to the best of my knowledge, there is no other example in late antique Gaul in which relics

---

[24] The church in Tours was rebuilt around 470 by Martin's successor, Bishop Perpetuus, who dug up Martin's sarcophagus and transported it to the apse of the new church, where the saint was reburied behind the altar. Gregory of Tours describes a large memorial basilica where the tomb of Martin was located behind the altar upon which a great marble stone was set, probably to enable the observance of the tomb from a distance; Gregory of Tours, *LH*, 2.14, 2.15. Perhaps a similar arrangement existed in the sixth-century church at Saint-Maurice d'Agaune, where it is possible that the tomb of St Maurice was placed inside the apse. This follows W. Jacobsen, 'Saints' Tombs in Frankish Church Architecture', *Speculum*, 72 (1997): 1107–43, esp. pp. 1108–10 with plans.

[25] Jacobsen, 'Saints' Tombs in Frankish Church Architecture'.

of a saint or a tomb were placed within a chamber behind the apse wall.[26] The uncommon space behind the apse may be the result of a special plan to enshrine the relic of the Cross. Based on comparisons with two other churches that contained the same relic, the Holy Sepulchre complex in Jerusalem and Sta. Croce in Rome, I would like to suggest that the chamber could visually and monumentally contextualise the relic with its own history and architectural group affiliation.

Egeria, the (Spanish?) nun who visited Jerusalem in the 380s, describes the Jerusalemite liturgy she experienced during her pilgrimage to the holy places in her itinerary. On the sixth day of the Great Week before Easter, for instance, she elaborates on the placement of the bishop's chair on Golgotha behind the Cross; people file past one by one to touch the holy wood and kiss it.[27] She is overwhelmed by the crowd filling the 'very spacious and beautiful courtyard between the Cross and the Anastasis'.[28] Later in the day, she writes, 'After the dismissal Before the Cross, they go directly in to the Great Church, the Martyrium, and do what is usual during this week between three o'clock and evening. After the dismissal they leave the Martyrium for the Anastasis where, once inside, they read the Gospel passage'.[29] Clearly there are three foci within the complex: the altar in the basilica, the Cross at Golgotha at the southern corner of the inner atrium, and the Sepulchre at the Rotunda of the Anastasis (Figure 12.2).[30] The inner atrium was located between the basilica and the rotunda. At its southern corner, Golgotha was closer to the altar within the basilica than to the tomb. In fact, Golgotha was located behind the southern curve of the basilica's apse. The two were separated by the apse's wall. This spatial relationship may have been reproduced in Rome as early as the fourth century.

A member of the Constantinian family, probably Constantine himself, was quite likely responsible for positioning the relic of the True Cross in the church of Sta. Croce in Gerusalemme, within the complex of the Sessorian palace (Fig. 12.3).[31] The palace was most probably the place

---

[26] Jacobsen, 'Saints' Tombs in Frankish Church Architecture', pp. 1126–9; for Merovingian architecture, see W. Jacobsen, L. Schaefer and H. R. Sennhauser, *Vorromanische Kirchenbauten: Katalog der Denkmäler bis zum Ausgang der Ottonen* (Munich, 1991).

[27] *Egeria Itiner.*, 37.1–2; trans. in J. Wilkinson, *Egeria's Travel to the Holy Land* (Jerusalem, 1981), pp. 136–7.

[28] *Egeria Itiner.*, 37.4; trans. in Wilkinson, *Egeria's Travel*, p. 137.

[29] *Egeria Itiner.*, 37.8; trans. in Wilkinson, *Egeria's Travel*, p. 138.

[30] For the possibility that a cross was erected on Golgotha as early as the fourth century, see S. Heid, *Kreuz-Jerusalem-Kosmos: Aspekte frühchristlicher Staurologie* (Münster, 2001), p. 230.

[31] The *Liber Pontificalis* attributes the foundation of the church to Constantine: 'Eodem tempore fecit Constantinus Augustus basilicam in palatio Sessorianum, ubi etiam de ligno sanctae Crucis domini nostri Iesu Christi posuit et in auro et gemmis conclusit,

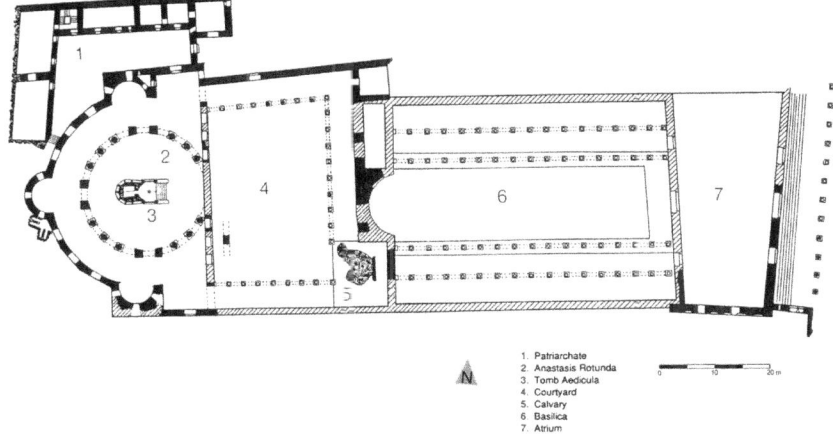

Figure 12.2 Plan of the Holy Sepulchre Church in Jerusalem, after Father Virgilio Corbo.

where the emperor's mother, Helena, resided prior to her journey to Palestine; in fact, she was buried on the same Sessorian territory.[32] The imperial architects, whether of Constantine or his son Constantius, used an existing third-century hall, 39 m long, 25 m wide, and 22 m high, within the palace complex. They added an apse on the south-east wall and divided the interior into three bays by means of transverse arches. Two original adjoining rooms, on the east, were preserved behind the apse, connected to the church by a corridor along the rounded wall. The remodelled church was open to the public; thus, the further room was probably a baptistery.[33] The nearer room, behind the apse wall, became

ubi et nomen ecclesiae dedicavit, quae cognominatur usque in hodiernum diem Hierusalem.' T. Mommsen (ed.), *Liber Pontificalis*, MGH Gest. Pont. Rom.I (Berlin, 1898), p. 34 c. 22; R. Krautheimer, *Corpus Basilicarum Christianorum Romae* I (Vatican City, 1937), pp. 165–95; R. Krautheimer, *Rome: Profile of a City, 312–1308* (Princeton NJ, 2000) p. 24. The description of the church follows S. de Blaauw, 'Jerusalem in Rome and the Cult of the Cross', in R. L. Colella and R. Krautheimer (eds.), *Pratum Romanum: Richard Krautheimer zum 100. Geburtstag* (Wiesbaden, 1997), pp. 55–73; S. de Blaauw, 'Gerusalemme a Roma e il culto della Croce', in R. Cassanelli and E. Stolfi (eds.), *Gerusalemme a Roma, la Basilica di Santa Croce e le reliquie della Passione* (Rome, 2012), pp. 27–39; S. de Blaauw, 'Translations of the Sacred City between Jerusalem and Rome', in J. Goudeau, M. Verhoeven and W. Weijers (eds.), *The Imagined and Real Jerusalem in Art and Architecture* (Leiden, 2014), pp. 136–66; H. Brandenburg, *Ancient Churches of Rome from the Fourth to the Seventh Century* (Turnhout, 2005), pp. 103–8.

[32] De Blaauw, 'Jerusalem in Rome', p. 60; Drijvers, 'Helena Augusta, The Cross and the Myth', p. 143; for Helena's mausoleum, see J. J. Rasch, *Das Mausoleum der Kaiserin Helena in Rom und der 'Tempio della Tosse' in Tivoli* (Mainz, 1998).

[33] R. Krautheimer, *Three Christian Capitals: Topography and Politics* (Berkeley, CA, 1983), p. 23, believed that the church was for the imperial family's private use. This view has

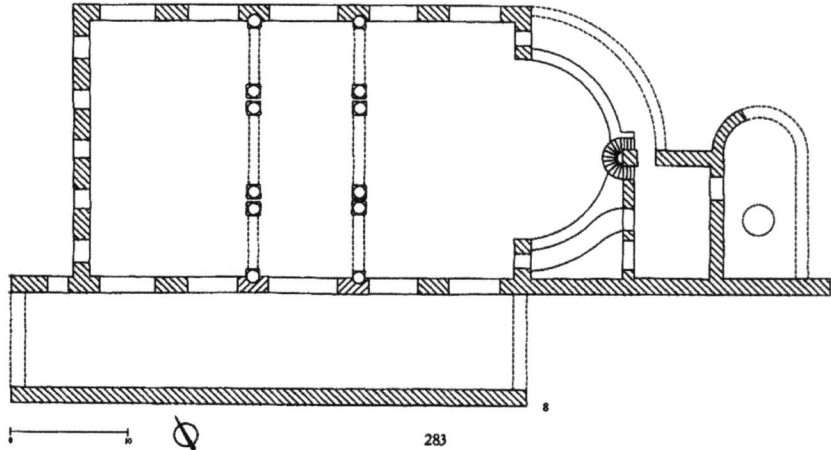

Figure 12.3 Plan of the basilica of S. Croce in Rome, after Richard Krautheimer and Hugo Brandenburg.

a shrine for the relic. There was thus a spatial separation between the church altar and the relic.

The basilica in the Sessorian Palace did not evoke the basilica of the Martyrium in Jerusalem, nor the atrium containing Golgotha. It was, however, named *Hierusalem* after the imported relic. The name held until at least the sixth century, suggesting an intention to link the location of the relic with the original sacred spot in Jerusalem by the specific spatial layout, i.e. depositing the relic of the Cross in an adjoining chapel.[34] A late-sixth-century source documents that Sta. Croce/*Hierusalem* was the location of the papal service on Good Friday.[35] Sta. Croce, therefore, may have been not only the earliest shrine of the True Cross outside Jerusalem but also the earliest implementation of the long and mostly later tradition of translating a part of the architectural setting of the Holy

---

been rejected. See de Blaauw, 'Jerusalem in Rome', p. 64. An alternative plan shows a variation in which the two adjoining rooms were both placed behind the apse, one leading to the second in which the relic was kept. See M. David, 'Da Gerusalemme a Ravenna. Il culto della croce e la corte imperial a Ravenna', in A. Coscarella and P. De Santis (eds.), *Martiri, santi, patroni: per una archeologia della devozione* (Arcavacata, 2012), pp. 687–95, Fig. 1.

[34] H. Grisar, *Analecta Romana: Dissertazioni, testi, monumenti dell'arte riguardanti principalmente la storia di Roma e dei papi nel medio evo* (Rome, 1899), pp. 556–8; de Blaauw, 'Jerusalem in Rome', p. 68.

[35] *Capitulare lectionum of Würzburg*, following S. de Blaauw, 'Jerusalem in Rome', p. 71.

Sepulchre complex from Palestine to Europe, thus creating a surrogate monument.[36]

The imperial patronage of Sta. Croce in Gerusalemme did not stop with the Constantinian dynasty; it continued into the fifth century. Between 425 and 444, Galla Placidia, her son, Valentinian III, and her daughter, Honoria, decorated the chapel of the Cross (later the Chapel of Sta. Helena) with a dedicatory inscription and new mosaics.[37] But the Constantinian foundation was kept in the formal collective Roman memory; the sixth-century *Liber Pontificalis* associates Sta. Croce with Pope Silvester and Constantine. However, the contemporary so-called *Gesta de Xysti* implies an established association between Helena and the Sessorian palace: *basilica Heleniana quae dicitur Sessorianum*,[38] an ideal phrasing for Radegund's intentions.

It is impossible to tell to what extent Radegund or the architect of the chapel in Poitiers aimed to visualise the Jerusalemite Golgotha. If Radegund, however, was seeking to shape a visual familiarity with the church enshrining the Cross in Rome, its imperial patronage, and its association with Helena, who was connected to Rome and to Jerusalem, all she needed to do was add a chamber behind the apse and celebrate the Finding of the Cross on the same day in May. Comparing the plan of the church in Rome with that of the chapel in Poitiers, it seems that the two constructions are closer to each other than they are to the original in Jerusalem: aside from the room behind or closer to the vertex of the apse, in both churches the apse's hemisphere wall is (Rome) almost as wide as, or (Poitiers) continues the walls that frame the basilica.[39]

---

[36] The 'copies' of the Holy Sepulchre is a vast field of research. See below, n. 40, and 42.

[37] Galla Placidia dedicated a church to the Holy Cross in Ravenna. It was a Latin-cross-shaped basilica with flanking rooms on both sides of the apse. For the possibility that the one on the north-east corner served as shrine for the relic of the Cross, see J. C. Smith, 'Form and Function of the Side Chambers of Fifth- and Sixth-Century Churches in Ravenna', *Journal of the Society of Architectural Historians*, 49 (1990): 181–204, at pp. 193–5. For a different view, see recently, M. David, *La basilica di Santa Croce: Nuovi contributi per Ravenna tardoantica* (Ravenna, 2013); M. David, 'Da Gerusalemme a Ravenna', pp. 687–95; A. Fiorini, 'Analisi stratigrafica della basilica di Santa Croce', in David, *La basilica di Santa Croce*, pp. 93–109.

[38] See de Blaauw, 'Jerusalem in Rome', p. 60.

[39] Vast literature has been written on the relation between architecture and liturgy. For a recent discussion of the relation of architecture and liturgy associated with specific relics, see E. Palazzo, 'Relics, Liturgical Space, and the Theology of the Church', in K. Bagnoli, H. A. Klein, C. G. Mann, and J. Robinson (eds.), *Treasures of Heaven: Saints, Relics and Devotion in Medieval Europe* (London, 2010), pp. 99–109; J.-P. Caillet, 'Reliques et architecture religieuse aux époques carolingienne et romane', in E. Bozóky and A.-M. Helvétius (eds.), *Les Reliques: Objets, cultes, symboles*, Actes du colloque international de l'Université du Littoral-Côte d'Opale, Boulogne-sur-Mer, 4–6 September 1997 (Turnhout, 1999), pp. 169–97.

The Church of the Holy Sepulchre in Jerusalem is the point of departure as well as the principal example for Richard Krautheimer's classical study 'Introduction to an "Iconography of Medieval Architecture"'.[40] He discusses, *inter alia*, St Michael's church in Fulda, the Church of the Holy Sepulchre in Paderborn and Cambridge, and St Stephen's church in Bologna, all of which consciously reproduce architectural elements associated with the Rotunda of the Anastasis in Jerusalem's Holy Sepulchre complex. The 'copies' are different from each other. Krautheimer clarifies that the 'architect of the medieval copy did not intend to imitate the prototype as it looked in reality; he intended to reproduce it *typice* and *figuraliter*, as a memento of a venerated site and simultaneously as a symbol of promised salvation'.[41] Following Krautheimer, in the succeeding years and especially in recent decades, Holy Sepulchre reproductions became an established field of research.[42] Most of them, indeed, are reconstructions of the Rotunda, the best extant original part of the complex from the fourth century. The possible correspondence of the Chapel of the Holy Cross in Poitiers with Sta. Croce in Rome suggests a parallel (and perhaps earlier) attitude, where in churches dedicated to the Cross the focus was on the Martyrium Basilica and Golgotha.

Perhaps the two chapels in Rome and Poitiers are not sufficient to define a separate group of reconstructions using the spatial separation between Golgotha and the Martyrium Basilica. I am not familiar with additional late-antique examples in the West. Perhaps the combination of Golgotha and the Martyrium Basilica was abandoned when this part of the complex was abolished in the tenth century, or earlier, leaving the Rotunda of the Anastasis as the main element in reconstructions of the church.[43]

I would like to think that Radegund's efforts to obtain a relic of the Cross and its *translatio* to Poitiers included the plan of the chapel and the rededication of the monastery to the Holy Cross. This makes Baudonivia's reference to Helena, as well as that made by Gregory of Tours, threefold – or, better yet, three-dimensional: the noble affiliation,

---

[40] R. Krautheimer, 'Introduction to an "Iconography of Medieval Architecture"', *Journal of the Warburg and Courtauld Institutes*, 5 (1942): 1–33, reprinted in R. Krautheimer, *Studies in Early Christian, Medieval and Renaissance Art* (New York, 1969), pp. 115–50; C. Carver McCurrach, '"Renovatio" Reconsidered: Richard Krautheimer and the Iconography of Architecture', *Gesta*, 50 (2011): 41–69.

[41] Krautheimer, 'Introduction to an "Iconography"'; the quote is found on p. 128.

[42] Recently, B. Kühnel, G. Noga-Banai and H. Vorholt (eds.), *Visual Constructs of Jerusalem* (Turnhout, 2014).

[43] For the history of the church before the crusaders conquered Jerusalem and of the new basilica they built, see D. Pringle, *The Churches of the Crusader Kingdom of Jerusalem: A Corpus* (Cambridge, 2007), vol. III, pp. 6–72, no. 283.

the *inventio/translatio* narrative and the monumental construction. Yet, the analogy between the empress and the queen, as much as it is multilayered, is but one tier of the present paper. Its consequences may be far-reaching for the field of architectural history in general and the historiography of Krautheimer's 'Iconography of Architecture' in particular. The comparison of the plan of Sainte-Croix in Poitiers with Sta. Croce in Rome suggests that during the late-antique period, the foci of Golgotha and the basilica of the Martyrium did not attract less attention than the Rotunda of the Anastasis. With Roman intervention, it may have been reconstructed in the Far West much earlier than architectural elements attributed to the Rotunda of the Anastasis.

Acknowledgements

I wish to thank Yitzhak Hen and Stefan Esders for inviting me to Berlin to participate in a conference focusing on 'Merovingian Kingdoms in Mediterranean Perspective'. I would also like to thank Werner Jacobsen (Münster) for taking the time (during another conference, in Hildesheim), to discuss the topic with me. I am grateful to the Mandel-Scholion Interdisciplinary Research Center in the Humanities and Jewish Studies at the Hebrew University of Jerusalem for its support of this study as well as the Research Cooperation Lower Saxony – Israel.

13 A Generic Mediterranean: Hagiography in the Early Middle Ages

Jamie Kreiner

Hagiography is a literature that narrates and celebrates the accomplishments of particular protagonists. It is ethics packaged as biography. Like any genre (SITCOM, ATLANTA TRAP MUSIC, PHARMACEUTICAL COMMERCIAL), hagiography can betray itself through familiar forms and structures.[1] But historians who work with hagiography are usually more interested in the *uncommon* features of their texts, the things that make them different from each other. Because hagiography comprises one of the largest corpora of late antique and medieval sources, that preference makes sense. If we want to recover the particular history that any text enfolds, the weird, idiosyncratic details matter a lot. And yet, somewhat counter-intuitively, the commonplaces we find among separate works that share a genre can also encapsulate historically specific ideas.

Certain features of Merovingian texts recur among the work of Gaul's near and distant neighbours around the Mediterranean, and some of the most striking similarities indicate that many early medieval writers saw their work as a kind of applied political and social science. These writers did not assume that readers would change their minds and actions simply by reading or hearing something. Persuasion was a problem that they took very seriously. They thought deeply about how cognitive and cultural processes worked, about the machinery and mechanisms that bound brains and individuals and groups together.

Merovingian hagiographers designed their texts to suit that science. They crafted narratives that would facilitate the process of thinking and perceiving and choosing particular ideas. But the strategies of persuasion that we find in their work, although essential to it, were not exclusive to it either. Many of them are visible in contemporary Greek, Syriac, Coptic, Middle Persian, and Arabic literature as well. In this chapter, I will discuss three of those shared structures: (1) rational persuasion, or

---

[1] Which is not to say that every element characteristic to a genre will be obvious to its audience: see T. Underwood, 'The Life Cycles of Genres', *Journal of Cultural Analytics* (23 May 2016), DOI 10.22148/16.005.

the idea that readers had to agree that an account's explicit arguments were believable and reasonable; (2) appealing to the memory as a mix of rational, emotional, and non-conscious cognition; and (3) the use of an episodic style to formulate and advocate political policies at the royal or imperial level. These patterns suggest that genre was not the only common denominator here. In the early Middle Ages, hagiography and other narrative practices seem to have been based on shared theories of literary representation and social transformation.

Most early medieval hagiographers, particularly if they were writing about persons who had recently died, were anxious to convince their audiences that their accounts were truthful and that a protagonist's reasons for acting as he or she had were legitimate. In Gaul, hagiographers established the credibility and rationality of their accounts by making arguments that were consonant with Merovingian law.[2] When they spoke about land transactions, for example, they echoed the language of the charters, or when they tried to justify or criticise a particular official's behaviour they nodded to the legal principles that informed it. And in order to be sure that their audiences would believe that the events they were reporting had really happened, they adopted contemporary legal procedures for producing credible testimony: they identified their witnesses by name. They cited their documentary sources or drew on the language of the law to defend their positions. Some could even say that they personally had seen something with their own eyes.[3]

Other hagiographical cultures employed very similar procedures. Some writers of late-antique Italian passions designed their texts to read like trial records, to convey the impression that they were the bureaucratic products of Roman prosecutors even though the events had transpired centuries earlier. Other Italian hagiographers took a different tack and explained that they were working with prior written sources.[4] Further east,

---

[2] J. Kreiner, *The Social Life of Hagiography in the Merovingian Kingdom* (Cambridge, 2014), pp. 52–87.

[3] Language of the law and reference to supporting documentation: Gregory of Tours, *Liber de passione et virtutibus Iuliani martyris*, 14, MGH SRM 1.2; *Vita Gaugerici episcopi Camaracensis*, 6, MGH SRM 3; *Vita Balthildis*, 7–9, MGH SRM 2; *Vita Sadalbergae abbatissae Laudunensis*, 29, MGH SRM 5. Naming informants: Baudonivia, *Vita Radegundis*, 15, MGH SRM 2; Florentius, *Vita Rusticulae sive Marciae abbatisse Arelatensis*, prologue, MGH SRM 4; Jonas of Bobbio, *Vita Columbani discipulorumque eius*, 1.15, MGH SRG 37; *Passio Praeiecti episcopi et martyris Arverni*, 39, MGH SRM 5. Hagiographers' own eyewitnessing: *Vita Sulpicii episcopi Biturigi*, prologue, MGH SRM 4; *Vita sancti Arnulfi*, 20, MGH SRM 2; *Vita Segolenae*, 1, AASS July V:630–1; *Vita Wandregiseli abbatis Fontanellensis*, 17, MGH SRM 5. For many more examples, see n. 2.

[4] C. Lanéry, 'Hagiographie d'Italie (300–550) I: Les Passions latines composées en Italie', in G. Philippart (ed.), *Hagiographies: Histoire internationale de la littérature hagiographique latine et vernaculaire en Occident des origines à 1550*, vol. V (Turnhout, 2010), pp. 15–369, at pp. 24–5. Quasi-judicial accounts include the passions of Agatha, Felix and

in northern Syria, Theodoret of Cyrrhus very self-consciously compared the fact-finding he had done for his hagiographical *Religious History* to the way that the Gospel writers had worked, as both eyewitnesses and as diligent researchers.[5] Christian hagiographers writing about individuals who had been crucified by the Umayyad caliphs were so attentive to the legal proceedings that (as Sean Anthony has pointed out) their accounts almost read like inverse commentaries on the very same details that would later interest early 'Abbāsid jurists when they outlined the proper parameters for this form of execution.[6] Muslim martyrologists and 'anti-martyrologists' made similar moves. In a unique pair of accounts that survive about the Qadarī Ghaylān al-Dimashqī, based on late Umayyad sources, each narrative constructs careful arguments for or against the justice of Ghaylān's crucifixion: one builds a case on political, economic, and religious grounds that Ghaylān was a martyr while the other appeals to exegetical and syllogistic reasoning to denounce him as heretical.[7] And in Egypt, a Coptic encomium for Apa Mena written at some point in the early Middle Ages tied several of these strategies together by asserting that it would put to rest the 'fictitious tales' that 'foolish men' had spread about the holy father by consulting reliable documents 'found lying in the library of the Church of the Patriarchate of Alexandria, written in Greek by the old chroniclers who lived at that time, [men] who saw with their eyes from the beginning and became officers of the word'.[8]

There was abundant precedent for adopting legalistic, rationalising arguments like these. The very earliest martyrdom accounts, written in various places around the Mediterranean from the second century

Fortunatus; and the passions of Primus and Felicianus. Texts that cite prior written sources include the passions of Gervasius and Protasius; Nazarius and Celsus; and Agnes and Emerentiana.

[5] D. Krueger, 'Early Byzantine Historiography and Hagiography as Different Modes of Christian Practice', in A. Papaconstantinou, with M. Debié and H. Kennedy (eds.), *Writing 'True Stories': Historians and Hagiographers in the Late Antique and Medieval Near East* (Turnhout, 2010), pp. 13–20, at pp. 14–15; P. Turner, 'Methodology, Authority and Spontaneity: Sources of Spiritual Truthfulness in Late Antique Texts and Life', in P. Sarris, M. Dal Santo and P. Booth (eds.), *An Age of Saints? Power, Conflict and Dissent in Early Medieval Christianity* (Leiden, 2011), pp. 11–35, at pp. 15–16.

[6] S. W. Anthony, *Crucifixion and Death as Spectacle: Umayyad Crucifixion in Its Late Antique Context* (New Haven, CT, 2014), pp. 55–9.

[7] *The Martyrology and Anti-Martyrology of Ghaylān of Damascus*, trans. S. W. Anthony, in *Crucifixion and Death as Spectacle*, pp. 76–82; on these genres more generally, see Anthony, *Crucifixion and Death as Spectacle*, pp. 40–64.

[8] *Apa Mena: A Selection of Coptic Texts Relating to St Menas*, ed. and trans. J. Drescher (Cairo, 1946), p. 129, quoted in G. Schenke, 'Creating Local History: Coptic Encomia Celebrating Past Events', in A. Papaconstantinou, with M. Debié and H. Kennedy (eds.), *Writing 'True Stories': Historians and Hagiographers in the Late Antique and Medieval Near East* (Turnhout, 2010), pp. 21–30, at p. 24.

onward, had co-opted the rhetoric of imperial trials to suggest that it was the Roman state, rather than the defendants they were prosecuting, that had done something unlawful.[9] In late antiquity, both Christian and pagan authors stressed that they had conducted responsible research, and they emphasised the correctness of their protagonists' actions by measuring them against the Bible, established philosophical models, or some other accepted authority.[10] Jerome had defended the truth of his hagiographical accounts in similar ways: he says he learnt about Malchus from Malchus personally; he says he learnt about Paul from the disciples of Antony as well as from the writings of Eusebius; and he says he got his information about Hilarion from a pre-existing biography and other unspecified sources. Jerome's three saints' lives were well known in the Latin world, and by the early Middle Ages they were available in Greek, Coptic and Syriac as well.[11]

But hagiography did not *have* to be this way. Not all of it was. For example, the northern Mesopotamian author Babai the Great, writing in Syriac in the late years of the Sasanian Empire, asks his audience to believe him not because he can point to specific informants or sources as credible testimony but because he himself is humble – just like his protagonist, George of Izla – and also because he is an established author with a long list of works to his credit.[12] The consistent methods of establishing trust that appear among many hagiographical traditions are more striking when we come across someone like Babai who worked very differently.

In Gaul, hagiographers were anxious to write believable and persuasive arguments because they believed that their texts could not possibly transform a reader's mind and actions without convincing the reader

---

[9] D. Liebs, 'Umwidmung: Nutzung der Justiz zur Werbung für die Sache ihrer Opfer in den Märtyrerprozessen der frühen Christen', in W. Ameling (ed.), *Märtyrer und Märtyrerakten* (Stuttgart, 2002), pp. 19–46; P. Buc, 'Martyre et ritualité dans l'Antiquité tardive: Horizons de l'écriture médiévale des rituels', *Annales: Histoire, Sciences sociales*, 48 (1997): 63–92. It should be noted that Nero's 'persecution' of Christians in Rome never actually happened, which helps explain Liebs' observation that this episode seems like a bizarre anomaly in terms of its legal protocols (or lack thereof). The 'Neronian persecution' was an anachronistic event patched together by Tacitus, who was relying on inaccurate information that made sense in the 110s/20s but could not have been true half a century earlier. See B. Shaw, 'The Myth of the Neronian Persecution', *Journal of Roman Studies*, 105 (2015): 73–100.
[10] Turner, 'Methodology, Authority and Spontaneity', pp. 15–21.
[11] A. A. R. Bastiaensen, 'Jérôme hagiographe', in G. Philippart (ed.), *Hagiographies: Histoire internationale de la littérature hagiographique latine et vernaculaire en Occident des origines à 1550*, vol. I (Turnhout, 1994), pp. 97–123.
[12] J. Walker, 'A Saint and His Biographer in Late Antique Iraq: The History of St George of Izla (†614) by Babai the Great', in A. Papaconstantinou, with M. Debié and H. Kennedy (eds.), *Writing 'True Stories': Historians and Hagiographers in the Late Antique and Medieval Near East* (Turnhout, 2010), pp. 31–41, at pp. 35–8.

that the accounts were legitimate. But there may have been an additional pressure to write in this mode by the late sixth and seventh centuries. This was a particularly sensitive time to be writing about miracles, especially miracles that saints seemed to perform posthumously. Matthew Dal Santo has shown that 'rationalist' circles in Constantinople in this period were suggesting not only that saints could not work miracles after they died but also that the entire premise of saints' cults was misguided. One popular counter-theory, for example, was that the cures that God allegedly performed through his saints were in fact the result of effective medical treatments. These arguments rattled the eastern Mediterranean world, and writers who still believed in the efficacy of saintly intervention responded by making hagiography more 'empirical', by reporting miracles in the carefully argued manner of a proof texts, to demonstrate that saints were actually responsible for the miracles attributed to them and that this in turn reflected a divine endorsement for the kinds of lives that the saints had lived.[13]

It is worth noting that Gregory the Great was intensely involved in these debates, and his work was popular in Gaul.[14] And yet, the Merovingian hagiographers who were reading Gregory were not fully convinced by his position. About 50 per cent of the hagiographical corpus that we can be sure was written in Gaul between 600 and 750 does not mention any post-mortem miracles or has very little to say about them.[15] The

---

[13] M. Dal Santo, *Debating the Saints' Cult in the Age of Gregory the Great* (Oxford, 2012), pp. 129–236; M. Dal Santo, 'The God-Protected Empire? Skepticism Towards the Cult of the Saints in Early Byzantium', in P. Sarris, M. Dal Santo and P. Booth (eds.), *An Age of Saints? Power, Conflict and Dissent in Early Medieval Christianity* (Leiden, 2011), pp. 129–49.

[14] See the individual text commentaries in W. Berschin, *Biographie und Epochenstil im lateinischen Mittelalter*, vol. II: *Merowingische Biographie; Italien, Spanien und die Inseln im frühen Mittelalter* (Stuttgart, 1988).

[15] No post-mortem miracles: Jonas, *Vita Columbani*; *Vita Geretrudis*, MGH SRM 2; *Vita Sadalbergae*; *Vita Wandregiseli*; *Vita Amandi episcopi* [prima], MGH SRM 2; *Passio Afrae vetustior*, MGH SRM 7. Minor treatment of post-mortem miracles: Baudonivia, *Vita Radegundis*, 26; Florentius, *Vita Rusticulae*, 26–7; Jonas of Bobbio, *Vita Iohannis abbatis Reomaensis*, 20, MGH SRM 3; Jonas of Bobbio, *Vita Vedastis episcopi Atrebatensis* 9–10, MGH SRM 3; *Vita Gaugerici*, 14–15; *Vita Balthildis*, 16; Bobolenus, *Vita Germani abbatis Grandivallensis*, 14–15, MGH SRM 5; *Vita Segolenae*, 35; *Vita Audoini episcopi Rotomagensis*, 17–19, MGH SRM 5; *Passio Iusti*, ed. M. Coens, 'Aux origines de la céphalophorie: Un fragment retrouvé d'une ancienne passion de S. Just, martyr de Beauvais', *Analecta Bollandiana*, 74 (1956): 86–114, at pp. 95–6; *Martyrium Prisci et sociorum*, 2, AASS May VI:367. Marc Van Uytfanghe came up with similar figures, although some of the texts he includes in his 'B' corpus – Merovingian texts that were revised in the Carolingian period as well as texts that could have been composed in either the Merovingian or Carolingian period – are generally accepted as Merovingian originals (*Vita Sadalbergae*, *Vita Segolenae*, *Passio Desiderii*, *Transitus Fursei*, and *Vita Landiberti*): 'Pertinence et statut du miracle dans l'hagiographie mérovingienne

statistical significance of that figure is not necessarily great because there are only thirty or forty hagiographical texts that historians feel confident in assigning to this century and a half. But the ways that writers did – and did not – treat post-mortem miracles suggests that they shared the doubts that rationalists in the eastern Mediterranean had about the ability of dead and even living persons to transmit God's power. And even when writers were not sceptics themselves, many of them felt obliged to address Gaul's concerns about whether particular miracles were genuine and should be attributed to the saints.[16]

I will give three telling examples. When Praeiectus of Clermont is credited for healing a man who had broken several limbs in a hunting accident, his hagiographer (writing in the late seventh century) emphasises that the man had first consulted several different doctors, and all of them had failed to fix him.[17] In the mid eighth century, Landibert of Maastricht's hagiographer reported that right after the bishop died, angels guarded his body in a basilica so that his murderers could not dispose of it. As proof that the angels were really there, the crowd that had gathered outside could hear them singing psalms, and Landibert's own voice was audible in that choir. But if anyone in the crowd got too close to the church, the singing would suddenly stop. When that person stepped back, the music would start again. This was a form of hypothesis testing, of demonstrating that the ethereal singing had everything to do with the bishop and the worthy goal of protecting his body. His hagiographer thought that the evidence could not be more straightforward. When God shows us things like this, he said, 'Who can make an investigation into his mercy?' It was a way of suggesting that there was no need to act like a detective, piecing together clues and causes, because God had laid out everything so clearly.[18] Or so he hoped it would seem.

A third example of argumentative miracle reporting is part of a set of eleven miracles that were written to supplement the *Vita Geretrudis* around 700.[19] (The original *Vita Geretrudis* did not contain any post-mortem miracles.) The last miracle functions as a defence for the whole

---

(600–750)', in D. Aigle (ed.), *Miracle et karāma* (Turnhout, 2000), pp. 67–144, at pp. 74–81, 86, 88.

[16] On the hagiographers' comparative disinterest in all kinds of miracles in contrast to their sixth-century antecedents, see Kreiner, *Social Life of Hagiography*, pp. 58–64, 103–4; Van Uytfanghe, 'Pertinence et statut du miracle', esp. pp. 74–81, 89–90.

[17] *Passio Praeiecti*, 38, p. 247.

[18] *Vita Landiberti episcopi Traeiectensis vetustissima*, 19, MGH SRM 6, pp. 372–3: 'Qui potest tua investigare misericordia, qui tanta dignatus es ostendere servis tuis, ut non solum animas eorum, sed et cadaver permittis custodire angelis tuis? Quis dubitare potest promissa tua, redemtor seculi, qui humanum non sinis genus perire?'

[19] *Virtutes Geretrudis*, 11, MGH SRM 2.

collection. It begins with a debate between a nun of Geretrude's monastery and a laywoman named Adula. The text characterises Adula as nobly born, rich and extremely nun-like in her actions. She was also one of those ultra-religious laypersons who thought she knew better than the clergy did. She thought it was wrong for the nuns to celebrate Geretrude's feast day with an actual feast because it fell during Lent. She also doubted that God actually worked miracles through Geretrude.

The dispute ends without a resolution, and the scene cuts to Geretrude's feast day. Monks and laypeople are there, men and women are there. Everyone is feasting and having a great time – except for Adula, who sits at the table and refuses to eat. She has brought her whole family with her, including her toddler, and the boy is running around playing, but nobody really notices him, and he falls into a fountain and drowns. When another nun discovers him, dead, the nun who had been arguing with Adula earlier says explicitly what the story sets us up to 'see' in this incident: 'Holy Geretrude, you did this because this child's mother was unwilling to believe in the miracles that the Lord worked through you.'[20]

But if Adula already disbelieved post-mortem miracles, a statement like that was not going to change her mind; it would only sting her. So the nun and the hagiographer get legal, and procedural. The nun swears several oaths: she formally pleads and adjures Geretrude to intercede with God and bring the boy back to life. She swears that if Adula will act as she (the nun) acts and believes what she (the nun) believes, Geretrude will revive her son. And finally she lays the boy in Geretrude's bed, which has been relocated into the monastery's church and has been a site of miracles in the past. The combination works on both mother and son. The child comes back to life, Adula believes in miracles and in Geretrude's role in miracle-working, and she is also happy to fully join the party in Geretrude's honour. And as proof that Adula was satisfied by all these proofs, the hagiographer notes that Geretrude's bed is now adorned with gold and gems that Adula supplied herself. They are material witnesses to what has already become an elaborate demonstration. On top of all this, the author ends by saying that she saw this with her own eyes.

These examples suggest that in the course of the seventh century, scepticism and even skittishness about post-mortem miracles had become as pervasive in Gaul as they were in Constantinople, Italy, Egypt, Syria and Cyprus. And when hagiographers who did believe in this particular power of the saints wanted to prove it, they amplified the rationalist rhetoric that pervades hagiography in this period.

---

[20] *Virtutes Geretrudis*, 11, p. 470: 'Sancta Geretrudis, tu hoc fecisti, quoniam nolebat mater huius infantis virtutibus credere, que per te Dominus operatus est'.

A second rhetorical strategy that many early medieval hagiographers employed was to write narratives that readers not only accepted as logical but which were meaningful and memorable, too. One sign that this was a shared concern is that writers across the Mediterranean paid great attention to the psychology of weeping. In Merovingian culture, weeping was both an intellectual act and a visceral one. You wept, or were capable of weeping, when you really understood and agreed with something. And ideas that elicited weeping, ideas that struck you as personally meaningful and triggered both your body and brain to react, were more memorable than things that did not provoke such strong reactions.[21] At the very least, weeping was valuable because it showed that an idea had the potential to become a real part of your mind's work.

But the Merovingians were not the only ones to appreciate that weeping was a sign of genuine communication. In the fourth century, Gregory of Nyssa had examined the biological processes that weeping involved to better understand how body and mind were working together through tears.[22] In the seventh century, Isaac of Nineveh identified tears as the hinge between the person you were – in the 'prison' of your old self – and the person you could become.[23] Tears were transformative. That is why the author of the Syriac *Chronicle of Zuqnīn*, when recounting the civil wars that unravelled the Umayyad Caliphate in the 740s, wished that the prophet Jeremiah would 'come now and cry' and that the whole earth would join him – not only to grieve but also to truly appreciate what missteps had ignited the Apocalypse.[24] Arabic traditions from the Umayyad and 'Abbāsid periods also emphasise weeping as an expression of sincere commitment, as for example al-Azdī does in his *Conquests of Syria*. That similarity was not a coincidence. Al-Azdī had drawn deeply

---

[21] M. Carruthers, *The Experience of Beauty in the Middle Ages* (Oxford, 2013), pp. 140–6; M. Carruthers, *The Book of Memory: A Study of Memory in Medieval Culture*, 2nd edn (Cambridge, 2008), pp. 246–9; M. Carruthers, *The Craft of Thought: Meditation, Rhetoric, and the Making of Images, 400–1200* (Cambridge, 1998), pp. 16–18, 66–9; Kreiner, *Social Life of Hagiography*, pp. 112–14.

[22] Carruthers, *Experience of Beauty*, pp. 142–4.

[23] Isaac, *Mystic Treatises*, Homily 14, trans. A. J. Wensinck (Amsterdam, 1923), p. 85; quoted in Ware, '"An Obscure Matter': The Mystery of Tears in Orthodox Spirituality', in K. C. Patton and J. S. Hawley (eds.), *Holy Tears: Weeping in the Religious Imagination* (Princeton, NJ, 2005), pp. 242–54, at p. 250; see also K. C. Patton, '"Howl, Weep and Moan and Bring It Back to God"': Holy Tears in Eastern Christianity', in K. C. Patton and J. S. Hawley (eds.), *Holy Tears: Weeping in the Religious Imagination* (Princeton, NJ, 2005), pp. 255–73, at pp. 260–4.

[24] *The Chronicle of Zuqnīn, Parts III and IV, AD 488–775*, trans. A. Harrak (Toronto, 1999), p. 168.

on Byzantine hagiographical traditions for his narratives about the Companions of Muḥammad.²⁵

In this psychological understanding, weeping was ideally an ongoing process rather than a momentary outburst, and so a text needed to stay in your memory if you were going to engage with it continuously and eventually be transformed by it. There were many ways to make a narrative memorable, but I will focus on one of them: vivid scene-setting. More than thirty years ago, Joaquín Martínez Pizarro characterised early medieval narratives as 'scenic', and the features of scenic narratives that he identified also happen to be mnemonic devices that were a standard part of the medieval cognitive-cultural repertoire. Texts written in this style represented complex arguments through striking and animated visualisations. They helped readers and listeners internalise the perspectives they encapsulated and to remember and reflect upon these images as they continued to 'warm' the mind.²⁶

Early medieval scenic stories give readers the impression that they are watching things move in live action rather than listening to a narrator present a carefully crafted piece of writing to them. The text unfolds as a set of stories set in distinct spaces, which we might compare to the frames of a graphic novel, but which members of medieval culture would have likened to the framed page of a codex, or an empty canon table, or a pictorial grid. There is direct speech and dialogue. There are highly visible objects or props, like goblets or treasure or swords, and there are also vivid gestures, like hitting or trembling or collapsing. There are generous doses of violence and humour, and even sex every once in a while. All these elements were part of the early medieval aesthetic, but they were also appreciated among medieval memory theorists as excellent memory aids.

Martínez Pizarro demonstrated that the literatures of early medieval Gaul, Italy, England and Byzantium shared these scenic properties. They are also characteristic of Syriac and Arabic literature. In the sixth century, Jacob of Sarug wrote a verse homily or *memra* called *On the Fall of the Idols* whose imagery was scenically vivid and violent, and he wrote it

---

[25] N. Khalek, "He Was Tall and Slender and His Virtues Were Numerous': Byzantine Hagiographical Topoi and the Companions of Muḥammad in Al-Azdī's Futūḥ al-Shām', in A. Papaconstantinou, with M. Debié and H. Kennedy (eds.), *Writing 'True Stories': Historians and Hagiographers in the Late Antique and Medieval Near East* (Turnhout, 2010), pp. 105–23, at pp. 118–19.

[26] J. Martínez Pizarro, *A Rhetoric of the Scene: Dramatic Narrative in the Early Middle Ages* (Toronto, 1989); for the mnemonic qualities of the aesthetic Martínez Pizarro identified see Kreiner, *Social Life of Hagiography*, pp. 92–104. On 'warming' as a Merovingian cognitive metaphor: *Vita Wandregiseli*, 1; *Vita Sadalbergae*, 6.

that way not because he was describing any actual event but because he thought it would more effectively persuade his Christian congregation to stop loving money so much. Dan Schwartz has shown that for Jacob it was greed among Christians that was the new 'idolatry', and his scenic narrative was a rhetorical device that made his point more forceful and memorable simultaneously – and, ideally, more effective.[27]

Early 'Abbāsid histories are unmistakably scenic, too, although there are some structural differences. Whereas some Umayyad histories (which no longer survive) were written in long-form narratives, 'Abbāsid historians who wanted to bring their work up to the standards set by ḥadīth scholarship broke their sources up into episode-sized units and introduced each report with an isnād or chain of transmission (which, incidentally, helped authenticate the narratives in a manner that hagiographers would have appreciated).[28] It is also common to find a mix of first- and third-person focalisation within each historical report, as the narrator toggles between the story and the authorities who transmitted it. But even so the historians favoured 'narrative and anecdote' as their main rhetorical modes,[29] and they packed their stories with the same features you find in Latin, Greek and Syriac narratives. There are scenic spaces, direct dialogue, prominent gestures and plenty of jokes and gags. Here is one example from al-Ṭabarī, who was still using many of these techniques in the late ninth and early tenth centuries:

It has been mentioned from Ismā'īl b. Ṣubayḥ, who said: I went into al-Rashīd's presence, and lo, there was a slave girl by his head with a bowl in one of her hands and a spoon in the other, and she was feeding him with it in successive spoonfuls. He related: I saw a thin, white substance and had no idea what it was. He related: He realized that I was eager to know what it was, so he said, 'O Ismā'īl b. Ṣubayḥ!' and I answered, 'Here I am, O my lord!' He said, 'Do you know what this is?' I replied in the negative. He said, 'It's a kind of gruel [ʿashīsh] made from rice, wheat, and the water in which the bran in white flour has been steeped. It's beneficial for contorted limbs and contraction of the tendons, it makes the skin clear, dispels red blotches on the face, puts fat on the body, and clears away

---

[27] D. L. Schwartz, 'Discourses of Religious Violence and Christian Charity: The Christianization of Syria in Jacob of Sarug's *On the Fall of the Idols*', in J. Kreiner and H. Reimitz (eds.), *Motions of Late Antiquity: Essays on Religion, Politics, and Society in Honor of Peter Brown* (Turnhout, 2016), pp. 129–49.

[28] F. Donner, *Narratives of Islamic Origins: The Beginnings of Islamic Historical Writing* (Princeton, NJ, 1998), pp. 255–71.

[29] H. Kennedy, *When Baghdad Ruled the Muslim World: The Rise and Fall of Islam's Greatest Dynasty* (Cambridge, MA, 2004), quotation p. xx; T. Sizgorich, '"Become Infidels or We Will Throw You into the Fire": The Martyrs of Najrān in Early Muslim Historiography, Hagiography, and Qur'ānic Exegesis', in A. Papaconstantinou, with M. Debié and H. Kennedy (eds.), *Writing 'True Stories': Historians and Hagiographers in the Late Antique and Medieval Near East* (Turnhout, 2010), pp. 125–47, at pp. 126–7.

impurities.' He related: When I returned homewards, the sole thought in my mind was to summon the cook. I said to him, 'Set before me each morning a dish of *jashīsh*.' He replied, 'What's that?' So I described to him the recipe I had heard. He said, 'You'll be fed up with it on the third day.' However, he made it on the first day, and I found it good; he made it on the second day, and it became less appetizing; he brought it on the third day and I told him, 'Don't offer it (to me) any more!'[30]

The aesthetics of a scene might seem to undermine the ethics that a story is supposed to communicate. Images of luxury might flood a scene with 'glamour and mystery' and foster greed rather than discourage it.[31] The same might go for watery porridge: because Hārūn al-Rashīd's food is so unappetising, readers might miss the point about his commitment to a healthful but difficult diet. But on the whole, early medieval writers did not think that images were counterproductive. Glamour and mystery and repulsion were not inherently hazardous. They were affective forces that could capture readers' attention and keep their memories revolving around those images and the meanings that the scenes created for them.

These 'meanings' were not merely biographical, although it was important that a reader accept a protagonist as legitimate. Early medieval characters offered an ethics that an audience was supposed to consider systemically. This is rarely obvious on first glance, not least because hagiographers filled their narratives with familiar motifs, a practice that today seems artificial. But if the experiences of the saints seem identical and ahistorical, the social visions their stories offered were not. Many heroes, for example, are praised for having endured the brutal torture of having their tongues cut out, on the orders of an unjust government. That 'motif' derives from what seem to have been actual practices. In 484, for example, the Vandal king Huneric had punished Catholics in the city of Tipasa this way, and the survivors who emigrated to Constantinople made such an impression there that for the next century Greek and Latin writers would boast of having either seen them personally, or met older informants who had.[32] And some writers may have also been thinking of popular legends such as the *Passio Ciryci et Iulittae*, in which a toddler named Cyricus (a.k.a. Cyr, or Quiricus) has his tongue cut out in the

---

[30] Muḥammad ibn Jarīr al-Ṭabarī, *The History of al-Ṭabarī (Ta'rīkh al-rusul wa'l-mulūk)*, trans. C. E. Bosworth, vol. XXX (Albany, NY, 1989), pp. 312–13.

[31] J. Bray, 'Christian King, Muslim Apostate: Depictions of Jabala Ibn Al-Ayham in Early Arabic Sources', in A. Papaconstantinou, with M. Debié and H. Kennedy (eds.), *Writing 'True Stories': Historians and Hagiographers in the Late Antique and Medieval Near East* (Turnhout, 2010), pp. 175–203, at 179.

[32] J. Conant, *Staying Roman: Conquest and Identity in Africa and the Mediterranean, 439–700* (Cambridge, 2012), pp. 76–8; V. Saxer, 'Afrique latine', in Philippart (ed.), *Hagiographies*, vol. I, pp. 23–95, at pp. 73–6.

course of an imperial prosecution. This *Passio*, which was probably first composed in the fourth or fifth century, was enthusiastically picked up by writers in Greek, Latin, Coptic, Syriac, Armenian, Arabic and Irish; it also forms the subject of a major mid-eighth-century fresco in Santa Maria Antiqua in Rome.[33]

But each hagiographer's choice to record another instance of the same mutilation was motivated by interests that were socially specific. In a Merovingian version of the Cyricus story, which is nearly identical to the Syriac and Arabic versions, it is a doctor who personally cuts out the little boy's tongue, and he is so astonished that Cyricus survived the ordeal and even continued to talk that he performs the exact same procedure on a live pig, as a 'controlled experiment': the pig dies instantly.[34] In the tradition of Galenic medicine, pigs were good subjects for thinking about human anatomy; Galen himself had performed theatrical vivisections on them using experiments of his own design.[35] Characteristic to its age, the early medieval tradition casts the motif as an empirical case for miracles.

By contrast, a Merovingian account of a more recent case of tongue-chopping had a different argument to make. In the *Passio Leudegarii* (written in the late seventh century, about events that had only transpired a decade or so earlier), a royal official named Ebroin ordered his men to blind a courtier and bishop named Leudegar of Autun and also to chop his lips and tongue off. The hagiographer suggests that these actions represented a criminal failure of the king and his right-hand adviser to keep political factionalism from overwhelming the crown's ability to deliver justice fairly.[36] Or in the context of Umayyad political culture, we can see the associations shift yet again. The state would cut out the tongues of Christians charged with capital crimes in order to keep them from cursing Muḥammad as they died, and it did the same to Shi'ite 'traitors' to prevent them from advancing their own political agendas in highly public spaces. Writers who mourned these victims did not necessarily object to this legal practice per se but instead disagreed

---

[33] F. Dolbeau, 'Introduction to *Passio Ciryci et Iulittae*', in M. Goullet (ed.), *Le Légendier de Turin: Ms. D.V.3 de la Bibliothèque Nationale Universitaire* (Florence, 2014), pp. 487–500, transcription of text pp. 500–14.

[34] *Passio Ciryci et Iulittae*, p. 509; A. Dillmann, 'Über die apocryphen Märtyrergeschichten des Cyriacus mit Julitta und des Georgius', *Sitzungsberichte der Königlich Preussischen Akademie der Wissenschaften zu Berlin*, 23 (1887): 339–56, at p. 343.

[35] S. Mattern, *The Prince of Medicine: Galen in the Roman Empire* (Oxford, 2013), pp. 149–55. One advantage of the pig, to Galen's mind, was that its loud voice made for better theatre. The doctor who severed Cyricus' tongue probably figured that if it were physically possible to speak after such an injury, a pig would prove it.

[36] *Passio Leudegarii episcopi et martyris Augustodunensis*, 29–30, MGH SRM 5; Kreiner, *Social Life of Hagiography*, pp. 71–83.

with its application, and their narratives represent these disfigurements as hallmarks of the Umayyads' misguided definitions of political and religious transgression.[37]

I would therefore suggest a third element that Merovingian hagiography shared with its literary cousins: the use of a biographical story to advocate political policy bearing on the highest levels of government. It was crucial that in addition to being rational and memorable, an individual hagiographical story was also comprehensible as an argument for the social order as a whole, because these texts were often written by, or written to address, elites who had a hand in steering the court and kingdom.

If early medieval narrative seems to exclude the wider world from its intimate portraiture, that is because we are ourselves removed from the political cultures that gave them meaning and because we do not expect this literary aesthetic to be a favoured mode for policy debate. John of Ephesus' *Lives of the Eastern Saints* (written in Syriac in 568) may seem parochial and archaising because John focuses on northern Mesopotamian holy men, some of whom seem to have stepped right out of the pages of hagiography from a century earlier. But, as Philip Wood has argued, such a narrative framework pointed straight to Constantinople. John was arguing that this region – the city of Amida in particular – featured the most competent ascetic leaders from Alexandria to Ctesiphon, and, as a result, the Chalcedonian emperors had no legitimate basis for involving themselves so deeply in the definition of orthodoxy.[38] In a similar way, the 'anecdotal' style of Muḥammad b. 'Abdūs al-Ǧahšiyārī's administrative history (written in the tenth century) seems to distil historically complex situations into idiosyncratic episodes. But the anecdote was al-Ǧahšiyārī's artful way of communicating both confidence and ambivalence about particular 'Abbāsid initiatives. In a study of al-Ǧahšiyārī's anecdotes about non-Muslim administrators, Nancy Khalek finds that the stories worked to justify the introduction of Arabic as the language of the imperial bureaucracy and the preference for Muslim officials while simultaneously representing that bureaucracy as a continuation of (and improvement upon) older administrative cultures, particularly the Sasanians'.[39]

Well before al-Ǧahšiyārī, when the Sasanian Empire still stood, the East Syrian hagiographer of the *Martyrdom of Narsai* embedded a

---

[37] Anthony, *Crucifixion and Death as Spectacle*, p. 59.
[38] P. Wood, *'We Have No King but Christ': Christian Political Thought in Greater Syria on the Eve of the Arab Conquest (c. 400–585)* (Oxford, 2010), pp. 175–208.
[39] N. Khalek, 'Some Notes on the Representation of Non-Muslim Officials in Al-Ǧahšiyārī's (d. 331/942) *Kitāb al-Wuzarā 'wa-l-kuttāb*', *Arabica*, 62 (2015): 503–20.

political commentary within a story that again seems at first to be singular. A member of the Sasanian aristocracy converts to Christianity, builds a church, then reverses on both counts and turns the church into a Zoroastrian fire temple. Narsai enters the picture as an ascetic Christian who dismantles the temple, refuses the opportunity a Sasanian official gives him to repair the damages and is executed for his non-compliance with royal policy. But Richard Payne has demonstrated that the Sasanian Empire never enacted blanket 'persecutions' of Christians but instead reserved execution as a punishment for subjects who flagrantly transgressed the state and its ritual responsibilities. In the Sasanian political model, Christians were not capable of restoring the cosmos to perfection, as Zoroastrians were, but they did have the power to help or hinder that process. And what seems to have particularly bothered the author of the *Martyrdom of Narsai* was that so many East Syrian Christians – possibly even a majority of them – agreed with such a model! On the contrary, this hagiographer objected: Iranian elites could not make true Christians as representatives of the court, and compliance with the state was an unforgivable compromise. So, in the end, the story was as much about Persian policy as it was about Narsai.[40]

I will stay in Persia for the last example, to consider the Sasanian version of the *Book of Kings*. Historical writing in Persia worked in very similar ways to hagiography, both within the Sasanian Empire and far west of it. The earliest version that we have of the Middle Persian *Book of Kings* is a string of episodic narratives that concentrate on modelling Iranian kingship. So, like a great deal of early medieval hagiography, this work telescopes between micro-scale storytelling and large-scale political vision: the goal here was to emphasise Persia as the supreme imperial power in the late antique world and to present the creation and maintenance of that power as a collaboration between the king of kings and the great aristocratic houses, whose lineages were not Sasanian at all but Parthian.[41]

The political orientation of the *Book of Kings* is strikingly consonant with the work Merovingian hagiographers were doing in Gaul, and I suspect that this has a lot to do with an even deeper similarity between the two kingdoms' political structures. In both Gaul and Persia in the seventh century, rulers explicitly acknowledged their reliance on the support of strong networks of elites who were unrelated to the royal family,

---

[40] R. Payne, *A State of Mixture: Christians, Zoroastrians, and Iranian Political Culture in Late Antiquity* (Berkeley, CA, 2015), esp. pp. 23–58.
[41] R. Payne, 'Cosmology and the Expansion of the Iranian Empire, 502–628 CE', *Past and Present*, 220 (2013): 3–33.

and, at the same time, elites valued the social and material capital that counsel and cooperation with the crown could bring.[42] The challenge in both cases was maintaining an equilibrium between those different interests and defining how exactly political collaboration should proceed in practice.

My reason for pushing past the Mediterranean and into Mesopotamia and the Iranian plateau is to suggest that it is worth comparing the structural features of only faintly connected early medieval societies in order to understand why their literatures look strikingly similar sometimes. It is important, of course, to look for direct influences and textual connections, to figure out what writers are reading or to whom they are listening and in the process track the literal movement of ideas from place to place. From the vantage point of Gaul, we have only scratched the surface in this regard. We know, for example, that when the legendary format first appeared, around 750, saints with Eastern pedigrees are surprisingly well represented. Of all the texts gathered together in one of the oldest Latin legendaries to survive in the world, an early Carolingian compilation now in Turin (Bibl. nat. univ., Ms. D. V3), 55 per cent of them were originally written in Greek, or possibly in other languages of the Mediterranean.[43]

But it is also worth asking what these early medieval societies had in common besides their reading material. In the case of Persia and Gaul, similar political cultures and similar ideas about narrative and representation encouraged historians and hagiographers to treat ostensibly biographical literary forms as an opportunity to offer suggestions for how a polity ought to function. Or, in the case of Syria and Mesopotamia before and after the conquests, similar concepts of cognition and behaviour shaped the style of poems and histories in ways that Merovingian hagiographers would have appreciated immediately. So, while it is true that hagiographers encountered many ideas from hearing and reading other hagiographers' work, the shared science of cultural practice clearly

---

[42] Payne, 'Cosmology'; R. Payne, 'Avoiding Ethnicity: Uses of the Ancient Past in Late Sasanian Northern Mesopotamia', in W. Pohl, C. Gantner and R. Payne (eds.), *Visions of Community in the Post-Roman World: The West, Byzantium, and the Islamic World, 300–1100* (Aldershot, 2012), pp. 205–21; J. Banaji, 'Aristocracies, Peasantries and the Framing of the Early Middle Ages', *Journal of Agrarian Change*, 9 (2009): 59–91, at pp. 62–6; for a case study that sharply underlines the interdependent politics of the crown and the elites in Gaul, see also I. Wood, 'Usurpers and Merovingian Kingship', in M. Becher and J. Jarnut (eds.), *Der Dynastiewechsel von 751: Vorgeschichte, Legitimationsstrategien und Erinnerung* (Münster, 2004), pp. 15–31.

[43] G. Philippart, 'Les Légendiers, des origines au début du IXe siècle', in M. Goullet (ed.), *Le Légendier de Turin: Ms. D.V.3 de la Bibliothèque Nationale Universitaire* (Florence, 2014), pp. 7–74, at p. 40.

moved through many channels that I have only barely indicated here – and which deserve much more substantial examination. One thing that does emerge clearly from these brief comparisons, however, is that hagiography's 'generic' features were not really a function of the genre at all but rather a sign that Gaul and its contemporaries to the south and east shared ideas about how culture worked – about how ideas could be created and communicated and eventually change a society's priorities and practices.

14 Defensor of Ligugé's *Liber Scintillarum* and the Migration of Knowledge

Yitzhak Hen

The so-called *Liber scintillarum* ('Book of Sparks') is perhaps the most neglected, underrated and consequently understudied Merovingian treatise that survives.[1] References to it in modern scholarship are sparse and normally do not exceed two or three lines acknowledging its existence and classifying it as a derivative and rather dull compilation.[2] One noteworthy exception in that respect is Michael Wallace-Hadrill, who described it as 'a remarkable product' of Merovingian Gaul that can profitably be studied as a reflection of late Merovingian religion and culture.[3] The reasons for the general dim view of the *Liber scintillarum* are complex. In part, the *Liber scintillarum* had fared badly because of its nature, which is not particularly original or imaginative. After all, the *Liber scintillarum* is nothing but a collection of excerpts and recycled material. But it was also because the cultural context in which the *Liber scintillarum* was produced is not at all clear, and certainly not self-evident. In what follows, I should like to explore the *Liber scintillarum* from a cultural perspective, arguing that in order to fully appreciate the scholarly achievement of the *Liber scintillarum* we must temporarily abandon familiar cultural territory and

---

[1] For its editions see Defensor of Ligugé, *Liber scintillarum*, ed. Hénri-Marie Rochais, CCSL 117 (Turnhout, 1957); Defensor de Ligugé, *Livre d'étincelles*, ed. and trans. Hénri-Marie Rochais, Sources chrétiennes 77 and 86 (Paris, 1961–2). Whereas in the *Corpus Christianorum* edition Rochais had preserved the Merovingian peculiarities of the Latin text, in the *Sources chrétiennes* edition he had standardised the Latin and added a French translation. Throughout this paper, I cited the *Corpus Christianorum* edition (hereafter cited as *LS*) and add a reference to the *Sources chrétiennes* edition in square brackets.

[2] See, for example, Max Manitius, *Geschichte der lateinischen Literatur des Mittelalters*, vol. I: *Von Justinian bis zum Mitte des zehnten Jahrhunderts* (Munich, 1959), pp. 422–3; Franz Brunhölzl, *Histoire de la littérature latine du Moyen Age*, vol. I: *De Cassiodore à la fin de la renaissance carolingienne*; 1 – L'époque mérovingienne, trans. Hénri-Marie Rochais, with a bibliographical update by J.-P. Bouhot (Turnhout, 1990), pp. 142–4; M. L. W. Lainster, *Thought and Letters in Western Europe, AD 500 to 900*, rev. edn (London, 1957), p. 176; Pierre Riché, *Education and Culture in the Barbarian West from the Sixth through the Eighth Century*, trans. J. J. Contreni (Columbia, SC, 1976), pp. 365–6; Ian N. Wood, *The Merovingian Kingdoms, 450–751* (London and New York, 1994), p. 254.

[3] John-Michael Wallace-Hadrill, *The Frankish Church* (Oxford, 1983), p. 77.

question received intellectual categories. Let me begin with some general remarks and numbers, which, in the case of the *Liber scintillarum*, are extremely indicative.

The *Liber scintillarum* is a collection of 2,505 short citations (normally not longer than one sentence) drawn from the Bible and from the works of the Church Fathers, and arranged thematically in eighty-one chapters.[4] Few of the chapters deal with theological matters, such as Chapter 35, which is entitled *De gratia*.[5] But the bulk of the chapters are dedicated to various moral issues, such as the vices and virtues, ethical dilemmas and social conflicts. Hence, one can find a chapter on drunkenness,[6] another one on medicine,[7] and even one on vain chatter.[8] Within each chapter, the chosen citations were arranged in more or less the same order: first to appear are the words of Jesus from the Gospels; then the words of the Apostles, followed by citations from the wisdom literature of the Bible, that is, the Books of Proverbs and Ecclesiastes, as well as the apocryphal Books of Ecclesiasticus (Ben-Sirah) and the Wisdom of Solomon; and finally excerpts from the works of the Church Fathers conclude each chapter.

Judging from its Latin, the *Liber scintillarum* was undoubtedly compiled in late Merovingian Gaul,[9] but *when* exactly and *where* is still open for debate. Numerous extracts from the work of Isidore of Seville, the latest author cited by the *Liber scintillarum*, set the *terminus post quem* to 636, the year of Isidore's death.[10] The *terminus ante quem*, on the other hand, is set to around 750, the approximate date of the earliest manuscript that transmits the *Liber scintillarum*, which is now preserved in Würzburg's Universitätsbibliothek.[11] A more precise date towards the end of the

---

[4] For the list of the chapters, see *LS*, pp. 1–2 [I, pp. 52–5].
[5] *LS*, 35, pp. 138–9 [II, pp. 18–25].
[6] *LS*, 28, pp. 113–16 [I, pp. 358–65].
[7] *LS*, 74, p. 218 [II, pp. 266–9].
[8] *LS*, 79, pp. 227–8 [II, pp. 296–9].
[9] See *LS*, pp. xix–xxviii.
[10] For a list of citations from Isidore, see the indices in both editions of the *LS* together with Hénri-Marie Rochais, 'Apostilles à l'édition du *Liber scintillarum* de Défensor de Ligugé', *Revue Mabillon*, 60 (1983): 267–93. See also Jacques Elfassi, 'Defensor de Ligugé, lecteur et transmitteur des *Synonima* d'Isidore de Séville', in G. Hinojo-Andrés and J. C. Fernández-Corte (eds.), *Munus quaesitum meritis: Homenaje a Carmen Codoñer* (Salamanca, 2007), pp. 243–53.
[11] Würzburg, Universitätsbibliothek, M.p.th.f.13. It was copied in a Continental scriptorium with some Insular influences, possibly in the region of Würzburg itself. On this manuscript see *Codices Latini Antiquiores: A Palaeographical Guide to Latin Manuscripts Prior to the Ninth Century*, 11 vols. with a supplement (Oxford, 1935–71; 2nd edn of vol. II, 1972) (hereafter cited as *CLA*), IX.1404; Bernhard Bischoff, *Die südostdeutschen Schreibschulen und Bibliotheken in der Karolingerzeit*, vol. I: *Die bayerischen Diözesen*, 3rd edn (Wiesbaden, 1974), pp. 45–6. Whereas Lowe and Bischoff have dated the manuscript to the second half of the eighth century, Ganz has dated it to the second third

Merovingian period can be postulated, and I shall get back to it in a moment.

Little is known of the *Liber scintillarum*'s compiler, whose identity remained hidden for almost a millennium. Many of the numerous manuscripts that transmit the work (more than 350) attribute it to a gallery of different late-antique and early medieval celebrities, among them Augustine, Basil of Caesarea, Cassiodorus, Caesarius of Arles, Isidore of Seville, Alcuin, Bede and even Paulus Alvarus of Cordoba.[12] It was only in 1675, during his manuscript-collecting campaign in Italy, that the Benedictine monk Jean Mabillon discovered a copy of the *Liber scintillarum* with an illuminating prologue in the library of Monte Cassino.[13] In this prologue, which is found in thirty-two rather late manuscript copies,[14] a certain Defensor reveals himself as the compiler and explains that he had operated at the instigation of his *nutritor*, Ursinus.[15] If this Ursinus is the same Ursinus who composed the second *Passio Leudegarii*, which was dedicated to Bishop Ansoald of Poitiers (c. 673/7–97), then a mid-eighth-century date of the *Liber scintillarum* is vindicated.[16] This date is indeed a bit later than the one postulated by Rochais and his followers, but it is still well within a Merovingian time frame. As for the geography, in the very same prologue, Defensor also dedicates the work to the monks of Saint-Martin of Ligugé, near Poitiers, where he himself was tonsured and where, as a child, he had benefited from the teaching of his masters.[17] Hence, it is most likely that Defensor operated in the region of Poitiers, if not at Ligugé itself.

---

of the eighth century, without explaining why. See David Ganz, 'Fragmentierung von patristischen Texten in der Merowingerzeit', in Christian Gastgeber, Christine Glassner, Kornelia Holzner-Tobisch and Renate Spreizer (eds.), *Fragmente: Der Umgang mit lückenhafter Quellenüberlieferung in der Mittelalterforschung* (Vienna, 2010), pp. 151–9, at p. 154.

[12] For a list of the various manuscripts, see Hénri-Marie Rochais, 'Les Manuscrits de "Liber scintillarum"', *Scriptorium*, 4 (1950): 294–309; Rochais, 'Defensoriana: Archéologie du "Liber scintillarum"', *Sacris Erudiri*, 9 (1957): 199–264.

[13] See Jean Mabillon, *Traité des études monastiques* (Paris, 1671), p. 174; Mabillon, *Annales OSB*, vol. I (Paris, 1703), p. 10; vol. II (Paris, 1704), pp. 92 and 704.

[14] See Hénri-Marie Rochais, 'Les Prologues du "Liber scintillarum"', *Revue Bénédictine*, 59 (1949): 137–56. For its edition, see *LS*, pp. xxxiii–xxxiv [I, pp. 48–51].

[15] *LS*, p. xxxiii: 'De domini et sanctorum suorum dictum est excerpta scintilla, nec mea extitit industria, sed Dei totum gratia, mei nutritori Ursini istud operari'.

[16] As Fouracre and Gerberding have clearly demonstrated, Ursinus, who composed the second *Passio Leudegarii*, could not have been contemporaneous with Ansoald, the late-seventh-century bishop of Poitiers. He was probably a monk, who operated around the middle of the eighth century. See Paul Fouracre and Richard A. Gerberding, *Late Merovingian France: History and Hagiography, 640–720* (Manchester, 1996), pp. 206–8.

[17] *LS*, pp. xxxiii–xxxiv: 'Cenobio locutiacinse Martini sancti, in quod coma mei totondi capitis, ipsum dono, donatum quae im perpetuum colligate aetatem, qua suam, ab adolescentia mea, ibi me dotaverunt mei degentes domini'. See also Hénri-Marie

Faithful to the rhetorical *topos* of humility, which is found in almost all prefaces of Merovingian texts from the sixth century onwards,[18] Defensor clarifies that nothing in this compendium is his own, apart from the goodwill and the labour he invested in amassing it.[19] Moreover, he entreats those who shall read it not to get angry if they find something wrong but to correct the mistakes with a benevolent mind.[20] Defensor, if that was indeed his name, further explains the rationale behind this enterprise. In order to save the trouble of browsing through numerous books, he culled for the reader 'the pearls and the gems', short sentences of wisdom, in a small and handy volume, and 'just as sparks come from a fire, so here short sentences from the many books of the scriptures will be found shining'.[21] To round up his prologue, Defensor rejoices at the completion of his mission, like a sailor that reaches the harbour, and he begs those who will read it to pray for him.[22]

Defensor's prologue is not a careless preface, written offhand in order to introduce a random collection of unrelated citations. It is, rather, an erudite written piece that reveals its author's learning, literary skills and rich world of idioms. Similarly, the *Liber scintillarum* itself is a thoughtful collection of carefully chosen excerpts, put together for didactic purposes, with a monastic and priestly audience in mind. As Defensor himself confesses, much time and effort were invested in choosing the

---

Rochais, 'Le "Liber scintillarum" attribué à Defensor de Ligugé', *Revue Bénédictine*, 58 (1948): 77–83. Felice Lifshitz's statement that Rochais 'invented an author and the conventional title for the work' is odd, at best, and her suggestion that the *Liber scintillarum* was composed in the region of Karlburg, which she calls 'the Anglo-Saxon cultural province of Francia', is based on extremely shaky ground. This is not the place to explain in detail why Lifshitz's assertions are untenable; suffice it to say that her arguments are emphatically circular, with no evidence to support them. See Felice Lifshitz, *Religious Women in Early Carolingian Francia: A Study of Manuscript Transmission and Monastic Culture* (New York, 2014), pp. 56–8 and *passim*; see also Felice Lifshitz, 'Demonstrating Gun(t)za: Women, Manuscripts, and the Question of Historical "Proof"', in Walter Pohl and Paul Herold (eds.), *Vom Nutzen des Schreibens: Soziales Gedächtnis, Herrschaft und Besitz* (Vienna, 2002), pp. 67–96.

[18] See T. Jason, *Latin Prose Prefaces: Studies in Literary Convention* (Stockholm, 1964), pp. 124–41; Yitzhak Hen, *Roman Barbarians: The Royal Court and Culture in the Early Medieval West* (Basingstoke and New York, 2007), pp. 6–9.

[19] *LS*, prologus, p. xxxiii [I, p. 48]: 'Voluntas bona et labor alius nihil fuit meum'.

[20] *LS*, prologus, p. xxxiv [I, p. 50]: 'Et si aliquid praeter id quod minus studiosae gessi, te oro legentem, non et emulus vituperes, sed ut benivolus emendes'.

[21] *LS*, prologus, p. xxxiii [I, p. 48]: 'Iussio et doctrina obtemperare volens, paginas quasque scrutans, sententiam repperiens fulgentem, sicuti inventas quis margarita aut gemma, ita avidus college; quemadmodum guttae multae fontem efficient, sic de diversorum voluminibus congregans testimoniis, hunc labellum condere temptavi. Veluti de igne procedunt scintilla, ita hunc minutae sententiae pluresque libri inveniuntus fulgentes'.

[22] *LS*, prologus, p. xxxiv [I, p. 50]: 'Sicut naviganti portus, ita et mihi versus fuit optabilis novissimo. Legentibus coniuro et audientibus implore pro me exorare'.

appropriate texts from a plethora of biblical and patristic works and in developing a comprehensible and useful scheme to present them.[23] This is not an intellectual enterprise to be taken lightly.

Combing through the pages of the *Liber scintillarum*, one can really get a sense of the rich learned world in which it was produced. As I have already mentioned, the *Liber scintillarum* consists of 2,505 citations, which is an enormous amount of material that had to be gleaned from a series of biblical and patristic texts, which, one may assume, were part of the library used by Defensor. Similar collections of excerpts became somewhat popular a genre in late-antique and early medieval Gaul.[24] Prosper of Aquitaine, for example, collected 392 citations from Augustine, and Eugippius prepared a compendium of 348 citations from Augustine.[25] A similar collection of excerpts from Jerome was prepared, most probably in sixth-century Lyons,[26] and two other florilegia from various sources were produced in Francia, one around 600 and the other one, which is indeed very reminiscent of the *Liber scintillarum*, can be dated to the first half of the eighth century.[27] Even if Defensor used such available collections of excerpts, which circulated around Merovingian Gaul, his exceptional achievement cannot be overestimated. Both in its scope and in its sophistication, Defensor's *Liber scintillarum* surpasses any of the florilegia known to us from late antiquity and the early Middle Ages.

Most *scintillae* collected by Defensor were identified by Hénri-Marie Rochais in his 1959 edition of the work.[28] Only 140 were left unidentified, and listing them at the end of his edition, gave philologists the cue

---

[23] *LS*, prologus, p. xxxiii [I, p. 48].

[24] See the discussion in Hénri-Marie Rochais, 'Contribution à l'histoire des florilèges ascétique du haut moyen-âge latin: Le *liber scintillarum*', *Revue Bénédictine*, 63 (1953): 246–91; Ganz, 'Fragmentierung'.

[25] On these collections, see Eligius Dekkers, 'Quelques notes sur des florilèges augustinniens anciens et médiévaux', *Augustiniana*, 40 (1990): 27–44. For their edition, see Prosper of Aquitaine, *Liber sententiarum*, P. Callens and M. Gastaldo, CCSL 68A (Turnhout, 1972), pp. 219–365; Eugipius, *Excerpta ex operibus sancti Augustini*, ed. P. Knöll, CSEL 9 (Vienna, 1885).

[26] On this collection, see Raymond Étaix, 'Un ancient florilège Hiéronymien', *Sacris Erudiri*, 21 (1972–3): 5–34.

[27] On these two florilegia, see Ganz, 'Fragmentierung', pp. 153–7. For an edition of the former, see *Testimonia divinae scriptuare et partum*, ed. H. Lehner, CCSL 108D (Turnhout, 1987), pp. 55–127. The latter, which is preserved in London, British Library, Harley 5041 [*CLA* II.202], is dated to the second quarter of the eighth century. According to Ganz ('Fragmentierung', pp. 155–6) it predates the earliest manuscript of the *Liber scintillarum* (Würzburg, M.p.th.f.13), and hence it is probable that Defensor had used this or a similar compendium. However, the dating of the two manuscripts is far from precise, and much more is needed to convince that Defensor had used this compendium, and not vice versa.

[28] *LS*, pp. 237–54.

they were waiting for to start looking for potential sources.²⁹ By the time Rochais had published his second edition in 1961, only forty citations were left unidentified,³⁰ and in 2002, after Leslie MacCoull used the Brepols' CETEDOC database, only nine unidentified citations were left and are still waiting to be salvaged by scholars from obscurity.³¹

A close look at the sources used by Defensor is extremely illuminating. Half of the citations were taken from the Bible, the vast majority of them from either the Book of Proverbs or from the apocryphal Book of Ecclesiasticus (Ben-Sirah), both of which are hardly cited in other Merovingian compositions.³² This peculiarity points to the didactic and contemplative purpose of the *Liber scintillarum*,³³ for both the Book of Proverbs and the Book of Ecclesiasticus were appreciated as wisdom literature throughout the early medieval West.³⁴ It seems that both a *Vetus Latina* and a Vulgate version of the Bible were in front of Defensor, and it is impossible to determine what made him chose one version over the other.³⁵

If knowledge of the Bible is to be taken for granted in a monastic milieu,³⁶ then Defensor's acquaintance with non-biblical texts is noteworthy, and quite unusual for a Merovingian scholar. More than thirty authors and no fewer than fifty treatises were used by Defensor for his *Liber scintillarum*.³⁷ This makes the library of Ligugé, if indeed it was in Ligugé that he compiled his treatise, larger and richer than any Merovingian library we can reconstruct,³⁸ and it was certainly larger and more diverse than the only Merovingian library whose inventory survives, that is, the library of Echternach.³⁹ The lion's share of Defensor's

---

²⁹ *LS*, pp. 254–6.
³⁰ See the list in Defensor de Ligugé, *Livre d'étincelles*, vol. I, pp. 343–4.
³¹ Leslie S. B. MacCoull, 'More Sources for the *Liber scintillarum* of Defensor of Ligugé', *Revue Bénédictine*, 112 (2002): 291–300.
³² See, for example, Pierre Riché, 'La Bible et la vie politique dans le haut Moyen Age', in Pierre Riché and Guy Lobrichon (eds.), *Le Moyen Age et la Bible* (Paris, 1984), pp. 385–400; Yitzhak Hen, 'The Uses of the Bible and the Perception of Kingship in Merovingian Gaul', *Early Medieval Europe*, 7 (1998): 277–90.
³³ See Rochais, 'Contribution à l'histoire'.
³⁴ See, for example, Cassiodorus, *Institutiones divinarum et saecularium litterarum*, ed. R. A. B. Mynors, 2nd edn (Oxford, 1961), I.5.
³⁵ See Defensor de Ligugé, *Livre d'étincelles*, vol. I, p. 13.
³⁶ See Jean Leclercq, *The Love of Learning and the Desire for God: A Study of Monastic Culture*, trans. Catherine Misrahi, 3rd edn (New York, 1982); Riché, *Education and Culture*, pp. 100–22.
³⁷ For a list of these works, see *LS*, pp. 245–54 [II, pp. 332–44].
³⁸ See, for example, David Ganz, 'The Merovingian Library of Corbie', in H. B. Clarke and M. Brennan (eds.), *Columbanus and Merovingian Monasticism* (Oxford, 1981), pp. 153–72.
³⁹ This inventory is preserved in Vatican, BAV, Pal. lat. 210, fol. 1r (*CLA*, I.84). On this inventory, see Michael Lapidge, *The Anglo-Saxon Library* (Oxford, 2006), pp. 83–4 and

scintillae was taken from Isidore of Seville, Jerome and Gregory the Great. Isidore's *Sententiae* is the most frequently cited work throughout the *Liber scintillarum*, but Defensor also used Isidore's *Synonymae*, his *De ecclesiasticis officiis*, and even his *De differentiis rerum*.[40] As far as the writings of Gregory the Great are concerned, Defensor quotes the *Moralia in Job*, the *Homilies on Ezekiel* and *On the Gospels*, the *Regula pastoralis*, the *Dialogues*, and even his letters.[41] From the works of Jerome, Defensor prefers his letters, but he also cites several of his biblical commentaries;[42] and Augustine is represented mainly by his *Ennarationes in Psalmos*, although other Augustinian treatises, such as his sermons or the *Enchiridion*, were also used.[43] To these one can add Ambrose, Cassian, Caesarius of Arles, Cyprian of Carthage, Eligius of Noyons, Eusebius Gallicanus, Faustus of Riez, Fulgentius of Ruspe, Hegessipus, Hilary of Poitiers, Julianus Pomerius, Maxim of Turin, Martin of Braga, Nilus, Palladius, Porcharius of Lérins, Prosper of Aquitaine, Rufinus, Taio of Saragossa and Gregory of Tours' *Vita Patrum*.[44] Yet the most dazzling citations are those taken from eastern authors, such as Basil of Caesarea,[45] Pseudo-Clemens,[46] Evagrius Ponticus,[47] Pseudo-Macarius,[48] Origen,[49] and Ephrem the Syrian.[50] Classical literature is also represented in the *Liber scintillarum*, with citations from Aristotle, Cicero, Hesiod and Terence, but it is negligible when compared with the massive presence of biblical and patristic texts.

The breadth of sources used by Defensor – from Spain in the west to Syria in the east and from Ireland in the north to North Africa in the south – is truly remarkable. These sources offer a rare glimpse of the

---

153–4; Yitzhak Hen, 'Wilhelm Levison's Willibrord and Echternach', in M. Becher and Y. Hen (eds.), *Wilhelm Levison (1876–1947): Ein jüdisches Forscherleben zwischen wissenschaftlicher Anerkennung und politischem Exil* (Siegburg, 2010), pp. 187–98, at pp. 196–7.

[40] See Defensor de Ligugé, *Livre d'étincelles*, vol. II, pp. 338–41; Elfassi, 'Defensor de Ligugé'.
[41] See Defensor de Ligugé, *Livre d'étincelles*, vol. II, pp. 334–6.
[42] See Defensor de Ligugé, *Livre d'étincelles*, vol. II, pp. 336–8.
[43] Defensor de Ligugé, *Livre d'étincelles*, vol. II, p. 332.
[44] See the relevant entries in Defensor de Ligugé, *Livre d'étincelles*, vol. II, pp. 332–44.
[45] Defensor de Ligugé, *Livre d'étincelles*, vol. II, p. 332.
[46] Defensor de Ligugé, *Livre d'étincelles*, vol. II, p. 333.
[47] Defensor de Ligugé, *Livre d'étincelles*, vol. II, p. 334.
[48] Defensor de Ligugé, *Livre d'étincelles*, vol. II, p. 332.
[49] Defensor de Ligugé, *Livre d'étincelles*, vol. II, p. 332. See also Henri Crouzel, 'Les Citations d'Origène dans le Livre d'Étincelles de Defensor de Ligugé', *Augustinianum*, 24 (1984): 385–94.
[50] Defensor de Ligugé, *Livre d'étincelles*, vol. II, p. 334. See also David Ganz, 'Knowledge of Ephrem's Writings in the Merovingian and Carolingian Ages', *Hugoye: Journal of Syrian Studies*, 2 (1999): 37–46.

diffusion of patristic texts into late Merovingian Francia,[51] and they also point at the availability of Greek (and maybe Syriac and Coptic) texts, most probably in Latin translation, in the pre-Carolingian West. This should come as no surprise. Eastern texts and intellectual traditions were constantly circulated around Merovingian Gaul, as clearly demonstrated by, for example, Gregory of Tours' Latin translation of *The Seven Sleepers of Ephesos*,[52] or the ample use of *The Apocryphal Collection of Pseudo-Abdias* by Merovingian authors and liturgists.[53] Bearing in mind the range of Defensor's bibliography, the *Liber scintillarum* seems like a heroic attempt to integrate Merovingian culture into a broader Mediterranean and Christian intellectual orbit. Whether the texts used by Defensor had reached the West in their original language and only then were translated into Latin (as in the case of Gregory's *Seven Sleepers of Ephesos*), or whether they had reached Gaul through the mediation of Italy, Spain or the British Isles, is impossible to gauge.[54] Nevertheless, their presence in the *Liber scintillarum* is extremely significant. Moreover, the literary genre to which the *Liber scintillarum* belongs, that is a florilegium of excerpts taken from numerous authors, may have been inspired by the eastern *Apophthegmata patrum*, which reached the West at a fairly early stage.[55]

But there is more to it. Defensor's *Liber scintillarum* was part of an intellectual and creative wave of scholarship that swept Merovingian Gaul towards the end of the seventh and the beginning of the eighth century.[56] Hence, its production coincided with an unprecedented

[51] The knowledge of patristic literature in the pre-Carolingian West still awaits a detailed comparative study. Some comments can be found in Riché, *Education and Culture*. For some specific case studies, see Luce Pietri, 'Venance Fortunat, lecteur des Pères latins', in Benoît Gain, Pierre Jay and Gérard Nauroy (eds.), *Chartae caritatis: études de patristique et d'antiquité tardive en homage à Yves-Marie Duval* (Paris, 2004), pp. 127–41; Martin Heinzelmann, 'The Work of Gregory of Tours and Patristic Tradition', in Alexander C. Murray (ed.), *A Companion to Gregory of Tours* (Leiden, 2016), pp. 281–336.
[52] Gregory of Tours, *Passio sanctorum septem dormientium apud Ephesum*, ed. Bruno Krusch, MGH SRM I.2 (Hanover, 1885), pp. 396–403, and MGH SRM VII (Hanover, 1920), pp. 757–69. See also Tamar Rotman, 'Miraculous History between East and West: Hagiography, Historiography and Identity in Sixth Century Gaul' (Ph.D. dissertation, Ben-Gurion University of the Negev, 2018).
[53] See Els Rose, *Ritual Memory: The Apocryphal Acts and Liturgical Commemoration in the Early Medieval West (c. 500–1215)* (Leiden, 2009).
[54] For some comments, see Pierre Courcelle, *Late Latin Writers and Their Greek Sources*, trans. Harry E. Wedeck (Cambridge, MA, 1969).
[55] On the *Apophthegmata patrum*, see Douglas Burton-Christie, *The Word in the Desert: Scripture and the Quest for Holiness in Early Christian Monasticism* (Oxford and New York, 1993), pp. 76–103. On its Latin version, see A. Wilmart, 'Le Receuil latin des Apophtemes', *Revue Bénédictine*, 34 (1922): 185–98; Wilhelm Bousset, *Apophthegmata* (Tübingen, 1923), pp. 1–208.
[56] Riché, *Education and Culture*, pp. 324–36 and 421–46; Wood, *The Merovingian Kingdoms*, pp. 239–54; Yitzhak Hen, *Culture and Religion in Merovingian Gaul, AD 481–751* (Leiden, 1995), pp. 43–60; Fouracre and Gerberding, *Late Merovingian France*, pp. 26–78. See

downpour of hagiography,[57] the composition of biblical exegesis, such as the commentary on the four gospels wrongly attributed to Theophilus of Antioch,[58] and the revision of the so-called *Collectio Vetus Gallica*, that is, the oldest and most important systematic canon-law collection from Merovingian Gaul.[59] This collection of more than 400 canons, drawn from both the decrees of the first ecumenical councils and the sixth-century Merovingian councils, is arranged in more than sixty chapters, and it is not impossible that the *Vetus Gallica* served as an inspiration, if not a concrete model, for Defensor's endeavour.

The production of the *Liber scintillarum* also coincided with the production and diffusion of a list of approved authors and their works, commonly known as *De libris recipiendis et non recipiendis*,[60] the copying of the Jerome-Gennadius *De viris illustribus*,[61] as well as the experimentation with and production of liturgical text (the earliest we have from Gaul), such as the *Gothic Missal*, the *Missale gallicanum vetus*, the *Bobbio Missal*, the *Old Gelasian Sacramentary*, and the *Lectionary of Luxeuil*.[62] These cultural tendencies were indeed more intense and apparent in the regions of Neustria and Burgundy, but they could also be observed in the region of Poitiers, where the *Liber scintillarum* and the *de-luxe* codex of the *Missale francorum* were produced.[63] All these reflect a late-Merovingian

also the various papers collected in H. Atsma (ed.), *La Neustrie: Les pays au nord de la Loire de 650 à 850*, 2 vols. (Sigmaringen, 1989), vol. II, pp. 297–432.

[57] See, for example, W. Berschin, *Biographie und Epochenstil im lateinischen Mittelalter*, vol. II: *Merowingische Biographie. Italien, Spanien und die Inseln im frühen Mittelalter* (Stuttgart, 1988); Fouracre and Gerberding, *Late Merovingian France*, pp. 26–58.

[58] See Yitzhak Hen, 'A Merovingian Commentary on the Four Gospels', *Revue des Études Augustiniennes*, 49 (2003): 167–87.

[59] Hubert Mordek, 'Kanonistische Aktivität in Gallien in der ersten Hälfte des 8. Jahrhunderts: eine Skizze', *Francia*, 2 (1974): 19–25; Hubert Mordek, *Kirchenrecht und Reform im Frankenreich: die Collectio Vetus Gallica, die älteste systematische Kanonessammlung des Fränkischen Gallien* (Berlin, 1975); Rosamond McKitterick, 'Knowledge of Canon Law in the Frankish Kingdoms before 789: The Manuscript Evidence', *Journal of Theological Studies*, 36 (1985): 97–117.

[60] See E. von Dobschütz, *Das Decretum Gelasianum de libris recipiendis et non recipiendis* (Leipzig, 1912); Rosamond McKitterick, *The Carolingians and the Written Word* (Cambridge, 1989), pp. 200–5.

[61] See Jerome-Gennadius, *De viris inlustribus*, ed. E. C. Richardson (Leipzig, 1896); Richard H. Rouse and Mary A. Rouse, 'Bibliography before Print: The Medieval *De Viris Illustribus*', in Peter Ganz (ed.), *The Role of the Book in Medieval Culture: Proceedings of the Oxford International Symposium, 26 September–1 October 1982*, 2 vols. (Turnhout, 1986), vol. I, pp. 133–53, at pp. 134–6; McKitterick, *The Carolingians and the Written Word*, pp. 200–5.

[62] See Hen, *Culture and Religion*, pp. 43–60; Yitzhak Hen, *The Royal Patronage of Liturgy in Frankish Gaul to the Death of Charles the Bald (877)* (London, 2001), pp. 28–64; Matthieu Smyth, *La Liturgie oubliée: La prière eucharistique en Gaule antique et dans l'Occident non romain* (Paris, 2003).

[63] Vatican, BAV, Reg. lat. 257 (*CLA* I.103). For its edition, see *Missale francorum*, ed. L. C. Mohlberg, L. Eizenhöfer and P. Siffrin (Rome, 1957).

preoccupation with authority, orthodoxy and correctness, and the *Liber scintillarum* fits that context extremely well.

In his prologue, Defensor unveils for us his *modus operandi*. He openly states that he will name the author of each excerpt in order to strengthen the authority of the passages he had collected.[64] This practice of indicating one's sources systematically and throughout the work, which is common to the *Liber scintillarum* and the *Collectio Vetus Gallica*, is quite unique and unusual for an early medieval author. One can find it in Regino of Prüm's *Libri duo de synodalibus causis*,[65] but I am aware of no other similar example before the twelfth century. That, I would argue, is one of the most powerful expressions of the late Merovingian craving for authority, orthodoxy and correctness, and it also reflects didactic and contemplative aims and objectives.

Defensor collected various excerpts from the Bible and the Church Fathers and arranged them thematically; the compiler of the *Vetus Gallica* collected canons and arranged them according to topics; compilers of sacramentaries and lectionaries amassed prayers and reading passages and arranged them according to liturgical cycles; and the various martyrologies and *calendaria* collected saints' feasts and fixed them in a Christian routine of celebration.[66] All these project a sense of authority, orthodoxy and correctness, but at the same time they are extremely careful not to limit the reader's freedom and choices.[67] The overarching didactic and contemplative objectives of these compilations, which can be classified as a late Merovingian peculiarity, determined much of the nature of the texts that were produced. This didactic context, and its monastic contemplative tint, is even more conspicuous when one juxtaposes the topics covered by Defensor's *Liber scintillarum* with the various masses in the third book of the Old Gelasian Sacramentary,[68] or with the topics of

---

[64] *LS*, p. xxxiii [I, p. 48]: 'Sed ne id opus, quasi sine auctore, putetur apocrifum, unicuique sententiae per singular propeium scripsi auctore'.

[65] See Regino of Prüm, *Libri duo de synodalibus causis et disciplinis ecclesiasticis*, ed. H. Wasserschleben (Leipzig, 1840). For a more recent edition, albeit incomplete, see W. Hartmann, *Das Sendhandbuch des Regino von Prüm* (Darmstadt, 2004), pp. 20–468.

[66] See, for example, Hen, *Culture and Religion*, pp. 82–120; Els Rose, 'Hagiography as a Liturgical Act: Liturgical and Hagiographic Commemoration of the Saints in the Early Middle Ages', in M. Barnard, P. Post and E. Rose (eds.), *A Cloud of Witness: Saints and Role Models in Christian Liturgy* (Louvain, 2005), pp. 161–83.

[67] On the issue of uniformity, or lack thereof, see Yitzhak Hen, 'Unity and Diversity: The Frankish Liturgy before the Carolingians', in Robert N. Swanson (ed.), *Unity and Diversity in the Church* (Oxford, 1996), pp. 19–31; Hen, *The Royal Patronage of Liturgy*, pp. 28–33.

[68] See *Liber sacramentorum Romanae aecclesiae ordinis anni circuli (Sacramentarium Gelasianum)*, ed. L. C. Mohlberg, L. Eizenhöfer and P. Siffrin (Rome, 1960), pp. 176–248.

Caesarius of Arles' sermons.[69] The overlap is astounding, and it is against this background that the *Liber scintillarum* should be understood and Defensor's scholarship appreciated.

Although the only piece that Defensor himself has written is his short introduction, still the *Liber scintillarum* appears to be a work of serious scholarship and thoughtful choices. We, as modern scholars, refrain from doing scholarship like that. Rather, we look for the broader picture and always strive to understand the context. For example, a pile of excerpts from Augustine's *Ennarationes in Psalmos*, like the one gathered by Defensor and scattered around the *Liber scintillarum*, can teach us very little about Augustine's theological stance and language.[70] But Defensor, one must constantly bear in mind, operated within a completely different cultural and intellectual framework. For him, forming a coherent book from bits and pieces of biblical and patristic literature was a work of pure scholarship, first and foremost because it answered some didactic and contemplative needs. With its 2,505 citations, the *Liber scintillarum* was a thoughtful reflection of biblical and patristic knowledge, and that is precisely how it was appreciated throughout the Middle Ages and the early modern period. Defensor's *Liber scintillarum* survives in more than 350 manuscripts,[71] which practically means that every medieval library that respected itself had a copy of it.[72] Moreover, it was edited and printed eleven times during the sixteenth century, twice in the seventeenth century, four times during the eighteenth century (once by Mabillon himself), four times during the nineteenth century, and it was reprinted in Migne's *Patrologia Latina*.[73] Finally, during the twentieth century it was edited twice by Henri-Marie Rochais, once for the *Corpus Christianorum* series (1957), and once for the *Sources chrétiennes* (1961).[74] It was constantly read, and there is plenty of evidence to demonstrate that it was used by some of the most illustrious scholars that the medieval world

---

[69] See Caesarius of Arles, *Sermones*, ed. Germain Morin, 2 vols. (Mardesous, 1937–42), reprinted in CCSL 103–4 (Turnhout, 1953).

[70] For an intriguing view on the usefulness of lists and collections of excerpts, see Umberto Eco, *The Infinity of Lists*, trans. Alastair McEwen (London, 2009).

[71] For a list of the various manuscripts, see Rochais, 'Les Manuscrits', pp. 294–309; Rochais, 'Defensoriana', pp. 199–250.

[72] For a list of some medieval catalogues that list the *Liber scintillarum*, see Rochais, 'Defensoriana', pp. 250–2. On its popularity in Anglo-Saxon England, where it was also translated into Old English, see Rolf H. Bremmer, 'The Reception of Defensor's *Liber scintillarum* in Anglo-Saxon England', in Patrizia Lendinara (ed.), ... *un tuo serto di fiori in man recandi: Scritti in onore di Maria Amalia D'Arcono* (Udine, 2008), pp. 75–89. On its popularity in Carolingian Francia, see Hénri-Marie Rochais, 'Le "liber de Virtutibus et Vitiis" d'Alcuin: Note pour l'étude des sources', *Revue Mabillon*, 41 (1951): 77–86.

[73] For a list of these editions, see Rochais, 'Defensoriana', pp. 252–9.

[74] See above, note 1.

had ever produced, such as Peter Abelard, Thomas Aquinas, Stephen Langton, or Erasmus of Rotterdam.

To sum up, Defensor's *Liber scintillarum*, unlike its common reputation among modern scholars, is perhaps the most eloquent witness to the dynamics and breadth of late Merovingian intellectual activity. Reading through it, one is stunned by the amount of scholarship crammed into this small volume. Not only did it render an enormous amount of theological scholarship readily available and accessible, it also introduced eastern patristic thought into the late Merovingian intellectual discourse. Defensor of Ligugé, so it seems, was a stupendous middleman between East and West, North and South, Merovingian times and future generations. If one looks for a true cultural broker in late Merovingian Francia, then Defensor of Ligugé is indeed a noteworthy one.[75]

---

[75] For a modern musical piece by Brian Ferneyhough that was inspired by the *Liber scintillarum*, see www.youtube.com/watch?v=xANR6U5CLG8.

15 Willibald in the Holy Places

Ora Limor

While Jerusalem has been remembered, longed for and commemorated by thousands of pilgrims, not many of them have been commemorated by her. One exception is St Willibald (c. 700–c. 787), a monk from South Anglia who later became the first bishop of Eichstätt in Bavaria, who visited the holy places in the twenties of the eighth century. Willibald's image is depicted in a splendid mosaic at one of the six side chapels surrounding the main altar of the Benedictine Dormition Abbey on Mount Zion (see Fig. 15.1), built in the first decade of the twentieth century.[1] The church is dedicated to the Virgin Mary and built on the spot where tradition located her home after Jesus' crucifixion, the place where her life upon earth ended. The chapel with Willibald's image is the second to the right from the centre. It shows Mary, holding the infant Jesus, surrounded by the patrons of Bavaria, one emperor, six church leaders and a small child. One of the church leaders is St Willibald, depicted kneeling to the left of the Virgin and gazing up at her. Like the other figures in the image, he too is hallowed. Indeed, in 938, he was canonised by Pope Leo VII. Yet, unlike the other five church leaders, who are fashioned as bishops, Willibald is depicted as a pilgrim.[2] In a blunt (probably conscious) anachronistic touch, he is shown with late-medieval pilgrimage attributes: a round hat is swinging from his arm, sandals on his feet, a staff in his hand, a shell on his garment. Willibald, as said above, was also to become a bishop, the founder of the diocese of Eichstätt in Bavaria. His role as a bishop, a position he held for the last fifty years of his life, is perhaps hinted at by the staff with a cross that he holds. Yet when the designer of the church made a decision about how to depict Willibald, he settled on a different role entirely: pilgrim.

---

[1] Research for this chapter was supported by the I-CORE Program (The Israel Science Foundation), Center for the Study of Conversion and Inter-Religious Encounters (No. 1754/12). I am grateful to Moshe Yagur for his help in writing this paper and to Iris Shagrir for her comments. The chapel was designed by a Munich atelier, probably in the 1930s.

[2] He is also the only figure depicted kneeling, perhaps because he is the only one who actually venerated the holy place of the Virgin.

Figure 15.1 Willibald, the Dormition Abbey, Jerusalem, c.1930? Photograph: Moshe Yagur.

The image of Willibald as pilgrim is based on his biography, the *vita*, written by the nun Hygeburg,[3] a young relative of Willibald who lived in the monastery of Heidenheim.[4] Hygeburg tells us that at around age twenty Willibald set out from his native Sussex in the early twenties of the eighth century. He spent more than three years in Rome and almost seven years in the East, of which more than two were in the Holy Land (spring 723–November 726).[5] After some two years in Constantinople and another ten in Monte Cassino, in around 740 Willibald settled as a missionary in Bavaria and became the first bishop of Eichstätt, a position he held for almost fifty years. There Willibald became known as a distinguished church leader and educator. Yet the pilgrimage makes up the major part of the biography (thirteen out of the twenty pages of the printed text). Was it Hygeburg's fascination with the remote, unreachable places of the Gospels that led her to lend such weight to the pilgrimage, or perhaps it was Willibald himself who considered his faraway travels, so rare in his day, the formative experience of his life? This brings us to the much-discussed question of authorship, that is, whose voice is heard in this and similar texts, where pilgrim and author are two different personalities. The question has been raised lately in connection with the treatise *De locis sanctis* by Adomnán of Iona, written in the eighties of the seventh century.[6] Like Hygeburg's biography of Willibald, *De locis sanctis* was written in the West, on the isle of Iona off the coast of Scotland, and, according to its author, it too was based, at least partially, on the experiences of a traveller to the East, a bishop from Gaul named Arculf. For years, Holy Land scholars related the information about the holy places included in the book to Adomnán's informant, the pilgrim Arculf, considering this information the book's most important contribution. Recently however, Irish scholars, in particular Thomas O'Loughlin, have

---

[3] Her name appears in research also as Hugeburc, Hugeberc, and Huneberc. I used 'Hygeburg' following M. Lapidge, 'Hygeburg', in M. Lapidge, J. Blair, S. Keynes and D. Scragg (eds.), *The Blackwell Encyclopedia of Anglo-Saxon England* (Oxford, 1999), p. 246.

[4] *Vitae Willibaldi et Wynnebaldi auctore sanctimoniali Heidenheimensis*, ed. O. Holder-Egger, MGH, SS, 15 (Hanover, 1887), pp. 80–117 (*Vita Willibaldi*, pp. 86–106); Hugeburc, *Vita Willibaldi*, ed. and tr. A. Bauch, Quellen zur Geschichte der Diözese Eichstätt I: Biographien der Gründungszeit (Eichstätter Studien nF. 19) (Regensburg, 1984), pp. 13–87. References in this article are to the MGH edition.

[5] *Vita Willibaldi*, p. 102; English translation: 'Huneberc of Heidenheim, *The Hodoeporicon of Saint Willibald*', trans. C. H. Talbot, in T. F. X. Noble and T. Head (eds.), *Soldiers of Christ: Saints and Saints' Lives from Late Antiquity and the Early Middle Ages* (University Park, PA, 1979), p. 160: 'And it was seven years since he first began his journey from Rome and ten years in all since he had left his native country'.

[6] *Adamnan's De locis sanctis*, ed. D. Meehan, Scriptores Latini Hiberniae 3 (Dublin, 1958); Adamnanus, *De locis sanctis libri tres*, ed. Ludwig Bieler, CCSL, 175 (Turnhout, 1965), pp. 175–234.

attempted to reclaim the book, arguing vigorously that the book is the creation of Adomnán alone, and that Arculf's part in it is negligible or even non-existent.[7] As I have suggested elsewhere, although this conclusion is based on a deep acquaintance with Adomnán's oeuvre and with the monastic culture of his time, effacing completely the contribution of the eyewitness's experience for the study of the holy places diminishes the value of the book and counters the author's express intent.[8]

Hygeburg's book is also a product of a cooperation of sorts between the oral evidence presented by a pilgrim and the output of an author. Yet her aim differs from that of Adomnán in *De locis sanctis*. While the latter is devoted to the holy places and the religious lessons one can glean from them, the former foregrounds the pilgrim – the person over the place. While putting the pilgrim at the centre, Hygeburg also does her best to minimise her own contribution, not only by concealing her identity but also by supplying many details about the creation of the book to the effect that the reader is hardly able to differentiate between writer and protagonist.[9] She tries hard to convince her readers that her report is the fruit of careful investigation, also confirmed by the book's principal actor, the aged and much-respected bishop who related his adventures of long ago. He dictated the story of his travels in the presence of witnesses – a few deacons and novices – and Hygeburg recorded it 'from his own lips'. If so, we must conclude that, although he had been living as a Christian missionary in Bavaria for almost forty years (the interview with Hygeburg took place in June 778), when he decided to tell the tale of his sacred work, he lavished attention on his early pilgrimage. Indeed, while the other parts of the biography are written in an embellished and rather artificial style, the itinerary is written in simple colloquial language, a result of Hygeburg's effort to pen the itinerary as Willibald told it.[10]

---

[7] O'Loughlin devoted some twenty articles and a full book to establish Adomnán's sole authorship of the work. See: T. O'Loughlin, *Adomnán and the Holy Places: Perceptions of an Insular Monk on the Location of the Biblical Drama* (London, 2007); See a summary of the debate over Arculf's historicity in R. Aist, 'Adomnán, Arculf and the Source Material of *De locis sanctis*', in J. M. Wooding, R. Aist, T. O. Clancy and T. O'Loughlin (eds.), *Adomnán of Iona: Theologian, Lawmaker, Peacemaker* (Dublin, 2010), pp. 162–80. See also recently: R. C. Hoyland and S. Waidler, 'Adomnán's *De locis sanctis* and the Seventh-Century Near East', *English Historical Review*, 129 (2014): 787–807; L. Nees, *Perspectives on Early Islamic Art in Jerusalem* (Leiden, 2015), pp. 33–57.

[8] O. Limor, 'Pilgrims and Authors: Adomnán's *De locis sanctis* and Hugeburc's *Hodoeporicon Sancti Willibaldi*', *Revue Bénédictine*, 114 (2004): 253–75.

[9] On Hygegurg's identity, see B Bischoff, 'Wer ist die Nonne von Heidenheim?', *Studien und Mitteilungen zur Geschichte des Benediktiner-Ordens*, 49 (1931): 387f. See also R. Schieffer, 'Hugeburc von Heidenheim', in *Die deutsche Literatur des Mittelalters. Verfasserlexikon*, 4 (Berlin, 1983), pp. 221–2.

[10] E. Gottschaller, *Hugeburc von Heidenheim: Philologische Untersuchungen zu den Heiligenbiographien einer Nonne des achten Jahrhunderts* (Munich, 1973), pp. 75–81.

Not only the language and style of the itinerary chapters but their very rhythm is dictated by linguistic traits characteristic of travel narratives, such as the frequent use of *inde, ibi* and *ille*.[11] As such, it is difficult, if not impossible, to distinguish between the voice of the itinerant monk and that of the sedentary nun.

Willibald's travel account raises many questions, some of which were recently dealt with in Rodney Aist's book, *The Christian Topography of Early Islamic Jerusalem*.[12] My own interest leads me in other directions, tackling mainly problems of memory, selection and transmission. The story of how Willibald's story was committed to writing in June 778, in the Heidenheim monastery, is a striking attestation to the transition from oral transmission to written text and to the actual moment in time when memory was sealed in writing. In the course of a single night, Willibald narrated his adventures, and Hygeburg took notes. Later, she turned these notes into what she describes as 'black tracks ploughed by a pen ... on the white plains of these fields [of parchment]'.[13] These 'pen-ploughed tracks' show that Willibald remembered his route and the stations on it quite well but forgot many details concerning the places he had visited. The lacunae in Hygeburg's text and the schematic quality of the description of the holy places and their traditions become especially evident when the work is compared to other, similar works. Adomnán, for example, supplies much more comprehensive information about the holy places, and the data collected for Charlemagne in the *Commemoratorium de casis Dei* in 808, eighty years after Willibald's visit, lists many churches and monasteries in and around Jerusalem that Willibald ignored.[14] Our protagonist stayed in Jerusalem for a while and returned there four times, no doubt fully familiarising himself with the city's Christian places. As he omits many of them from his review, we can assume that either he considered them sufficiently famous to require no specification or that his memory betrayed him.[15] In view of the five

---

[11] L. Spitzer, 'The Epic Style of the Pilgrim Aetheria', *Comparative Literature*, 1 (1949): 225–58.
[12] R. Aist, *The Christian Topography of Early Islamic Jerusalem: The Evidence of Willibald of Eichstätt (700–787 CE)* (Turnhout, 2009).
[13] *Vita Willibaldi*, p. 88; English translation: *Soldiers of Christ*, p. 145.
[14] M. McCormick, *Charlemagne's Survey of the Holy Land: Wealth, Personnel, and Buildings of a Mediterranean Church between Antiquity and the Middle Ages*, with a critical edition and translation of the original text (Washington, DC, 2011).
[15] Another possibility, although less plausible, is that Hygeburg had not been able to note everything down while the journey was related to her. If Willibald rather narrated and less dictated what he had seen and learnt, this could explain in part the incomplete information in the final text.

decades that elapsed between the travel and the interview with Hygeburg, we should in fact not be surprised by the details he forgot but rather by those he remembered. How indeed did he manage to keep the travel alive in his mind for such a long time? Written notes are a possibility, although there is no hint to this in the text.[16] Another explanation would be that Willibald had repeatedly recounted the trip over the years. So, while the half century that elapsed since the journey may have obscured details, the verbal formulation, rehearsed again and again, kept it lively and fresh. Hygeburg describes one such recounting. It took place on the occasion of Willibald's interview with Pope Gregory III (731–41) during his visit to Rome and before his departure for Germany. This interview, a lovely vignette about a memory of recounting memories, also took place long after Willibald left the Holy Land and holds no additional information about the holy places recounted in the pilgrimage chapters.[17] It would seem that while the repetition of memories kept them alive, it also resulted in a fossilised narrative (as retellings often do), which may also account for the many lacunae.

But ought all lacunae to be blamed on memory? Without doubt, Willibald's remembered landscape is quite selective. It tends towards exotic traditions and emphasises the heroic and wondrous aspects of pilgrimage. The places and deeds carved in his mind were conveyed not only for religious and didactic purposes but, even more, for transmitting to posterity the sense of excitement and awe experienced by a young monk from a faraway land when encountering the sites of venerated history.

Willibald describes only seven holy places in Jerusalem: the compound of the Holy Sepulchre, where he mentions the Finding of the Cross, the Sepulchre and Calvary, but not many other traditions connected with the church (like the tomb of Adam and the Centre of the World); Holy Zion, without mentioning any of the many traditions connected to it (such as the Last Supper, Pentecost, the column of the flagellation, St Stephen's stones); the sheep's pool, without mentioning the nearby house of Mary; the column commemorating the miracle of Mary's funeral; Mary's empty tomb; the place of Agony, without indicating the name of the place – Gethsemane – and without mentioning the nearby place of Betrayal; and the Church of the Ascension, without pointing out its most prominent feature – Jesus's footprints. At the same time, while failing to note central traditions, Willibald supplies information on

---

[16] M. McCormick, *Origins of the European Economy: Communications and Commerce AD 300–900* (Cambridge, 2001), p. 129.
[17] *Vita Willibaldi*, p. 103; *Soldiers of Christ*, p. 161.

marginal sites, markers of local, non-canonical traditions, unfamiliar to travellers from far away: the column commemorating Mary's funeral and the two columns at the Church of the Ascension.

Mary's Funeral Column

One of Willibald's most detailed accounts refers to the column at the place where the Jews attempted to harm Mary's body during her funeral. Willibald is the first Western traveller to mention the place, and it is clear that it made a marked impression on him.

He himself said, that in front of the gate of the city stood a tall pillar, on top of which rose a cross, as a sign and memorial of the place where the Jews attempted to take away the body of Saint Mary. For when the eleven apostles were bearing the body of holy Mary away from Jerusalem the Jews tried to snatch it away as soon as they reached the gate of the city. But as soon as they stretched out their hands toward the bier and endeavoured to take her their arms became fixed, stuck as it were to the bier, and they were unable to move, until, by the grace of God and the prayers of the apostles, they were released, and then they let them go.[18]

Memories of pilgrims such as Willibald are our best witnesses to the evolution of the Christian sacred map and to the way it reflected cult and belief throughout the Christian world. A distinctive example is the evolution of Mary's sacred map.[19] When traced chronologically, pilgrimage accounts show clearly how Mary's topography developed and changed over time, serving as a mirror for the growing devotion to her in both East and West. While accounts from the fourth century scarcely mention any site commemorating Marian traditions, from the sixth century on pilgrims provide evidence for the formation of a sacred map of Mary alongside that of Jesus. Mary's map took shape side by side with the recognition of her elevated status in Christian theology, and, from the sixth century on, sites related to her became a decisive component of

---

[18] *Vita Willibaldi*, pp. 97–8: 'Similiter et ipse dixit, quod ante portam civitatis staret magna columna, et in summitate columne stat crux ad signum et ad memoriam, ubi Iudei volebant tollere corpus sanctae Mariae. Cumque illi 11 apostoli tollentes corpus sanctae Mariae portaverunt illum de Hierusalem, et statim cumque ad portam venerunt civitatis, Iudaei voluerunt conprehendere illum. Statimque illi homines qui porrigebant ad feretra et eam tollere conabant, retentis brachiis quasi glutinati inherebant in feretro et non poterant se movere, antequam Dei gratia et apostolorum petitione iterum resoluti fuerant, et tunc eos reliquerunt'. English translation: *Soldiers of Christ*, p. 156.

[19] O. Limor, 'Mary in Jerusalem: An Imaginary Map', in B. Kühnel, G. Noga-Banai and H. Vorholt (eds.), *Visual Constructs of Jerusalem* (Turnhout, 2014), pp. 11–22, and the bibliography there.

the sacred landscape in Jerusalem and elsewhere. Indeed, three of the seven Jerusalem sites described by Willibald are associated with Mary.

The story of Mary and the Jews is much older than the commemorative column and probably dates to the third century.[20] Its most widespread versions tell how the Jews of Jerusalem tried to harm Mary's body during her funeral. Coming out of the city's gate they were all struck blind, yet one of them managed to get to the bier and get hold of it. As soon as he touched it, his hands were affixed to it as if with glue (or even cut off according to other versions). He was saved only after praying to Mary. The importance that this apocryphal legend acquired in Jerusalem of the seventh century could be seen as a reaction to the return of the Jews to the city after the Muslim conquest and the renewal of old rivalries over the holy city and the holy places. The lesson learnt from this story was more than just a curiosity. Already in late antiquity, in the apocryphal texts relating Mary's biography, her life story was depicted as analogous to the life of Jesus and her body as a focal point in the history of salvation. Like the body of Jesus, his mother's body too was considered holy and free of sin. As such, Christian imagination perceived it as a battlefield between the old and the new law, as so well dramatised in the funeral story, where Mary's flesh provoked the Jews' wrath and they schemed to destroy it. The result of their act is opposite to their intention: instead of destroying Mary's body, they prove its power and sanctity.[21] In the last scene, when the Jew who attacked the body is saved by Mary after praying to her, Mary serves for the first time as *mater mediatrix*, an intercessor even for the sinning Jews, when they repent.[22]

From the length of the description of the funeral legend, we may surmise that it was new both to Willibald as well as to Hygeburg. The column was first mentioned in the Armenian Guide, a short text probably written after the Persian and before the Muslim conquest as a guide for Armenian pilgrims. It mentions the place outside the city where the Jew tried to snatch the bier of the Holy Virgin. 'There is a dome resting on four marble columns and surmounted by a bronze cross'.[23] The structure with four columns is mentioned also by the account of

---

[20] S. J. Shoemaker, *Ancient Traditions of the Virgin Mary's Dormition and Assumption* (Oxford, 2002).

[21] O. Limor, 'Mary and the Jews Story, Controversy, and Testimony', *Historein*, 6 (2006): 55–71.

[22] M. J. Kinservik, 'The Struggle over Mary's Body: Theological and Dramatic Resolution in the N-Town Assumption Play', *The Journal of English and Germanic Philology*, 95 (1996): 193–6.

[23] J. Wilkinson, *Jerusalem Pilgrims before the Crusades* (Warminster, 2002²), p. 166.

Epiphanius Hagiopolita, written in Greek in the late seventh century.[24] As the memorial structure existed even before the Muslim conquest, it was probably shown also to Arculf, Adomnán's informant. Yet Adomnán does not mention it. As a distinguished educator and a renowned scholar, associating himself with the tradition of great authorities such as Jerome, he must have been suspicious of extra-canonical traditions. Even if such traditions had been brought to his attention, he likely would not have seen fit to include them in his text. Willibald seems to be more receptive to local, apocryphal traditions. The special interest in the funeral legend might be accounted for by the appeal of an unfamiliar story about an amazing miracle performed in faraway Jerusalem. With stories like this, new to his listeners, the traveller built his fame as a daring explorer and a hero, risking himself for his faith. Hygeburg, for her part, communicated to the world both the traveller's fame and the wondrous nature of the holy places. Thus, the special place of the funeral story reflects the interest of both pilgrim and author in new and wondrous tales. It also resonates with the growing importance of Mary in Jerusalem as well as the increasing veneration of her in Bavaria, where Willibald built a church of St Mary to replace the smaller church that already stood on the site when he arrived there.[25]

The Two Pillars at the Church of the Ascension

Willibald's selective memory and his attraction to colourful traditions are also salient in his description of the Church of the Ascension. While not mentioning the most significant element in the church, the stone bearing the footsteps of Jesus, he does pay attention to a local tradition he encountered there:

> The church has no roof and is open to the sky, and two pillars stand there inside the church, one against the northern wall, the other against the southern wall. They are placed there in remembrance and as a sign of the two men who said: 'Men of Galilee why do you stand looking into heaven?' (Acts 1:11). Any man who can squeeze his body between the pillars and the wall is freed from his sins.[26]

---

[24] H. Donner, 'Die Palästinabeschreibung des Epiphanius Monachus Hagiopolita', *Zeitschrift des Deutschen Palästina-Vereins (ZDPV)*, 87 (1971): 87–8; Wilkinson, *Jerusalem Pilgrims*, p. 212.
[25] *Vita Willibaldi*, p. 104; *Soldiers of Christ*, p. 162.
[26] *Vita Willibaldi*, p. 98: 'Illa aecclesia est desuper patula et sine tectu; et ibi stant duas columnas intus in aecclesia contra parietem aquilonis et contra parietem meridialis plage. Illa sunt ibi in memoriam et in signum duorum virorum qui dixerunt: 'Viri Galilei, quid aspicitis in caelum'; et ille homo, qui ibi potest inter parietem et columnas

Willibald is the sole Christian witness from the early Middle Ages to the practice of squeezing in the Church of the Ascension, but, interestingly, the habit is mentioned also in Muslim texts. An ancient Muslim teaching, dating to the eighth century (just when Willibald was visiting Jerusalem), attributed to Ka'b al-Akhbar, a Yemenite Jew who had converted to Islam and accompanied 'Umar on his visit to Jerusalem, instructs the Muslims, 'Do not come to the Church of Mary or approach the two pillars, for they are idols. Whoever goes to them, his prayers will be as naught'. Or, in another text: 'Do not come to the Church of Mary ... , nor go into the two pillars in the church of the Mount of Olives (Kanisat al-Tur), for they are both idols and whoever enters there in a spirit of devotion, his act shall be annulled.'[27]

Willibald here shares with his listeners and readers a local custom, not mentioned elsewhere. Even the Piacenza Pilgrim, in around 570, who was an avid collector of traditions and beliefs, did not discuss it. Yet the Muslim prohibition attests its existence in eighth-century Jerusalem. Placed side by side, Willibald's description and the Muslim prohibitions illuminate a shared Jerusalem custom: to visit the Church of the Ascension, pray near the columns, and pass between them and the wall as a penitential act, a proof of forgiveness for one's sins. Islam, like Judaism and Christianity, held the Mount of Olives to be the scene of the Last Judgment and the resurrection of the dead. In Christianity, the Church of the Ascension was considered the closest place on earth to Heaven: 'the Gate of Heaven', 'God's footstool'.[28] The squeezing custom must have impressed Willibald because of the prospect to be freed from sin and its special significance in that particular location – the place from which Jesus ascended to Heaven and where he was destined to return to earth to judge the living and the dead.

The insistence of the traveller and the author on dwelling on the penitential practice is probably evidence of its novelty, a belief unknown to them and thus worthy of recording. The obsession with sin and its repentance, and the gathering of indulgences as a result of this obsession, are traits of late-medieval pilgrimage, yet the notion of privileged places, close to Heaven, where prayers are better heard and accepted, is quite early. We can also say that the idea of pilgrimage as a penitential way of

---

repsere, liber est a peccatis suis'.; English Translation: *Soldiers of Christ*, p. 156 (with some changes).

[27] A. Elad, *Medieval Jerusalem and Islamic Worship: Holy Places, Ceremonies, Pilgrimage* (Leiden, 1995), pp. 139–41.

[28] O. Limor, 'The Place of the End of Days: Eschatological Geography in Jerusalem', in B. Kühnel (ed.), *The Real and Ideal Jerusalem in Jewish, Christian and Islamic Art*, Jewish Art, 23–4 (Jerusalem, 1997/8), pp. 13–24.

life was surely familiar to Willibald and that it had special import in significant places, such as the Mount of Olives, the place of the expected Last Judgment.[29] Herein lies the secret of the attraction that the two columns held: the gap between them and the wall was like the entrance to paradise, and only people who managed to squeeze through the narrow passage would be granted entry.[30]

The two above-discussed traditions indicate the degree to which marvels and miracles were an integral part of the contemporary world picture and the extent to which they were intertwined with pilgrimage and holy places. In this vein, Francesca Vitrone holds that the miracle motive is central to the biography of Wynnebald, Willibald's brother who also acted as a missionary in Germany. In Willibald's text, by contrast, such motive has only a minor place, with travel taking pride of place, and the fact that the hero was still alive when the biography was written.[31] I tend to disagree with this assessment. Willibald's journey was full of wonders: struck blind, he was cured when entering the Holy Sepulchre; he met a lion but was saved, and he had managed to escape for such a long a time 'the wickedness of the pagans', as the pope put it.[32] As François Hartog has noted, 'Any traveler's tale that claims to be a faithful report must contain a category of *thoma* (marvels, curiosities) ... It is as if it were postulated that far away, in these other countries, there were bound to be marvels/curiosities'.[33] Hygeburg's text, in which pilgrimage and marvels are so of a piece, is a fine example of this position.

The Tale of the Balsam

One of the most widespread pilgrimage customs, a distinct characteristic of Christian pilgrimage from its beginnings, was to collect relics and sacred objects and to bring them back home. These objects represented

---

[29] M. Dietz, *Wandering Monks, Virgins, and Pilgrims: Ascetic Travel in the Mediterranean World AD 300–800* (Philadelphia, PA, 2005), pp. 189–212.

[30] After Saladin's conquest of Jerusalem in 1187, when the Church of the Ascension became a mosque and was drastically reduced in size, the pillars, together with many other attractions, disappeared, and only the footprints remained in situ. In the thirteenth century, we first hear that the squeezing 'devotional sport' moved to the neighboring tomb of Pelagia, where it remains to the present day. O. Limor, 'Pelagia's Tomb on the Mount of Olives: Sin, Repentance, Salvation', *Cathedra*, 118 (2006): 13–40 (Hebrew).

[31] F. Vitrone, 'Hugeburc di Heidenheim e le *Vitae Willibaldi et Wynnebaldi*', *Hagiographica*, 1 (1994): 43–79, especially pp. 56, 64.

[32] *Vita Willibaldi*, p. 103; *Soldiers of Christ*, p. 161.

[33] F. Hartog, *The Mirror of Herodotus: The Representation of the Other in the Writing of History*, trans. J. Lloyd (Berkeley, CA, 1988), pp. 230, 231.

the sublime nature of the holy places and served as a metonym for them.[34] The more wealthy pilgrims brought back with them rare items, such as a scrap of the Holy Cross or of the crown of thorns or relics of saints, but the common travellers had to do with more mundane objects, such as geological or botanical fragments, or fruits grown in the holy ground.[35] The collection of Holy Land objects assembled by the Piacenza Pilgrim in around 570, is a conspicuous example of the urge felt by pilgrims to bring back some physical traits of the holiness they encountered.[36] The Piacenza Pilgrim seems to have been singular only with respect to the volume of his collection and the documentation of his catch; the act of collecting itself was rather diffused.

Hygeburg does not mention relics Willibald may have brought with him from the East. In a sole sentence at the end of her text, she writes, 'And all through the land of Bavaria, now dotted about with churches, priests' houses, and the relics of saints, he amassed treasures worthy of our Lord'.[37] It is hard to connect this general phrase with any items Willibald himself may have brought from the Holy Land. However, in a recent article, analysing the relic collections in eleventh-century Eichstätt and Exeter, Julia Smith tried to make such a connection.[38] The Eichstätt collection was assembled by Bishop Gundechar of Eichstätt (1057–75), who worked hard to promote the reputation and resources of his diocese. 'As in other major eleventh-century churches', writes Smith, 'Eichstätt's multiple altars transported the specific history of the diocese with its own patronal saints onto the universal narrative of Christian salvation'.[39] In 1060, Bishop Gundechar marked 22 July, the day on which Willibald's priestly ordination was commemorated, by consecrating the

---

[34] J. M. H. Smith, 'Relics: An Evolving Tradition in Latin Christianity', in C. Hahn and H. A. Klein (eds.), *Saints and Sacred Matter: The Cult of Relics in Byzantium and Beyond* (Washington, DC, 2015), pp. 41–60; J. M. H. Smith, 'Portable Christianity: Relics in the Medieval West (c.700–1200)', *Proceedings of the British Academy*. 181 (2012) 143–67; J. Strong, 'Relics', in L. Jones (ed.), *Encyclopedia of Religion* (Detroit, MI, 2005), pp. 7686–92.

[35] For such natural objects, see O. Limor, 'Earth, Stone, Water and Oil: Objects of Veneration in Holy Land Travel Narratives', in R. Bartal, N. Bodner and B. Kühnel (eds.), *Natural Materials of the Holy Land and the Visual Translation of Place, 500–1500* (London and New York, 2017), pp. 3–18.

[36] *Itinerarium Antonini Piacentini: Un viaggio in Terra Santa del 560–570*, ed. Celestina Milani (Milan, 1977); Antoninus, *Itinerarium*, ed. P. Geyer, CCSL 175, pp. 127–74; English translation by Wilkinson, *Jerusalem Pilgrims*, pp. 129–51.

[37] *Vita Willibaldi*, p. 106: 'sanctorumque reliquiis dignas Domino delibat dona'; English translation: *Soldiers of Christ*, p. 164.

[38] J. M. H. Smith, 'Eleventh-Century Relic Collections and the Holy Land', in R. Bartal, N. Bodner and B. Kühnel (eds.), *Natural Materials of the Holy Land and the Visual Translation of Place, 500–1500* (London and New York, 2017), pp. 19–35.

[39] Smith, 'Eleventh-Century Relic Collections', p. 22.

Willibald altar in the choir. The altar held seventy-four relics, five of which referenced the Holy Land. Another four were kept in the St Willibald western crypt. These sacred objects made Jerusalem present in Eichstätt and commemorated Willibald: a pilgrim, a monk and a bishop.[40]

Among the relics mentioned in the Eichstätt list is vegetation from the Holy Land: fronds from a palm which Jesus had carried and a piece of the tree 'under which the shepherds were when the angel appeared to them'.[41] This exceptional object, Smith suggests, may have derived from Willibald's own pilgrimage to the Holy Land, for Hygeburg reports that his itinerary included 'the place where the angel appeared to the Shepherds'.[42] Although Smith herself asserts that the channels through which Holy Land relics circulated are usually hard to identify, and consequently none of the relics in the Eichstätt list can be connected to Willibald with any confidence, Smith's suggestion about the piece from the tree of the shepherds can be substantiated by one of the most peculiar vignettes in the pilgrimage story, the tale about the balsam. This vignette attests that Willibald indeed took out of the Holy Land some valuable objects.

Towards the end of the Holy Land section of the book, Hygeburg deviates from the sequence of Willibald's pilgrimage to tell in great detail a smuggling story that she represents as an outstanding and risky adventure. Willibald, according to the story, acquired in Jerusalem some valuable balsam and put it in a calabash.[43] He then took a hollow reed[44] that had a bottom to it and filled it with petrol oil. Next, he cut the reed equal to the calabash so their surface was even and closed the mouth of the calabash. Upon reaching Tyre, Willibald was detained for examination and his belongings were checked. The punishment for smuggling was death, we are assured, or better in Hygeburg words: 'and if they had found anything they would immediately have punished them with a martyr's death'.[45] Luckily, when the authorities in Tyre sniffed the calabash, they smelt the petrol oil which was in the reed on the top and did not discover the balsam hidden inside.

---

[40] Quoting the title of the exhibition held in Eichstätt in 1987, marking Willibald's 1200 day of death: B. Appel, E. Braun and S. Hofmann (eds.), *Hl. Willibald 787–1987: Künder des Galubens, Pilger, Mönch, Bischof* (Eichstätt, 1987).
[41] Smith, 'Eleventh-Century Relic Collections', p. 25.
[42] *Vita Willibaldi*, p. 98; *Soldiers of Christ*, p. 156.
[43] *Vita Willibaldi*, p. 101: 'replevit unam munerbam'. *Soldiers of Christ*, p. 159: A calabash is a dried gourd used as a container.
[44] Canna, *Vita Willibaldi*, p. 101; *Soldiers of Christ*, p. 159.
[45] *Vita Willibaldi*, p. 101: 'et si aliquid invenissent, cito illos punientes martyrizarent'. *Soldiers of Christ*, p. 159.

The story may support McCormick's assumption that Willibald was also involved in commercial activity, an assumption that may explain his many travels back and forth: four times to Jerusalem, three times to Damascus.[46] But what is interesting from the narrative point of view is the way Hygeburg tells the story. Willibald's balsam adventure is framed as a heroic story that combines the protagonist's resourcefulness with the unfailing help that God provided his believer, the devout pilgrim, who was ready to suffer a martyr's death for the sake of the balsam. Balsam was the most celebrated product of Judea during the Roman and early Byzantine period and the most valuable one.[47] Willibald's story is very late evidence of its production there, perhaps the latest one. Exquisite, exotic and important for liturgical use, balsam here also holds a symbolic meaning, which may explain the place this episode acquires in the pilgrimage narrative. Willibald's pilgrimage took place not long after the Muslim conquest of Palestine, shedding some light on the conditions in the country and the state of the Christian holy places at a time for which there is relatively sparse evidence. After more than 300 years of Christian exclusivity, Jerusalem became again a shared space, hosting Christians, Muslims and Jews, and ruled by the Muslims. This may explain the place, length and tone of the balsam story. On an allegorical level, the balsam may stand for Jerusalem itself, as if Willibald managed to smuggle the holy city out, under the very noses of the Muslims, as it were. For this, he was ready even to risk his life and die a martyr's death.

In a historical perspective, all three stories – Mary's funeral columns, the two Mount of Olives columns and the tale of the balsam – resonate with the religious and political situation in eighth-century Jerusalem and draw their significance from it. While the funeral story revitalises the old rivalry with the Jews who were allowed by the Muslims to return to the city after hundreds of years of absence, the balsam story reflects the new rivalry with the Muslims, who replaced the Christians as rulers and who also claimed ownership to the holy city. Conversely, the squeezing habit reveals a shared practice by Christians and Muslims that reflects both local expressions of religious conversations and the very possibility of sharing the sacred.

We are left with many questions concerning the pilgrimage narrative. For instance, Willibald's long stay in the East and his travelling back and

---

[46] McCormick, *Origins of the European Economy*, p. 133. See also J. Sumption, *Pilgrimage: An Image of Medieval Religion* (London, 1975), p. 209.

[47] On its reputation in the early Middle Ages, see the ninth-century text *Anonymi Leidensis de Situ Orbis Libri Duo*, ed. R. Quadri (Padova, 1974), pp. 74–5; see also A. Grabois, *Le Pèlerin occidental en Terre Sainte au Moyen Âge* (Paris, 1998), p. 121, note 15.

forth remain a mystery. McCormick believes that he was some kind of petty merchant while Dietz, for her part, thinks that he was studying monastic life (he does mention many monasteries on his route, and probably lodged in them).[48] Certainly, his long stay in the East does not support Hygeburg's emphasis on the cruelty of the Saracens.[49] For her, his encounters with them were an integral part of his adventures and the harsh experiences that he had to endure. It is the pope himself who provides the strongest evidence for the prestige that accompanied the heroic pilgrim, as recorded by Hygeburg from Willibald's mouth. The pope admired him for spending seven years travelling 'to the ends of the earth' and for 'contriving to escape for so long a time the wickedness of the pagans'.[50]

From a distance of two generations, Willibald recounted his travel to the Holy Land as an adventure in a far-off, foreign land, dotted with exotic yet theologically important experiences. The illnesses, the blindness, the courage, the unsatiated longing for Jerusalem, and also the appeal of unknown places and of Holy Land objects, all these remained fixed in the traveller's mind and served the hagiographic purpose of the work and its heroic dimension as both Willibald and Hygeburg strived to design it. Now we can understand the place of the pilgrimage in the narrative. Willibald achieved great things in Christian Bavaria during the long years he acted there, yet it was precisely the youthful pilgrimage period that was constitutive of his identity. This is the image of him Hygeburg left for posterity, and this is the image the artists of the Dormition Abbey in Jerusalem learnt from her when depicting him as a pilgrim. As for Willibald himself, we can be quite sure that being brought to Jerusalem for the fifth time and portrayed there as a lifelong pilgrim would have been much to his liking.

---

[48] Dietz, *Wandering Monks*, pp. 200–12.
[49] Willibald was held prisoner in Emesa (Homs). He was careful to get proper documents in his second visit to Syria: *Vita Willibaldi*, pp. 94, 100.
[50] *Vita Willibaldi*, p. 103; *Soldiers of Christ*, p. 161.

Part V
Rethinking the Late Merovingians

16 'Great Security Prevailed in Both East and West': The Merovingian Kingdoms and the Sixth Ecumenical Council (680/1)

Stefan Esders

Naturally, the idea of an 'ecumenical' council revolved around the question of how Christians of the whole inhabited world could be represented by the Christian church in defining dogmas and essential rules of the Christian faith.[1] The Roman emperor's responsibility to maintain the unity of the faith among his Christian subjects became fixed under Constantine at the Council of Nicaea, later classified as the first ecumenical council.[2] Constantine also took care of the Christians in Persia, but the integration of Christians under non-Roman rule was only conceptualised as *ecclesia in barbaricis gentibus* by the second ecumenical council held in 381.[3] The emergence of the barbarian kingdoms in the Roman West made things more complicated, as can be observed for Gaul. Having adopted Catholicism, the Merovingian kings governed former Roman provinces with well-established ecclesiastical structures and presided over synods whose decrees they confirmed by their legislation.[4] In so doing, they apparently also accepted their Christian subjects' representation within the Christian Roman Empire through the bishop of Rome as the Western patriarch.[5] This changed only in the early Carolingian period when under Charlemagne indignation arose at court that Frankish bishops had not been invited to the seventh ecumenical

---

[1] E. R. Fairweather, and E. R. Hardy, *The Voice of the Church: The Ecumenical Council* (Greenwich, CT, 1962); C. Lange, *Einführung in die allgemeinen Konzilien* (Darmstadt, 2012).
[2] *Conciliorum oecumenicorum generaliumque decreta, editio critica*, vol. I: *The Oecumenical Councils from Nicaea I to Nicaea II (325–787)* (CC COGD 1), ed. G. Alberigo (Turnhout, 2006), pp. 1–34.
[3] First Council of Constantinople a. 381, c. 2: *Conciliorum oecumenicorum generaliumque decreta*, pp. 35–70, at p. 36. R. W. Mathisen, 'Barbarian Bishops and the Churches *in barbaricis gentibus* in Late Antiquity', *Speculum*, 72 (1997): 664–95.
[4] O. Pontal, *Die Synoden im Merowingerreich* (Paderborn, 1986); G. I. Halfond, *The Archaeology of Frankish Church Councils, AD 511–768* (Leiden, 2010).
[5] See H. Mordek, *Kirchenrecht und Reform im Frankenreich. Die Collectio Vetus Gallica, die älteste systematische Kanonessammlung des fränkischen Gallien. Studien und Edition* (Berlin and New York, 1975), p. 82.

council of Nicaea in 787. Consequently, he commissioned the writing of the *Libri Carolini* as a theological statement[6] and convoked a large synod that referred to the ecumenical council bluntly as the 'synod of the Greeks'.[7] His imperial coronation in 800 effectively ended the pope's role as Western patriarch of an imperial church governed from Constantinople.[8]

It may thus be asked what precise role could be attributed to the Merovingian kings with regard to an ecumenical council. From the perspective of Constantinople, a loyal, Catholic Frankish king had to ensure that bishops under his rule could communicate with their fellow bishops inside and outside his realm and travel to Rome, and also had to enforce an ecumenical council's decisions in his realm. The importance of such long-distance, inner-ecclesiastical communication becomes visible for the first time during the preparations for the controversial fifth ecumenical council convoked for the purpose of condemning the Three Chapters. While the pope was detained in Constantinople, ecclesiastical networks operated on various scales and even linked up to diplomacy between emperor and kings.[9] The sixth ecumenical council held at Constantinople in 680/1, which is at the heart of the following contribution, finds the emperor and the pope willing to restore their long lost harmony, disrupted by Monotheletism and the Lateran Council of 649, as Constantine IV was seeking to establish peace and Pope Agatho, as Western patriarch, to forge a consensus among the churches under barbarian rule.[10] While the theological issues of the council[11] and the Latin transmission of its acts[12] are beyond the scope of this paper, a closer look at diplomatic gestures and episcopal mobility in the 660s and 670s reveals that even in the later Merovingian period, which is often portrayed as one of political decline, internal strife and isolation,[13]

---

[6] *Opus Caroli regis contra synodum (Libri Carolini)*, ed. A. Freeman (MGH Concilia 2, Supplementum I) (Hanover, 1998).

[7] Synodus Francofurtensis a. 794, c. 2: *Capitularia regum Francorum 1*, ed. A. Boretius (MGH LL Sect. II, 1) (Hanover, 1883), no. 28, pp. 73–4.

[8] See R. Schieffer, 'Der Papst als Patriarch von Rom', in M. Maccarrone (ed.), *Il primato del vescovo di Roma nel primo millennio* (Vatican City, 1991), pp. 433–51, at p. 446.

[9] See I. N. Wood, 'The Franks and Papal Theology, 550–660', in C. Chazelle and C. Cubitt (ed.), *The Crisis of the Oikoumene. The Three Chapters Controversy and the failed quest for unity in the sixth-century Mediterranean* (Turnhout, 2007), pp. 223–41, at pp. 223–33.

[10] J. Herrin, *The Formation of Christendom* (Oxford, 1987), pp. 275–80.

[11] On the theological background and the sources, see F. Winkelmann, *Der monenergetisch-monotheletische Streit* (Frankfurt, 2001); C. Lange, *Mia Energeia: Untersuchungen zur Einigungspolitik des Kaisers Heraclius und des Patriarchen Sergius von Constantinopel* (Tübingen, 2012).

[12] See R. Riedinger, *Kleine Schriften zu den Konzilsakten des 7. Jahrhunderts* (Turnhout, 1998), nos. 5, 7, 16 and 18.

[13] For example, E. Ewig, *Die Merowinger und das Imperium* (Opladen, 1983), p. 56.

kings, mayors of the palace and the episcopate were struggling hard to find a position for themselves in the wider Mediterranean world of the Christian Oikoumene.

Episcopal Mobility and Networks, and Suspicion against Clerics in the 660s

Coinciding with the Arab expansion, the Christological dogma of Monotheletism, introduced in 638 by Emperor Heraclius' *Ekthesis* and confirmed by Constans II's *Typos* in 648, caused enormous episcopal activity and mobility across the Mediterranean. It culminated in the Lateran synod of 649,[14] which, as it was directed against both emperors' religious policies, cannot really be regarded as an ecumenical council though the pope and his advisers were seeking to convey exactly this impression.[15] It intended to bring about a general reaffirmation of Western religious solidarity under the papacy, whose primacy subsequently even came to be accepted by some Palestinian bishops.[16] Merovingian Gaul appears to have been involved in the exchange of religious ideas connected to this as early as in the 640s.[17] When the Lateran synod condemned Monotheletism in 649, Pope Martin transmitted the synodal acts to Bishop Amandus of Maastricht, requesting that he encourage the Austrasian king, Sigibert III, to send a delegation of bishops to Rome who 'may act as delegates of the apostolic see and transmit without fail the proceedings of our council together with these our synodical letters to our most clement prince', the emperor, Constans II.[18] However, as it seems, Sigibert III was not willing to follow the pope's policy towards Constantinople. He forbade the bishops of his Aquitanian possessions to participate in a synod to be convoked by their metropolitan bishop, Vulfoleudes of

---

[14] P. Booth, *Crisis of Empire: Doctrine and Dissent at the End of Late Antiquity* (Berkeley, CA, 2013).
[15] C. Cubitt, 'The Lateran Council of 649 as an Ecumenical Council', in R. Price and M. Whitby (eds.), *Chalcedon in Context: Church Councils 400–700* (Liverpool, 2009), pp. 133–47.
[16] Booth, *Crisis of Empire*, pp. 273–4.
[17] Vita Eligii episcopi Noviomagensis I, 35–6, ed. B. Krusch, in *Passiones vitaeque sanctorum aevi Merovingici* 2 (MGH SS rer. Mer. 4) (Hanover, 1902), pp. 691–5; see L. Sarti in this volume.
[18] *Concilium Lateranense a. 649 celebratum*, ed. R. Riedinger (*Acta conciliorum oecumenicorum* II,1) (Berlin, 1984), pp. 422–4; *The Acts of the Lateran Synod of 649*, trans. R. Price (Liverpool, 2014), pp. 40–412, at p. 411. See G. Scheibelreiter, 'Griechisches – lateinisches – fränkisches Christentum: Der Brief Martins I. an den Bischof Amandus von Maastricht aus dem Jahre 649', *Mitteilungen des Instituts für Österreichische Geschichtsforschung*, 100 (1992): 84–102, and C. Mériaux's chapter in this volume.

Bourges, apparently to deal with this matter.[19] Vulfoleudes, along with all other bishops subject to King Clovis II (Sigibert's brother), seems to have adopted the position of the Lateran synod, since a Neustrian synod was assembled at Chalons, probably in 650, whose first canon echoed the Lateran synod's position in condemning Monotheletism.[20] While Bishop Eligius of Noyon was for some reason prevented from travelling to Rome, it seems possible that Wandregisil took over his job and went to the eternal city.[21] The impression that the two Merovingian kingdoms took up a different stance concerning the Lateran synod of 649 seems to be confirmed by the fact that in Austrasia Amandus resigned from his position as bishop of Maastricht soon after.[22]

Constans II's move to southern Italy and Sicily in 663,[23] launched after having held trials against his ecclesiastical opponents in the 650s[24] and signing a peace treaty with the Arabs, had a profound impact on the West. Theodore of Tarsus, who was appointed archbishop of Canterbury in 668, had to stop at Arles on his way to Britain, since travel documents issued by Pope Vitalian were not accepted by Archbishop John of Arles, a loyal supporter of the Frankish mayor of the palace, Ebroin.[25] Having received his travel permission,[26] Theodore continued to Paris, where he wintered with Bishop Agilbert before continuing from Quentovic to Britain, with the permission of Ebroin and the help of King Egbert of

---

[19] Desiderius of Cahors, *Epistulae* II, 17: 'Desiderii episcopi Cadurcensis epistolae', ed. W. Arndt, in *Epistulae Merowingici et Karolini aevi 1* (MGH Epp. III,1) (Berlin, 1892), pp. 192–214, at p. 212.
[20] Synod of Chalon, Preface and c. 1: *Concilia Galliae A. 511–A. 695*, ed. C. de Clercq (CC SL 148A) (Turnhout, 1963), p. 303. The synod revealingly omits any reference to the fifth ecumenical council that had condemned the Three Chapters.
[21] *Vita Eligii*, I, 33: *Passiones vitaeque sanctorum aevi Merovingici 2*, pp. 689–90. See J. Semmler, 'Die Friesenmission und der Eintritt den in der alten Provinz Germania II gelegenen Bistümer in die karolingische Reichskirche', *Annalen des Historischen Vereins für den Niederrhein*, 212 (2009): 1–43, at p. 7. On Wandregisil's role, see A. Borias, 'Saint-Wandrille et la crise monothélite', *Revue Benedictine*, 97 (1987): 42–67.
[22] On Amandus' resignation, see R. Price, in *The Acts of the Lateran Synod of 649*, p. 393. For the interpretation given here, see in more detail S. Esders, 'King Chindasvinth, the "Gothic Disease" and the Monothelite Crisis', *Millennium-Jahrbuch* (forthcoming).
[23] P. Corsi, *La spedizione italiana di Costante II* (Bologna, 1983), pp. 79–105; V. Prigent, 'La Sicile de Constant II: l'apport des sources sigillographiques', in A. Nef and V. Prigent (eds.), *La Sicile byzantine de Byzance à l'Islam* (Paris, 2010), pp. 157–87.
[24] W. Brandes, '"Juristische" Krisenbewältigung im 7. Jahrhundert? Der Prozess gegen Papst Martin I. und Maximus Homologetes', in L. Burgmann (ed.), *Fontes Minores* X (Frankfurt, 1998), pp. 141–212.
[25] Beda Venerabilis, *Historia ecclesiastica gentis Anglorum*, IV, 1: *Bede's Ecclesiastical History of the English People*, ed. B. Colgrave and R. A. B. Mynors (Oxford, 1969), pp. 328–32.
[26] For travel documents granting royal protection, see for example, Formula Marculfi I, 24 (*Carta de mundeburde regis et principis*): *Marculfi formularum libri duo*, ed. A. Uddholm (Uppsala, 1962), pp. 98–100.

Kent. His companion, Hadrian,[27] took a more easterly route via Sens, where he met Archbishop Emmo,[28] and Meaux, where he visited Bishop Faro, both important figures operating in various aristocratic and ecclesiastical networks that extended beyond the Channel. Agilbert, a former bishop of Wessex and close ally of Wilfrid of York, had become bishop of Paris probably in 667. He was related to the noble family of the Faronids, of Burgundian origin, and connected to the royal courts of Kent and East Anglia, as was Bishop Faro of Meaux, a former *referendarius* of King Dagobert I, associated with the Columbanian movement and in close contact with Hadrian.[29] Indeed, the Merovingian church appears to have been very open to different external influences in the seventh century.[30] For reasons untold by Bede, Ebroin began to suspect Hadrian of forging a Byzantine–Anglo-Saxon political alliance[31] against the Frankish kingdom of which he had the chief charge. Ebroin's suspicion may have arisen from the fact that Emperor Constans resided in Sicily at that time and that Hadrian had been abbot of a monastery in Naples, where Constans' troops and fleet were positioned in his war against the Lombards.[32] From a Frankish perspective, Constans' image as a heretical ruler did not rule out such a diplomatic alliance. Theodore came from Tarsus and certainly was thinking in terms of an imperial church, while Hadrian had already travelled to Gaul twice before he was asked to

---

[27] They were also accompanied by Benedict Biscop, later founder of the monastery of Jarrow, who had some sort of network near Vienne. See I. N. Wood, 'The Continental Connections of Anglo-Saxon Courts from Æthelberht to Offa', in *Le relazioni internazionali nell'alto medio evo* (Spoleto, 2011), pp. 443–78, at p. 459.

[28] On Emmo, see E. Ewig, 'Die Klosterprivilegien des Metropoliten Emmo von Sens, das Reichskonzil von Mâlay-le-Roi (660) und der Sturz des Metropoliten Aunemund von Lyon (661/62)', in G. Jenal (ed.), *Herrschaft, Kirche und Kultur: Beiträge zur Geschichte des Mittelalters* (Stuttgart, 1993), pp. 63–82.

[29] R. Le Jan, *Famille et pouvoir dans le monde franc (VIIe–Xe siècles): Essai d'anthropologie sociale* (Paris, 1995), pp. 390–1; Wood, 'The Continental Connections', pp. 462 and 470; Y. Fox, *Power and Religion in Merovingian Gaul: Columbanian Monasticism and the Frankish Elites* (Cambridge, 2014), pp. 80–1 and 205–13.

[30] See I. N. Wood, 'Reform and the Merovingian Church', in R. Meens, D. van Espelo, B. van den Hoven van Genderen, J. Raaijmakers, I. van Renswoude and C. van Rhijn (eds.), *Religious Franks: Religion and Power in the Frankish Kingdoms* (Manchester, 2016), pp. 95–111, at p. 111.

[31] On Byzantine and Anglo-Saxon relations, see R. S. Lopez, 'Le Problème des relations anglo-byzantines du septième au dixième siècle', *Byzantion*, 18 (1946–8): 139–62; C. Morrison, 'Byzantine Coins in Early Medieval Britain: A Byzantinist's Assessment', in R. Naismith, M. Allen and E. Screen (eds.), *Early Medieval Monetary History: Studies in Memory of Mark Blackburn* (Farnham, 2014), pp. 207–42.

[32] S. Esders, 'Konstans II. (641–668), die Sarazenen und die Reiche des Westens: Ein Versuch über politisch-militärische und ökonomisch-finanzielle Verflechtungen im Zeitalter eines mediterranen Weltkrieges', in J. Jarnut and J. Strothmann (eds.), *Die Merowingischen Monetarmünzen als Quelle zum Verständnis des 7. Jahrhunderts in Gallien* (Munich, 2013), pp. 189–241, at pp. 190–1.

accompany Theodore so that, according to Bede, he 'would not contrary to the true faith introduce Greek habits into the church'.[33] As Theodore had fled from Constantinople and possibly became aware of the Lateran Council when he was a monk in Rome,[34] Bede's remark cannot refer to Monotheletism but nevertheless may have 'reflected a persistent undercurrent of uneasiness among a large segment of Western ecclesiastics about the orthodoxy of their Eastern brethren'.[35]

Such external connections should be kept in mind when considering Ebroin's conflicts with bishops attested from c. 660 onward. According to his biography, Wilfrid, later bishop of York, visited his colleague and friend, Archbishop Aunemund of Lyons while on his way to Rome, probably in 662. Aunemund offered his brother's daughter to Wilfrid, who was still a layman, and mysteriously promised him the rule over 'a good part of Gaul' (*bonam partem Galliarum ad regendam in saeculum*), which Wilfrid wisely declined.[36] On his way back to Britain he found the archbishop of Lyon together with his brother, prefect of the same city, accused of treason (*pro infidelitatis crimine*). According to the acts of his martyrdom, Aunemund responded to the royal judge in his defence: 'I have not become so wildly mad that I would envy the glory of the one whose name I took from the font, and of whose Christianity I stand as a witness, and secretly try to bring in a foreign people' (*extraneam gentem occulte invitare*).[37] We cannot prove whether this charge was correct or not, but it seems clear that it must have referred to either Byzantine or Anglo-Saxon connections (or both).[38] Loyalty mattered much to Ebroin, who is reported to have issued a tyrannical edict:

> that no one from the region of Burgundy was to come to the palace unless he had ordered him to come. Because of his fear now all the leading men were suspect,

---

[33] Beda, *Historia*, IV, 1: *Bede's Ecclesiastical History*, p. 331.
[34] It is not clear whether Theodore while being a monk in Rome took part in the Lateran Council. For a positive vote, see Booth, *Crisis of Empire*, pp. 271 and 299.
[35] A. J. Ekonomou, *Byzantine Rome and the Greek Popes: Eastern Influences on Rome and the Papacy from Gregory the Great to Zacharias, AD 590–752* (Lanham, MD, 2007), p. 164.
[36] *Vita Wilfridi*, 4: *The Life of Bishop Wilfrid by Eddius Stephanus*. Text, translation and notes by B. Colgrave (Cambridge, 1927), pp. 10–11. On the biblical modeling of this passage, see T. Foley, *Images of Sanctity in Eddius Stephanus' 'Life of Saint Wilfrid', an Early English Saint's Life* (Lewiston, NY, 1992), p. 30; P. Fouracre, 'Wilfrid and the Continent', in N. J. Higham (ed.), *Wilfrid of York: Abbot, Bishop, Saint* (Donington, 2013), pp. 186–99, at pp. 187–8.
[37] *Acta Aunemundi*, cc. 3 and 8; *Vita S. Aunemundi* 2, AA SS 7. Sept. (Antwerp, 1760), p. 744; trans. P. Fouracre and R. A. Gerberding, *Late Merovingian France: History and Hagiography, 640–720* (Manchester, 1996), pp. 183 and 186–7, referring this to Chlothar III's baptism.
[38] See Ewig, 'Die Klosterprivilegien', pp. 81–2.

because he thought to increase his crime either by condemning certain people to death by cutting off their head or by taking away their lands.[39] The double sanction mentioned here – decapitation along with confiscation – clearly refers to trials of treason, as two further sources report that several members of the ecclesiastical and lay aristocracy of Burgundy were executed on this charge, with the bishops among them becoming venerated as martyrs soon thereafter.[40] Even the fairly balanced Passio of Praeiectus of Clermont records that Ebroin was 'at other times energetic, but too cruel in his killing of priests' (*in nece sacerdotum nimis ferocem*),[41] while, according to another source, under 'the wicked queen Jezebel' (Balthild) in the early 660s, a total number of nine bishops were killed.[42] The mayor, while seeking to monopolise access to the royal court, may have become suspicious as he found it difficult to see southern aristocratic bishops act in purely ecclesiastical terms. Among Constans' predecessors, even the Roman emperor Heraclius, despite being a heretic in papal eyes, and contrary also to the Frankish chronicler Fredegar's verdict,[43] was capable of being seen in much more positive terms in Merovingian Gaul. Heraclius' victory over the Persians and his return of the True Cross to Jerusalem in 630 were commemorated through the liturgical feast of the exaltation of the Cross, which spread quickly in the West in the mid seventh century.[44] Apparently a relic of the True Cross came to Saint-Denis as part of a treaty concluded between

---

[39] *Passio Leudegarii episcopi Augustodunensis* I, 4, ed. B. Krusch, in *Passiones vitaeque sanctorum aevi Merovingici* 3 (MGH SS rer. Mer. 5) (Hanover, 1910), p. 287. Transl. Fouracre and Gerberding, *Late Merovingian France*, p. 221 (slightly altered).

[40] P. Fouracre, 'Why Were So Many Bishops Killed in Merovingian Francia?', in N. Fryde and D. Reitz (eds.), *Bischofsmord im Mittelalter – Murder of Bishops* (Göttingen, 2003), pp. 13–35.

[41] *Passio Praeiecti* c. 26: *Passio Praeiecti episcopi et martyris Averni*, ed. B. Krusch, in *Passiones vitaeque sanctorum aevi Merovingici*, 3, p. 241; trans. Fouracre and Gerberding, *Late Merovingian France*, p. 291.

[42] *Vita Wilfridi*, 6: *The Life of Bishop Wilfrid*, pp. 14–15. J. L. Nelson, 'Queens as Jezebels: The Careers of Brunhild and Balthild in Merovingian History', in D. Baker (ed.), *Medieval Women* (Oxford, 1978), pp. 31–77.

[43] Fredegar's depiction of Emperor Heraclius, written in the 650s, echoes the Lateran council of 649: Fredegar, *Chronicon*, IV, 66: *Chronicarum quae dicuntur Fredegarii scholastici libri IV cum continuationibus*, ed. B. Krusch, in *Fredegarii et aliorum chronica. Vitae sanctorum* (MGH SS rer. Mer. II) (Hanover, 1888), p. 154. See S. Esders, 'Herakleios, Dagobert und die "beschnittenen Völker": Die Umwälzungen des Mittelmeerraums im 7. Jahrhundert in der fränkischen Chronik des sog. Fredegar', in A. Goltz, H. Leppin and H. Schlange-Schöningen (eds.), *Jenseits der Grenzen. Studien zur spätantiken und frühmittelalterlichen Geschichtsschreibung* (Berlin and New York, 2009), pp. 239–311, at pp. 291–2.

[44] S. Borgehammar, 'Heraclius Learns Humility: Two Early Latin Accounts Composed for the Celebration of *Exaltatio crucis*', *Millennium*, 6 (2009): 145–201.

Heraclius and King Dagobert around 630.[45] A related document of communication is a relic tag from the eighth-century collection of Sens, once attached to a relic of St Anastasius the Persian,[46] who served in the Persian army when Chosroe II captured Jerusalem and carried off the True Cross to Ctesiphon in 614. The Cross caused Anastasius to desert the Persian army, convert to Christianity and become a monk, resulting in his execution. At Rome, the monastery of Aquae Salviae kept the head of Anastasius, which had been transferred by Cilician monks from the Near East to Italy already in the 640s.[47] Theodore of Tarsus seems to have translated the *Life of Anastasius* into Latin, shortly later used by Bede.[48] Most likely Theodore also took a relic of Anastasius to Gaul,[49] which Hadrian could have brought to Sens. Bringing a relic to Gaul did not make Hadrian a traitor or spy, but we should bear in mind that the cult of Anastasius the Persian attributed a prominent role to the Roman emperor as a religious champion in the fight against non-Christians by placing emphasis on the True Cross. This might explain why Ebroin wanted to find out to what extent the two clerics' religious affiliation to Rome also implied political loyalty to Syracuse and Constantinople.[50]

Theophanes' Account of the Run-Up to the Sixth Ecumenical Council

Despite this picture of intense and vibrant communication ranging from the Mediterranean to Britain in the 660s, Frankish historiography, that is the continuations of the Chronicle of Fredegar, remained silent on the sixth ecumenical council of 680/1, while the authors of hagiographical works paid much attention to the conflicts of Ebroin with the bishops and to King Childeric II (673–5). This may also have led most scholars

---

[45] H. Vierck, 'Werke des Eligius', in G. Kossack and G. Ulbert (eds.), *Studien zur vor- und frühgeschichtlichen Archäologie* (Munich, 1974), vol. II, pp. 309–80, at pp. 319–21 and 368–72.

[46] ChLA XIX, no. 682/52. See M. McCormick, *Origins of the European Economy: Communications and Commerce, AD 300–900* (Cambridge, 2002), p. 295 n. 34 and p. 307 n. 69, and C. Vircillo Franklin *The Latin Dossier of Anastasius the Persian: Hagiographic Translations and Transformations* (Toronto, 2004), p. 24.

[47] B. Flusin, *Saint Anastase le Perse et l'histoire de la Palestine au début du VIIe siècle* (Paris, 1992), vol. II, pp. 354–6.

[48] C. Vircillo Franklin, 'Theodore and the *Passio S. Anastasii* (BHL 410b)', in M. Lapidge (ed.), *Archbishop Theodore. Commemorative studies on his life and influence* (Cambridge, 1995), pp. 175–203.

[49] That Theodore may have brought relics of Anastasius to Britain is suggested by Booth, *Crisis of Empire*, p. 299.

[50] Wood, 'The Continental Connections', p. 205, suggests that Ebroin let Hadrian only pass after news of the murder of Constans in September 668 had reached Francia.

of Merovingian matters[51] to ignore the world chronicle of Theophanes Confessor, who, writing in the early ninth century, sought to present a coherent narrative of political events that ultimately led to the pacification of the world as a precondition of the re-establishment of religious unity through the sixth ecumenical council. Starting with the year 676/7, Theophanes presents the Mardaites, a tribe in the Nur Mountains (southern Turkey),[52] as Byzantine allies ominously about to recover Jerusalem from the Arabs, causing the caliph, Muawiyah, to realise 'that the Roman Empire was guarded by God' and to negotiate a sworn and written long-term peace treaty with Constantinople promising the yearly payment of a huge tribute to the Roman state so that 'complete peace prevailed between the Romans and the Arabs'.[53] For Theophanes, it was Emperor Constantine IV's success against the Arabs that enabled him to revise imperial diplomacy by acknowledging the status of the Lombards in Italy and concluding peace treaties with the Western rulers. In 678/9, after Bulgarian assaults on Thrace, the emperor likewise made peace with them,[54] by which, according to Theophanes, 'the Romans were put to shame for their many sins'. By contrast, the emperor 'believed that this had happened to the Christians by God's providence and made peace in the spirit of the Gospels; and until his death he remained undisturbed by all his enemies'. Accordingly, Constantine even regarded the Bulgars as sent 'by God's providence', as his 'particular concern was to unite God's holy churches which had been everywhere divided from the days of the emperor Heraclius'. Constantine thus

convened at Constantinople an ecumenical council of 289 bishops. He confirmed the doctrines previously established by the five earlier holy and ecumenical councils and joined in promulgating the pious dogma of the two wills and two energies at this holy and most accurate sixth ecumenical council, which was presided by the same most pious emperor Constantine and the pious bishops.[55]

[51] See, for example, Ewig, *Die Merowinger und das Imperium*; J. Semmler, 'Spätmerowingische Herrscher: Theuderich III. und Dagobert II.', *Deutsches Archiv für Erforschung des Mittelalters*, 55 (1999): 1–28, at pp. 23–8.
[52] J. Howard-Johnston, 'The Mardaites', in T. Goodwin (ed.), *Arab-Byzantine Coins and History* (London, 2012), pp. 27–38.
[53] See A. Kaplony, *Konstantinopel und Damaskus. Gesandtschaften und Verträge zwischen Kaisern und Kalifen 639–750. Untersuchungen zum Gewohnheits-Völkerrecht und zur interkulturellen Diplomatie* (Berlin, 1996), pp. 77–97.
[54] See D. Ziemann, *Vom Wandervolk zur Großmacht: Die Entstehung Bulgariens im frühen Mittelalter (7. bis 9. Jh.)* (Cologne, 2007), pp. 161–3.
[55] Theophanes, *Chronographia*, AM 6169 (677/8) and AM 6171 (678/9): *Theophanis Chronographia*, ed. K. de Boor (Leipzig, 1885), vol. II, pp. 355–9; *The Chronicle of Theophanes Confessor: Byzantine and Near Eastern History* AD *284–813*, trans. C. Mango and R. Scott (Oxford, 1997), pp. 495–500.

Theophanes' chronicle is often characterised as a collection of excerpts from different sources which the author rather loosely associated. However, his account of the years 676–81 is teleologically constructed around a divine plan to achieve religious unity at an ecumenical council.[56] Despite chronological rearrangements, there seems to be no reason to doubt Theophanes' information that

the Chagan of the Avars as well as the kings, chieftains, and *castaldi* who lived beyond them (ὅ τε Χαγάνος τῶν Ἀβάρων καὶ οἱ ἐπέκεινα ῥῆγες ἔξαρχοί τε καὶ κάσταλδοι) and the princes of the western nations (οἱ ἐξοχώτατοι τῶν πρὸς τὴν δύσιν ἐθνῶν) sent ambassadors and gifts to Constantine to confirm peace and friendship and that the emperor eventually ratified an imperial peace (δεσποτικὴν εἰρήνην) with them. Thus, great security prevailed in both East and West.

His mentioning of the office of *castaldi* clearly points to the Lombard kingdom here (and very likely also to a Western source),[57] whose position in Italy Constantine acknowledged for the first time in general terms.[58] Theophanes' emphasis that, in addition to the Avars and Lombards, several Western rulers (ἐξοχώτατοι) also concluded peace treaties with Constantinople, most likely referred to Frankish, Anglo-Saxon and perhaps also Visigothic kings. Although no Western source records such a treaty,[59] this would make the most sense, as will be shown later, in light of their role in preparing their churches for the ecumenical council.

---

[56] I. Rochow, 'Die monenergetischen und monotheletischen Streitigkeiten in der Sicht des Chronisten Theophanes', *Klio*, 63 (1981): 669–82, at pp. 674–5, 677 and 679–80 on Theophanes' contradictions and inaccuracy; see also M. Jankowiak, 'The First Arab Siege of Constantinople', in C. Zuckerman (ed.), *Constructing the Seventh Century* (Paris, 2013): 237–320; C. Zuckerman, 'Theophanes the Confessor and Theophanes the Chronicler, or, A Story of Square Brackets', in M. Jankowiak and F. Montinaro (eds.), *Studies in Theophanes* (Paris, 2015), pp. 31–52.

[57] As does the account of Nikephoros, *Historia syntomos*, 34: *Nikephoros, Patriarch of Constantinople, Short History*, text, trans. and comm. by C. Mango (Washington, DC, 1990), p. 86, not mentioning *gastaldi*. On *gastaldi* see C. G. Mor, '*Gastaldi* con potere ducale nell'ordinamento publico longobardo', in Id., *Scritti di storia giuridica altomedievale* (Pisa, 1977), pp. 465–72.

[58] The exact date is not clear, but 680 appears to be too late. See J. Jarnut, *Geschichte der Langobarden* (Stuttgart, 1982), pp. 62–3; K. P. Christou, *Byzanz und die Langobarden: Von der Ansiedlung in Pannonien bis zur endgültigen Anerkennung (500–680)* (Athens, 1991), pp. 219–25; W. Pohl, *Die Awaren: Ein Steppenvolk in Mitteleuropa 567–822 n. Chr.* (Munich, ²2002), p. 278, also on the Avar chagan mentioned.

[59] A reference about foreign relations under Pippin II refers to c. 690: 'Confluebant autem ad eum circumstarum gentium legationes, Grecorum sicilicet et Romanorum, Langobardorum, Hunorum quoque et Sclavorum atque Sarracenorum': *Annales Mettenses priores*, ed. B. von Simson (MGH SS rer. Germ. in us. schol. 10) (Hanover, 1905), p. 15. See Y. Hen, 'The Annals of Metz and the Merovingian Past', in Y. Hen and M. Innes (eds.), *The Uses of the Past in the Early Middle Ages* (Cambridge, 2000), pp. 175–90.

Undoubtedly, in the years preceding the ecumenical council the constellation of Mediterranean politics changed profoundly in political as well as in ecclesiastical terms.[60] Constantine IV would eventually promulgate the decrees of the council in all parts of the Roman Empire by his imperial edict; however, it was by treaties as well as by papal intervention that the Western rulers came to accept the involvement of their bishops in the council's preparation and to agree to enforce the conciliar decisions for the churches under their rule. This represents a new degree of political 'contractualism' in the process of implementing a universally conceived, imperial, religious policy with the help of an ecumenical council.

Pope Agatho (678–81) and the Western Synods of 679/680

While Theophanes focused on secular rulers, Western sources credit Pope Agatho with having negotiated the treaty between the empire and the Lombards.[61] In order to make the council in Constantinople ecumenical from a Western perspective, Agatho sought to integrate the churches under barbarian rule. In October 679,[62] or possibly even earlier,[63] he ordered synods to be held in the Western kingdoms to prepare a joint Roman statement, which should be accorded at a synod in Rome and thereafter serve to instruct the ecumenical council at Constantinople. In his address to Constantine IV, written in March 680, the pope apologises for his belated writing to Constantinople, mentioning the huge size of his patriarchate, which made assembling a general synod difficult, and the fact they had been waiting for Theodore of Canterbury and other British bishops to attend. The pope, it is stated, did not want to exclude anyone from such a general synod 'and especially because among the peoples (*in medio gentium*), as the Lombards, and the Sclavi, as also the Franks, the Gauls (*Galli*), the Goths, and the Britains, there are known to be very many of our fellow-servants (*confamuli nostri*) who do think in unison with us regarding the faith (*in consonantia fidei nobiscum tenentur*)' and might be 'found troublesome

---

[60] E. K. Chrysos, 'Conclusion: *De foederatis iterum*', in W. Pohl (ed.), *Kingdoms of the Empire: The Integration of Barbarians in Late Antiquity* (Leiden, 1997), pp. 185–206, at p. 200; J. Meyendorff, *Imperial Unity and Christian Divisions: The Church, 450–680 AD* (Crestwood, NY, 1989).

[61] See L. M. Hartmann, *Geschichte Italiens im Mittelalter, II/1: Römer und Langobarden bis zur Teilung Italiens* (Leipzig, 1900), pp. 272 and 280.

[62] See W. Levison, 'Die Akten der römischen Synode von 679' (1912), in Id., *Aus rheinischer und fränkischer Frühzeit: Ausgewählte Aufsätze* (Düsseldorf, 1948), pp. 267–94, at pp. 287–8.

[63] Jankowiak, 'The First Arab Siege', pp. 307–8, n. 324.

and contrary, if (which may God forbid!) they stumble at any article of the faith'. The pope thus proclaims that

> we strive with all our might that the commonwealth of your Christian empire may be shown to be more sublime than all the nations (*christiani vestri imperii res publica ... omnium gentium sublimior esse monstretur*), for in it has been rounded the See of Blessed Peter, the prince of the Apostles, by the authority of which all Christian nations (*omnes Christianae nobiscum nationes*) venerate and worship with us.[64]

Agatho's main point here is that a 'harmony of faith' with the peoples and their bishops could only be achieved through the agency of St Peter in Rome who could make the Western 'nations' think of themselves as belonging to the Roman Empire.[65]

The pope's mention of 'Franks' *and* 'Gauls' is also striking; it most likely refers to the Frankish kingdoms of Austrasia and Neustro-Burgundia ruled by Dagobert II and Theuderic III, respectively.[66] This is confirmed by the synodal acts, as the joint statement is subscribed by three representatives titled 'legate of the synod for the provinces of Gaul' (*legatus per Galliarum provincias*). These were Bishop Deodatus of Toul, Archbishop Felix of Arles and Deacon Taurinus of Toulon.[67] While the latter two had obviously been sent by the Neustro-Burgundian mayor of the palace Ebroin and King Theuderic III, Deodatus of Toul clearly represented the Austrasian kingdom of Dagobert II. Their subscriptions thus document the division of the episcopate between the two kingdoms. Deodatus had come along with Bishop Wilfrid of York, who subscribed as the 'legate of the synod for Britain',[68] while Theodore of Canterbury,

---

[64] *Concilium Universale Constantinopolitanum Tertium (680–681): Concilii actiones I–XVIII*, ed. R. Riedinger (*Acta conciliorum oecumenicorum*, II,2,1) (Berlin, 1992), pp. 132–5 (quoted here from the Latin translation); 'The Seven Ecumenical Councils of the Undivided Church', trans. H. R. Percival, in P. Schaff and H. Wace (eds.), *Nicene and Post-Nicene Fathers II/14* (Peabody, MA, 1995), pp. 352–3 (altered). On the Slavic groups referred to by Agatho, see R. Bratož, 'Die römische Synode 680 und die Frage der Kirchenorganisation "in gentibus" im 7. Jahrhundert', *Acta Congressus Internationalis Archaeologiae Christianae*, 13 (1998): 587–602, at pp. 588–90.

[65] Agatho's focus on the *gentes* lets him leave North Africa unmentioned, as no African bishops subscribed the Roman synod of 680. According to W. E. Kaegi, *Muslim Expansion and Byzantine Collapse in North Africa* (Cambridge, 2010), pp. 76–7 and 221–3. Constantine IV's efforts for religious reconciliation had no positive effect on African resistance against the Arabs.

[66] J.-P. Poly, '*Agricola et ejusmodi similes*: La noblesse romaine et la fin des temps mérovingiens', in M. Sot (ed.), *Haut moyen âge: Culture, education et sociéte. Études offertes à Pierre Riché* (Paris, 1990), pp. 197–228, at pp. 223–6; J. Semmler, 'Spätmerowingische Herrscher', pp. 23–8. On Agatho's policy towards the Frankish church see also Epistolae Viennenses spuriae no. 10, ed. W. Gundlach, *Epistolae Merowingici et Karolini aevi* (MGH Epp. 3) (Berlin, 1902), pp. 91–2; see I. N. Wood, 'Between Rome and Jarrow: Papal relations with Francia and England, from 597 to 716', in *Chiese locali e chiese regionali nell'alto medioevo* (Spoleto, 2014), vol. 2, pp. 297–317, at pp. 311–12.

[67] *Concilium Universale Constantinopolitanum Tertium*, 2, p. 149, nos. 48, 51 and 55.

[68] *Concilium Universale Constantinopolitanum Tertium*, 2, p. 149, no. 49.

who had assembled a synod at Hatfield to prepare his church's statement on Monotheletism,[69] had been long awaited in vain in Rome according to the letter of Pope Agatho. Deodatus and his Anglo-Saxon associate, Wilfrid, also had Lombard connections, as the Catholic King Perctarit, of Agilolfing origin and formerly in Britain in exile,[70] welcomed Wilfrid on his way to Rome in Pavia in 679.[71] Following the treaty concluded with Constantine IV, Perctarit had allowed a provincial synod to take place in Milan in 679 or 680, so that many bishops from the Lombard kingdom took part in the Roman synod of 680. Consequently, at Rome right after the delegates from Gaul subscribed Archbishop Mansuetus of Milan,[72] whose bishops had previously been invited by Pope Agatho, as becomes clear from a letter of Mansuetus written directly to the emperor.[73] Moreover, the pope had also invited the prelates from the archbishopric of Ravenna.[74]

Although Constantine IV in his 'sacred letter' to Rome from August 678 had stated that times did not permit the convoking of a general council,[75] Agatho seems to have interpreted this as a first step towards an ecumenical council by making preparations for a Western statement to be made in March 680. In September 680, after the arrival of a

---

[69] Beda, *Historia*, IV, 1: *Bede's Ecclesiastical history*, pp. 384–6. See H. Chadwick, 'Theodore, the English Church and the Monothelete Controversy', in *Archbishop*, pp. 88–95, at pp. 92–3.

[70] Paulus Diaconus, *Historia Langobardorum*, V, 32: ed. L. Bethmann and G. Waitz, in *Scriptores rerum Langobardicarum et Italicarum saec. VI–IX* (MGH SS rer. Lang. 1) (Hanover, 1878), pp. 154–5.

[71] *Vita Wilfridi*, 28: *The Life of Bishop Wilfrid*, pp. 54 and 56.

[72] *Concilium Universale Constantinopolitanum Tertium*, p. 149, no. 53.

[73] *Epistula Mansueti episcopi Mediolanensis*: G. D. Mansi, *Sacrorum Conciliorum Nova et Amplissima Collectio* 11 (Florence, ²1765), pp. 203–8. See also Paulus Diaconus, *Historia Langobardorum*, VI, 4: ed. Bethmann and Waitz, pp. 165–6. I have not been able to consult F. Furciniti, 'Mansueto, Damiano e il Basileus. La Suggestio e l'Expositio Fidei della sinodo milanese a Costantino IV', doctoral thesis, Università Cattolica del Sacro Cuore, Facoltà di lettere e filosofia, dipartimento di scienze storiche, XXIII ciclo, a. 2009/10.

[74] From the Roman perspective, Ravenna was subdued again to the Roman see with God's help: *Liber pontificalis*, *Vita Doni*, c. 1: *Le Liber pontificalis. Texte, introduction et commentaire*, ed. L. Duchesne (Paris, ²1955), vol. I, p. 348. For Ravenna, the ecumenical council was only a pretext to restore Roman control: Agnellus, *Liber pontificalis Ravennatae ecclesiae* c. 124: *Agnelli Ravennatis Liber pontificalis ecclesiae Ravennatis*, ed. D. Mauskopf-Deliyannis (CC CM 199) (Turnhout, 2006), p. 237. See V. Ortenberg West-Harling, 'The Church of Ravenna, Constantinople and Rome in the Seventh Century', in J. Herrin and J. Nelson (eds.), *Ravenna: Its Role in Medieval Change and Exchange* (London, 2016), pp. 199–210, at pp. 207–9. On the north Italian bishops at the Roman synod, see R. Bratož, 'Das Patriarchat Grado im monotheletischen Streit', in R. Bratož (ed.), *Slowenien und die Nachbarländer zwischen Antike und karolingischer Epoche: Anfänge der slowenischen Ethnogenese* (Ljubljana, 2000), vol. II, pp. 609–58, at pp. 631–3.

[75] *Concilium Universale Constantinopolitanum Tertium*, pp. 2–10. Jankowiak, 'The First Siege', pp. 254–5, 283–5.

long-awaited delegation from Rome, Constantine convoked the ecumenical council, which opened in November 680 and was completed after eighteen sessions in September 681. While the emperor reported this in letters to the new pope, Leo II (682–3), and to the churches of the Western patriarchate in December 681, the acts of the ecumenical council were finally accepted by the pope in 682.[76]

While in his letter to Constantine IV Pope Agatho claimed to speak on behalf of Spain, no Visigothic bishop is recorded to have taken part in the Roman synod in 680. King Wamba, who had refrained from convoking a general synod in Spain,[77] was deposed and replaced in October 680 by Ervig, the son of a man called Artabasdos, a high-ranking immigrant from Constantinople, who had married a niece of the Visigothic king, Chindasvinth.[78] Ervig was strongly supported by the bishops of his kingdom and ordered a synod to be held in Toledo in January 681, which met too early to account for the ecumenical council's decisions. Nonetheless, it formulated a definition of the Holy Trinity that was to be accepted by any newly elected king and to convoke a general synod by the archbishop of Toledo.[79] This was confirmed by Pope Agatho and his successors. With some delay, and after a long series of quarrels, the Visigothic episcopate, backed by King Ervig, finally adapted the ecumenical council's resolutions in 684.[80]

The Merovingian Kingdoms, the Synod of Rome (680) and the Murder of Ebroin

To some extent, the split in the Merovingian episcopate between the two kingdoms may have also been due to the fact that King Dagobert II in Austrasia (676–9) and Theuderic III of Neustria-Burgundy (675–91) turned out to be capable rulers.[81] While we could already observe a separate religious policy pursued by the two kingdoms thirty years earlier

---

[76] *Concilium Universale Constantinopolitanum Tertium*, pp. 857–66 and 866–86.
[77] J. Orlandis and D. Ramos-Lisson, Die *Synoden auf der Iberischen Halbinsel bis zum Einbruch des Islams (711)* (Paderborn, 1981), p. 240. However, M. Vallejo Girvés, *Hispania y Bizancio: Una relación desconocida* (Madrid, 2012), pp. 418–20, suggests that Wamba and Constantine IV could have concluded a treaty before, referring to the above quoted report of Theophanes.
[78] Chronica de Alfonso III, c. 2: *Crónicas Asturianas*, ed. J. Gil Fernández, J. L. Moralejo and J. Ruíz de la Peña (Oviedo, 1985), p. 114.
[79] Twelfth council of Toledo, cc. 1 and 6: *Concilios visigóticos e hispano-romanos*, ed. J. Vives (Barcelona and Madrid, 1963), pp. 385 and 393.
[80] Fourteenth council of Toledo: *Concilios visigóticos*, pp. 441–8. See in more detail Orlandis and Ramos-Lisson, *Die Synoden*, pp. 272–7, Riedinger, *Kleine Schriften*, no. 18, and Vallejo Girvés, *Hispania y Bizancio*, pp. 420–7.
[81] See Semmler, 'Spätmerowingische Herrscher'.

in reacting to the Lateran synod of 649, it seems that in 680, when both kingdoms' prelates eventually accepted the Roman (and ecumenical) position, this only happened following a series of conflicts that again seem to reflect inner divisions. As it seems, the Austrasian court was the first to become involved in the preparations for the ecumenical council. The *Vita Wilfridi* contains a long sequence about Wilfrid of York's expulsion from his see, his journey to Rome and his restoration in York.[82] It provides the interesting detail that when Wilfrid left Britain for Rome, his Anglo-Saxon opponents requested Ebroin to apprehend him. Ebroin caught the wrong person, Bishop Winfrid of Lichfield, who was also on his way to Rome, whereas Wilfrid took the eastern route, with the duke of Frisia supporting his travel against Ebroin's machinations, followed by friendly reception at the courts of the Austrasian king, Dagobert II, and the Lombard king, Perctarit.[83] There was a clear perception among the Anglo-Saxon clergy of the political divisions between Neustria and Austrasia after King Dagobert II's retrieval from exile in Ireland,[84] allowing Anglo-Irish, Frisian, Austrasian and Lombard networks to operate as far as Rome. If the chronology is correct, Deodatus of Toul and Wilfrid had come to Rome in 679, as Wilfrid intended to negotiate on the status of the episcopal see of York.[85] However, his biographer reports that King Dagobert II, after Wilfrid refused to accept his offer to become bishop of Strasbourg, sent him to Rome with Deodatus as guide.[86] It seems most likely that Dagobert II in sending Deodatus also responded to Pope Agatho's plans to prepare in Rome a coordinated statement on Monotheletism. Dagobert would not have dispatched an important bishop along with Wilfrid were he not expecting him to participate in the Roman synod under preparation.

It may not be without significance that the bishopric of Toul had strong personal connections to the Neustrian abbey of Saint-Jean in Laon at that time, whose abbess Anstrudis, niece of a former bishop of Toul, along

---

[82] *Vita Wilfridi*, 24–34: *The Life of Bishop Wilfrid*, pp. 48–70, with original documents on which see Levison, 'Die Akten'; M. E. Gibbs, 'The Decrees of Agatho and the Gregorian Plan for York', *Speculum*, 48 (1973): 213–46.

[83] *Vita Wilfridi*, 25–8: *The Life of Bishop Wilfrid*, pp. 50–6.

[84] J.-M. Picard, 'Church and Politics in the Seventh Century: The Irish Exile of King Dagobert II', in J.-M. Picard (ed.), *Ireland and Northern France, AD 600–850* (Dublin, 1991), pp. 27–52; P. Fouracre, 'Forgetting and Remembering Dagobert II: The English Connection', in P. Fouracre and D. Ganz (eds.), *Frankland: The Franks and the World of the Early Middle Ages* (Manchester, 2008), pp. 70–89.

[85] See I. N. Wood, 'The Continental Journeys of Wilfrid and Biscop', in *Wilfrid of York: Abbot, Bishop, Saint*, pp. 200–11, at pp. 208–10; É. Ó Carragáin and A. Thacker, 'Wilfrid in Rome', in *Wilfrid of York: Abbot, Bishop, Saint*, pp. 212–30, at pp. 222–5.

[86] *Vita Wilfridi*, 28: *The Life of Bishop Wilfrid*, p. 54.

with her brother came into dramatic conflict with Theuderic III and his mayor Ebroin very probably in 679 for her and her family's staunch support of the Pippinids.[87] For while the Austrasian delegation headed by Bishop Deodatus of Toul was in Rome already in 679 and stayed there over winter,[88] Neustria and Burgundy, under King Theuderic III and his mayor Ebroin, experienced the peak of the conflict between ruler and Burgundian bishops precisely at that time. A charter issued by Theuderic III on 15 September 679 records a decision of a Neustro-Burgundian synod held at Mâlay-le-Roi (near Sens), where several bishops were accused of treason (*infidelitas*) against the king and deposed from their sees.[89] Chramlin of Embrun, it was stated, had been illegally appointed bishop without royal approval by a false charter and in a rebellious act (*per revellacionis audacia*). The charter claims that the bishops were judged according to canon law, meaning that they first had been deprived of their status as clerics and were handed over to the king's criminal jurisdiction afterwards. Chramlin was imprisoned in the monastery of Saint-Denis, but since his property was guaranteed to him, the charter was addressed to the *patricii* of Provence and Burgundy being under Ebroin's control at this time.[90] Among the participants mentioned are the metropolitan bishops Genesius of Lyons, Adon of Bourges, Blidram of Vienne, Terniscus of Besançon and Landobert of Sens. At it seems, Ebroin had placed the episcopal hierarchy of Burgundy firmly under his control, as the final deposition, condemnation and execution of Bishop Leodegar of Autun accused of having been involved in the murder of King Childeric II likely took place at the same synod,[91] while the deposition of Burgundian

---

[87] *Vita Anstrudis*, c. 5–14: *Vita s. Anstrudis abbatissae Laudunensis*, ed. W. Levison, in *Passiones vitaeque sanctorum aevi Merovingici IV* (MGH SS rer. Mer. 6) (Hanover, 1913), pp. 64–78, at pp. 68–72; see R. Le Jan, 'Convents, Violence and Competition for Power in Seventh-Century France', in M. De Jong and F. Theuws (eds.), *Topographies of Power in the Early Middle Ages* (Leiden, 2001), pp. 243–69, at pp. 259–61, and Fox, *Power and Religion*, pp. 84–5 and 150–8. (I owe this information to the kindness of Yaniv Fox.)

[88] See Semmler, 'Spätmerowingische Herrscher', pp. 25–6.

[89] *Die Urkunden der Merowinger*, ed. T. Kölzer (MGH Diplomata regum Francorum e stirpe Merovingica) (Hanover, 2001), no. 122, p. 312 n. 1. On the date, see M. Weidemann, 'Zur Chronologie der Merowinger im 7. und 8. Jahrhundert', *Francia*, 25 (1998): 177–230, at pp. 189–90. An image of the charter (ChLA 13, No. 565, p. 69) shows a Tironian note *ordinante Ebroino majore domus*.

[90] See H. Ebling, *Prosopographie der Amtsträger des Merowingerreiches von Chlothar II. (613) bis Karl Martell (741)* (Munich, 1974), pp. 64 and 211–12. On Chramlin's networks, see P. J. Geary, *Aristocracy in Provence: The Rhône Basin at the Dawn of the Carolingian Age* (Stuttgart, 1985), pp. 136–40, and Fox, *Power and Religion*, pp. 210–11.

[91] *Passio Leudegarii*, I, 33: *Passiones vitaeque sanctorum aevi Merovingici*, 3, pp. 314–15. See H. Mordek, 'Bischofsabsetzungen in spätmerowingischer Zeit: *Justelliana, Bernensis* und das Konzil von Mâlay (677)', in H. Mordek (ed.), *Papsttum, Kirche und Recht im Mittelalter* (Tübingen, 1991), pp. 31–53, at pp. 39–43; I. N. Wood, *The Merovingian Kingdoms, 450–751* (London, 1994), pp. 230–1.

bishops was followed by a flight of Burgundian lay nobles to the duke of Aquitaine.⁹² The dispatch of Archbishop Felix of Arles as the representative of Theuderic III's kingdom, along with Taurinus of Toulon to the Roman synod, thus must have followed shortly after the shake-up carried out among the Burgundian episcopate in September 679.⁹³ Two months later, on 23 December 679, Dagobert II was assassinated, allegedly by malicious Neustrian dukes instigated by Ebroin with the consent of his bishops: *Degoberthto rege per dolum ducum et consensum episcoporum – quod absit – insidiose occiso*.⁹⁴ By adding Austrasia to his rule, King Theuderic III now became sole ruler over all three kingdoms. Wilfrid of York, on his way back from Rome, was now caught by one of Ebroin's bishops, who charged him with having been a friend of Dagobert II and calling him back from exile. Wilfrid was threatened with imprisonment and with extradition to Ebroin.⁹⁵ While this apparently did not happen, Ebroin now sought to extend his influence over Austrasia by military means and successfully defeated troops led by the Austrasian mayor, Pippin II, and Duke Martin, the latter being closely associated to the above-mentioned abbess of Saint-Jean of Laon, Anstrudis. However, in 680 or 681, Ebroin was assassinated by a man called Ermenfried, who sought refuge with Pippin soon after.⁹⁶

Was Ebroin's murder just another turnabout in the enduring struggle between Austrasia and Neustria whose climatic conclusion would take place in Tertry in 687? The Frankish mayor has often been portrayed as a radical fighter for a centralist kingship against aristocratic regionalism pursuing an uncompromising *Kirchenpolitik*,⁹⁷ while conflicts were interpreted as internal strife between aristocratic factions, bishops and their local clergy who called upon the mayor to pursue their interests.⁹⁸

---

⁹² See E. Ewig, *Die Merowinger und das Frankenreich* (Stuttgart, 2001), p. 169; Wood, *The Merovingian Kingdoms*, pp. 175–6.
⁹³ Poly, 'Agricola et eiusmodi similes', pp. 223–6, takes the subscription list of the Roman synod of 680 as 'la dernière manifestation d'insoumission épiscopale connue en Provence' (p. 224).
⁹⁴ *Vita Wilfridi*, 33: *The Life of Bishop Wilfrid*, pp. 68–9.
⁹⁵ For the date, see Weidemann, 'Chronologie', p. 196.
⁹⁶ *Continuatio Fredegarii*, 4; *Liber historiae Francorum*, 47; *Fredegarii et aliorum chronica*, pp. 170 and 320–1. For the date, see J. Fischer, 'Der Hausmeier Ebroin', dissertation, Bonn 1953 (Wilkau-Hasslau, 1954), p. 172 (May 680) and Weidemann, 'Chronologie', p. 193 (autumn 681). See Fox, *Power and Religion*, p. 191.
⁹⁷ Fischer, *Der Hausmeier Ebroin*, pp. 182–3; P. Fouracre, 'Merovingians, Mayors of the Palace and the Notion of a "Low-Born" Ebroin', *Bulletin of the Institute of Historical Research*, 57 (1984): 1–14; H. H. Anton, 'Ebroin', *Reallexikon der germanischen Altertumskunde*, 6 (1986): 346–8; Wood, *The Merovingian Kingdoms*, p. 221.
⁹⁸ P. Fouracre, 'Merovingian History and Merovingian Hagiography', *Past and Present*, 127 (1990): 3–38.

However, it should also be seen against the background of the rapid changes unfolding in the Mediterranean constellation, with which the Merovingian kingdoms appear, in various ways, to have been more closely connected than is often assumed. As it seems, Constans II's move to Italy and fight against the Lombards could easily bring bishops under suspicion as imperial spies or traitors in the 660s, while the conflicts between 675 and 680 after Ebroin's resurgence to power may have been influenced by a growing expectation that Constantine IV would restore orthodoxy.

Conclusion

As Emperor Constantine IV paved the political way for a dogmatic reconciliation between Rome and Constantinople in the later 670s, this happened politically on a contractual basis, while we find the papacy quickly activating its ecclesiastical networks to prepare an ecumenical council. The dynamic of this process developed rapidly and involved a multitude of actors: kings, diplomats and higher clerics, connecting the British Isles via Frisia and Austrasia to Lombard Italy and Rome, and also including Visigothic Spain soon after. The Merovingian kings could permit bishops to communicate with the pope and their episcopal brethren by exchange of letters and through travel to Rome. The bishops, locally based and connected to wide-ranging monastic and aristocratic networks, were the only functional elite in the West that could still imagine the Roman Empire as having an impact on their actions. However, bishops emphasising their external responsibilities and networks could also fall under suspicion – at least under Ebroin – and lose their position through trials of infidelity, often in connection with internal conflicts. As most bishops under Frankish rule seem to have adopted Rome's position on Monotheletism, as formulated in 649, in the run-up to the sixth ecumenical council they could attribute the Roman emperor with the role of governing and protecting a Christian Roman Empire or 'Byzantine commonwealth', of which the barbarian kingdoms, their rulers and churches in some respects willingly considered themselves to be a part.[99]

---

[99] G. Fowden, *Empire to Commonwealth: Consequences of Monotheism in Late Antiquity* (Princeton, NJ, 1994), pp. 100–36; W. Pohl (ed.), *Kingdoms of the Empire: The Integration of Barbarians in Late Antiquity* (Leiden, 1997). I would like to thank Patrick Griffith for improving the English of this chapter.

17 In the Circle of the Bishop of Bourges: Bern 611 and Late Merovingian Culture

David Ganz

It is important to acknowledge quite how little we can know about Merovingian libraries and Merovingian manuscript culture. We have five seventh-century manuscripts from Lyon which may have been copied there: Origen on Genesis, Exodus and Leviticus,[1] Jerome on Jeremiah,[2] Jerome Against Jovinian,[3] excerpts from Jerome's letters,[4] and works of Augustine.[5] Lyon is the one Merovingian centre that preserves late antique manuscripts, some of which were most probably copied locally. Seventh-century Merovingian manuscripts also survive from Autun: Isidore on the Old Testament,[6] Augustine on the Psalms,[7] and John Cassian.[8] There are some thirty manuscripts copied at Luxeuil, which I believe were copied there for other houses; they include letters and sermons of Augustine,[9] Augustine on the Epistles of John,[10] on the Psalms,[11]

---

[1] Lyon Bibl. Ville 443 (372), Origen. For palaeographical accounts of these manuscripts, I give the reference to E. A. Lowe's *Codices Latini Antiquiores*, CLA 6. 774a. The Lyon manuscripts can now be viewed online at the Bibliothèque Municipale website. For brief surveys of Merovingian manuscripts, see D. Ganz, 'La Diversité des écritures', in I. Bardiès-Fronty, C. Denoël and I. Villela-Petit (eds.), *Les Temps merovingiens: trois siècles d'art et de culture* (Paris, 2016), pp. 172–4; I. Wood, 'The Problem of Late Merovingian Culture', in S. Dusil and G. Schwedler (eds.), *Exzerpieren – Kompilieren – Tradieren: Transformationen des Wissens zwischen Spätantike und Frühmittelalter* (Berlin and Boston, MA, 2016), pp. 199–222.
[2] 6. 776, Lyon Bibl. Ville 468 (397) and Paris BN nouv. acq. lat. 602, Jérôme sur Jérémie (Lyon?).
[3] Lyon BM 602, CLA 6 782.
[4] Lyon BM 600, CLA VI, 781.
[5] Lyon Bibl. Ville 426 (352) and Paris BN Lat. 1629, Augustine, *Enarrationes in Psalmos*, 6. no. 773a: Lyon Bibl Ville 604 (521) and Paris BN Lat. nouv acq lat 1594, Augustine Opuscula, CLA 6. 783.
[6] Autun BM 27 S 29, CLA 6, 727
[7] Autun, Bibl. Mun. 107 and Paris BN Lat. nouv. acq. 1629: 15–16, Augustine, *Enarrationes in Psalmos*, CLA 6, no 724.
[8] Autun Bibl Mun 24 and Paris BN nouv. acq, lat 1629 ff. 17–20.
[9] Paris BN Lat. 11641, Geneva I 16 and St Petersburg F1.1, Augustine, *Letters, Sermons, Excerpta*, CLA 5. 614.
[10] New York Pierpont Morgan Library M 334, Augustine on the Epistle of John (this manuscript has a colophon dating it to 669), CLA 11. 1659.
[11] Würzburg Univ. M P Th. F 64 a, Augustine Ennarationes in Psalmos, CLA 9. 1419.

De Genesi ad Litteram,[12] Jerome on Ecclesiastes,[13] Isidore, *Synonima* and Ambrose,[14] Ambrose on Psalm 118,[15] Sedulius,[16] two copies of parts of Gregory's *Moralia*,[17] Gregory's *Regula Pastoralis*,[18] the Chronicle of Eusebius-Jerome,[19] and two homiliaries.[20] There is an important group of Merovingian manuscripts from Corbie, founded around 661, which includes manuscripts of Gregory on Ezekiel,[21] an abridged version of the *Histories* of Gregory of Tours,[22] a New Testament,[23] letters of Jerome,[24] the Rule of Basil,[25] exegetical works by Jerome,[26] Jerome-Gennadius *De Viris Illustribus*,[27] Cassian's Collations,[28] Isidore,[29] Origen[30] and the Breviary of Alaric.[31] From Fleury, founded around 640, there is an important group of fragments of biblical books and patristic texts,[32] but they

[12] Bern, Burgerbibl A 91 (8) and Paris BN Lat. 9377, Augustinus, *De Genesi ad Litteram*, CLA 7. 855.
[13] St Paul in Carinthia, Stift 3, Jerome on Ecclesiastes, CLA 10. 1454.
[14] Fulda Landesbibl. Boniface 2, *Epistula Dogmatica Leonis Papae*, Faustus, *De ratione Fidei*, Decretum Gelasianum, Ambrosius, *De bono mortis*, Isidore Synonyma, CLA 8. 1197.
[15] The scrap in Oxford Bodleian Library Lat. Misc. a 3 Ambrose on Psalm 118, CLA Supp. 1739 is probably from the same volume as a fragment in Strasbourg, Archives du bas Rhin 151 J 108 which is not in CLA.
[16] Munich CLM 29033, Sedulius, Carmen Paschale, CLA 9. 1328.
[17] London, British Library Add 11878, Add 41567, Harvard Typ 592 and BN nouv. acq. Lat 2243 and 2388; Gregory, Moralia Books XXIII–XXIV, CLA 2. 163: Verona XL 38, Gregory, Moralia Books XXVII–XXIXV, CLA 4. 497.
[18] Ivrea Bibl. Cap. 1, Gregorius, *Regula Pastoralis* with dedication to Bishop Desiderius, CLA 3. 300.
[19] Valenciennes Bibl. Mun. 495 (455), Eusebius-Jerome, *Chronicon*, CLA 6. 841.
[20] Yale Beinecke Library, BL Addit MS 29972 and Metz Bibl. Mun. Salis 140 (1), Augustin, Caesarius. 7. 173; New York Pierpont Morgan M 17, Caesarius, CLA 11. 1658. I have argued that these were originally part of the same book.
[21] St Petersburg Publ. Lib. Q v I. 14, copied in the script of Luxeuil, CLA 11. 1617. I discuss the earliest Corbie manuscripts in D. Ganz, *Corbie in the Carolingian Renaissance* (Sigmaringen, 1990).
[22] Paris BN Lat. 17655, Gregory of Tours, *Historiae*, Books I–VI, CLA 5. 671.
[23] Paris BN nouv. acq. Lat. 1063, Gospels and Pauline Epistles by the scribes of BNF Lat. 17655, CLA 5. 679. For this volume, D. Ganz, 'A Merovingian New Testament Manuscript and Its Liturgical Notes: Paris BNF Nouv. acq. Lat 1061', *Revue Benedictine*, 126 (2016): 122–37.
[24] St Petersburg Publ. Lib. Q v 1.13; Gennadius, *De Ecclesiasticis Dogmatibus*, Jerome Letters, CLA 11. 1616.
[25] St Petersburg Publ. Lib. F v 1.2, *Regula Basilii*, CLA 11. 1598.
[26] Jerome, *Quaestiones in Genesim, De Situ et Nominibus*. CLA 5. 655. Paris BN Lat. 13348, Jerome, *Questiones in Genesin*, Eucherius, Ephraem, Scarapsum, Pseudo Methodius, CLA 5. 656. Paris BN Lat. 13349, Jerome in Ecclesiasten, CLA 5. 657.
[27] Paris BN Lat 12161, CLA 5, 624. This manuscript is a palimpsest.
[28] St Petersburg Publ Lib O v I 4, Cassian, Collationes XI–XVII, CLA 11. 1625.
[29] Paris BN Lat. 13028 Isidore, *Etymologiae* XVI–XX, CLA 5. 647.
[30] London BL Burney and St Petersburg F v 1.4, Origen, *Homilies on Balaam*, John Chrysostom, *De reparatione lapsi*, CLA 2. No 182.
[31] Paris BN Lat 4403A, CLA 5 556.
[32] Orleans BM 19 and BM 192. The separate items are CLA 6, 797–801 and 804–19.

were probably not copied there. The earliest books of Tours date from c. 725: Eugippius,[33] Isidore on the Old and New Testament,[34] Jerome's letters,[35] Jerome on Isaiah,[36] the grammarian Pompeius on Donatus with the preface to Cassidorus on Divine letters, a short Greek-Latin glossary, treatises on metre,[37] an abridged version of Gregory of Tours' *Histories*[38] and Phillipus' commentary on Job.[39] From Soissons we have a manuscript with a colophon stating that it was copied for Bishop Numedius.[40] We can place a manuscript of canon law in Toulouse in 666[41] and a manuscript of the Gospels with portions of a commentary was copied in 754 for an abbess at Vosevio, probably somewhere in Burgundy but so far unlocalised.[42] So the assemblage of booklets in Bern 611 (with a detached quire now in Paris), is an important witness to a portion of a Merovingian library.

The collection comprises twenty-seven quires in six parts, copied in a Merovingian cursive script by several scribes, with later Merovingian and Carolingian additions.[43] A quire has been detached, and is now Paris BnF Lat 10756 ff. 62–9. Folios 116–45 are palimpsested: the lower text is the *Passio sancti Sebastiani* thought to be seventh century. A single folio [ff. 143–4] has a fifth-century copy of the Vetus Latina text of Mark 1:2–23, 2:22–7 and 3:11–18. Both lower texts are copied in uncial.

The manuscript belonged to Jacques Bongars (1554–1612)[44] who owned a part of the library of the Bourges jurist Jacques Cujas

---

[33] CLA 5. 682, Paris BN Lat. nouv acq 1575, Eugippius Excerpta Augustini. The earliest Tours manuscripts were identified and discussed by B. Bischoff, 'Ein wiedergefundener Papyrus und die ältesten Handschriften der Schule von Tours', *Mittelalterliche Studien I* (Stuttgart 1966), pp. 6–16.
[34] Cologne Dombibl 98, Isidore, CLA 8. 1157.
[35] Epinal, Bibl. Mun. 149 (68), Jerome Letters (this manuscript is dated 744/5) CLA 6. 762.
[36] London British Library, Egerton 2831 CLA 2 196.
[37] Wolfenbuttel, Herzog August Bibl. Weissenburg 86, Pompeius etc. CLA 9. 1394.
[38] Leiden Univ Voss Lat. Qu. 63, Gregory of Tours, *Decem Libri Historiarum*, 10, 1584.
[39] The Hague, Museum 10 A 1, Phlippus, *Expositio in Iob*, CLA 10. 1571.
[40] CLA 10. 1547a, Brussels Bibl. Roy 9850–2, Caesarius, Homelies, *Commentaire sur les Evangiles* (St Médard pour Nomedius s VII ex).
[41] Toulouse Bibl Mun 364 and Paris BN Lat. 8901, Canons (Albi, 666/7), CLA 6. 836.
[42] Autun BM 3. L. Nees, *The Gundohinus Gospels* (Cambridge, MA, 1987).
[43] I am grateful to Dr Anna Dorofeeva for sharing her photographs of the manuscript when I was writing this paper. Her work on the manuscript is contained in her Cambridge doctoral thesis. The reception and manuscript context of the early medieval Latin prebestiary 'Physiologus' (Bern, 611) may now be viewed online, at e-codices Virtuelle Handschriftenbibliothek der Schweiz, with an excellent description, analysis of the scripts, and a full bibliography, which draws on the contents list I prepared for this paper.
[44] Bongars's signature is on f 5r and f 153 v. M. Mostert, *The Library of Fleury: A Provisional List of Manuscripts* (Hilversum, 1989), pp. 30–1, 81, 228.

(1522–90).⁴⁵ The Paris portion belonged to Pierre Pithou and contains a document dated to 1571 relating to Pierre Daniel, who may have owned it.⁴⁶

The manuscript has certainly lost one quire, for it contains a contents list that includes items now missing. It has been severely damaged at the start of the first booklet, and the glossary leaves with entries for A–C are missing. The contents list reveals that at least one quire is lost after folio 72, the quire which followed that was detached and is now in Paris. Most leaves have been trimmed by the sixteenth-century binder. The first booklet (ff. 1–19) is the Abba Glossary, followed by a short and incomplete second glossary listing a small number of words beginning with A to H. The second booklet (ff. 20–41) contains two substantial sections from Isidore's *Etymologiae*, the first listing the six ages of the world from Adam to Emperor Heraclius and the second on the seventy-three nations of the world descended from the sons of Noah. The third (ff. 42–93 and Paris BnF Latin 10756 ff. 62–9) contains the grammar of Asper or Aspor with a set of verse riddles and various short texts, some in shorthand, for which we have a contents list. The volume also contains Isidore's history of Latin shorthand on f. 72v, immediately following the grammar. The list reveals that the volume originally contained an account of literary genres,⁴⁷ a sermon about the Magi,⁴⁸ a text about weights and measures, and a text about the three languages by which the Holy Spirit is called.⁴⁹

The fourth part (ff. 94–115) contains a computus for 727 and the Pseudo-Methodius, the fifth (ff. 116–45) the Physiologus, and the final part (ff. 146–53), which is not complete, a set of medical recipes. It is not clear whether these parts were bound. Part III (ff. 40–86v) has quire signatures that run from I to VIII,⁵⁰ suggesting that it was a separate volume, as the contents list implies. It remains unclear whether the separate parts were kept together,⁵¹ or whether we have a series of books which were all copied at around the same time in very similar scripts; because of this uncertainty, I shall refer to the present Bern 611 as a

---

⁴⁵ R. Kohldorfer-Fries, *Diplomatie und Gelehrtenrepublik: Die Kontakte des französischen Gesandten Jaques Bongars (1554–1612)* (Tübingen, 2009); X. Prévost, *Jacques Cujas (1522–1590), Jurisconsulte humaniste* (Geneva, 2015).
⁴⁶ The document is now Ms 847.9 according to the e-codices description.
⁴⁷ Item III in the contents list on f 92 v reads III. *Quid est antifrasin, enigma, parabula, paradigma, prosa, bucolica epitalamia, trenos epitafium, fabulas, sillogismi*. Item IV: *confectio amforalis*.
⁴⁸ V. *Sermo de tribus magis*. VI. *de ponderibus et mensuris*. VII. *De drumeta vel citeris quaenam omnibus clarent*.
⁴⁹ VIIII. *De trebus principalibus linguis quibus spiritus sanctus appellatur*.
⁵⁰ The last leaf of quire IV, all of quire V and the first and last leaves of quire VII are missing. Quire VI, which has a signature, is now in Paris.
⁵¹ There seems to be no evidence for a binding before the sixteenth century.

collection rather than as a single manuscript. The separate sections are ruled differently, with between fourteen and twenty-seven lines per page.

The sections are copied in various types of Merovingian cursive script, with the chapter list and the opening of the Physiologus in uncial (f 116v–117v) and each subsequent chapter opening with an uncial title in a much darker ink. Several pages are in Latin shorthand. On ff. 68v–69r in the copy of Asper's grammar, half uncial is used. I believe that the hand that copied the passage from Palladius on ff. 40v–41v also copied ff. 98–9 and ff. 138v–140v. The hand that copied the historical and geographical excerpts from Isidore is very similar to the hands in the canon-law collection Berlin Phillipps 1743. Red ink is used for some initials on ff. 42–93, and there are red titles and text openings on ff. 94–145. Blank spaces in the original collection were filled with short passages, some in shorthand, in the eighth and ninth centuries.

The cursive scripts are very close to those found in Merovingian royal and private charters, and on relic labels.[52] Cursive script is far less common as the main text hand of manuscripts.[53] The use of cursive script, and the frequent use of shorthand, suggests that the collection was assembled in a centre where documents were being drawn up, and that is confirmed by the presence of the formulae, which are also copied in cursive charter scripts. So the Latin being taught in this collection is Christian Latin, but it is not simply learnt for teaching and researching. The extensive use of Tironian notes is the work of clerics used to administration, and possibly even to taking dictation.

Using the manuscript, we can suggest what sort of education the clerics in the entourage of the bishop of Bourges in the first third of the seventh century might have received. As catechumens, they would first have learnt the words of the Lord's Prayer, and the manuscript contains an elementary explanation of that text. An extract from Isidore lists all of the books of the Bible. They learnt a Christian vocabulary from the Abba Glossary, which includes a definition of *monachus* and interpretations of biblical names but also material derived from Virgil. *Himnus* is defined as *Carmen in laudem Dei*. The vocabulary includes *Hirographum* (a handwritten document), and the Nomina Sacra HIS *Salvator* and XPS *unctus*. The Latin of the glossary has abandoned standard case endings, reading *sine dubium, ad pugna, ad Gloria*.

---

[52] For photographs of the charters and relic labels, H. Atsma and J. Vezin, *Chartae Latinae Antiquiores*, Parts XIII–XIX (Zurich, 1981–7).
[53] Note the copies of Gregory's *Dialogues* in stylised minuscule. Autun BM 20, CLA 6 719 and St Gall Stiftsbibliothek 214, CLA 7, 924.

Asper's Grammar includes examples of proper names: Michael, Petrus, Stephanus, Esaias, Aaron, Ezechiel, and of appellative nouns: *angelus, apostolus, martyr, propheta, sacerdos, rex.*[54] The first three verbs are *ieiunio, oro* and *lego.*[55] This is a Christian world very different from that of Donatus: the examples of verbs with a preposition are *in ecclesia sto, in charta scribo, in populis praedico.*[56] *Benedictus qui venit in nomine Domini* is used as an example of a particular ablative. A possible clue to the place of origin of the grammar is the sentence *Lugduni vel Augustoduni legebam.* The grammar was supplemented by definitions of various figures of speech: definitions of *Ars, Oratoria* with *Cacotecnia* and *Feudotecnia* – rare terms – *Latinitas, Vox, Orthographia, Analogia, Ethimologia,*[57] *Glossa, Deferentia, Solecismus, Metaplasmus, Scemata.*[58] The contents list reveals that the collection originally included a section which has not survived: *III. Quid est antifrasin enigma, parabula, paradigma, prosa, bucolica epitalamia, trenos epitafium, fabulas, sillogismi.* These topics are also found in the first book of Isidore's *Etymologiae.*[59]

Latin was also learnt from the riddles, which cover household objects, but also parchment and papyrus, wax tablets and letters, and then the sun, moon, sky and stars. There is no clearly Christian content, and the same collection is found in several Carolingian manuscripts. They probably served to teach verse composition, and the brief epitaphs for abbesses found on f. 86v show verse being composed. The abbesses, whose names are not recorded, may have been in charge of the nunnery at Bourges founded by Berthoara at the start of the seventh century.[60] In that case there would be evidence of contact between the bishop and other religious houses in his city.

The collection contains a number of brief passages from Jerome and Gregory the Great, probably taken from the *Sententiae* of Taio of Saragossa, and Christian teaching is also found in the Physiologus, a

---

[54] *Anecdota Helvetica*, p. 39.
[55] *Anecdota Helvetica*, p. 48.
[56] *Anecdota Helvetica*, p. 59.
[57] The definition quotes *Nam cum videris unde ortum est, cicius vim eius intelligis*, Isidore, *Etymologiae*, I XXIX, 2.
[58] *Analogia, Etymologia Glossa Differentia Soloecismus Metaplasmus* and *Schemata* at *Etymologiae* I chapters XXVIII, XXIX XXX, XXXI, XXXIII, XXXV and XXXVI, though Isidore has a much fuller treatment.
[59] *Antiphrais* I XXXVII 24, *Aenigma* XXXVII 26, *Parabola* XXXVII 33, *Prosa* I XXXVIII, *Bucolicum* I XXXIX 16, *Epithalamia* I XXXIX 18, *Threnos* I XXXIX 19, *Epitaphium* I XXXIX 20, *Fabula* I XL and *Syllogismus* II IX.
[60] Vita Columbani II 10 ed. Krusch p. 256. The nunnery is discussed by Y. Fox, *Power and Religion in Merovingian Gaul: Columbanian Monasticism and the Frankish Elites* (Cambridge, 2014) p. 119. A second nunnery was founded and endowed by Eustadiola (see Fox, *Power and Religion*, p. 121).

spiritual bestiary. Like the Pseudo-Methodius, this is a text originally translated from Greek, which explains the allegorical significance of birds, animals and even stones mentioned in the Bible, generally starting with a biblical quotation. The guiding principle is set out in chapter XXIX *De Panthere: Nihil ergo sine intentione de volatilibus et animalibus scriptura dixerunt.*[61]

The version here has forty chapters, most of which come from Carmody's Y version but which include chapters on the unicorn and the ape found in his B version. The flavour of the text is well conveyed by the following passage:

De Serra Marina Mare saeculum dictum est, naues prophetas et apostolos, qui pertransierunt saeculum hoc; et uirtutes aduersarii, haec autem serra, que non permansit cum nauibus transeuntibus, horum sunt similitudines qui ad tempus sunt abstinentes, et cursu bono currentes non permanserunt – incipientes opere bono, non permanserunt in fine, propter cupiditatem et superbiam et turpis lucri gratiam, aut fornicationes aut mechias aut odio: in quibus fluctibus maris (hoc est contrarie uirtutes) sunt que eos deducunt in infernum.[62]

The chapters on the Ibex and the Beaver offer explicit moral lessons for the reader.

De Hibice

Si uis ascendere in altitudinem, et mysteria domini Ihesu Christi discere, disce spiritaliter natare. Nisi enim duas manus extenderis et feceris typum crucis, non poteris pertransire mare; et nisi tu uolueris pertransire seculum ad deum per typum crucis, omnia scandala non uitabis: nescient enim natare neque orare scientes, foris depascuntur ab ecclesia.[63]

Et separa te opera carnis, quod est uectigal et tributum diaboli; et adipiscamur fructus spirituales, id est: caritatem, gaudium, pacem, patientiam, bonitatem, fidem, mansuetudinem, continentiam, castitatem in operibus bonis, id est in elemosinis, in uisitationibus infirmorum, in curis pauperum, in laudibus dei, in orationibus, in gratiarum actione, et caeteris qui dei sunt.

There is an explicit warning against heretical teaching:

De Herodion: O et tu, homo polionomene, una tibi sit nutrix et sempiterna ecclesia catholica, ut spiritalis esca et celestis panis digestibilis fiat in te: noli querere multa loca aliene glorie (hoc est hereticorum).[64]

The collection reveals a clear interest in world history and geography. Isidore Etymologiae V 39 *De descriptione temporum*, his history of the

---

[61] F. J. Carmody, *Physiologus Latinus Versio y* (Berkeley, CA, 1933–4), pp. 95–134, at p. 124.
[62] Carmody, *Physiologus*, p. 105.
[63] Carmody, *Physiologus*, p. 115.
[64] Carmody, *Physiologus*, p. 122.

six ages, ending with Emperor Heraclius. It is followed by Isidore Etymologiae IX 2 *De gentium vocabulis* (On the Nations of the World).

The interest in geography is also present in the Pseudo-Methodius, a Syrian text which was rapidly translated first into Greek and then into Latin. Pseudo-Methodius is an unusual combination of world chronicle and prophetic vision.[65] Starting with Adam, it gives a brief history of the world with prophecies about the fate of the Romans and Byzantium, the rise of the sons of Ishmael, and the destruction of Persia. During the seventh week, honour will be taken away from the priests and the ministry of God will be ended and the priests will be just as the laity. The King of the Romans will place his crown on the Cross, which will be taken up into Heaven, the king of Romans then dies and all rule and authority are destroyed. The Son of Perdition pretends to be God, occupies the Temple in Jerusalem until the Second Coming, with which the work ends.

Within the collection this text may be linked to the passages from Jerome's commentary on Daniel which also relate to the world empires and the end of the world.

The added text from Palladius' account of Pachomius and his rule shows an explicit interest in monasticism, which is also presented as originally Eastern. Several texts are directly related to bishops: the extracts from the *Regula Pastoralis* in Gregory's letter to Queen Brunhild about the election of laymen as bishops, and the excerpts from church councils on the election of bishops and the prohibition on bishops changing town. The shorthand passage from Jerome on Matthew refers to the clandestine ordination of clerics.

The Paris portion contains five formulae for documents comprising a charter recording an exchange of property, the renewal of a precarial grant, a mandatum asking someone to record a donation to a monastery in the *gesta municipalia*, a *securitas* guaranteeing a grant to a bishop and a document asking an archdeacon to support a newly ordained priest. Document no. 6, which is later, begins with a dating clause in the fourteenth year of an unnamed king[66] and records the words to be spoken by the Defensor and the Ordo curiae in recording a donation. These documents give a remarkable insight into late-antique municipal administration. They may be supplemented by further documents referring to Bourges in which there is mention of the clergy of St Stephen and the

---

[65] For the text, and this manuscript, cf. J. T. Palmer, *The Apocalypse in the Early Middle Ages* (Cambridge, 2014), pp. 113–14, and all of his chapter 4.

[66] For possible dates which this might refer to, see A. Rio, *Legal Practice and the Written Word in the Early Middle Ages Frankish Formulae, c. 500–1000* (Cambridge, 2009), p. 111.

viri magnifici.⁶⁷ As Rio has shown, almost all Merovingian formulae have survived in law books, but St Gallen Stiftsbibliothek 125 contains exegetical works, sermons and patristic excerpts.⁶⁸

Patristic passages relate to spiritual life: Isidore VI xix on prayers three times a day, fasting and penance; Jerome on the need for almsgiving; Prosper on penance and the Last Judgment; and a homily on penance which also mentions the Last Judgment.⁶⁹ Concern for the Last Judgment is also found in a passage from a letter of Jerome, and the extract from Gregory's Dialogues is concerned with Purgatory.

The small format of the Bern collection makes it clear that it was always a set of teaching texts, and therefore it would never have included substantial patristic texts. Some two-thirds of the works which are included, in full or as excerpts, were composed no more than a century before they were copied. Isidore, Taio composed 653–4, and Pseudo-Methodius around 700; Mordek thought that the extracts from church councils were assembled in the 690s, and the computus passages are dated to 727.

The grammar of Asper is a Christian Latin grammar probably dating to the sixth or seventh century. Louis Holtz thought it was an Irish work,⁷⁰ but Vivien Law took the references to Lyons and Autun as evidence that an earlier version was composed on the Continent.⁷¹

If the *Differentias* in the contents lists is the work of Isidore, then even more of his works were known at Bourges, making the links to Spain especially interesting.

The presence of the prefatory poem to Taio of Saragossa's collection of passages from the works of Gregory the Great suggests that Taio may be the source of the excerpts from Gregory in the collection. Apart from a passage from the Dialogues on Purgatory, all of the excerpts from Gregory are also in Taio. This is the earliest evidence of knowledge of Taio's *Sententiae*. The excerpts from Jerome on Matthew on f 87v are a selection which follows the order of the Lyon florilegium edited by Etaix.⁷²

---

⁶⁷ MGH Formulae, p. 171 no 7. from Paris BN Lat 4629. A further mention of a manumission ceremony taking place in front of the altar of St Stephen in the presence of bishops, priests and deacons is found in document 9 from the early-ninth-century manuscript Leiden BPL 114, pp. 172–3.
⁶⁸ Rio, *Legal Practice and the Written Word*, pp. 241–71, with the contents of St Gallen 125 listed on pp. 263–4.
⁶⁹ The text was transcribed by A. Mentz, *Die Tironischen Noten* (Berlin, 1944), pp. 161–3.
⁷⁰ Louis Holtz, *Donat et la tradition de l'enseignement grammatical: Étude sur l''Ars Donati' et sa diffusion (IVe–IXe siècle) et édition critique* (Paris, 1981), pp. 278–9, 286, 422.
⁷¹ V. Law, *The Insular Latin Grammarians* (Woodbridge, 1982), pp. 35–41, at p. 41.
⁷² R. Etaix, 'Un ancien florilège hiéronymien', *Sacris Erudiri*, 21 (1972–3), pp. 5–34, nos. 1, 2, 3, 4, 6, 8, 9, 13, 15, 16, 19, 22, 23, 24, 27, 32, 33, 37, 46, 48 and 52, followed by 62, 66, 96, 97, 98, 114 and 115.

The collection may be securely dated because of the computistical dialogue on ff. 94–6r: *Iterum a principio mundi usque in presente anno in unum collecti fiunt anni |V| DCCCCXXVIII et restant adhuc de isto sexto miliario anni LXXII indictione X.* The Easter table on f. 96r covers the years 727–48.

The computus is in question-and-answer form, again suggesting the schoolroom.[73]

The manuscript was made to instruct the clerics around the bishop of Bourges, who would have been trained in Latin vocabulary and Christian Latin grammar. In addition to grammar and two glossaries, they were familiar with riddles, verse composition and the brief moral instruction furnished by the interpretation of the natural world in the Physiologus. Isidore provided them with a brief history of the world and an account of the peoples who inhabited it. There were model formulae for these clerics to record transfers and sales of property, for the bishop had become the chief civic magistrate. Several texts relate to the proper election of bishops, and there is even some rudimentary canon law, apparently assembled at Bourges, as well as an exposition of the Lord's prayer and discussions of fasting and penance.

Were the texts of Isidore and Taio brought by refugees from Spain, like those who brought Visigothic manuscripts to Autun?

The collection is most probably from Bourges, because of the mention in the Formulae III *ut ad vicem meam Beturegas civitate accedes*. The collection allows us to see the bishop of Bourges and his entourage, some presumably married, who made up the *ordo curiae*, people who would have been called *boni homines*, as in the formulae.[74] Gregory of Tours mentions a *mensa canonica* at Bourges in his life of St Patroclus.[75] Our first record of canons is a charter of archbishop Hugh dating to 978.[76]

Our knowledge of seventh- and eighth-century Bourges depends largely on the *Vita Sulpicii*.[77] That text shares the concern for fasting and almsgiving which is found in the Bern collection. There is an eleventh-century episcopal list on the reverse of a consular diptych, discussed by Duchesne,[78] and the presence of bishops of Bourges is attested at

---

[73] A. Borst, *Schriften zur Komputistik im Frankenreich von 721 bis 818*, MGH Schriften 21 (Hanover, 2006), pp. XXIX, 348–74.
[74] MGH Formulae, p. 169.
[75] Gregory of Tours, *Vitae Patrum*, IX 1. MGH SRM I.2, p. 253.
[76] J. Péricard, *Ecclesia Bituricensis: le diocèse de Bourges des origines à la réforme grégorienne* (Clermont-Ferrand, 2006), p. 171.
[77] MGH SRM IV, pp. 364–80.
[78] L. Duchesne, *Fastes épiscopaux de l'ancienne Gaule*, vol. II: *L'Aquitaine et les Lyonnaises* (Paris 1910), pp. 21–31 with further discussion by Péricard.

church councils from 453. Bourges was captured by Charles Martel in 731. The city had a palace[79] and was described as *Caput Acquitaniae* in the continuation of Fredegar's Chronicle.[80] It clearly had a tradition of schools, for Amandus supposedly studied there.[81] It also had a mint. Stefan Esders has drawn my attention to a letter of Sigibert III to Desiderius of Cahors, forbidding him from attending a synod summoned by Vulfoleudes of Bourges, presumably in 650. Several of the bishops in the see of Bourges were subjects of Sigibert, but Bourges itself was in the territory of Clovis II, and the archbishop attended the synod of Chalons which Clovis had summoned.[82] Because the archbishop had to deal with bishops who were subject to a rival ruler, he may have had a particular interest in canon law.

The other late-eighth-century manuscripts associated with Bourges are a copy of the Lex Salica, capitularies of Charlemagne, the Lex Ribuaria and a formula relating to Bourges Paris BN Lat 4629, which Mordek and Bischoff associated with Leiden BPL 114 containing the Epitoma Aegidii of Lex Romana Visigothorum and the Formulae of Marculf,[83] a copy of the Collectio Sancti Mauri Hague Meerm Westr 10 B 4 (CLA X 1572), a copy of texts by Isidore and Martin of Braga and a letter of Leo I, Kassel 4o 10 (CLA VIII 1141), Paris BnF Lat 2034 (CLA V, 540) Augustinus, Enchiridion, and Ps Augustinus, Hypomnesticon from St Martial, and Paris BnF Lat. 1960 Augustinus in Ev. Johannis LV–CXXIV from St Martial and, lastly, the collection of canon law known as the Collectio Remensis, Berlin Phillipps 1743. They are all copied in a distinctive Merovingian cursive minuscule and show a development in this script from the scripts used in Bern 611.

Bern 611 came from Bourges, but it shows an awareness of a Mediterranean world. Isidore's history refers to Byzantine emperors, and the geographical extracts cover the whole world. The riddles include mention of papyrus, imported from Egypt, and the Physiologus describes exotic animals. The Pseudo-Methodius has been seen as a response to

---

[79] *Rex Pippinus in Betoricas per hiemen totum cum regina sua Bertradane in palatium resedit* Cont. Fredegarii c. 50 SRM II, p. 191.
[80] Fredegar Continuatio c. 13 SRM II, p. 175 c. 25 MGH SRM II, p. 180 c. 47, p. 189. For the history of Merovingian Bourges, see D. Claude, *Topographie und Verfassung der Stadte Bourges und Poitiers bis in das 11. Jahrhundert* (Lübeck and Hamburg, 1960) and Péricard, *Ecclesia Bituricensis*.
[81] Vita Amandi I c 5–6, MGH SRM 5, p. 433. Austrigisil *in pueritia litteris sacris fuerat instructus* MGH SRM IV p. 191.
[82] MGH Epistolae III pp. 192–214 at p. 212.
[83] For a full description, see H Mordek, *Bibliotheca capitulcrium regum Francorum manuscripta* (Munich, 1995), pp 502–7.

the rise of Islam and the Arab conquests. Another Bourges manuscript, in Kassel, contains the Apocalypse of Thomas, which also deals with the approaching end of the world. The clerics of Bourges had texts from Spain and from Rome, but also Latin translations of Greek medical texts.

Acknowledgements

I am grateful to Stefan Esders and Alain Stoclet for advice about Bourges, to Anna Dorofeeva for photographs of Bern 611, to Gerald Schwedler for discussion of the manuscript and to the editors of this volume for their help in making this paper more lucid. None of them are responsible for errors.

Appendix: The Contents of Bern 611

Originally Six Separate Parts

1r–18v Latin glossary (D–Z)[84]
18v–19r Latin glossary (A–H)
19v–20r Birth lunarium (later ninth-century addition)[85]
20v–26r Isidore of Seville, *Etymologiae* V, 39, *De descriptione temporum*. (on world history)
26r–40v Isidore of Seville, *Etymologiae* IX, 2 (sections 2–135), *De gentium uocabulis*
40v–41v Excerpts from Palladius, *Historia Lausiaca* 32 (on Pachomius and his rule)[86] (later addition) *De libro qui apellatur Paradisus*
42r Carmen de ventis (later addition)[87]
42v–72v *Ars Asporii*[88]
72v Isidore of Seville, *Etymologiae*, I.22 (*De notis vulgaribus*)

---

[84] From the Abba glossary as edited by M. Warren, *Transactions of the American Philological Association*, 15 (1884): 141–87 from St Gallen 912.

[85] This appears to be the same text as that in the following British Library manuscripts: Cotton Tiberius A.iii (s. ix^{med}); Harley 3017 (s. ix^2); Cotton Titus D.xxvi, xxvii (s. xi^1); and in Biblioteca Apostolica Vaticana, Pal. lat. 235 (s. xi); edited as part of a group of similar lunaria in R. Liuzza (ed.), *Anglo-Saxon Prognostics: An Edition and Study of Texts from London, British Library, MS Cotton Tiberius A. iii*, Anglo-Saxon Texts 8 (Cambridge, 2010), pp. 158–63.

[86] Text family 1 a according to A. Wellhausen, *Die lateinische Übersetzung der Historia Lausiaca des Palladius* (Berlin, 2003), pp. 356–8.

[87] Paulo Farmhouse Alberto (ed.) 'The Textual Tradition of the "Carmen de uentis" ("AL" 484): Some Preliminary Conclusions with a New Edition', *Aevum: Rassegna di scienze storiche, linguistiche e filologiche*, 83 (2009): 341–75.

[88] The section of the text from fol. 71r appears to be unique to Bern 611. The text of Asper is edited by H. Hagen, *Anecdota Helvetica* (Leipzig, 1870), pp. 39–61.

Paris BnF Lat 10756 ff. 62–9

62r–64r Formulary with five documents, no. 3 mentions Bourges;[89] these are numbered as in the contents list
64r(a) Jerome, *Contra Vigilantium*, chapter XIV in Tironian notes (5 lines)[90]
64v–67r Table of a nineteen-year lunar cycle
67r Section from a paschal cycle, attributed in the manuscript to Victorius of Aquitaine[91]
67v–68r Verses on the creation and end of the world, mainly in Tironian notes[92]
68v–69r Dionysius Exiguus, *Argumenta paschalia* (argument 16 de ratione bissexti); ends with two lines on 69r
69v Pope Gregory I the Great, *Regula pastoralis* III:12 (*PL* 77.66D–68A = Taio III lii) in shorthand[93]

Bern 611

73r–80v Aenigmata Bernensia[94] (the first leaf is lost, a leaf is missing after f. 78)
80v–81r Metrical *sententiae*, arranged alphabetically (A–T) written partly in Tironian notes[95] (later addition)
81v List of measurements for Noah's Ark; uncial *Descriptio arcae Noae*
81v–82r List of various measurements based on the stadium; Isidore *Etymologiae* XV 16. 2–3
82r Excerpt from Jerome on Daniel 10:12 (later addition)

---

[89] Text edited in full from this manuscript in K. Zeumer (ed.), *Formulae merowingici et karolini aevi accedunt ordines iudiciorum dei* (Hanover, 1886), pp. 169–71; and in Pardessus, 'Notice sur les manuscrits de formules relatives au droit observé dans l'empire des Francs, suivis de quatorze formules inédites', *Bibliothèque de l'École des Chartes*, 4 (1843): 10–11, 20–2.

[90] *PL* XXIII.350. Edited from Bern 611 and discussed in W. Schmitz, 'Tironianum', *Mélanges Julien Havet: recueil de travaux d'érudition dédiés à la mémoire de Julien Havet (1853–1893)* (Paris, 1895), pp. 77–80.

[91] B. Krusch, 'Chronologisches aus Handschriften', *Neues Archiv der Gesellschaft für Ältere Deutsche Geschichtskunde*, 10 (1885): 81–94, at p. 93.

[92] Edited in E. Chatelain, *Introduction à la lecture des notes tironiennes* (Paris, 1900), pp. 226–9.

[93] Discussed in W. Schmitz, 'Tironische Noten aus der Pariser lateinischen Handschrift 10756', *Franz Xaver Gabelsberger und seine Kunst* (Munich, 1890), pp. 116–20.

[94] *Aenigmata Bernensia* ed. F. Glorie, *Variae collectiones aenigmatum Merovingicae aetatis*, CC SL 133A (Turnhout, 1968), A 547–610 (ms. H). There is an earlier edition in MGH Poetae IV pp. 737–59.

[95] Edited by K. Strecker (ed.), *Monumenta Germaniae Historica. Poetae Latini aevi Carolini* 4 (Berlin, 1899), pp. 648–51.

82v–85v Galen, *Letter on Fevers*[96]

86r Jerome, *In Danielem* III 5 (extracts); (later addition) Taio *Sententiae* II 37

86v Epitaph of an anonymous abbess[97]

87r Prognostics for a good or bad summer or winter (seven lines in Tironian notes); the remainder of the page left blank[98]

87v Jerome, extracts (*In Matthaeum* V.12, 18, 29, 30; *In Jonam* II.2, Epistola 123.14)

88r(a) Anonymous compilation of questions and answers on grammar, in eighteen lines of Tironian notes; verse epigram by Taio of Saragossa (the start of his *Sententiae*)[99]

88v–89r Exposition of the Lord's Prayer as in the Gelasian sacramentary (*PL* 74:1091–3) (later addition)[100]

89v Most of the *In aurium apertione* Lent service for the induction of catechumens; largely written in Tironian notes

89v Pope Gregory I the Great, *Moralia in Iob* XII.52 (4 lines) followed by his *Regula pastoralis* III.11 (2.5 lines) (Taio III liv, III xxviii)

90r(a) Pope Gregory I the Great, *Regula pastoralis* III.3 (7 lines) (*PL* 83.1156C) = Taio II xliv; (b) Isidore, *Sententiae* III. 57, 1–4. 6–7 *De oppressoribus pauperum* (10.5 lines); (c) Pope Gregory I the Great, *Moralia in Iob* XX.21 (9 lines) Taio IV xxii

90v–91r Brief sentences from Jerome in Isai XVI, 58, 66, Augustine and Isidore, Etymologiae VI 19 largely written in Tironian notes[101]

91v(a) Julianus Pomerius *de Vita contemplativa* II vii and III xxix; (b) unidentified homily on penitence (line 4 onwards)[102]

---

[96] K.-D. Fischer's Typ I text also in Paris, Bibliothèque nationale, lat. 11218 (s. viii/ix) and Berlin, Preussische Staatsbibliothek, Phillipps 1790 (s. ix¹) and St Gallen 759. edited by H. Hagen, De Oribasii versione latina Bernensi commentatio, (Bern, 1875).

[97] B. Bischoff 'Epitaphienformeln für Äbtissinnen (Achtes Jahrhundert)', *Anecdota novissima. Texte des 4. bis 16. Jahrhunderts*, 11 (1984): 151–3. Two epitaphs quote Hieronymus Ep. 39, 1.

[98] W. Schmitz, 'Schnellschriftliches aus der Berner Handschrift 611', *Deutsche Stenographenzeitung*, 3 (1888): 360–7.

[99] Edited from Bern 611 in H. Hagen, *Carmini medii aevi maximam partem inedita* (Bern, 1877), p. 12.

[100] Cf Ordo Romanus XI, 69.

[101] Edited from Bern 611 in W. Schmitz, 'Notenschriftliches aus der Berner Handschrift 611', *Commentationes Woelfflinianae: Eduard Woelfflino natalicia sexagesima gratulantur qui colligendo thesauro linguae latinae eo auctore per VII annos operam dederunt* (1891), pp. 7–13.

[102] Edited from Bern 611 in P. Legendre, *Études tironiennes: Commentaire sur la VIe églogue de Virgile tiré d'un manuscrit de Chartres* (Paris, 1907), pp. 48–50 (with notes on the Tironian elements on pp. 85–7).

92r Unidentified homily in Tironian notes; quotations from Amos, Zacharias questions on penitence; this includes a passage from Taio, *Sententiae* III, 34–5

Inc. 'In amos propheta ...'[103]

92v–93r Original contents list to the manuscript listing the following texts in uncial: 'I. Ars donati ab aspero. II. De notis uulgaribus. III. Quid est antifrasin enigma, parabula, paradigma, prosa, bucolica epitalamia, trenos epitafium, fabulas, sillogismi. IV. Confectio amforalis. V. Sermo de tribus magis. VI. De ponderibus et mensum. VII. De drumeta uel citera quaendam omnibus clarent. VIII. Pauca nomina. VIIII. De trebus principalibus linguis quibus spiritus sanctus appellatur. X. Indicolos diuersos pauci. XI. Carta conmutationis. XII. Praecaria. XIII. Mandatum. XIIII. Securitas. XV. Ad archepresbyterum instituendum. (large gap) XVI. Quid sanctus hieronimy de antidotis dixit. XVII. Differentias. XVIII. De olla de lucerna de sale de mensa de calice de litteris. XVIIII. De arca noe. XX. De stadiis. XXI. Epistula gallieni de febribus'

92v At base, Gregory the Great's *Moralia in Iob* V.22, on the ant-lion.

94r–96v *Computus*, in dialogue form based on the table of Victorius of Aquitaine[104]

97r–v Excerpt from Isidore, *De ecclestiasticis officiis* I XI 4–7, XII 1–7 *Sanctus isidorus*

98r–99r Pope Gregory I the Great, *Epistola* IX.213 to Brunhildis on the ordination of laymen as bishops (in the same shortened form as in the *Collectio Vetus Gallica*)[105]

99r–100r Pope Gregory I the Great, *Dialogues* IV.25.2–41.3 (On Purgatory) This has the titles *De Anime iustorum si anti restutione corporum in celo recipiuntur De Infernum Utrum unus Gehenne ignis an diverse*

100r Pope Gregory I the Great, *Moralia in Iob* XVIII.54.88 (=Taio I xxxviii)

[103] Transcribed by A. Mentz, *Die Tironischen Noten* (Berlin 1944), pp. 161–3.
[104] Edited A. Borst, *Schriften zur Komputistik*, pp. XXIX, 348–74 cf. I. Warntjes, *The Munich Computus: Text and Translation – Irish Computistics between Isidore of Seville and the Venerable Bede and Its Reception in Carolingian Times* (Stuttgart, 2010), pp. xxiv–xxv.
[105] MGH *Epistolae*, II, p. 199. The version of the letter in Bern 611 is discussed in H. Mordek, *Kirchenrecht und Reform im Frankenreich. Die Collectio Vetus Gallica, die älteste systematische Kanonessammlung des fränkischen Gallien* (Berlin and New York, 1975), pp. 108–9.

101r–113r Pseudo-Methodius, *De initio et fine saeculi*;[106] *Incipit facciuncola vel sermo Sancti Methodii epsicopi de regnum gentium et novissimis temporibus certa demonstratio*

114r–115r Excerpt from Jerome, *Epistula de uirginitate seruanda ad Eustochium* (*epistola* 22 cap 30)

116v–138v *Physiologus* versio y with sections from versio b in forty chapters;[107] *Incipit Tractatus Episcopi ortodoxi de Natura animalium*

138v–145v Excerpts from church councils on the election of bishops (*Collectio Bernensis*); headings given in uncial for each extract;[108] f. 145v is widely and clumsily spaced

146r–153v Medical recipes; Gargilius Martialis 72–97 Pseudo-Oribasius commentary on the Hippocratic aphorisms (by the scribe of Pseudo-Methodius); *Incipit de arte medica ad stomachum*

---

[106] W. J. Aerts and G. A. Korteaas (eds.), *Die Apokalypse des Pseudo-Methodius: die ältesten griechischen und lateinischen Übersetzungen* (Louvain, 1998) with an account of this manuscript, pp. 50–4. Cf. B. Garstad, *Apocalypse of Pseudo-Methodius: An Alexandrian World Chronicle* (Cambridge, MA, 2012).

[107] This version was edited by Carmody, *Physiologus Latinus Versio y*, pp. 95–134. Cf F. Sbordone, 'La tradizione manoscritta del Physiologo latino', *Athenauem*, NS 27 (1949): 246–80.

[108] The collection is called the Sammlung von Bern in Mordek, *Kirchenrecht und Reform im Frankenreich*, pp. 107–9. It was edited by. H. Mordek, 'Bischofsabsetzungen in spätmerowingischer Zeit. Justelliana, Bernensis und das Konzil von Mâlay (677)', in Id (ed.), *Papsttum Kirche und Recht im Mittelalter. Festschift für Horst Fuhrmann* (Tübingen, 1991), pp. 31–53.

18 Contact with the Eastern Mediterranean in the Late Merovingian Period

Ian Wood

In 1970, Peter Brown was in the habit of asking first-year students why the horizons of the sixth-century bishop and historian Gregory of Tours were apparently more limited than those of the seventh-century compilation known as Fredegar. This is not a question that would be asked today, and it was posed before Brown himself worked on Gregory's hagiography, which of course gives an impression of substantially wider horizons than do the *Histories*. Nevertheless, the range of Fredegar's interests still remains remarkable, not least his concerns with Heraclius, and the coming of the Saracens, the circumcised people, which culminate in the chronicler's apocalyptic reading of the defeat of the emperor, following his opening of the Caspian Gates.[1] Fredegar continues his account of events in the East with a discussion of the problems of Emperor Constans following the Saracen capture of Jerusalem, Alexandria and Africa, as well as the seizure of the Mediterranean islands, and he even promises to take the story up to at least 658,[2] although he never gets that far. The next reference to the Saracens in the Fredegar compilation comes in the eighth-century continuations, with their arrival in Gaul in the 720s.[3]

The best-known evidence for links between Francia and Egypt in the early seventh century is to be found in the *Life of John the Almsgiver*, patriarch of Alexandria from 606 to 616.[4] One further indication of a Frankish

---

[1] Fredegar, *Chronicle*, IV, 66, ed. J. M. Wallace-Hadrill, *The Fourth Book of the Chronicle of Fredegar* (Edinburgh, 1960), pp. 54–5: S. Esders, 'Herakleios, Dagobert und die "beschnittenen Völker": Die Umwälzungen des Mittelmeerraums im 7. Jahrhundert in der Chronik des sog. Fredegar', in A. Goltz, H. Leppin and H. Schlange-Schöningen (eds.), *Jenseits der Grenzen: Beiträge zur spätantiken und frühmittelalterlichen Geschichtsschreibung* (Berlin, 2009), pp. 239–311; A. Fischer, 'Rewriting History: Fredegar's Perspectives on the Mediterranean', in A. Fischer and I. N. Wood (eds.), *Western Perspectives on the Mediterranean: Cultural Transfer in Late Antiquity and the Early Middle Ages, 400–800 AD* (London, 2014), pp. 55–75.
[2] Fredegar, *Chronicle*, IV, 81, ed. Wallace-Hadrill, pp. 68–9.
[3] Fredegar, cont. 13, ed. Wallace-Hadrill, pp. 90–1.
[4] S. Loseby, 'The Mediterranean Economy', in P. Fouracre (ed.), *The New Cambridge Medieval History*, vol. I: *c. 500–c. 700* (Cambridge, 2005), pp. 605–38, at p. 627.

interest in, and even of direct contact with, the eastern Mediterranean in the first half of the century is the presence in Francia of numerous pilgrim flasks depicting St Menas.[5] These were no doubt brought back by pilgrims to the Holy Land from Abu Mina in Egypt, prior to the Arab conquest in 642, when the site seems to have ceased to be a focus of pilgrimage. The flasks are an important indication of the visits of Franks to Egypt before the middle of the seventh century, but even if the pilgrimage route was disrupted thereafter, it is unlikely that interest in the region ended with its takeover by the Muslims.

Historians have been unwilling to accept that there was much continuing knowledge of the eastern Mediterranean in Francia between the composition of the Fredegar Chronicle and the early Carolingian area – and this despite the likelihood that the Merovingians were among 'the most eminent members of the Western peoples' who sent envoys with gifts to Constantine IV following the repulse of the Muslim siege of Constantinople in 678, which would suggest a significant channel of communication.[6] After Fredegar, the next text from the Frankish world to show interest in the Middle East is often thought to be the *Hodoeporicon* by Hygeburg, describing the visit of the Anglo-Saxon Willibald to the Holy Land, a journey that began in 723, although the account of it was only set down shortly before 787.[7] Since Willibald settled in southern Germany in 741 at Boniface's request, the information he brought back to Francia can be seen as part of the history of contacts between the Merovingian world and the eastern Mediterranean. We will return to the more problematic pilgrim account of the Frankish bishop Arculf, which dates to the second half of the seventh century.

My concern in what follows is to ask whether there really was a gap in communication between Byzantium and Francia in the years between Fredegar and Willibald. As regards indirect patterns of connection, the Frankish church had at least intermittent knowledge of the eastern Mediterranean, as is clear from the admittedly fragmentary evidence of the papal lobbying of Western churches in the half century prior to the third council of Constantinople in 680/1.[8] We have evidence for the 660s,

---

[5] W. Anderson, 'Pilgrimage and Trade at the End of Antiquity', *Ancient West and East*, 6 (2007): 221–43, at pp. 235–8.

[6] Theophanes, *Chronographia*, 6169, in *The Chronicle of Theophanes: Anni Mundi 6095–6305 (AD 602–813)*, trans. H. Turtledove (Philadelphia, PA, 1982), p. 54. See also Stefan Esders' chapter in this volume.

[7] Hugeburc, *Vita Willibaldi*, ed. A. Bausch, *Biographien der Gründungszeit, Quellen der Diözese Eichstätt* (Eichstätt, 1952) See also Ora Limor's chapter in this volume.

[8] I. N. Wood, 'Between Rome and Jarrow: Papal Relations with Francia and England, from 597–716', in *Chiese locali e chiese regionali nell'alto medioevo* (Spoleto, 2014), vol. I, pp. 297–320, at pp. 310–15.

670s and 680s, from Spain, England and also from Francia, showing a sequence of concerted efforts by the popes to gain support against the church of Constantinople over Monotheletism, and one might guess that such lobbying also occurred before the Council in Trullo of 692, with its hostile position over various points of Western theology and liturgy. Pope Sergius' liturgical reforms may have attracted attention in England, and it would be surprising if the relevant information reached the Anglo-Saxons without being noted in Francia.[9] The lobbying of Western churches by popes in the late seventh century would seem to have been the continuation of a policy which had been pursued in 649, when Pope Martin sought support for the Lateran Council in its opposition to the *Ecthesis* of Patriarch Sergius and the *typos* of Patriarch Paul, both of which were upheld by Emperor Constans.[10] And Constans is the major player in Fredegar's final entries on Byzantium and the Arabs. The chronicler's attention might have been drawn to the emperor partly as a result of his move to the West in 663:[11] we can infer that the Merovingian court had noted the move from the fact that Abbot Hadrian was detained by the Franks as a potential spy, on his journey from Rome to England in 668.[12]

There is further evidence for Frankish knowledge of the East in the first half of the eighth century. In an article on Latin translations of Pseudo-Methodius, Richard Pollard stressed the remarkably early transmission of that apocalyptic text to the West.[13] The *Revelationes* of Pseudo-Methodius would appear to have been written shortly after, and perhaps in response to, the erection of the Dome of the Rock in Jerusalem by

---

[9] É. Ó Carragáin, 'Liturgical Innovations Associated with Pope Sergius and the Iconography of the Bewcastle and Ruthwell Crosses', in R. T. Farrell (ed.), *Bede and Anglo-Saxon England* (Oxford, 1978), pp. 131–47; F. Orton, I. N. Wood and C. Lees (eds.), *Fragments of History: Rethinking the Ruthwell and Bewcastle Monuments* (Manchester, 2007), pp. 176–7, and 139–92.

[10] R. Price, *The Acts of the Lateran Synod of 649* (Liverpool, 2014), pp. 5–108; Wood, 'Between Rome and Jarrow', pp. 310–11.

[11] I. N. Wood, 'Fredegar's Fables', in A. Scharer and G. Scheibelreiter (eds.), *Historiographie im frühen Mittelalter* (Vienna, 1994), pp. 359–66, at p. 366.

[12] Bede, *Historia Ecclesiastica*, IV, 1, ed. B. Colgrave and R. A. B. Mynors, *Bede's Ecclesiastical History of the English People* (Oxford, 1969), pp. 332–3: I. N. Wood, 'The Continental Connections of Anglo-Saxon Courts from Æthelberht to Offa', *Settimane* 58, *Le relazione internazionali nell'alto medioevo* (Spoleto, 2011), pp. 443–80, at p. 458. On this, see Stefan Esders' chapter in this volume.

[13] R. Pollard, 'One "Other" on Another: Petrus Monachus' *Revelationes* and Islam', in M. Cohen and J. Firnhaber-Baker (eds.), *Difference and Identity in Francia and Medieval France* (Farnham, 2010), pp. 25–42; J. T. Palmer, *The Apocalypse in the Early Middle Ages* (Cambridge, 2014), pp. 107–29.

Abd al-Malik in 691/2.¹⁴ The original text seems to have been written in Syriac, but it appears that the Latin translation undertaken by a man who identifies himself as Petrus was made from a Greek intermediary. The earliest manuscript of the Pseudo-Methodius is Bern 611, a section of which is dated to 727.¹⁵ Whether the folios containing the *Revelationes* are of that year, or slightly later in date, is unclear. On the other hand, the Bern manuscript is definitely not an authorial copy: indeed, the text is corrupt, in that the preface is misplaced, being inserted into the main body of the work.¹⁶ We are, therefore, faced with an original Syriac work written after 691/2, which was probably translated first into Greek and was already available in a Merovingian Latin translation by or shortly after 727. This suggests some reasonably direct line of contact between the eastern Mediterranean and Francia in the years immediately before Willibald's journey to the holy places.

Pollard doubted that late Merovingian linguistic knowledge was good enough to be responsible for the translation of Pseudo-Methodius. He wondered whether Petrus might have been linked with the School of Canterbury and pointed to some similarities of opinion between the *Revelationes* and the Anglo-Latin *Liber Monstrorum*.¹⁷ It has to be said that there is no obvious reason for thinking that the School of Canterbury was involved in the translation of Pseudo-Methodius, other than an assumption that no one in Francia could have managed it. The same objection can be raised against James Palmer's preference to see the translator as a Greek living in Rome.¹⁸ The Latin of the text exhibits elements of *Merovingika*, which might rather suggest that Petrus was a Frank.¹⁹

If we turn to the Bern manuscript, we may get a little closer to identifying the context in which the translation was copied, if not originally prepared. David Ganz has stressed the fact that the manuscript of the Bourges *formulae* (Paris BN Lat 10756) was once attached to Bern 611, which itself contains the Grammar of Asporius, with its references to Lyon and Autun. In addition, he has also pointed to the likelihood that some of the texts in Bern 611 were derived from the works of Taio

---

[14] G. J. Reinink, 'Pseudo-Methodius: A Concept of History in Response to the Rise of Islam', in A. Cameron and L. I. Conrad (eds.), *The Byzantine and Early Islamic Near East*, vol. I: *The Literary Sources* (Princeton, NJ, 1992), pp. 149–87.
[15] *CLA*, VII, p. 604.
[16] W. J. Aerts and G. A. A. Kortekaas, *Die Apokalypse des Pseudo-Methodius: Die ältesten greischichen und lateinischen Übersetzungen*, 2 vols. (Louvain, 1998), vol. I, p. 28.
[17] Pollard, 'One "Other" on Another', p. 39.
[18] Palmer, *The Apocalypse in the Early Middle Ages*, p. 113.
[19] Aerts and Kortekaas, *Die Apokalypse des Pseudo-Methodius*, vol. I, pp. 28–31.

of Saragossa.[20] We might guess that various sections of the compilation were copied in Bourges or somewhere on the fringes of Aquitaine, in a centre where there were refugees from Spain. This would provide an ideal context not just for the creation of the manuscript which contained the Pseudo-Methodius but also for the preparation of a translation, in which, as Pollard has remarked, the savagery of the Ishmaelites is emphasised much more than in the Greek text on which it was based.[21] A crucial passage of the *Revelationes* reads:

And after the tribulation caused by the sons of Ishmael, when all men will have been endangered and suffered tribulation, having no hope of safety (salvation?) or any redemption from their hands, having been persecuted and tormented by them, and when they, who have been reduced to hunger, thirst and nakedness, have been afflicted by the barbarians, those nations will be there eating and drinking and joking, glorying in their victories and in the desolation into which they have reduced Persia, Romania, Cilicia and Syria, Cappadocia and Isauria, Africa as well, and Sicily, and those who live near Rome and the islands, replying to those round them, and blaspheming, they say 'The Christians will never find an escape from our hands.'[22]

Rather than rule out the possibility of a translation being made within Merovingian Gaul, one might note the presence of Easterners in the Loire valley not just in the days of Gregory of Tours,[23] but also after 610. On being forced out of Luxeuil, Columbanus and his Irish and British disciples were escorted to Nantes. At Orléans, where Gregory records the presence of Jews, they met a Syrian woman and her husband, who are explicitly said to have come from the East and, given their support for Columbanus and his monks, are unlikely to have been Jewish.[24] It is not inconceivable that there was a Syrian community in the Loire valley and that it continued to attract Easterners in the aftermath of the Islamic expansion in the Holy Land.

---

[20] Personal communication. See also David Ganz's chapter in this volume. This MS was also discussed by Alice Rio.
[21] Pollard, 'One "Other" on Another', p. 32.
[22] Pseudo-Methodius, 13, 6, ed. Aerts and Kortekaas, pp. 169–71: 'Et post tribulationem, quae fit a filiis Ismahel, cumque periculati fuerint homines tribulatione passi, nequaquam habentes spem salutis aut redemptionem aliquam de manibus eorum, persecuti et tribulati ab eis, afflicti, qui fuerint in famem et sitem et nuditate, barbaris vero nationes erunt hi commedentes et bibentes et iocundantes, in victoriis eorum gloriantes et in desolationibus, quibus desolaverunt Persidamque et Romaniam, Ciliciam quoque et Syriam, Cappadociamque et Isauriam, Africam quoque vel Siciliam et eos, qui habitant proximae Romam et insulas, circumamicti quemadmodum sponsi, et blasphemantes dicunt quia: "Nequaquam habebunt christiani ereptionem de manibus nostris"'. See also B. Garstad, ed., *Apocalypse, Pseudo Methodius: An Alexandrian World Chronicle* (Cambridge, Mass., 2012), p. 127.
[23] Gregory of Tours, *Decem Libri Historiarum*, VIII, 1, ed. B. Krusch and W. Levison, MGH SRM, I, 1 (Hanover, 1951), pp. 370–1.
[24] Jonas, *Vita Columbani*, I, 21, ed. B. Krusch, MGH, SRG, 37 (Hanover, 1905), pp. 199–200.

286   Ian Wood

Such a milieu would also seem to be appropriate for an abridged version of the *Revelationes*, although its text differs so often from Petrus' translation that one may wonder whether the redactor was drawing on a different recension of the work. As Pollard notes, this second version obviously interpreted the *Revelationes* in local terms, substituting Aquitaine for Pseudo-Methodius' original Rome, Sicily and Greece.[25]

God hands us over to the barbarians because we have been forgetful of his precept; thus he hands us to the barbarians and they did much wrong to the Christians, because they are polluting themselves, which is dreadful to say. So God hands them over to the Saracens: Persia will be put to the sword and captured, Aurania[26] will be put to sword and captured, Epficius[27] will be put to sword and captured, Sicily will be strangled, the land of Syria will be a desert and its people taken away as captives, Cilicia likewise and its people put to the sword, Greece will be put to the sword and made captive, Egypt and the East and the Assyrians will be subject to heavy tribute of immense weight of silver and gold, Spain has perished by the sword and its people are led away captive, Gaul, Germany, Aquitaine have been swallowed up in various battles and many of their people are led away captive, Romania will be put to the sword, and is turned to flight, and they will take the islands of the sea, which will be devastated; Italy is partly defeated, and part will remain intact, the mountains of Auriolis (Alpes Maritimes) in their upland areas[28] are devastated, but they will remain intact along the sea coast, the Roman people will not be captured, but the sons of Ishmael will gain access to the North, the East, the South and the West, and Jerusalem will be filled with many peoples, who are led captive, and the Promised Land will be filled with all peoples, and their yoke will be heavy on many peoples and everything will be under their yoke.[29]

---

[25] Pollard, 'One "Other" on Another', p. 33.
[26] Identified as Armenia, O. Prinz, 'Eine frühe abendländische Aktualisierung der lateinischen Übersetzung des Pseudo-Methodios', *Deutsches Archiv für Erforschung des Mittelalters*, 41(1985): 1–23, at p. 19.
[27] Identified as Cappadocia, Prinz, 'Eine frühe abendländische Aktualisierung', p. 19.
[28] Prinz, 'Eine frühe abendländische Aktualisierung', p. 21: *oriis* is derived from ορος/ορειος.
[29] Prinz, 'Eine frühe abendländische Aktualisierung', pp. 12–13, ll. 119–37: 'Tradit nobis Deus in manus barbarorum, quia obliti sumus praeceptum Domini, propterea tradit nobis Deus ad populis barbaris et facient christianis multa inlicita, quia inmaculant semetipsos, quod turpissimum est dicendum. Propterea tradit illos Deus in manus Sarracinorum. Persida autem erit in captivitatem et occisionem, Aurania in occisionem erit et captivitatem, Epficium erit in occisionem et captivitatem, Sicilia erit in iuculacionem, terra Siria erit in solitudinem et habitatores eius captivi ducuntur, Cilicia similiter et habitatores eius gladio pereunt, Grecia in occisionem erit et captivitatem, Egyptus et orientem et Assirii erunt sub tributum grave in argentum et aurum pondera inmensa, Spania gladio periit et habitatores eius captivi ducuntur, Gallia, Iermania, Aquitania variis praeliis devorati et multi ex eis captivi ducuntur, Romania in occisione erit et convertitur in fuga et insulas maris erunt desolacione et obtinebunt, Italia parte

Although the earliest manuscript of this text (Zurich Zentralbibliothek C. 65) has been dated to the period 750–850, and its provenance identified as Alemannia, the description of the state of Gaul has been taken as an indication that the recension had already been made before Charles Martel's success at Poitiers – although this has been queried by Palmer in the light of Hannes Möhring's suggestion that it might belong after Charlemagne's attack on Spain in 778.[30] It is nevertheless worth noting the possible early date for this recension, because, if it is accepted, the text becomes the earliest witness to the impact of the Muslims on Gaul – and it also suggests that the arrival of the invaders was genuinely horrifying. The introduction of Gaul, Germany, Aquitaine and the Alpes Maritimes surely locates this abridgement of the *Revelationes* in Francia, and perhaps, like the translation of Petrus, on the fringes of Aquitaine.

Both these versions of this section of the *Revelationes* are curiously reminiscent of Fredegar's account of the devastation caused by the Saracens following the death of Heraclius' son Constantine III in 641:

In his [Constans'] time the Empire was savagely devastated by the Saracens. Jerusalem was captured by the Saracens, and other cities overthrown. Upper and Lower Egypt were invaded by the Saracens, and Alexandria taken and sacked. The whole of Africa was devastated and quickly occupied by the Saracens, and there the patrician Gregory was killed by the Saracens. Only Constantinople, together with the Thracian province and a few islands, and the Roman province had remained under the jurisdiction of the Empire, for the whole Empire had been greatly and gravely diminished by the Saracens. And finally the emperor Constans, confined and under pressure, was even made tributary to the Saracens, so that only Constantinople and a few provinces and islands were reserved for his authority. For around three years and more it is said till now that Constans filled the treasury of the Saracens with a thousand gold solidi a day.[31]

---

vincitur, parte intacta erit, Montes Auriolis per loca oriis devastatur et in longo lithore maris intacte erunt, Romana gentes non capietur et obtinebunt filii Ismahel introitum aquilonis et orientem et meridie et occidentem et replebitur Hierusolima de cunctis gentibus, qui captivi ducuntur, et replebitur terra repromissionis de omnes gentes et erit iugus eorum gravis super cunctas gentes et erit omnia sub iugu eorum.'

[30] Palmer, *The Apocalypse in the Early Middle Ages*, p. 122.

[31] Fredegar, *Chronicle*, IV, 81, ed. Wallace-Hadrill, pp. 68–9: 'Idem eius tempore grauissime a Sarracinis uastatur imperiom. Hierusolema a Saracinis capta ceterasque ciuitates aeuersae. Aegyptus superiur et inferior a Saracines peruadetur, Alexandria capetur et praedatur. Afreca tota uastatur et a Saracines possedetur paululum ibique Gregorius patricius a Saracinis interfectus. Constantinopolis tantum cum Traciana prouincia et paucis insolis, etiam et Romana prouincia emperiae dicione remanserat, nam maxeme totum emperium a Saracines grauetr fuit adtritum; etiam et in postremum emperatur Constans constrictus adque conpulsus, effectus est Saracinorum tributarius, ut uel Constantinopoles cum paucis prouincies et insolis suae dicione reseruaretur. Trebus annis circeter et fertur adhuc amplius per unumquemque diem mille soledus auri aeraries Saracinorum Constans emplebat.'

One might even wonder whether the translator of either of the versions of the *Revelationes* was influenced by the Fredegar compilation, which has been shown to belong to a remarkable historiographical debate taking place within Francia in the wake of Gregory of Tours' *Decem Libri Historiarum*.[32] Such influence would be entirely plausible if the writer responsible for the abridgement was working in the border area between Burgundy and Aquitaine.

Petrus' translation of Pseudo-Methodius implies that there was someone in Francia in the 720s or 730s who had access to the Greek version of Pseudo-Methodius, and was able to translate it into Latin. This is clearly a point that one needs to factor into a reading of late Merovingian culture.[33] Late Merovingian knowledge of and interest in Eastern apocalyptic texts is confirmed by the *Cosmographia of Aethicus Ister*, a work that indeed uses the Pseudo-Methodius, which as a result provides a *terminus post quem* for the composition of the cosmography.[34] This strange work provides an account of the world, supposedly as written by an Istrian philosopher (*Aethicus Ister*) and claiming to be redacted by Jerome. Most remarkable for its fantastic account of the monstrous peoples and their shipping in the North (apparently the Baltic),[35] it tends to be regarded as an oddity, and to be omitted from accounts of late Merovingian culture. The *terminus ante quem* of its composition is the earliest manuscript attestation, in the Admont fragments of the later eighth century,[36] and on linguistic grounds, Michael Herren would place the composition of the text in the second quarter of the century.[37] Certainly, it needs to be squeezed into the time frame between the translation of Pseudo-Methodius and the earliest manuscript fragments. Of course, the provenance of *Aethicus Ister* remains unclear: Michael Herren has firmly ruled out an Irish origin,[38] but has argued instead for a composition at

---

[32] H. Reimitz, *History, Frankish Identity and the Framing of Western Ethnicity, 550–850* (Cambridge, 2015), pp. 127–239.

[33] I. N. Wood, 'The Problem of Late Merovingian Culture', in S. Dusil, G. Schwedler and R. Schwitter (eds.), *Exzerpieren – Kompilieren – Tradieren: Transformationen des Wissens zwischen Spätantike und Frühmittelalter* (Berlin, 2017), pp. 199–222.

[34] I. N. Wood, 'Aethicus Ister: An Exercise in Difference', in W. Pohl and H. Reimitz (eds.), *Grenze und Differenz im frühen Mittelalter* (Vienna, 2000), pp. 197–208.

[35] I. N. Wood and G. Indruszewski, 'An Eighth-Century Written Source on Ships and Navigation: The Cosmography of Aethicus Ister', in A. Englert and A. Trakadas (eds.), *Wulfstan's Voyage: The Baltic Sea Region in the Early Viking Age* (Roskilde, 2009), pp. 220–34.

[36] M. Herren, *The Cosmography of Aethicus Ister: Edition Translation and Commentary* (Turnhout, 2011), p. ciii.

[37] Herren, *The Cosmography of Aethicus Ister*, p. civ.

[38] Herren, *The Cosmography of Aethicus Ister*, pp. lxxiii–lxxxviii.

Bobbio.[39] Although there is no Bobbio manuscript of the work (which, given our knowledge of books from the Italian monastery must raise a doubt about the work originating there), there may be a reference to a copy of the text in the ninth- or tenth-century catalogue.[40] One striking aspect of the catalogue entry, however, is the fact that a *cosmographia* is placed alongside histories of Troy and of Alexander. In the late seventh and early eighth centuries, the Western centre that was most interested in Troy was Francia, as is shown above all by Fredegar (who also had a strong interest in Alexander) and the *Liber Historiae Francorum*.[41] The Bobbio catalogue certainly provides an indication of the sort of library that the Cosmographer used, but it is unlikely to have been the only early eighth-century centre that held the works used in the *Cosmographia* that are identified by Herren as appearing in the catalogue.[42] In any case, while the work of *Aethicus Ister* may not have originated from Francia, the manuscript distribution suggests that it was in the Frankish world, and especially Bavaria, that it was most appreciated.[43]

In addition to Pseudo-Methodius, the author of *Aethicus Ister* had access to at least two Greek sources for which we lack any surviving early Latin translation, the sixth-century *Christian Topography* of Cosmas Indicopleustes and material related to the *Alexander Romance* of Pseudo-Callisthenes.[44] The *Cosmographia* thus fits into the same cultural world as that of the Latin translations of Pseudo-Methodius, not only because it made use of a translation of the *Revelationes* but also because it had access to other Greek texts which may not have been available in translation, or which had only recently been translated. In chronological terms, the Latin translation of Pseudo-Methodius antedates the *Hodoeporicon* of Willibald by no more than a generation, and so it does not radically alter our knowledge of Merovingian interest in the East, but it does suggest that we should not simply see Merovingian interest as being triggered by the adventurousness of Anglo-Saxons.

---

[39] Herren, *The Cosmography of Aethicus Ister*, pp. lxi–lxxiii. Palmer, *The Apocalypse in the Early Middle Ages*, p. 124.
[40] Herren, *The Cosmography of Aethicus Ister*, p. lxvii. A. Zironi, *Il monastero Longobardo di Bobbio: Crocevia di uomini, manoscritti e culture* (Spoleto, 2004), pp. 139–57; M. Richter, *Bobbio in the Early Middle Ages* (Dublin, 2008), pp. 140–56.
[41] Reimitz, *History, Frankish Identity*, passim; N. K. Yavuz, *Transmission and Adaptation of the Trojan Narrative in Frankish History between the Sixth and Eleventh Centuries*, unpublished Ph.D. thesis, University of Leeds (2015). On Alexander in Fredegar, I. N. Wood, 'Iocundus in Fabulis: The Value of Friendly Advice', in L. Jégou, S. Joye, T. Lienhard and J. Schneider (eds.), *Splendor Reginae: Passions, genre et famille* (Turnhout, 2015), pp. 327–38, at pp. 337–8.
[42] Wood, 'The Problem of Late Merovingian Culture'.
[43] Wood, 'Aethicus Ister: An Exercise in Difference', pp. 206–8.
[44] Herren, *The Cosmography of Aethicus Ister*, pp. xlv–li.

As Pollard has pointed out, of the four eighth-century manuscripts of Petrus' version of Pseudo-Methodius, two also include texts of Pseudo-Ephraem.[45] For Pollard, this is an indication that the Franks read the *Revelationes* as an apocalyptic text, which is scarcely surprising given its contents. As Palmer has noted, moreover, the *Scarpsum* of Pseudo-Ephraem is to be found in a manuscript with Pseudo-Methodius.[46] The popularity of the writings of Ephraem or Pseudo-Ephraem is surely a further indication of Merovingian interest in the East.[47] If we limit ourselves to manuscripts of Latin translations of his works from before 750, written within the Frankish world, we only have a paltry haul of one fragmentary *Vita Abrahae*.[48] If, however, we turn to the *Liber Scintillarum* of Defensor of Ligugé, we find two citations of the *De dei iudicii*, two from Pseudo-Ephraem's *Adhortatio ad Monachos*, and nine other citations of Ephraem or Pseudo-Ephraem.[49] Of course, much, if not all, of this was probably circulating in Gaul long before Defensor added the excerpts to his collection, probably in the late seventh century. David Ganz has pointed to Caesarius of Arles' apparent knowledge of Ephraem's sermons.[50]

Even more striking are the sixth-century Greek papyrus fragments of a work on Patriarch Joseph supposedly by Ephraem, found in the binding of a Tours manuscript. Sebastian Brock has made the intriguing suggestion that one should think of Tours as a centre of the dissemination of Ephraem's work and has proposed that the fragments might be linked to the Syrian who translated the *Legend of the Seven Sleepers of Ephesus* for Gregory of Tours.[51] This, of course, is to take us back to the sixth century, and to Gregory's Greek sources, which Averil Cameron discussed in 1975, having noticed some remarkable similarities between Gregory's accounts of Justin II and Tiberius and comments in John of Antioch and Evagrius Scholasticus.[52] One might note the possible relation of

---

[45] Pollard, 'One "Other" on Another', pp. 32–3. D. Ganz, *Corbie in the Carolingian Renaissance* (Sigmaringen, 1990), pp. 42 and 131.
[46] Palmer, *The Apocalypse in the Early Middle Ages*, p. 121; Ganz, *Corbie in the Carolingian Renaissance*, p. 131.
[47] S. Brock, 'The Changing Faces of St Ephrem as Read in the West', in J. Behr, A. Louth and D. Conomos (eds.), *Abba: The Tradition of Orthodoxy in the West* (Creswood, NY, 2003), pp. 65–80: D. Ganz, 'Knowledge of Ephraem's Writings in the Merovingian and Carolingian Age', *Hugoye: Journal of Syriac Studies*, 2 (2010): 37–46.
[48] Ganz, 'Knowledge of Ephraem's Writings', p. 40.
[49] Ganz, 'Knowledge of Ephraem's Writings', pp. 38–9. See also Yitzhak Hen's chapter in this volume.
[50] Ganz, 'Knowledge of Ephraem's Writings', p. 39.
[51] Brock, 'The Changing Faces of St Ephrem as Read in the West'.
[52] A. Cameron, 'The Byzantine Sources of Gregory of Tours', *Journal of Theological Studies*, 26 (1975): 421–6.

this material to Tiberius' recruiting drive among the Franks, identified by Benjamin Fourlas.[53] Stefan Esders has recently deepened our understanding of what Gregory has to say about the cult of St Polyeuktos in Austrasia in the days of Sigibert I.[54] From the same period there is also the evidence of Venantius Fortunatus,[55] and the *Epistolae Austrasicae*.[56] Defensor's use of Ephraem, then, does not necessarily tell us anything new about Merovingian contacts with the East in the late seventh or early eighth century, though it does unquestionably point to a continuing interest in works of Ephraem and Pseudo-Ephraem.

If we wish to explore the period closer to the time of Fredegar than to that of the translation of Pseudo-Methodius, we have the already mentioned evidence for papal lobbying against the Byzantine theological position, in the days of Pope Martin, in the 660s and 670s, as well as in the run-up to the Third Council of Constantinople in 680/1.[57] In addition, and more intriguingly, we have another text: Adomnán of Iona's *De locis sanctis*.[58] This purports to be Adomnán's transcription of an account of bishop Arculf's pilgrimage to the Holy Land. The claim has been much criticised in recent years.[59] Certainly, there is something odd about Bede's reference to Adomnán's encounter with Arculf, 'a bishop of Gaul who had visited Jerusalem to see the holy places':

He had wandered all over the Promised Land and had been to Damascus, Constantinople, Alexandria, and many islands of the sea. Returning home by ship, he was cast by the violence of the tempest on the west coasts of Britain. And after a great deal he came to the servant of Christ Adomnán.[60]

---

[53] See above.
[54] S. Esders, '"Avenger of All Perjury", in Constantinople, Ravenna and Metz: Saint Polyeuctus, Sigibert I, and the Division of Charibert's Kingdom in 568', in A. Fischer and I. N. Wood (eds.), *Western Perspectives on the Mediterranean: Cultural Transfer in Late Antiquity and the Early Middle Ages, 400–800 AD* (London, 2014), pp. 17–40.
[55] Esders, '"Avenger of All Perjury"', pp. 34–5.
[56] G. Barrett and G. Woudhuysen, 'Assembling the Austrasian Letters at Trier and Lorsch', *Early Medieval Europe*, 24 (2016) 3–57.
[57] Wood, 'Between Rome and Jarrow', pp. 310–15.
[58] Adamnan's *De locis sanctis*, ed. D. Meehan (Dublin, 1958).
[59] D. Woods, 'Arculf's Luggage: The Sources for Adomnán's *De locis sanctis*', *Ériu*, 52 (2002): 25–52: T. O'Loughlin, 'The *De locis sanctis* as a Liturgical Text', in J. M. Wooding (ed.), *Adomnán of Iona: Theologian, Lawmaker, Peacemaker* (Dublin, 2010), pp. 181–92: R. Aist, 'Adomnán, Arculf and the Source Material of the *De locis sanctis*', in J. M. Wooding (ed.), *Adomnán of Iona: Theologian, Lawmaker, Peacemaker* (Dublin, 2010), pp. 162–80.
[60] Bede, *Historia Ecclesiastica*, V, 15, ed. Colgrave and Mynors, pp. 506–9. I have altered the translation following the comments of D. Woods, 'On the Circumstances of Adomnán's Composition of *De locis sanctis*', in J. M. Wooding (ed.), *Adomnán of Iona: Theologian, Lawmaker, Peacemaker* (Dublin, 2010), pp. 192–204, at pp. 201–2, nn. 27–3. See also Bede, *De locis sanctis*, XIX, 5, ed. I. Fraipont, *Itineraria et alia geographica*, CCSL CLXXV (Turnhout, 1965), p. 280.

Bede seems to have understood the landing in Britain as occurring in the course of the journey back to Francia, which is improbable. Adomnán, however, does not combine the return journey from the Holy Land with the shipwreck on the coast of Britain:

> The holy bishop, Arculf, a Gaul by race, versed in divers far-away regions, and a truthful and quite reliable witness, sojourned for nine months in the city of Jerusalem, traversing the holy places in daily visitations. In response to my careful inquiries he dictated to me, Adamnan, this faithful and accurate record of all his experiences which is to be set out below. I first wrote it down on tablets: it will now be written succinctly on parchment.[61]

Thereafter, Arculf's name appears intermittently, but frequently, throughout the text. Both David Woods and Thomas O'Loughlin have argued that the text is largely a florilegium of citations put together for some liturgical or theological purpose.[62] The exposé of the work as a text made up of quotations, masquerading as a genuine account of a journey, is surely irrefutable – although that does not necessarily mean that there was no journey at all.

Neither O'Loughlin or Woods has gone so far as to deny that Arculf ever existed, although Woods suggests that the traveller should be called Arnulf.[63] However, the elements in the original name are authentically Frankish, even if the name itself is unattested. If one were to emend it, one might just as well argue for a change to Marculf: after all, the name Arnulf in this period is rare outside the Arnulfing family. As for the date of Arculf's supposed visit to the Holy Land, it used to be claimed that this must have taken place during the caliphate of Muawiyah (661–80), on the grounds of the pilgrim's mention of a ruler called Mauias,[64] thus dating the visit of Arculf to Iona to the mid 660s at the earliest. But, as Woods points out, the reference to Muawiyah may belong to his time as emir of al-Sham (Syria and Palestine), which began in c. 639.[65] The written text of the *De locis sanctis* can only be dated to the years before Adomnán's death in 704.[66] A long interval between his interview with Arculf and the final composition of his account of the holy places could explain not only some of the oddities of the descriptions in the text but

---

[61] Adomnán, *De locis sanctis*, pref., ed. Meehan, pp. 36–7.
[62] Woods, 'Arculf's Luggage'; O'Loughlin, 'The *De locis sanctis* as a Liturgical Text'. Among the responses to these arguments, see R. Hoyland and S. Waidler, 'Adomnán's *De locis sanctis* and the Seventh-Century Near East', *English Historical Review*, 129 (2014): 787–807.
[63] Woods, 'Arculf's Luggage', p. 49.
[64] Adomnán, *De locis sanctis*, I, 9, 11, ed. Meehan, pp. 54–5.
[65] Woods, 'Arculf's Luggage', p. 40.
[66] Woods, 'On the Circumstances of Adomnán's Composition of *De locis sanctis*', pp. 192–9.

also how it could be that the abbot of Iona's account was believed by his community. Even so, the traditional date of Arculf's journey may be worth consideration. If we place the visit of Arculf to Iona closer to 676, then we might set it in the context of the Frankish search for the young Dagobert II, who was discovered and returned to Francia at that moment, having been exiled to an Irish monastery (perhaps Slane, or Rathmelsigi), probably in 657.[67]

Another issue that is surely worth considering is the importance of Constantinople. Adomnán places the visit to the imperial city at the end of Arculf's journey.[68] Given the liturgical and exegetical concerns of the text identified by Woods and O'Loughlin, one can well understand that Adomnán deliberately placed Jerusalem at the start of Arculf's journey. Perhaps, however, the pilgrim first went to Constantinople. One might guess that, as a bishop, he went east on a diplomatic mission, such as that attested by Theophanes for 678,[69] though relations between Byzantium and Damascus in that particular year can scarcely have encouraged a visit to Jerusalem. The journey to the holy places could have been added to a formal visit to the East, as has been suggested for the itinerary of the Bordeaux Pilgrim in the fourth century.[70]

I would argue, therefore, that Arculf was a genuine figure, that he did indeed visit Constantinople and the Holy Land, and that he brought back some genuine information: Ora Limor has noticed information in the *De locis sanctis* which would seem to have derived from an eyewitness rather than any written source.[71] Even so, he might well have couched his account of his travels in terms derived from written sources – such an approach is not unknown in the early Middle Ages.

If we accept that Arculf both visited the eastern Mediterranean and brought back written material relating to Constantinople and the Holy Land,[72] we must assume that he transmitted his information to his colleagues in Francia, just as he did to Adomnán. Woods has suggested

---

[67] I. N. Wood, *Fursey and His Brothers: Their Contribution to the Irish Legacy on the Continent*, Fursey Lecture (Norwich, 2016), pp. 7–9.

[68] Adomnán, *De locis sanctis*, III, 1–6, ed. Meehan, pp. 106–19. On this Constantinopolitan section, see Hoyland and Waidler, 'Adomnán's *De locis sanctis* and the Seventh-Century Near East', pp. 799–805.

[69] Theophanes, *Chronographia*, 6169, trans. Turtledove, p. 54.

[70] B. Salway, 'There but Not There: Constantinople in the *Itinerarium Burdigalense*', in L. Grig and G. Kelly (eds.), *Two Romes: Rome and Constantinople in Late Antiquity* (Oxford, 2012), pp. 293–324.

[71] O. Limor, 'Pilgrims and Authors: Adomnán's *De locis sanctis* and Hugeburc's *Hodoeporicon sancti Willibaldi*', *Revue Bénédictine*, 114 (2004): 253–75; Aist, 'Adomnán, Arculf and the Source Material of the *De locis sanctis*'.

[72] For a fair assessment of the journey, see Hoyland and Waidler, 'Adomnán's *De locis sanctis* and the Seventh-Century Near East'.

that the *De locis sanctis* drew on a Byzantine *Life of Constantine*, as well as a collection of miracles of St George.[73] Neither text survives in a version that could have been the source for Arculf, but the fact that Adomnán's text boasts similarities with later Byzantine accounts of Constantine and also with miracle stories related by the Coptic monk Epiphanius gives some indication of works that might have been available to Arculf. Similarly, we get further glimpses of written sources used by Arculf in the story relating to Muawiyah.[74] Significantly, one of these stories may indicate that Arculf or Adomnán failed to understand what a Greek text actually said. Thus, Woods has pointed to the fact that Arculf/ Adomnán apparently mistranslated the Greek word ϛτηλη as *tabula* rather than *columna*, resulting in the notion that the original Al-Aqsa mosque was built of timbers rather than stone[75] – not that either suggestion is supported by any archaeological evidence.

Arculf, or rather the *De locis sanctis* of Adomnán, is rarely cited within Merovingian scholarship,[76] yet the work seems to fit neatly into the picture that we can deduce from a number of late Merovingian sources, beginning with Fredegar and ending with the *Cosmographia of Aethicus Ister* – and the *Cosmography*, perhaps like Adomnán, attests to an interest in fictional journeys. There were clearly people in Francia who were interested in the East, and especially in Constantinople and Jerusalem. If we leave aside Theophanes' comment on the presence of Western envoys in Constantinople in 678,[77] we have little evidence for the visit of a Frank to the eastern Mediterranean in the seventh century. Yet, even if we consign Arculf's visit to the realm of literary fiction (which we probably should not), we can have no doubt about the acquisition of information and especially of written information relating to Constantinople and the Holy Land.

There was clearly interest in such Eastern texts as the works of Ephraem throughout the late Merovingian period. Moreover, while it may well be true that there was no regular contact between Francia and Byzantium in the last decades of the seventh and first decades of the eighth century, it would seem that there were moments when there was a particular

---

[73] Woods, 'Arculf's Luggage'.
[74] Adomnán, *De locis sanctis*, I, 9, 11, ed. Meehan, pp. 54–5.
[75] Woods, 'Arculf's Luggage', p. 41. But see also the suggestion of Hoyland and Waidler, 'Adomnán's *De locis sanctis* and the Seventh-Century Near East', p. 798, that *tabula* means 'slab' rather than 'plank' in this context, although it would not be a standard translation of the Latin.
[76] Y. Hen, 'Holy Land Pilgrims from Frankish Gaul', *Revue Belge de Philologie et d'Histoire*, 76 (1998): 291–306, is exceptional.
[77] Theophanes, *Chronographia*, 6169, trans. Turtledove, p. 4.

interest in the East or in matters Eastern. Fredegar, for instance, gathered information on both Heraclius and Constans. If Heraclius did indeed write to Dagobert, instructing him to have all Jews in the Frankish kingdom baptised,[78] the arrival of the instruction was surely an occasion for gathering information about the East, and this situation may have continued down to the time of the expansion of Islam. From 649 we have the evidence of Pope Martin's lobbying of the Frankish church against the Monotheletism of Constans and his Byzantine clergy at the time of the Lateran synod.[79] Constans' arrival in Sicily in 663 might well have been what prompted Fredegar's interest in the East: Constans would remain in Italy and the Italian islands from 663 until his murder in 668. The same year saw the sending of Theodore through Francia to take over the archdiocese of Canterbury. Interestingly, his companion, Hadrian, was detained for a year as a Byzantine spy.[80] How we should understand this is unclear, but since Constans was based in Italy and Sicily until 15 September 668, Ebroin's concern was not about a distant power but was focused on the current presence of the emperor in the West. No doubt, Theodore and Hadrian were both questioned about their knowledge of the East. As I have suggested, the search for Dagobert in an Irish monastery in 676 might account for Arculf's visit to Iona. Only two years later, Frankish envoys may have been in Constantinople to congratulate Constantine IV on the repulse of the Muslim siege of the city.

In 679, it would appear that Pope Agatho was lobbying the Western churches to ensure support in his opposition to the Monotheletes in the East, and he surely did not ignore the Merovingian church. This was a further opportunity for the Franks to learn about the eastern Mediterranean. We may guess that there was similar activity in the run-up to the Quinisext Council of 692.[81] Certainly there was an awareness of the liturgical reforms of Pope Sergius that came from this context. However, it is not until we come to the arrival of the Muslims in Aquitaine that Merovingian interest in the East comes back into clear focus. The completion of the Dome of the Rock in 691/2 seems to have prompted the writing of the *Revelationes* of Pseudo-Methodius: there was certainly interest in his text at the time of the Muslim arrival in Aquitaine, and this

---

[78] Fredegar, *Chronicle*, IV, 65, ed. Wallace-Hadrill, p. 54.
[79] Wood, 'Between Rome and Jarrow', pp. 310–11.
[80] Bede, *Historia Ecclesiastica*, IV, 1, ed. Colgrave and Mynors, pp. 332–3: Wood, 'The Continental Connections of Anglo-Saxon Courts', p. 458.
[81] There is an obscure reference to the holding of a Frankish synod in c. 690 in *Annales Mettenses Priores*, s.a. 692, ed. B. de Simson, MGH, SRG, 10 (Hanover, 1905) p. 14, which is followed by an equally obscure reference (p. 15) to legations of Greeks, Romans, Lombards, Huns, Slavs and Saracens attending on Pippin II.

would seem to account both for the translation of the text by the monk Petrus, for which our earliest manuscript evidence may be dated to c.727 and also of the near-contemporary abridgement of the Latin *Revelationes*, which may date before 732. This flurry of interest, which was unquestionably apocalyptic in its outlook,[82] and was linked to the activities of the Muslims in the West, and perhaps with their arrival in Aquitaine, would seem to have continued on to the time of the composition of the *Cosmographia of Aethicus Ister*. By that time, we have almost reached the date of the *Hodoeporicon* of Willibald, when we have what is effectively an eyewitness account of the Holy Land written in Francia, although both the pilgrim and the hagiographer were Anglo-Saxon by birth.

This is not a history of close contacts. Given what we now know about links between the Merovingians and Constantinople in the late sixth century, from Venantius Fortunatus and from the *Epistulae Austrasicae*, and of an interest in the East to be found in Tours, not only in the writings of Gregory but also in the papyrus fragments of Ephraem, we cannot argue that the Merovingian world had wider horizons in the seventh century than in the late sixth, even if a comparison between the *Histories* of Gregory of Tours and the *Chronicle* of Fredegar gives that impression. But equally there is enough here to suggest that interest in and contact with the East never completely vanished in Merovingian Francia. Moreover, there would seem to have been individuals in Francia who knew enough Greek as well as Latin to translate Greek texts, as did Petrus. We do not need to call in the Anglo-Saxons to explain a translation from the Greek: nor do we need an Irishman to write the *Cosmography of Aethicus Ister*. In other words, it is not just the horizons of Fredegar that were broad: he had successors, admittedly not among the writers of hagiography or history but certainly in those with more theological and apocalyptic interests.

---

[82] Palmer, *The Apocalypse in the Early Middle Ages*, pp. 112–14.

19 'Merovingian' Illuminated Manuscripts and Their Links with the Eastern Mediterranean World

Lawrence Nees

Art historians have long posited various types of 'Eastern influence' on the art of Merovingian Francia, for example suggesting a link between manuscripts produced in Francia and Eastern, particularly Sasanian, textiles.[1] This approach always troubled me, and not only because terming such posited examples as the Gellone Sacramentary, from the 790s, 'Merovingian' on account of its style seemed bizarre. The approach formed part of a much wider art historical disposition to see the western Eurasian world as steeply inclined from a high East to a low West, with everything not nailed to the ground moving downhill on a one-way path:[2] '*Ex oriente lux*.'[3]

---

[1] A. Grabar and C. Nordenfalk, *Early Medieval Painting* (Geneva, 1957), pp. 126–35 and pl. p. 130. Nordenfalk illustrates this leaf but does not make the comparison, which stems from C. R. Baldwin, 'Sasanian Ducks in a Western Manuscript', *Gesta*, 9 (1970): 3–10. Some compelling comparisons are available. A bird, probably an eagle, in a fragment in the Kulturhistoriska Museet in Lund (no. 37.651; see C. J. Lamm, *Cotton in Mediaeval Textiles of the Near East* (Paris, 1937), pp. 68–9 and Fig. 41) has the kind of patterned torso found in manuscripts such as the Book of Durrow and Echternach Gospels. I am grateful to the organisers and participants in the Minerva Stiftung – Gentner Symposium on 'East and West in the Early Middle Ages: The Merovingian Kingdoms in Mediterranean Perspective' at the Freie Universität in Berlin, 17–20 December 2014. The earliest version of this presentation was in my graduate seminar at the University of Delaware, and a preliminary version of some portions were presented at the Historians of Islamic Art Association conference in Philadelphia, October 2008. I am grateful to my students for their patience, and to Finbarr Barry Flood for having permitted me to participate in the session that he organised for HIAA.

[2] For an overview of the earlier scholarship on the topic, see L. Nees, *From Justinian to Charlemagne: European Art, AD 565–787* (Boston, MA, 1985), pp. 122–38. For a recent attempt to see direct influence from the East on Western authors of the seventh and eighth centuries, in this case Irish authors, see P. Weeda, 'The Irish, the Virgin Mary and Proclus of Constantinople', *Peritia*, 22–3 (2011–12): 83–106, and the convincing rebuttal by D. Woods, 'Once More on Proclus, the Virgin Mary, and the Irish', *Peritia*, 24–5 (2013–14): 173–80. That this particular 'Eastern connection' hypothesis proved unconvincing should not, of course, be taken to mean that the possibility of such a direct link is in general terms to be rejected.

[3] The earliest occurrence of the phrase is unknown to me. For variations on the theme, see the three-volume catalogue *Ex Oriente: Geschichte und Gegenwart christlicher, jüdischer und islamischer Kulturen* (Mainz, 2003).

Several times I have sought to challenge the vague invocation of 'Eastern influence', for example seeking to point out that Italian art often furnished less exotic and far more plausible analogues than did invariably lost Eastern works, for which the evidence was flimsy at best.[4] Still, in my doctoral dissertation and first book, devoted to the wonderful Gospels manuscript written and illuminated by Gundohinus in the third year of King Pippin, probably 754 but possibly 757, much of my thinking ran along similar lines.[5] I found that although script and decorated initials were wholly Frankish, much of the programme of fullpage illuminations derived in large part from lost Eastern sources, albeit most likely transmitted through Italy, probably Ravenna. Thus, the best comparisons for the figures of the standing Evangelists, a type rare in the West, were offered by works such as later ninth- or tenth-century works from the eastern Mediterranean in Greek or Georgian or Armenian or Syriac manuscripts that depended, I presumed, upon much older and now lost exemplars dating from the sixth century.[6] The addition of the Evangelist symbols I took for a Western transformation, as was, in my view, the miniature of Christ in Majesty with the Evangelist symbols.[7]

Since the publication of my book on Gundohinus in 1987 new information has emerged that at first seemed to me to support, and then seemed to me to challenge my earlier views. For example, I probably overvalued the importance of 'early' sources and undervalued the importance of continuing artistic contacts of various kinds between East and West during the eighth century.[8] For example, the names of the Three Magi

---

[4] L. Nees, 'A Fifth-Century Book Cover and the Origin of the Four Evangelist Symbols Page of the Book of Durrow', *Gesta*, 17 (1978): 3–8. I would therefore be cautious in accepting that the ill-fitting leather cover of a recently discovered eighth- to ninth-century psalter was an import from Egypt based in large part on the discovery of papyrus used as a lining, since papyrus was also extensively used in Merovingian Francia, especially for charters, and its presence is not *ipso facto* conclusive evidence that the associated material was imported from Egypt. See A. Read, *The Faddan More Psalter: Discovery, Conservation and Investigation* (Dublin, 2014), pp. 54–5 and 77–8.

[5] Autun, Bibliothèque municipale, cod. 3; see L. Nees, *The Gundohinus Gospels* (Cambridge, MA, 1987). I should alert the reader to two important studies on the unique texts in the manuscript, Y.-M. Duval, 'Le "Liber Hieronymi ad Gaudentium": Rufin d'Aquilée, Gaudence de Brescia et Eusèbe de Crémone', *Revue bénédictine*, 97 (1987): 163–86, and P. Meyvaert, 'An Unknown Source for Jerome and Chromatius: Some New Fragments of Fortunatianus of Aquileia?', in S. Krämer and M. Bernhard (eds.), *Scire litteras: Forschungen zum mittelalterlichen Geistesleben* (Munich, 1988), pp. 277–89.

[6] Nees, *Gundohinus Gospels*, pp. 83–120, figs. 24–44 and pls. 32–5.

[7] Nees, *Gundohinus Gospels*, pp. 120–9 and 165–73, respectively.

[8] On the possible connection of the Gundohinus Gospels with Iconoclasm, see T. F. X. Noble, *Images, Iconoclasm and the Carolingians* (Philadelphia, PA, 2009), esp. pp. 139–49, as a possibly isolated piece of evidence for, and first response to, Iconoclasm in the East, followed by the Roman Synod of 769.

occurring in one of the *exposiciones* in the Gundohinus Gospels apparently derive from an Eastern source through some means other than the unique later-eighth-century *Excerpta Latina Barbari* manuscript (Paris, BnF lat. 4884), so named by Joseph Justus Scaliger in the sixteenth century.[9] I certainly failed to give due attention to the Gundohinus Gospels' likely early connection with Flavigny, and thus with Pippin, thereby likely missing the royal role in making possible extensive contacts with the East.[10] When I wrote the book, such contacts were generally considered rare and at best intermittent, but abundant evidence, including studies in this volume, shows more intense contact.[11] For example, in regard to artistic works, recent discoveries such as the narthex fresco at S. Sabina in Rome demonstrate not only contacts across the Mediterranean but artists and their patrons responding to immediate contemporary issues.[12] Most pertinent for this study is the discovery of new manuscripts of great interest. Hidden away in the monastery of Saint-Catherine at Mount Sinai until 1975 was a treasure trove of manuscripts, including an Arabic gospels dated 859, and thus almost certainly earlier than any of the other Eastern analogues to the Gundohinus Evangelists.[13] Although the manuscript is in Arabic, the inscriptions of the Evangelist portraits are in Greek, and very likely the painting is the work of someone trained in

---

[9] See most recently on that manuscript and the text from which it derived B. Garstad, ed. and trans., *Apocalypse Pseudo-Methodius. [and] An Alexandrian World Chronicle* (Cambridge, MA, 2012), pp. xviii–xxx. On the still unedited *exposiciones* in the Gundohinus Gospels, see Meyvaert, 'An Unknown Source for Jerome and Chromatius'.

[10] C. B. Bouchard, *Rewriting Saints and Ancestors: Memory and Forgetting in France, 500–1200* (Philadelphia, PA, 2015), p. 159, suggests that the manuscript came to Autun from the monastery of Flavigny in the ninth century along with some other manuscripts when the bishops took over control of the abbey of Flavigny, where both manuscripts had likely been kept, since, in Bouchard's view, the Flavigny Gospels directly copied the Gundohinus Gospels.

[11] See, among many studies, M. McCormick, *Origins of the European Economy: Communications and Commerce AD 300–900* (Cambridge, 2001).

[12] See M. Gianandrea, 'Un inedita committenza nella chiesa romana di Santa Sabina all'Aventino: il dipinto altomedievale con la *Vergine e il Bambino, santi d donatori*', in A. C. Quintavalle (ed.), *Medioevo: I committenti. Atti del Convegno internazionale di studi Parma 21–26 settembre 2010* (Milan, 2011), pp. 399–410; and M. Gianandrea, 'Politica delle immagini al tempo di Papa Costantino (708–715): Roma *versus* Bisanzio?', in G. Bordi, I. Carlettini, M. L. Fobelli, M. R. Menna and P. Pogliani (eds.), *L'Officina dello Sguardo: Scritti in onore di Maria Andaloro*, 1: *I luoghi dell'Arte: Immagine, Memoria, Materia* (Rome, 2014), pp. 335–42.

[13] Mount Sinai, Holy Monastery of St Catherine, NF Arab. memb. 14 and NF Arab. Memb. 16 and St Petersburg, Library of the Russian Academy of Sciences, MS Q no. 537. See I. E. Meïmarē, *Catalogos tōn Neōn Arabikōn Xeirographōn tēs Ieras Monēs Hagias Aikaterinēs tou Orous Sina* (Athens, 1985), p. 27 and pp. 24–5 and 164–6, pls. 19–21, colour pls. 5–6, M. P. Brown (ed.), *In the Beginning: Bibles before the Year 1000* (Washington, DC: Freer Gallery of Art, 2006), no. 35; and R. S. Nelson and K. M. Collins (eds.), *Holy Image, Hallowed Ground: Icons from Sinai* (Los Angeles, CA: Getty Museum, 2006), no. 32.

the Greek tradition. It would be easy to see this as just another example of the widespread influence of the art of Constantinople, the centre from which such imagery was diffused to the 'provinces'. Easy, but perhaps too easy.

Compare two manuscript pages dominated by ornamental patterns executed in a similar palette, predominantly red and yellow with some green and sometimes a bit of blue, one a manuscript from northern Francia, the other a Qur'an, most likely from Syria or Iraq (Figs. 19.1 and 19.2). The patterns are primarily knotwork of various kinds, used to create a frame for a rectangular field. In the Frankish manuscript, the framed field contains only another ornamental panel, while in the Qur'an the framed field contains text. The pages serve similar functions, one a frontispiece and one a finispiece with colophon. The Frankish page is the frontispiece image in a manuscript of Augustine now in Paris, probably already in the ninth century in the Corbie library, and likely made at Corbie or somewhere in its network in the eighth century.[14] The Qur'an is less well known, probably dating from the ninth century, with ornamental pages as frontispiece and finispiece, and a careful layout of the text on the page with fine calligraphy and notable strips of ornament serving as headpieces to show the beginning of each new sura, a new chapter of the text.[15] The similarities to the Corbie Augustine manuscript are not of course precise, and I am certainly not suggesting that one depends directly on the other, but I have come to see both as responding to similar challenges, serving similar functions, and doing so in similar ways. It is not easy to understand how this might have come about, how exchanges might play a role in the similarities, but one big problem with my earlier approach, and that of many others, is that I envisaged disembodied 'influence' from earlier 'models' in the form of manuscripts, often much earlier in date, and did not even consider the possibility of a living and shared tradition and development.[16]

---

[14] Paris, BnF lat. 12190, fol. Av, Augustine, *De Consensu Evangelistarum*. See C. Nordenfalk, 'Corbie and Cassiodorus', *Pantheon*, 32 (1974): 225–31 with colour plate. Nordenfalk saw the page as a sixth-century Italian product inserted into the eighth-century Frankish book, which on codicological grounds is highly unlikely. Nordenfalk's theory was rejected by M. Gorman, 'The Codex Amiatinus: A Guide to the Legends and Bibliography', *Studi medievali*, 44 (2003): 863–910, at p. 906, and doubted by B. Tewes, *Die Handschriften der Schule von Luxeuil: Kunst und Ikonographie eines frühmittelalterlichen Skriptoriums* (Wiesbaden, 2011), pp. 62–3 and Fig. 64.

[15] M. F. Abu Khalaf, *Islamic Art through the Ages: Masterpieces of the Islamic Museum of al-Haram al-Sharif (al-Aqsa Mosque) Jerusalem* (Jerusalem, 1998), pp. 15–19 and figs. 1–4.

[16] See J. Lowden and A. Bovey (eds.), *Under the Influence: The Concept of Influence and the Study of Illuminated Manuscripts* (Turnhout, 2007) for various criticisms of this approach.

Figure 19.1 Ornamental frontispiece, Paris BnF lat. 12190, fol. Av. Photograph: Bibliothèque nationale de France.

When we look a little more closely, we can indeed find evidence for other ties, with Merovingian Francia playing a significant role. St Catherine's monastery at Mount Sinai also has among recent finds a fragmentary psalter in Latin which certainly looks 'Merovingian', as demonstrated by a comparison of one of its initials to the Augustine manuscript dated 669 in the Morgan Library,[17] and to the Gundohinus Gospels.[18] This portion of the psalter was found only in 1975,[19] but twenty years earlier

---

[17] New York, Pierpont Morgan Library, cod. M. 334; P. Salmon, *Le Lectionaire de Luxeuil* (Vatican City, 1944), pp. xxxi, xliii, xlix; C. Charlier, 'Note sur les origines de l'écriture dite de Luxeuil', *Revue Bénédictine*, 68 (1948): 150–1; R. Branner, 'The Art of the Scriptorium of Luxeuil', *Speculum*, 29 (1954): 678–90, at p. 680 n. 14; J. J. Putnam, 'Evidence for the Origin of the "Script of Luxeuil"', *Speculum*, 38 (1963): 256–66, at p. 256; 5; Nordenfalk, *Die spätantiken Zierbuchstaben*, p. 130, Fig. 58; David Ganz, *Corbie in the Carolingian Renaissance* (Sigmaringen, 1990), p. 15.

[18] Nees, *Gundohinus Gospels*, pls. 24–7.

[19] Mount Sinai, Holy Monastery of St Catherine, Latin New Finds MS 1 and Slavonic MS 5; see E. A. Lowe, 'An Unknown Latin Psalter on Mount Sinai', *Scriptorium*, 9 (1955): 177–99, pls. 18–23; M. Kamil, *Catalogue of all Manuscripts in the Monastery of*

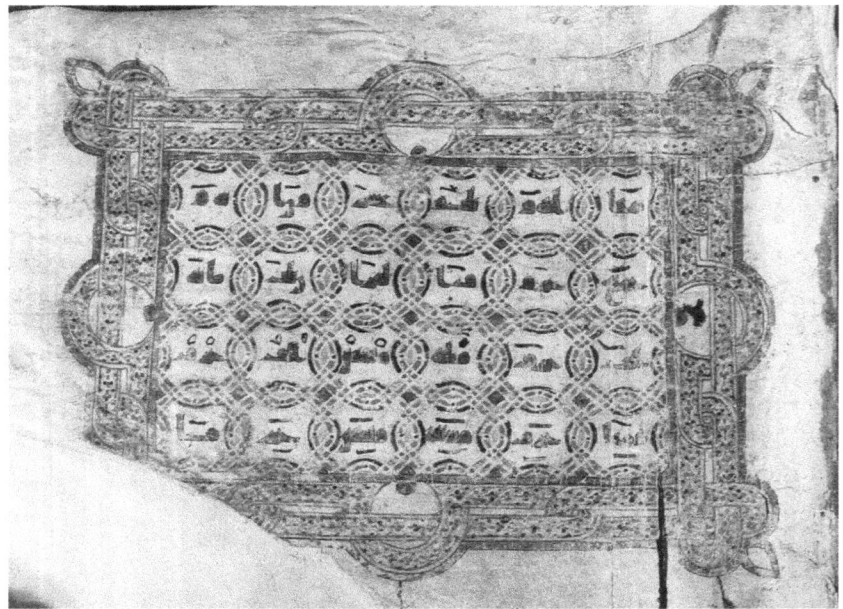

Figure 19.2 Ornamental finispiece, Qur'an from al-Haram al-Sharif Museum, fol. 173v (after M. F. Abu Khalaf, *Islamic Art through the Ages. Masterpieces of the Islamic Museum of al-Haram al-Sharif (al-Aqsa Mosque) Jerusalem* [Jerusalem, 1998], Fig. 4).

E. A. Lowe had published another portion of the same manuscript, kept as Sinai MS Slavonic 5. Lowe suggested that it might be dated to the ninth century, drew on a variety of script traditions and was likely written in the East, at Sinai itself or perhaps in Jerusalem, by a monk trained in Latin language and script. Recently, Michelle Brown observed the obvious links between its recently discovered initials and pre-Carolingian manuscripts, although she suggested a tenth-century dating for the book for reasons she did not give.[20] Much more remains to be learnt from this rich new fund of material, now only beginning to be published.[21]

St *Catherine on Mount Sinai* (Wiesbaden, 1970), p. 144; M. Altbauer, *Psalterium latinum hierosolymitanum: Eine frühmittelalterliche lateinische Handschrift Sin. Ms. No. 5* (Jerusalem, 1977, also Vienna, 1978).

[20] Brown, *In the Beginning*, no. 48 (with colour plate fols. 19v–20r) compared the script to 'pre-Carolingian scriptoria of Gaul and of Irish foundations on the continent, such as Luxeuil, St Gall and Bobbio'.

[21] M. P. Brown, 'The Bridge in the Desert: Towards Establishing an Historical Context for the Newly Discovered Latin Manuscripts of St Catherine's Sinai', in A. Dottone (ed.), *East and West: Proceedings of a Symposium at La Sapienza, Rome, 2014=Rivista degli*

The psalter should not, therefore, be regarded as an isolated freak. It is a modest book, small and easily portable, and, as the indispensable book for prayer very likely the kind of thing that Willibald and the other Western pilgrims would have carried.[22] I am not sure whether we can tell where it was written, and of course we do not know when it entered the Sinai collection,[23] but around the time of its creation seems the likeliest scenario. The manuscript, whatever its origin, tells us something new and important about artistic links between the Frankish world and the eastern Mediterranean.[24]

Sadly, few people want to spend large amounts of time studying minor initials and other ornaments, but such material provides other intriguing analogies and links between Latin and Islamic manuscripts during the seventh and eighth centuries. From the Islamic world, the only manuscripts that could possibly be dated to this period are copies of the Qur'an, none of which are securely dated or localised before 873, and they are as difficult and confusing as they are fascinating, their study still in its early days in some respects. François Déroche published what he termed 'A First Overview' of the *Qur'ans of the Umayyads* in 2014, the kind of corpus publications available for early Latin manuscripts such as the *Codices latini antiquiores* series being unavailable, and rich new troves of manuscripts still being discovered.[25] Déroche made a strong case for the first appearance of elaborately decorated and hugely impressive manuscripts around the year 700, during the caliphate of 'Abd al-Malik. None of the manuscripts are complete, but the surviving fragments have

---

studi Orientali, Supplemento 1, new series, 90 (2017): 73–94; and M. P. Brown, *Art of the Islands: Celtic, Pictish, Anglo-Saxon and Viking Visual Culture c. 450–1050* (Oxford, 2016), p. 137.

[22] See the chapter by Ora Limor in this volume, and on Willibald see D. Lohrmann, 'Geographie und Reisen im 8. bis 9. Jahrhunderts', in *Ex Oriente* (as above n. 2), pp. 36–55 esp. pp. 43–7 with map, and for a convenient translation of the text by C. H. Talbot in T. F. X. Noble and T. Head (eds.), *Soldiers of Christ: Saints and Saints' Lives from Late Antiquity and the Early Middle Ages* (University Park, PA, 1995), pp. 141–64.

[23] Lowe, 'Unknown Latin Psalter'. That such decoration is commonly termed 'Merovingian' and sometimes 'Bird and Fish initial style' is misleading, and it was by no means limited to Merovingian Francia; C. Nordenfalk, *Die spätantiken Zierbuchstaben* (Stockholm, 1970).

[24] On manuscripts moving the other way during this period, from East to West, see D. N. Dumville, 'The Importation of Mediterranean Manuscripts into Theodore's England', in Michael Lapidge (ed.), *Archbishop Theodore: Commemorative Studies on His Life and Influence* (Cambridge, 1995), pp 96–119.

[25] F. Déroche, *Qur'ans of the Umayyads: A First Overview* (Leiden, 2014). For a splendid overview of this issues in a broader context, see S. S. Blair, *Islamic Calligraphy* (Edinburgh, 2006), and for a succinct overview of approaches going back to the eighteenth century, see A. George, *The Rise of Islamic Calligraphy* (London, Berkeley, CA and Beirut, 2010), pp. 15–17.

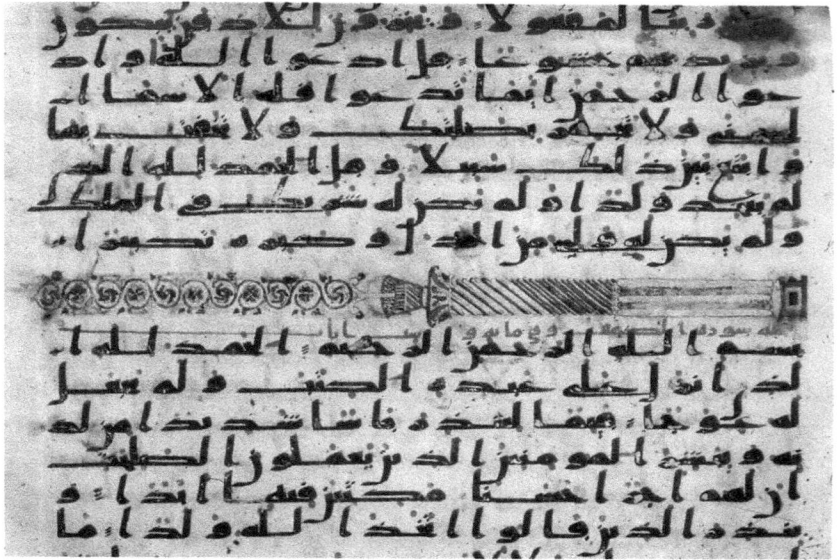

Figure 19.3 Qur'an manuscript with sura divider, St Petersburg, National Library of Russia, cod. Marcel 13, fol. 1r. Photograph: National Library of Russia, St Petersburg.

leaves measuring up to and even beyond 50 cm in height, truly giant volumes.

One of these grand books, cod. Marcel 13 in St Petersburg,[26] in a number of places uses columns laid upon their sides as sura dividers (Fig. 19.3), and Déroche suggested that the origin of this motif might be sought in contemporary Islamic architecture, specifically the Dome of the Rock also built by 'Abd al-Malik. The vine scroll springing from a basket atop the column does have nice analogues in the Dome of the Rock,[27] but the represented columns also pose problems, even beyond the oddity of imagining a scribe or patron looking at the Dome of the Rock's great spoliated columns and saying to himself, 'Aha, turned on their sides these would be great sura dividers!' A few columns in Marcel 13 seem to imitate coloured marbles,[28] like those in the Dome of the Rock, but early Islamic architecture offers few, possibly no,[29] parallels for

[26] Fol. 1v; see Déroche, *Qur'ans of the Umayyads*, fig. 25.
[27] S. Nuseibeh and O. Grabar, *The Dome of the Rock* (New York, 1996), with the most complete photographic record of the mosaic decoration.
[28] Fol. 33r; see George, *Rise of Islamic Calligraphy*, fig. p. 148.
[29] The mihrab under the Rock has such columns but has been dated by a consensus of recent scholars to a significantly later period. For discussion and earlier bibliography on

Figure 19.4 Title page, Paris BnF lat. 10593, fol. Av. Photograph: Bibliothèque nationale de France.

columns like the lower one of the two from the Marcel 13 manuscript, its bottom part with vertical (here of course horizontal) fluting, and the upper part with diagonal, twisted, fluting. Latin manuscripts of this time and earlier do provide good parallels, however, as in a late-sixth- or seventh-century book probably from northern Italy (Fig. 19.4),[30] and vegetal patterns spring from atop these columns too. Moreover, we are looking at book art in both cases, and perhaps even more significant at book art that uses ornament to articulate and clarify texts. It is easy to find more parallels in Latin manuscripts, where columns are frequently used in canon table in Gospels manuscripts, as in a wonderful book from

---

this controversial work, see L. Nees, *Perspectives on Early Islamic Art in Jerusalem* (Leiden, 2016), pp. 70–1, with earlier literature.

[30] E. H. Zimmermann, *Vorkarolingische Miniaturen* (Berlin, 1916), pp. 39 and 147–8 and pl. 3, and Tewes, *Handschriften der Schule von Luxeuil*, fig. 142.

Figure 19.5 Canon table page, Trier Domschatz, cod. 61, fol. 11r. Photograph: Franz Ronig.

Echternach or Trier now in the latter's Domschatz (Fig. 19.5), a manuscript certainly from the core lands of Merovingian Francia.[31]

Other decorative devices used in early Qur'an manuscripts include frames for pages of text, as in leaves in the David Collection in Copenhagen, and notably a Qur'an formerly in the Great Mosque at Kairouan,[32] providing a precedent or at least an analogue for the appearance of such frames in the Godesscalc Evangelistary presented to Charlemagne in

---

[31] Trier, Domschatz, cod. 61, fol. 11r; see N. Netzer, *Cultural Interplay in the Eighth Century: The Trier Gospels and the Making of a Scriptorium at Echternach* (Cambridge, 1994), pl. 5.

[32] Copenhagen, David Collection, inv. No. 26/2003, for which see Déroche, *Qu'rans of the Umayyads*, p. 121 and fig. 40; and S. S. Blair and J. M. Bloom, *Cosmophilia: Islamic Art from the The David Collection, Copenhagen* (Boston, MA, 2006), no. 33. Kairouan, Musée des arts islamiques (R 38, fol. 132v), for which see Déroche, *Qu'rans of the Umayyads*, pp. 121–6 and fig. 43 with the author's drawing, no photograph having yet been published to the best of my knowledge.

Figure 19.6 Ornamental page, drawing by François Déroche, Kairouan Raqqada R 38 (after François Déroche, *Qur'ans of the Umayyads* [Leiden, 2014], Fig. 43, with the author's permission).

781–3,[33] but space precludes looking at those. The Kairouan page is significant, for it is entirely given over to ornament, serving as the frontispiece page to a giant Qur'an dated by Déroche to the early eighth century. A dramatic eight-pointed star comprised of two superimposed squares contains at its centre a small medallion with an eight-petal rosette (Fig. 19.6). The star is then contained within a large medallion, which

---

[33] Paris, BnF, cod. n.a. lat. 1203, for which see now the digital reproduction in colour at http://gallica.bnf.fr/ark:/12148/btv1b60007 18s/f43.image.r=Evangeliarium%20 Evang%C3%A9liaire%20dit%20de%20Charlemagne%20ou%20de%20Godescalc, and the recent facsimile publication *Godescalc Evangelistar* (Lucerne, 2011). Note that

is set within a square frame, having rinceaux on each of the four sides and a different pattern at the corners, at least on the two corners that survive in part. The only other Qur'an with some of its end leaves extant assigned by Déroche and many other scholars to this early period is the famous manuscript discovered a few decades ago at the Great Mosque in Sana'a, in Yemen. It has a similar eight-pointed star pattern, without the outer frame, and was compared by Alain George to the plan of the Dome of the Rock.[34] The Sana'a frontispiece may also be compared to the page depicting Juliana Anicia in the great Vienna Dioscurides manuscript produced at Constantinople in 512, which also uses the motif of the eight-pointed star made by two superimposed squares, and also uses this as one of the pages opening the book.[35] That the Roman image sets the star within a medallion actually makes it even closer to the frontispiece in the Kairouan Qur'an than to that from Sana'a. The outer frame of the Kairouan page is absent from the other two, but a remarkably good comparison is furnished by another of the prefatory miniatures in the Vienna Dioscurides, which also has loose rinceaux on the four sides and distinctively different corner ornaments.[36] One could argue that the artists of these grand Qur'ans, which Déroche and George, and others, have linked to caliphal patronage, got hold of an older Roman manuscript rather like the Vienna Dioscurides, which became their 'model', after stripping away the figural scenes which are, after all, the main point of the Roman manuscript. Such an interpretation would highlight the 'imperial' quality of the great Qur'an manuscript. However, no imperially connected (East) Roman manuscript offers an analogue for a page given over entirely to ornament. We do have such analogues in the early medieval West.

First and foremost among those analogues is an ornamental frontispiece page in the Orosius from the Bobbio library now in the Ambrosiana, which has the central rosette, here much larger, and the large medallion set in a frame with distinctive corner ornaments, albeit no rinceaux on the sides (Fig. 19.7). The Ambrosiana manuscript is not dated, but scholars

---

the traditional spelling of the scribe's name as Godescalc with a single 's', used in these titles, is not the spelling in the manuscript itself in the colophon on fol. 127r, which manifestly uses double 's' rather than single, as pointed out to me by David Ganz, and we ought to use the man's own spelling for his name.

[34] George, *Rise of Islamic Calligraphy*, pp. 80–3, with earlier literature, and fig. 55.
[35] Vienna, Österreichische Nationalbibliothek, cod. Med. Gr. 1, fol. 6v; see O. Mazal, *Der Wiener Dioskurides: Codex medicus graecus 1 der Österreichischen Nationalbibliothek* (Graz, 1998), pp. 25–6.
[36] Vienna, Österreichische Nationalbibliothek, cod. Med. Gr. 1, fol. 5v; see Mazal, *Wiener Dioskurides*.

Figure 19.7 Ornamental page, from the Bobbio Orosius, Milan, Biblioteca Ambrosiana cod. D. 23 sup, fol. 1v. Photograph: Biblioteca Ambrosiana, Milan.

have uniformly accepted its close association with another Bobbio manuscript probably datable to 615–22,[37] and the only controversy about this ornamental page has involved not its date but its origin, whether created in Ireland and imported to Italy or made there, most likely at Bobbio itself, which in my view is surely correct based on this ornament, which has parallels in the Mediterranean world but none in the Insular.[38] My thinking in making this comparison, admittedly less striking at first glance than that between the Islamic and Constantinopolitan images, is that the similarity between the Western and Islamic miniatures is not

[37] Milan, Biblioteca Ambrosiana, cod. D. 23 sup, fol. 1v; see M. L. Gengaro and G. V. Guglielmetti, *Inventario dei codici decorate e miniati della Biblioteca Ambrosiana* (Florence, 1968), pp. 3–4, pls. 1–2, and J. J. G. Alexander, *Insular Manuscripts: Sixth to the Ninth century* (London, 1978), no. 3, p. 28, figs. 6, 7.
[38] L. Nees, 'Ethnic and Primitive Paradigms in the Study of Early Medieval Art', in C. Chazelle and F. Lifshitz (eds.), *Paradigms and Methods in Early Medieval Studies* (Basingstoke, 2007), pp. 41–60

merely the negative one that neither involves images but rather the positive one that both are not so much illustrations set into a book as they are illuminations integrated in various ways with the book as text, and designed to clarify as well as embellish it.

In the seventh century, we can see both the Islamic and Frankish writing centres struggling to produce a radically new kind of book, based upon similar inherited writing traditions and similar problems of conveying knowledge in written form. Both in the Latin West and in the Islamic world scribes and readers are experimenting with ways of making the written text more clearly legible and at the same time more visually attractive. In the case of the Latin manuscripts, it seems clear that this new form of manuscript is at least associated with, if not necessarily dependent upon, a shift from oral to silent reading,[39] and perhaps also anxiety that oral reading from a written text should be accurate.[40] This anxiety was also central to the very existence of the Qur'an in written form, and the Islamic tradition specifies that early caliphs (stories are told of both 'Umar ibn al Khattab and especially of 'Uthman) were prompted to commission authoritative written texts precisely because they heard, or heard of, alternate version of the prophetic revelation being spoken.[41]

Latin manuscripts up to approximately the seventh century lacked the familiar aids to the reader that we take for granted. The text being transmitted was presented without word division, without separation of sentences or phrases, with very limited punctuation, without colour or ornament, offering visually undifferentiated and at least to my eyes intimidating blocks of text. Decoration, where it was present at all, was generally restricted to non-textual material such as incipits, title pages or in a very few instances figural decoration. Much the same might be said of the earliest manuscripts of the Qur'an datable to roughly the third quarter of the seventh century, which present the same uniform

---

[39] P. Saenger, *Space between Words: The Origins of Silent Reading* (Stanford, CA, 1997), and on the development of punctuation in these manuscripts see M. B. Parkes, *Pause and Effect: An Introduction to the History of Punctuation in the West* (London, 1992).

[40] Writing at the end of the eighth century in a poem to Charlemagne, Alcuin emphasised the importance of punctuation for the proper reading of the scriptures: E. Dümmler (ed.), *Poetae latini aevi carolini*, MGH, Poetarum latinarum medii aevi 1 (Berlin, 1881), vol. I, no. 94, p. 320, verses 7–10, quoted by J. Vezin, 'Les Livres dans l'entourage de Charlemagne et d'Hildegarde', in P. Riché, C. Heitz and François Héber-Suffrin (eds.), *Actes du colloque 'Autour d'Hildegarde'* (Paris, 1987), pp. 63–71, at p. 69. Alcuin returns to the importance of punctuation for oral reading in a different poem, Dümmler, *Poetae*, p. 292; see David Ganz, 'Mass Production of Early Medieval Manuscripts: The Carolingian Bibles from Tours', in R. Gameson (ed.), *The Early Medieval Bible: Its Production, Decoration, and Use* (Cambridge, 1994), pp. 53–62, at p. 56.

[41] Déroche, *Qur'ans of the Umayyads*, p. 35 with sources.

and intimidating block of text.[42] These Qur'an pages have virtually no margin at all and are written continuously with no spaces between words, and even with single words carried over from one line to the next. They use a *scriptio* highly *defectiva*, with no marking of short vowels or other diacriticals. As I mentioned before, these manuscripts have recently been the subject of François Déroche's book on Umayyad period Qur'ans. The scholarly term 'Hijazi' used for them is a stylistic descriptor, and not by any means a regional term indicating that such books were necessarily made in Mecca and Medina; indeed, Syria seems more likely, for they seem to emerge during the caliphate of Muawiyah, the first ruler of the Umayyad dynasty, who was acclaimed as caliph in 661 in Jerusalem. As it happens, 661 is also the usual date given for the foundation of the monastery of Corbie, and the admittedly scanty evidence at our disposal suggests that Luxeuil and/or its daughter house at Corbie were producing 'new style' minuscule manuscripts during the last third of the seventh century. There are many parallels between the Luxeuil books and those of this early Islamic period, which are in other words probably closely contemporaneous, and time permits me only to mention a few.

Some early manuscripts share codicological features, unusual in later period. A few of the earliest Qur'an manuscripts can be shown to have been constructed as is the rule with Western books, with hair side facing hair, and flesh facing flesh, although even by the later Umayyad period it seems that the different standard was adopted that would be followed in later Islamic parchment books, with all the leaves stacked in the same manner, so that hair always faces flesh within an opening.[43] Some Latin manuscripts and some early Qur'ans that can probably be dated to the later seventh or early eighth century use coloured script in similar ways. For example, a Qur'an in Istanbul and a Prophets manuscript from Luxeuil now in New York both use very much the same palette of colour, a dark brown ink, tending to black in the Islamic books as one moves towards the eighth century, with the beginning of red and green being employed for headings or other not strictly textual features, including headings in which groups of two or three letters in red alternate with

---

[42] Notable examples are the well-known manuscripts in St Petersburg, NLR cod. Marcel 18, and Paris BnF Arabe 328a; see Déroche, *Qur'ans of the Umayyads*, pp. 17–73 with discussion and earlier bibliography, and figs. 1–5 for colour reproductions of some pages.

[43] See Déroche, *Qur'ans of the Umayyads*, p. 109 and fig. 35, writing about the 'caliphal' Qur'an fragment in Dublin, Chester Beatty Library, cod. Is 1404; and François Déroche (ed.), *Islamic Codicology: An Introduction to the Study of Manuscripts in Arabic Script* (London: Al-Furqān Islamic Heritage Foundation, 2005), pp. 71–6, preferring alternative explanations to the impact of Greek (or Latin) traditions.

two or three letters in green.[44] Most intriguing, in my view, is similarity between the marks that begin to appear in this period in the Qur'an manuscripts, serving to separate groups of five or ten verses of text,[45] and elaborate quire marks that occur commonly in Latin manuscripts especially from and around Luxeuil. In his important book on the early Qur'an manuscripts in the Khalili collection, Déroche wrote that the origin of the Qur'anic verse markers is unknown.[46] Latin manuscripts need to be considered as a parallel if not necessarily as a source. Similar graphic signs appear in a manuscript produced at Luxeuil in 669 now in the Morgan Library,[47] with an exuberantly baroque expansion of dots, hearts and other motifs around the quire mark, and in the Ivrea Gregory from Luxeuil, datable c. 680, with triangles of coloured dots around the number.[48] The latter makes a striking comparison to the motif used in an early Qur'an in London,[49] with six dots in circles stacked to make an equilateral triangle; the Qur'an also shows an early stage in shifting towards a *scriptio* more nearly *plena*, with the addition of dots to marks vowels. The Latin quire marks make many interesting comparisons with the sura dividers in the great Qur'an manuscript discovered in the 1970s in Sana'a,[50] but, as I have published another study devoted to these marks in Latin and Arabic manuscripts, I will not give more details here, referring the interested reader to that other study.[51]

---

[44] Istanbul TIEM SE 63, fol. S.n., for which see Déroche, *Qur'ans of the Umayyads*, fig. 30, and New York, Pierpont Morgan Library cod. M. 17, fol. 25v, for which see CLA no 1658; Nordenfalk, *Zierbuchstaben*, p. 193, fig. 56.
[45] For example, Paris BnF Arabe 328a, fol. 50v, and London BL Or. 2165, fol. 19v; for this manuscript see C. Baker, *Qur'an Manuscripts: Calligraphy, Illumination, Design* (London, 2007), pp. 15–18, and fig. 5.
[46] Déroche, *Abbasid Tradition*, p. 22.
[47] New York, Pierpont Morgan Library, cod. M. 334, fol. 180v; P. Salmon, *Le Lectionaire de Luxeuil* (Vatican City, 1944), pp. xxxi, xliii, xlix; 5; Nordenfalk, *Die spätantiken Zierbuchstaben*, p. 130, fig. 68; David Ganz, *Corbie in the Carolingian Renaissance* (Sigmaringen, 1990), p. 15.
[48] Leproni, *Il Liber Regulae Pastoralis*, pl. 8a, and Tewes, *Handschriften der Schule von Luxeuil*, p. 173 (not illustrated).
[49] London Or. 11737, fol. 3r; the manuscript is mentioned and one page (not this one) reproduced in Baker, *Qur'an Manuscripts*, p. 18, fig. 6.
[50] See U. Dreibholz, *Frühe Koranfragmente aus der Grossen Moschee in Sanaa/Early Quran Fragments from the Great Mosque in Sanaa* (Sana'a, 2003), the discussion of these marks pp. 31–3 and figs. 2 and 10–12. This is a rare volume, difficult to find, so for a more accessible example in a probably slightly later manuscript see the leaf in a private collection published by D. J. Roxburgh, *Writing the Word of God: Calligraphy and the Qur'an* (Houston, 2007), fig. 3.
[51] L. Nees, 'Graphic Quire Marks and Qur'ānic Verse Markers in the Seventh and Eighth Century', in M. Brown, I. Garipzanov and B. Tilghman (eds.), *Graphic Devices and the Early Decorated Book* (Woodbridge, 2017), pp. 80–99.

I should hasten to say that I am not really suggesting 'influence' from one end of the Mediterranean upon the other in terms of book art. Quite the reverse, it seems to me that the developments are more or less synchronous, or overlapping, and suggest some kind of ongoing engagement or exchange very much on the level of craft, not of high patronage. This is scribal work, not command from the abbot, much less the caliph. In certain respects I am reminded of the rapid development and wide distribution of new methods of working silk textiles during the seventh and eighth centuries, which requires highly sophisticated technical expertise on the part of craftsmen collaborating, whether at a single location or separately, and not simply the exchange of objects or models or materials.[52]

Can we really suggest direct links of some sort between scribes working in the Latin West and in the Islamic East during the later seventh and early eighth century? Had we more extensive surviving manuscripts in Syriac and Coptic and Greek, we might find that there is a broader pan-Mediterranean development. At this point, the most compelling comparisons and analogies link Islamic and Latin book production, with the Merovingian world very much at the centre of the phenomenon. I hope that someone will look at this issue, neglected too long.

A final example shows another way in which we might have missed something significant because we have tended to regard the Frankish and Islamic worlds as separate rather than linked, or at least 'entangled'.[53] One of the best-known examples of what is commonly termed 'Merovingian' manuscript illumination is the Gelasian sacramentary from Chelles now in the Vatican, generally dated c. 750, which has elaborately decorated openings for the three different sections of the text, wonderful variations on the theme of the Cross under frame and the Cross isolated but surrounded by decorated text.[54] Looking more closely at the first and

---

[52] See N. Kajitani, 'A Man's Caftan and Leggings from the North Caucasus of the Eight to Tenth Century: A Conservator's Report', *Metropolitan Museum Journal*, 36 (2001): 85–124 at pp. 109–12 and n. 76. Recently M. C. Miller, 'The Sources of Textiles and Vestments in Early Medieval Rome', in V. L. Garver and O. M. Phelan (eds.), *Rome and Religion in the Medieval World: Studies in Honor of Thomas F. X. Noble* (Farnham, 2014), pp. 83–99, at pp. 88–9, on fabrics woven in western Europe probably using imported silk thread, and now preserved in Maaseik and at the Vatican.

[53] See E. H. Gould, 'Entangled Histories, Entangled Worlds: The English-Speaking Atlantic as a Spanish Periphery', *American Historical Review*, 112 (2007): 764–86, esp. pp. 765–7 and nn. 10–12, and J. Cañizares-Esguerra, 'AHR Forum: Entangled Histories – Borderland Historiographies in New Clothes?' *American Historical Review*, 112 (2007): 787–99, which criticises some other treatments of 'entangled histories' as concentrating too much on the borderlands or margins of different cultural/political areas and 'not at the core', a point that seems to me important for considering Frankish and Islamic connections in the seventh and eighth century.

[54] Zimmermann, *Vorkarolingische Miniaturen*, pp. 87–8, cat. p. 224, pls. 146, 148–9, and J. Hubert, J. Porcher and W. F. Volbach, *Europe of the Invasions* (New York, 1969), pp. 165, 178, figs. 188 and 190.

Figure 19.8 Paris BnF lat. 12168. Vatican City, Biblioteca Apostolica Vaticana, cod. Reg. lat. 216, fol. 3v (© Biblioteca Apostolica Vaticana, by permission, all rights reserved)

largest of the cross pages (Fig. 19.8), one can see the profusion of animal ornament often dismissed as birds and fishes. The pearled border around the medallion at the centre of each cross is a motif that has been derived directly or indirectly, from Eastern textiles, the phenomenon with which I began, but I want to direct attention to something else, which has never been commented upon, namely the capitals supporting the arch over the cross. The capital at each side features a large bird with curved beak, piercing eye and short tail. It is a spread eagle. Is it significant? It is certainly not a common motif, and I cannot claim to have gone through the corpus of Merovingian illumination looking for others. There is one notable parallel from just across the Channel in Anglo-Saxon Canterbury. The famous frontispiece miniature of the Vespasian Psalter, commonly dated c. 725, but in my own view more likely a bit later and thus roughly contemporary with the Chelles Sacramentary, has the same motif, a spread eagle, in both capitals (and also of course pairs of affronted

'Merovingian' Illuminated Manuscripts 315

Figure 19.9 David and Musicians, London British Library MS (© British Library Board, London BL Cotton Vespasian A. 1, fol. 30v).

quadrupeds as bases) (Fig. 19.9). No one has ever commented on the eagle capitals in the Vespasian Psalter either, dismissed it would seem as mere ornament.[55]

Placing eagles, generally spread eagles, on capitals, was not rare in the Roman world, and Eugen von Mercklin collected dozens of examples, dating generally from the second to the fifth century.[56] One could thus see the eagle capitals in our two manuscripts as just another genuflection to the Roman tradition. Possible, of course. However, also ignored by scholars are the Roman eagle capitals installed in the Dome of the Rock in or about 692, some of which are spread eagles (Fig. 19.10).[57]

---

[55] D. H. Wright, *The Vespasian Psalter: British Museum, Cotton Vespasian A.I.* (Copenhagen, 1967), and for discussion of the date of the manuscript, and more recent literature, see L. Nees, 'Recent Trends in Dating Works of Insular Art', in C. Hourihane (ed.), *Insular and Anglo-Saxon: Art and Thought in the Early Medieval Period* (University Park, PA, 2011), pp. 14–30, at p. 25.

[56] E. von Mercklin, *Antike Figuralkapitelle* (Berlin, 1962), pp. 221–35 and figs. 1020–98.

[57] For this passage, see Nees, *Perspectives on Early Islamic Art in Jerusalem*, for extended discussion with references and illustrations.

Figure 19.10 Eagle capital in the Dome of the Rock. Photograph: L. Nees.

They are not closely linked to the Vespasian Psalter capital in style, but is this analogy of eagle capitals a coincidence? The eagle capitals are not randomly disposed in the Dome of the Rock but are given prominent position around the Rock itself, one in the centre on the east side, facing the doorway that leads to the Dome of the Chain, which is associated with the judgement rendered here by David and Solomon. The other two eagle capitals form a pair on the inner colonnade, bracketing the central column on the north side. We have abundant evidence for intense interest in Jerusalem during the early Islamic period, from Adomnán and Bede, who wrote his commentaries on the Temple and the Tabernacle, and the only early medieval commentary on Ezra and Nehemiah,[58] to Willibald of Eichstätt, discussed elsewhere in this volume. The appearance of

---

[58] On Bede and the East, see C. B. Kendall, 'Bede and Islam', in P. Darby and F. Wallis (eds.), *Bede and the Future* (Farnham, 2014), pp. 93–114. Kendall discussed Bede's version of Adomnán's *De locis sanctis*, which he dates 702–3. W. T. Foley and H. Holder, *Bede: A Biblical Miscellany* (Liverpool, 1999) discuss the term Saracens used by both Adomnán and Bede, which seems to follow the usage of Jerome and or Isidore in the *Etymologiae*, 9.2.57. Bede also has three mentions of Saracen actions in his *Chronica maiora*, which is the final chapter 66 of his *De temporum ratione*, including the final entry in the work, on the siege of Constantinople, dated to 725, referring to the siege of Constantinople in 717–18.

eagle capitals on miniatures in a psalter, flanking David himself, and in a sacramentary seems likely to me to be a reference to the Temple in Jerusalem and to the new construction on its former site. As we begin together to further explore the contacts between the people living in this period in East and West, consider them as entangled worlds, we will no doubt learn a great deal more.

20 'Sons of Ishmael, Turn Back!'

Ann Christys

The campaigns of the Muslims in western Europe slowed at the Pyrenees but did not stop. In 720, the governor of al-Andalus, al-Samḥ, destroyed the remnants of Visigothic power in Septimania with the capture of Narbonne. The ruler of Aquitaine, Eudo (d. c. 735) defeated and killed al-Samḥ at Toulouse in the following year, but Carcassonne, Nimes and Autun fell into Andalusi hands in the 720s and Provence experienced frequent raiding into the 740s.[1] The Muslim–Christian frontier is poorly defined in sources for this period,[2] but archaeological evidence suggesting Muslim occupation has recently been discovered in Nimes.[3] Control of Septimania was disputed until it came under the Carolingians in 760. Campaigns into Francia continued under the Umayyads; the twelfth-century historian Ibn al-Athīr described the campaign of Hishām I in Francia in 793 as 'one of the most celebrated expeditions of the Muslims of al-Andalus'.[4] There seemed to be no obvious bar to the conquest of Francia. Only in retrospect could the encounter between the Andalusi governor 'Abd al-Raḥmān al-Ghāfiqī and Charles Martel, somewhere near Poitiers, c. 732, be seen as one of the 'Fifteen Decisive Battles of the World'.[5] Yet the Muslims never did take Paris, and, to provide future generations with an explanation for this failure, Islam's final frontier had to be reimagined.

---

[1] R. Collins, *The Arab Conquest of Spain* (Oxford, 1989), p. 87.
[2] E. Manzano, *La frontera de Al-Andalus en época de los Omeyas* (Madrid, 1991), pp. 44–50.
[3] Y. Gleize, F. Mendisco, M.-H. Pemonge, C. Hubert, A. Groppi, B. Houix, M-F. Deguilloux and J-Y. Breuil 'Early Medieval Muslim Graves in France: First Archaeological, Anthropological and Palaeogenomic Evidence', *PLoS ONE*, 11/2 (2016): e0148583. doi:10.1371/journal.pone.0148583.
[4] Ibn Al-Athīr, *Al-Kamil fi al-tār'īkh*, 11 vols. (Beirut, 1966), vol. V, p. 174.
[5] H. Kennedy, *The Great Arab Conquests. How the Spread of Islam Changed the World We Live in* (London, 2007), p. 32; U. Nonn, 'Das Bild Karls Martells in mittelalterlichen Quellen', in J. Jarnut, U. Nonn and M. Richter (eds.), *Karl Martell in seiner Zeit* (Sigmaringen, 1994), pp. 9–21; D. G. König, *Arab-Islamic Views of the Latin West: Tracing the Emergence of Medieval Europe* (Oxford, 2015), pp. 190–1.

The battle near Poitiers has been much discussed but, since nearly all the evidence come from Latin sources, almost entirely from the winners' perspective. The most important of these is the *Chronica muzarabica*, also known as the *Chronicle of 754*, composed at about that date, possibly in Toledo.[6] Many of the chroniclers writing in Arabic about this period failed to mention the battle at all and passed quickly over the failure of the Muslim armies to deal with the Franks as they had done with the Visigoths.[7] In an attempt to change the balance, this article uses Arabic narratives of campaigns in *Ifranja*, the land of the Franks, during the Merovingian period and references to the frontier with Francia in the work of Andalusi geographers such as al-Bakrī (1019–94).[8] It will be argued that it seemed inevitable to many of these authors that the Islamic empire ended where it did.

The first scholar writing in Arabic to mention the battle near Poitiers was probably Ibn 'Abd al-Ḥakam (803–71),[9] who, with Ibn Ḥabīb (c. 790–c.853)[10] provide the earliest Arabic narratives of this period – although their value to historians and their relationship to variant accounts of the conquest in the works of later historians is controversial.[11] Ibn 'Abd al-Ḥakam, an Egyptian, was more famous in his own day for his knowledge of Islamic law, but he is remembered today for the *Conquest of Egypt* (*Futūḥ miṣr*), an account of Egypt from creation to the Islamic conquest, with a postscript on the conquests of the Maghreb and Hispania. Ibn 'Abd al-Ḥakam may have been the first to record the well-known fables associated with the conquest of Hispania. They include the revenge that a certain Count Julian took on Rodrigo, the last Visigothic ruler, for Rodrigo's mistreatment of his daughter, Rodrigo's opening of the House of Bolts in Toledo, where his predecessors were supposed to have deposited their crowns under lock and key, where Rodrigo saw a picture of the men who would conquer Hispania, and the discovery in Spain of the Table of Solomon. The *Conquest of Egypt* gives an annalistic account of the governors who ruled al-Andalus on behalf of the

---

[6] *Chronica muzarabica*, ed. J. Gil Fernández, *Corpus Scriptorum Muzarabicorum*, 2 vols. (Madrid, 1973) vol. I, pp. 15–54

[7] H. Péres, 'Balāṭ al-shuhadā', in *Encyclopaedia of Islam*, 4 vols. (Leiden, 1913–38), vol. I, pp. 988–9.

[8] Al-Bakri, *Jughrāfiyyat al-andalus wa-'urūbba min kitāb 'al-masalik wa-l-mamalik*', ed. 'A. A. El-Ḥajjī (Beirut, 1968).

[9] Ibn 'Abd al-Ḥakam, *Kitāb futūḥ miṣr wa-l-magrib wa-l-andalus*, ed. C. Torrey (New Haven, CT, 1922).

[10] Ibn Habib, *Kitab al–Ta'rīkh*, ed. J. Aguadé (Madrid, 1991).

[11] E. Manzano, 'Las fuentes árabes sobre la conquista de al-Andalus: una nueva interpretación', *Hispania*, 202 (1999): 389–432; E. Manzano, *Conquistadores, Emires y Califas: Los Omeyas y la formación de al-Andalus* (Barcelona, 2006), pp. 32–6.

Umayyads in Damascus. Here Ibn 'Abd al-Ḥakam devoted a few lines to the second period of governorship of 'Abd al-Raḥmān al-Ghāfiqī (731–c. 733): "Abd al-Raḥmān campaigned against Francia, the most distant enemy of al-Andalus, and took much booty and was victorious over them ... [Ibn 'Abd al-Ḥakam described the booty and how it was divided and concluded] ... Then he made another expedition against them and was martyred with all his companions.'[12]

Ibn 'Abd al-Ḥakam dated this battle to 115 AH, i.e. between 21 February 733 and 9 February 734.[13] Following Arabic historiographical practice, he gave the name of his informant: an Egyptian Ibn Layth (d. 791). Ibn Layth was remembered for a work of history, now lost.[14] Makkī argued that Ibn Layth was a link in a chain of oral transmission going back to eyewitnesses to the conquest.[15] Other segments of Ibn 'Abd al-Ḥakam's narrative came from compilations by Eastern historians, most notable among them Ibn Isḥāq (d.760s), the biographer of Muḥammad, from whom Ibn 'Abd al-Ḥakam said he taken the story of the House of Bolts,[16] and al-Wāqidī (d. 823), active at the court of Hārūn al-Rashīd. The process of compilation led to the preservation of discrepant accounts of the battle near Poitiers in the works of late medieval historians. Ibn al-Athīr (1160–1233) copied Ibn 'Abd al-Ḥakam's passage on the defeat of 'Abd al-Raḥmān al-Ghāfiqī, although he amended the date to the previous year.[17] Ibn 'Idhārī, writing c. 1300, named the site of the battle as *Balāṭ al-Shuhadā'*. *Al-shuhadā'*, the martyrs, are the Muslim fallen; the place where they met their end should probably be translated 'the paved road of the martyrs', which could locate the battle on or near the Roman road to Poitiers from the south.[18] It is always disconcerting to find a later historian adding details of which his predecessors had apparently been ignorant. Ibn 'Idhārī does not seem to have read Ibn 'Abd al-Ḥakam's account, and it is not clear where he got his information. Apart from

---

[12] Ibn 'Abd al-Ḥakam, *Kitāb futūḥ miṣr*, pp. 216–17.
[13] On variant dating, see G. V. Sumner, 'The Chronology of the Governors of al-Andalus to the Accession of ᶜAbd al-Rahman I', *Mediaeval Studies*, 48 (1986): 422–69.
[14] N. Clarke, *The Muslim Conquest of Iberia: Medieval Arabic Narratives* (Abingdon and New York, 2012), p. 3.
[15] Makkī, 'Egipto y los orígines de la historiografía árabe–española', *Revista del Instituto Egipcio de Estudios Islámicos*, 5 (1957): 157–248, trans. M. Kennedy in M. I. Fierro and J. Samsó (eds.), *The Formation of the Classical Islamic World*, vol. XLVII: *The Formation of al-Andalus, Part II: Language, Religion Culture and the Sciences* (Aldershot, 1998), pp. 173–233.
[16] Ibn 'Abd al-Hakam, *Kitāb futūḥ miṣr*, p. 206.
[17] Ibn al-Athīr, *Kāmil*, vol. V, p. 174.
[18] E. Lévi-Provençal, *Histoire de l'Espagne musulmane*, 2nd edn, 3 vols. (Paris, 1950, reprinted 1999), vol. I, pp. 61–2; Peres, 'Balāṭ al-shuhadā'.

variant names for the battlefield, the Arabic sources provide no further details of the Muslims' defeat.

The historians seem to have had only the vaguest notion how far the armies of Islam had marched. Further on in his account of the conquest, Ibn 'Abd al-Ḥakam noted that:

> Narbonne (*Ārbūna*) is the furthest border (*thugr*) of al-Andalus. It was conquered during the reign of 'Umar ibn 'Abd al-Azīz (the caliph Umar II, 717–20); then the polytheists[19] (*ahl al-shirk*) conquered it and it is [still] in their hands today. But Ṭāriq [ibn Ziyād] acquired the Table [of Solomon] there.[20]

Narbonne is almost certainly being used to mean the former Roman province of Narbonesis – Visigothic Septimania – rather than the city. It is unlikely that Ṭāriq ibn Ziyād, the first Muslim commander to reach the peninsula, went as far north as Septimania. Indeed, Ibn 'Abd al-Ḥakam also said that Ṭāriq found the Table of Solomon somewhere near Toledo, the former Visigothic capital;[21] in later sources this morphed into a wholly imaginary city, named *al-Mā'ida* (the Table).[22] Ibn 'Abd al-Ḥakam said that the story of the Table came from the Egyptian historian al-Layth;[23] his relocation of the discovery of the Table looks like a literary response to a liminal situation. Indeed, for this author, al-Andalus itself was at the end of the world. In the opening passage of the *Conquest of Egypt*, he compared the world to a figure of a bird, across which the different countries are distributed, ending at the tail which extends to the Maghreb (North Africa and Spain).[24] He acknowledged the political reality that Muslim gains here had been short-lived; the mixture of fantasy and reality is a characteristic response to this frontier in the Arabic sources, as we shall see.

The second ninth-century historian of the conquest, Ibn Ḥabīb, was an Andalusi who spent three years in Egypt, where he met 'Ibn 'Abd al-Ḥakam, before returning to al-Andalus; he served as a legal adviser to the court of the emir 'Abd al-Raḥmān II.[25] The *Book of History* attributed to him survives in a single manuscript copied in the thirteenth century. It is a history that begins with the creation and the prophets from Adam

---

[19] This was a term that historians writing in Arabic commonly applied to Christians.
[20] Ibn 'Abd al-Ḥakam, *Kitāb futūḥ miṣr*, p. 208.
[21] Ibn 'Abd al-Ḥakam, *Kitāb futūḥ miṣr*, p. 207.
[22] *Ajbār Majmuā (Colección de tradiciones)*, ed. and trans. E. Lafuente y Alcántara (Madrid, 1867), pp. 14–15, 19; *Fath al-Andalus (La conquista de al-Andalus)*, ed. L. Molina (Madrid, 1994), p. 23; M. J. Rubiera Mata, 'La Mesa de Salomon', *Awraq*, 3 (1980): 26–31.
[23] As did Ibn Ḥabīb, although his telling is different: *Kitab al-Ta'rīkh*, p. 141.
[24] Ibn 'Abd al-Ḥakam, *Kitāb futūḥ miṣr*, p. 1.
[25] Ibn Ḥabīb, *Kitāb al-ta'rīkh*, commentary, pp. 15–56.

to Muḥammad, continues with the expansion of the Islamic empire and ends with a brief narrative of the conquest of al-Andalus and the rule of the governors and emirs. To call Ibn Ḥabīb the author of this text is misleading; it must have been compiled at the very earliest in the generation after Ibn Ḥabīb (d. c. 853) since it extends to the reign of the emir 'Abd Allāh (888–912). Nor does it include all the information about the conquest which later historians attributed to Ibn Ḥabīb.[26] Not surprisingly, given their close association, Ibn Ḥabīb's *History* shares some of its attitudes and fantastic tales with Ibn 'Abd al-Ḥakam's *Conquest of Egypt*. Yet the relationship between the two historians is far from simple. They seem to make different use of information that they shared, citing the same authority for contradictory statements and telling the same story from different sources. Ibn Ḥabīb's account of the conquest of al-Andalus and its immediate aftermath is dominated by the deeds of Ṭāriq ibn Ziyād, and Mūsā ibn Nuṣayr, the governor of North Africa who followed his subordinate across the Straits in 712 and extended his gains in the peninsula. Ibn Ḥabīb listed most of Mūsā's successors with little more than the length of their rule. He noted that al-Samḥ ruled al-Andalus for two years and nine months and 'Abd al-Raḥmān al-Ghāfiqī for two years and eight months without referring to their campaigns in Francia or their deaths at the hands of the Franks. This may be because, in Ibn Ḥabīb's moralising version of events, it was under Mūsā's governorship that the Islamic conquests in the west came to a halt.

Ibn Ḥabīb described Mūsā's entry into Toledo, where he found the crowns of the Visigothic kings and the House of Bolts. Advancing northwards,

> he conquered the towns, and the people of Christian Spain (*Jillīqīya*) came to him asking for peace and he made peace with him. He attacked the Basques (*al-B.shāk.sa*) and advanced deep inside their country ... Then he turned towards the Franks. He reached Saragossa and took from there a quantity [of booty] which cannot be counted.[27]

This account is very similar to that in the *Chronicle of 754*; the chronicler noted that, after Mūsā had imposed 'a fraudulent peace' on Toledo, 'he devastated ... Hispania Citerior up to and beyond the ancient and once flourishing city of Zaragoza, which was now, by the judgement of God, openly exposed to the sword, famine and captivity'.[28]

---

[26] E.g., *Fath al-Andalus*, pp. 21–2.
[27] Ibn Ḥabīb, *Kitāb al-ta'rīkh*, p. 142.
[28] *Cronica muzarabica*, I, 32; trans. K. B. Wolf, *Conquerors and Chroniclers of Early Medieval Spain*, 2nd edn (Liverpool, 1990), p. 133.

Ibn Ḥabīb noted that Mūsā went on to capture an unnamed fortress, perhaps a certain Lūdlūn, near the river Rhône, named by Ibn 'Idhārī (fl. c. 1300), who also credited him with the capture of Barcelona, Narbonne and Avignon.[29] But although 'Mūsā's army was never defeated until he died',[30] he faced opposition from within his own ranks. In recounting this episode, as elsewhere in the *History*, Ibn Ḥabīb or his continuator deployed some of the stock techniques of storytelling to add verisimilitude to a narrative that may be an invention.[31] First, the account of Mūsā's failed advance into Francia came from the best of authorities: one of Ibn Ḥabīb's own teachers, 'Abd al-Ḥamīd (d. c. 846), a famous scholar of Medina.[32] Second, the story was recounted in the words of the participants:

Musa ibn Nusayr advanced into the land of the enemy until the people became more and more weary. They said 'Where do you want to go with us? We have considered what is before us. Where do you want to take us – out of the world to seek greater things than God has [already] conquered for us?' Musa laughed and said 'By God! ... I will go on to Constantinople and conquer it if God wills it.'[33]

Shortly afterwards, Mūsā was recalled to Damascus,[34] perhaps because his patron, Caliph al-Walīd, was dying. He arrived in time to present the caliph with 'precious things made of pearls and sapphires and chrysolite, together with female and male servants and the Table of Solomon ... and crowns adorned with wreaths of pearls and sapphires'.[35] This is a shopping list of *topoi*; the *Chronicle of 754* has another: 'gold and silver ... valuable ornaments, precious stones, ointments to kindle women's desire and many other things from all over Spain that it would be tedious to record'.[36]

Both Ibn Ḥabīb and Ibn 'Abd al-Ḥakam included anecdotes about the excessive booty that the conquerors seized in al-Andalus; a ship carrying Muslims back to North Africa was so overladen that it sank and all on

---

[29] Ibn 'Idhārī, *Al-Bayān al-Mughrib*, ed. G. Colin and E. Levi-Provençal, 2 vols. (Leiden, 1948), vol. II, p. 12.
[30] Ibn Ḥabīb, *Kitāb al-ta'rīkh*, p. 141.
[31] R. Hoyland, 'History, Fiction and Authorship in the First Centuries of Islam', in J. Bray (ed.), *Writing and Representation in Early Islam* (Abingdon and New York, 2007), pp. 16–46; S. Leder and H. Kilpatrick, 'Classical Arabic Prose Literature: A Researcher's Sketch Map', *Journal of Arabic Literature*, 23 (1992): 2–26.
[32] Ibn Ḥabīb, *Kitāb al-ta'rīkh*, commentary, p. 72; the same authority gave an eyewitness description of the Table of Solomon from his father: *Kitāb al-ta'rīkh*, p. 141.
[33] Ibn Ḥabīb, *Kitāb al-ta'rīkh*, p. 142.
[34] Ibn Ḥabīb, *Kitāb al-ta'rīkh*, p. 147; Ibn 'Abd al-Ḥakam, *Kitāb futūḥ miṣr*, p. 216; *Chronica muzarabica*, vol. I, p. 34.
[35] Ibn Ḥabīb, *Kitāb al-ta'rīkh*, p. 147.
[36] *Cronica muzarabica*, vol. I, p. 33, trans. Wolf, *Conquerors and Chroniclers*, p. 134.

board were drowned.[37] Such greed undermined the legitimacy of the conquest by offending Islamic norms that the property of indigenous populations should be respected and the caliph given one-fifth of the profits of conquest.[38] Mūsā was particularly at fault in this respect, accumulating much treasure and a huge army whose loyalty was to himself rather than the caliph. A courtier in Damascus warned Mūsā of the price he would have to pay for overreaching himself.[39] Yet Mūsā flaunted his wealth before the new caliph Sulaymān:

> [Mūsā and the Sulaymān] were passing through a country estate with a flock of sheep estimated at about one thousand strong. Sulayman was astonished at the number of them and he turned to Musa and said: 'Do you have anything like this?' Mūsā laughed and said, 'If you saw what the least of my clients has, it is many times as much as this.' Sulayman questioned him again: 'The least of your clients?' [Mūsā] responded: 'Yes, by God!' and repeated it several times.[40]

Mūsā boasted of his conquests:

> [Caliph Sulaymān] said, 'Tell me about the Christians (Rum)'. [Mūsā] said, 'In their fortresses, eagles display the courage of lions; women ride on horseback in their mounted escorts. Whenever they see a chance [of victory] they take it and when they face defeat, then like mountain goats they retreat to the mountains'. [The caliph] went on: 'Tell me about the people of al-Andalus.' [Mūsā] replied, '[They are] kings living in luxury and horsemen who are not cowards.' [The caliph] said, 'And tell me about the war between you and them.' [Mūsā] boasted, 'No banner of mine was ever defeated' ... And Sulaymān laughed and was amazed at what he said.[41]

Ibn 'Abd al-Ḥakam saw Mūsā's end as the nemesis attendant upon hubris. Goaded into action by Mūsā's boasting, Sulaymān imposed upon his subordinate a public humiliation and a fine of 100,000 dinars.[42] The story of Mūsā's nemesis was popular with Arabic historians, who retold many versions of it. It may either be based on an outline of fact or have developed much of its content within half a century of the conquest. Mūsā's conflict with the caliph was another element of Mūsā's history that the author of the *Chronicle of 754* recorded – although in this version it was Walīd rather than Sulaymān who brought down his

---

[37] Ibn 'Abd al-Ḥakam, *Kitāb futūḥ miṣr*, pp. 209–10.
[38] A. Christys, 'From *Gihād* to Diwān in Two Providential Histories of Hispania/Al-Andalus', in M. Di Branco and K. Wolf (eds.), *Guerra santa' e conquiste islamiche nel Mediterraneo (VII–XI secolo)* (Rome, 2014), pp. 79–94.
[39] Ibn Ḥabīb, *Kitāb al-ta'rīkh*, p. 148.
[40] Ibn Ḥabīb, *Kitāb al-ta'rīkh*, p. 149.
[41] Ibn Ḥabīb, *Kitāb al-ta'rīkh*, p. 148.
[42] Ibn 'Abd al-Ḥakam, *Kitāb futūḥ miṣr*, p. 213.

'Sons of Ishmael, Turn Back!' 325

over-mighty subordinate. In spite of all the gifts Mūsā had brought for Walīd, the caliph was angry, and 'Mūsā was ignominiously removed from the prince's presence and publicly paraded with a rope around his neck'; he was pardoned only after paying a fine of 2 million *solidi*.[43] Chastened, Mūsā died shortly afterwards while on pilgrimage with Sulaymān.[44]

Ibn Ḥabīb's tales of the conquest, particularly those relating the misappropriation of booty contributed to his stated purpose to make the conquest and settlement of the Iberian peninsula the culmination of his scheme of history: 'I will mention the governors of al-Andalus up to the present day, and who will govern up to its destruction, and who will govern after its destruction up to the Day of Judgement, with *ḥadīths* and signs [of the End of World]'.[45] The *History* makes extensive use of *ḥadīth*: sayings attributed to the prophet Muḥammad and his Companions, often accompanied by chains of transmitters of oral or written information going back to its alleged source. They included a prediction that the rule of the Umayyads would come to an end, which his continuator applied to the reign of 'Abd Allāh:

Cordoba will be destroyed until no one lives there except crows ... Constantinople will be conquered ... the Christians of Cordoba and her region will be killed and no Christian will remain and imprisonment will fall on her children until even the servant will be punished with a spur and the beardless with a whip.[46]

Predictions of the fall of al-Andalus originated within a century of the conquest. Ibn 'Abd al-Ḥakam, citing his Egyptian informant, noted that when Mūsā entered al-Andalus, he said, 'It is not a conquest, but the Day of Resurrection (*al-Ḥashr*).'[47] At about the same period, an association developed between the conquest and settlement of al-Andalus and the fall of Constantinople to the Arabs, and both were written into the scenario of the Last Days.[48] Muslim preoccupation with Constantinople may be derived from the earlier Christian apocalyptic focus on the city.[49] It seems to have originated with attacks under Yazīd I in 669 and by

---

[43] *Cronica muzarabica*, vol. I, p. 35, trans. Wolf, *Conquerors and Chroniclers*, p. 134.
[44] Ibn 'Abd al-Ḥakam, *Kitāb futūḥ miṣr*, p. 213; Ibn Ḥabīb, *Kitāb al-ta'rīkh*, p. 149.
[45] Ibn Ḥabīb, *Kitāb al-ta'rīkh*, p. 26.
[46] Ibn Ḥabīb, *Kitāb al-ta'rīkh*, p. 153.
[47] Ibn 'Abd al-Ḥakam, *Kitāb futūḥ miṣr*, p. 208; M. I. Fierro, 'Sobre al-Qarmuniyya', *Al-Qantara*, 11 (1990), 83–9; M. I. Fierro, 'Doctrinas y movimientos de tipo mesiánico en al-Andalus', in J.-I. de la Iglesia Duarte (ed.), *Milenarismos y Milenaristas en la Europa Medieval: IX Semana de Estudios Medievales Nájera, del 3 al 7 de agosto de 1998* (Logroño, 1999), pp. 159–76; A. Christys, 'Al-Andalus in the Last Days' (Berlin, forthcoming).
[48] Makki, 'Egipto y los historiadores', pp. 177–8; M. Cook, 'The Heraclian Dynasty in Muslim Eschatology', *Al-Qantara*, 13 (1992): 3–24.
[49] P. Magdalino, 'The History of the Future and Its Uses: Prophecy, Policy and Propaganda', in R. Beaton and C. Roueché (eds.), *The Making of Byzantine History: Studies Dedicated to Donald M. Nicol on His Seventieth Birthday* (Aldershot, 1993), pp. 3–34.

Mu'āwiya in the 670s and been reinforced by Maslama ibn Abd al-Malik's failure to take the city in 715–17; later tradition included an account of Maslama's entering Constantinople and desecrating Hagia Sophia. It is however difficult to disentangle early medieval components of these stories from accretions in the period of the Crusades when the conquest of Constantinople was 'predicted' as punishment for the Christians' desecration of the Temple area.[50] The third caliph, 'Uthmān (644–56) was said to have written a letter to the leaders of an army raised to conquer al-Andalus, more than half a century before the event, saying, 'Constantinople will not be taken until we are assured of the possession of al-Andalus. If you take al-Andalus, you will be the associates of (i.e. deserve the same reward as) those who subsequently have the honour to take Constantinople.'[51] The letter of Uthmān was first recorded in the eleventh century,[52] but al-Ṭabarī (d. 923) recorded a prediction that Constantinople would be conquered from al-Andalus.[53] Ibn Ḥabīb did not report mention this prediction, but it is likely that he was aware that some of the eschatological qualities of Constantinople had been transferred to the frontier between al-Andalus and Francia. Yet Mūsā made an unsuitable agent of divine purpose for the Last Days. Mūsā's hubris in setting out across this frontier to conquer Constantinople was the first step in his nemesis. Mūsā was forced to turn back because, Ibn Ḥabīb implies, at this period al-Andalus extended thus far and no farther.

Something of this view emerges from descriptions of al-Andalus in the works of Arabic geographers. It would be a mistake to consider that all these authors were 'armchair' geographers, simply recycling the Ptolemaic world view of their predecessors.[54] Ibn Ḥawqal, who visited al-Andalus in 949, noted that there were two frontiers, one fronting the ocean, the other with the unbelievers, of whom the Franks (*al-Ifranj*) were tractable, while the Galicians of Northern Spain (al-*Ghalījashkash*) were not.[55] In c. 1068, an Andalusi, al-Bakrī, composed a *Book of Roads and Kingdoms*, a geography of al-Andalus and the Maghreb based on a

---

[50] P. Soucek, 'The Temple of Solomon in Islamic Legend and Art', in J. Gutmann (ed.), *The Temple of Solomon: Archaeological Fact and Medieval Tradition in Christian, Islamic and Judaic Art* (Missoula, MT, 1976), pp. 73–124; D. Cook, 'Muslim Apocalyptic and *Jihād*', *Jerusalem Studies in Arabic and Islam*, 20 (1996): 66–104.

[51] Ibn al-Athīr, *Kāmil*, vol. III, p. 93; Al-Bakrī, *Kitab al-masalik wa-l-mamalik*, ed. A. van Leeuwen and A. Ferré, 2 vols. (Qarta, 1992), vol. II, p. 526.

[52] M. I. Fierro and S. Faghia, 'Un nuevo texto de tradiciones escatológicas sobre al-Andalus', *Sharq al-Andalus*, 7 (1990): 99–111.

[53] Al-Ṭabarī, *Ta'rīkh al-rusūl wa-l-mulūk*, ed. M. J. De Goeje (Leiden, 1879–1901), vol. IV, p. 255.

[54] König, *Arab-Islamic Views*, pp. 268–322.

[55] Ibn Ḥawqal, *Kitāb ṣūrat al-arḍ*, ed. J. Kramers, 2 vols. (Leiden, 1967); trans. J. Kramers and G. Wiet, *Configuration de la terre*, 2 vols. (Beirut, 1964), vol. I, p. 108; trans. vol. I, p. 107.

number of earlier texts that do not survive. Its gazetteer of towns and cities roughly coincides with the extent of al-Andalus at the time of writing.[56] The complicated relationship with areas beyond this 'frontier' may be glimpsed in the Arabic sources on regions such as the kingdom of Navarre which had once been under Muslim control and were still under Muslim influence.[57]

Yet this was only one way of conceptualising al-Andalus. Al-Bakrī himself noted that:

The ancients delimited al-Andalus in different ways. Constantine divided [the country] into six parts: he created the first from Narbonne, and this is the border between Gaul and al-Andalus; he added to [Narbonne] seven cities that were around it (although al-Bakrī listed only 5): Béziers (Battarish), Toulouse (Tulyūsha), Maguelonne (Maqalūna), Nimes (Nūmshū) and Carcassonne (Qarqashūna).[58]

Four versions of this so-called Division of Constantine are extant, in Arabic and in Latin, although its ultimate origin is not clear. It was probably well known in the Iberian peninsula, since a list of cities in the *Chronica pseudo-isidoriana*, a Latin chronicle that may have been translated from Arabic,[59] lists the first five of seven cities in the same order as al-Bakrī.[60] A further instance of the interplay between Latin and Arabic sources is reflected in al-Bakrī's use of an Arabic translation of Orosius' *Seven Books of History against the Pagans*.[61] In common with other Arabic geographers, al-Bakrī used only the geographical introduction,[62] which also circulated independently in Latin; an eighth-century manuscript survives from Iberia or Septimania.[63] Al-Bakrī copied Orosius' famous description of Spain, beginning 'The land of al-Andalus is triangular.' He went on to describe the three angles, which, according to

---

[56] E. Tixier du Mesnil, *Géographes d'al-Andalus: De l'inventaire d'un territoire à la construction d'une mémoire* (Paris, 2014), pp. 329–31.

[57] J. J. Larrea and J. Lorenzo, 'The Barbarians of the Dār al-Islām', in G. Vannini and M. Nuccioti (eds.), *La transgiordania nei secoli XII-XIIIe e le 'frontiere' del Mediterraneo medievale* (Oxford, 2012), pp. 277–88.

[58] Al-Bakri, *Jughrāfiyyāt*, pp. 59–60.

[59] A. Christys, '"How Can I Trust You Since You Are a Christian and I Am a Moor?" The Multiple Identities of the *Chronicle of Pseudo-Isidore*', in R. Corradini, R. Meens, C. Pössel and P. Shaw (eds.), *Texts and Identities in the Early Middle Ages* (Vienna, 2006), pp. 359–72.

[60] *La chronica gothorum pseudo-isidoriana (ms Paris BN 6113)*, ed. F. González Muñoz (A Coruña, 2000), p. 138.

[61] Al-Bakrī could have known an interpolated version of Orosius, which may have been translated into Arabic at the end of the ninth century: *Kitāb Hurūshiyūsh (Traducción Árabe de las Historiae Adversus Paganos de Orosio)*, ed. M. Penelas (Madrid, 2001).

[62] L. Molina, 'Orosius y los geógrafos musulmanes', *Al-Qantara*, 5 (1984): 63–92.

[63] *Mappa mundi e codice Albigensi 29 accedunt indeculum quod maria vel venti sunt et (Pauli Orosii) Descriptio terrarum ex eodem codice* ed. F. Glorie (1965), *Itineraria et alia geographica*, CCSL 175, pp. 467–8.

Arabic cartographic practice, are viewed from the north. At the top stood what al-Bakrī called 'the idol of Cádiz'[64] – the tower built by Hercules – and at the third, near present-day A Coruña, was a lighthouse which 'is similar to the idol of Cádiz'.[65] Al-Bakrī added another idol at the second angle, sited at Tarragona. He may be the first to mention this idol, which derives from a number of Arabic traditions relating to the presence of the Greeks, and in particular Hercules, in pre-Islamic Hispania.[66] In geographical scholarship, al-Andalus was the whole peninsula, whatever its political realities;[67] the three idols and the Division of Constantine defined the frontiers of al-Andalus in a way that was just as meaningful as a gazetteer of the places one might actually visit.[68]

For almost a century, Islamic armies had boldly gone with barely a thought for what they might find in the lands into which they were marching, or so it appears. But the border between the Muslims and the land of the Franks was given a different significance to that bordering the Galicians of northern Spain, against whom Cordoba's armies campaigned almost every year. Stepping beyond the Pyrenees, Muslim armies were on their way to an apocalyptic confrontation in Constantinople. The dangers of taking this step, which Mūsā had scorned, were matched only by those posed by entering the cold, dark and fathomless waters of the Atlantic, against which Hercules had warned when he erected the idols at Cádiz and A Coruña. In the words of an anonymous chronicler of the twelfth century:

At the beginning of the year 712, Mūsā b. Nuṣayr ... entered the lands of the Franks. He went on until he came to a great desert, a plain where there were the remains of ancient monuments. Among them was a huge statue erected on a column on which there was an inscription written in Arabic ... [saying] 'Sons of Ishmael, if you have reached here, turn back!'[69]

---

[64] Al-Bakri, *Jughrāfiyya*, p. 65.
[65] Al-Bakri, *Jughrāfiyya*, p. 67.
[66] H. de Carlos Villamarín, *Las Antigüedades de Hispania* (Spoleto, 1996), pp. 241–70; Clarke, *Muslim Conquest*, pp. 82–3.
[67] Although, as we have seen, Ibn Ḥawqal and others also equated al-Andalus with its current situation and defined its frontiers: Ibn Ḥawqal, *Kitāb ṣūrat al-arḍ*, vol. I, p. 108; Tixier du Mesnil, *Géographes*, p.45.
[68] A. García Sanjuán, 'El significado geográfico del topónimo al-Andalus en las fuentes árabes', *Anuario de Estudios Medievales*, 33 (2003): 3–36; A. García Sanjuán, 'La caracterización de al-Andalus en los textos geográficos árabes Orientales (siglos ix-xv)', *Norba, Revista de Historia*, 19 (2006): 43–59.
[69] *Fatḥ al-Andalus*, p. 29; the episode also appears in later accounts see, e.g., Ibn al-Athīr, *Kāmil*, vol. IV, p. 565; Ibn 'Idhārī, *Al-Bayān*, vol. II, p. 17.

21 Carolingian Kingship, Apostolic Authority and Imperial Recognition: Pippin the Short's *Italienpolitik* and the Quest for Royal Legitimacy

Erik Goosmann

With the Greek proverb 'Have a Frank as a friend, not as a neighbour', Einhard ended his account of Charlemagne's diplomatic exploits in a minor key.[1] For, according to Einhard, Charlemagne had subjected the king of Galicia and Asturias and the kings of Ireland through diplomacy, and he had garnered such respect from Caliph Harun-al-Rashīd that he allegedly gave him his only elephant, but Charlemagne had failed to win the trust of the emperors of Byzantium.[2] The Byzantine rulers had ample reason to look to their Western neighbour with suspicion: not only was Frankish influence expanding into territories traditionally claimed by Byzantium, but in taking up the imperial *nomen*, Charlemagne also challenged the Byzantine political order.[3] On top of that, there were serious doctrinal disagreements, most famously regarding the veneration of the images of the saints, to further weigh down relations between East and West.[4]

'If Italy was the key to Byzantine and western interaction, Rome was the key to Italy', as Michael McCormick stated.[5] In 754, when Pippin the

---

[1] Einhard, *Vita Karoli*, c. 16, ed. and trans. R. Rau, *Quellen zur karolingischen Reichsgeschichte* (Darmstadt, 1987): 'ΤΟΝ ΦΡΑΝΚΟΝ ΦΙΛΟΝ ΕΧΙC, ΓΙΤΟΝΑ ΟΥΚ ΕΧΙC.', trans. D. Ganz, *Two lives of Charlemagne / Einhard and Notker the Stammerer* (London, 2008), p. 30.
[2] Einhard, *Vita Karoli*, c. 16.
[3] *Annales regni Francorum*, s.a. 774, 786–8, 806–7, 809–14, ed. and trans. R. Rau, *Quellen zur karolingischen Reichsgeschichte* (Darmstadt, 1987); J. L. Nelson, 'Why Were There So Many Different Accounts of Charlemagne's Imperial Coronation?', in J. L. Nelson (ed.) *Nelson, Courts, Elites, and Gendered Power in the Early Middle Ages: Charlemagne and Others* (Aldershot, 2007), pp. xii, 1–27, at pp. 16–20; M. McCormick, 'Western Approaches (700–900)', in J. Shepard (ed.), *The Cambridge History of the Byzantine Empire, c. 500–1492* (Cambridge, 2009), pp. 395–432, at p. 409; J. Herrin, 'Constantinople, Rome and the Franks in the Seventh and Eighth Centuries', in J. Shepard and S. Franklin (eds.), *Byzantine Diplomacy: Papers from the Twenty-Fourth Spring Symposium of Byzantine Studies, Cambridge, March 1990* (Aldershot, 1992), pp. 91–107, at pp. 103–4.
[4] T. F. X. Noble, *Images, Iconoclasm, and the Carolingians* (Philadelphia, PA, 2009).
[5] M. McCormick, 'Byzantium and the West, 700–900', in R. McKitterick (ed.), *The New Cambridge Medieval History*, vol. II: *c. 700–c. 900* (Cambridge, 1995), pp. 349–80, at p. 361; C. Gantner, 'Eighth-Century Papacy', in C. Gantner, R. McKitterick and

Short (r. 741–68) crossed the Alps at Rome's behest to fight off Lombard oppression, he was the first Carolingian to step onto this stage.[6] Pippin knew that Italy was a Byzantine province, the pope the emperor's subject, and that a military intervention would likely trigger a response from Constantinople. When it comes to explaining the emergence of a trilateral relationship between Franks, Romans and Byzantines in the 750s and 760s, the papal–imperial dialectic tends to dominate at the expense of Frankish agency. In a climate of trans-Mediterranean doctrinal disputes and increased Lombard aggression, the Franks were called upon by the papacy to help it achieve greater political autonomy and security, and by the emperor to maintain imperial hegemony in its westernmost province. In this contribution, Frankish agency will be brought to the fore, focusing on the motives behind Pippin's so-called *Italienpolitik* and its perception on the basis of (near-) contemporary sources.

These sources are predominantly Roman and Frankish in origin. Because of this, Pippin is presented as Rome's unyielding supporter, immune to the supplications of the empire as these interfered with papal interests. It is doubtful that this was the case, however. We are dealing with a highly stylised rendering that was meant to convey the idea of an exclusive pact between the papacy and the Carolingian king to a Frankish and Roman audience. Papal letters, recited at court, reminded the Frankish leadership of its moral and spiritual obligations towards the papacy and its apostolic patron, whereas the language in the *Life of Stephen* may initially have served to warm a Roman elite to the idea of an alliance with the Franks.[7] It was not until much later, when this alliance had proved successful, that it came to be incorporated in the Frankish historical canon.[8] However, Pippin had also successfully

---

S. Meeder (eds.), *The Resources of the Past in Early Medieval Europe* (Cambridge, 2015), pp. 245–61.

[6] T. F. X. Noble, *The Republic of St Peter: The Birth of the Papal State, 680–825* (Philadelphia, PA, 1984), p. 77, referring in n. 69 also to: C. Erdmann, *Die Entstehung des Kreuzzugsgedankens* (Darmstadt, 1935).

[7] *Codex epistolaris Carolinus*, ed. W. Gundlach, *MGH Epp.*, vol. III (Berlin, 1826), pp. 282–313; *Liber Pontificalis*, ed. L. Duchesne, *Le liber pontificalis: Texte, introduction et commentaire*, 2 vols. (Paris, 1886–92), trans. R. Davis, *The Lives of the Eighth-Century Popes (Liber Pontificalis): The Ancient Biographies of Nine Popes from AD 715 to AD 817* (Liverpool, 2007). The *Liber pontificalis* is exclusively known through copies that had circulated in the Frankish world, making the question if this text had originally been intended for a Roman or papal audience difficult. R. McKitterick, *History and Memory in the Carolingian World* (Cambridge, 2004), pp. 145–6; C. Gantner, *Freunde Roms und Völker der Finsternis: Die päpstliche Konstruktion von Anderen im 8. und 9. Jahrhundert* (Vienna, Cologne and Weimar, 2014), pp. 28–38.

[8] F. C. W. Goosmann, 'Memorable Crises. Carolingian Historiography and the Making of Pippin's Reign, 750–900', unpublished Ph.D. thesis, University of Amsterdam (2013), pp. 163–74.

pursued diplomatic relations with Emperor Constantine V (r. 741–75). Driven by opportunism rather than blind devotion, Pippin therefore actively engaged with both parties, allowing him to use both apostolic and imperial authority to bolster his claim to the royal title, which may have been disputed in Francia because of the illicit manner in which he seized the throne in 751.[9] It was only in retrospect that the apostolic see became an obvious source of royal legitimation. The use of apostolic authority to sanction Carolingian kingship, linking it to Old Testament models through the rite of anointing, was a bold experiment to which, at first, there may even have been considerable Frankish opposition. Within this climate of political opposition, ideological experimentation and the creation of new precedents, imperial authority, as an alternative source of Carolingian royal legitimacy, became an enticing idea.

Motives

In his 1912 address to the German historical society, Johannes Haller argued that Pippin's oath to restore and protect the patrimony of St Peter had encumbered him with a monumental responsibility, which hardly gained Pippin any material or territorial advantage. Based on the language of the *Liber Pontificalis* and the *Codex Carolinus*, Haller argued that Pippin's actions were not governed by political or secular motives but by a deep-felt devotion towards St Peter and the Holy Roman Church.[10] If we ignore that Pippin's campaigns against the Lombards (in 754/5 and 756) had yielded a veritable fortune in plunder and tribute, we must concede that Pippin had not expanded the borders of his realm south of the Alps.[11] Moreover, despite incessant papal pleas, Pippin's armies would not intervene in Italy a third time, supposedly because he faced more pressing matters at home.[12] However, to equate a lack of territorial expansion with political ineptitude presupposes that it was Pippin's objective to conquer – an assumption seemingly based on the knowledge that Charlemagne would eventually annex the Lombard kingdom in 774. Likewise, the conclusion that Pippin must have been unable to eliminate the Lombard threat to the nascent papal state foregoes the possibility that it may have been in the Frankish interest to preserve a Lombard threat in northern Italy.

---

[9] R. McKitterick, 'The Illusion of Royal Power in the Carolingian Annals', *English Historical Review*, 115 (2000): 1–20.
[10] J. Haller, 'Die Karolinger und das Papsttum', *Historische Zeitschrift*, 108 (1912): 38–76, at pp. 53–60; Cf. Noble, *Republic*, p. 77; McKitterick, 'Illusion', p. 11.
[11] Haller, 'Karolinger', pp. 50–2.
[12] Haller, 'Karolinger', p. 50.

In 1940, Martin Lintzel argued that Haller had taken the papal letters too literally. Not only had he understood that for Pippin and his contemporaries there was no clear dividing line between politics and religion, but, more importantly, Lintzel argued that the content of these and other writings was by definition selective, determined by circumstances, conventions and expectations of both the author and his intended audience.[13] On account of this methodological critique, Lintzel suggested that Pippin might well have had additional motives to aid the papacy, beyond the ones stated in the extant sources.

Pippin's bold claim to the Frankish kingship may help to explain his decision to aid the papacy, especially since Stephen II offered him an apostolic sanction, in the form of an anointing ritual, in return. What makes the idea of an exchange problematic is that, according to the *Continuations to the Chronicle of Fredegar* and the *Royal Frankish Annals* (*Annales regni Francorum, ARF*), Pippin had allegedly already obtained papal permission for his coup from Stephen's predecessor.[14] More recently, however, Rosamond McKitterick has reassessed the version of events as presented in these Frankish texts, arguing that Pippin's alleged petition to Pope Zacharias in 749 had been a clever and later fabrication made with the intent of suggesting that papal approval had already been gained prior to the coup, rather than in 754.[15] Its aim was to expunge the notion of illegitimate dynastic change from the historical record. A major advantage of this interpretation is that it explains the problematic circumstance of Pippin's 'double anointing': first by the Frankish bishops or by Boniface, depending on the source, in 751 and once more by Pope Stephen in 754. It also casts a different light on Pippin's negotiations with Stephen in Ponthion: if Pippin's position was indeed affected by the way he had procured the royal *nomen*, then legitimate status through apostolic mediation may have been something well worth pursuing.

Technically speaking, there is no evidence that Pippin contended with charges of usurpation. Nevertheless, contemporary and later sources are conspicuously silent regarding the coup and the events surrounding it.[16] In fact, the formal establishment of the Carolingian royal dynasty

---

[13] M. Lintzel, 'Der *Codex Carolinus* und die Motive von Pippins Italienpolitik', *Historische Zeitschrift*, 161 (1940): 33–41, at pp. 39–41.

[14] *Continuations to the Chronicle of Fredegar*, c. 33, ed. and trans. J. M. Wallace-Hadrill, *Fredegarii chronicorum liber quartus cum continuationibus/The Fourth Book of the Chronicle of Fredegar with Its Continuations* (London, 1960); *Annales regni Francorum*, s.a. 749 and 750; Noble, *Republic*, p. 71. Noble's argument is founded on the premise that Pope Zacharias sanctioned Pippin's coup in 751.

[15] McKitterick, 'Illusion'; cf. J. Semmler, *Der Dynastiewechsel von 751 und die fränkische Königssalbung* (Düsseldorf, 2003), pp. 1–29 and 45–6.

[16] McKitterick, *History and Memory*, p. 151.

attracted surprisingly little attention in Carolingian historiography. By cleverly separating the royal *postestas* from the royal *nomen*, Frankish history-writers were instead able to situate Carolingian royal ascendance in the late seventh century, effectively reducing the coup to little more than its formal recognition.[17] We are thus poorly informed about the event itself, but, instead of interpreting this silence as a sign of disinterest or as an attempt to stress greater continuity with the Merovingian past, it ought perhaps to be interpreted as a sign of controversy and as a testament to the skill with which Frankish history-writers were able to repress unfavourable memories from the public record.[18]

If Pippin's promise to defend the papacy was, in part, a *quid pro quo* for having been publicly anointed by Pope Stephen in Saint-Denis in 754, the plan to solicit papal support in order to legitimise Carolingian kingship may not have been a Frankish initiative, nor will it have entered the Frankish agenda before 752, when a papal messenger arrived at Pippin's court carrying Stephen's request for support.[19] That year and the next, Frankish and papal delegations travelled between Rome and the Frankish court to prepare for Stephen's visit, at which occasion both leaders entered into a treaty in which Frankish military aid was exchanged for an apostolic sanction. As per agreement, Pippin attacked the Lombards in 754/5 and again in 756, forcing King Aistulf to concede to Franco-papal demands, most notably to restore Lombard conquered territories to Rome. By entering Italy, Pippin had led the Franks onto an already cramped stage occupied by the Lombard, Roman and Greek peoples.

Not everyone supported Pippin's commitment to the papal cause. Prominent among Frankish opponents was Pippin's brother, Carloman (d. 754), who had left Francia in 737 to become a monk in Monte Cassino, where King Aistulf recruited him to subvert Stephen's plans. Carloman was unsuccessful in his mission, and he died in custody in Vienne, as Pippin marched on Pavia.[20] His death, however, does not

---

[17] Goosmann, 'Memorable Crises', c. 5; P. J. Fouracre, 'The Long Shadow of the Merovingians', in J. Story (ed.), *Charlemagne: Empire and Society* (Manchester, 2005), pp. 5–21.

[18] M. J. Innes and R. McKitterick, 'The Writing of History', in R. McKitterick (ed.), *Carolingian Culture: Emulation and Innovation* (Cambridge, 1994), pp. 193–220; Y. Hen and M. J. Innes (eds.), *The Uses of the Past in the Early Middle Ages* (Cambridge, 2000).

[19] Angenendt, A., 'Pippins Königserhebung und Salbung', in M. Becher and J. Jarnut (eds.), *Der Dynastiewechsel von 751: Vorgeschichte, Legitimationsstrategien und Erinnerung* (Münster, 2004), pp. 179–209, at p. 185; McKitterick, 'Illusion'.

[20] Goosmann, 'Memorable Crises', pp. 144–51; F. C. W. Goosmann, 'Politics and Penance: Transformations in the Carolingian Perception of the Conversion of Carloman', in C. Gantner, R. McKitterick and S. Meeder (eds.), *The Resources of the Past in Early Medieval Europe* (Cambridge, 2015), pp. 51–67.

appear to have silenced the opposition. According to Einhard, resentment lingered among the Frankish nobles, who threatened to abandon their king during the Lombard campaign.[21] Although Einhard does not disclose their motives, some members of the elite may have felt uncomfortable breaking a long-standing and mutually beneficial alliance with the Lombards, despite papal accusations that they were enemies of the Church.[22] It also was not the first time that Rome had asked the Franks for help against the Lombards. In 739, Pope Gregory III had sent a similar petition to Charles Martel, who replied with a formal delegation bearing gifts, but not weapons.[23] Political circumstances instead of pious devotion can explain why Stephen's petition met a more favourable response in 754.[24] The point to stress, however, is that Charles's reluctance to help Pope Gregory and Carloman's opposition to Pope Stephen suggests that Pippin and his contemporaries saw through papal rhetoric and were able to distinguish between the interests of St Peter and those of the papacy. This, therefore, argues against the idea that the Franks acted out of blind devotion towards the apostolic see.[25] Pippin's resolve to come to Rome's aid in the face of domestic opposition suggests that, in addition to spiritual reprieve, the papacy had more to offer, namely the moral authority to endorse Pippin's royal title within the Frankish community. Because the Franks had come to accept the papacy as the highest spiritual authority in the West, it was an obvious source of royal legitimacy. But so, too, was the emperor.[26]

---

[21] Einhard, *Vita Karoli*, c. 6. Einhard's account probably inspired Notker's story of Pippin proving himself before his nobles by fighting wild animals: Notker Balbulus, *Gesta Karoli*, l. 2, c. 15, ed. H. H. Haefele, *MGH SRG NS*, 12 (Berlin, 1959). Trans. D. Ganz, *Two Lives of Charlemagne/Einhard and Notker the Stammerer* (London, 2008).

[22] Contemporary Frankish sources are silent about this pact. The earliest reference is in Paul the Deacon, *Historia Langobardorum*, l. 6, c. 53, ed. L. Bethmann and G. Waitz, *MGH SS RL* (Hanover, 1878). An alternative version, that was friendlier to Pippin's remembrance, was Adrevald of Fleury, *Miracula sancti Benedicti*, l. 1, c. 14, ed. O. Holder-Egger, *MGH SS* 15:1 (Hanover, 1887). This work was composed in the 860s. Adrevald identified it as a *foedus* between Charles and Liutprand. For discussion, see R. Holtzmann, *Die Italienpolitik der Merowinger und des Königs Pippin* (Darmstadt, 1962), pp. 5–7 and 39–42; J. Jarnut, 'Die Adoption Pippins durch König Liutprand und die Italienpolitik Karl Martells', in J. Jarnut, U. Nonn and M. Richter (eds.), *Karl Martell in seiner Zeit* (Sigmaringen, 1994), pp. 217–26; G. G. Wolf, 'Nochmals zur "Adoption" Pippins d.J. durch den Langobardenkönig Liutprand 737', *Zeitschrift der Savigny-Stiftung für Rechtsgeschichte: Germanistische Abteilung*, 117 (2000): 654–8.

[23] Jarnut, 'Adoption', pp. 221–5.

[24] McCormick, 'Byzantium and the West', p. 365.

[25] T. Hodgkin, *Frankish Invasions: Italy and Her Invaders, 744–74* (Oxford, 1880–9), p. 215; Lintzel, '*Codex Carolinus*', pp. 36–7. Lintzel points to the *Annales Mettenses priores*, s.a. 743, ed. B. v. Simson, *MGH SRG*, 10 (Hanover and Leipzig, 1905), on Pippin's dealings with the papal legate Sergius, who is captured during a Frankish campaign against the Bavarians.

[26] McCormick, 'Western Approaches', p. 409.

The Italian Stage

Information about Frankish diplomatic activities in the Apennine peninsula in the period 751–68 derives exclusively from papal and Frankish sources. However, the latter are hardly contemporary and mostly date to the late eighth and early ninth centuries. Moreover, these Frankish texts were composed at a time when Franco-Byzantine relations were at a low point, which significantly affected the manner in which these events came to be written down. As a result, reconstructions of these events tend to lean heavily on two contemporary papal sources, although they, too, ended up being transmitted in a Frankish context. The first of these is the *Life of Pope Stephen II*. It was composed shortly after the pope's death in 757 and came to be included in the papal serial biography known as the *Liber Pontificalis*. Although Stephen's pontificate lasted only five years, it merited a lengthy biography with a focus that was political rather than pastoral. The second source is the papal letter collection known as the *Codex epistolaris Carolinus*, assembled by order of Charlemagne in 791.[27] The Codex consists of ninety-nine papal letters that date to the reigns of Charles Martel (two), Pippin the Short (forty-one) and Charlemagne (fifty-six).[28] Of the letters dating to Pippin's reign, eight were composed during the pontificate of Pope Stephen II and thirty during that of his brother and successor Pope Paul I (757–67). These letters form an invaluable source of information for the formation of the papal state and, in connection to this, the bond between the papacy and the Carolingians. Although they discuss a wide-ranging set of issues, the majority of the letters composed during Pippin's reign express concern for the Lombard and Byzantine threat to Rome's territories. What follows is merely intended as a basic outline of the events in Italy, as more detailed reconstructions are easily available elsewhere.[29]

In July 751, the Lombards conquered the exarchate of Ravenna and the duchy of the Pentapolis, and Rome was next on their list. Unable to negotiate a peace treaty with the Lombard king, Aistulf, Stephen turned to the emperor for help.[30] Emperor Constantine V, having

---

[27] D. van Espelo, 'A Testimony of Carolingian Rule: The *Codex epistolaris Carolinus* as a Product of Its Time', unpublished Ph.D. thesis, Utrecht University (2014); Gantner, *Freunde*, pp. 38–43; Hack, *Codex Carolinus*.

[28] Only ninety-eight letters survive, because only the lemma of letter 15 exists. Regarding the dates of these letters, see Hack, *Codex Carolinus*, pp. 1074–9.

[29] Noble, *Republic*, pp. 71–112; W. Brandes, 'Das Schweigen des Liber pontificalis: Die "Enteignung" der päpstlichen Patrimonien Siziliens und Unteritaliens in den 50er Jahren des 8. Jahrhunderts', *Fontes minores*, 12 (2014): 97–203, at pp. 164–78.

[30] *Liber pontificalis*, no. 94, cc. 5–7; McCormick, 'Byzantium', p. 360.

committed his military resources to securing the Balkans, resorted to diplomacy and sent John *silentiarios* to Pavia, but with little effect.[31] It was Constantinople's inability to protect Rome while demanding heavy imperial taxation, rather than doctrinal disputes, that made the papacy turn to the king of the Franks.[32] As discussed above, this would lead to the famous meeting between Stephen and Pippin at Ponthion in 753, where the latter promised to restore the patrimony of St Peter and where Stephen, in turn, anointed Pippin and his sons as kings of the Franks and conferred onto them the title of *patricius Romanorum*.[33] However, on the eve of Stephen's departure, John returned to Rome with orders for a final round of negotiations with Aistulf, and it was only when these negotiations had failed that Stephen continued north to Francia.[34] John, at this point, presumably returned to Constantinople. Because Byzantine and papal legates had acted in concert in seeking a solution to the Lombard threat, John, and therefore also the emperor, would probably have been aware of Stephen's plans to visit Francia.[35] In fact, now that diplomacy had run its course, it may even have been possible that the emperor had signed off on the idea to call in outside help.[36] An indication for this is that Stephen, in addition to anointing Pippin and his sons, also bestowed upon them the title of *patricius Romanorum*, which, under normal circumstances, would have been the prerogative of the emperor.[37]

The *Continuations* provide an elaborate and triumphant account of Pippin's Lombard campaigns in 754/5 and 756.[38] Aistulf had to promise to surrender his conquests to Rome, and much of his treasury to the Franks. Constantinople may have foreseen Pippin's intention to concede

---

[31] Brandes, 'Schweigen', pp. 164–5; L. Brubaker, *Inventing Byzantine Iconoclasm* (London, 2011), pp. 45–6.

[32] *Liber pontificalis*, no. 94, cc. 8–9, 15; Herrin, 'Constantinople', p. 98; Brandes, 'Schweigen', pp. 105–10.

[33] *Liber pontificalis*, no. 94, cc. 26–7. The *Life of Stephen* only mentions that Stephen anointed Pippin. That he had allegedly also given him the title *patricius Romanorum* is recorded in the *Annales Mettenses priores*, s.a. 754 and the so-called *Clausula de unctione Pippini*, ed. B. Krusch, *MGH SRM*, I (Hanover, 1885), pp. 15–16. The papal letters address Pippin with this title, but he never used it himself. See below, no. 37.

[34] *Liber pontificalis*, no. 94, c. 17.

[35] A. Lombard, *Études d'histoire byzantine: Constantin V, Empereur des Romains (740–775)* (Paris, 1902), p. 72; Brandes, 'Schweigen', p. 167.

[36] This was a common Byzantine strategy. McCormick, 'Byzantium and the West', p. 360; cf. Herrin, 'Constantinople', p. 99.

[37] By arguing that these were extraordinary circumstances, and because the addition *Romanorum* was unique, many historians have concluded that Stephen must have acted alone. For an overview of the debate, see Van Espelo, 'A Testimony of Carolingian Rule', pp. 152–3; Noble, *Republic*, pp. 278–9, esp. n. 3; Brandes, 'Schweigen', 168–9.

[38] *Continuations*, cc. 37–8. Compare with *Liber Pontificalis*, no. 94, cc. 31–47. On the date, see Noble, *Republic*, p. 88, n. 113.

the exarchate to papal control, which would explain why Emperor Constantine dispatched a high-profile delegation to Pippin, led by John and chief-secretary George, to prevent this from happening. They arrived in Marseille in 756 only to learn that Pippin had already crossed the Alps.[39] George caught up with Pippin near Pavia and petitioned the king to restore the exarchate to imperial control. But, according to the *Life of Stephen*,

> [George] was totally unable to sway the stalwart heart of the Christian and kindly Pippin king of the Franks, who was loyal to God and devoted to St Peter, to grant those cities and places to imperial control. The God-worshipping gentle king stated there was absolutely no way at all that these cities could be alienated from St Peter's power and the ownership of the Roman church and the apostolic see's pontiff.[40]

Pippin's resolve may have been somewhat overstated. While George hurried after Pippin, John had remained in Francia to await Pippin's return. In a letter sent the following year, Stephen warned Pippin to protect the purity of the Catholic Church against Greek influences. More specifically he added that Pippin 'should deliver to us what you have discussed with the *silentiarius* [i.e. John], or how your goodness has absolved him, along with a copy of the letter that you will have given him, so that we know how we are to act in joint concord.'[41] Stephen assumed that Pippin had remained loyal to the papal cause, but there also seems to have been some concern about Pippin's exposure to such prominence Byzantine officials without there being any papal representatives present. In fact, Wolfram Brandes has argued that John may not have returned from Pippin's court empty-handed; in exchange for conceding the exarchate of Ravenna to Rome, Pippin may have agreed not to interfere with the recent imperial confiscation of papal territories in Calabria and Sicily.[42]

Moreover, Frankish sources imply that Pippin had established friendly relations with Constantine in 757. According to the *Continuations*, composed between 768 and 786, Pippin had taken the initiative by sending a Frankish delegation to Constantinople 'pro amicitiis causa et salutem patrie sue'.[43] Constantine reciprocated by sending a Greek

---

[39] *Liber Pontificalis*, no. 94, c. 44. See also Noble, *Republic*, p. 93.
[40] *Liber Pontificalis*, no. 94, c. 45, trans. Davies, p. 71.
[41] *Codex Carolinus*, no. 11, pp. 506–7: 'Qualiter autem cum silentiario locuti fueritis vel quomodo eum tua bonitas absolverit una cum exemplare litterarum, quas ei dederitis, nos certiores reddite, ut sciamus, qualiter in commune concordia agamus.'
[42] Brandes, 'Schweigen', pp. 172–5.
[43] *Continuations*, c. 40. Cf. D. H. Miller, 'Byzantine-Papal Relations during the Pontificate of Paul I: Confirmation and Completion of the Roman Revolution of the Eighth Century', *Byzantinische Zeitschrift*, 1 (1975): 47–62, at p. 51, n. 14.

delegation that carried 'many gifts' in return. But although king and emperor 'through their legates promised each other friendship (*amicitia*) and loyalty (*fides*)', the chronicler concluded his passage with the words: 'What happened, that afterwards the friendship they had mutually promised between them had no effect, I do not know.'[44] The events in the *Continuations* are rarely clearly dated. In this case, they are said to have occurred 'dum haec ageretur', referring to Pippin's Lombard campaigns, followed by Aistulf's death in 756. The concluding statement, on the other hand, appears to point to a later development, although the text holds no clue as to why the *amicitia*-pact had failed in the end. The author may have been referring to events outside the scope of his narrative, or to events that were not to be discussed.[45]

The first section of the *ARF* was composed during the late 780s or early 790s. According to the entry for 757, the year in which Stephen wrote the above-mentioned letter, 'Emperor Constantine sent King Pippin, along with other gifts, an organ that had come all the way to Francia.'[46] A later revision of these annals adds that the organ arrived during an assembly at Compiègne.[47] The organ was a novelty in Francia, and its arrival appears to have been quite a spectacle, since it came to be recorded in a score of 'minor annals' (see Fig. 21.1).[48] In Byzantium, organs were predominantly used in secular ceremonies, from sporting events in the Hippodrome to imperial advent ceremonies.[49] According to Judith Herrin, the organ was 'a symbol of ancient royalty', and, as a gift, it was unprecedented in the West.[50] Indeed, as Michael McCormick has stated, 'its ostentatious presentation to the usurper king at the assembly of his unruly magnates suggests that the Byzantines curried royal favour by supplying the means to magnify a nascent monarchy.'[51]

---

[44] *Continuations*, c. 40: 'Nescio quo faciente, postea amicitias quas inter se mutuo promisserant nullatenus sortita est effectu.'

[45] Note the remark by R. McKitterick, *Charlemagne: The Formation of a European Identity* (Cambridge, 2008), pp. 9–10.

[46] *Annales regni Francorum*, s.a. 757: 'Misit Constantinus imperator regi Pippino cum aliis donis organum, qui in Franciam usque pervenit.'

[47] Revised-*Annales regni Francorum*, s.a. 757, ed. and trans. R. Rau, *Quellen zur karolingischen Reichsgeschichte* (Darmstadt, 1987).

[48] *Annales Mettensis priores*, s.a. 757: 'quod antea visum non fuerat in Francia.' So-called minor annals that recorded the organ's arrival s.a. 757 are: *Annales Laureshamenses*, ed. G. H. Pertz, *MGH SS*, vol. I (Hanover, 1826), pp. 22–39; *Annales Alamannici*, ed. W. Lendi, *Untersuchungen zur frühalemannischen Annalistik: die Murbacher Annalen. Mit Edition* (Freiburg, 1971), pp. 145–93; pp. 145–93; *Annales Nazariani*, ed. G. H. Pertz, *MGH SS*, vol. I (Hanover, 1826), pp. 23–44; *Annales Petaviani* (A, B), G. H. Pertz (ed.), *MGH SS*, vol. I (Hanover, 1826), pp. 7–18.

[49] Brandes, 'Schweigen', p. 177; Herrin, 'Constantinople', pp. 104–7.

[50] Herrin, 'Constantinople', pp. 100 and 106.

[51] McCormick, 'Byzantium and the West', p. 365.

Pippin the Short's *Italienpolitik*

Figure 21.1 Organ depicted in the Utrecht Psalter (Rheims, 825–50), illustrating Psalm 150:4: 'Praise him with strings and organs.' Utrecht, Universiteitsbibliotheek, Hs. 32, f. 83r. Printed with permission of the Utrecht University Library.

Assuming that Pippin understood and copied the instrument's function in Byzantine court culture, as a symbol of Carolingian royal majesty it may well have rivalled the papal anointing ritual (not least because an organ could be sounded again and again, whereas the anointing ritual was a one-time affair), regardless of the fact that they drew on different symbolic registers. Of course, that the organ features prominently in histories composed around 800, but not in the more contemporary *Continuations*, may also indicate that the instrument's symbolic potential was only fully realised when Charlemagne revived the empire in the West.

Both Aistulf and Stephen died the year the organ arrived in Francia. Stephen was succeeded by his brother Paul (d. 767). Unfortunately, Paul's biography contains no information about the political circumstances in Italy, for which we have to rely on his letters, although these at best offer glimpses of the complex political constellation between Franks,

Lombards, Romans and Greeks.⁵² Two main concerns become clear from Paul's letters: first, Paul was terrified of a Lombard or Byzantine military invasion. Aistulf had been succeeded by Desiderius (r. 757–74), whose election had the support of Stephen and Pippin, on the condition he would honour the Pavia treaty. But once in power, Desiderius had failed to make good on his promise, resulting in more papal missives demanding Frankish military intervention.⁵³ Papal apprehension peaked in 758, when Desiderius made a pact with George, who had taken up residence in Naples.⁵⁴ Paul now feared that a Lombard–Byzantine invasion was imminent, but Desiderius above all wanted to regain control over the Lombard duchies of Spoleto and Benevento.⁵⁵ In reality, neither Desiderius nor Constantine was in much of a position to launch a serious offensive against Rome, which enjoyed Frankish protection. Paul's second concern therefore was that Pippin would turn his back on Rome. In particular, he feared that Byzantine diplomacy would succeed in destabilising the Franco-papal pact.⁵⁶ To this end, one letter speaks of a Byzantine mole in the papal administration: Paul informed Pippin that the priest Marinus, who acted as papal liaison in Francia, was colluding with George and demanded that he be sent back to Rome.⁵⁷ In addition to infiltration, Constantinople also pursued a disinformation campaign, spreading rumours of armies being assembled, of the papacy secretly supporting Pippin's enemies and of Pippin being unwilling to protect the Roman Church, were it to come under attack.⁵⁸

The bond of *amicitia* and *fidelitas* between Pippin and Constantine did not prevent Pippin from further strengthening relations with the papacy the following year, when he accepted Paul's invitation to act as the baptismal sponsor of his daughter Gisela (b. 757), establishing a spiritual bond of compaternity between Paul and Pippin.⁵⁹ Perhaps in an attempt to counter this pact, the emperor proposed a marriage between Gisela and Leo IV, the imperial heir apparent. This proposition

---

[52] Noble, *Republic*, pp. 108 and 111.
[53] *Codex Carolinus*, no. 14.
[54] *Codex Carolinus*, no. 15.
[55] Desiderius used his pact with George to negotiate better terms with the papacy: *Codex Carolinus*, nos. 15–17.
[56] Noble, *Republic*, p. 112.
[57] *Codex Carolinus*, no. 25.
[58] *Codex Carolinus*, nos. 29–31 and 36; Miller, 'Byzantine–Papal Relations', p. 56; Noble, *Republic*, p. 109; Herrin, 'Constantinople', p. 92.
[59] *Codex Carolinus*, no. 14 (758); A. Angenendt, '*Mensa Pippini regis*: Zur liturgischen Präsenz der Karolinger in Sankt Peter', in A. Angenendt, Th. Flammer and D. Meyer (eds.), *Liturgie im Mittelalter: Ausgewählte Aufsätze zum 70. Geburtstag* (Münster, 2004), pp. 89–109, at p. 91; Van Espelo, 'Testimony of Carolingian Rule', pp. 172–3; Herrin, 'Constantinople', pp. 91–2.

is known through a letter by Pope Stephen III (768–72), written shortly after Pippin's death.⁶⁰ In this letter, Stephen warns Charlemagne and Carloman not to marry foreign women and not to act against the will of the papacy. It then recalls Constantine's proposal to Pippin, but it does not inform us about Pippin's response – and it is perhaps remarkable, to say the least, that no evidence for this proposition is found in contemporary letters by Paul. If Pippin had indeed turned down the emperor's proposal, it could explain why Franco-Byzantine relations broke down.⁶¹ By contrast, Noble's view is that Pippin had looked favourably to the emperor's proposal and considered it the main reason for intensified diplomatic exchange between the Frankish and Byzantine courts in the period *c.* 760–7.⁶²

Others have argued that the intensified diplomatic exchange, which can be reconstructed on the basis of various papal letters, was mostly connected to doctrinal matters and to preparations for the Synod of Gentilly in 767.⁶³ However, doctrinal disputes, most notably the one regarding the images of the saints, are no longer believed to be the be-all and end-all of Franco-Byzantine relations in the mid eighth century.⁶⁴ In fact, that the Franks considered religious doctrine to be an issue at all in their interaction with the Byzantine court is based entirely on papal correspondence. Paul repeatedly complimented Pippin on his spiritual integrity and urged him to defend Catholic orthodoxy, in particular against the 'nefandissimi Greci, inimici sanctae Dei ecclesiae et orthodoxae fidei expugnatores'.⁶⁵ There can be no doubt that religious orthodoxy was important to the Carolingians, but whether it also affected Frankish foreign policy is a different matter.⁶⁶ Noble's reconstruction is

---

[60] *Codex Carolinus*, no. 45, p. 562; P. Classen, *Karl der Große, das Papsttum und Byzanz. Die Begründung des karolingischen Kaisertums* (Düsseldorf, 1968), p. 26, n. 73 proposed a date of 766/7. This date has been accepted by M. McCormick, 'Textes, images et iconoclasme dans le cadre des relations entre Byzance et l'Occident carolingien', in *Testo e immagine nell'alto medioevo, 15–21 aprile 1993* (Spoleto, 1994), pp. 96–162, at pp. 130–1.
[61] Cf. Herrin, 'Constantinople', pp. 100–1.
[62] *Codex Carolinus*, nos. 20, 28 and 37. Noble, *Iconoclasm*, p. 143.
[63] P. F. Kehr, 'Über die Chronologie der Briefe Papst Pauls I. im Codex Carolinus', *Nachrichten von der Gesellschaft der Wissenschaften zu Göttingen: Philologisch-Historische Klasse*, 2 (1896): 104–57, p. 125; Miller, 'Byzantine–Papal Relations', pp. 59–60. Cf. McCormick, 'Textes', pp. 130–1.
[64] Brandes, 'Schweigen', pp. 97–203; Brubaker, *Byzantine Iconoclasm*, p. 46; Herrin, 'Constantinople', p. 98.
[65] *Codex Carolinus*, no. 30. See also Gantner, *Freunde*, pp. 111–12
[66] M. J. Innes, '"Immune from Heresy": Defining the Boundaries of Carolingian Christianity', in P. J. Fouracre and D. Ganz (eds.), *Frankland: The Franks and the World of the Early Middle Ages – Essays in Honour of Dame Jinty Nelson* (Manchester, 2008), pp. 101–25, at p. 122.

appealing in this respect, because it argues that Paul, by raising the issue of doctrinal orthodoxy, forced Pippin to choose in favour of the papacy, reminding him that Carolingian royal ideology ultimately rested on the papal definition of religious orthodoxy.[67]

The Synod of Gentilly and the End of Franco-Byzantine Relations

The *ARF* state that in the year 767 'Lord Pippin convened in the above-mentioned villa [Gentilly] a great synod between Romans and Greeks on the Holy Trinity and on the images of the saints.'[68] Apart from this single entry, we are not informed of the proceedings of this assembly, nor of its political consequences. Two papal letters, now presumed to have been written shortly before and after the synod, merely refer to the importance of maintaining Catholic orthodoxy.[69] Regardless, historians traditionally regard the synod of Gentilly to have been the turning point in Frankish-Byzantine relations, which appear to have been good prior to 767. With no further reports of delegations crossing the Adriatic and because Gisela never married Leo IV, diplomatic activity between Francia and Byzantium is thought to have ceased after 767, its likely cause being the doctrinal differences between Eastern and Western Christianity.[70]

According to the *ARF*, the synod of Gentilly revolved around two major doctrinal issues: 'de sancta Trinitate' and 'de sanctorum imaginibus'. According to Noble, if the issue of the Holy Trinity should be interpreted as an early reference to the *filioque* debate, then it probably was 'a later confection designed to add historical precedent to the theological concerns of a later time'.[71] Perhaps the same can also be argued for the issue of the proper worship of the images of the saints. Unlike the *filioque* controversy, the dispute about images already had a long history. However, the reference in the *ARF* is the first sign that the dispute had also spread to Francia. It would furthermore have been an isolated event, as the debate on images does not appear to have been particularly prominent at the Frankish court prior to 787. That year, Empress Irene (d. 802) convened Nicaea II, at which the iconoclast position of her predecessors was retracted, allowing for the images of the saints to be

---

[67] Noble, *Iconoclasm*, p. 143. See also McCormick, 'Textes', p. 131.
[68] *Annales regni Francorum*, s.a. 767: 'Tunc habuit domnus Pippinus rex in supradicta villa synodum magnum inter Romanos et Grecos de sancta Trinitate vel de sanctorum imaginibus.'
[69] McCormick, 'Textes', pp. 116–23.
[70] Noble, *Iconoclasm*, p. 143.
[71] Noble, *Iconoclasm*, p. 144.

once more venerated in the East. But whereas the papacy welcomed the Byzantine about-face and celebrated a church reunited, the acts of this synod, poorly translated from the Greek into Latin, met with fierce critique at the court of Charlemagne, whose theologians instead preached a *via media* that condemned both the veneration *and* the destruction of images. Ultimately, the acts of Nicaea II were condemned at the Synod of Frankfurt in 794.[72]

The *ARF* were thus composed in a climate of doctrinal arguments, border disputes and failed marriage alliances. Intended to celebrate the triumph of Carolingian rule, the annals' authors wrote in support of the then-current political agenda, which had significant repercussions for the way in which they presented the Carolingian past.[73] The attention that was given to the Synod of Gentilly – attention almost entirely absent in the more contemporary *Continuations* – was not meant to celebrate the orthodoxy of Pippin's reign but Carolingian orthodoxy in general. Specifically, with regard to the doctrinal controversies that had risen to such prominence at the time these annals were composed, the annalist may well have considered the Synod of Gentilly a fitting canvas on which to back-project the Frankish concern for orthodoxy, giving these issues undue historical precedence.

If these issues had indeed been debated at Gentilly, their effect on Franco-Byzantine relations nonetheless remains unclear. Regardless of the synod's outcome, for Pippin to even stage such a 'great synod' that hosted delegations from all corners of Christendom (not just Romans and Greeks but also representatives of the Christian communities of the Levant)[74] was already a powerful display of royal majesty with distinct imperial overtones – imagine only the ceremonious bellowing of the organ, announcing the king's arrival!

But if religious doctrine did not cause relations to break down, what had? An alternative option is Pippin's death in 768, after which the Frankish realm was divided between his sons, Charlemagne and Carloman. As is so often the case, this succession was not problem-free.[75] Political factions needed to be realigned and the Frankish court – now courts – had to be put in order. In light hereof, a marriage alliance between Gisela and Leo IV may have been inconvenient at this time.

---

[72] Noble, *Iconoclasm*, p. 159.
[73] McKitterick, *History and Memory*, p. 132; J. L. Nelson, 'History-Writing at the Courts of Louis the Pious and Charles the Bald', in J. L. Nelson (ed.), *Rulers and Ruling Families in Early Medieval Europe: Alfred, Charles the Bald and Others* (Farnham, 1999), pp. IX:435–42, at pp. 437–8.
[74] *Codex Carolinus*, no. 40; Miller, 'Byzantine–Papal Relations', p. 61.
[75] Einhard, *Vita Karoli*, c. 3; *Revised-ARF*, s.a. 769.

Something similar may have occurred a generation earlier, when Franco-Bavarian relations abruptly ended after Charles Martel's death in 741. Although this is not the place to go into detail about the complex history between the Carolingian and Agilolfing families, marriage had been a strategy by which Charles hoped to strengthen his ties with the Bavarian ducal house. Towards the end of his life, Charles may have arranged or consented to a marriage between his daughter Chiltrud and the Bavarian duke Odilo. However, as soon as Charles had died, Carloman and Pippin forbade this marriage but could not prevent Chiltrud from eloping with her Bavarian prince, causing great scandal.[76] Pippin's own sons may have been similarly opposed to their sister Gisela's marriage to Leo IV.[77]

Moreover, early medieval foreign relations, like modern ones, often appeared to be founded on personal connections and their maintenance. Paul continually felt he had to remind Pippin of the promise he had made to his brother. Was Paul afraid that Pippin had forgotten about his promise to Stephen, or was he perhaps emphasising his close personal connection to the former pope, presenting himself not just as Stephen's apostolic successor but also as the heir to Stephen's bond with the Frankish king? Stephen had established a close personal connection with the Frankish king and his sons by performing the rite of anointing. Paul lacked such a bond, at least until he entered into a bond of compaternity with Pippin through the confirmation of Gisela's baptism. Likewise, Carloman and Charlemagne may not have felt obliged to honour their father's agreement with Constantine. Successions, after all, meant the shifting of a political balance in Francia, which in turn rendered the best-laid plans obsolete.

Conclusion

The argument that Pippin was able to differentiate between the interests of St Peter and those of the papacy should not be mistaken for an attempt to downplay the significance of religious motivation as a force driving Carolingian action. To characterise Pippin's *Italienpolitik* as opportunistic and pragmatist does not make him a 'Bismarckian *Realpolitiker*'.[78]

---

[76] Goosmann, 'Memorable Crises', p. 96; A. Fischer, *Karl Martell: Der Beginn karolingischer Herrschaft* (Stuttgart, 2012), at pp. 102–3; U. Nonn, 'Die Nachfolge Karl Martells und die Teilung von Vieux-Poitiers', in M. Becher and J. Jarnut (eds.), *Der Dynastiewechsel von 751: Vorgeschichte, Legitimationsstrategien und Erinnerung* (Münster, 2004), pp. 61–73, at pp. 66–7.

[77] W. Pohl, 'Why Not to Marry a Foreign Woman: Stephen III's Letter to Charlemagne', in V. L. Garver and O. M. Phelan (eds.), *Rome and Religion in the Medieval World: Studies in Honor of Thomas F. X. Noble* (Farnham, 2014), pp. 47–64, at p. 50.

[78] Miller, 'Byzantine–Papal Relations', p. 58, n. 45.

Rather, it means that Pippin acted on a complex set of motives and circumstances. The Carolingian attraction to imperial and apostolic Rome is well attested: in the course of the eighth century, through agents such as Willibrord and especially Boniface, the apostolic see had become the highest authority in matters of religious doctrine and church organisation in the West. Taking into account that, like late-antique imperial rule, early medieval kingship was an office with a great religious significance, the idea to invoke Rome's apostolic authority to sanction dynastic change may appear to have been only a small step. However, that Pippin was able to take this step in 754 is not self-evident but owed above all to the circumstance that the papacy was at that point in dire need of a strong, secular ally to protect the patrimony of St Peter from Lombard expansion and imperial fiscal policy. In this contribution, I have therefore not only attempted to argue that there were other steps possible for a Carolingian usurper in search of legitimacy, but that these were also actively explored. If Rome could dazzle the Frankish mind, then so could Constantinople.

When Pippin entered Italy in 754, he did so newly anointed and with a pope at his side. Two years later, Pippin hosted high-ranking imperial officials at his court, signing a formal treatise of friendship with the emperor and receiving the latter's formal recognition in return, most audibly in the form of an imperial organ. While it is compelling to view Constantinople and Rome as two diametrically opposed centres, from an eighth-century Frankish perspective, Old and New Rome inhabited the same Mediterranean world, though Pippin's crossing of the Alps greatly stimulated the decline of imperial hegemony in Italy.[79] Through skilful diplomacy, Pippin had been able to acquire potent symbols of both the emperor's and the pope's formal recognition of Carolingian kingship. That he was able to obtain their recognition was because of his unique ability to keep the Lombards in check. The threat of Lombard hostility – real, imagined or fabricated – continued to permeate the papal letters sent to Pippin's court, but after 756 it no longer incited a Frankish military response. Constantinople also realised that Pippin held the key to maintaining order on the Italian peninsula and diverted the full force of its diplomatic potential to persuade Pippin to protect Byzantine interests in Venice, Calabria and Sicily. By allowing Desiderius to remain a threat to both papal and Byzantine interests in the region, Pippin was able to exploit his relationship with Rome and Constantinople. Had Pippin ended the Lombard threat once and for all in compliance with papal

---

[79] Herrin, 'Constantinople', p. 98.

demands, his leverage over pope and emperor would be gone. This precarious balance must have shifted around the time of Pippin's death: in 774, Charlemagne's armies annexed the Lombard kingdom and replaced Pippin's carefully maintained balance of power with direct Frankish control. What had triggered this change in policy – a dispute over religious doctrine or perhaps a shift in the political balance in Francia due to Pippin's death – will remain unclear. What does seem clear, however, is that before the Franks became difficult neighbours, they had already been questionable friends.

Acknowledgements

I am grateful to Mayke de Jong, Janneke Raaijmakers and Dorine van Espelo for having commented on an earlier version of this paper.

Index

A Coruña, city, 328
Abba Glossary, 269
Abbāsid Caliphate, 204, 209, 211, 214
Abd al-Ḥamīd, scholar, 323
Abd Allāh, emir, 322, 325
Abd al-Malik, caliph, 284, 303, 304
Abd al-Raḥmān al-Ghāfiqī, governor of Andalusia, 318, 320, 322
Abd al-Raḥman, emir, 321
Abelard, Peter, 229
Abu Mina, Egypt, 282
Acacian schism, 168, 175
Acta Sancti Silvestri, 183
Ado, bishop of Lyon, 186
Adomnán of Iona, 232, 233, 238, 291, 292, 293, 294, 316
  De locis sanctis, 232, 233, 291, 292, 293, 294
Adon, bishop of Bourges, 262
Adriatic, sea, 342
Adula, 208
Aenigmata Bernensia, 277
Africa, 3, 21, 22, 22n51, 23, 32, 33n5, 37, 42, 69, 75, 78, 80, 212, 224, 258n65, 281, 285, 287, 321, 322, 323
Agathias, Byzantine historian, 56, 57, 58, 62, 101, 117
Agatho, Pope, 147, 174, 248, 249, 257, 259, 260, 261
Agilbert, bishop of Paris, 250, 251
Agnes, abbess, 173, 190
Agnus Dei, 178
Aist, Rodney, 234
Aistulf, Lombard king, 333, 335, 336, 338, 339, 340
Alamanni, 11, 34, 114, 116
al-Andalus, 318, 319, 319n11, 320n13, 320n15, 321, 321n22, 322, 322n26, 323, 324, 324n38, 325, 325n47, 326, 326n52, 327, 328n67, 328n68, 328n69
Alans, 34

Al-Aqsa, mosque, 294
al-Bakrī, geographer, 319, 327, 328
  Book of roads and kingdoms, 326
Alcuin of York, 185, 220
Alemannia, 287
Alexander Romance, 289
Alexander the Great, 58, 289
Alexander, Pope, 171
Alexandria, city, 183, 214, 281, 287
al-Ğahšiyāri, 214
Alps, 14, 31, 97, 98, 107, 167, 286, 287, 330, 331, 337, 345
al-Rashīd, 211
al-Samh, governor of al-Andalus, 318
al-Ṭabarī, historian, 211, 326
al-Walīd I, caliph, 323, 324, 325
Amalafrida, Ostrogothic princess, 37
Amalasuntha, Ostrogothic queen, 38, 43, 44
Amalfrid, Thuringian prince, 41
Amals, 33, 39
Amandus, missionary and bishop, 6, 138, 139, 160, 161, 163, 249, 250, 275
Ambrose, bishop of Milan, 180, 183, 193, 224, 266
Amida, city, 214
Amingus, *dux*, 116, 119
Anastasius, emperor, 72
Anastasius, papal legate, 135
Anastasius, Pope, 175
Anastasius, saint, 254
Anglo-Saxons, viii, 6, 9, 10n7, 17, 20fl.4, 116, 221n17, 223, 228n72, 232n3, 251, 251n27, 251n31, 252, 256, 259, 261, 276n85, 282, 283, 283n12, 295n80, 296, 303, 314, 315
Anicia Juliana, 308
Annales regni Francorum, 332, 338, 342, 343, 343n75. *See* Royal Frankish Annals
Ansoald, bishop of Poitiers, 220
Anstrudis, abbess, 261, 262n87, 263

347

Anthony, Sean, 204
Antony, monk, 205
Apocryphal Collection of Pseudo-Abdias, 225
Apollinaris, bishop of Valence, 40
Apophthegmata patrum, 225
Aquitaine, 28, 249, 285, 286, 287, 288, 295
Arab
 conquest, 2, 3, 88, 237, 238, 243, 249, 250, 255, 276, 281, 282, 283, 286, 287, 295, 321, 323, 325, 328
 language, 213, 214, 299, 319, 327, 328
 people, 3
 sources, 6, 202, 204, 210, 213, 239, 299, 309, 312, 319, 320, 321, 324, 326, 327
 traditions, 209, 328
 in the West, 287, 295, 296, 318, 319, 320, 321, 327, 328
 world, 3, 214, 239, 243, 244
Arculf, bishop, 232, 233, 238, 282, 291, 292, 293, 294, 295
Areagni, Burgundian queen, 38, 40
Arianism, 39, 41, 47
Aristotle, 224
Arles, city, 129, 131, 133, 137, 250
Armenian Guide, 237
Arnulfings, 292
Arrhenius, Birgit, 14
Asia Minor, viii, 16, 17, 107, 186
Assyrians, 286
Asturias, 329
Athalaric, Ostrogothic king, 51
Atlantic, ocean, 328
Audoin, bishop of Rouen, 143, 146, 150, 151, 152, 157, 158, 162
Augustine, bishop of Hippo, 220, 222, 228, 265, 278, 300, 301
 Enchiridion, 224
 Ennarationes in Psalmos, 224, 228
 Sermones de Symbolo, 180
Aunemund, bishop of Lyons, 252
Aurelian, bishop of Arles, 135
Austrasia, viii, 4, 17, 20fl.4, 22, 28, 52, 55, 59, 61, 116, 119, 125, 147, 250, 258, 260, 261, 262, 263, 264, 291
Austrasian Letters, 55, 61, 80, 118n35, 119, 291, 296
Autharius, Lombard *dux*, 114
Autun, city, 146, 184, 185, 186, 273, 274, 284, 318
Auxerre, city, 165
Avars, 141, 145, 146, 256
Avignon, city, 323
Avitus, bishop of Vienne, 34, 35, 40, 42, 47

Babai the Great, Syrian author, 205
Bacchus, saint, 71
Balkans, 336
Balthild, Merovingian queen, 11, 253, 253n42
Basil, bishop of Caesarea, 220, 224
Basques, 322
Baudonivia, nun, 190, 191, 192, 193, 194, 200
Bavaria, viii, 12, 13fl.1, 230, 233, 238, 241, 244, 289
Bavarians, 11, 334n25, 344
Bayer, Clemens, 143, 151, 152
Bede the Venerable, 29, 159, 169, 220, 251, 252, 254, 291, 292, 316
Belisarius, Byzantine general, 32, 56, 129, 130, 131, 133, 170, 175
Benedict III, Pope, 174
Benevento, Duchy, 112, 340
Bernard Gui, inquisitor, 145
Berschin, Walter, 152
Berthoara, abbess of Bourges, 270
Béziers, city, 327
Biqā valley, Lebanon, 87, 88, 95, 96, 101
Bischoff, Bernhard, 178, 275
Blidram, bishop of Vienne, 262
Bobbio Missal, 226
Bobbio, monastery, 289, 308
Bodegisel, *dux*, 53
Bohemia, 22
Böhme, Horst Wolfgang, 14
Bongars, Jacques, 267
Boniface I, Pope, 174, 176
Boniface II, Pope, 170
Boniface IV, Pope, 174
Boniface, missionary, 282, 332, 345
Book of Kings, 215
Bordeaux Pilgrim, 293
Bourges, city, 267, 275, 276, 284, 285
Brandes, Wolfram, 337
Breviary of Alaric, 266
Britain, 225, 250, 252, 257, 259, 264, 283, 285, 291, 292
Brock, Sebastian, 290
Brown, Michelle, 302
Brown, Peter, 183, 281
Brown, Warren, 179
Brunhild, Merovingian queen, 52, 59, 272, 279
Bruttium, region in Italy, 175
Bulgarians, 72, 255
Burgundian
 diplomacy, 34, 41, 42, 44, 116, 120
 Frankish conquest, 32, 35, 36, 43
 Gibichung kingdom, 5, 32, 34, 35, 36, 37, 39, 41, 43, 47, 49

Merovingian kingdom, 4, 44, 251, 253, 258, 262, 263, 288
 sources, 185
Burgundy, region, 267
Byzacena, 37
Byzantine
 Africa, 80
 archaeology, 12, 13, 14, 16, 17, 18, 29, 78, 87, 89, 90, 99, 103, 109, 121
 army, 32, 56, 69, 71, 75, 76, 80, 82, 99, 104, 114, 115, 117, 170, 340
 Church, 75, 84, 86, 103, 140, 146, 210, 291, 295, 343
 culture, 57, 69
 diplomacy, 37, 41, 42, 43, 58, 60, 62, 115, 118, 119, 123, 251, 252, 255, 295, 330, 335, 336, 340, 341, 342, 343
 emperors, 6, 33, 48, 55, 59, 60, 61, 62, 108, 122, 126, 149, 161, 164, 175, 190, 275, 329, 339, 341
 Empire, 5, 16, 56, 58, 59, 60, 61, 68, 69, 70, 71, 82, 95, 98, 101, 105, 107, 144, 152, 189, 264
 influence, 70
 Italy, 112, 329, 330
 people, 40, 57, 62
 politics, 75, 77, 78, 80, 81, 82, 83, 84, 109, 111, 114, 115, 125, 146, 329, 335, 337, 338, 345
 sources, 106, 107, 110, 111, 113, 117, 202, 205, 209, 210, 211, 213, 214, 225, 272, 284, 290, 294, 298, 313
 trade, 11, 19, 24, 28
 traditions, 76, 146, 152, 243
 tributes, 111, 114, 115, 116, 117, 118, 123, 124, 125, 126

Cádiz, city, 328
Caesarea, city, 96
Caesarius, bishop of Arles, 129, 132, 220, 224, 290
 Sermones, 228
Calabria, region in Italy, 175, 337, 345
Callistus, Pope, 171
Cambridge, 200
Cameron, Averil, 57, 70, 290
Canones Gregorii, 181
Canterbury, 250, 284, 295
Carcassonne, city, 318, 327
Carloman, king, 185, 333, 334, 341, 343, 344
Caspian Gates, 281
Cassian, 224, 265
 Collationes, 266
Cassiodorus, statesman and scholar, 33, 43, 48, 51, 220, 267

Cassiodorus-Epiphanius
 Historia ecclesiastica tripartita, 183
castaldi, 256
Chagan, Avar ruler, 256
Chalcedonian Christianity, 62, 158, 180, 214
Chamingus. *See* Amingus, *dux*
Chapel of the Cross, 192, 199
Charibert I, Merovingian king, 53, 59
Charlemagne, 144, 148, 182, 185, 234, 247, 275, 287, 306, 329, 331, 335, 339, 341, 343, 344, 346
Charles Martel, Pippinid ruler, 4, 275, 287, 318, 334, 335, 344
Chelles Sacramentary, 314
Childebert I, Merovingian king, 32, 41, 55
Childebert II, Merovingian king, 6, 55, 61
Childeric I, Merovingian king, 14, 15, 47
Childeric II, Merovingian king, 254, 262
Chilperic I, Merovingian king, 55, 60
Chilperic, Burgundian leader, 33
Chiltrud, princess, 344
Chindasvinth, Visigothic king, 260
Chlodomer, Merovingian king, 35, 40, 42
Chlothar I, Merovingian king, 32, 41, 52, 55, 189
Chlothar II, Merovingian king, 4
Chlothar III, Merovingian king, 29
Chlothild, nun, 190
Chosroe II, Persian ruler, 254
Chramlin, bishop of Embrun, 262
Chramnichis, *dux*, 117
Chrodebert, bishop of Tours, 149, 150
Chrodinus, *dux*, 53
Chronica muzarabica, 319, 319n6, 322, 323, 323n34, 324
Chronica pseudo-isidoriana,, 327
Chronicle of 754. *See Chronica muzarabica*
Chronicle of Fredegar. *See* Fredegar, chronicle
Church of the Ascension, 235, 238, 239, 240n30
Church of the Patriarchate, Alexandria, 204
Cicero, 224
Cilicia, 285, 286, 286n29
Cleph, Lombard king, 112
Clermont, city, 43, 124
Clothild, Frankish queen, 36, 37, 40
Clovis I, Merovingian king, 3, 33, 34, 35, 46, 47, 48, 49, 50, 54
Clovis II, Merovingian king, 4, 12, 143, 145, 153, 157, 161, 250, 275
Codex Carolinus,, 331, 335
Collectio Flaviniacenis, 179
Collectio Herovalliana, 181, 182, 182n40, 184

350   Index

Collectio Sancti Mauri, 275
Collectio Vetus Gallica, 182, 184, 226, 247, 280
Cologne, city, 165
Columbanian monasticism, 251, 285
Column of the flagellation, 235
Commemoratio, 156
Commemoratorium de casis Dei, 234
Conon, Pope, 166, 169, 177, 178
Cononian epitome. See Cononian recension
Cononian recension, 166, 167, 169, 170, 171, 177, 179, 180, 183, 184, 186
Constans II, emperor, 17, 141, 143, 146, 153, 157, 158, 159, 160, 175, 249, 250, 251, 253, 264, 281, 283, 287, 295
Constantine I, emperor, 183, 197, 199
Constantine II, Pope, 166, 186
Constantine III, emperor, 287
Constantine IV, emperor, 248, 255, 256, 257, 258n65, 259, 260, 260n77, 264, 282, 295
Constantine V, emperor, 331, 335, 338, 340
Constantius I, emperor, 174, 197
Coptic, 9, 17, 106, 202, 204, 205, 213, 225, 294, 313
Corbie, abbey, 29, 266, 311
Cordoba, city, 328
Cosmas Indicopleustes
  Christian Topography, 289
Cosmographia of Aethicus Ister, 288, 289, 294, 296
Councils
  Attigny 760/2, 185
  Bourges 453, 275
  Carthage 418, 182
  Chalcedon 451, 131, 132, 133, 134, 181
  Chalon 647/53, 146, 250, 275
  Constantinople 381, 133, 247
  Constantinople 553, 136
  Constantinople 680, 155, 248, 254, 255, 256, 257, 260, 261, 264, 282, 291
  Épaone 517, 35, 40
  Ephesus 431, 133
  Frankfurt 794, 343
  Gentilly 767, 341, 342, 343
  Hatfield 680, 258
  in Trullo 692, 175, 178, 283, 295
  Lateran 649, 6, 139, 140, 141, 142, 143, 146, 148, 157, 158, 160, 161, 162, 168, 175, 179, 180, 248, 249, 250, 252, 264, 283
  Mâlay-le-Roi 679, 262
  Nicaea 325, 133, 247
  Nicaea 787, 248, 342

Orléans 549, 134, 135, 146
Rome 769, 166, 185, 186
Toledo 580, 78
Toledo 589, 84, 85
Crimea, 155, 163
Cherson, 146, 155
Crusades, 326
Ctesiphon, city, 214, 254
Cumae, ancient city in Campania, Italy, 117
Cyprian of Carthage, 224
Cyrus, patriarch of Alexandria, 162

Dagobert I, Merovingian king, 4, 29, 140, 143, 144, 145, 146, 148, 251, 254
Dagobert II, Merovingian king, 255n51, 258, 260, 261, 261n84, 263, 293, 295
Dailey, Erin T., 38
Dal Santo, Matthew, 206
Damascus, city, 87, 243, 291, 293, 320, 323, 324
Damasus I, Pope, 171, 174
Daniel, Pierre, 268
Danube, river, 15, 96, 98, 145, 146
Datius, bishop of Milan, 135
De libris recipiendis et non recipiendis, 182, 226
Declercq, Georges, 145
Defensor of Ligugé, 220, 221, 222, 223, 224, 225, 226, 227, 228, 229, 272, 290, 291
Deodatus, bishop of Toul, 258, 259, 261, 262
Déroche, François, 303, 304, 307, 308, 311, 312
Desiderius, bishop of Cahors, 275
Desiderius, Lombard king, 340, 345
Dierkens, Alain, 141
Dietz, Maribel, 244
Dionysius Exiguus
  Argumenta paschalia, 277
Dionysius, Pope, 176
Dioscorus, antipope, 176
Dome of the Rock, Jerusalem, 283, 295, 304, 308, 315, 316
Donatus, grammarian, 267, 270
do-nothing kings. See rois fainéants
Drôme, river, 41
Duchesne, Louis, 166, 169, 274
Durance, river, 41

East Anglia, 251
Ebroin, maior domus, 29, 213, 250, 251, 252, 254, 258, 260, 261, 262, 263, 264, 295
Echternach, city, 223

Index 351

Ecthesis. See *Ekthesis*
Effros, Bonnie, 3
Egbert, king of Kent, 251
Egeria, nun, 196
Egypt, 9, 17, 23, 72, 98n41, 204, 208, 275, 281, 282, 286, 287, 319, 320, 321, 325
Eichstätt, Bavaria, 230, 232, 242
Einhard, scholar, 334
  Life of Charlemagne, 329
Ekthesis, 159, 249, 283
Eligius, bishop of Noyon, 143, 146, 150, 153, 154, 155, 157, 161, 163, 224, 250
Emmo, bishop of Sens, 251
Ephrem the Syrian, scholar, 224
Epiphanius Hagiopolita, author, 238
Epiphanius, monk, 294
Epistolae Austrasicae. See *Austrasian Letters*
Epitoma Aegidii, 275
Erasmus of Rotterdam, 229
Ervig, Visigothic king, 260
Esders, Stefan, 144, 275
Eudo, governor of Aquitaine, 318
Eugippius, hagiographer, 222, 267
Eulalius, bishop, 174
Eusebius Gallicanus, 224
Eusebius, bishop of Caesarea, 68, 103, 173, 183, 205, 266
Eusebius-Rufinus
  Historia ecclesiastica, 183
Eutyches, presbyter, 132, 134, 141, 171, 174
Evagrius Ponticus, theologian, 224
Evagrius Scholasticus, historian, 97, 290
Evangelist, 298, 299

Faro, bishop of Meaux, 251
Faronids, 251
Faustus, bishop of Riez, 224
Feissel, Denis, 102
Felician epitome, 169, 170, 175
Felix III, Pope, 175
Felix IV, Pope, 171
Felix V, Pope, 175
Felix, bishop of Arles, 258, 263
Flavigny Formulary, 183
Flavigny, abbey, 165, 166, 178, 179, 182, 184, 185, 186, 299
Florus of Lyons, author, 86
Fontanelle. See St Wandrille, abbey
Formularies of Marculf. See *Marculf, formulary*
Formulary, Tours, 182
Fos-sur-Mer, city, 30
Fourlas, Benjamin, 291

Framarich, 89, 94, 95, 96, 101, 104, 107
Fredegar, chronicle, 144, 145, 149, 152, 253, 254, 281, 282, 283, 287, 288, 289, 291, 294, 295, 296, 332
  continuations, 254, 275, 281, 332, 336, 337, 338, 339, 343
Frisia, 261, 264
Fritze, Wolfgang, 144
Fulda, city
  St Michael's church, 200
Fulgentius, bishop of Ruspe, 224

Galen, physician, 213
  Letters on fevers, 278
Galicia, 329
Galilee, 238
Galla Placidia, empress, 43n57, 199, 199n37
Ganz, David, 284, 290
Gelasian Sacramentary, 313
Gelasius, Pope, 172, 175, 182
Gelimer, Vandal king, 32
Gellone Sacramentary, 297
Genesius, bishop of Lyons, 262
Geneva, city, 38
Gennadius of Marseilles
  De ecclesiasticis dogmatibus, 180
  De viris illustribus, 226, 266
Gentilly, villa, 342
George of Izla, Syrian author, 205
George, Alain, 308
Geretrude, abbess, 208
Gesta de Xysti, 199
Gethsemane, 235
Ghaylān al-Dimashqī, martyr, 204
Gibich, Burgundian king, 33
Gibichungs, 32, 33, 34, 35, 43, 44, 47, 48, 49
Gisclahad, Burgundian prince, 36
Gisela, Carolingian princess, 340, 342, 343, 344
Godesscalc Evangelistary, 306
Godomar, Burgundian king, 32, 35, 36, 39, 40, 42, 43, 44
Golgotha, 191, 196, 198, 199, 200, 201
Gothic Missal, 226
Gothic wars, 168
Grammar of Asper, 268, 273, 284
Grammar of Asporius. See *Grammar of Asper*
Great Mosque, Kairouan, 306, 307
Great Mosque, Sana'a, 308
Greeks, 95, 149, 248, 328, 340, 342, 343
Gregory I, Pope. See Gregory the Great, Pope
Gregory II, Pope, 158, 169

Gregory III, Pope, 235, 334
Gregory of Nyssa, Byzantine bishop, 209
Gregory the Great, Pope, 74, 75, 77, 78, 85, 86, 114, 115, 122, 137, 172, 174, 181, 206, 224, 270
Dialogues, 86, 224, 273, 279
Letters, 279
Letters, 224
Morals, 84, 224, 266, 278, 279
Pastoral Rule, 224, 266, 272, 277, 278
Gregory, bishop of Tours, 35, 37, 42, 43, 51, 52, 53, 54, 55, 57, 58, 59, 60, 61, 62, 67, 68, 69, 72, 73, 74, 86, 108, 110, 111, 116, 119, 123, 126, 170, 190, 194, 200, 281, 285, 291
Historiae, 35, 36, 38, 39, 40, 53, 54, 55, 59, 60, 67, 79, 169, 266, 267, 281, 285, 288, 290, 296
Lives of the Fathers, 224, 274
Seven Sleepers of Ephesos, 225, 290
Gregory, Byzantine patrician, 287
Gundechar, bishop of Eichstätt, 241
Gundioc, Burgundian leader, 33
Gundobad, Burgundian king, 5, 33, 34, 35, 36, 38, 39, 40
Gundohinus, illuminator, 298, 299, 301
Guntram, Merovingian king, 55

Hadrian I, Pope, 166, 170, 178
Hadrian, monk, 29, 251, 254, 283, 295
Hagia Sophia, Constantinople, 71, 326
Haller, Johannes, 331, 332
Hartog, François, 240
Hārūn al-Rashīd, calif, 212, 320, 329
Hasdings, 33
Heather, Peter, 37
Hegessipus, historian, 224
Heidenheim, monastery, 232, 234
Helena, mother of Constantine I, 173, 183, 191, 192, 193, 194, 197, 199, 200
Heraclius, emperor, 18, 71, 120, 140, 144, 145, 157, 158, 159, 160, 161, 249, 253, 254, 255, 268, 272, 281, 287, 295
Hercules, God, 328
Hermenegild, Visigothic prince, v, 74, 74n1, 75, 75n6, 76, 76n7, 77, 78, 79, 79n27, 79n30, 80, 81, 81n40, 81n41, 82, 82n43, 83, 84, 85, 85n53, 86, 109n3
Herren, Michael, 288
Herrin, Judith, 338
Hesiod, 224
Hilary, bishop of Poitiers, 175, 180, 224
Hilderic, Vandal king, 37

Hishām I, emir of Córdoba, 318
Historia Augusta, 168
Hodges, Richard, 2
Holy Sepulchre, Jerusalem, 104, 196, 199, 200, 235, 240
Holy Spirit, 180, 268
Holy Zion, 235
Homilies on Ezekiel, 224
Honoria, princess, 199
Hormisdas, Pope, 132, 175
Huneric, Vandal king, 212
Huns, 16, 175
Hygeburg, nun, 232, 232n3, 233, 234, 234n15, 235, 237, 238, 240, 241, 242, 244, 282
Hodoeporicon, 282, 289, 296
Hygelac, Danish king, 41
Hypomnesticum, 156

Ibas, bishop of Edessa, 131
Ibn 'Abd al-Ḥakam, historian, 319, 320, 320n12, 320n16, 321, 321n20, 321n21, 321n24, 322, 323, 323n34, 324, 324n37, 324n42, 325, 325n44
Book of History, 321
Conquest of Egypt, 319, 321, 322
Ibn 'Idhārī, historian, 320, 323, 323n29, 328n69
Ibn al-Athīr, historian, 318, 320, 320n17, 326n51, 328n69
Ibn Ḥabīb, scholar, 319, 321, 321n23, 321n25, 322, 322n27, 323, 323n30, 323n32, 323n33, 323n34, 323n35, 325, 326
Ibn Ḥawqal, historian, 326, 328n67
Ibn Isḥāq, historian, 320
Ibn Layth, historian, 320
India, 22, 23
Inventio sanctae Crucis, 192
Iona, island, 232, 292, 293, 295
Ireland, 224
Irish, 213, 232, 261, 261n84, 273, 279, 285, 288, 293, 295, 296, 297n2, 302n20, 329
Isaac of Nineveh, 209
Ishmael, vii, 272, 285, 286, 318, 328
Ishmaelites, 285
Isidore of Seville, 74, 82, 85, 181, 219, 220, 224, 265, 266, 267, 268, 269, 270, 273, 274, 275
De differentiis rerum, 224
De ecclesiasticis officiis, 224, 279
Etymologiae, 181, 183, 268, 271, 272, 276, 277, 278
Sententiae, 224, 278
Synonymae, 224

Ismā'īl b. Ṣubayḥ, 211
Iudicia Theodori, 181

Jacob of Sarug, 210
Jacobsen, Werner, 194
James, apostle, 173
Jeremiah, prophet, 209
Jerome, 171, 205, 222, 224, 226, 238, 265, 266, 267, 270, 272, 273, 277, 278, 280, 288
   Contra Vigilantium, 277
   Epistolae, 266
   Liber quaestionum Hebraicarum in Genesin, 178
Jerome, pseudo
   Expositio IV evangeliorum, 178
Jesus Christ, 219, 230, 235, 236, 237, 238, 239, 242
Jews, 83, 144, 182, 236, 237, 239, 243, 285, 295
John I, Pope, 175
John IV, Pope, 174
John of Antioch, 290
John of Biclaro, Visigothic bishop, 55, 74, 79, 83, 85, 110, 126
John of Constantinople, abbot, 180
John of Ephesus
   Lives of the Eastern Saints, 214
John of Ravenna, Exarch, 176
John the Almsgiver, Life of, 281
John the Almsgiver, patriarch of Alexandria, 281
John the Baptist, 173
John V, Pope, 176
John VI, Pope, 177
John XVII, Pope, 178
John, Pope of Arles, 250
Judas, 193
Julian, count, 319
Julianus Pomerius, 224
   de Vita contemplativa, 278
Julius, Pope, 183
Justin II, emperor, 18, 59, 60, 190, 290
Justinian I, emperor, 18, 32, 38, 44, 70, 96, 97, 129, 130, 131, 132, 134, 136, 137, 168, 191
Justinian II, emperor, 175

Ka'b al-Akhbar, convert, 239
Kairouran, Musée des arts islamiques, R 38, 306n32
Karilos, 89, 90, 91, 93, 94, 95, 96, 101, 104, 107
Keefe, Susan, 180
Kent, 251
Khalek, Nancy, 214

Khalili collection, 312
Krautheimer, Richard, 200, 201
Kurth, Godefroid, 1

Landibert, bishop of Maastricht, 207
Landobert, bishop of Sens, 262
Langton, Stephen, 229
Laon, city, 139, 140, 148, 165
Laurence, saint, 173
Laurentian schism, 168
Laurentius, antipope, 175
Law, Vivien, 273
Lectionary of Luxeuil, 226
Leo I, Pope, 134, 136, 174, 180, 275
Leo II, Pope, 174, 260
Leo III, Pope, 170, 178
Leo IV, emperor, 340, 342, 343, 344
Leo the Deacon, 71
Leo VII, Pope, 230
Leudegar, bishop of Autun, 213, 262
Leuthari, *dux*, 116
Lex Ribuaria, 275
Lex Romana Visigothorum, 275
Lex Salica, 275
Liber Historiae Francorum, 68n4, 289
Liber Monstrorum, 284
Liber Pontificalis, 155, 159, 161, 165, 166, 167, 168, 169, 170, 171, 172, 173, 174, 175, 176, 177, 178, 180, 186, 199, 331
   Epitome, 179
   Life of Agapetus, 175
   Life of Agatho, 175, 178
   Life of Alexander, 176
   Life of Benedict, 174
   Life of Boniface III, 174
   Life of Boniface V, 174
   Life of Celestine, 177
   Life of Conon, 175
   Life of Constantine I, 177
   Life of Deusdedit, 174
   Life of Eleutherius, 176
   Life of Eusebius, 176
   Life of Felix II, 173
   Life of Felix IV, 169, 170
   Life of Gregory I, 173
   Life of Hilarus, 173
   Life of Honorius, 174
   Life of Hormisdas, 175
   Life of Innocent I, 176
   Life of John I, 175
   Life of John II, 175
   Life of John III, 173, 175
   Life of Leo II, 175
   Life of Liberius, 174
   Life of Mark, 173

Liber Pontificalis (cont.)
  Life of Paul I, 339
  Life of Pope Constantine, 168
  Life of Pope Martin, 156, 159, 160, 162
  Life of Pope Stephen II, 335
  Life of Sextus I, 176
  Life of Siricius, 173
  Life of Sixtus III, 173
  Life of Stephen II, 330, 337
  Life of Symmachus, 175
  Life of Vigilius, 167, 175
  Life of Ygenus, 177
Liber scintillarum, vi, 218, 219, 220, 221, 222, 223, 225, 226, 227, 228, 229
Libri Carolini, 248, 248n6
Life of Amandus, 140, 142, 144, 160
Life of Eligius of Noyon, 143, 145, 146, 149, 150, 151, 152, 154, 155, 158, 160, 161, 162, 163
Life of Geretrude of Nivelles, 147, 207
Life of Lambert, 151
Life of Remigius of Rheims, 151
Life of Sulpicius of Bourges, 274
Life of Wilfrid of York, 261
Ligugé, abbey, 220, 223
Limor, Ora, 293
Lintzel, Martin, 332
Loire, 285
Loire, river, 285
Lombard, Maurice, 2
Lowe, Elias Avery, 302
Lucania, region in Italy, 175
Lucius I, Pope, 176
Lupus, *dux*, 53
Luxeuil, monastery, 285
Lyon, city, 33, 42, 181, 184, 185, 222, 252, 265, 273, 284

Maas, Michael, 57
Maastricht, city, 140, 141, 142, 143, 145, 148, 250
Mabillon, Jean, 220, 228
MacCoull, Leslie, 223
Maghreb, 319, 321, 326
Maguelonne, city, 327
Mainz
  Römisch-Germanisches Zentralmuseum, 99
maior domus, 4, 6, 147. *See also* Ebroin
Makkī, scholar, 320
Malchus, monk, 205
Manasses, abbot of Flavigny, 185
Manicheans, 141
Mansuetus, bishop of Milan, 259
manuscripts
  Autun BM 107, 265n7

Autun BM 20, 269n53
Autun BM 24, 265n8
Autun BM 27 S 29, 265n6
Autun BM 3, 267n42, 298n5
Berlin SB Phillipps 1743, 269, 275
Berlin SB Phillipps 1790, 278n96
Bern Burgerbibl A 91 (8), 266n12
Bern Burgerbibl. 611, 265n1, 267, 267n43, 268, 273, 274, 275, 276n88, 277, 277n90, 278n101, 278n102, 278n96, 278n99, 279n105, 284
Boston, Harvard University Library Typ 592, 266n17
Brussels BR 5374–5, 151n18, 157n47
Brussels BR 9850–2, 267n40
Copenhagen, Museum of Fine and Applied Art, David Collection 26/2003, 306n32
Dublin Chester Beatty Library Is 1404, 311n43
Epinal BM 149 (68), 267n35
Fulda Landesbibl. Boniface 2, 266n14
Geneva Bibl. publique et universitaire I 16, 265n9
Istanbul TIEM SE 63, 312n44
Ivrea BC 1, 266n18
Ivrea BC XLII s.IX1/4, 182n40
Leiden Universiteitsbibl. BPL 114, 273n67, 275
Leiden Universiteitsbibl. Scaliger MS 49, 169n15
Leiden Universiteitsbibl. Voss Lat. Qu. 63, 267n38
London BL Add 11878, 266n17
London BL Add 29972, 266n20
London BL Add 41567, 266n17
London BL Burney, 266n30
London BL Egerton, 267n36
London BL Harley 5041, 222n27
London BL Or. 11737, 312n49
London BL Or. 2165, 312n45
Lyon BM 426 (352), 265n5
Lyon BM 468 (397), 265n2
Lyon BM 600, 265n4
Lyon BM 602, 265n3
Lyon BM 604 (521), 265n5
Metz BM Salis 140, 266n20
Munich BSB Clm 29033, 266n16
Munich BSB Clm 6430, 184
Naples Biblioteca Nazionale IV.A.8, 165n2, 169n14
New York Morgan Library M 17, 266n20, 312n44
New York Morgan Library M 334, 265n10, 301n17, 312n47
Orléans BM 19, 266n32

Index 355

Orléans BM 192, 266n32
Oxford Bodleian Library Lat
  Misc. a 3, 266n15
Paris BnF Arabe 328a, 311n42, 312n45
Paris BnF Lat 10756, 267, 277, 284
Paris BnF Lat 11218, 278n96
Paris BnF Lat 11641, 265n9
Paris BnF Lat 1203, 307n33
Paris BnF Lat 12161, 266n27
Paris BnF Lat 13028, 266n29
Paris BnF Lat 13348, 266n26
Paris BnF Lat 13349, 266n26
Paris BnF Lat 1451, 170
Paris BnF Lat 1629, 265n5
Paris BnF Lat 17655, 266n22, 266n23
Paris BnF Lat 2034, 275
Paris BnF Lat 2123, 166, 171, 177, 178, 179, 181, 182, 184, 186
Paris BnF Lat 4403A, 266n31
Paris BnF Lat 4629, 273n67, 275
Paris BnF Lat 5287, 154
Paris BnF Lat 6113, 327n60
Paris BnF Lat 8901, 267n41
Paris BnF Lat 9377, 266n12
Paris BnF nouv. acq. 1063, 266n23
Paris BnF nouv. acq. 1575, 267n33
Paris BnF nouv. acq. 1594, 265n5
Paris BnF nouv. acq. 1629, 265n7, 265n8
Paris BnF nouv. acq. 2243, 266n17
Paris BnF nouv. acq. 2388, 266n17
Paris BnF nouv. acq. 602, 265n2
St Gallen Stiftsbibliothek 125, 273
St Gallen Stiftsbibliothek 214, 265n53
St Gallen Stiftsbibliothek 759, 278n96
St Paul in Carinthia, Stiftsbibl. 3, 266n13
St Petersburg Publ. Lib. F.v.1.1, 265n9
St Petersburg Publ. Lib. F.v.1.2, 266n25
St Petersburg Publ. Lib. F.v.1.4, 266n30
St Petersburg Publ. Lib. O.v.1.4, 266n28
St Petersburg Publ. Lib. Q.v.1.13, 266n24
St Petersburg Publ. Lib. Q.v.1.14, 266n21
Strasbourg AbR 151 J 108, 266n15
The Hague Museum Meermanno-Westreeanum MS 10.A.1, 267n39
The Hague Museum Meermanno-Westreeanum MS 10.B.4, 170
Toulouse BM 364, 267n41
Turin Biblioteca Nazionale D.V.3, 216
Turin Biblioteca Nazionale F.IV.18, 165n2
Valenciennes BM 495 (455), 266n19
Verona Biblioteca Capitolare LII, 166
Verona Biblioteca Capitolare LII (50), 179
Verona Biblioteca Capitolare XL 38, 266n17
Verona Biblioteca Capitolare XXII (20), 165n2
Wolfenbuttel, HAB Weissenburg 8, 267n37
Würzburg UB M P Th. F 64 a, 265n11
Yale Beinecke Library (frag.), 266n20
Marcellinus, Pope, 171, 173
Marcellus, Pope, 171
Marculf, formulary, 182, 275
Mardaites, tribe, 255
Marinus, priest, 340
Maris, bishop of Hardashir, 131
Marius of Avenches, historian, 32, 42, 44
Marseille, city, 16, 29, 120, 121, 122, 337
Martin I, Pope, 6, 139–42, 143, 145, 146, 147, 148, 153, 154, 155, 156, 157, 158, 159, 160, 161, 162, 163, 164, 175, 249, 283, 291, 295
Martin, bishop of Braga, 224, 275
Martin, bishop of Tours, 194
Martin, *dux*, 263
Martyrdom of Narsai, 214, 215
Martyrium, basilica in Jerusalem, 196, 198, 200, 201
Martyrologium Hieronymianum, 191
Maslama ibn Abd al-Malik, Muslim general, 326
Masona, bishop of Mérida, 83
Mathisen, Ralph, 69
Maubeuge, abbey, 147
Mauias, ruler, 292
Maurice, *cartularius*, 175
Maurice, emperor, 61, 70, 80, 97, 99, 108, 110, 116, 120, 121, 126
Maxim, bishop of Turin, 224
Maximus the Confessor, theologian, 142
mayor of the palace. *See maior domus*
McCormick, Michael, 2, 243, 244, 329, 338
McKitterick, Rosamond, 332
Meaux, city, 251
Mecca, city, 311
Medina, city, 311, 323
Megalous, 89, 91
Mena, Apa, 204
Menander the Guardsman, historian, 113, 118, 125
Menas, martyr, 282
Mériaux, Charles, 160
Mérida, city, 75
Merovingika, 284
Mesopotamia, 23, 96, 205, 214, 216

Migne, Jacques-Paul, 228
Milan, Biblioteca Ambrosiana, cod. D. 23 sup, 309n37
Milan, city, ix, 44, 135, 136, 259
miles, 151
Milo, monk of Saint-Amand, 138, 140
Miltiades, Pope, 171
Milvian Bridge, battle, 105
Missale francorum, 226
Missale gallicanum, 184, 226
Missale gothicum, 184
Moderannus, bishop of Autun, 185
Möhring, Hannes, 287
Monoenergism, 141
Monophysitism, 131, 134, 141, 158
Monotheletism, 6, 143, 146, 148, 158, 159, 161, 162, 163, 168, 248, 249, 250, 252, 259, 261, 264, 283, 295
Monte Cassino, abbey, 220, 232, 333
Moralia in Job, 224
Mordek, Hubert, 181, 182, 273, 275
Mount of Olives, 239, 240, 243
Mount Sinai, 299, 301
Mount Zion, 230
Muawiyah, caliph, 255, 292, 294, 311, 326
Muhammad, prophet, 210, 213, 320, 322, 325
Mummolinus of Soissons, Frankish noble, 123
Mummolus, *patricius*, 67
Mundell Mango, Marlia, 95, 102, 103
Mūsā ibn Nuṣayr, Muslim governor, 322, 323, 324, 325, 326, 328
Muslim. *See* Arab

Nantes, city, 285
Naples, city, 251, 340
Narbonesis, province, 321
Narbonne, city, 318, 321, 323, 327
Narsai, fire temple, 215
Narses, Byzantine general, 175
Navarre, kingdom, 327
Nephisana, city, 174
Nestorianism, 132, 134, 174
Neustria, 4, 28, 29, 79, 125, 142, 143, 146, 161, 226, 260, 261, 262, 263
New Testament, 266, 267
Nicolas I, Pope, 72
Nilus, monk, 224
Nimes, city, 318, 327
Nivelles, abbey, 147
Nordulf, Lombard noble, 114, 115
Noricum, province, 116
Northumbria, 169
Notitia Galliarum, 181
Noyon, city, 154

O'Loughlin, Thomas, 232, 292, 293
Odilo, *dux*, 344
Old Gelasian Sacramentary, 226, 227
Old Testament, 265, 267, 331
Origen, theologian, 224, 265, 266
Orléans, city, 285
Orontes, valley, 87
Orosius, historian, 308
  Seven Books of History Against the Pagans, 327
Ostia, city, 176
Ostrogotho-Areagni. *See* Areagni, Burgundian queen

Pachomius, abbot, 272, 276
Pacificus of Verona, Carolingian scholar, 166
Paderborn, city
  Church of the Holy Sepulchre, 200
Palestine, 17, 23, 28, 197, 199, 243, 249
Palladius, bishop of Helenopolis, 269, 272
  Historia Lausiaca, 276
Palmer, James, 284, 287
Pange Lingua, 190
Pantheon, Athens, 174
Paris, BnF Lat. 12190, 300n14
Paris, BnF Lat. 4281, 182n40
Paris, BnF Lat. 4884, 299
Paris, city, ix, 11, 29, 130, 137, 171, 250, 251, 268, 300, 318
Passio sancti Sebastiani, 267
Passion od Cirycus and Iulitta, 212, 213
Passion of Leudegar of Autun, 213, 220
Passion of Praeiectus of Clermont, 253
Paul I, Pope, 335, 339, 340, 341, 344
Paul the Deacon, historian, 108, 111, 112, 113, 114, 116, 117
Paul, Apostle, 137, 172, 173, 174
Paul, hermit, 205
Paul, patriarch of Constantinople, 141, 159, 162, 283
Paulus Alvarus, scholar, 220
Pavia, city, 111, 259, 333, 336, 337, 340
Payne, Richard, 215
Pelagianism, 180
Pelagius I, Pope, 133, 136, 137, 175
Pelagius II, Pope, 109
Pentapolis, duchy, 335
Perctarit, Lombard king, 259, 261
Persia, 286
  Christianity, 131, 247, 254
  culture, 216, 297
  elite, 215
  literature, 215
  military, 70
Parthian Empire, 215

Persian language, 202, 215
Persian wars, 87, 98, 104, 105, 106, 237, 253, 254
politics, 215
Sasanid Empire, 3, 141, 214, 215, 272, 285
Peter, Apostle, 137, 142, 165, 171, 172, 173, 174, 177, 185, 258, 331, 334, 336, 337, 344
Philip II, king of Spain, 75
Philippicus, Byzantine general, 70
Phillipus, author, 267
Phoenicia Libanensis, province, 96, 101
Phokas, emperor, 18
Physiologus, 6, 268, 269, 270, 274, 275, 280
Piacenza Pilgrim, 239, 241
Pippin II, *maior domus*, 263
Pippin III, Carolingian king, 6, 185, 298, 299, 329, 330, 331, 332, 333, 334, 335, 336, 337, 338, 339, 340, 341, 342, 343, 344, 345, 346
Pippinids, 262
Pirenne, Henri, 1–3, 138
  Mahomet et Charlemagne, 1
Pithou, Pierre, 268
Pius I, Pope, 171, 176
Pizarro, Joaquín Martínez, 210
Placidus, *patricius*, 137
Poitiers, city, 59, 124, 189, 190, 191, 192, 193, 194, 199, 200, 201, 220, 226, 320
  battle, 287, 318, 319, 320
  Chapel of the Holy Cross, 200
Polemius Silvius, author, 181
Pollard, Richard, 142, 283, 284, 285, 286, 290
Polyeuktos, martyr, 291
Pompeius, grammarian, 267
Ponthion, royal estate, 332, 336
Porcharius, abbot of Lérins, 224
Praeiectus, bishop of Clermont, 182, 185, 207, 253
Price, Richard, 142
Priscilla, cemetery, 173
Procopius of Caesarea, historian, 32, 37, 56, 57, 96, 131
Prosper of Aquitaine, scholar, 222, 224, 273
Provence, 120, 121, 139, 262, 318
Psalter, 301, 303, 317
  St Catherine, 301
  Utrecht, 339f21.1
  Vespasian, 314, 316
Pseudo-Callisthenes, 289
Pseudo-Clemens, 224

Pseudo-Ephraem, 290, 291, 294
  Adhortatio ad Monachos, 290
  Scarpsum, 290
Pseudo-Macarius, 224
Pseudo-Methodius, 6, 58, 268, 271, 272, 273, 275, 280, 283, 284, 284n14, 284n19, 285, 285n22, 286n26, 288, 289, 290, 291, 299n9
  Petrus, translator, 284, 286, 287, 288, 290, 296
  Revelationes, 283, 284, 285, 286, 287, 288, 289, 290, 295, 296
Pyrenees, 318, 328
Pyrrhus, patriarch of Constantinople, 141, 162

Quentovic, emporium, 250
Qur'an, 300, 303, 306, 307, 308, 310, 311, 312

Radegund, Merovingian queen, 59, 189, 190, 191, 192, 193, 194, 199, 200
Raetia, province, 116
Rathmelsigi, abbey, 293
Ravenna, city, 33, 37, 39, 42, 44, 114, 175, 259, 298, 337
  Exarchate, 335
Reccared, Visigothic king, 76, 80, 81
Recceswinth, Visigothic king, 82
Reginald, bishop of Autun, 186
Regino, abbot of Prüm
  Libri duo de synodalibus causis, 227
Reimitz, Helmut, 33
Remigius, bishop of Rheims, 47
Rheims, city, 40, 165, 339f21.1
Rhine, river, 16, 31, 46, 94, 97, 121n47
Rhône, river, 17, 31, 34n11, 262, 323
Ricimer, general, 35
Riedinger, Rudolf, 139, 141
Rigunth, Merovingian princess, 30
Rio, Alice, 179, 273
Rochais, Hénri-Marie, 220, 222, 228
Roderic, Visigothic king, 319
Rodrigo. *See* Roderic, Visigothic king
rois fainéants, 4
Rotunda of the Anastasis, 196, 200, 201
Rouen, city, 143, 150
Royal Frankish Annals, 332
Rufinus of Aquileia, historian, 72, 224
Rule of Basil, 266
Rule of St Benedict, 179

Sadovec, fortress, 99
Sagittarius, bishop of Gap, 69
Salonius, bishop of Embrun, 69
Salzburg, city, 140, 145

Samo, king of the Slavs, 145
San Lorenzo-in-Palatio, church in Rome, 148
Sana'a, city, 308, 312
Sant'Agnese fuori le mura, church in Rome, 174
Santa Maria Antiqua, church in Rome, 213
Sapaudus, bishop of Arles, 137
Saracen. *See* Arab
Saragossa, city, 322
Sardinia, island, 35
Saxons, 98, 144
Scaliger, Joseph Justus, 299
Schäferdiek, Knut, 84
Scheibelreiter, Georg, 143, 160
Scheldt, river, 17, 144, 145
Schmitz, Herman J., 181
Schreiner, Peter, 58
Schwartz, Dan, 211
Sens, city, 251
Septimania, 76, 318, 321, 327
Sergius I, Pope, 178, 283, 295
Sergius, martyr, 71
Sergius, patriarch of Constantinople, 140, 141, 160, 162, 176, 283
Sergius, saint, 67
Sessorian palace, 196, 198, 199
Sevastopol, city, 155
Severinus, Pope, 174
Seville, city, 84
Shanzer, Danuta, 38
Shi'ite, 213
Sicily, 133, 175, 250, 251, 285, 286, 295, 337, 345
Sigibert I, Merovingian king, 52, 59, 75, 76, 116, 118, 291
Sigibert III, Merovingian king, 4, 6, 141, 144, 145, 160, 249, 275
Sigismund, Burgundian king, 5, 33, 34, 35, 36, 37, 38, 39, 40, 41, 42, 43
Sigistrix, Burgundian prince, 35, 36, 37, 38, 39, 40, 41
Silverius, Pope, 167, 175
Silvester, Pope, 172, 176, 199
Simon Magus, 171
Simplicius, Pope, 175
Sinai collection, 303
Sisbert, 80
Sixtus I, Pope, 171
Sixtus II, Pope, 172
Sixtus III, Pope, 177
Sixtus V, Pope, 75
Slane, abbey, 293
Slavs, 145, 146, 148, 257
Smith, Julia, 241, 242

Sophia, empress, 189, 190
Soter, Pope, 171
Spain, 225, 276, 285, 286, 287, 319, 322, 325, 326, 327, 328. *See also* al-Andalus
Spoleto, Duchy, 112, 114, 340
Sri Lanka, 22, 23
St Agatha, 174
St Apollinaris, church in Rome, 174
St Pancratii, church in Rome, 174
St Stephen stones, 235
St Amand, abbey, 138, 139, 140, 147, 148, 165
St Benigne de Dijon, abbey, 185
St Catherine's, abbey, 299, 301
St Denis, Paris, 11, 12, 29, 253, 262, 333
St Jean de Laon, abbey, 261, 263
St Maurice d'Agaune, abbey, 34, 39
St Stephen's, church in Bologna, 200
St Symphorien, Autun, 184
St Wandrille, abbey, 146
Sta. Croce, church in Jerusalem, 196, 198, 199
Sta. Croce, church in Rome, 200, 201
Sta. Sabina, church in Rome, 299
Ste. Croix, abbey, 194
Ste. Croix, abbey in Poitiers, 201
Stephanus, treasurer, 35
Stephen I, Pope, 176
Stephen II, Pope, 166, 178, 332, 333, 334, 335, 336, 337, 339, 340, 344
Stephen III, Pope, 341
Strasbourg, city, 261
Sueton, Roman author, 168
Suevi, 114
Sulaymān, caliph, 324, 325
Sulpicius, bishop of Bourges, 144
Sussex, 232
Sutton Hoo, 14
Symmachus, Pope, 132
Syria, 6, 28, 67, 71, 87, 88, 95, 96, 101, 107, 204, 208, 209, 214, 215, 216, 224, 285, 286, 300, 311
  al-Sham, 292
  people, 95, 285

Taio, bishop of Saragossa, 224, 270, 273, 274, 278, 279, 285
Ṭāriq ibn Ziyād, Muslim general, 321, 322
Tarragona, city, 328
Taurinus, deacon of Toulon, 258, 263
Teilreiche, 4, 52n30
Telesphorus, Pope, 176
Terence, playwright, 224
Terniscus, bishop of Besançon, 262
Tertry, battle, 263
Theoderic, Ostrogothic king, 37, 42, 43, 48, 51, 175

Theodora, empress, 130
Theodore of Tarsus, bishop of Canterbury, 29, 181, 250, 251, 252, 254, 257, 258, 295
Theodore, bishop of Mopsuestia, 131
Theodore, bishop of Pharan,, 162
Theodore, Pope, 174
Theodoret, bishop of Cyrus, 131, 136, 204
Theodorus Spudaeus, 156
Theodosius I, emperor, 72, 193
Theophanes Confessor, historian, 255, 256, 257, 293, 294
Theophilus, patriarch of Antioch, 226
Theudebald, Merovingian king, 131
Theudebert I, Merovingian king, 32, 42, 44, 55, 116, 117, 130
Theuderic I, Merovingian king, 40, 41, 42, 55
Theuderic III, Merovingian king, 185, 258, 260, 262, 263
Thomas Aquinas, 229
Thrace, 255, 287
Three Magi, 298
Three-Chapters Controversy, 6, 129, 131, 132, 133, 134, 135, 136, 137, 139, 248
Thuringians, 189
  Christianity, 41
  Frankish conquest, 41
Tiberius II, emperor, 18, 60, 80, 95, 97, 101, 103, 104, 105, 107, 113, 116, 118, 120, 123, 290, 291
Tipasa, city, 212
Toledo, city, 76, 319, 321, 322
  House of Bolts, 319
Tomb of Adam, 235
Totila, Ostrogothic king, 117
Toul, city, 261
Toulouse, city, 318, 327
Tournai, city, 14
Tours, city, 124, 165, 169, 290, 296
  St Martin's basilica, 194
Traguilla, slave, 38
Transformation of the Roman World, 2
Trier, Domschatz, cod. 61, 306n31
Trinity, 180, 260, 342
Trishagion, 42
Troy, 289
True Cross, 59, 70, 71, 103, 173, 176, 189, 190, 191, 192, 193, 194, 196, 198, 199, 200, 235, 241, 253, 254
Typos, 141, 159, 249, 283
Typus. See *Typos*
Tyre, 242

Umar ibn al-Khattab, caliph, 239, 310
Umar II, caliph, 321

Umayyad Caliphate, 3, 5, 204, 209, 211, 213, 303, 311, 318, 320
Umbria, 143
Ursinus, monk, 220
Uthman ibn Affan, caliph, 310, 326
Uzès, city, 120

Valdonne, city, 17
Valencia, city, 80
Valenciennes, city, 138
Valentinian II, emperor, 183
Valentinian III, emperor, 199
Vandals, 32, 37, 42, 44, 75, 96, 174
Venantius Fortunatus, poet, 51, 52, 53, 54, 55, 59, 119, 190, 291, 296
Venetia, province, 116
Venice, city, 345
Verhulst, Adriaan, 145
Vespasian Psalter, 315
Vetus Gallica, 226, 227, 279
Vetus Latina, 223, 267
Vexilla Regis, 190
Vézeronce, battle, 42, 43
Via Aurelia, 173
Victor I, Pope, 171
Victorine cycle, 177
Victorius of Aquitaine, author, 277, 279
Vienna Dioscurides, 308
Vienne, city, 333
Vigilius, Pope, 129, 130, 132, 133, 134, 135, 175, 177
Vincentius, bishop of Saragossa, 79
Virgil, 269
Virgin Mary, 174, 191, 230, 235, 236, 237, 238, 239, 243
Visigoths, 6, 43, 49, 50, 52, 59, 68, 70, 71, 74, 75, 76, 77, 82, 83, 84, 85, 86, 256, 260, 264, 274, 318, 319, 321, 322
Vita Abrahae, 290
Vita Eligii. See *Life of Eligius of Noyon*
Vita Geretrudis. See *Life of Geretrude of Nivelles*
Vitalian, Pope, 250
Vitrone, Francesca, 240
von Mercklin, Eugen, 315
von Ranke, Leopold, 1
Vosevio, abbey, 267
Vouillé, battle, 41
Vulfoleudes, bishop of Bourges, 250, 275

Wallace-Hadrill, Michael, 218
Wamba, Visigothic king, 260
Wandrille, abbot, 146, 250
Wascones, 145
Werner, Joachim, 16

Wessex, 251
Whatley, E. Gordon, 192
Whitehouse, David, 2
Wickham, Chris, 2
Wideradus, donor, 183, 185
Wilfrid, bishop of York, 251, 252, 258, 259, 261, 263
Willibald, bishop of Eichstätt, 230, 232, 233, 234, 235, 236, 237, 238, 239, 240, 242, 243, 244, 282, 284, 289, 296, 303, 316
Willibrord, missionary, 345
Winfrid, bishop of Lichfield, 261
Witigis, Ostrogothic king, 170
Wolfram, Herwig, 41

Wood, Ian, 33
Wood, Philip, 214
Woods, David, 292, 293, 294
Wynnebald, missionary, 240

Yazīd I, caliph, 325
Yemen, 308
York, city, 261

Zacharias, Pope, 86, 332
Zacho, abbot of Flavigny, 185
Zaragoza, city. *See Saragossa*
Zephyrinus, Pope, 171
Zoroastrian, 215
Zuqnīn, chronicle, 209

For EU product safety concerns, contact us at Calle de José Abascal, 56–1°,
28003 Madrid, Spain or eugpsr@cambridge.org.